"Here is a vigorous, juicy, engaging, life-centered, God-honoring set of sermons, brilliantly overviewing the entire New Testament: a truly rich resource from which to benefit and borrow. Dr. Dever is a Puritan in twenty-first-century clothing, and it shows."
— J. I. PACKER
Professor of Theology, Regent College

"Mark Dever knows that Christians cannot be powerfully influenced by the Bibles they do not know. So here is the antidote: a biblical flyover that reveals the contours and glories of the New Testament landscape so that it becomes familiar geography to the soul. This book will grace many lives."
— R. Kent Hughes,
Pastor, College Church, Wheaton, Illinois

"In our transient age, one of the pressing responsibilities of the faithful expository preacher is to, within a reasonably short span of years, walk his congregation through the whole canon of Scripture. One of the best ways to accomplish this is through preaching one-sermon whole-Bible-book overviews. Mark Dever is a master at this, and his gifts (first given to his own flock) are now here made available to preachers and congregants everywhere who want a thorough survey of the New Testament literature, not in the form of a scholarly introduction, but instead as a pastoral overview from the heart of a preacher who wants his people to know and live the truth. These expositions are theologically rich, biblically faithful, loaded with superb introductions, illustrations, and applications, and a model for how to preach didactically, practically, apologetically, and evangelistically all at once."
— J. Ligon Duncan III
Senior Minister, First Presbyterian Church, Jackson, Mississippi
President, Alliance of Confessing Evangelicals
Adjunct Professor, Reformed Theological Seminary
Chairman, Council on Biblical Manhood and Womanhood

"Whether you are a pastor seeking to preach the 'whole counsel of God' or simply an individual wanting to understand your whole Bible, this unique and invaluable resource provides a wealth of insight that will serve you for years to come. We can never know our Bibles too well or preach them too fully. This wonderful book will help individual Christians and pastors do both."
— C. J. Mahaney
Sovereign Grace Ministries
Author, *The Cross Centered Life*

"This outstanding series of bird's-eye studies of the New Testament books will enable all Christians to feed deeper from God's Word and equip teachers to feed others. They expand the mind, warm the heart, and challenge the will."
— Vaughan Roberts
Rector, St. Ebbe's Church, Oxford, England
Author, *God's Big Picture*

"Unusually prophetic utterances from the heart of the nation's capital, these overview introductions to the most salient truths of each book of the New Testament are vintage Mark Dever. Dever's scholarship abounds as all of his knowledge is here poured into truths that will transform a person, a church, or a nation."
— Paige Patterson
President, Southwestern Baptist Theological Seminary,
Fort Worth, Texas

"Is biblical exposition a lost art? Not if this book is any indication. Dr. Mark E. Dever is a masterful expositor who combines stellar scholarship with a tremendous ability to communicate God's revealed truth. These sermons and essays represent more than brief introductions to the books of the New Testament. Mark Dever helps draw the reader into the text and texture of each book, while providing a constant frame of reference that sees the New Testament not only as a collection of books but as a book in itself—telling the Christian story and grounding the church in God's truth. This book is a gem—and it belongs on every Christian's bookshelf."

 —R. Albert Mohler, Jr.
  President, The Southern Baptist Theological Seminary,
  Louisville, Kentucky

"Many Bible readers know individual verses and sometimes even chapters but often do not see the message of books as a whole. They are familiar with individual trees while failing to see the forest. They are in great danger of misinterpreting the parts of the Bible they read because they do not see the entire structure of a Gospel like John or an epistle like Ephesians. Mark Dever fills a gaping need with his sermons on each of the individual books. Readers will be given a vision of the landscape of each of the New Testament books. Pastors will see the importance of preaching sermons that cover an entire book. All will be strengthened by the biblical truth, the insightful introductions, and the relevant application found in this work."

 —Thomas R. Schreiner
  Teaching Minister, Clifton Baptist Church
  Professor of New Testament, Associate Dean for
  Scripture and Interpretation, The Southern Baptist
  Theological Seminary, Louisville, Kentucky

"The heart of biblical preaching is exposition: explaining what the text of Scripture is saying and applying it. But sometimes this approach is allowed to degenerate into laborious verse-by-verse expositions in which the larger view of the forest easily becomes lost to the minute details of the trees. This book provides an encouragement for another way which complements the systematic exposition of whole units of the biblical literature. Mark Dever's approach is thematic without ignoring the literary and theological structure of the books and is thus a stimulus to doctrinal preaching. This is not only a book for preachers but a challenging read for all who listen to sermons."

 —Graeme Goldsworthy
  Moore Theological College, Sydney

THE MESSAGE OF
THE NEW TESTAMENT

THE MESSAGE OF
THE NEW TESTAMENT

PROMISES KEPT

MARK DEVER

FOREWORD BY
JOHN MACARTHUR

CROSSWAY BOOKS

A PUBLISHING MINISTRY OF
GOOD NEWS PUBLISHERS
WHEATON, ILLINOIS

The Message of the New Testament: Promises Kept

Copyright © 2005 by Mark Dever

Published by Crossway Books
   a publishing ministry of Good News Publishers
   1300 Crescent Street
   Wheaton, Illinois 60187

Cover design: Josh Dennis

Cover photo: Getty Images

First printing 2005

Printed in the United States of America

Unless otherwise indicated, references are from *The Holy Bible: New International Version.*® Copyright © 1973, 1978, 1984 by International Bible Society. Used by permission of Zondervan Publishing House. All rights reserved.

The "NIV" and "New International Version" trademarks are registered in the United States Patent and Trademark Office by International Bible Society. Use of either trademark requires the permission of International Bible Society.

Scripture quotations marked ESV are from *The Holy Bible, English Standard Version*®, copyright © 2001 by Crossway Bibles, a publishing ministry of Good News Publishers. Used by permission. All rights reserved.

Scripture quotations marked KJV are from the King James Version of the Bible.

All emphases in Scripture citations have been added by the author.

Library of Congress Cataloging-in-Publication Data
Dever, Mark.
 The message of the New Testament : promises kept / Mark Dever.
  p. cm.
 Includes bibliographical references and index.
 ISBN 13: 1-58134-716-6 (HC : alk. paper)
 ISBN 10: 1-58134-716-2
 1. Bible. N.T.—Criticism, interpretation, etc. 2. Bible. N.T.—Sermons.
3. Baptists—Sermons. 4. Sermons, American—21st century. I. Title.
BS2361.3.D48 2005
225.6—dc22
                  2005013979

SH / M-L		15	14	13	12	11	10	09	08	07	06
15	14	13	12	11	10	9	8	7	6	5	4	3	2

To my colaborers in the gospel

MATT SCHMUCKER,
BRUCE KEISLING,
and AARON MENIKOFF,

who, like Phoebe, have
"been a great help to many people, including me"
ROMANS 16:2

CONTENTS

LIVING IN THE REAL WORLD

FOREWORD

THERE IS, OF COURSE, more than one valid approach to biblical exposition. When the preacher surveys a long section of biblical text, he is able to expound on large ideas and present the grand flow of biblical logic in a panoramic way. When he deals with smaller sections in more careful detail, he can home in on specific issues and explain them in greater depth. There are advantages and disadvantages to both styles. Both methods have a legitimate place in biblical preaching.

From time to time, I have done surveys of large passages of Scripture. I once preached through the entire New Testament in six day-long sessions in one week for a group of Russian pastors. On other occasions, I have surveyed whole chapters, groups of chapters, or entire books of Scripture in a single sermon. (One of the most popular sermons I have preached was a single message covering the whole book of Revelation, titled "A Jet Tour Through Revelation.")

Yet these types of overviews have been the rare exceptions to my normal approach. For most of my ministry, as I have preached through the New Testament, I have given careful attention to words, phrases, and verses, usually devoting whole sermons to a select phrase from a single verse. That is how I have worked my way systematically through book after book of Scripture: phrase by phrase, verse by verse, line upon line, precept upon precept. By that method, it has taken me thirty-five years to cover most of the New Testament, and I am not yet finished.

In stark contrast, Mark Dever used twenty-eight sermons in the early years of his ministry at Capitol Hill Baptist Church in Washington, D.C. to preach through the entire New Testament—one sermon for each of the twenty-seven books of the New Testament and one extra sermon that surveys the whole New Testament. He is uniquely and supremely gifted to teach in this manner.

Fortunately for us, Pastor Dever's sermons on the whole New Testament have been collected in this book, and I think it will give you a new and deep appreciation for how valuable the overview approach can be. This is a wonderful survey of the entire New Testament, unfolding its big picture—and the central themes of each book—with amazing clarity and accuracy. I found the book hard to put down.

Having done relatively little of this type of survey-style exposition, I know how difficult it is to do well. Mark Dever does it superbly. He covers a broad range of topics, always succinctly, accurately, and with remarkable care and clarity. He is very good at seeing the big picture, which is not always an easy thing to do. But he makes it look easy, and the result is a valuable tool that I know will help thousands to understand the New Testament more accurately.

I am grateful for Mark Dever's obvious love for God's Word, his commitment to handling Scripture carefully, his willingness to take the truth of the Bible seriously, and his ability to teach it so clearly. All of that comes through powerfully in this book. My prayer is that the Lord will bless these pages to the hearts of thousands of readers.

—John MacArthur
Pastor, Grace Community Church,
Sun Valley, California
President, The Master's College and Seminary

ACKNOWLEDGMENTS

RICHARD SIBBES once observed, "what the heart liketh best, the mind studieth most."[1] When I realized how large this volume was going to be, I wondered who would read it. Regardless of who belongs to that company, I know that I have been helped by many others to understand and present the truth of the Bible through these sermons.

Four groups of people especially require my thanks for helping me with these sermons. First and most immediately are the editors, and chief among them is Jonathan Leeman. After many friends had transcribed these sermons, it fell to Jonathan to spend months comparing those transcripts to my own manuscripts. Jonathan—a friend and brother in the ministry—has used his own understanding of the Bible, his theological education, and his experience as an editor to make these sermons tighter, clearer, more accessible, and better for you the reader. You owe him more than you know!

But these sermons had a long life before Jonathan ever saw them, and that brings me to another group of people that require my thanks: the congregation and especially the elders of the Capitol Hill Baptist Church with whom I have been privileged to serve. The congregation as a whole has been a wonderful family to preach to. And each one of my brother elders has had a careful and loving influence on me and my preaching. Chief among those who have affected my preaching would have to be Bill Behrens, and this for two reasons: first, he has given his time Saturday after Saturday for years now to sit down and make my sermons better; second, it was Bill who encouraged me to make sure the gospel was in every sermon. If the gospel is clearly present in my preaching, it was not the schools I attended who made it so. No, Bill was the human instrument God used in this.

Another group of people that God used to encourage me were those teachers who—through their books—taught me to look at the great sweep of biblical history. Chief among these authors would have to be Graeme

---

[1] Richard Sibbes, *The Bruised Reed*, Works, I.89.

Goldsworthy and Bill Dumbrell. Along with Don Carson, they have helped supply whatever biblical theology informs these sermons.

Finally and most profoundly, I must thank my family. Sermons for me happen at inconvenient times, and Connie, Annie, and Nathan have surely been inconvenienced most. In eternity, I pray that all of us will feel that the inconveniences were worthwhile and the time well spent. In the meantime, I express my love and thanks.

Many others deserve thanks. A special thanks to Duncan Rein, who first showed enthusiasm and gave time and effort to get my sermons into print. Bill Deckard and the good folks at Crossway have believed in this project and shepherded it through to completion. Various friends have encouraged me. I could go on thanking others who have contributed, but the responsibility for these sermons lies finally with me. Credit for good I happily and rightly share with others; fault for what is amiss truly must be my own. They are now offered to you with the prayer that your heart will "best like" God and so your mind will most be given to studying his Word.

—Mark Dever
Capitol Hill Baptist Church
Washington, D.C.
June 2005

INTRODUCTION:
GETTING A WINDOW SEAT

SOME THINGS CAN BE seen only from a great height. Go to the highest point in a city and what do you see? Sweeping vistas that both delight and inform. "Wow, look how far the city stretches out." "Oh, that's how the street system works."

If you are anything like me, you love these views. When out-of-town friends visit, I like to take them to the roof of our church building. Looking out, we can see the Capitol Hill neighborhood as well as numerous landmarks of both Capitol Hill and the city of Washington. The view reminds me of the unusual community God has placed us in. And by this view we are thrilled and challenged and inspired.

Back in college, I enjoyed reading my Bible and praying out on a dormitory fire-escape that had a good view of the campus.

The window seat on an airplane is also a must for me. "That's Chicago!" "Look at the Grand Canyon!" "Did you have any idea this area had so many lakes?"

I remember the first time I flew back to America with my family after living in England for a few years. Once the airplane was over the American landscape, I peered out the window and was reminded of how vast and unpeopled the American continent is, especially compared to the quilt-work cultivation you see when you glance out the window over Great Britain. Seeing the two landscapes from a great height put them into a different perspective and gave me a far richer understanding of them.

That is what I hoped these "overview sermons" would do for my congregation, and what I hope they will do for you.

When you compare these sermons to most sermons you have heard, I think you will find them unusual. Sermons typically come in a couple of varieties. Some people preach *topical* sermons, which focus on a particular topic such as money, parenting, heaven, or repentance. The sermons in this book are not topical in that sense.

Other people preach *expositional* sermons. An expositional sermon takes a portion of Scripture, explains it, and then applies it to the life of the congregation. The sermon text might be something like "Honor your father and mother" or "Jesus wept" or Ephesians 2:1-10 or Psalm 23.

The sermons in this book are more expositional than topical, but they are expositional with a difference. Rather than looking at particular Scripture passages through a microscope, we are looking down from an airplane.

Some expositional preachers may feel that their seriousness in preaching God's Word shows itself in how many years they spend in one particular book. Maybe you have heard someone say, "Our church just spent eighteen weeks in Jude!" or a pastor testifying, "When I arrived at the church two-and-a-half years ago, I began in Matthew chapter 1, and we are just now getting to the Sermon on the Mount." Then, of course, there are the Puritan ministers like Joseph Caryl or William Gouge, who spent several decades in Job and Hebrews, respectively! Can you imagine being in Job on Sunday morning for decades?

Do not misunderstand me. God's Word is inspired and worth a lifetime of study. We can legitimately preach for decades on any book of the Bible. God's Word contains beauties to be seen through careful consideration that the more impatient among us will never see. I do worry that such preaching runs the danger of becoming topical preaching under the guise of expositional preaching. It can also deprive people of learning about all the different parts of God's Word.

There is another kind of expositional preaching that is, I think, more rare, but that also serves the church well. This is what I call an "overview sermon," like the ones contained in this volume. An overview sermon attempts to give the burden of one particular Bible book in a single message. If a typical expositional sermon makes the point of the biblical text the point of the sermon, an overview sermon simply makes the point of a whole book the point of the sermon. I have preached these sermons based on the conviction that aspects of God and his plans can be seen most clearly not only when studying the microscopic structure of one phrase in one verse but when examining a book as a whole.

Now, preparing these sermons is more difficult than preparing a sermon on smaller portions of Scripture. But like an invigorating hike up a mountain, they provide views that are rarely seen, views breathtaking in their beauty and stunning in their usefulness.

I cannot remember when I first thought of preaching sermons like this. It may have been when I was discipling a recent Muslim convert and asked him to teach me the book of Hebrews in three meetings (I thought he would learn it better by teaching me). At each meeting, I would read a sentence or two from Hebrews and ask him where the verse fit into the book's argument. I did not so much care if he could tell me chapter and verse references; I was more concerned about whether he understood the overall flow of the book, and how any one idea from the book fit into that flow.

As we worked through Hebrews this way, I found that an overview was beneficial not just for my friend but also for me as a pastor. When I preach a passage like Ephesians 2, do I approach the chapter in context? That is, am I using chapter 2 in the same way Paul uses chapter 2 within his larger argument as it unfolds in Ephesians?

The Hebrews overview also got me to thinking about my congregation. I want the members of my church to become so familiar with the books of the Bible that they know how to turn there as easily as they turn to popular Christian books. So when members of the church struggle with conflict, I will encourage them to read the book on conflict resolution by Ken Sande, but I also want them to have been trained by an overview sermon to immediately ask themselves, "I wonder what James says about this situation?" When members want to learn about the Christian life, let them read C. S. Lewis and J. I. Packer; but let them also think to read 1 Peter and 1 John! When people struggle with discouragement, by all means read Ed Welch on depression; but also read Revelation! When people worry they are slipping into legalism, I hope they know to reach for Martin Luther or C. J. Mahaney on the cross-centered life; but I also hope they know to reach for Galatians. I am even happy for the congregation to read Dever on the church, but I would prefer for them to know Paul's argument in 1 Corinthians.

Obviously, I can preach this kind of sermon in my own church only sixty-six times. This volume presents the twenty-seven sermons I preached on the twenty-seven books of the New Testament (with one more sermon thrown in that I preached on the New Testament as a whole). Hopefully, these sermons are not just dry lectures; nor, hopefully, are they just random thoughts on my favorite verses from each book. Rather, I preached each of these sermons with the conviction that they were genuine expositions of God's Word—except that the passages were a little larger than the passages I normally expound. In each sermon, I attempted to present the weight and balance of the Bible book, with applications that represent the original thrust of the book but that also applied to our congregation at the time I first preached the sermon. In recognition of how time-bound the sermons are, we have included the date on which each sermon was first preached at the beginning of every chapter. Yet in recognition of the continuing relevance of God's Word, these sermons are offered for your consideration as well.

I hope you are encouraged by how the various Gospels hold up the life of Jesus Christ, or how Paul presents the church in 1 Corinthians, or what Peter says is normal for Christian lives in 1 Peter, or what the elderly prisoner John perceives in his triumphant vision of God's sovereignty over the world in Revelation.

What a benefit I have known in my own life from preparing these studies! How they have familiarized me with the arguments of the various books, so that I understand each of their parts more in context! How I pray they have blessed our own congregation!

Now, we commit them to you, with our prayers and wishes that you, too, will be surprised, delighted, and edified as long-familiar books take on new aspects of coherence and power and conviction.

—Mark Dever
Capitol Hill Baptist Church
Washington, D.C.
May 2005

THE MESSAGE OF THE NEW TESTAMENT: PROMISES KEPT

THE MESSAGE OF THE NEW TESTAMENT: PROMISES KEPT

PROMISES KEPT[1]

In 1858, the Illinois legislature elected Stephen A. Douglas to the office of U.S. senator instead of Abraham Lincoln. Afterward, a sympathetic friend asked Lincoln how he felt, to which he responded, "Well, a little bit like the boy who stubbed his toe; I am too big to cry and too badly hurt to laugh." As a pastor on Capitol Hill, I am struck every election season by how one person's political victory is someone else's political loss. No matter who wins an election, a vast number of people—up to half—are disappointed. People become so involved in partisan politics that election seasons can be a time of great hope for some and, just as surely, great disappointment for others.

Sometimes we can bear disappointment well. Some people are so given over to disappointment they actually seem to thrive on it. Like the character Eeyore in the Winnie-the-Pooh tales, they take comfort in looking for the dark cloud around every silver lining. For most of us, however, disappointment can feel like a sharp thrust to the heart. We do what we can just to get by.

Did you ever see the movie *Shadowlands*—the story about C. S. Lewis's late-in-life marriage to Joy Davidman? In an opening scene of the movie, Lewis is sitting amid several of his students at Oxford and he refers to a piece of poetry that mentions the image of a perfect rosebud. Lewis asks what the image of the bud represents. One of the students responds, "Love?"

"What kind of love?" says Lewis impatiently.

"Untouched," says a student.

"Unopened, like a bud?" says another student.

"Yes, more?"

Another student says anxiously, "Perfect love."

"What makes it perfect?" says Lewis, "Come on, wake up."

"Is it the courtly ideal of love?"

Now, that is a little inside Lewis joke, because Lewis had written a thesis

[1] This sermon was originally preached on September 6, 1996, at Capitol Hill Baptist Church in Washington, D.C.

on the courtly ideal of love. Still, Lewis replies, "Okay, what is that, though? What is the courtly ideal's one essential quality?"

The students are quiet. They don't know the answer. So Lewis himself answers: "Unattainability. The most intense joy lies not in the having, but in the desiring. The delight that never fades. Bliss that is eternal is only yours when what you most desire is just out of reach."

Well, is that true? It sounds fine as an artistic and romantic ideal, but is life like that? Is the only lasting bliss the bliss of desire rather than fulfillment? If so, how can we have hope without the possibility of actually attaining that for which we hope? After all, the pain of disappointment is acute because the object of our desires comes close and then we miss it. Whether it is a lost election, a collapsed business scheme, a disproved theory, a canceled vacation, a piece of defeated legislation, a failed job prospect, or a departed loved one, we understand what the writer of the proverb means when he says, "Hope deferred makes the heart sick!" (Prov. 13:12). In other words, we cannot overlook what our hearts are set upon.

What do you set your hopes upon? If you cannot answer that question, you may not be able to benefit from the rest of this study. It is crucial for you and me both to answer that question: What are our hopes set upon? Many of our problems come from attaching our hopes to things that were not made to bear them. Some things hold out great promise but they prove to be passing fancies as life goes on. Other things are actually dangerous and destructive. In this old world, it is not only in politics that promises made are not necessarily promises kept.

Of course, this is where God comes in. As the one who made us, he knows how we work best. He knows what we should hope for, and he has set those very things in the Bible so that we can fix our hopes upon them. In the companion to this volume, *The Message of the Old Testament: Promises Made*,[2] we looked at the "big picture" of the Old Testament. Now we will do a similar overview of the New Testament.

In the Old Testament, we saw that God created the earth and then patiently bore with a people who rebelled against him. Beginning with Abraham, he chose a special people of his own. Those people, the nation of Israel, waxed and waned for almost two millennia until their once high hopes almost vanished when their nation was crushed a final time by an alien invader—the mighty Roman Empire. When this final defeat occurred, they felt disappointed to the point of heartsickness and despair. Would their deliverer never come? Would they never be restored to the fellowship with God for which they longed? Would the world never be put right?

---

[2] Mark Dever, *The Message of the Old Testament: Promises Made* (Wheaton, Ill.: Crossway, 2006).

The New Testament tells the story of how all the promises made in the Old Testament were actually kept. And as we understand what God is doing in the grand scheme of history, our own disappointments and hopes will begin to fall into perspective.

In order to view the whole New Testament, we will look first at *Christ*, then at God's *covenant people*, and finally at the renewal of all of *creation*. Think of three concentric circles. First, we focus on Christ; then we expand outward to the new covenant people; and, finally, we take in all creation.

CHRIST

The first question that must be addressed concerning the New Testament is, did the deliverer whom God promised in the Old Testament actually come? The New Testament answers that Old Testament question with a resounding yes! And he is not just an ordinary human deliverer, he is God come in the flesh. The one and only Son, Jesus, perfectly displayed the Father, so that God's people might know him and be delivered from their sins. The New Testament squarely focuses on Christ. He is the heart of it all. He is the center of its message.

God has always had a plan for creation. Before history even began, the New Testament teaches, God planned to send his Son as a human to die for the sins of his people. After God created the universe and humankind, Adam and Eve rebelled against God's rightful rule. God then called a special people to himself in Abraham. Through Abraham's descendent Jacob, or Israel, the family grew to be a great nation. The majority of this nation was then destroyed by invading armies because of its sin, while the survivors were taken captive, exiled, dispersed, and only partly regathered from exile. Yet God's plan remained firmly in place through all of this. In this tattered remnant would be found the coming deliverer, the anointed one—in Hebrew, the "Messiah"; in Greek, the "Christ."

The collection of twenty-seven books that comprise the New Testament begins with four accounts of the life of this Messiah—Jesus of Nazareth. Look at the contents page in your Bible. Under the New Testament heading you will see four books at the top of the list—Matthew, Mark, Luke, and John. Following these four is a fifth—Acts. All five of these books argue that Jesus of Nazareth is the Messiah. These books are documentaries, as it were, of Jesus' life, and they make the case for his Messiahship. They presented to their readers the tremendous news that the promised deliverer had actually come! The one for whom God's people were waiting had come! Where Adam and Israel had failed and been unfaithful, Jesus proved faithful. He survived the temptations. He lived a life without sin. Furthermore, Jesus fulfilled God's promise to Moses of a coming prophet (Deut. 18:15, 18-19). Jesus fulfilled God's promise to David of a coming king (2 Sam. 7:12-13). Jesus fulfilled the prophecy of the divine Son of Man witnessed by Daniel (Dan. 7:13-14). All of these promises and more were fulfilled, say these four Gospels, in Jesus of Nazareth. In fact, according to John chapter 1, Jesus was the Word of God made flesh—God himself living in human form.

Turning to these Gospels individually, we note that Matthew was probably written for a Jewish community. He stresses Jesus' fulfillment of Old Testament prophecies, such as the many prophecies about his birth. Matthew includes five major teaching sections, each of which shows Jesus to be the great prophet promised by Moses.

Mark chronicles, perhaps, the apostle Peter's recollections. The book does not say that but various things in the book make us think Mark compiled Peter's recollections about Jesus for the Roman Christians, maybe around the time Peter was killed for being a Christian. Seeing the first apostles killed, the church may have wanted to commit these things to writing. Mark's account is the shortest of all the Gospels and it may be the oldest.

Luke, the third Gospel, is sometimes called the Gospel to the Gentiles. Luke stresses that the Messiah has come not just for the Jewish people but for all the nations of the world, and he puts to good use the Old Testament prophecies that make this promise. Luke also wrote a second volume, the book of Acts. Acts is "part two" of Luke's work. It shows how Jesus actively expanded his church through his Spirit. So even after Jesus' crucifixion, resurrection, and ascension, his work continued as the church grew and as God established this new society. Luke concluded his narrative with Paul imprisoned—but still ministering—in Rome.

The fourth book is the Gospel of John, which may be the most beloved of the Gospels. It is different from the other three Gospels in some ways. It does not teach a different theology but it has an especially clear emphasis on both Jesus' identity as the Messiah and the fact that the Messiah is God himself. John explicitly states this purpose for his Gospel in chapter 20: "these are written that you may believe that Jesus is the Christ [that is, the Messiah], the Son of God, and that by believing you may have life in his name" (20:31).

These are the four Gospels and the book of Acts. They begin the New Testament by showing us that the promises made about the Messiah in the Old Testament have been fulfilled in Christ.[3] They proclaim the good news that God has kept his promises to deliver not just his Old Testament people

---

[3] Among many other designations, Jesus is also described as the New Adam (2 Cor. 15:45-47); the Righteous One (2 Pet. 2:15; Acts 3:14; 1 John 2:1); greater than Moses (John 1:17; 5:45-46; Heb. 3:1-6); and greater than David (Matt. 22:41-45; Acts 2:29-36). Abraham also rejoiced to see his day (John 8:56-58).

but you and me as well, if we repent of our sins and follow his Son. If the collection of the Gospels and Acts strikes you as just a few more musty old history books, you have not read them very well. Read them again. I think you will find there is more than you suspect, even as I did when I began reading them carefully as an agnostic. The Gospels show that Jesus the Messiah is not just the Lord of people who lived two thousand years ago but is the Lord that you need in your life.

COVENANT PEOPLE

This brings us to our second concentric circle for understanding the overall message of the New Testament. Christ is at the heart of the New Testament's message, and then we move outward to his special covenant people. Glimpses of Christ's work among his people can be seen in the Gospels, especially among the disciples. Yet it really picks up momentum in the book of Acts and then in the New Testament Epistles. God himself took on human form in order to display his image in Jesus Christ, as we will consider in the Gospels. Yet the Old Testament teaches that God made human beings—all of us—in his image to display his image to creation. So as we read along in the New Testament, the transforming, image-clarifying work of Christ among his special covenant people emerges as a second dominant theme.

Now, I know the word "covenant" is not used very often these days. If anything, it sounds like a legal term. In our study of the Old Testament, we thought about the "covenant" language used in ancient Israel and we found that it is not cold, legal language; it is the language of relationship. Then in the Gospels, Jesus used the language of covenant when he shared the Last Supper with his disciples: "This cup is the new covenant in my blood, which is poured out for you" (Luke 22:20). Covenants are used to form new relationships, which is why Jesus came: to make a new relationship for his people with God, because that relationship had been destroyed by sin.

Jesus said very strangely, toward the beginning of John, "Destroy this temple, and I will raise it again in three days" (John 2:19). At the time, he was standing in the temple in Jerusalem; but then he told his disciples he was talking about his body (2:21-22). He himself was the temple that would be destroyed and rebuilt. He would be the new meeting place for God and his people, just as the temple in Jerusalem had been in former days. He would be the mediator between God and man. As we have already considered, Jesus Christ fulfilled the Old Testament promise that the Messiah would come as a prophet and a king. But in order to deliver his people from their sin and establish his new covenant, Jesus also fulfilled the promise that the Messiah would come as a priest. Like the Levitical priests of the Old Testament, he would intercede between God and man with a blood sacrifice. The rescue needed by God's people, ultimately, was a rescue from their sins.

The Old Testament temple, priests, and sacrifices could not effectually accomplish (and were never intended to accomplish) that work of intercession and reconciliation, which brings us to the riddle of the Old Testament. In Exodus 34 God revealed himself as the Lord who "forgives wickedness" (see 34:7). Then in the same sentence, he said he "will not leave the guilty unpunished." The riddle is this: how can God "forgive wickedness" and yet "not leave the guilty unpunished"? The Levitical priests could not solve the riddle by sacrificing bulls and goats (Heb. 10:4). The answer is found, of course, in Jesus. Jesus came as priest, sacrifice, temple, and substitute, in order to intercede between God and man by taking upon his body God's punishment for sin. God could then forgive the wickedness of his people and yet ensure that their wickedness is punished. The New Testament provides the answer to the riddle posed in the Old. Jesus' death on the cross allowed God to both forgive and punish. Christ forms the new covenant—he reestablishes a relationship between God and his people—with his blood.

Not that the Old Testament did not foresee this. Through the prophet Isaiah, the LORD promised,

> Surely he took up our infirmities
>   and carried our sorrows,
> yet we considered him stricken by God,
>   smitten by him, and afflicted.
> But he was pierced for our transgressions,
>   he was crushed for our iniquities;
> the punishment that brought us peace was upon him,
>   and by his wounds we are healed.
> We all, like sheep, have gone astray,
>   each of us has turned to his own way;
> and the LORD has laid on him
>   the iniquity of us all (Isa. 53:4-6).

Isaiah said these things centuries before the birth of Christ. Yet that is exactly what God did for us in Christ! It is clear from the Gospels that Jesus had meditated on the Isaiah passage and knew he would fulfill those very prophecies. So he taught his disciples, "the Son of Man did not come to be served, but to serve, and to give his life as a ransom for many" (Mark 10:45). After his resurrection, "beginning with Moses and all the Prophets, he explained to them what was said in all the Scriptures concerning himself." He also told them,

"This is what is written: The Christ will suffer and rise from the dead on the third day, and repentance and forgiveness of sins will be preached in his name to all nations, beginning at Jerusalem" (Luke 24:27, 46-47).

Christ did not come for himself. He came for his people. As you read through the whole New Testament, you will not only find that Jesus is the Messiah, you will find what this means for you. As Paul wrote, "God sent his Son, born of a woman, born under law, to redeem those under law, that we might receive the full rights of sons" (Gal. 4:4-5). Christ came to make a people for himself.

One of the New Testament's most amazing passages is Revelation 5. The apostle John is given a vision of the great throne room of God in heaven. As John looks, God's decrees for the rest of history are brought into the room on a scroll. John desperately wants to know what history contains. What has God decreed? But the scroll is sealed, so he begins to weep. An elder approaches John and says, "Do not weep! See, the Lion of the tribe of Judah, the Root of David, has triumphed. He is able to open the scroll and its seven seals" (Rev. 5:5). John looks up to see this lion of the tribe of Judah, this mighty king of the beasts, but what does he see? "Then I saw a Lamb, looking as if it had been slain, standing in the center of the throne" (5:6). The ferocious lion that God sends to devour his enemies is a Lamb that he sends to be slain. It is not the way you or I would have rescued a people. If we had been made director and producer of the Messianic coming, we would have sent somebody who would clean up in the polls, who would win all his battles, and who would bring everything our flesh desired. But that is not the way God did it. The enemy to be devoured is sin. So he sent a sacrifice to die on our behalf. The lion of the tribe of Judah is the Lamb that was slain.

God would be completely justified to leave us all eternally separated from him in hell under the penalty of our sin, yet in his great love, God has not done that. He sent his Son, who came and lived a perfect life and who therefore deserved no wrath or punishment for sin. Christ died on the cross specifically to take the place of everyone who turns and trusts in him. In exchange for our sinfulness, we are given his holiness. In Christ, then, we are declared holy before God and are brought into a reconciled, everlasting relationship with him!

The very thing the letter of Hebrews says never happened in the Old Testament has now come to pass in the New. In the Old Testament, God's people were only ceremonially clean. The covenant in the Old Testament was real, but partial. The prophets knew this and promised that a new covenant would come. Speaking through the prophet Jeremiah, God said,

"The time is coming," declares the LORD,
   "when I will make a new covenant
with the house of Israel
   and with the house of Judah.
It will not be like the covenant
   I made with their forefathers
when I took them by the hand
   to lead them out of Egypt,
because they broke my covenant,
   though I was a husband to them," declares the LORD.
"This is the covenant I will make with the house of Israel
   after that time," declares the LORD.
"I will put my law in their minds
   and write it on their hearts.
I will be their God,
   and they will be my people. . . .
For I will forgive their wickedness
   and will remember their sins no more" (Jer. 31:31-33, 34b).

Now, in the New Testament, God finally has a people who are not just cere-monially clean; the guilt of their sins has actually been removed because of Christ's death on the cross.

As Christians, we are counted as completely righteous in Christ, and we are being made holy in our lives *today*, as attested to by our manner of living and interactions with one another. We are not perfect by any means. If you have any doubt about that, get a mirror. Nevertheless, we are growing and improving with the help of God, dealing with life in a way that brings him glory and honor, not pretending we have no disappointments, but knowing where to turn in those disappointments and where to set our hopes. God is making us his own, and we wait for the completion of his work. For on that day, we will be fully, finally, and personally holy in the way that we are now holy in Christ.

In all this, a Christian's salvation is past, present, and future. So Paul can tell the Ephesian Christians they have been saved (Eph. 2:8-9), the Corinthian Christians they are being saved (1 Cor. 1:18), and the Roman Christians they shall be saved (Rom. 5:9). This accomplished, ongoing, and promised salva-tion distinguishes the covenanted people of God from the rest of humanity.

What all this means occupies almost the rest of the New Testament. If you look back at the table of contents for the New Testament, you will see the first four Gospels. Following these is the book of Acts, which is really the transi-tion from these Gospels to the books about living as God's people. In Acts, the gospel expands outward from Jerusalem, to Judea, to Samaria, and, with Paul's three missionary journeys, to the ends of the world. After Acts, the rest of the New Testament books are letters written to early Christians about what it means to live as the special covenant people of God, who are distinct from the rest of the world.

The first thirteen letters were written by the apostle Paul, a former rabbi and Pharisee who was remarkably converted by God while traveling to persecute some Christians "to their death," as he puts it (Acts 22:4). His letters are ordered in the New Testament from longest to shortest—first letters to churches and then letters to individuals. In his first letter, Romans, Paul explains that God has been faithful to his covenant through Christ. Through Christ, God has provided a righteousness for his people, which is accounted to us by faith, as was the case with Abraham.

Then 1 and 2 Corinthians were written to a church with a lot of troubles. The church lived within a very secular society, so Paul tried to help them sort out how to live holy, special, distinct lives in an unholy culture. You will find a lot of very interesting parts in these two letters, such as a famous chapter on love (1 Corinthians 13). In the second letter to the Corinthians, Paul passionately defends his own ministry.

If you want just the sharp edge of Paul's teaching, Galatians is a good summary. He is clear about what he is saying, and he is clear about what he is not saying.

Then in Ephesians Paul writes about the church God is creating. God had always planned to create the church, and it is a new society calling together both Jews and Gentiles in Christ.

Philippians—often called the happiest book in the New Testament because Paul does not seem to have a cross word to say—encourages its readers to rejoice in the Lord. It includes that beautiful hymn in chapter 2 describing how Christ, though being equal with God, made himself nothing and gave himself to die on the cross (Phil. 2:6-11).

Colossians is about Christ's supremacy over all, and some implications this has for our lives.

First and Second Thessalonians are two of Paul's earliest letters. Apparently, a number of people in Thessalonica had heard about Christ's second coming and, misunderstanding it, had quit their jobs. They were just hanging around like fanatics, waiting for God to do something. So Paul writes and tells them to get a job.

Next are Paul's personal letters, written to his individual friends. Paul wrote 1 and 2 Timothy to Timothy, a young minister he discipled and trained.

The letters were intended to encourage this young associate in his work as an elder. Second Timothy is probably the last letter Paul ever wrote.

The letter to Titus was written to a ministerial friend Paul left on the island of Crete to establish elders in the new churches and to complete other unfinished business.

Finally, Paul wrote a very short letter to Philemon, which you could easily read in the next five minutes. Philemon was the owner of an escaped slave who had found Paul and become a believer. It is interesting to see how Paul deals with a slave owner.

The rest of the New Testament is comprised of a second set of letters, none of which were written by Paul. There are nine of them, and again they are basically in order of length. The author of the first letter in this second set, Hebrews, is unknown. Hebrews helps us understand the relationship between the Old and New Testaments as well as what it means for us to be the new covenant people of God. Evidently some Christians were considering going back to some version of the older covenant God had made with Moses. After all, these plain Christian assemblies meeting in people's homes, devoid of any great ceremony, felt unimpressive. Back in the temple in Jerusalem, there was incense, sacrifices, fancy garments, great horns, and so forth. All that felt special, maybe even religiously satisfying. So people were beginning to turn back. The author of Hebrews responded by saying, "Look very carefully. Under the old covenant, you have priests who died because of their own sin. And their endless sacrifices of bulls and goats only made people ceremonially clean. But look at what you have in Christ! The eternal, sinless Son of God gave himself once forever to make his people truly clean and holy. The blood of the former sacrifices merely points to him."

James is a very practical letter. He describes how to live the Christian life with a practical concern for others.

First and Second Peter are relevant for the church today because they were written to Christians who were beginning to undergo difficulties for being Christians. This confused them. I think they were assuming, "If I am living rightly, won't life go well?" Peter responded, "Actually, if you look at the life of Jesus, you will see this is not a good assumption. In fact, living rightly can mean life does not go well, at least not in this world." Both of these letters encourage Christians to persevere in the faith, with Christ as their example. The second letter also warns about the danger of false teachers.

First, Second, and Third John are three brief letters written to encourage Christians in their lives of love and faithful obedience to the Lord.

Jude is a brief letter, similar to 2 Peter, warning against false and immoral teachers.

These are the New Testament's instructions for us about what it means to be the covenant people of God. In the New Testament, the promises made to the holy people in the Old Testament are kept in God's new covenant people. If we are Christians, they are kept in us today.

CREATION

In many church services, you will hear the prayer, "Thy kingdom come. Thy will be done on earth as it is in heaven." Have you ever wondered what that means? It falls off our tongues so easily. Many of us have said it since childhood.

"Thy kingdom come. Thy will be done on earth as it is in heaven."

Consider for a moment the kind of people who carefully tend their hearts because they want to avoid hurt or disappointment. The only hopes they allow themselves are the hopes they are able to make happen. The only promises they hear or make to themselves are the promises they have the power to keep. Yet limiting your hopes in this fashion is the complete opposite of Christianity. If you tend your heart in this way, I encourage you to look at the gospel. As Christians, Peter says, "we are looking forward to a new heaven and a new earth, the home of righteousness" (2 Pet. 3:13), and this is entirely beyond our power to effect. No elected party, no economic scheme, no job promotion, and no successful relationship can bring about the great thing we as Christians wait for. We wait for the fulfillment of our first and final hope: the whole world being put right, as God's plan in the New Testament extends from Christ to his covenant people to the outermost circle—his whole creation. In other words, we wait for his kingdom to come and his will to be done, on earth as it is in heaven.

This is what we find at the end of the New Testament in the book of Revelation. It is a letter too, but it is an unusual letter in which the apostle John describes a number of visions God gave him. In certain respects, John's apocalyptic letter picks up on the Old Testament prophetic tradition by focusing on great events that lie in store for the earth's inhabitants. More specifically, Revelation describes the consummation of God's people, in God's place, in right relationship to him. The church militant becomes the church triumphant—the victorious church in heaven. And the whole heavens and earth are re-created forever (see Rev. 21:1-4; 21:22–22:5).

The Bible does not present Christians as Platonists or Gnostics—people who think this world and material things do not matter, that only the spiritual afterlife matters. Throughout the book of Revelation and the whole New Testament, the biblical authors stress the bodily nature of the resurrection. Jesus was bodily resurrected, and his resurrection is called "the firstfruits." It begins what we will experience in the final resurrection from the dead. We will be taken up to be with God forever, but that is no world-denying proposition. God's plan for the world does not exist on some ethereal plain, far away from concrete reality. There is an interesting verse in Revelation that reads, "The nations will walk by [Christ's] light, and the kings of the earth will bring their splendor into" the city of heaven (Rev. 21:24). In the final consummation of creation, the kings of the earth will present their splendors and all the cultural grandeur of the world before the gathered heavenly assembly; and all these things will display God's glory as we discover what he meant for creation. Not only what Mark the preacher or Mary the Sunday school teacher brings will be counted worthwhile. Rather, the things you and I do in our daily lives in business, education, government, health care, or our families—if we have done them unto the Lord—will be presented and appear on the last day as adding to the luster of God's glory. These things are part of God's plan for the world. And here at the end, the holiness of God's people will finally be complete, as they are at home with him. John wrote in his first letter, "Dear friends, now we are children of God, and what we will be has not yet been made known. But we know that when he appears, we shall be like him, for we shall see him as he is" (1 John 3:2). The end will be like the beginning, only better. The Garden of Eden, in some sense, will be restored. God will dwell with his people. The whole heavenly city is presented in Revelation as a perfect cube, which recalls the Most Holy Place in the Old Testament temple. The Most Holy Place, which represented the presence of God on earth, was also in the shape of a cube. Only now, this heavenly cube is not restricted to the high priests once a year, as in ancient Israel; all the children of God will enter his presence, and we will live there with him forever! That is how the book called the New Testament ends.

It is a good way for the New Testament to end, I think. It gives us as Christians great news to offer the world. We presently live in a time of waiting, but we wait with God and we wait for God. After all, Revelation was written by a man in his nineties who had been exiled on an island by the mightiest power on earth, the Roman Empire. At the time, Christians were being killed for their faith. He was utterly desperate and dependent upon God. Yet he was full of hope because his hope did not rest on external circumstances. It rested on the sovereign God who ruled above the Roman emperors. That's when the curtain of the New Testament drops.

God promises in Scripture that the earth will be filled with the knowledge of his glory, and the promise is certain to be kept in his new creation.

Promises made; promises kept.

CONCLUSION

Of course, some disappointments have their uses. The ruins of our own cherished plans often become the steps we take toward the true good that God has waiting for us. Some of the very things you hope for right now are what God in his great love wants to pry from your fingers, so that you can receive what is better from him. Paul learned that when he prayed three times for God to remove the thorn from his flesh. God told Paul that his strength would be made perfect in Paul's weakness. So Paul rejoiced to become weak for the glory of God. And this is what we find in our own lives. When we cling to the world with all our might, we soon realize we cannot hold on. As Jesus said, "What good is it for a man to gain the whole world, yet forfeit his soul?" (Mark 8:36). God has something even better than the whole world for his children.

In the last paragraph of the last book of C. S. Lewis's series *The Chronicles of Narnia,* Lewis captures something of the nature of Christian hope. He writes, "And as Aslan spoke, he no longer looked to them like a lion; but the things that began to happen after that were so great and beautiful that I cannot write them. And for us this is the end of all the stories, and we can most truly say that they all lived happily ever after. But for them it was only the beginning of the real story. All their life in this world and all their adventures in Narnia had only been the cover and the title page: now at last they were beginning Chapter One of the Great Story which no one on earth has read: which goes on forever: in which every chapter is better than the one before."[4]

After considering the mysteries of God, his mercies to us in Christ, and the hope we have as his covenant children, Paul dissolves into doxology and says, "Oh, the depth of the riches of the wisdom and knowledge of God! How unsearchable his judgments, and his paths beyond tracing out!" (Rom. 11:33).

So I hope I have been clear: the *point* of the New Testament, indeed, the *point* of the whole Bible, is that God has made promises to us, he has kept those promises to us, and we are called to trust him because he is the keeper of promises! God has revealed himself to humanity through his promises. And that is why faith is so important. At the end of the day, the Bible does not lie on the shelf like a passive object for us to investigate. At the end of the day, it turns and looks at us and says, will you believe and trust? Or as Lady Wisdom cries out in the book of Proverbs, "Who will trust? Who will follow? Who will believe what I say?"

God gives his Word and his promises to us. He calls us to trust his Word and to believe his promises. Adam and Eve did not believe in the Garden of

---

[4] C. S. Lewis, *The Last Battle* (New York: Collier, 1956), 183.

Eden. Jesus believed throughout his life, and particularly in the Garden of Gethsemane. And as you and I hear and believe God's Word, we are restored to the relationship with him for which we were made. This is the hope in which we can trust, because this hope will not disappoint. This is what the Bible— Old Testament and New—is all about.

Let us pray:

Lord, we praise you that you have not left us alone, even though we asked you to get out of our lives. We praise you that you sent Jesus as the Messiah, and that he came not just to display your holiness and exclude us, but to incorporate us into your holiness and to make us your people. With love, mercy, and forgiveness he has come and told us of your love by giving himself completely, so that we might be made acceptable to you. Lord God, we praise you for the love you show us in Christ and for the people you are making for yourself. We pray that you will put in our hearts a hope that compels us to live as the new people you have made us to be, trusting you and your Word. Lord, you have given yourself fully for us. We pray that you would come and take our whole lives, and use them to your glory, for Jesus' sake. Amen.

Questions for Reflection

1. Have you ever been given or achieved something you had sought for a long time, only to find yourself disappointed? When? Why were you disappointed? Is there anything in this world worth desiring that is *not* that way?

2. What is the main argument of the four Gospels?

3. What does "Christ" mean? What does "Messiah" mean?

4. Explain the riddle of the Old Testament. Explain how Christ alone solves that riddle.

5. As we have seen, Jesus, the lion of the tribe of Judah, came to devour the enemy, sin. How was this lion able to devour this enemy?

6. What do the New Testament Epistles, generally speaking, attempt to accomplish?

7. What does it mean to refer to Christ as our "priest"? How does he act as our priest?

8. As we have seen, Christians are counted as perfectly righteous today, even though we are by no means perfect. Is this a contradiction? How does this work?

9. Earlier, we considered the kind of people who try to protect their hearts by hoping only for things that they have the power to control or make happen. Then we saw that Christianity calls for the exact opposite. How? Why?

10. Why is it significant that the heavenly city is shaped like a cube?

11. As we have considered, some of the very things you hope for right now are what God in his great love wants to pry from your fingers, so that you can receive what is better from him. What might he want to pry from your fingers? What dream, hope, ambition, demand, expectation, possession, person are you tightly clutching that he might ask you to surrender?

12. Surrendering the things we long for requires a kind of death—the death of a desire. And willfully choosing that death is hard to do. It requires us to believe—really believe!—that what God promises is even better. Can you remember a time in your life when God proved himself faithful to his promise of something better? Do you think he would do otherwise next time?

13. The end of Lewis's *The Last Battle* is marvelous, isn't it? A stanza in John Newton's hymn *Amazing Grace* evokes a similar sentiment when it begins, "When we've been there ten thousand years, bright shining as the sun . . ." Take a few moments to consider, what will all the things that have seemed so important to you over this last week look like in ten thousand years? Ten thousand years from now, what do you think you will want to have done this coming week?

14. In sixty seconds or less, what's the good news of Christianity?

PART ONE
THE TRUTH ABOUT JESUS

THE MESSAGE OF MATTHEW: JESUS, THE SON OF DAVID

1

THE MESSAGE OF MATTHEW: JESUS, THE SON OF DAVID

WHY ARE THERE SO MANY GOSPEL ACCOUNTS?[1]

This month, the world population is projected to reach 6 billion people for the first time ever. Out of that 6 billion, about 14 million people claim to be Jews, 22 million claim to be Sikhs, and 350 million claim to be Buddhists. Various new religions claim around 100 million adherents, and about 250 million people are adherents of various tribal religions. There are also supposed to be about 150 million atheists. Everyone I have mentioned so far, then, totals about 900 million people.

The statisticians who compiled these figures describe about 800 million people as nonreligious. They do not explain how they compiled that category. If these particular researchers have defined mild Confucianism and Shintoism not as religions but as life customs, the great bulk of these "nonreligious" must be Chinese and Japanese.

Of those that are left, about 800 million are Hindu, a little more than one billion are Muslim, and about two billion are professing Christians.

I wonder how you react to such statistics. Those of us who are professing Christians may see something of the great challenge still before us for reaching the unreached. Some less spiritual types may feel a vague reassurance, a strangely satisfied feeling that "our team is on top!" Some may feel a despair of ever knowing the truth for themselves. Such a great variety of perceptions of ultimate reality seals their case—that the whole world is as confused and divided as they are.

An inquiring historian appearing on the scene might well ask, where did this largest of all the world's religions come from? Perhaps knowing a bit about

[1] This sermon was originally preached on June 6, 1999, at Capitol Hill Baptist Church, Washington, D.C.

religion, the historian realizes that Christianity is not a political or military movement like Islam that can expand by the sword. (The Crusades were a failed error on the part of a minority.) Nor is Christianity simply the life customs and mythology of a populous culture, emerging slowly out of the mists of common practice and lore, like Hinduism.

Christianity burst onto the scene, like Minerva emerging fully formed from Zeus's head. True, our understanding of various doctrines has developed through the church's history, but we trace them all back to our one teacher, Jesus Christ. His life and teaching, his death and his victory over death are together the exploding nucleus which has propelled this faith across Asia, Europe, Africa, and the globe. It all began in him.

It is this One, easily the most influential figure ever to live, who will be the subject for our studies in Matthew, Mark, Luke, John, and Acts—the section we have called "The Truth About Jesus." To learn this truth, we will display one of the strange riches of the Christian faith: the accounts of four men who were contemporaries of Jesus—John, the disciple; Luke, the historian friend of the apostles; Mark, the young, well-placed friend in Jerusalem; and perhaps the strangest one of the lot, Matthew, the bureaucrat, the tax-collecting, pencil-pushing scribbler. Matthew was a tortured combination—Jewish by birth and Roman by employment. More important, he was one of the twelve disciples called by Jesus.

All four authors include in their accounts the same basic themes about the mission and message of Jesus, and you will find no disagreement between them. For example, our discussion of Mark is titled "Jesus, the Son of Man," because this is a title Jesus uses to refer to himself that is very prominent in Mark's Gospel. But we should not conclude that "Son of Man" is not used in Matthew. Indeed, it is used about thirty times in Matthew.[2] And just one more example: where would an experienced Bible reader guess the following verse is from? "All things have been committed to me by my Father. No one knows the Son except the Father, and no one knows the Father except the Son and those to whom the Son chooses to reveal him." An experienced Bible reader may think this sounds like John's Gospel, but it is Matthew 11:27.

These four verbal portraits of Jesus clearly present a unified picture. They are talking about the same person. And yet the Bible provides four separate accounts for a reason. The Lord did not leave just one testimony. Each Gospel writer emphasizes slightly different themes, and we can learn something fresh

---

[2] See Matt. 8:20; 9:6; 10:23; 11:19; 12:8, 32, 40; 13:37, 41; 16:13, 27-29; 17:9, 12, 22; 19:28; 20:18, 28; 24:27, 30, 37, 39, 44; 25:31; 26:2, 24, 45, 64.

about Jesus from each one. Ultimately, all four will enrich our understanding of Jesus himself.

INTRODUCING MATTHEW

We begin where the New Testament begins, with Matthew, who presents the new with an understanding of its rootedness in the past. Everyone agrees that Matthew's Gospel was written in the decades immediately following the life of Jesus. Matthew's name is at the top of the book, but nowhere is Matthew named in the text itself. Nevertheless, it seems likely that the apostle Matthew was the author. From the earliest history of the church, other writers quoting from the text cite him as the author. And nothing in the book would lead us to think he did not write it. The book is written in fairly good Greek, which a tax collector and scribal official such as Matthew would be trained in. No other name has been closely associated with the book. And, honestly, there would be little reason for an anonymous writer to ascribe anything to Matthew. Matthew's background was not prestigious. A number of books were written right after the New Testament period under the assumed identity of someone famous. But these pseudonymous writers picked Peter, or Paul, or John. Nobody would have picked Matthew.

Pulling down Matthew's document from the shelf of history, what do we find? What does Matthew tell us about Jesus?

Some people expect to find the religious inventor *par excellence*. Jesus, they like to imagine, really knew how to make up a religion. He discovered the key to the human psyche and could market himself, or let himself be marketed, better than anyone ever.

Other people expect to find a Horatio Alger story, some self-made hero who has pulled himself up by his own bootstraps.

But if either group were to take up Matthew's Gospel and begin reading it carefully, they would not find someone who was a religious innovator with a product to sell or a self-made man, though Jesus certainly did teach some new things. Rather, they would find someone who thought and taught—indeed, who embodied and personified—what people had been taught not just for decades or centuries, but for millennia before him. It was as if history itself had been prepared for *him*.

Matthew provides a deeply textured portrait of Christ. What does this portrait portray? Was Jesus about something new? That is what the religious leaders at the time thought. We must go back two thousand years and listen to Matthew tell us what caused this startling phenomenon of *Christ*-ianity.

Specifically, we want to ask three questions: 1) What does this book say? 2) Was Jesus more *new* or more *Jew*? 3) Who is Jesus?

WHAT DOES THIS BOOK SAY?

First, what does this book say? When you read Matthew's Gospel, which took me two hours to read aloud, you encounter many familiar things. You find the Golden Rule and the Lord's Prayer, the Sermon on the Mount and the Great Commission, the baby Jesus and Peter's declaration that Jesus is the Christ. You find Jesus' teaching on the church, discipline, and divorce.

Matthew presents Jesus' ministry in seven sections. The first four chapters provide an introduction. They include a genealogy and an account of Jesus' infancy, his baptism, and his preparation for ministry. The three concluding chapters in Matthew, chapters 26 to 28, recount his suffering, his death on the cross, and his resurrection.

The great bulk of the book is the middle section, chapters 5 though 25, which comprises the body of Jesus' ministry. These middle chapters easily divide into five sections. Each of these sections begins with a long teaching block, followed by narrative. Matthew is the only Gospel with this structure. We get the longest sermons of Jesus in this book.

Let me take you through those five sections. The first covers chapters 5–9, and comprises the Sermon on the Mount and accounts of a number of Jesus' healings. In this first section, Matthew appears to be establishing Jesus' authority as a teacher and healer. Jesus is someone we are supposed to hear, trust, and obey.

Chapters 10–12 make up the second section, which shows a rising opposition to Jesus' ministry. In chapter 10 Jesus prepares his disciples for this opposition, some of which they experience in chapters 11 and 12. This section is helpful for the Christian who is experiencing opposition to his or her faith.

From chapter 13 through the middle of chapter 16, this opposition leads to the formation of two camps—those who are beginning to see that Jesus is the Christ, as Peter acknowledges, and those who do not. Jesus teaches in the block of parables in chapter 13 that a polarization happens when the kingdom of heaven comes. This polarization is then acted out in the remaining chapters. This section is helpful for reorienting us outward for evangelism. God has a concern that is going to push us out even amid people who may disagree with us about who Jesus is.

The fourth section begins at what people say is the turning point in the

Gospel. The hinge of Matthew is Peter's confession of Jesus as the Messiah, which ends the previous section. We then read,

> From that time on, Jesus began to explain to his disciples that he must go to Jerusalem and suffer many things at the hands of the elders, chief priests and teachers of the law, and that he must be killed and on the third day be raised to life (16:21).

In the rest of chapter 16 and then throughout chapters 17 and 18, Jesus teaches about discipleship, corrects misunderstandings, and shows his disciples how to live together. The block of parables in chapter 18 does this by teaching about the church. Jesus answers questions like, How are we to deal with sin in the church? How are we to forgive one another? It is almost as if Jesus, seeing the opposition in chapters 10–12 and the division into two camps in 13 to 16, now turns and directly instructs those who have decided to follow him. This section is helpful for dealing with wrong expectations in the church.

Then there is the final, large section of Matthew's Gospel—chapters 19 to 25—that focuses on judgment. The conflict grows as the opposition to Jesus intensifies in the first half of the section, and then Jesus' promise of judgment upon Israel for rejecting the Messiah becomes obvious in a long teaching section in the second half. Here it is clear that God will judge the leaders of the people, the temple will be destroyed, and, according to Jesus' parables in chapter 25, everybody will finally be judged by God. Those words can be more difficult to hear, but they are also helpful, especially when we as Christians feel discouraged, thinking that God will never win. He doesn't seem to be winning in our life, or in the world around us. This section is a reminder from Jesus that God intends to bring the whole world into judgment. It is helpful for encouraging us even when we see no ground for hope.

There you have the five main sections in the middle: Jesus' authority in 5–9, opposition to him in 10–12, polarization concerning him in 13–16, teaching about discipleship in 16–18, and a promise of judgment on those who reject him in 19–25. Add the introductory chapters 1–4 about his birth and beginning of his ministry, and the concluding chapters 26–28 about his arrest, trial, suffering, crucifixion, and resurrection, and you have the story of Jesus as presented by Matthew.

All of it is laid out to bring us to the core of Matthew's message, and the core of our concern for understanding who Jesus is. Which brings us to our second question.

WAS JESUS MORE NEW OR MORE JEW?

Jesus the New

With all this opposition from the Jewish leadership, including their final rejection of him and his rejection of them, was Jesus more new or more Jew? Stepping back and looking at the whole of Matthew's Gospel, we find the tremendous story of a teacher and preacher, a rabbi, a faithful Jew, and one who knew the Old Testament and was certain it would be fulfilled in his ministry. As he taught and performed miracles, his mission caught the imagination of the Hebrew people, and they began calling him by titles close to their hearts—Son of Man, Son of David, Messiah, the Christ. This figure was not so much the founder of a new religion as he was the inheritor and interpreter of a deep, ancient stream of God's special revelation of himself to his special people.

Not that there was *nothing* new about Jesus and his ministry. Whole books have been written about what was new in the ministry of Jesus. My own Bible has a table of contrasts between the Old and New Testaments (it does not provide a table of continuities!). Certainly there is a lot of newness in Matthew. Jesus talked about new wine, new wine skins, and new treasures. In Matthew 24, Jesus taught that the temple, the gigantic building in which he was standing, was going to be destroyed. This destruction would have huge implications. Think about how the Judaism of the time would be rearranged. Animal sacrifices would end. Elsewhere in the Gospel, Jesus described his own body as the temple, and said that he would die as the ransom for the sins of many. The vision Jesus presented was one of considerable change.

The replacement of the temple had other implications, including the end of the priesthood and a decline in the significance of the earthly city of Jerusalem. Matthew, like the other three Gospel writers, shows that Jesus worked to include people from all nations, not just Israel. This is clear from the Gospel's beginning, when Gentile wise men came to worship him, to the Gospel's end, when Jesus instructed his disciples to "go and make disciples of all nations." The good news Jesus brought and proclaimed was meant for all nations. His mission had a global reach. While we will look at this more clearly in Luke's Gospel, only Matthew contains the statement that "the kingdom of God will be taken away from you [ethnic Israel] and given to a people who will produce its fruit" (21:43). Only Matthew uses the parable of the sheep and the goats to picture a universal judgment. And only Matthew records this final call of Jesus to preach the gospel to all *ethne*, all nations.

Jesus the Jew

Yet having said all this, we notice from the first sentence of Matthew's Gospel how Jewish this Jesus was. You can hear the plaintive, haunting note of the *shofar,* the ram's horn, blowing as you read, "A record of the genealogy of Jesus Christ the son of David, the son of Abraham" (1:1). Mark does not begin with a sentence like this, nor does Luke or John.

Matthew is the most Jewish of the Gospels. It was written in the first century A.D., a formative time for Judaism. After the destruction of the temple in A.D. 70, the ancient religion of Judaism was bound to change. In fact, only two main branches of Judaism survived after the Roman invasion and destruction—Rabbinic Judaism, which directly descended from the Pharisees of the New Testament Gospels, and Jewish Christianity. A century earlier, before the time of Jesus, there were many variations of Judaism. And Matthew's Gospel appears to have been written at a time when the break either loomed just ahead or had just happened. Issues of what it meant to be Jewish were both critical and problematic for those who followed Jesus. So it is no surprise that Jesus taught and Matthew recorded much about the Jews' reaction to Jesus during his ministry.

Some of those reactions were quite severe. For example, toward the end of Matthew we find what has been called the most anti-Semitic statement in the New Testament. Jesus had been handed over to the Roman governor Pilate, who was trying to find a way to let him off because he did not find anything wrong with Jesus. He certainly did not want to kill Jesus. Yet the people yelled back, "'Crucify him!' When Pilate saw that he was getting nowhere, but that instead an uproar was starting, he took water and washed his hands in front of the crowd. 'I am innocent of this man's blood,' he said. 'It is your responsibility!' All the people answered, 'Let his blood be on us and on our children!'" (27:23b-25). Is retelling this account anti-Semitic? When we hear the conflict recounted in Matthew between Jesus and many Jewish leaders, we can well imagine something like this being said. And if this happened, is it wrong to recount it as history just because it is unpleasant or difficult to read? Shall we not have any books on slavery or the Holocaust? Matthew is honest about the conflict between Jesus and the Jewish leaders.

Matthew makes it clear that Jesus taught new things. But he shows that Jesus was not simply about something new. This Gospel is full of references to Old Testament Scriptures that were being fulfilled in the life and ministry of Jesus. We read that the virgin birth of Jesus was predicted in the Old Testament (1:22-23), as was the flight from Egypt (2:15), the slaughter of the Innocents (2:17-18), the fact that Jesus was from Nazareth (2:23), and his ministry in

Galilee (4:13-16). His healings fulfilled prophecy (8:16-17), as did the fact that he did not talk much about his healings publicly (12:15-21). The people's lack of understanding was predicted (13:14), as was the fact that Jesus taught in parables (13:34-35). Jesus' riding a donkey's colt was predicted (21:4-5). Jesus also taught that his arrest and suffering had to happen so that "the Scriptures be fulfilled" (26:54) and so that "the writings of the prophets might be fulfilled" (26:56). We find that even Judas's betrayal of Jesus for thirty pieces of silver had been predicted (27:9).

Many more Old Testament prophecies are mentioned both in this Gospel and in the others. The Old Testament came to fulfillment in the ministry of Jesus. Indeed, Jesus taught in the Sermon on the Mount that he had come to fulfill the whole of the Law and the Prophets (5:17). Jesus was not an innovator, but the answer. He was not an inventor, but the fulfillment.

In Matthew, Jesus presents himself as the key to understanding the Old Testament Scriptures. If you were to rip your Bible in half and take away the Old Testament and read it, Jesus would say to you, "You won't understand that book without me. It all serves as a pointer to me." He is the authoritative interpreter of Israel's religious writings and traditions. He explains them. From Genesis to Malachi, from teaching on marriage and divorce to the Ten Commandments and love, Jesus quotes the Old Testament and tells us what it means.

Sometimes people see Jesus' conflict with the Jewish leaders and say, "Wow, he went in there and smashed up Judaism!" Well, no, Jesus restored Judaism to its full glory. He displayed why the Law, the Prophets, the temple, and its customs were there—for the glory of God through the display of God's holiness, the conviction of human sin, and the provision of mercy in the form of a sacrifice. Ultimately, it all points to Christ who is holy God, perfect man, and merciful sacrifice. Indeed, beginning with his forty days and nights in the wilderness—mirroring Israel's forty-year Exodus wanderings—Jesus displays himself as the obedient and true Israel throughout his ministry. He is the obedient son that Jacob was supposed to be but never was.

But to finally settle the question of whether Jesus is more new or more Jew, we have to turn to our third question.

WHO IS JESUS?

Jesus and Old Testament Figures

Who is Jesus? Jesus' ministry is deeply rooted in the history and life of the nation of Israel. We see a glimmer of Old Testament figures in Jesus' ministry, as if those figures lived and ruled and prophesied for the purpose of helping us understand Jesus more than they lived for themselves or their own times! In Jesus we see the fruition of the lives of these great men of the Old Testament.

We see Abraham, dimly in the background. He shows up first in Matthew's opening genealogy: "A record of the genealogy of Jesus Christ the son of David, the son of Abraham." He is treated as the progenitor of the faith in chapters 3 and 8, and Jesus invokes God's own name in relation to his covenant with Abraham in chapter 22: "I am the God of Abraham . . ." (22:32). The faith that began with God's call to Abraham is brought to culmination in Jesus.

Even more clearly, the figure of Moses looms across Matthew's picture of Jesus. In 8:4, Jesus enjoined obedience to the commands given through Moses. Moses stood with Elijah at the Transfiguration, signifying the Law and the Prophets' testimony to Jesus. Moses' teaching was Christ's reference point for discussing with the Pharisees everything from divorce to the resurrection.[3] And many subtle parallels to the life of Moses are scattered throughout the Gospel: miracles surrounding Jesus' infancy; turmoil with the ruler of the land; a massacre of male babies his age; his journey to and from Egypt; and his forty-day sojourn in the wilderness. Jesus even begins his teaching ministry on a "Mount," subtly reminding readers of another mountain—Mount Sinai. Some have seen a parallel between the five teaching sections we have noted and the five Old Testament books of the Law. Whether Matthew intended to make this parallel or not, I do not know. But certainly Matthew intends to present Jesus as the new Moses, because Jesus appears to have understood himself as the new Lawgiver for Israel.

Beside Abraham and Moses is one other Old Testament figure: David. David was the planner of the temple, the greatest king, and the psalmist who probably wrote more of the Old Testament than anyone except Moses. Perhaps more than anyone else from the Old Testament, David prefigures Jesus in Matthew's Gospel.

One interesting feature of the Gospel is the frequent occurrence of statements of comparison, statements that quickly refute any notion that Jesus was just a humble moral teacher. He was not. Matthew writes,

> At that time Jesus went through the grainfields on the Sabbath. His disciples were hungry and began to pick some heads of grain and eat them. When the Pharisees saw this, they said to him, "Look! Your disciples are doing what is unlawful on the Sabbath."
>
> He answered, "Haven't you read what David did when he and his companions were hungry? He entered the house of God, and he and his companions

---

[3] Matt. 19:7-8 and 22:24; cf. 23:2.

ate the consecrated bread—which was not lawful for them to do, but only for the priests. Or haven't you read in the Law that on the Sabbath the priests in the temple desecrate the day and yet are innocent? I tell you that one greater than the temple is here" (12:1-6).

Well, that last comparison would have gotten the attention of Jesus' Jewish audience. It is unclear how exactly the Greek pronoun for "one" (in the phrase "one greater than the temple") should be translated into English, whether as "one" or as "someone." But it is very clear in the narrative to whom Jesus was referring: he was referring to himself. Here is a first-century Jew referring to himself as greater than the temple!

Yet he was not done. A few lines later we read,

> Then some of the Pharisees and teachers of the law said to him, "Teacher, we want to see a miraculous sign from you."
>
> He answered, "A wicked and adulterous generation asks for a miraculous sign! But none will be given it except the sign of the prophet Jonah. For as Jonah was three days and three nights in the belly of a huge fish, so the Son of Man will be three days and three nights in the heart of the earth. The men of Nineveh will stand up at the judgment with this generation and condemn it; for they repented at the preaching of Jonah, and now one greater than Jonah is here" (12:38-41).

Again it is clear to whom he was referring with this comparison: himself. He was describing himself as greater than the prophet Jonah.

And in the next verse, we read, "The Queen of the South will rise at the judgment with this generation and condemn it; for she came from the ends of the earth to listen to Solomon's wisdom, and now one greater than Solomon is here" (12:42). Again, Jesus was referring to himself in comparison with King Solomon.

Jesus presented himself as greater than the temple, greater than the prophet Jonah, and greater than King Solomon. He was the priest, prophet, and king. Matthew's message about Jesus is no more than Jesus' own message—Jesus is the priest to end all priests, the prophet to end all prophets, and the king who will one day end all other kings. These others are mere foreshadows of him.

Jesus as Son of David

This is why Jesus is referred to as "Son of David." We have seen how the Gospel begins: "A record of the genealogy of Jesus Christ, the son of David." Several lines later, the angel of the Lord addresses Jesus' earthly father as "Joseph son of David" (1:20), because the Messiah was supposed to be of the line of David.

It is interesting to notice who recognized Jesus as the Son of David and called him by this name. In chapter 9, two blind men shouted out, "Have mercy on us, Son of David" (9:27). When Jesus healed a blind, mute man in chapter 12, the people were astonished and asked each other, "Could this be the Son of David?" (12:23). In chapter 15, a Canaanite woman with a demon-possessed daughter cried out, "Son of David" (15:22). Another two blind men called out to Jesus as "Son of David" in 20:30-31. And in chapter 21 the crowds greeted Jesus at his triumphal entry into Jerusalem with "Hosanna to the Son of David" (21:9). Evidently, in 21:15, the chief priests and teachers of the law became alarmed when children began shouting these words.

And there is this interesting exchange:

> While the Pharisees were gathered together, Jesus asked them, "What do you think about the Christ? Whose son is he?"
>
> "The son of David," they replied.
>
> He said to them, "How is it then that David, speaking by the Spirit, calls him 'Lord'? For he says,
>
> > "The Lord said to my Lord:
> > "Sit at my right hand
> > until I put your enemies
> > under your feet."'
>
> If then David calls him 'Lord,' how can he be his son?" (22:41-45).

This is one of the most frequently quoted passages from the Old Testament in the New, and Jesus used it often to explain his ministry to people.

How do we understand this quotation? Jesus was quoting Psalm 110:1, where David wrote, "The LORD said to my Lord . . ." Since David calls someone "my Lord" who was not Yahweh, Jesus understood that David knew the Messiah would be one of his descendants. Yet David would not normally refer to a descendant as greater than himself with a title like "My Lord." David knew—and Jesus knew—that David's son would be greater than he was.

The people understood that Jesus was something more. Those who called out to Jesus as "Son of David" often did so in connection with healing. In Matthew 12:22-23 they wondered if he was the Son of David explicitly on the basis of his miraculous healings. And in 15:31 we read, "The people were amazed when they saw the mute speaking, the crippled made well, the lame walking and the blind seeing. And they praised the God of Israel." These types of miracles were associated with the great day to come, which the Israelites hoped for. And they were seeing it! So they began to wonder, is this the one?

Another shepherd had arisen in Israel, one even greater than David, or as the hymn says, "Great David's greater son." Matthew says of Jesus at one point, "When he saw the crowds, he had compassion on them, because they were harassed and helpless, like sheep without a shepherd" (9:36). This Son of David was compassionate and caring. In a surprising fulfillment of David's great psalm, "The Lord is my Shepherd," Peter finally realized that this shepherd he had come to know was in fact the Messiah: "You are the Christ" (16:16).

Jesus as Messiah

Matthew makes it clear that Jesus is the Christ (the Greek word for Messiah). Four times in the first chapter he uses this title for Jesus, indicating that he is the Anointed One for whom the people of God have waited long (1:1, 16, 17, 18). The rest of the Gospel continues this theme. When the Magi came looking for the king of the Jews in chapter 2, Herod knew they were looking for "the Christ."

The first person Matthew quotes to give voice to this title in Jesus' adult ministry is the imprisoned John the Baptist: "When John heard in prison what Christ was doing, he sent his disciples to ask him, 'Are you the one who was to come, or should we expect someone else?'" (11:2-3). John clearly knew that Jesus was special, indeed, that he was the Lamb of God. We know that from the account of his baptism of Jesus. It seems that John knew the Messiah so well from the Old Testament that he expected the Messiah's ministry to look like Jesus' ministry. Yet it seems he only half-recognized Jesus as the Messiah because of Christ's teaching, preaching, and healing. Perhaps this partly explains why Jesus called John the greatest of the prophets but the least in the kingdom of God (11:11). God had not yet revealed to anyone that Jesus was the Messiah. That happened in chapter 16 with Peter. Nor had God yet given the Spirit-filled baptism of the resurrected and seated Messiah. That began to happen in Acts 2. Yet through the grace he had been given, John the Baptist so knew the Old Testament he could dimly perceive the Messiah in Jesus.

Then, of course, Matthew records in Peter's mouth the words that everyone agrees provide the hinge of Matthew's Gospel.

> When Jesus came to the region of Caesarea Philippi, he asked his disciples, "Who do people say the Son of Man is?"
>
> They replied, "Some say John the Baptist; others say Elijah; and still others, Jeremiah or one of the prophets."
>
> "But what about you?" he asked. "Who do you say I am?"
>
> Simon Peter answered, "You are the Christ, the Son of the living God."
>
> Jesus replied, "Blessed are you, Simon son of Jonah, for this was not

revealed to you by man, but by my Father in heaven." . . . Then he warned his disciples not to tell anyone that he was the Christ (Matt. 16:13-17, 20).

Jesus accepted Peter's statement that he was the Messiah. And Peter understood that Jesus was more than David's son and Messiah—he was the Son of the living God. This was what the Pharisees did not understand when confronted with Psalm 110.

Interestingly, the title Messiah, or Christ, is used more sparingly in Matthew than the title Son of David. Behind this is what we call the messianic secret. Throughout the Gospels as here in Matthew 16, we find Jesus telling his disciples and others not to tell people he is the Messiah. The people had a lot of false ideas about the Messiah, mostly thinking of him in his political aspects and little more (e.g., Isa. 9:6-7). They believed this person would come and liberate them from the rule of Rome, but they did not combine the promise of Isaiah 9 with the promise of Isaiah 53. The king would also be a suffering servant, bearing the sins of his people. Other sections of prophecy were also ignored. Not wanting them to be confused by the word, Jesus did not use the title very much. But Jesus pulled these different prophecies together in his person—king and servant—as the true Messiah.

During Jesus' trial, the high priest told him, "'I charge you under oath by the living God: Tell us if you are the Christ, the Son of God'" (Matt. 26:63). And his response was not received well: "Then they [the chief priests] spit in his face and struck him with their fists. Others slapped him and said, 'Prophesy to us, Christ. Who hit you?'" (26:67-68). Clearly, the Jewish leadership understood who Jesus was presenting himself to be. Pilate too, though more disinterestedly, referred to Jesus by this title, almost as if to avoid unnecessarily offending frenzied partisans of Jesus who might be lurking about, a bit like addressing a deranged person as "Zerco, Lord of the universe" because the individual refers to himself that way. Or maybe that is too cynical. Maybe Pilate saw something in Jesus as well. If so, he only becomes more culpable. Matthew writes, "So when the crowd had gathered, Pilate asked them, 'Which one do you want me to release to you: Barabbas, or Jesus who is called Christ?'" (27:17). Then in verse 22, "'What shall I do, then, with Jesus who is called Christ?' Pilate asked. They all answered, 'Crucify him!'"

The irony is almost unimaginable—the people asked their oppressors to kill the one who had come to liberate them more fully than they could ever imagine.

So Matthew and the Magi, John the Baptist and Peter, the priests and Pilate all gave some recognition that Jesus was or claimed to be the Messiah. But did Jesus call himself the Messiah? The answer is a clear yes. In chapter 16, he basically admitted it to his disciples after Peter's confession: "Then he warned his disciples not to tell anyone that he was the Christ" (16:20). And in chapter 22, Jesus asked the Pharisees whose son the Christ would be. "'The son of David,' they replied" (22:42). They understood something about his human descent, but they did not see that he was something more. So Jesus took them to Psalm 110:1 to show them the truth about the Messiah.

Jesus also taught that there is only one true Messiah: "Nor are you to be called 'teacher,' for you have one Teacher, the Christ" (23:10). False messiahs would abound: "For many will come in my name, claiming, 'I am the Christ' and will deceive many" (24:5). And again, "At that time if anyone says to you, 'Look, here is the Christ!' or, 'There he is!' do not believe it" (24:23). Finally, when the high priest directly asked Jesus, "'I charge you under oath by the living God: Tell us if you are the Christ, the Son of God,'" Jesus answered clearly and unambiguously, "'Yes, it is as you say'" (26:63-64).

Jesus of Nazareth taught that he was the Christ, the Messiah. He knew he was the one who God had promised would fulfill his age-old plan to have a people for himself.

People's Response to Jesus

Not that everyone understood that, or does today!

One of the most interesting parts of these Gospels, and one thing that inspires our confidence in them, is their honesty with details that are not very neat. Consider how slowly the disciples came to belief. Small-in-faith Peter sunk into the Sea of Galilee (14:30). A group of the disciples unwittingly threatened to bog Jesus down with the worry that "the Pharisees were offended" by his teaching (15:12). Peter confessed Jesus as the Messiah, and then told this Messiah his plans were wrong (16:22). The disciples failed to heal an epileptic boy for lack of belief (17:16-17). I could go on, but the point is clear. The disciples—who had become the leaders of the church by the time Matthew wrote this account—were faith-midgets during the ministry of Jesus. They did not seem to understand him.

Who did understand Jesus? A strange assortment of people.

In chapter 11 Jesus prayed, "I praise you, Father, Lord of heaven and earth, because you have hidden these things from the wise and learned, and revealed them to little children. Yes, Father, for this was your good pleasure" (11:25).

There were only two people in Matthew's Gospel whose faith evoked a positive reaction—even astonishment—from Jesus: a Roman centurion and a Canaanite woman, representing two groups with whom the Jews were at particular enmity. The centurion said to Jesus,

"Just say the word, and my servant will be healed. For I myself am a man under authority, with soldiers under me. I tell this one, 'Go,' and he goes; and that one 'Come,' and he comes. I say to my servant, 'Do this,' and he does it" (8:8-9).

Jesus was astonished at how well this Roman occupier understood Jesus' own authority. He also praised the Canaanite woman, whom he first rebuffed by calling her a dog—to which she replied, "'Yes, Lord, . . . but even the dogs eat the crumbs that fall from their masters' table'" (15:27). Both of these Gentiles accepted without question Jesus' authority and mission as he defined it. And they were certain he could meet their need because they saw him for who he really was: one who had authority over all and a concern for all.

Rightly, then, we find people worshiping Jesus throughout this Gospel. The Magi worshiped him at the beginning (2:2-11). Jesus told Satan that God alone is to be worshiped (4:10) and then he accepted worship three times: from the disciples in the boat who had seen him walk on water (14:33), from the woman at the tomb after his resurrection (28:9), and from the disciples who saw the resurrected Jesus (28:17). "But," the always-honest Matthew writes, "some doubted."

The message of Matthew is that Jesus is the Christ, the Son of David, and the long-predicted Messiah.

CONCLUSION

In the last twenty-five years, there has been a scientific theory gaining ground called the "anthropic principle" (after *anthropos,* the Greek word for man). Named at a conference in 1973 by Cambridge astrophysicist Brandon Carter, this principle says that "the seemingly unrelated constants in physics have one strange thing in common—these are precisely the values you need if you want to have a universe capable of producing life. In essence, the anthropic principle came down to the observation that all the myriad laws of physics were fine-tuned from the very beginning of the universe for the creation of man—that the universe we inhabit appeared to be expressly designed for the emergence of human beings."[4] This is not coming from a Christian group or even individual scientists who are Christians; increasingly it is coming from nonbelieving scientists. A good book on this is Patrick Glynn's *God: The Evidence,* particularly the first chapter.[5] The "anthropic principle" relates to phenomena such as the exact strength of gravity, the nuclear force, the difference in mass between a proton and a neutron, and how all of these attributes are necessary

---

[4] Patrick Glynn, *God: The Evidence: The Reconciliation of Faith and Reason in a Postsecular World* (Rocklin, Calif.: Forum, 1997), 22-23.
[5] Ibid.

for a world like ours to exist and, particularly, for human life to exist. Scientists give striking examples of how the slightest change of some force in the universe would make everyone flat or make stars explode or otherwise make life unsustainable. Everything is here for a purpose, it seems, from the synthesis of carbon to the weight of ice versus water.

For Christians, of course, the existence of such an intelligent, purposeful designer comes as no surprise. It is his work we perceive not just in chemistry, biology, physics, and astronomy but also in history. We think there is an anthropic principle at work through history too. Through history, God has worked purposely in Israel. He had a purpose in calling Israel, and he sovereignly disposed her history to that end. According to Jesus, that end was Jesus himself. Abraham and Moses, David and Solomon, Jonah and Elijah, John the Baptist and even Judas were all there for him.

And why is he here? Why did Christ come? For us!

This message is clear in Matthew. Jesus is the Messiah, the Christ. And if you want one verse for practical application, do not take a verse on mercy or humility. Consider why Jesus said he came: "The Son of Man did not come to be served, but to serve, and to give his life as a ransom for many" (20:28).

Matthew teaches that you and I have sinned. We have separated ourselves from God. And now we are under his just judgment. Every single one of us. But Christ has come in love to take the punishment for our sins on himself and to rise in victory over death. And then he has come to us, calling us to repent and believe, to trust in him, to turn from our sins, and to have a new life in him.

You cannot understand Jesus finally without understanding something of yourself. In chapter 9 of his Gospel, Matthew recounts his own calling by Jesus, and the celebration dinner he threw for his tax collector friends and Jesus:

> While Jesus was having dinner at Matthew's house, many tax collectors and "sinners" came and ate with him and his disciples. When the Pharisees saw this, they asked his disciples, "Why does your teacher eat with tax collectors and 'sinners'?"
> On hearing this, Jesus said, "It is not the healthy who need a doctor, but the sick. . . . I have not come to call the righteous, but sinners" (9:10-12, 13b).

What a beautifully economical, self-interpreting response! A person's heart is revealed through the person's ears, how he or she hears—just as your response to this sermon is revealing something about you right now, about what you love or long for, about what bores you or simply does not concern you.

Jesus is so straightforward and unaffected in this passage. "The sick," he says. "Sinners," he says. That is whom the doctor comes for. Righteous, healthy people are not his immediate concern. If you think you are pretty righteous and healthy before God, then in a funny way you are not his immediate concern. No, Jesus has come for the sinners.

Who were the sinners in the room that day? Were they only those tax collectors?

I wonder, when Jesus said to the Pharisees, "It's not the healthy who need a doctor, but the sick . . . I have not come to call the righteous, but sinners," did these Pharisees consider, just for a moment, that *they* might be sick, that *they* might be sinners? Or did they simply think, "Good answer, Rabbi. Those people are pretty bad off," and walk away self-satisfied?

I wonder about us: Are you among the sinners? Are you among the sick? Are you among the spiritually needy?

I promise you this. You will finally realize who Jesus is only when you realize who you are. You will understand his fullness only when you come to see your own need.

Let us pray:

Lord God, we praise you for your love shown by coming and taking on our frail flesh. By suffering in the Garden of Gethsemane. By agreeing to death, even death on a cross, to be the ransom for us. We praise you as the one who so loves the church that you laid down your life for her. O God, we pray that your Holy Spirit would require our hearts to give up ourselves to you in worship. For Jesus' sake. Amen.

Questions for Reflection

1. Why does the New Testament present four different accounts of the life of Jesus (Matthew, Mark, Luke, and John)? This chapter mentions a few possible answers. Find them and then reflect further on your own.

2. What are some of the ways people today characterize who Jesus is? On what authority do they typically base their opinions?

3. Who do you say Jesus Christ is?

4. If you belong to a church, who does your church teach Jesus Christ is? How often and in what ways does it teach this? If someone who has never heard of Christianity spent a Sunday at your church, would they be able to say who Jesus is? If you are an ordinary (non-staff) member of a congregation, what role do you see yourself playing within your church (reading Galatians 1:6-9 might help you answer this last question)?

5. According to the Gospel of Matthew, can we just rip our Bibles in half and walk away with just the New Testament in our hands? Why not?

6. Matthew clearly emphasizes the Jewish heritage of Jesus Christ and, we might say, of Christianity generally. Abraham, Moses, and David all point to Jesus! Why did God not simply begin the Bible with Jesus, or even place him shortly after the Fall? What did God use all of this history to teach us about himself? About ourselves? How does Jesus Christ then *complete* or *fulfill* what we can learn about God and ourselves from the Old Testament?

7. Matthew also teaches that Jesus fulfills the Old Testament role of prophet (who brings God's word to God's people), priest (who intercedes before God on behalf of God's people), and king (who exercises God's rule over God's people). How does Jesus fulfill the role of prophet? Priest? King?

8. We have seen that Matthew paints the deeply ironic picture of the Jewish people asking their oppressors to kill the very one who came to liberate, or free, them more fully than they could ever imagine. What did Jesus really come to liberate them from? What liberation do we all ultimately need?

9. What are some other areas of life in which we seek liberation, or freedom? How can these ambitions deceive us from recognizing the true liberation that we need?

10. Did Peter and the disciples understand right away who Jesus was? What does this teach us about the growth of faith in individuals' lives? What implications does this have for how we disciple others, whether our own children or other members of our church?

11. Jesus said, "It is not the healthy who need a doctor, but the sick. . . . I have not come to call the righteous, but sinners" (Matt. 9:10-12, 13b). Do you perceive yourself as among the spiritually sick? How does this show itself in how you interact with your family? With members of your church? With non-Christians?

THE MESSAGE OF MARK: JESUS, THE SON OF MAN

WHO IS HE, REALLY? INTRODUCING MARK

JESUS AND MARK: THE STORY OF JESUS

Source: Peter

Structure

Style

JESUS AND OTHERS: RESPONSES TO JESUS

Some Believed

Some Were Confused

Some Were Antagonistic

The Secret

JESUS ON JESUS: THE TEACHING OF JESUS

What "Son of Man" Means

 Himself

 Human

 More than human

 Messenger

 Messiah

What the Son of Man Will Do

 Bear authority

 Suffer

 Return to judge

JESUS AND YOU: THE REASON FOR JESUS

A Ransom for Sinners

The Example of Peter

2

THE MESSAGE OF MARK: JESUS, THE SON OF MAN

WHO IS HE, REALLY? INTRODUCING MARK[1]

Everyone wants to know all about him. You see his face everywhere. People wonder, what does he really do? What does he really think? Does he care about war in Kosovo or have an answer to the slayings of students at Columbine High School? On social issues, you almost wonder if he is more than one person: some people talk about him as taking this position; others are sure he takes that position.

People want to know, if I give him the opportunity, will he improve my life?

Perhaps most intriguing to journalists and scholars is the question, what is his relationship like with the one he claims is his father?

He is regularly on the cover of magazines. You see him on the cover of *Time* and *Newsweek* sometime in December or in the spring, and maybe once more during the year for marketing purposes. After all, he's so good for sales. Do you know what two covers of *Time* have generated more reader mail than any others? In April 1966, 3,430 letters were sent in reply to the question "Is God Dead?" while in August 1998, 2,121 letters were sent in reply to "Who was Jesus?"

Who was Jesus? I understand the interest in the question, and I can understand why *Time* would pose it. In this last decade, bookstore shelves have creaked under the burgeoning number of books claiming to uncover the true, unvarnished figure of Jesus from the ancient world. All of them are based on the assured results of modern, dispassionate scholarship and previously unavailable evidence, and all of them provide the definitive portrait—Jesus the

---

[1] This sermon was originally preached June 20, 1999, Capitol Hill Baptist Church, Washington, D.C.

Jew, or Jesus the sectarian fanatic Jew, or Jesus the Cynic philosopher, or Jesus the healer, or Jesus the sage, or Jesus the teacher, or Jesus the social justice man, or Jesus the rabbi, or Jesus the Pharisee, or Jesus the humanist, or Jesus the end-of-the-world-is-coming guy, or Jesus the rationalist, or Jesus the visionary. I could go on and on. Historian Paul Johnson commented a few years ago that "using the same texts and scholarly apparatus, dozens, perhaps hundreds, of different Jesuses can be constructed."[2] But there were not hundreds, or even dozens, of Jesuses. There is just one.

What is the truth about this Jesus?

In this series of studies in Matthew, Mark, Luke, John, and Acts, we are not calling on recent historians to creatively reconstruct Christ from the extant materials. No, we are listening to the accounts of first-century followers of Jesus, who either knew those who knew Jesus or who knew him themselves and heard him.

In this study, we turn to what many think was the first Gospel written, the Gospel of Mark. We will begin by looking at:

Jesus and Mark: The Story of Jesus
Then, Jesus and Others: Responses to Jesus
Then, Jesus on Jesus: The Teaching of Jesus
And finally, Jesus and You: The Reason for Jesus

In this, I pray that the truth about Jesus will become clearer to us all.

JESUS AND MARK: THE STORY OF JESUS

Source: Peter

First, where did Mark learn everything he included in his Gospel? Well, Mark was probably an eyewitness to at least some of Jesus' life. Yet Mark's Gospel has also been associated with the apostle Peter. The late-first- and early-second-century church leader Papias, who knew the disciples themselves, said that Mark wrote down everything the apostle Peter told him about the sayings and deeds of Jesus,[3] an idea which the New Testament supports. John Mark (Mark being his Roman name, John being his Jewish name) first became associated with Peter when Peter was freed from prison and went to the home of Mark's mother (Acts 12:12). And then Peter, in his first letter, mentioned that Mark was with him (1 Pet. 5:13). According to tradition, Mark wrote down Peter's account near the end of Peter's ministry in Rome. And that is what we have as the Gospel of Mark.

---

[2] Paul Johnson, *Daily Telegraph* (London), September 13, 1992.
[3] See Papias's *Fragments of Papias,* in Alexander Roberts and James Donaldson, eds., *Ante-Nicene Fathers* vol. 1. (1885; repr. Peabody, Mass.: Hendrickson, 2004), vi.

We do not know exactly when Mark was written. Presumably, Peter either had just died or was fast approaching death. Mark probably felt that time was running out, and the gospel message had to be preserved and published.

Structure

The structure of Mark's Gospel is pretty straightforward. It contains the quickest beginning of any of the Gospels. John's Gospel starts with a prologue about the beginning of creation and the role of "the Word." Luke and Matthew begin their Gospels with genealogies and stories about the birth of Jesus. Not Mark. Mark jumps right in with the ministry of John the Baptist. By 1:16, Jesus is already calling his first disciples.

Chapters 1–8 provide a record of Jesus' ministry in Galilee, where he established himself as a teacher and a miracle-worker. As in Matthew's Gospel, a turning point occurs in the middle of chapter 8 when Peter confessed that Jesus is the Messiah. After this confession, Jesus focused more intently on his closest followers. He warned them of his coming death and resurrection and taught them about the cost of following him. This teaching continued through chapter 10 as they traveled toward Jerusalem. They arrived in Jerusalem in chapter 11 and were greeted with cries of "Hosanna." Chapters 11 to 13 contain Jesus' teaching in Jerusalem over the last week of his life. Chapter 14 contains the Last Supper as well as Jesus' betrayal, arrest, and arraignment before the Sanhedrin. Chapter 15 describes his appearance before Pilate, his conviction, his being mocked, as well as his crucifixion, death, and burial. Chapter 16 then provides a brief account of Jesus' resurrection.

Style

Mark gives us a vigorous and lively account of Jesus' life. It is the shortest of the four Gospels. It has sixteen chapters and takes about one hour to read. The prose is spare.

More than any other Gospel, Mark highlights action over teaching, which leaves us with the impression of a dramatic story. Mark's favorite word is *euthus,* which means "straightway" or "immediately." For instance, Mark writes in chapter 1, "And immediately, they left their nets . . ." (1:18); "And immediately, he called them . . ." (1:20); "And immediately . . . he entered . . ." (1:21); "And immediately there was . . ." (1:23).[4] Again and again, he cuts to a different camera shot. Like a fast-paced movie, Mark keeps the interest of his readers.

---

[4] *English Standard Version.*

Compared to the other Gospels, Mark does not contain much teaching. Consider Jesus' parables: Luke has twenty-five, Matthew has twenty, while Mark has only seven. Mark presents two parables in chapter 2 about new cloth and new wine, each of which takes up one verse (2:21 and 22). He presents three in chapter 4 about the kingdom: the parables of the sower (4:2-20), the seed which grows (4:26-29), and the mustard seed (4:30-32). And in Jerusalem he presents the parables of the wicked tenants (12:1-11) and the householder (13:34-37). That is all. There is no good Samaritan, no prodigal son, no rich man and Lazarus, no talents, no ten virgins, no house on the rock, and no lost sheep.

But in Mark's account of the events, the details are vivid, sometimes more vivid than what is provided in the other Gospels. We can read through a few passages from his Gospel to gain a feel for his writing before we consider the substance.

Beginning in chapter 5, we read,

> When Jesus got out of the boat, a man with an evil spirit came from the tombs to meet him. This man lived in the tombs, and no one could bind him any more, not even with a chain. For he had often been chained hand and foot, but he tore the chains apart and broke the irons on his feet. No one was strong enough to subdue him. Night and day among the tombs and in the hills he would cry out and cut himself with stones.
>
> When he saw Jesus from a distance, he ran and fell on his knees in front of him (5:2-6).

If we were to compare Mark's account with Matthew or Luke's version of the same story, the differences would be immediately clear—Mark provides far more details (see Matt. 8:28-29; Luke 8:27-28). You can almost feel the vigorous, impetuous Peter recounting this story to Mark.

Or consider this account in chapter 6:

> The apostles gathered around Jesus and reported to him all they had done and taught. Then, because so many people were coming and going that they did not even have a chance to eat, he said to them, "Come with me by yourselves to a quiet place and get some rest."
>
> So they went away by themselves in a boat to a solitary place. But many who saw them leaving recognized them and ran on foot from all the towns and got there ahead of them. When Jesus landed and saw a large crowd, he had compassion on them, because they were like sheep without a shepherd. So he began teaching them many things (6:30-34).

Or this account in chapter 7:

> Then Jesus left the vicinity of Tyre and went through Sidon, down to the Sea of Galilee and into the region of the Decapolis. There some people brought to him a man who was deaf and could hardly talk, and they begged him to place his hand on the man.
>
> After he took him aside, away from the crowd, Jesus put his fingers into the man's ears. Then he spit and touched the man's tongue. He looked up to heaven and with a deep sigh said to him, "Ephphatha!" (which means, "Be opened!"). At this, the man's ears were opened, his tongue was loosened and he began to speak plainly.
>
> Jesus commanded them not to tell anyone. But the more he did so, the more they kept talking about it. People were overwhelmed with amazement. "He has done everything well," they said. "He even makes the deaf hear and the mute speak" (7:31-37).

Then a passage from chapter 8:

> They came to Bethsaida, and some people brought a blind man and begged Jesus to touch him. He took the blind man by the hand and led him outside the village. When he had spit on the man's eyes and put his hands on him, Jesus asked, "Do you see anything?"
>
> He looked up and said, "I see people; they look like trees walking around."
>
> Once more Jesus put his hands on the man's eyes. Then his eyes were opened, his sight was restored, and he saw everything clearly. Jesus sent him home, saying, "Don't go into the village" (8:22-26).

Or this one in chapter 9:

> When they came to the other disciples, they saw a large crowd around them and the teachers of the law arguing with them. As soon as all the people saw Jesus, they were overwhelmed with wonder and ran to greet him.
>
> "What are you arguing with them about?" he asked.
>
> A man in the crowd answered, "Teacher, I brought you my son, who is possessed by a spirit that has robbed him of speech. Whenever it seizes him, it throws him to the ground. He foams at the mouth, gnashes his teeth and becomes rigid. I asked your disciples to drive out the spirit, but they could not."
>
> "O unbelieving generation," Jesus replied, "how long shall I stay with you? How long shall I put up with you? Bring the boy to me."
>
> So they brought him. When the spirit saw Jesus, it immediately threw the boy into a convulsion. He fell to the ground and rolled around, foaming at the mouth.
>
> Jesus asked the boy's father, "How long has he been like this?"

"From childhood," he answered. "It has often thrown him into fire or water to kill him. But if you can do anything, take pity on us and help us."

"'If you can'?" said Jesus. "Everything is possible for him who believes."

Immediately the boy's father exclaimed, "I do believe; help me overcome my unbelief!"

When Jesus saw that a crowd was running to the scene, he rebuked the evil spirit. "You deaf and mute spirit," he said, "I command you, come out of him and never enter him again."

The spirit shrieked, convulsed him violently and came out. The boy looked so much like a corpse that many said, "He's dead." But Jesus took him by the hand and lifted him to his feet, and he stood up.

After Jesus had gone indoors, his disciples asked him privately, "Why couldn't we drive it out?"

He replied, "This kind can come out only by prayer" (9:14-29).

Then there is this account of the moments following Jesus' arrest in the Garden of Gethsemane: "Then everyone deserted him and fled. A young man, wearing nothing but a linen garment, was following Jesus. When they seized him, he fled naked, leaving his garment behind" (14:50-52). We think the fleeing figure was the young John Mark, and that this vignette is kind of like his signature in the book.

Most of the details in these stories are not in the other Gospels even if the stories themselves are present, leading many to think the book recounts what Peter remembered from the events. It has that sort of eye-witness feel.

One more passage is worth mentioning here, one that points to something I like about Mark: Jesus remained freshly strange to those who encountered him, and Mark recorded honestly how people responded to Jesus. So only Mark reported this incident: "Then Jesus entered a house, and again a crowd gathered, so that he and his disciples were not even able to eat." It's almost like Peter's stomach had grumbled so much that he remembered this incident. Yet the story continues: "When his family heard about this, they went to take charge of him, for they said, 'He is out of his mind'" (3:20-21). The fact that Mark included this account is amazing. After all, some critics regard the Gospels as propaganda written by Jesus' followers. They accuse the Gospel writers of trying to dress up the truth and present Jesus as someone who immediately impressed everyone with the idea that he was God. But this is not how the Gospels were written. Jesus' own family thought he was crazy and tried to have him committed. Mark honestly recounted that fact, and his Gospel is popular exactly because of such indicators of historic authenticity.

So Mark's source is impeccable, his structure is clear, and his style is engaging—all of which makes his Gospel a good one to use for evangelism. It is a great book for introducing the gospel and Jesus to non-Christians.

JESUS AND OTHERS: RESPONSES TO JESUS

But we must look into the Gospel and think about what it says. This is the story of Jesus and his life, and a first question to ask is, how did people respond to Jesus?

Some Believed

Some believed Jesus was who he said he was, like the friends of the paralyzed man (2:5), the woman subject to bleeding (5:34), Jairus the synagogue ruler (5:23), the Syrophoenician woman (7:29), blind Bartimaeus (10:52), and the Roman centurion at the cross (15:39). However, when you think about who believed Jesus, you are struck by the fact that, by and large, they were not the religious professionals of the time. Rather, they were individuals on "the outs" of society, like women, foreigners, and the disabled.

Some Were Confused

You would think the disciples would be among those who believed. At best, they believed haltingly. Indeed, many people have noticed that Jesus is most critical of the disciples' failings in this Gospel, which may have something to do with the fact that Peter was the Gospel's source.

The disciples' slowness to believe is most evident in the middle of the Gospel. When the disciples did not understand the parable of the sower and asked Jesus to explain it, he responded, "Don't you understand this parable? How then will you understand any parable?" (4:13). When they were surprised by his ability to calm the storm on the lake, he asked, "Why are you so afraid? Do you still have no faith?" (4:40). They also failed to understand how he could instruct them to feed the five thousand (6:37, 52). And later that same day, "they saw him walking on the lake, [and] they thought he was a ghost. They cried out, because they all saw him and were terrified. Immediately he spoke to them and said, 'Take courage! It is I. Don't be afraid'" (6:49-50). When they asked Jesus about the parable of the clean and unclean cup, he responded, "Are you so dull? . . . Don't you see?" (7:18). Apparently, Jesus did not regard what he was saying as complicated. When he fed a large crowd of people a second time, the disciples were just as uncomprehending and surprised. Immediately following this miracle, Mark writes, "The disciples had forgotten to bring bread except for one loaf they had with them in the boat. 'Be careful,' Jesus warned them. 'Watch out for the yeast of the Pharisees and that of Herod'" (8:14-15). Notice how the disciples did not immediately go to Jesus with their uncertainty:

> They discussed this with one another and said, "It is because we have no bread."
>
> Aware of their discussion, Jesus asked them: "Why are you talking about having no bread? Do you still not see or understand? Are your hearts hardened? Do you have eyes but fail to see, and ears but fail to hear? And don't you remember? When I broke the five loaves for the five thousand, how many basketfuls of pieces did you pick up?"
>
> "Twelve," they replied.
>
> "And when I broke the seven loaves for the four thousand, how many basketfuls of pieces did you pick up?"
>
> They answered, "Seven."
>
> He said to them, "Do you still not understand?" (8:16-21).

And the pattern continues: The disciples did not understand Jesus' teaching about his death and resurrection (9:10). They were shocked by his teaching on wealth and heaven (10:22-27). Again and again this Gospel describes the disciples as amazed or astonished. The reader is tempted to imagine them walking around with their mouths constantly open in amazement.

Yet this did not keep them from acting foolishly. Peter may have been frightened at the eerie glory of the Transfiguration (9:6), but that did not mean he maintained a reverential silence. Instead he blurted out, "It is good for us to be here. Let us put up three shelters—one for you, one for Moses and one for Elijah" (9:5). Then, walking toward Jerusalem, several disciples began to compare their future prospects and even got into a fight over their comparative importance (10:35-45). They didn't seem to get it. When people brought children to Jesus, the disciples rebuked them. But "when Jesus saw this, he was indignant" (10:14), and he told them so!

In all of this, the disciples are symbolized by the blind man whom Jesus healed in stages. Jesus first put spit in the man's eyes, and the man responded, "I see people; they look like trees walking around" (8:24). The disciples' vision, like this man's vision, was half-formed, and the effect was sometimes comical, sometimes tragic. As with the blind man, Jesus had to keep working with them.

Now do not misunderstand me. In all this flaying of the disciples, I am not suggesting you or I could have done better! Rising from the dead was certainly a novel concept, and difficult to get one's head around. Certainly it is still unusual, even if we have become more accustomed to talking about Christ's resurrection.

But when all is said and done, Mark is clear: the disciples were confused and slow to learn.

Some Were Antagonistic

Not everyone in Mark's Gospel was as confused as the disciples. Some clearly understood what Jesus was saying, and they opposed him. The opposition begins in chapters 2 and 3. There is a bit in the middle of chapters 5, 6, and 7. It recedes as Mark focuses on Jesus' interactions with his disciples in chapters 8, 9, and 10. But it recurs in chapters 11 and 12. In chapter 14, it hijacks the story and almost finishes it off.

Plots to take Jesus' life started early, coming in response to his claims. In chapter 2, Jesus made several provocative claims. He professed to be the one who could forgive sins (2:7, 10), the bridegroom of the nation of Israel (2:19-20), and the Lord of the Sabbath (2:28). Of course, all of these were jobs that belonged to God alone. The teachers of the law responded to his claim to forgive sins by charging him with blasphemy (2:7). And the Pharisees objected to his eating with sinners and to his statements about the Sabbath (2:16, 24). Therefore, they watched for Jesus to heal on a Sabbath so that they might bring charges against him. As early as chapter 3, we read, "The Pharisees went out and began to plot with the Herodians how they might kill Jesus" (3:6).

Later in chapter 3, Jesus' family thought he was crazy and tried to take custody of him (3:21), and the teachers of the law thought he was demon-possessed (3:22, 30).

The Gerasenes were so scared after Jesus did a miracle that they asked him to leave their region (5:15-17). The residents of his hometown were offended by him (6:4-5). Herod worried about him (6:16), and the Pharisees kept on challenging him (7:5).

When Jesus entered Jerusalem—and effectively "went national"—the chief priests and the teachers of the law joined the Pharisees and Herodians in the conspiracy to kill him. Hearing what he did and said in the temple, they "began looking for a way to kill him, for they feared him, because the whole crowd was amazed at his teaching" (11:18). They challenged him publicly (11:28-33), but this prompted Jesus to expose their murderous intentions by telling the parable of the tenants (12:1-11). In response to this parable, the chief priests and teachers of the law "looked for a way to arrest him because they knew he had spoken the parable against them. But they were afraid of the crowd; so they left him and went away. Later they sent some of the Pharisees and Herodians to Jesus to catch him in his words. They came to him and said, 'Teacher, we know you are a man of integrity. You aren't swayed by men, because you pay no attention to who they are; but you teach the way of God in accordance with the truth. Is it right to pay taxes to Caesar or not? Should we pay or shouldn't we?' But Jesus knew their hypocrisy. 'Why are you trying to trap me?' he asked. 'Bring me a denarius and let me look at it.' They brought the coin, and he asked them, 'Whose portrait is this? And whose inscription?' 'Caesar's,' they replied. Then Jesus said to them, 'Give to Caesar what is Caesar's and to God what is God's.' And they were amazed at him" (12:12-17). No matter how hard they tried, they couldn't entrap him.

Then the liberal Sadducees took their turn. In the very next passage, they tried to embarrass Jesus by challenging his fundamentalist, literal, and credulous reading of the Jewish holy texts. You can almost hear the barely concealed snickers as they questioned him:

> Then the Sadducees, who say there is no resurrection, came to him with a question. "Teacher," they said, "Moses wrote for us that if a man's brother dies and leaves a wife but no children, the man must marry the widow and have children for his brother. Now there were seven brothers. The first one married and died without leaving any children. The second one married the widow, but he also died, leaving no child. It was the same with the third. In fact, none of the seven left any children. Last of all, the woman died too. At the resurrection whose wife will she be, since the seven were married to her?" (12:18-23).

Maybe they thought a question of this complexity would stymie him.

It did not, and the plotting continued. In chapter 14, we read,

> Now the Passover and the Feast of Unleavened Bread were only two days away, and the chief priests and the teachers of the law were looking for some sly way to arrest Jesus and kill him. "But not during the Feast," they said, "or the people may riot" (14:1-2)

When Judas decided to help these conspirators (14:10-11), the whole story turned in a tragic direction. The opposition to Jesus became so comprehensive it engulfed Pharisees and Sadducees, Jews and Gentiles, foes and even friends. Not only Judas but Peter and the rest of the disciples played their parts in betraying, denying, and deserting Jesus. After Christ's arrest in the Garden of Gethsemane (14:43-49), the disciples melted away into the night, deserting their rabbi and leaving him—literally—to die. "Then everyone deserted him and fled" (14:50).

The Secret

One further thing is worth noting about the response to Jesus. Through the first half of Mark's Gospel, Jesus occasionally attempted to hide his identity as the Messiah, what scholars refer to as "the messianic secret."

In chapter 1, he told the evil spirit who recognized him to "Be quiet!"

(1:25). A few verses later, after driving out many demons, "he would not let the demons speak because they knew who he was" (1:34). One is almost tempted to wonder if the Bible has a misprint—"because they knew who he was"? But the command is repeated. Jesus ordered a leper he healed not to tell anyone about him (1:44), and later in the story he again "gave [the evil spirits] strict orders not to tell who he was" (3:12). Apparently, Jesus even taught in parables partly to reveal, partly to conceal his message (cf. 4:11-12). He downplayed a little girl's sickness (5:39); and when he raised her from the dead, he gave "strict orders not to let anyone know about this" (5:43). When Jesus healed a deaf and mute man, he then told him not to tell anyone (7:36). He gave sight to a blind man from Bethsaida and told him not to enter the village (8:26). And he warned his own disciples "not to tell anyone about him" after Peter confessed him to be the Messiah (8:30).

What was Jesus doing? Was this an "aw, shucks" humility? Was he wiping his feet in the dirt and saying, "Well, it's really not much, being that I'm God and all. Don't think anything of it." I think not. I believe this was a teaching strategy.

His purpose was to shield himself from the attention of the crowds long enough to teach the disciples what the Messiah had really come to do. He was buying time in order to reeducate them and to point to the particular Scriptures that taught about the Messiah but had gone unnoticed. Shortly after the Transfiguration in chapter 9, Jesus left with all his disciples and "did not want anyone to know where they were, because he was teaching his disciples" (9:30-31). He then taught them who he was and what he had come to do.

Once the disciples were reeducated, the "messianic secret" theme evaporated. In chapter 12, Jesus taught publicly in the temple about the Messiah from Psalm 110. His time had nearly come, and he knew it. The disciples' confused assent in the middle chapters gave way to pitched opposition by others in the later chapters. As we have seen, chief priests, the teachers of the law, the Pharisees, and the Sadducees all understood what Jesus was saying, and they made their final moves to kill him.

And what was this secret that led first to confusion and then to opposition? The centerpiece of Mark's Gospel: the truth about who Jesus is.

JESUS ON JESUS: THE TEACHING OF JESUS

If you listen to Jesus' own words in Mark's Gospel, you will find he did teach about matters of morality. But that is not mainly what he taught about. The main thing he taught about was himself. Whatever else Mark was doing with his Gospel, he clearly wrote about who Jesus is.

What "Son of Man" Means

Some people believe that Jesus is simply a humble figure from the past—a rural carpenter-philosopher, someone of accidentally gigantic influence like the movie character Forrest Gump. For evidence, they might point to the title Jesus used to refer to himself, "Son of Man." After all, it sounds like a humble title, as if Jesus is saying, "I'm nobody special. I'm just another run-of-the-mill guy." But when you study the texts themselves you find that Jesus clearly meant more than that with this strange phrase "Son of Man." What did he mean? Well, it is a composite picture.

Himself. Jesus certainly used the phrase "Son of Man" to refer to himself. He meant "I" by it. So while Mark uses the phrase "Son of Man" to refer to Jesus' coming to serve (10:45), Luke uses "I" in an equivalent phrase (22:27). On the other hand, Matthew puts "Son of Man" in Jesus' mouth when he asks for Peter's confession (16:13-15), while Mark uses "I" in his account of the same incident (8:27-30). Except for the name "Jesus," the title "Son of Man" is the most frequent phrase used to refer to Jesus in Mark.

Human. Jesus knew himself to be truly human. This phrase "son of man" was used in the first half of the Old Testament to distinguish between man and God. The poetry of Numbers 23:19, for instance, uses what is called Hebrew parallelism—in which a second line repeats, explains, or amplifies a first line—to define "son of man" as "man" for the reader: "God is not a man, that he should lie, nor a son of man, that he should change his mind." The point is clear: God is not like man. When God speaks, God acts. When he promises, he fulfills. In the book of Job, Bildad uses the same poetic device to offer similarly humbling words for the human race: ". . . how much less man, who is but a maggot—a son of man, who is only a worm!" (25:6).

More than human. But Jesus also understood himself to be more than a normal human. In our discussion of Matthew's Gospel, we saw that Psalm 110:1 was one of Jesus' favorite Old Testament verses for teaching about himself. In the psalm, David says, "The LORD says to my Lord: sit at my right hand." Jesus then asked the Pharisees in Matthew's Gospel how David could call "Lord" someone who was his son (22:41-45). David must have had in mind someone who was more than merely human. Mark also records Jesus' quotation from David (12:36). And Jesus seems to allude to the verse again when he promises the Sanhedrin they "will see the Son of Man sitting at the right hand of the Mighty One" (14:62).

Yet Psalm 110 would not have been the only psalm familiar to Jesus that refers to the Son of Man. Psalm 80:17 reads, "Let your hand rest on the man at your right hand, the son of man you have raised up for yourself." And Psalm

144:3 reads, "O LORD, what is man that you care for him, the son of man that you think of him?" Now the psalmist may not be referring to anything more than God's concern for humanity. But the writer to the Hebrews uses a similar phrase from Psalm 8 to refer to Jesus: "What is man that you are mindful of him, the son of man that you care for him?" (Heb. 2:6; quoting Ps. 8:4). Where would this New Testament writer have learned this? Probably from Jesus. Jesus used the ambiguity in the Psalms to teach about himself.

Psalm 110 and other Psalms make it clear that the coming one is greater than David. How is he greater? Another book in the Old Testament uses the title "Son of Man" to point toward Jesus as a special messenger.

Messenger. The book of Ezekiel uses the title "son of man" more than any other Bible book. God calls the prophet Ezekiel "son of man" ninety-three times. And notice the characteristics that the ministries of Ezekiel and Jesus share. Both were called to ministry at age 30. Both were God's messenger. Both found the people unresponsive. Both came to give a message anyway. Both brought a message of judgment. Great personal cost came to both in giving the message. And both gave what was finally a message of redemption.

Messiah. To the first-century Hebrew mind, the Son of Man was more than a prophet. "Son of Man" was another title for the Messiah. In the Gospel of John, the crowd says to Jesus, "We have heard from the Law that the Christ will remain forever, so how can you say, 'The Son of Man must be lifted up'?" (12:34). The crowd treats the two titles as synonymous. Jesus, when he calls himself the Son of Man, means that he is the Messiah.

What the Son of Man Will Do

What does Mark say the Son of Man—this unique prophet and Messiah—came to do?

Bear authority. Jesus came to bear amazing authority. He taught with authority: "The people were amazed at his teaching, because he taught them as one who had authority" (1:22). He had the authority to cast out demons: again amazed, the people remarked, "A new teaching—and with authority! He even gives orders to evil spirits and they obey him" (1:27; cf. 3:15; 6:7). He had authority to forgive sin: "But that you may know that the Son of Man has authority on earth to forgive sins . . ." (2:10). He also had the authority to be the bridegroom of the people of Israel (2:19) and the authority to be the Lord of the Sabbath (2:28). Who had that kind of authority? No one but God.

Suffer. If you or I were to become convinced that we were God, our first thought would not be, "Therefore, I must suffer." It would probably be, "Therefore, do what I say." But at the same time Jesus taught that he had unusual authority, he also taught that he must suffer. So his instruction to his disciples concerning his identity was as full of the servant language of Isaiah 53 as it was full of the lord language of Psalm 110. Isaiah 53:3 reads, "He was despised and rejected by men, a man of sorrows, and familiar with suffering. Like one from whom men hide their faces he was despised, and we esteemed him not."

When the disciples became excited about the Transfiguration, Jesus told them the Son of Man must suffer much and be rejected (Mark 9:12). When Judas dipped his bread in the bowl during the Last Supper, Jesus said the Son of Man would go just as it was written about him (14:21). And later that night, when Judas led the armed crowd to Jesus, Jesus told the disciples the Son of Man was betrayed into the hands of sinners (14:41).

As we have noted, Jesus began to reeducate his disciples in chapters 8, 9, and 10 immediately after Peter confessed him to be the Messiah (8:29). His teaching was punctuated in these chapters by three great predictions of suffering, predictions that take us to the heart of Jesus' understanding of himself as the Son of Man and Messiah. In 8:31, Jesus told his disciples, "that the Son of Man must suffer many things and be rejected by the elders, chief priests and teachers of the law, and that he must be killed and after three days rise again."

In 9:31, Jesus again privately told them, "The Son of Man is going to be betrayed into the hands of men. They will kill him, and after three days he will rise."

And in 10:32-34, Jesus again took the Twelve aside and told them, "We are going up to Jerusalem . . . and the Son of Man will be betrayed to the chief priests and teachers of the law. They will condemn him to death and will hand him over to the Gentiles, who will mock him and spit on him, flog him and kill him. Three days later he will rise."

Do you realize how strange this is? Jesus has come to teach with the authority of God and to forgive sins. Yet he says the religious leaders of the people will reject him.

Return to judge. So who is Jesus? He taught from Psalm 110 that he is great David's greater son who has come to bear authority. He taught from Isaiah 53 that he has come to be rejected and to suffer to the point of death. But did you notice the twist in the story? He also taught them he would rise from the dead and return to bring judgment. We can see his promise to rise from the dead in the verses quoted above: Mark 8:31; 9:31; and 10:34. He also told Peter, James, and John after the Transfiguration "not to tell anyone what they had seen until the Son of Man had risen from the dead" (9:9).

In Mark's Gospel, Jesus appears to draw from a third great Old Testament passage—Daniel 7—for teaching his disciples about himself. Daniel wrote,

"In my vision at night I looked, and there before me was one like a son of man, coming with the clouds of heaven. He approached the Ancient of Days and was led into his presence. He was given authority, glory, and sovereign power; all peoples, nations and men of every language worshiped him. His dominion is an everlasting dominion that will not pass away, and his kingdom is one that will never be destroyed" (Dan. 7:13-14)

Three times Jesus appears to invoke this passage. First, shortly after Peter rebuked Jesus for saying that the Son of Man must suffer and die, Jesus said, "If anyone is ashamed of me and my words in this adulterous and sinful generation, the Son of Man will be ashamed of him when he comes in his Father's glory with the holy angels" (Mark 8:38).

Second, while Jesus was teaching in the temple courts during his last week in Jerusalem, his disciples marveled at the massive stones (13:1). But Jesus promised that the temple would be destroyed (13:2), that great chaos and judgment would follow (13:5-25), and that "men will see the Son of Man coming in clouds with great power and glory" (13:26).

Third, after his arrest, Jesus was asked directly by the high priest whether he was the Messiah (14:61). Jesus answered, "I am. . . . And you will see the Son of Man sitting at the right hand of the Mighty One and coming on the clouds of heaven" (Mark 14:62).

In Mark's Gospel, Jesus knows who he is. He is David's greater son. He is the suffering servant. And he is the one who will come again to bring judgment. This is Mark's teaching about Jesus: God came in the flesh, was rejected, and will come again in judgment.

JESUS AND YOU: THE REASON FOR JESUS

Now what about Jesus and you? At the very beginning of his book, Mark writes, "The beginning of the gospel about Jesus Christ" (1:1). The word gospel means "good news." So what is the good news? We have seen who Jesus is—David's greater Son, the rejected and despised one, and the one who will return in judgment. But where is the good news in this for us? An understanding of God through the Incarnation? The assurance of final justice? Both of those things are good and important, but there is something more.

A Ransom for Sinners

We see the good news for us when we notice why Jesus came. So far we have read these words from Isaiah about the Messiah: "He was despised and rejected by men, a man of sorrows, and familiar with suffering. Like one from whom men hide their faces he was despised, and we esteemed him not" (53:3). Yet Isaiah goes on in his fifty-third chapter:

> Surely he took up our infirmities
>   and carried our sorrows,
> yet we considered him stricken by God,
>   smitten by him, and afflicted.
> But he was pierced for our transgressions,
>   he was crushed for our iniquities;
> the punishment that brought us peace was upon him,
>   and by his wounds we are healed.
> We all, like sheep, have gone astray,
>   each of us has turned to his own way;
> and the LORD has laid on him
>   the iniquity of us all (53:4-6).

Right before Jesus entered Jerusalem for that final week of his earthly ministry, he told his disciples, "The Son of Man did not come to be served, but to serve, and to give his life as a ransom for many" (Mark 10:45). This one who had come to serve is the one about whom Isaiah was talking in chapter 53. The one who would be pierced for our transgressions and crushed for our iniquities, and the one who would bring us peace and healing by his wounds, is the one who came and gave his life as a ransom for many. Jesus knew Isaiah 53 was about him. He was God come in the flesh both to be rejected by people and to give his life as a ransom for all of those who would repent of their sins and believe in him.

Isaiah further says this promised one would be a guilt offering, and he would justify many by bearing their iniquities.

> It was the LORD'S will to crush him and cause him to suffer,
>   and though the LORD makes his life a guilt offering,
> he will see his offspring and prolong his days,
>   and the will of the LORD will prosper in his hand.
> After the suffering of his soul,
>   he will see the light of life and be satisfied;
> by his knowledge my righteous servant will justify many,
>   and he will bear their iniquities (Isa. 53:10-11).

Listen to Jesus' words again in Mark 10:45: "the Son of Man did not come to be served, but to serve, and to give his life as a ransom for many." Jesus came to serve by being crushed. He came to give his life as a ransom by becoming a guilt offering, and by bearing their iniquities.

The Example of Peter

If the Gospel of Mark is about who Jesus is, it is also about who we are and his claim on our lives. His claim is total. How does Jesus put it in 8:34? "If anyone would come after me, he must deny himself and take up his cross and follow me." To know what denying oneself and taking up one's cross looks like, we can look to the disciples for examples. We can look especially to the chief of the disciples, Peter. (If Peter was not the chief, at least he was the loudest!)

As we have seen, tradition associates Mark's Gospel with the Christian community at Rome. Based on evidence from Mark's Gospel itself, we think it was written in Rome. He takes extra care in explaining Jewish customs[5] and in translating Aramaic expressions into Greek.[6] He uses Latin terms and measurements like "legion," "denarius," "Praetorium," and more.[7] He even recounts the fact that a Roman centurion confessed Jesus as the Son of God. Evidently, Mark related all of this to fortify the Roman Christians during what may have been a time of persecution, maybe the time of Nero's reign. It may even have been written around the time when persecution cost them their pastor, Peter. So it is not so surprising that Peter features prominently in this Gospel.

And what a figure Peter was! This Gospel's first hearers could hear about their late beloved pastor with all the full vigor of his young manhood restored to him—the Peter of thirty years before. Look at him in chapter 8. There he was at Caesarea Philippi, the first one of the disciples to confess that Jesus is the Messiah. Can you imagine the joy of discovering the Desire of Ages?

And then look at him a few verses later: after Jesus said the Son of Man must be killed, "Peter took him aside and began to rebuke him" (8:32). He tried to correct Jesus concerning God's eternal plan; he tried to instruct the One who had planned it all from before the creation of the world; he tried to tell him how to be the Messiah! Here in the flush of the most newsworthy scoop of all time, Peter erred so egregiously in counseling Jesus, that Jesus addressed him as if he were the devil incarnate: "Get behind me, Satan" (8:33).

Then in chapter 14, when Jesus told his disciples that they would desert him, who protested the loudest? Peter! "Even if all the others desert you, I never will!" Just as when he stepped out of the boat and began to sink, or drew a sword and sliced off a man's ear, Peter acted sincerely but thoughtlessly with this boast. A few verses later, Peter fell asleep in the Garden of Gethsemane in spite of Jesus' warning, and then he did it again, and then he did it again. You can hear Peter's words still ringing—"Even if all desert you, I will not."

---

[5] E.g., 7:3-4; 14:12; 15:42.
[6] 3:17; 5:41; 7:11, 34; 15:22, 34.
[7] 5:9; 6:27, 48; 12:15, 42; 13:35; 15:16, 39.

Then Jesus was arrested, and "everyone deserted him and fled" (14:50). And Peter's words still rang—"Even if all desert you, I will not."

As if that were not enough, Peter's tragedy deepened. The words that follow are cold and harsh on the page of Mark's Gospel. What one would not give to be able to go back and un-speak the words Peter spoke when the servant-girl asked him if he was with Jesus: "I don't know or understand what you're talking about" (14:68). The question was asked a second time, and a second time Peter denied knowing Christ. But the awful words were most clearly stated after the third questioning: "I don't know this man you're talking about" (14:71).

Who was the greater traitor? Judas or Peter?

Yet the story in Mark's Gospel is not quite over. Do you see that last sentence in the chapter? "And he broke down and wept" (14:72). This is not an insignificant detail, or the addition of a little color. In those tears was Peter's hope. True repentance often begins with realizing the weight of your sins and the greatness of your need. It can come like a thunderclap. Then it can cause showers of regretful weeping. If it is godly sorrow, it brings change.

It brings the kind of change that transforms a boastful traitor like Peter into a faithful pastor, who, according to church history, would one day walk onto a Roman road, take up his cross, and follow Christ. Tradition tells us that Peter would not let himself be crucified in the same way Christ was. He did not feel worthy. So he was crucified upside down.

Peter may have been the leader of the disciples in confusion and confession, as well as in cowardly denials and bold promises. But he could also weep. If you want to see Jesus for who he is, you must see yourself for who you are. And if you are seeing clearly, you will begin by weeping.

May God give us eyes to see the truth about ourselves, and then the truth about Jesus who came to lay down his life as a ransom for many. This was the good news for Peter, and it is the good news for us too.

Let us pray:

Lord God, we praise you for the good news of peace through Jesus Christ, who is Lord of all. We praise you for everything recounted in Mark's Gospel beginning in Galilee after John's baptism of Jesus: how you anointed Jesus of Nazareth with the Holy Spirit and power, how the Lord Jesus went around doing good and healing all who were under the power of the devil, how he was killed and hanged on a tree, and how you raised him from the dead on the third day. Lord, we know this is the good news, the message that you have commanded us to believe and to preach, so that all will know that the Lord Jesus

is the one whom you have appointed as the judge of the living and the dead.
Lord, we pray that we would believe in him, and so receive forgiveness of sins
through his name. We pray for his glory's sake. Amen.

Questions for Reflection:

1. What makes Mark's Gospel unique when considered alongside the other Gospels?

2. Three different responses to Jesus have been described in this chapter: some people believed, some were confused, and some were antagonistic. Can you think of times when each one of these responses characterized you?

3. Did you notice what types of people tended to believe Jesus when he said who he was? They tended to be people on "the outs" of society, like women, foreigners, and the disabled. Why would these types of people believe Jesus? What *heart* characteristics do those who respond in belief to Jesus all share?

4. Do you share the heart characteristics of such a believer on "the outs" of society? Or are you preoccupied with being on the "inside"? Really, what is your heart like? What does it want? Is there a connection between our *beliefs* and our *heart's desires?* Does this have any implications for evangelism?

5. Maybe you have heard people say, "Ah, religion is just a crutch for the weak. What we need is more self-reliance." If Jesus does in fact appeal to people with the heart characteristics of someone on "the outs" of society, what can you say to such skeptics?

6. As we have seen, Jesus used something we call the "messianic secret" to shield himself from the attention of crowds long enough to teach the disciples what the Messiah had really come to do. The disciples, like many people in that day, had wrong expectations and hopes for the Messiah. What wrong expectations might you have about what God promises to do in your life? What kinds of "salvation," or saving, do you hope for from day to day? What salvation does the Gospel of Mark teach that you really need?

7. Among other things, the Gospel of Mark teaches that Jesus came to suffer. Reflect for a moment on the idea of the Son of God—who bears all authority and will return to judge—*suffering.* What leaders like this have you known in your own life? What does this say about the character of God? What does it

suggest about his love for repentant sinners? What does this suggest about the Christian pilgrimage?

8. The Gospel of Mark also teaches that Jesus will return to judge. What implications does that have for your local church, particularly in terms of the responsibilities members of a church have for one another?

9. According to Mark's Gospel, Peter broke down and wept. Was this a moment of true repentance or just emotionalism? How do we know? If you consider yourself a Christian, what in your life would suggest that your repentance is real and not merely self-deceiving emotions? How can the members of a church encourage one another toward true repentance and not mere displays of emotions in our public gatherings and in our lives together?

10. Who do you say Jesus is?

THE MESSAGE OF LUKE: JESUS, THE SON OF ADAM

WHAT WAS IT REALLY LIKE?

INTRODUCING LUKE

JESUS THE MAN'S MAN?

Jesus' Concern for Women

Jesus' Concern for Children

JESUS THE CULTURE-SHAPER?

Jesus' Concern for the Poor

Warnings to the Wealthy

JESUS THE POPULAR GUY?

Jesus' Concern for the Disreputable

JESUS THE NATIONALIST?

Jesus' Concern for the Nations

Judgment

Consolation

JESUS THE MANAGER?

Jesus' Concern for the Lost

The reality of judgment

Salvation

Forgiveness of sins

Pictures of Faith

3

THE MESSAGE OF LUKE: JESUS, THE SON OF ADAM

WHAT WAS IT REALLY LIKE?[1]

Richard Sibbes was a brave martyr for the cause of truth. For decades in early seventeenth-century England, Sibbes preached the gospel faithfully, refusing to bow to the tyrannical decrees that came down from the heights of Anglican hierarchy. The university asked him to sign statements of faith and conduct in order to keep both his teaching position at Cambridge University and his popular weekly public lectureship, paid for by the town. Though Sibbes had been connected with Cambridge for more than twenty years, and though his Sunday afternoon preaching bore much fruit, he courageously refused to sign his name and therefore suffered persecution. He was fired from his college job and his public lecture. He was forced to move from his home. And only because of some unusually powerful friends he escaped to a position down in London. His reputation was not rehabilitated in Cambridge for a decade.

This is the story you will find about Sibbes in everything from popular books about him, such as *The Bruised Reed and Smoking Flax*, all the way to the scholarly encyclopedias in college libraries. And they are all wrong.

The truth is, Sibbes was never fired from his college, because he *did* sign his name to the documents. He hesitated at first, but he did sign. He left Cambridge not because he was fired as a principled martyr but because he was offered a great position as preacher at one of the most powerful locations in London at the time—Gray's Inn, a kind of combination of Yale Law School and the upper-crust Watergate Apartments in Washington, D.C.

My own academic work was done, in part, in this area of Sibbes's life. Such work requires a careful analysis of the evidence. It is part examination, part

---

[1] This sermon was originally preached June 27, 1999, Capitol Hill Baptist Church, Washington, D.C.

detective work, and part historical empathy (being able to imagine yourself in the historical setting). One of the telltale clues that led me to realize that the commonly accepted and published story about Sibbes was false was that none of Sibbes's own contemporaries told this tale. The story of his supposedly great suffering emerged only years later.

Of course I'm not alone in my interest in historical investigation. When *Washington Post* reporter Bob Woodward publishes books describing details of the Watergate scandal, people wanted to find out what *really* happened. Were the hunches they had when watching the news correct? Biographies also remain as popular as ever. People read biographies to see if some famous individual matches what they imagined him or her to be like. Did Nero really order persecutions against the Christians? What did Freud himself dream about? What did the Wright brothers actually think would happen with their invention? Whatever happened to Mrs. Spurgeon after her husband died?

The more interesting a historical figure is, the more interpretations of their lives we can find on the shelves of libraries and bookstores. And who has been the center of more interest than Jesus of Nazareth? Perhaps a billion people around the globe think about him every Sunday, week after week!

INTRODUCING LUKE

So what was Jesus of Nazareth *really* like? Luke is the third book in the New Testament. More than the other Gospel writers, Luke wrote his Gospel based on his own historical investigations. It begins, "Many have undertaken to draw up an account of the things that have been fulfilled among us, just as they were handed down to us by those who from the first were eyewitnesses and servants of the word. Therefore, since I myself have carefully investigated everything from the beginning, it seemed good also to me to write an orderly account for you, most excellent Theophilus, so that you may know the certainty of the things you have been taught" (Luke 1:1-4).

To this end, Luke wrote two books that are in the New Testament: the Gospel of Luke and the book of Acts. Acts, you will notice, begins by referring back to Luke:

> In my former book, Theophilus, I wrote about all that Jesus began to do and to teach until the day he was taken up to heaven, after giving instructions through the Holy Spirit to the apostles he had chosen (Acts 1:1-2).

So Luke and Acts are the first and second volumes of one larger work.

In both books, Luke gives evidence of being a careful researcher who talked with eyewitnesses, read other accounts, compared stories, and compiled and investigated data. And he was in a good position to do so. As a traveling companion to Paul,[2] he would have known the apostles and would have been introduced to everybody. In a very quiet way, he is present in Acts. Every time the narrator refers to the action in terms of "we," it indicates that Luke was present with Paul.

Indeed, I wonder if Luke's involvement with Paul on his missionary journeys, and the opposition they encountered among some of the Jews, is what made Luke want to investigate the roots of Paul's message to the Gentiles. Some Jews said Paul should not tell the Gentiles about the Messiah. And perhaps Luke wondered, what did Jesus himself say about evangelizing the Gentiles? Did he intend to come as the Messiah for the Jewish people only or for all nations? And what was Jesus really like? What did he do and say? For one reason or another, Luke decided to hunt down and examine the evidence that would answer these types of questions. And perhaps this Greek-speaking nobleman Theophilus found Luke's investigations interesting enough to fund them.

Luke was not Jewish, and he appears to have been a doctor (Col. 4:14). He wrote in Greek quite well—maybe because it was his native language, maybe because he was well educated, maybe both. Whatever the explanation, he avoided Aramaic words like "Rabbi" and "Abba" that are in the other Gospels.

Luke probably undertook his investigations sometime in the late 50s or early 60s A.D. We base this estimation on the fact that the book of Acts concludes before the onset of the persecution that took the lives of Peter and Paul in the late 60s. It is hard to imagine that Luke would have failed to mention their deaths had either one of them already been killed.

Luke wrote more of the New Testament than anyone else, even Paul or John. The Gospel of Luke is the longest book in the New Testament. Twice as long as Mark's Gospel, it takes about two hours to read silently.

As for the quality of Luke's Gospel, Ernst Renan, a famous scholar in the nineteenth century and a harsh critic of Jesus, called Luke's Gospel the most beautiful book in the world.

Luke's structure is fairly simple:

CHAPTERS 1–3 describe Jesus' birth, boyhood, baptism, and genealogical descent.

CHAPTERS 4–9 tell about Jesus' ministry of teaching and healing in Galilee. The book's key turning point occurs in chapter 9 with these words: "As the time approached for him to be taken up to heaven, Jesus resolutely set out for Jerusalem" (9:51).

---

[2] Col. 4:14; 2 Tim. 4:11; Philem. 24.

CHAPTERS 10–19 then follow Jesus' course toward Jerusalem. Luke uses these middle chapters to recount what Jesus taught about being a disciple and about what he was going to do in Jerusalem.

CHAPTERS 19–21 recount Christ's teachings in Jerusalem.

CHAPTER 22 records Jesus' arrest, while chapter 23 describes his trial, crucifixion, and burial.

CHAPTER 24 then reports his resurrection, his post-resurrection appearances, and his ascension.

When you read this book, you find Luke doing something different from the other Gospel writers. Since this Gospel is the first half of a larger work, he provides a fuller account of what happened after the resurrection in order to bridge the storyline from Luke to Acts. So in addition to a number of other stories that are unique to Luke, he includes the story of Jesus' ascension into heaven.

Of course, Luke shares much in common with the other Gospels. The basic story is the same, and many of the verses match what is in Matthew or Mark word for word. In fact, about 60 percent of Mark's Gospel is reproduced verbatim in Luke's. And like Matthew, Luke devotes much attention to how Jesus fulfilled Old Testament prophecy. The Gospel writers clearly tell the same basic story and use some of the same basic sources from the same people. And we expect such basic agreement between these four Gospels. If they are describing the same life, many of the same events, and some of the same teachings, the overlap confirms their authenticity. Yet each Gospel also has its own special flavor, which mutually supplements and rounds out the story of Jesus' life, death, and resurrection.

So again, the question we put to Luke is, what was Jesus really like?

This is an important question, in part because of the confused state of modern scholarship on Jesus. As we saw in our study of Mark, modern scholarship presents multiple Jesuses to us: Jesus as sectarian fanatic Jew, as Cynic philosopher, as healer, as sage, as teacher, as advocate for social justice, as rationalist, as mystic, and so forth.

It is also an important question because our own hearts are easily misled. Who do you think Jesus is?

Consider what has informed your picture of Jesus: perhaps a few TV specials, an article or two, some memories of sermons, your desires of what you want him to be like. How have these sources informed what you imagine the world's greatest religious leader was like?

Maybe Jesus was a man's man, who set out to build up the smashed self-esteem of the conquered Jewish males. Or maybe he was a culture-shaper who, being knowledgeable in the ways of the shapers of public policy in Jerusalem, tried to redirect Israel's thinking in crucial areas of social significance. Or perhaps he was more savvy with the people—a real populist: born in the hill country of Bethlehem, reared on the wide-open plains of northern Israel, schooled at his father's knee in hard work and industry, a teacher of wide acclaim who knew how to inspire confidence and change. Or maybe Jesus was a nationalist—someone who could inspire politically charged cries of "Hosanna! Son of David!" when entering the occupied nation's capital city.

If you have thought about Jesus in any of these categories, what we discover about Jesus in Luke's Gospel might surprise you.

So what is the truth about Jesus?

JESUS THE MAN'S MAN?

Was Jesus a man's man? We have been told that since Jesus was represented for so long in Sunday school pictures as a slender, soft figure, men have stopped following him. So in the last few decades, Sunday school drawings have recharacterized Jesus as burly and rough—the manly carpenter, hardened by long hours of lifting beams and swinging hammers. You can see the veins on his hands!

And this makes sense, right? In most societies, men have provided most of the public leadership. A religious leader who wants to succeed must therefore go for the men. Certainly Jesus understood this dynamic.

I can think of one religious leader today who parades well-dressed, carefully coiffed young men as role models for the community. Recent evangelical men's rallies have stressed the importance of keeping men involved in leadership. And books we recommend in our own church remind husbands and fathers that what goes on in the family is ultimately the husband's responsibility.

So it makes sense that, if we are going to reconstruct the real Jesus, we should emphasize the fact that he was male, that his twelve apostles were male, and that all of the New Testament was written by males. In short, Jesus clearly appreciated the importance of giving attention to men, right?

Jesus' Concern for Women

Jesus did give much time to discipling men. Yet Luke's Gospel shows he had great compassion and concern for women as well. To see this, consider first Luke's attention to Jesus' infancy and youth. He recounts the celebration shared by the two pregnant mothers, Mary and Elizabeth, as well as Mary's song of praise following the angel's amazing announcement. It is also hard to miss the fact that John the Baptist's mother, Elizabeth, appears to have had more faith than his father, Zechariah. Mary's faith is evident as well in her song of jubilation. She trusted and believed.

Throughout his Gospel, Luke recounts Jesus' expressions of concern for women. In chapter 7, Jesus' "heart went out" to a widow who had lost her son, a loss which would have caused more than emotional hardship in that society (7:13). Later in the chapter, "a woman who had lived a sinful life" came and washed Jesus' feet with tears and perfume (7:37-50). Contrary to the orthodoxy of the day's religious leaders, Jesus accepted her offering. Chapter 8 mentions the crucial ministry of support several women contributed to Jesus' work:

> After this, Jesus traveled about from one town and village to another, pro-claiming the good news of the kingdom of God. The Twelve were with him, and also some women who had been cured of evil spirits and diseases: Mary (called Magdalene) from whom seven demons had come out; Joanna the wife of Cuza, the manager of Herod's household; Susanna; and many others. These women were helping to support them out of their own means (8:1-3).

Chapter 10 highlights Mary and Martha's friendship with Jesus. As Martha busied herself with meal preparations and Mary sat and listened to Jesus' teaching, Jesus invited Martha to give attention to his teaching as well (10:38-42). Of course, inviting a woman to sit and learn was a radical idea in those days. In chapter 13, Jesus saw a crippled woman and had compassion on her. She didn't approach him, but he saw her, approached her, and healed her (13:10-13). Over and over Jesus displayed a special compassion toward women.

Jumping to the end of the story, we find that a group of women followed Jesus to Calvary, while even his male disciples abandoned him. The women wailed and mourned for Jesus, yet he turned and instructed them to weep for their own future, not his (23:27-31). These same women witnessed the cruci-fixion (23:49), and then they followed Joseph of Arimathea "and saw the tomb and how his body was laid in it. Then they went home and prepared spices and perfumes" (23:55-56). It is interesting that Luke takes the time to mention these details.

All told, Luke refers to more women than any other Gospel. This might reflect something about Luke, but it also reveals something of what Jesus considered important.

Jesus' Concern for Children

Even the way Jesus demonstrates concern for children throughout Luke's Gospel shows something of his unusual care for women. We have noticed that Luke begins the story— unusually—with two pregnant women—the once-barren Elizabeth and the virgin Mary. This would not have been an auspicious beginning for a story set in that culture. Yet Jesus' special awareness of children continues throughout the Gospel. He healed children (8:41-42, 51-55). He said they should be welcomed (9:47-48). He described them as recipients of God's grace in understanding: "I praise you, Father, Lord of heaven and earth, because you have hidden these things from the wise and learned, and revealed them to little children. Yes, Father, for this was your good pleasure" (10:21). He even rebuked his disciples for keeping the children from him, and then pointed to them as models of trust: "'I tell you the truth, anyone who will not receive the kingdom of God like a little child will never enter it'" (see Luke 18:17; cf. 17:2).

What other religious leader has been concerned with children? Perhaps you are a Buddhist or a Muslim, and you know of such stories involving Buddha or Muhammad. But I have not yet seen them, and I have looked for them. Jesus seems to have been unusual in his attitude towards children.

More generally, what other religious leader has been so concerned with the vulnerable? Jesus was, and he called his followers to demonstrate concern not only for the strong and healthy but for the young, old, weak, and vulnerable. In a recent interview, Christian ethicist Stanley Hauerwas speculated that, "within a hundred years, Christians may be known as those odd people who don't kill their children or their elderly."[3] As Christians, we do not love like this because of our own personal predilections toward loving. Rather, we see that Jesus loved in this way, and we follow him.

I cannot do justice here to all the gender-relevant concerns people might have when reading Luke, but let me say that Jesus taught and exemplified love and benevolence toward women when too often they had been ignored or abused in the name of religion. Sadly, many today try to address some of these larger concerns about the way women are treated in society by reconceiving of God as a woman. Interestingly, Tikva Frymer-Kensky, professor of Hebrew Bible at the University of Chicago, recently observed, "The existence and power of a goddess, particularly of Ishtar, is no indication or guarantee of a high status for human women. In Assyria, where Ishtar was so prominent, women were not. The texts rarely mention any individual women, and, according to the Middle Assyrian laws, married women had to be veiled, had no rights to their husband's property . . . and could be struck by their husbands at will."[4]

If you are a woman who is unsure of what Jesus has to do with your life, I urge you to read Luke's Gospel. Find out the truth about Jesus.

---

[3] Stanley Hauerwas, in an interview with Rodney Clapp, "What Would Pope Stanley Say?" *Books and Culture* (November/December 1998): 16.

[4] Tikva Frymer-Kensky cited in Cullem Murphy, "Is the Bible Bad News for Women?" *Wilson Quarterly* 22, no. 3 (Summer 1998): 30-31.

So was Jesus a man's man? Well, Jesus was certainly manly, and part of that masculinity was expressed in his concern for women and for those who were vulnerable in his society. If you are a man, I wonder how you think about your own manliness. Is your manliness expressed like his?

JESUS THE CULTURE-SHAPER?

Maybe you think of Jesus primarily as a culture-shaper. You know, one who makes friends with the wealthy and powerful in order to wield influence? Certainly, our church in Washington, D.C., understands something about this.

For Jesus to have been a successful religious initiator, he must have known how to tap into financial resources. All great leaders must do so. Money speaks all languages. And Jesus' example teaches us that if we want Christianity to survive in our culture today, we must bring the gospel to the people who have the money—their billions contain the direction and resources for the future, right?

Not long ago, I listened to a tape published by one of America's largest and most influential evangelical churches. It included a discussion about ministry to the wealthy. Part of this discussion was devoted to teaching the wealthy how to be good stewards of their assets. The other part was devoted to encouraging the rest of us to reach the wealthy. In short, the tape emphasized the special responsibility we have as Christians to reach out to the wealthy in ways that are culturally appropriate.

Surely Jesus came to the same conclusions about what makes ministry work, don't you think?

Jesus' Concern for the Poor

Well, if you think this is true, you might be surprised when you open Luke's account of the life and ministry of Jesus. Jesus appears to demonstrate a greater concern for the poor than for the rich.

In Mary's opening song of praise, she sings that God "has filled the hungry with good things but has sent the rich away empty" (1:53). This is a funny verse to stick on page one or two of a book to be sent to wealthy Theophilus, unless Mary really said that. Luke must have been an honest historian.

Mary's upside-down values seems to typify Jesus' ministry more than the American evangelical tendency to cater to the wealthy does. Jesus' own family was poor. In fact, his standard of living was probably beneath the standards of most people following this study. When Mary and Joseph made a sacrifice of purification for Mary, in keeping with the law, they brought "a pair of doves or two young pigeons" (2:24). If you turn back to Leviticus 12, you will find the law actually prescribes a year-old lamb for this type of sacrifice, unless the lamb is a budget-buster. "If she cannot afford a lamb, she is to bring two doves or two young pigeons" (Lev. 12:8). That is what Mary and Joseph did.

Years later, after Jesus grew up, he returned to his home synagogue, took the Isaiah scroll, and taught that the Messiah would "preach good news to the poor" (Luke 4:18; cf. Isa. 61:1-2). He cited the same passage again to John the Baptist's disciples when they asked him, "Are you the Messiah?" Jesus responded, "Go back and report to John what you have seen and heard . . . the good news is preached to the poor" (7:22). In chapter 12, Jesus told his disciples, "Sell your possessions and give to the poor" (12:33). And to a Pharisee hosting a feast at his house he said, "invite the poor" (14:13; cf. 14:21)

Amid an age in which the poor were more despised than in our own, Jesus told the story of the rich man and Lazarus (16:19-31). And his hearers' expectations were turned on their heads. The rich man went to hell, and the poor beggar Lazarus went to heaven!

Christ's hearers would have been equally surprised by his words to his disciples several chapters later:

> Jesus saw the rich putting their gifts into the temple treasury. He also saw a poor widow put in two very small copper coins. "I tell you the truth," he said, "this poor widow has put in more than all the others. All these people gave their gifts out of their wealth; but she out of her poverty put in all she had to live on" (21:1-4).

Jesus did not condemn the widow for her lack of financial prudence and planning; he commended her for the reality and fullness of her devotion to God.

Warnings to the Wealthy

Rather than teaching his disciples how to identify and enlist wealthy backers for their movement, Jesus taught them, "Blessed are you who are poor, for yours is the kingdom of God." In fact, he issued warnings to the wealthy: "Woe to you who are rich, for you have already received your comfort" (6:20, 24).

And the pattern continues. To a man worried about the apportionment of his inheritance, Jesus cautioned, "A man's life does not consist in the abundance of his possessions" (12:15). Then he told the parable of the rich fool, where a man shows himself to be rich in stuff but poor toward God (12:16-21). Several verses later, Jesus said, "Sell your possessions and give to the poor" (12:33a). Then, substantiating the advice, he warned, "where your treasure is, there your heart will be also" (12:34). In chapter 16 Jesus warned, "No servant can serve two masters. Either he will hate the one and love the other, or he will be devoted to the one and despise the other. You cannot serve both God and Money" (16:13).

In Jesus' day, worldly wealth and religious respectability often went together. So he warned the money-loving Pharisees not to confuse the two: "You are the ones who justify yourselves in the eyes of men, but God knows your hearts. What is highly valued among men is detestable in God's sight" (16:15). That is when he told the story of the Rich Man and Lazarus.

Perhaps the most shocking and upending story about wealth is found in Matthew, Mark, and Luke. If there was ever a seeker, the rich ruler was a seeker. He asked Jesus what he must do to inherit eternal life, and Jesus responded with a number of evidences of repentance and belief in God: do not commit adultery, do not murder, do not steal, and so forth, to which the man responded, "All these I have kept" (18:21). Then Jesus, knowing the man's heart, said, "You still lack one thing. Sell everything you have and give to the poor, and you will have treasure in heaven. Then come, follow me" (18:22). But the rich seeker could not do it. When he got the real bill, he basically said, "That's too much. I didn't really want it that much." So he turned away, refusing to part with his wealth and follow Christ. At the end of the conversation, Jesus concluded, "How hard it is for the rich to enter the kingdom of God" (18:24). The disciples were shocked. Surely, if anyone was a shoo-in to heaven, it was the wealthy. After all, isn't wealth a sign of God's blessing? Rich people are rich because they are good, and poor people are poor because they are bad, right? Jesus blew up these misconceptions: "How hard it is for the rich to enter the kingdom of God." The disciples responded in sincere desperation: "Who then can be saved?" (18:26).

The answer to that question comes in the next chapter, when another rich man approached Jesus. Yet this rich man did not have the influence and respect of the first rich man. No, it was the slimy, disreputable, traitor-to-the-nation tax collector, Zaccheus. Zaccheus was given the same choice—Jesus or wealth. And he, the one who was scorned in his culture, chose Jesus over everything else (19:1-10).

Do not misunderstand me here. Jesus was not a Marxist fixated on redistributing material goods. Nor was he not an ascetic fixed on ignoring them. Jesus was a spiritual realist who knew that good things become distorted and deceptive in a fallen world. They allure us with promises of fulfillment they can never fulfill.

After the death of the Grateful Dead's Jerry Garcia, his wife reportedly said, "Jerry died broke. We only have a few hundred thousand dollars in the bank." That's an interesting definition of "broke"! As the book *Bold Purpose* says, "Acquiring things is a slippery slope. The more you get, the more you want. The more you want, the more dissatisfied you feel when you can't get it. Money and work expose the depths of our depravity. Like relationships, work and money satisfy us initially but then leave us disillusioned, hungry for what no person or object can give us. Money and work are like a purgative that brings up all the ill inside of us, leaving us hungry for good food—a food that money and work can't possibly provide."[5]

Jesus was wary of the wealthy and concerned for the poor.

JESUS THE POPULAR GUY?

Was Jesus the "popular guy"? You know, the guy everyone wants to be with? Not necessarily the guy with money, but the guy with influence just the same. Surely Jesus knew how to work a crowded room and get in with the right people. Some religious ministries work this way. I know of one that pays people to hang around and make themselves "available." Whom do they make themselves available to? People in positions of influence. And that makes sense, doesn't it? If you want to influence a culture, go for its leaders and icons, the shapers of public opinion, the heroes, the admired. One of these heroes just might score a touchdown, get down on one knee, and thank God in silent prayer. Then 30,000 watching fans will get converted!

Jesus' Concern for the Disreputable

Interestingly, Jesus spent most of his time with people who were not well regarded in his society. He surrounded himself with sinners and tax collectors. (Do not be alarmed if you work at the IRS! First-century Jewish disgust with tax collectors was related to Rome's occupation and not with giving a portion of one's income to the government, per se. A tax collector, especially a Jewish one, would have been viewed as selling out to these occupiers.) Jesus ate in tax collectors' homes. And they accompanied him into the homes of the respectable class. The respectable class responded predictably: "Now the tax collectors and 'sinners' were all gathering around to hear him. But the Pharisees and the teachers of the law muttered, 'This man welcomes sinners and eats with them'" (15:1-2). This was Jesus' pattern. He kept company with the outcasts, from Zaccheus the tax collector to the blind man whom Jesus ordered brought to him (18:39-40).

Consider also what shepherds represented in Jesus' day, and the fact that they were the first to hear the announcement of his birth. We think of shepherds in terms of charming Christmas pageants, with cute children dressed in

---

[5] Dan Allender and Tremper Longman III, *Bold Purpose* (Wheaton, Ill.: Tyndale, 1998), 106-107.

nicely pressed robes. Yet in the ancient world, shepherds were thought of as shifty, untrustworthy, even thieving migrant-workers. Yet they were some of the first to greet Jesus! That was typical, I think, of Jesus' whole ministry.

The nineteenth-century English preacher Charles Spurgeon once said to his hearers in London, "You are the same sort of person as those whom Jesus used to welcome. They were good-for-nothing bodies; they were persons that were full of need, and could not possibly bring a price with which to purchase his favour. Are you not just like them? Are you a very special sinner? I am sure I could find another special sinner like you whom Jesus has received. I will not go into detail; but I will venture to ask you—Are you a thief? The dying thief rejoiced to see in Christ salvation full and free. Have you been unchaste? David was an adulterer and was pardoned; and Jesus forgave a woman that was a sinner, who therefore loved him much. The untruthful, the unclean, the ungodly, are the sort of people that Jesus came to seek and save."[6]

In the first century, the nineteenth century, and today, Jesus builds his kingdom not upon the reputation people have when they enter the kingdom but on the change that occurs in their lives once they are there. And that gave Jesus—and it gives us—all the more reason to have a concern for the disreputable.

JESUS THE NATIONALIST?

Maybe Jesus was a nationalist, as some have said. One way to begin a religious movement is to appeal to common boundaries and prejudices. Is that what Jesus did? Maybe he was like one of those leaders who holds rallies with lots of bunting and chants of "Our Nation; Our Race"? Perhaps this was how he made his movement succeed.

Several recent TV specials have proposed this theory. Jesus was concerned with the fate of his own nation, the theory goes; Paul was the one who reshaped Jesus' teaching into a movement that included Gentiles.

Maybe this portrait of Jesus seems far-fetched to you at first glance. But haven't you ever belonged to some group for a long time and then had newcomers enter the picture and disrupt your comfortable environment? Perhaps you have been a member of a church for ten or twenty years and then have found yourself thinking of newcomers as intruders, threatening your nice we-all-know-each-other circle. After all, this is your church, not theirs. These are natural feelings to have. Feelings of closeness and commonality make people feel relaxed. People can be themselves. Leaders can easily build churches and organizations on these feelings.

---

[6] Charles H. Spurgeon, *The Metropolitan Tabernacle Pulpit* (London : Passmore & Alabaster, 1885), 27.588 (sermon for October 16, 1881, A.M.).

Maybe Jesus was an early exponent of what is called the homogeneous unit principle: if you want to grow a church or Christian ministry, target people who are alike, affirm them in their alikeness, and then build them in the direction you want to take them. Did Jesus try to cultivate his own group's sense of identity? Did he appeal to the national-family feel?

Jesus' Concern for the Nations

Well, this is not how we see Jesus in Luke's Gospel. Jesus affirmed God's special concern for Israel, but he also clarified Israel's purpose: to be a light for all nations. To those in Israel who understood its true purpose, Jesus brought consolation. But there was another Israel whom Jesus addressed: those who had nationalistic prejudices and treated the nation as an end in itself. To this Israel, Jesus brought judgment. Simeon promised the young mother Mary that Jesus would separate the one Israel from the other: "This child is destined to cause the falling and rising of many in Israel (2:34).

Judgment. Throughout his ministry, Jesus was in conflict with the Pharisees over the Sabbath. Luke emphasizes this disagreement in chapters 6, 13, and 14, one of which we will consider. In chapter 13, the Sabbath stands in for the whole picture of Jewish identity:

> On a Sabbath Jesus was teaching in one of the synagogues, and a woman was there who had been crippled by a spirit for eighteen years. She was bent over and could not straighten up at all. When Jesus saw her, he called her forward and said to her, "Woman, you are set free from your infirmity." Then he put his hands on her, and immediately she straightened up and praised God.
>
> Indignant because Jesus had healed on the Sabbath, the synagogue ruler said to the people, "There are six days for work. So come and be healed on those days, not on the Sabbath."
>
> The Lord answered him, "You hypocrites! Doesn't each of you on the Sabbath untie his ox or donkey from the stall and lead it out to give it water? Then should not this woman, a daughter of Abraham, whom Satan has kept bound for eighteen long years, be set free on the Sabbath day from what bound her?" (13:10-16; cf. 6:1-11; 14:1-6).

The Pharisees' misunderstanding of the Sabbath points to the way many people in Israel mistook Israel's role. God intended for Israel to be a means for reaching the whole world. But the Pharisees treated Israel as an end in itself, and so they bound up the people with unnecessary and overzealous regulation. This is why Jesus likened the Pharisees to guests who had been invited to a great banquet but who ignored their invitations and therefore would not "get a taste of my banquet" (14:24). Later he likened them to servants who had been given gifts and opportunities but did not use them to reach others and therefore would be judged (19:26-27).

In chapter 12, Jesus taught his disciples,

> "That servant who knows his master's will and does not get ready or does not do what his master wants will be beaten with many blows. But the one who does not know and does things deserving punishment will be beaten with few blows. From everyone who has been given much, much will be demanded; and from the one who has been entrusted with much, much more will be asked" (12:47-48).

Consider what this meant for Israel. Israel had been given God's Word and teaching and the opportunities these gifts afford. But by rejecting Jesus, Israel threw away those opportunities forever. They were more interested in protecting their own little fiefdom.

In chapter 20, Jesus tells a harsh parable about wicked and murderous tenants who wrongly use their master's property for themselves and their own ends. Listening to Jesus, "The teachers of the law and the chief priests looked for a way to arrest him immediately, because they knew he had spoken this parable against them" (20:19).

Consolation. Other Israelites anticipated the "consolation of Israel" (2:25); these were the same people who knew that God intended the light of Israel to shine to the Gentiles. Simeon, one such character, praised God saying, "my eyes have seen your salvation, which you have prepared in the sight of all people, a light for revelation to the Gentiles and for glory to your people Israel" (2:30-32). Likewise, John the Baptist's ministry prepared the way for "all mankind [to] see God's salvation" (3:4-6).

It is also worth remarking that chapter 3's genealogy of Jesus does not stop with Abraham, as the genealogy in Matthew does; it goes back to the father of all nations, "Adam" (3:38). Jesus' ministry is not concerned merely with ethnic Israel but with the whole world.

Jesus demonstrated this concern throughout Luke's Gospel. In chapter 4, Jesus observed that God blessed foreigners in the Old Testament and excluded the Israelites whenever they rejected God's Word through his prophet (4:26-30). In chapter 10, Jesus told the parable of the good Samaritan, where a Samaritan performs the act of faith that several Israelites fail to perform (10:30-37). In chapter 17, Jesus healed ten lepers, but only one, a Samaritan, returned to thank him. Jesus asked, "'Was no one found to return and give praise to God except this foreigner?' Then he said to him, 'Rise and go; your faith has made you well'" (17:18-19). The Samaritans were despised and hated by Jesus' countrymen but loved by Jesus.

Jesus was concerned not just for his own people but for the nations. This was no adaptation thought up by Paul. This was in the ministry and the heart of Jesus. As he said in chapter 13, "People will come from east and west and north and south, and will take their places at the feast in the kingdom of God" (13:29).

JESUS THE MANAGER?

Was Jesus a manager? Was he a religious organizer and promoter who was wrapped up in his own organization and was always looking for people who agreed with the organization's own agenda—like a Baptist Student Union worker looking for Baptist students? A lot of religious groups are like that. Somehow they sniff out those who agree with them and pull them together. Is that what you think Jesus did?

Jesus' Concern for the Lost

Even if Jesus was, in obvious ways, a man's man, or a culture-shaper, or a popular guy, the notion of Jesus as "manager" is thoroughly misconceived. His concern for the lost, rather than a preoccupation with some private agenda, is blazingly obvious as you read through Luke.

The reality of judgment. Jesus knew that people were lost, and so he clearly taught about the coming judgment. God would judge whole cities and whole generations for rejecting his words (10:14; 11:31-32). And the teachers of the law who used God's religion for their own ends would be "punished most severely" (20:47). Indeed, God would judge everyone for their sins, which is why people stand in need of salvation.

Salvation. Luke uses various forms of the word "salvation" more than any other book in the New Testament. Luke's Gospel begins with Mary praising God as "my Savior" (1:47). Zechariah praised God for the salvation he was bringing (1:71, 77). The angels proclaimed to the shepherds, "Today in the town of David a Savior has been born to you; he is Christ the Lord" (2:11). And Simeon recognized Jesus as God's salvation (Luke 2:30).

Jesus taught the same thing in his ministry. He said at one point, "For whoever wants to save his life will lose it, but whoever loses his life for me will save it" (9:24). What does Jesus mean by "will save it"? Zaccheus learned the answer in chapter 19, when he saw his choice between two ways of living. He could keep his money and mastery over his own life, or he could love and follow Christ. Zaccheus chose the second way, to which Jesus responded, "Today salvation has come to this house, because this man, too, is a son of Abraham. For the Son of Man came to seek and to save what was lost" (19:9).

How did Jesus bring this salvation? He told his disciples at the Last Supper, "I have eagerly desired to eat this Passover with you before I suffer. For I tell you, I will not eat it again until it finds fulfillment in the kingdom of God" (22:15-16). Bringing salvation means Jesus had to suffer. Breaking the bread and pouring the wine, he said, this is "my body given for you" and "my blood . . . poured out for you" (22:19-20). He then quoted from Isaiah, who prophesied, "he poured out his life unto death, and was numbered with the transgressors. For he bore the sin of many, and made intercession for the transgressors" (Isa. 53:12). Jesus observed, "Yes, what is written about me is reaching its fulfillment" (Luke 22:37). Jesus then offered his body as the sacrifice for the sins of many that Isaiah promised, making intercession for the transgressors.

Forgiveness of sins. The prophet Jeremiah had promised the forgiveness of sins (Jer. 31:34; Luke 1:77), and now Jesus fulfilled that promise (5:20-24; 7:47-49). So Jesus taught his disciples to proclaim this message: "repentance and forgiveness of sins will be preached in his name to all nations, beginning at Jerusalem" (24:47).

The great message is that we, who were made to know God, have separated ourselves from God by our sin; we deserve his judgment by the way we live; but God, by his great love in Christ, has come and lived a life deserving no punishment. He has taken our sins on his body on the cross—the sins of all those from every nation who repent and believe in him. He calls us now to repent and believe.

Pictures of Faith

Who believed? Many believed, even in Luke's Gospel: Elizabeth and Mary (1:45), the Roman Centurion (7:7-9), the sinful woman (7:50), the Samaritan leper (17:19), and the blind beggar (18:42). It was a strange lot, but these are the pictures of faith Luke provides for us. They looked, they trusted, and they relied.

Luke also presents pictures of individuals who were conscious of their own righteousness and looked down on others. Both types are represented in the parable of the Pharisee and the tax collector:

> To some who were confident of their own righteousness and looked down on everybody else, Jesus told this parable: "Two men went up to the temple to pray, one a Pharisee and the other a tax collector. The Pharisee stood up and prayed about himself: 'God, I thank you that I am not like other men—robbers, evildoers, adulterers—or even like this tax collector. I fast twice a week and give a tenth of all I get.'

"But the tax collector stood at a distance. He would not even look up to heaven, but beat his breast and said, 'God, have mercy on me, a sinner.'

"I tell you that this man, rather than the other, went home justified before God. For everyone who exalts himself will be humbled, and he who humbles himself will be exalted" (18:9-14).

We do not always understand why bad things happen to us, nor do we always understand why we choose bad things. This tax collector made a bad choice to be a tax collector. But do you see how God used it? He drove him to cry out for mercy! The word for "mercy" in this passage, literally translated, means "be propitiated." The man did not just ask for mercy. He cried out for God's just wrath against him to be assuaged. The mercy he desired was the mercy that could be given only when a sacrifice stood in his place and took away God's wrath. This man was a sinner who knew he needed forgiveness. So he stood up from his tax collector's booth, walked to the temple, and prayed, "God, be propitiated so that you can love me. My sins mean you cannot love me and remain just."

One last picture of saving faith, at least its beginning, is presented after the resurrection. The women found the tomb empty and were told by the angel that Jesus had risen. The women then returned to the disciples and told them what they had seen, but only one disciple began to believe right away: "But the [disciples] did not believe the women, because their words seemed to them like nonsense. Peter, however, got up and ran to the tomb" (24:11-12).

Peter got up and ran to the tomb.

Peter was the one who boasted that he would not deny Christ even if all the others did, which was where Mark's Gospel left him—denying Christ and weeping bitterly. But Luke tells us a bit more. These two women came and told a confused tale that nobody believed, except Peter. Peter did not entirely understand what getting up from the dead meant. But like that tax collector, he was so desperate that he stood up in the middle of all the apostles and ran to the tomb looking for Jesus. He believed in him. He had faith in him. He trusted him.

The story line in Luke's Gospel points to Jerusalem like one big arrow, because Jerusalem is where Jesus was hanged on the cross, where he became as vulnerable to abuse as a woman or a child, where he was made poorer than a beggar, where he was despised as a traitor, and where he was cast out like a Samaritan or a failed disciple. And he did it not for himself alone; he did it for you and for me, whoever we are, if we will find in Jesus our only hope.

Let us pray:

Dear God, we thank you for Luke's great message of your love for us in Christ, even though we know that we are not an assembly of the righteous. Regardless of how long we have taught Sunday school, or how much we know about Luke, or how much money we have given, or how many people we have witnessed to, we are an assembly who need the salvation that only you can bring. Every one of us. O God, forgive us for our coldness of heart, for our sense of self-sufficiency, for our sense of self-righteousness. O God, we pray that none of us would be like that Pharisee who is so tragically and foolishly blind to his own need for you. O God, give us hearts like that tax collector, who knows something of the extent of his need. And we pray this so that we might find all of our needs met in you and you alone. For Jesus' sake we ask it. Amen.

Questions for Reflection:

1. How many books of the Bible did Luke write? How did he write them? What is the relationship between them?

2. Why is the question "Who is Jesus?" so important? Who/what often informs people's views today of who Jesus is? Who/what has informed your own view?

3. An underlying theme throughout this chapter is our tendency to refashion Jesus, or God, in our own image. We want God to value the things we value and denigrate the things we denigrate. If you were tempted to refashion God in your own image, what attributes might you give him? What attributes might your culture at large give him? How would you (or your culture) know if you were right or wrong about your assumptions?

4. What role should the Bible play in answering the question of who Jesus is?

5. What would you do if your church or favorite church leader said something contrary to what the Bible says?

6. According to Luke, Jesus displayed a concern for women, children, and the vulnerable that was uncommon in his day. What does this teach us about God's heart? What does *your* treatment of people in positions of vulnerability teach people about God? What implications does this have for husbands? Parents? Employers? Politicians? Pastors? Teachers? Citizens?

7. Why was Jesus wary of wealth? Is being rich sinful? If you were to show your personal/family budget to your non-Christian neighbors, would they commend your spending patterns as being similar to their own? Or would your budget provoke them to think that Christians were a little strange? If you showed your church's budget to non-Christian financial consultants, would they notice anything different about your church compared to the other businesses they examine?

8. We have seen that Jesus builds his kingdom not upon the reputation people have when they enter the kingdom but on the change that occurs in their lives once they are there. What does this teach us about whose glory God is interested in promoting? Where should we expect to find the power to change and grow in godliness? What implications does this have for how we do ministry?

9. Luke shows that Jesus is passionate about reaching the nations. Do your private prayers reflect his concerns? How? Do the prayer meetings at your church reflect these concerns? How can you personally encourage your fellow church members to begin praying about kingdom concerns publicly and privately? Aside from your prayers, in what practical ways do you work to reach the nations? In answering this last question, you might want to think about who your friends are. Are they all similar to you in age, race, socioeconomic class, and professional interests? Or are you learning to befriend, encourage, and love people who are different from you? How?

10. How did Jesus bring salvation? Another way of asking this question would be, how can a holy God *forgive* sinners without simply "overlooking sin," thereby impugning his own righteousness?

THE MESSAGE OF JOHN: JESUS, THE SON OF GOD

4

THE MESSAGE OF JOHN: JESUS, THE SON OF GOD

IS HE JUST HUMAN?[1]

"Nothing of importance happened today." Those were the words King George III of Great Britain wrote in his diary. Just one more humdrum diary entry in the life of a king.

The day was July 4, 1776.

On that day, another man, who had the motto "Rebellion to tyrants is obedience to God," published a document called "The Declaration of Independence." That document gave formal expression to the increasingly widespread belief that King George had ruled the American colonies unjustly and that they must be independent. The Continental Congress had passed a resolution calling for independence two days earlier. But on "the Glorious Fourth" the forceful words of Thomas Jefferson were published before the world as the Congress's justification for their action.

The kind of leadership exercised in these small, sparsely populated colonies during the late-eighteenth century has been the marvel of teachers and writers, lawyers and politicians, jurists and scholars ever sense. We think of Madison, Monroe, Jefferson, Washington, Franklin, Adams, Hamilton, and others. The demands of the day were severe, but there were great leaders aplenty to meet them.

Now, I wonder if this is how you think of Jesus—a heroic leader who challenged the establishment of his day; someone who provokes feelings of nostalgia as we recount sometimes-true, sometimes-mythologized school-day stories? It is popularly believed that Jesus was a great religious leader. Thomas Jefferson in fact wrote this about Jesus: "His parentage was obscure; his con-

---

[1] This sermon was originally preached on July 4, 1999, at Capitol Hill Baptist Church in Washington, D.C.

ditions poor; his education null; his natural endowments great; his life correct and innocent; he was meek, benevolent, patient, firm, disinterested and of the sublimest eloquence."[2]

If Jefferson had said those words about a contemporary, his remarks would be generous. If he had said them of himself, they would be immodest. But to say them about Jesus, well, have you ever heard the phrase "damning with faint praise"?

Don't misunderstand me. It is not that I disagree with anything Jefferson said about Jesus in these words. Rather, he seems to have missed the point of who Jesus really was.

His error is common. Much scholarship since Jefferson's time has proposed that Jesus was merely human—maybe a great human, but merely human. The proposal that Jesus is God is treated as an overlay on actual history. Richard Rubenstein's book *When Jesus Became God*,[3] for example, chronicles the struggle between Arius and Athanasius in the fourth-century church and ascribes the Christian conviction that Jesus was God incarnate almost solely to Athanasius. Several years ago, the PBS Easter special "From Jesus to Christ" had the same basic thesis, only it placed responsibility for the deification of Jesus at the feet of Paul, who needed a stronger product to market Christianity in the competitive Greek religion market. So Jesus became Christ; he became deified.

INTRODUCING JOHN

It is all very well to have questions about who Jesus is. Jesus' own contemporaries asked such questions. For example, we read in John 7 that "after his brothers had left for the Feast, he went also, not publicly, but in secret. Now at the Feast the Jews were watching for him and asking, 'Where is that man?' Among the crowds there was widespread whispering about him. Some said, 'He is a good man.' Others replied, 'No, he deceives the people'" (7:10-12). Like today, opinions in Jesus' own time varied greatly.

But in order to find the correct answer of who Jesus was, we turn once again a primary source, the account of someone who lived nearer Jesus' time than modern scholars or screenwriters, Jefferson, Arius, or Athanasius. We turn to the Gospel of John.

John's Gospel is longer than Mark's and shorter than Luke's. It takes about an hour and a half to read. Christians have traditionally believed it was writ-

---

[2] Thomas Jefferson, "Syllabus of an Estimate of the Merit of the Doctrines of Jesus, Compared with Those of Others," in *The Letters of Thomas Jefferson: 1743–1826*, April 1803.
[3] Richard E. Rubenstein, *When Jesus Became God : The Epic Fight over Christ's Divinity in the Last Days of Rome* (New York: Harcourt Brace, 1999).

ten by John, "the disciple whom Jesus loved" (13:23; 19:26; 21:7; 21:20). The structure of John's Gospel is simple. A prologue (1:1-18) and an epilogue (chapter 21) begin and end the book, and everything in between falls into two parts. The first half is about Jesus' teaching and ministry leading up to his final week in Jerusalem (1:19–12:10). The second half is devoted to the final week in Jerusalem, including his death and resurrection (12:12–20:31). The Gospel bears certain resemblances with the other three Gospels, but there are clear differences. For example, John does not record as many healing miracles, and he does not record any teaching parables or exorcisms.

All four Gospels focus on the identity of Jesus, but John does so especially. It seems like every time Jesus speaks, he speaks about himself, why he came into the world, or what he will do for those who believe in him.

Why did John write this book? He tells us at the end of chapter 20, in what might be described as the theme verses of John's Gospel:

> Jesus did many other miraculous signs in the presence of his disciples, which are not recorded in this book. But these are written that you may believe that Jesus is the Christ, the Son of God, and that by believing you may have life in his name (20:30-31).

In this study, we will search through all of John's Gospel, and 20:31 will act as our guide. We will look first at *what* John says we should believe: "But these are written that you may believe *that Jesus is the Christ, the Son of God,* and that by believing you may have life in his name."

Second, we will look at *why* we should believe: "But *these* are written that you may believe that Jesus is the Christ, the Son of God, and that by believing you may have life in his name." We will learn in a moment what "these" refers to.

Finally, we will look at the *results* of believing: "These are written that you may believe that Jesus is the Christ, the Son of God, and *that by believing you may have life in his name."*

In doing this, we hope to learn more of the truth about Jesus.

WHAT WE SHOULD BELIEVE

"But these are written that you may believe *that Jesus is the Christ, the Son of God,* and that by believing you may have life in his name" (20:31).

"Christ" is the Greek word for "Messiah," and like the other Gospels John presents Jesus as the one who fulfills the Old Testament promise of a coming Messiah. As 20:31 says, "Jesus is the Christ." Some scholars have suggested that John's Gospel was specifically written for Jews looking for the Messiah.

Whether or not the book was written with this audience in mind, the center of John's Gospel is the message of who the Messiah is and what he came to do.

Who the Messiah Is

One of the most interesting parts of these early records of Jesus' ministry, and particularly of John's Gospel, is the strength of the opposition to Jesus. When Jesus taught about who he was, people reacted strongly. Many of his contemporaries not only rejected his teaching, they rejected it violently. It is ironic that so many books these days will refer to Jesus kindly. One calls him a model chief executive officer. Another calls him a reflection of God. John Meier has called him an "insufferably ordinary" Galilean layman.[4] But many of those who actually knew Jesus, who walked with him and heard him teach, did not perceive him as an ordinary layman, a model businessman, or a mere reflection of God's character. They hated him.

John describes many people as being defensive and skeptical from the beginning of Jesus' ministry. They took offense at him (2:12-25; 6:61). They grumbled at his provision of bread (6:41, 61), like the Israelites who grumbled about the Lord's provision of manna in the wilderness. A number of Jesus' disciples abandoned him (6:66). His own brothers did not believe in him (7:5). Some people called him a liar (7:12, 47). Others said he was a foreigner fraudulently posing as Jewish (8:48), or that he was demon-possessed (7:20; 8:48, 52; 10:20), or that he was raving mad (10:20). They repeatedly attempted to seize and arrest him (7:30-32, 44; 8:20) and even to stone him (8:59; 11:8). They plotted to take his life (11:53, 57). They harassed his disciples (9:22; 12:42; 16:2). They even sought to kill Lazarus after Jesus raised him from the dead (12:10-11)! Finally, of course, Jesus was betrayed, arrested, bound, deserted, denied, interrogated, struck, flogged, mocked, crowned with thorns, made the center of what amounted to a lynching, and was crucified, causing him to suffocate to death. Mildly previewing the response many had to Jesus, John introduces his book by writing, "He came to that which was his own, but his own did not receive him" (1:11).

As I have reflected on this Gospel, one thing is so obvious it is easy to miss. If you want to know who Jesus is, consider one indisputable clue: the strength of the opposition Jesus received when he talked about who he is. The fate that every historian agrees befell Jesus and the fate that every local church remembers in the practice of the Lord's Supper—violent rejection and crucifixion—suggests that something was going on that we would not expect surrounding

---

[4] John Meier, *A Marginal Jew: Rethinking the Historical Jesus*, 3 vols., Anchor Bible Reference Library (New York: Doubleday, 1991), I.350-352.

a Galilean layman who had "no power base," as Meier argues, nor surrounding one who was merely a pedestrian, itinerate sage. He was making some kind of claim that proved inflammatory among the people of his day and, no doubt, does the same within our own culture's pluralistic belief in the equality of all religions. In short, the ire that accrues around Jesus in John's Gospel appears to result from how he described his relationship with God: he presented himself as the unique *Son of God*.

From the beginning of his public ministry, Jesus was surrounded by individuals who recognized his unique status. John the Baptist (not the author of the Gospel) witnessed the Holy Spirit descending on Jesus and then said, "I have seen and I testify that this is the Son of God" (1:34). When Nathanael first met Jesus, he was surprised by Jesus' intimate knowledge of him and stated, "Rabbi, you are the Son of God" (1:49).

Jesus himself said to Nicodemus in the famed John 3:16, "For God so loved the world that he gave his one and only Son, that whoever believes in him shall not perish but have eternal life." Clearly, Jesus perceived his sonship as unique; he was the "one and only Son." And he perceived himself as specially given, or sent, by God: "For God did not send his Son into the world to condemn the world, but to save the world through him" (3:17).

I once had a conversation about Jesus with a follower of the Hare Krishna religion in front of a department store in England. He tried to assure me that he believed Jesus was "god" like I did. I said, "I believe that Jesus of Nazareth is actually God." He looked relieved and said, "Well, I believe that too." I responded, "No, you believe Jesus is god in a Hindu, monistic way. You think that everything is part of god, and I don't believe that at all. I believe that Jesus taught that he was God in an utterly unique sense, and that he was right. He was the big one, the capital "G" God. He came to earth and took on flesh in a unique one-time-only way." Well, that is an idea that seems very strange today, but it is what Jesus himself taught.

To a number of his countrymen, Jesus said,

> "I tell you the truth, a time is coming and has now come when the dead will hear the voice of the Son of God and those who hear will live. For as the Father has life in himself, so he has granted the Son to have life in himself" (5:25-26).

The Father has *life in himself,* Jesus said, which means that no one gives him life and that his life is entirely self-sufficient. And then Jesus said the Father "grants" the Son life, which makes it sound as if the Son's life is not self-sufficient. But then we notice Jesus said the Father grants the Son "life in himself," like the Father! How the son is *granted life in himself* is a remarkable mystery to us. But this special reciprocal arrangement of equality between Father and Son is at the very heart of Jesus' self-understanding. The Father glorifies the Son and the Son glorifies the Father in a way that is absolutely unique. Look at the way Jesus began His prayer in John 17: "Father, the time has come. Glorify your Son, that your Son may glorify you" (17:1).

Jesus' contemporaries clearly understood he was claiming to have this kind of special relationship with God, a claim considered heretical, blasphemous, and dangerous by the Jews. In John 19, Pilate, a nervous Roman official, examined Jesus and then tried to dismiss the seriousness of the charges brought against him. In response, "The Jews insisted, 'We have a law, and according to that law he must die, because he claimed to be the Son of God'" (19:7).

Now maybe you want to read John's Gospel for your own reasons, and maybe you want to read that phrase "Son of God" as an enlightened way of saying we are all sons and daughters of God. You can do that. We live in a free country. But you must understand this was not how Jesus meant it, nor is this how his contemporaries took it. You can live in your own constructed world that makes you feel comfortable, but should you decide to investigate honestly the facts, you will find that Jesus spoke of himself as the Son of God in an utterly unique way, and that his contemporaries understood this very clearly.

This is why John places "the Son of God" appositionally to "Christ" in John 20:31: "But these are written that you may believe that Jesus is the Christ, the Son of God, and that by believing you may have life in his name."

Do not misunderstand this "sonship" kind of language. Jesus did not use this language to mean he is secondary to, or created by, the Father. He used it in the opposite way—to associate himself with God in his very nature, as if to say, "I am of the same essence, of the same stuff, as God." We see this particularly in the famous "I am" sayings of John's Gospel: "I am the true vine" (15:1, 5), "I am the good shepherd" (10:11, 14), "I am the gate" (10:7, 9), "I am the way" (14:6), and so forth. All of these would have prompted the Hebrew mind to recall Yahweh's words to Moses by the burning bush: "I AM WHO I AM" (Ex. 3:14). And notice what Jesus said at the end of one heated exchange: "'I tell you the truth,' Jesus answered, 'before Abraham was born, I am!'" (John 8:58). The people who heard him knew exactly what he was saying. You can tell by their response: "At this, they picked up stones to stone him, but Jesus hid himself, slipping away from the temple grounds" (8:59). Even if higher critics in today's academy or our Muslim friends deny it, we can hear what those pious Jews heard at the time: Jesus was claiming to *be* God. He was claiming to be the same one who revealed himself to the Old Testament Israelites as "I AM."

Jesus, in this tenaciously monotheistic culture that haltingly but doggedly withstood the siren call of Roman and Greek polytheism, was claiming to be the equal of God! Now, our own culture is increasingly saturated with mystical Eastern thought, and Jesus' claim to be the equal of God may seem less and less surprising since we have higher and higher thoughts of ourselves (as we understand ourselves, I think, less and less). But Jesus was brought up in a culture that understood many truths our culture does not understand, and one of those truths is the great distinction between God, the Creator of the universe, and ourselves, creatures in this universe. It was in the context of such a culture that Jesus claimed to be equal with God. Consider his statement and the people's response in chapter 5:

> Jesus said to them, "My Father is always at his work to this very day, and I, too, am working." For this reason the Jews tried all the harder to kill him; not only was he breaking the Sabbath, but he was even calling God his own Father, making himself equal with God (5:17-18).

A similar exchange occurs in chapter 10:

> "I and the Father are one."
> Again the Jews picked up stones to stone him, but Jesus said to them, "I have shown you many great miracles from the Father. For which of these do you stone me?"
> "We are not stoning you for any of these," replied the Jews, "but for blasphemy because you, a mere man, claim to be God" (10:30-33).

Jesus issued no denial of this accusation.

In fact, Jesus later reinforced the point privately with his disciples. Thomas asked where he was going, and Jesus replied,

> "I am the way and the truth and the life. No one comes to the Father except through me. If you really knew me, you would know my Father as well. From now on, you do know him and have seen him" (14:6-7).

The disciple Philip, not getting it, spoke up,

> "Lord, show us the Father and that will be enough for us." Jesus answered, "Don't you know me, Philip, even after I have been among you such a long time? Anyone who has seen me has seen the Father. How can you say, 'Show us the Father'?" (14:8-9).

Because Jesus is God, John can unabashedly record the worship of Jesus as God. A blind man whom Jesus healed worshiped him (9:38), as did Thomas, who formerly doubted: "'My Lord and my God!'" (20:28). And Jesus accepted these acts of worship.

The disciple Andrew proclaimed early in the Gospel, "'We have found the Messiah' (that is, the Christ)" (1:41). And John says who this Messiah is through Nathaniel only a few verses later: "'Rabbi, you are the Son of God'" (1:49). Of course, John had said as much already, in the very first verse of his Gospel: "In the beginning was the Word, and the Word was with God, and the Word was God" (1:1).

What Jesus Came to Do

A central part of who Jesus is and therefore what we are to believe is found in Jesus' teaching about what he came to do. He came to do a number of things.

Expose misunderstanding and disobedience. Jesus clearly came to reveal misunderstanding and disobedience among the Jewish people and their leaders. One interesting way to see this is to examine the three Sabbaths mentioned in the book. Jesus regularly attended synagogue on the Sabbath, and sometimes he took his turn as an adult male by reading from the scroll. But beyond that, he exposed misunderstanding and disobedience by acting contrary to what his religious peers required for Sabbath observance.

We noticed a moment ago in 5:18 that the Jews charged Jesus with making himself equal with God. But did you also notice the other charge in the line above that: "breaking the Sabbath." What prompted this charge? Jesus had seen a man who had been paralyzed for thirty-eight years lying on his mat, and said to him, "'Get up! Pick up your mat and walk.' At once the man was cured; he picked up his mat and walked" (5:8-9a). The story continues: "The day on which this took place was a Sabbath, and so the Jews said to the man who had been healed, 'It is the Sabbath; the law forbids you to carry your mat'" (5:9b-10). Really, it was Jesus they were after: "So, because Jesus was doing these things on the Sabbath, the Jews persecuted him" (5:16). Indeed, the Jews were good at remembering the smaller laws and reminding others of those laws, but they had forgotten why the law had been given in the first place. Jesus called further attention to their misuse of the law when he said,

> "I did one miracle, and you are all astonished. Yet, because Moses gave you cir-
> cumcision (though actually it did not come from Moses, but from the patriarchs),
> you circumcise a child on the Sabbath. Now if a child can be circumcised on the
> Sabbath so that the law of Moses may not be broken, why are you angry with
> me for healing the whole man on the Sabbath?" (7:21-23).

The second Sabbath is mentioned in chapter 9, where a man born blind receives his sight from Jesus:

> Now the day on which Jesus had made the mud and opened the man's eyes was a Sabbath. Therefore the Pharisees also asked him how he had received his sight. "He put mud on my eyes," the man replied, "and I washed, and now I see."
>
> Some of the Pharisees said, "This man is not from God, for he does not keep the Sabbath" (9:14-16).

Again, the Pharisees missed the point of the Sabbath. I think Jesus deliberately picked the Sabbath as an opportunity to expose their hypocrisy and jolt them out of their self-righteousness. Jesus did not come to help anyone keep up the pretence of holiness and love; he came to bring the real thing.

John's third mention of the Sabbath especially demonstrates what a sham the people's understanding of the day had become. In chapter 19 he writes,

> Now it was the day of Preparation, and the next day was to be a special Sabbath. Because the Jews did not want the bodies left on the crosses during the Sabbath, they asked Pilate to have the legs broken and the bodies taken down (19:31).

Do you see the irony in this? The chief priests were so mindful of the law's obligations, they literally dogged Jesus to death for healing on the Sabbath. So mindful were they that they cleaned up after the murder they had committed to avoid ceremonial uncleanness on the Sabbath.

Provide a sacrifice for the salvation of sinners. More fundamentally, Jesus came to save sinners. As he said, "I did not come to judge the world, but to save it" (12:47). And he came to save the world by acting as God's provision for their sins. He told the Pharisee Nicodemus,

> "Just as Moses lifted up the snake in the desert, so the Son of Man must be lifted up, that everyone who believes in him may have eternal life.
>
> "For God so loved the world that he gave his one and only Son, that whoever believes in him shall not perish but have eternal life" (3:14-16; cf. 8:28; 12:32).

Just as the bronze snake was God's provision for Israelites bitten by poisonous serpents (Numbers 21), Jesus came as God's provision for the salvation of sinners.

How, specifically, does God's provision in Christ save sinful humanity? John the Baptist points toward the answer near the beginning of the Gospel: "Look, the Lamb of God, who takes away the sin of the world!" (1:29). Jesus is the Passover sacrifice, who was killed in the stead of sinful human beings.

Jesus then says in chapter 6, "I tell you the truth, unless you eat the flesh of the Son of Man and drink his blood, you have no life in you. Whoever eats my flesh and drinks my blood has eternal life, and I will raise him up at the last day" (6:53-54). Jesus did not intend for his disciples to grab his arm and begin to chew on him. Rather, he intended for his blood to be shed and his body to be broken when he was lifted up on the cross. And sinners must put their confidence, their faith, in his substitutionary sacrifice.

Bring light into the world. Through his life, death, and resurrection, Jesus came to shed light upon God, man, and God's plan of salvation (1:4-9). As John says, "This is the verdict: light has come into the world . . . whoever lives by the truth comes into the light, so that it may be seen plainly that what he has done has been done through God" (3:19, 21). Jesus himself said to the crowds in Jerusalem, "I have come into the world as a light, so that no one who believes in me should stay in darkness" (12:46; also 8:12; 9:5, etc.).

Be glorified by the Father. And how did this light present itself? By the glory of the Father shining upon the Son. John writes, "We have seen his glory, the glory of the One and Only, who came from the Father, full of grace and truth" (1:14). And Jesus clearly said his glory came directly from the Father: "My Father, whom you claim as your God, is the one who glorifies me."[5]

Interestingly, throughout John's Gospel the reader is told that Jesus' time had "not yet come" (2:4; 7:6, 8, 30; 8:20). What is meant by this is not entirely clear at first, except that it is given as the reason for why no one could seize or stone him. The great dividing point in the Gospel comes in Jesus' last week, when he entered Jerusalem and announced that his time had come:

> "The hour has come for the Son of Man to be glorified. . . . Now my heart is troubled, and what shall I say? 'Father, save me from this hour'? No, it was for this very reason I came to this hour. Father, glorify your name!" (12:23, 27-28; also, 17:1).

The time that had come was the time of his glorification, and his glorification, we learn, happened at the cross! At the same moment, Jesus gave all glory to the Father: "Father, glorify your name!" Jesus the Son was in a unique position to bring glory to God the Father, by effecting the Father's merciful salvation and showing the Father's perfect love.

So John writes with a majestic simplicity, "Jesus knew that the time had come for him to leave this world and go to the Father. Having loved his own who were in the world, he now showed them the full extent of his love" (13:1).

---

[5] 8:54; also 2:11; 8:50; 11:4; 12:41; 13:32; 16:14; 17:4-5, 22, 24.

This is what we are to believe: Jesus is the Christ, the Son of God, who came into the world to expose disobedience, provide a sacrifice for sins, bring light to the world, and be glorified by the Father. In so doing he in turn gave glory to the Father.

WHY WE SHOULD BELIEVE

"But *these* are written that you may believe that Jesus is the Christ, the Son of God, and that by believing you may have life in his name" (20:31).

Why does John say we should believe that Jesus is the Christ? Again, John tells us, "These are written that you may believe . . ." What does the pronoun "these" in verse 31 refer to? It refers to the miraculous signs mentioned in verse 30. So to quickly answer our question, we should believe because of the miraculous signs John has written about that testify to the authenticity of everything he is saying.

What are these signs, and what exactly does it mean to believe?

What the Signs Are

John has been called the book of signs because he uses this word and because he gives careful attention to showing how those signs demonstrate Jesus is the Christ, the Messiah of God.

The first "miraculous sign" was Jesus' changing of the water to wine at the wedding in Cana (2:11). Later, Nicodemus came to him because of these "miraculous signs," believing they were indisputable evidence that Jesus was from God (3:2). The "second miraculous sign" was his healing of the royal official's son (4:54). And later, we learn that great crowds "followed him because they saw the miraculous signs he had performed on the sick" (6:2). But Jesus had little regard for his popularity. He was not out to win an election or begin a promo tour for some new religion.

Still, in these early days, people viewed Jesus as a celebrity rather than as a Savior, as a philanthropist rather than as the Son of Man. When crowds greeted him after the feeding of the five thousand, Jesus said, "I tell you the truth, you are looking for me, not because you saw miraculous signs but because you ate the loaves and had your fill" (6:26). They were more interested in what they could get from the miracles than in what the miracles meant about who he was. But Jesus performed these signs in order that people might see them and believe.

You may wonder if the miracles really happened. Interestingly, even Jesus' bitterest opponents, the Pharisees, conceded the miracles were real. Consider John 11:47: "Then the chief priests and the Pharisees called a meeting of the

Sanhedrin. 'What are we accomplishing?' they asked. 'Here is this man per-forming many miraculous signs.'"

Jesus raised Lazarus from the dead as his last great sign. Immediately after-ward he entered Jerusalem, and we read,

> Now the crowd that was with him when he called Lazarus from the tomb and raised him from the dead continued to spread the word. Many people, because they had heard that he had given this miraculous sign, went out to meet him (12:17-18).

So John recorded many of these miraculous signs in order to testify to an even larger claim. As he said,

> Jesus did many other miraculous signs in the presence of his disciples, which are not recorded in this book. But these are written that you may believe that Jesus is the Christ, the Son of God, and that by believing you may have life in his name (20:30-31).

What Believing Means

What does it mean to believe? At one point, the people directly asked Jesus what they must do to please God: "'What must we do to do the works God requires?' Jesus answered, 'The work of God is this: to believe in the one he has sent'" (6:28-29). Perhaps after reading this, you are thinking, "I would love to believe, if only I understood what it means. How do you do it?"

Well, let's examine the matter. In chapter 1, John writes that many did not "receive" Jesus (1:11), "Yet to all who received him, to those who believed in his name, he gave the right to become children of God—children born not of natural descent, nor of human decision or a husband's will, but born of God" (1:12-13). So believing is a kind of receiving, and apparently this receiving is worked out in our hearts by God.

Going through the Gospel, then, we find people believed in Jesus by receiv-ing him and his words, like the Samaritans in chapter 4. Jesus conversed with the woman at the well, she returned to her village, and, "Many of the Samaritans from that town believed in him because of the woman's testimony, 'He told me everything I ever did'" (4:39). The Samaritans then "urged him to stay with them" for two days (4:40),

> And because of his words many more became believers.
>   They said to the woman, "We no longer believe just because of what you said; now we have heard for ourselves, and we know that this man really is the Savior of the world" (4:41-42).

Notice the importance given to Jesus' words throughout this account: *"because of his words* many more became believers." Jesus later described unbelief as the failure to have God's "word dwell in you" (5:38). Positively, he described belief as bound up with valuing God's praise above man's (5:44), as well as with believing both Moses' words and his own words (5:46-47).

In chapter 6, Jesus hinted at what belief is not. He said, "'There are some of you who do not believe.' For Jesus had known from the beginning which of them did not believe and who would betray him" (6:64). Presumably, Judas, who spent three years in a close discipleship relationship with Jesus, thought he believed, or agreed, with Jesus' claims. But the kind of belief Jesus was talking about was not a probationary test drive. It was not mere armchair speculation or a passive religious gamble concerning the afterlife, which one may barely value anyway. I fear this is the fatal mistake many people make about the nature of belief, and they will perish because of this mistake. Saving belief is belief that lasts. Jesus said as much in chapter 8: "To the Jews who had believed him, Jesus said, 'If you hold to my teaching, you are really my disciples'" (8:31).

Furthermore, true belief does not simply mean *believing* Jesus, that is, believing that he is telling the truth and is not speaking lies. Rather, the work God requires is this: to *believe in* the one he has sent. Or as Jesus says elsewhere, "He who *believes in* me will live, even though he dies; and whoever lives and *believes in* me will never die" (11:25-26).[6] To believe, then, is to rely completely on his person and to trust totally what he teaches about himself. True believers see Jesus for who he says he is, *and they rely on him.*

Lazarus's resurrection released a flood of such belief in the environs of Jerusalem. Meeting in conclave, the desperate Jewish leaders responded, "If we let him go on like this, everyone will believe in him" (11:48). But the effects of Lazarus's resurrection continued: "for on account of [Lazarus] many of the Jews were going over to Jesus and putting their faith in him" (12:11). Not that everyone believed. "Even after Jesus had done all these miraculous signs in their presence, they still would not believe in him" (12:37). Apparently, the battle for faith was intense: "Yet at the same time many even among the leaders believed in him. But because of the Pharisees they would not confess their faith for fear . . ." (12:42).

The word that most helps us understand what Jesus meant by "believe" is the word "love." Jesus said to his disciples, "The Father himself loves you because you have loved me and have believed that I came from God" (16:27).

---

[6] See also 7:5; 9:35-36; 11:48; 12:37, 44; 16:9; 17:20.

The word that helps us understand "love" is the word "obey": "Whoever has my commands and obeys them, he is the one who loves me" (John 14:21).

Please hear the words of Jesus here. Do not think you love him because you know what he says. Everybody in John's Gospel hears Jesus. Do not think you love him because you have an emotional attachment to him. Do not think you love him because you know his teaching and affirm that it is true and would even defend it to a skeptical friend or family member. Do not deceive yourself. Hear the word of God: Jesus says, "Whoever has my commands and obeys them, he is the one who loves me."

We are to believe the facts about Jesus—that he came from God, lived, died, and rose again. And we are to believe in the person and work of Jesus— that we can rely on his love and sacrifice for us on the cross. But when we receive these things through God's work in our hearts and lives, we will believe in him with persevering love and obedience.

THE RESULTS OF BELIEVING

"But these are written that you may believe that Jesus is the Christ, the Son of God, *and that by believing you may have life in his name*" (20:31).

What are the results of believing? As John states in 20:31, by believing we will be given life in Jesus' name. Several stages are involved in this process.

Our Present State: We Are Condemned

As we have seen, Jesus did not come to condemn the world, but to save it. The condemnation had already happened—at the Fall, through the curse. And in another sense condemnation is reserved for the day of Christ's promised return in power and glory (12:48). Yet Jesus also provided a grotesque preview of how the final judgment already appears among us: in our natural selves, we stand condemned already. More than that, we are all spiritually dead, and we dwell among the spiritually dead. Jesus warned, "Whoever believes in [God's Son] is not condemned, but whoever does not believe stands condemned already because he has not believed in the name of God's one and only Son" (3:18). Before we believe, Jesus says we dwell by nature in "death" (5:24). We are born dead! *Life* comes through hearing and believing (5:24). Apart from such life, we can expect final condemnation (5:29). The devil, the prince of this world, "stands condemned" (16:11), and all who follow his evil rebellion will share his ultimate fate. This is the grim picture that Jesus presents. It is one of darkness and death. If you do not understand this, you will not understand anything that follows.

We Can Be Saved

The good news that follows this grotesque and dark picture is that Jesus came this first time to save all those who believe. Once more, "God did not send his Son into the world to condemn the world, but to save the world through him" (3:17).

When Jesus met with the Samaritans in John 4, he taught that salvation is *from* the Jews but *for* the world! And they recognized how good the news was (4:22, 42). Jesus came to save. "I am the gate; whoever enters through me will be saved. He will come in and go out, and find pasture" (10:9).

Ironically, we can be saved because Jesus *did not* save himself from the wrath of God. Since he absorbed God's wrath, we who believe his Word are saved from God's wrath (12:27). However, those who reject his Word will themselves be judged: "Whoever believes in the Son has eternal life, but whoever rejects the Son will not see life, for God's wrath remains on him" (3:36; cf. 12:47-48). We are given a choice: believe in his Word and let him absorb God's judgment on our behalf; or reject his Word and absorb it ourselves.

We Can Have Life

Being saved from wrath means being saved to life. John writes of Jesus, "In him was life, and that life was the light of men" (1:4).

The theme resonates loudly and melodiously through the entire Gospel. Jesus gave life to the royal official's son (4:50). Jesus called himself the "bread of God" who gives life to the world (6:33). And again, he is the "bread of life," and whoever "comes to me will never go hungry, and he who believes in me will never be thirsty" (6:35). His words are Spirit-filled words that give life (6:63).

Ironically, as Jesus was giving life, his opponents were skulking about trying to take his life. "Jesus went around in Galilee, purposely staying away from Judea because the Jews there were waiting to take his life" (7:1). A bit later, Jesus summarized the difference between his work and the efforts of the skulkers: "The thief comes only to steal and kill and destroy; I have come that they may have life, and have it to the full" (10:10). He was not a thief, but a shepherd: "I am the good shepherd. The good shepherd lays down his life for the sheep. . . . just as the Father knows me and I know the Father—and I lay down my life for the sheep" (10:11, 15).

Despite opposition, the theme of life plays on. When Lazarus died, Jesus found Martha mourning and said to her, "I am the resurrection and the life. He who believes in me will live, even though he dies" (11:25). He then raised

Lazarus from death to life! Not that the forces of death gave up the fight: "So from that day on they plotted to take his life" (11:53).

Later Jesus said to his disciples, "I am the way and the truth and the life. No one comes to the Father except through me" (John 14:6).

And, "Greater love has no one than this, that he lay down his life for his friends" (15:13).

And, "But these are written that you may believe that Jesus is the Christ, the Son of God, and that by believing you may have life in his name" (20:31).

We Can Have Eternal Life

What kind of life does Jesus promise for those who believe? He promises eternal life. "For God so loved the world that he gave his one and only Son, that whoever believes in him shall not perish but have eternal life" (3:16). As we have already seen, our acceptance or rejection of the Son makes the difference: "Whoever believes in the Son has eternal life, but whoever rejects the Son will not see life, for God's wrath remains on him" (3:36).

Eternal life is the gift of Christ: "I give them eternal life, and they shall never perish; no one can snatch them out of my hand" (10:28; cf. 4:14).

Eternal life comes through belief: "For my Father's will is that everyone who looks to the Son and believes in him shall have eternal life, and I will raise him up at the last day" (6:40). And a few verses later: "I tell you the truth, he who believes has everlasting life" (6:47).

Eternal life is otherworldly: "The man who loves his life will lose it, while the man who hates his life in this world will keep it for eternal life" (12:25).

But what does eternal life look like? Jesus defines it beautifully in his final prayer:

> "You granted him [that is, Jesus, the Son] authority over all people that he might give eternal life to all those you have given him. Now this is eternal life: that they may know you, the only true God, and Jesus Christ, whom you have sent" (17:2-3).

We Can Have Full Life

Jesus' own life was "full of grace and truth" (1:14). And Jesus came to give those who believe the same fullness of life: "The thief comes only to steal and kill and destroy; I have come that they may have life, and have it to the full" (10:10). He can give us full life because he gives us *his* life, a life full of grace and truth and joy! As he prayed to the Father, "I am coming to you now, but I say these things while I am still in the world, so that they may have the full measure of my joy within them" (17:13).

We Can Have a Life of Love

Jesus said that loving him is a sign of being a child of God. "If God were your Father, you would love me, for I came from God and now am here. I have not come on my own; but he sent me" (8:42). Certainly love typified Jesus' life, as we have already seen in chapter 13: "Jesus knew that the time had come for him to leave this world and go to the Father. Having loved his own who were in the world, he now showed them the full extent of his love" (13:1). And since we have been the recipients of such boundless love, we who are believers are called to the same life of love: "A new command I give you: Love one another. As I have loved you, so you must love one another. By this all men will know that you are my disciples, if you love one another" (13:34-35). Being his disciples in our own day and age demands that we hear Jesus' teaching on love. Some time ago, I was asked to speak at a conference, and before the event I received a piece of correspondence from one of the other speakers. He and I were presenting one part of the conference together, and he wanted to consider with me how we could explain the gospel in a way that would be less offensive. But after looking at John's Gospel, I have to say it is a perilous thing to make the Christian message less offensive. It pretty much lives on its offensiveness. It says we are spiritually dead. It says Jesus is our only hope for life. But there is a powerful dynamic at work between the Christian message and the Christian life, because Christian lives should be attractive. Christian lives should be full of love, not to mention grace, truth, and joy. The message of the Gospel is hard for all of us to hear at first. But when people made in the image of God—however distorted the image has become—observe us living attractive lives that increasingly image the love of our Savior, they come to a place where they are prepared to hear this message and to say, "I want to know more about that."

How do you know if you love Jesus like this? Jesus answers that question for his disciples in chapter 14: "If you love me, you will obey what I command" (14:15). And again, "Whoever has my commands and obeys them, he is the one who loves me" (14:21a). The rest of the verse contains a promise: "He who loves me will be loved by my Father, and I too will love him and show myself to him" (14:21b). Apparently, this is important because Jesus repeats all of it: "If anyone loves me, he will obey my teaching. My Father will love him, and we will come to him and make our home with him" (14:23). Behind these instructions and promises is Christ's example of loving the Father through obedience: "The world must learn that I love the Father and that I do exactly what my Father has commanded me" (14:31).

There was much discussion of love on Jesus' final night with his disciples.

As the night wore on, Jesus came back to love again and again: "As the Father has loved me, so have I loved you. Now remain in my love" (15:9).

"If you obey my commands, you will remain in my love, just as I have obeyed my Father's commands and remain in his love" (15:10).

"My command is this: Love each other as I have loved you. Greater love has no one than this, that he lay down his life for his friends" (15:12-13).

"This is my command: Love each other" (15:17).

"If you belonged to the world, it would love you as its own. As it is, you do not belong to the world, but I have chosen you out of the world. That is why the world hates you" (15:19).

CONCLUSION

Jesus is God the eternal Son, who has come to give us who believe life by his death. John writes, "But these are written that you may believe that Jesus is the Christ, the Son of God, and that by believing you may have life in his name."

Do you believe?

As suggested at the beginning, we should not be shocked when authors today who write about Jesus expose their unbelief. Many of Jesus' own contemporaries did not believe in him, and many excuses were given for that unbelief. Publicly, they said he was from the wrong place, or that he disregarded God's laws, or that he was blasphemous. Privately, they said something a little different. They admitted that he threatened their imperfect but comfortable *status quo*. They had worked out with Rome a decent power base for themselves (5:16; 9:14-16; 5:18; 11:45-50). Yet John reveals the chilling but ultimate reality: God had already begun his judgment upon them for their unbelief (12:37-43).

Of course, anyone who reads John's Gospel today, or who is reading this message right now, still has the opportunity to believe. As we have seen, some scholars believe this book was an evangelistic piece written for Jews looking for the Messiah. Whether or not this is correct, John's Gospel presents the same challenge to us today. John has laid out the facts with the explicit goal of convincing us that Jesus is the Messiah and Lord who is worthy of our whole lives: "But these are written that you may believe that Jesus is the Christ, the Son of God." Not that it is just facts John says we must submit to. It is *him* we submit to.

We have concluded the last two studies in Mark and Luke with the apostle Peter, and we close with Peter yet again, as John's Gospel does. In God's providence, Peter is a great example for us. In our study of Mark, we left him weeping bitterly for his denials of Jesus. In our study of Luke, we left him running toward the tomb, after the women said they had seen him. In John, we pick up Peter's story after the resurrection, when Jesus appeared to the disciples by the lake in Galilee to eat with them:

> When they had finished eating, Jesus said to Simon Peter, "Simon son of John, do you truly love me more than these?"
>
> "Yes, Lord," he said, "you know that I love you."
>
> Jesus said, "Feed my lambs."
>
> Again Jesus said, "Simon son of John, do you truly love me?"
>
> He answered, "Yes, Lord, you know that I love you."
>
> Jesus said, "Take care of my sheep."
>
> The third time he said to him, "Simon son of John, do you love me?"
>
> Peter was hurt because Jesus asked him the third time, "Do you love me?"
>
> He said, "Lord, you know all things; you know that I love you."
>
> Jesus said, "Feed my sheep" (21:15-17).

Why did Jesus ask Peter the same basic question three times? Some have focused on the slight variations in the way Jesus puts the question. Different words and tenses were used. But I don't think much can be found in that direction. It was still the same question: "Do you love me?" Instead, I think—and this is speculation in part because the text does not say—he asked three times because Peter had denied knowing him three times.

Jesus did not forever bar Peter from serving him. He told him, "Feed my lambs, take care of my sheep, feed my sheep." He challenged Peter to give evidence of his belief in and love for Christ through loving Christ's people. He was not to assume some grand office like pope or even senior pastor; he was to give himself again and again in love to Christ's people.

And then Jesus made this prediction about Peter's life:

> "I tell you the truth, when you were younger you dressed yourself and went where you wanted, but when you are old you will stretch out your hands, and someone else will dress you and lead you where you do not want to go." Jesus said this to indicate the kind of death by which Peter would glorify God. Then he said to him, "Follow me!" (21:18-19).

Did Peter follow him? Earlier Jesus had said, "This is to my Father's glory, that you bear much fruit, showing yourselves to be my disciples" (15:8). And we know that Peter went on and became a great apostle who bore much fruit. He was the first apostle to take the gospel to the Gentiles. We also know he again stumbled badly and Paul had to make a public example of him (Gal. 2:11ff.). Peter had so misconstrued the gospel by his actions that Paul had to give him a dressing-down in front of everyone.

But it seems that Peter obediently heard Paul's rebuke. Peter's letters in the New Testament are gems, filled with instruction and encouragement for following Christ through times of suffering. And Peter lived up to his own instruction and encouragement. John, writing his Gospel probably a couple of decades after Peter's death, could look back and see "the kind of death by which Peter would glorify God." Tradition has it that around A.D. 67 in Rome, Peter was crucified upside down, because he did not consider himself worthy to be crucified right side up like Christ.

Peter did believe in Christ finally, and he did love him finally with his life. Jesus said, "I am the resurrection and the life. He who believes in me will live, even though he dies; and whoever lives and believes in me will never die. Do you believe this?" (John 11:25-26).

I wonder what you will write in your diary tonight? "Nothing of importance happened today"?

Let us pray:

Lord, there are so many things we think are of such great importance, until we see what you have done for us and until we understand our need. Lord, then we see that above all we must give attention to following you. We pray that you would teach our hearts to believe in what you have done in love for us. And we pray that you would win our hearts in love for you even today. For Jesus' sake. Amen.

Questions for Reflection

1. What do you say to someone who says the Bible's teachings about Jesus are at least partly, if not wholly, mythological, like some of the tales about America's founding fathers?

2. As we have seen, Thomas Jefferson once said Jesus' "natural endowments [were] great, his life correct and innocent; he was meek, benevolent, patient, firm, disinterested, and of the sumblimest eloquence." Why is this *damning* Jesus *with faint praise*, as the cliché goes? In other words, why should we *not* be encouraged as Christians when someone refers to Jesus as merely a "great teacher," "an inspired prophet," or even "an example for all humankind"?

3. Why did so many of Jesus' contemporaries hate him? What does this suggest about the audience Jesus was playing to? What implications does this have for the Christian life? What audience do you play to?

4. According to the Gospel of John, whom does Jesus intend to glorify above all others? Whom should we intend to glorify in our own lives and in the life of our church? Is this priority reflected in the sermons at your church? How? What about the Bible studies you attend? In your own life, was this priority reflected in the way you lived last week? Would God, who can read your thoughts, agree?

5. How, specifically, is Christ "God's provision" for sinful humanity? In other words, how does Christ's sacrifice provide for the salvation of sinners?

6. When is Jesus "glorified" in John's Gospel? Why then? If we are Christians, what in our day-to-day lives will bring him the greatest glory?

7. What is the biblical purpose of miraculous signs?

8. What does John's Gospel mean by "believe"? What does John's Gospel *not* mean by "believe"? What does true believing look like in a Christian's life? What does *false* believing look like in someone's life? Are false believers typically aware of the fact that their belief is false? If you consider yourself a Christian, how can you be sure you are not a false believer? What practical steps can a church take to help cultivate true believers, and not false ones, in its public gatherings? In its sermons? In its music? In its evangelism? In its practice of church discipline?

9. The sins *you* have committed either will receive or already have received the infinite wrath of God. This fact is as certain as anything else in the universe. Are you then necessarily condemned to enduring God's punishment? Why or why not? Are you clear about this fact with non-Christians in your evangelism? Or do you consider this just a scare tactic?

10. According to John's Gospel, how do you know if you love Jesus? If you consider yourself a Christian, how have you loved Jesus, practically speaking, during this past month?

THE MESSAGE OF ACTS: JESUS, THE RISEN LORD

5

THE MESSAGE OF ACTS: JESUS, THE RISEN LORD

THE REASSURANCE OF PREDICTABILITY[1]

"It pleased the Lord to take to himself, my dear and faithful wife, with whom I had lived nearly forty-two years; whose tenderness to me, and faithfulness to God, were such as cannot, by me, be expressed, as she constantly sympathised with me in all my afflictions. I can truly say, I never heard her utter the least discontent under all the various providences that attended either me or her; she eyed the hand of God in all our sorrows, so as constantly to encourage me in the ways of God: her death was the greatest sorrow to me that ever I met with in the world." So said English Baptist minister William Kiffin in 1682 about the death of his wife, Hanna.[2]

Kiffin's grief over his wife's death was both profound and common. It was unique to him yet a widely shared experience. People experience grief differently, yet there is a sameness that surrounds our attitudes toward death. As the years pass by, we grapple with the inevitability of the death of our loved ones and of ourselves. So we resign ourselves to it and make our uncomfortable peace with it.

Perhaps what helps us bear the prospect of our death is the universality of it. Everyone dies. Death is a one-way street, right? The rule to which there are no exceptions? The verdict against which there is no appeal? As the eleventh-century *Rubaiyat* of Omar Khayyam put it, "The Moving Finger writes, and, having writ, moves on."

Yet this is where a careful look at the truth about Jesus may unsettle us. He died, yes, but a number of early witnesses tell us he also rose from the dead.

---

[1] This sermon was originally preached on July 11, 1999, at Capitol Hill Baptist Church in Washington, D.C.
[2] William Kiffin, quoted in Michael Haykin, *Kiffin, Knollys, and Keach: Rediscovering English Baptist Heritage* (Leeds, England: Reformation Today, 1996), 51.

He defied the natural order! He was the exception to the rule! What do we make of this?

Many refuse to acknowledge it. They assume Jesus of Nazareth is just like them, except that he lived and died a long time ago. It is much easier to look back at Jesus and make him like us. It is natural to admire an individual for traits that we value in ourselves rather than for what may or may not be true of the person.

Some have suggested that the long effort by liberal scholars in the last century, referred to as the "quest for the Historical Jesus," was always doomed to failure because scholars who abandon the written record of Scripture will inevitably reconstruct a picture of Jesus that looks like themselves and their own hopes idealized. As Albert Schweitzer once said, they "looked down the well of human history and saw in the bottom a reflection of their own face."

But we do not have to be scholars to do that. We all have a tendency to hear what we like to hear and to see what we like to see. And we tend to do that with Jesus. Perhaps you have noticed all the different pictures of Jesus hanging in different kinds of churches. There are white and black Jesuses (even though he was from the Middle East), burly and holy Jesuses, happy and somber Jesuses, fun and responsible Jesuses, certain and questioning Jesuses, resolved Jesuses, and responsible Jesuses. In a similar vein, I noticed long ago that you can tell what a pastor really values by listening to him talk about Jesus.

Recently, I read that more than 1,500 books had been published on Jesus in the preceding twelve months—all of them with their own portrait and slant. Lutheran theologian Carl Braaten said it well: "There is no lack of Jesusology in America; American religion of all kinds retains its fascination with Jesus, as one of the most unforgettable personalities of all time."[3] But it is only on the level of personality that most people pay any attention to him. After all, he is very interesting. And he is just enigmatic and complex enough that something can be found for everyone. So we look to him, see something of ourselves, and are assured that reality is as we imagine it to be.

But what if you desire more than an immediate reassurance of what you already believe? What if you are interested in knowing the truth, even if the truth sounds surprising?

INTRODUCING ACTS

In the event that you are interested in knowing the truth, we come to the book of Acts. We have been examining the earliest historical sources about Jesus—

---

[3] Carl E. Braaten, in Carl E. Braaten and Robert W. Jenson, eds., *Either/Or: The Gospel or Neopaganism* (Grand Rapids, Mich.: Eerdmans, 1995), 10.

Matthew, Mark, Luke, and John—in order to find the truth about him. Despite all the interest in Jesus these days, there is remarkably little written at a popular level that draws from the primary sources.

Luke wrote both the book of Luke and the book of Acts. In fact, they are the two parts of one larger work that scholars believe were separated when the Gospels were put together in one volume and the Gospel of John was inserted between the two. In addition to similarities of word usage and writing style, both books are addressed to Theophilus, perhaps Luke's wealthy Greek patron. The book of Luke begins "it seemed good also to me to write an orderly account for you, most excellent Theophilus, so that you may know the certainty of the things you have been taught" (Luke 1:3-4). The book of Acts follows right in step: "In my former book, Theophilus, I wrote about all that Jesus began to do and to teach until the day he was taken up to heaven" (Acts 1:1-2). The book of Luke presents Luke's account of the birth, life, ministry, death, and resurrection of Jesus. The book of Acts provides Luke's account of what happened next in history: Jesus ascended to heaven, and the apostles led the church through its earliest days and initial growth.

The book of Acts has 28 chapters. Chapters 1–12, roughly, comprise the first half of the book. They focus mostly on Jerusalem and its environs. Chapters 13–28, the second half, follow the ministry of Paul on his three missionary journeys through the areas we now call Turkey, Greece, and Italy.[4] Acts takes about two-and-a-half hours to read silently, which is a good investment of time. Think of all the things you are willing to sit and do for two and a half hours—watch a movie, read a couple of magazines, chat on the phone, run an errand. Let me encourage you to find one two-and-a-half-hour segment in your week to read Acts. It is a wonderful and exciting story.

In this last study of section 1, seeking out the truth about Jesus from these earliest witnesses, we will observe three aspects of this truth:

> First, what is the message about Jesus?
> Then, what is the mission of Jesus?
> Finally, what means are used to accomplish this mission?

I think we will find that Jesus is not just like us, and that that is a good thing, too.

THE MESSAGE ABOUT JESUS

Athens might have been known as the center of learning in the ancient world, but Luke described the city as filled with people who "spent their time doing

---

[4] Journey 1: 13:4–14:27; journey 2: 15:36–18:22; journey 3: 18:23–20:38.

nothing but talking about and listening to the latest ideas" (Acts 17:21). Having lived in Washington, D.C., for a number of years, I am not unfamiliar with that kind of city. But you do not need to visit ancient Athens or present-day Washington to find such endless talk. The subject of Christianity itself has given rise to excessive chatter wherever it is discussed. If you spend time in bookstores or take courses on Christianity or comparative religion, you will find Christianity examined and debated in terms of everything from its social implications to its psychological ramifications; from its impact on Western history to the sense of self it provides. People love to wade through Christianity's rich tradition. Yet all this talk can obscure the real message.

What is the core message of Christianity?

Witnesses to the Message

The book of Acts is an important witness to help us discern the core message of Christianity because it provides accounts of many of the earliest statements about Jesus. You might say that Acts has forty-two "testimonies" to the gospel. There are ten sermons, which I define as at least several sentences in a row of someone preaching (Peter preaches five sermons, Paul preaches four, and Stephen preaches one).[5] There are thirty preaching summaries.[6] And there are two commissions given by Jesus.[7] Partially overlapping with these forty-two testimonies are the descriptions of Christianity provided by its opponents. The Jews believed the Christians were preaching against the temple, the law, their customs, and circumcision.[8] The Greek philosophers suggested that the Christian message concerned foreign gods (17:18). And the Greek silversmiths and idol manufacturers saw in Christianity the "danger not only that our trade will lose its good name, but also that the temple of the great goddess Artemis will be discredited" (19:27).

Throughout the book, the apostles displayed an ability to present the gospel in an amazing diversity of ways, yet always pointing to the same gospel. When Paul preached to the Greek philosophers in Athens, he argued from the basis of their experience and reason. He did not cite Scripture; he started with creation and reasoned from there (17:22-23, 24-29). When the apostles spoke to the Jewish crowds in Jerusalem, or in synagogues around the Mediterranean

---

[5] By Peter: 2:22-39; 3:12-26; 4:8-12; 5:29-32; 10:36-43; by Paul: 13:15-41; 17:22-31; 22; 26:2-23; by Stephen: 7:2-53.
[6] 4:33; 5:28; 5:42; 6:13-14; 7:52-53; 8:12; 8:30-36; 9:20, 22; 15:11; 17:2-3; 17:8a; 17:8b; 18:5; 18:13; 18:15; 18:28; 19:8; 19:26; 20:21, 24, 25, 27; 21:19-21; 21:28; 23:6; 23:29; 24:5-6; 25:19; 26:6-9, 18, 20, 22-23; 28:20; 28:23; 28:31.
[7] To the apostles in 1:8; to Paul in 9:15.
[8] 6:13-14; 18:13, 15, 28-29; 21:21; 24:6.

world, they began by rehearsing Old Testament history (7:2-50; 13:17-22) or by arguing that the prophecies of Scripture had been fulfilled in their time.[9]

Substance of the Message

The message preached by these earliest Christians in the book of Acts was about Jesus (1:8; 8:35; 9:15; 17:18b; 22:15; 26:16). This is exactly what Jesus commissioned his disciples in chapter 1 and Paul in chapter 9 to do—to go all around the world and be witnesses to his life, death, and resurrection.[10] Jesus knew he was the focus of God's saving activity in the world.

Jesus' life. Occasionally, these early Christians preached about Jesus' life (2:22; 10:37-39; 19:24-25). But on the whole the sermons were not filled with such biographical details. Perhaps the hearers of the day would have already known the particulars of Jesus' life. Or perhaps the author Luke left those details out, knowing his reader would find them in his first book, the Gospel of Luke. For whatever reason, Luke's account of these early preachers does not present them as placing their primary emphases on the particulars of Jesus' life.

Jesus' death. The main emphasis of the message about Jesus in Acts, interestingly, was unlike the main emphasis you will find in most biographies of great people. In most biographies, everything noteworthy an individual did over his or her life is recounted, followed by a description of retirement or perhaps a tragic death. But with Jesus, the end of the story was the focus! The death and resurrection of Jesus were what these early Christians talked about! Again and again, they referred to his death and its significance.[11] They did not try to win people over with glowing endorsements of Jesus' life: "he was the greatest rabbi since Shimmei" or "the most profound prophet since Malachi." In fact, they were honest and straightforward about the fact that very often Jesus' teachings and public pronouncements were rejected (e.g., 4:11).

Not only did these early witnesses refer often to Christ's death; again and again, as they tried to win Jewish people to Christianity, they said, "you killed him"! (2:36; 3:13, 15; 4:10; 5:30; 7:52). These early preachers do not pull punches. Jesus' terrible death, they said, fulfilled Old Testament prophecy that God's people would reject the one he sent. Stephen forcibly made this point in his sermon (7:35, 39-43, 51-52). And while Jesus' suffering must have been, for many, a stumbling block to belief in his Messiahship, these preachers actually used Jesus' sufferings as evidence *for* his Messiahship (3:18; 8:32; 13:27-29; 17:2-3; 26:22-23). Evidently most first-century Jews had never noticed that

[9] 2:25-28, 34; 3:22-25; 4:11; 7:37; 10:43; 13:23, 27, 29, 32-37, 39-41; 17:2-3; 18:28; 26:6-7, 22-23, 27; 28:20, 23.
[10] 1:8, 22; 4:33; 5:32; 9:15; 10:39, 41-42; 13:3-11; 18:5; 20:24; 22:14-15; 26:16, 22.
[11] 2:23; 3:13-15; 4:10; 5:28, 30; 7:52; 8:32; 10:39; 13:27-29.

Isaiah 53 promised the Messiah would come and suffer. But these disciples had finally learned that truth from Jesus, and now they used it as another piece of evidence for his Messiahship (e.g., 8:32).

Jesus' resurrection. If you read through the book of Acts, though, you will find that the undisputed center of the early Christians' message was the resurrection of Jesus. Again and again they preached that Jesus was raised from the dead.[12] Notice how Luke summarized what they preached early in the book: "With great power the apostles continued to testify to the resurrection of the Lord Jesus, and much grace was upon them all" (4:33). As we have seen, this is what Jesus told them to do. Before he ascended, he said, "You will receive power when the Holy Spirit comes on you; and you will be my witnesses in Jerusalem, and in all Judea and Samaria, and to the ends of the earth" (1:8). When the disciples set about to replace Judas, they looked for someone who could be a "witness with us of his resurrection" (1:22).

After all, Jesus' resurrection from the dead proved beyond a shadow of a doubt that Jesus of Nazareth was the Son of God, the Messiah, the Christ, the Promised One.[13] This is what Peter argued in the first recorded Christian sermon, preached in Jerusalem at Pentecost (2:14-36). He cited Old Testament Scriptures as well as some of the recent events involving Jesus of Nazareth, including his resurrection, for proof. What is interesting, however, is that Peter treated the resurrection as a given. Though the resurrection was central to his message, the resurrection was not argued *for,* as if people were skeptical about it, so much as it was argued *from.* The fact that it happened was not treated as a matter of dispute. Rather, it seems to have been assumed that everyone in Jerusalem knew the resurrection had happened. Too many people saw Jesus crucified and then saw him alive after his death. And even if they did not personally see him, they knew many people who did. It is worth noting that one of the stronger arguments for the resurrection is the fact that these early Christians could assume that nonbelievers believed in the resurrection.

Significance of the Message

The great question concerning the resurrection is, what does it mean? What was the significance of the fact that Jesus of Nazareth, after being crucified, got up from the dead? At Pentecost, Peter argued from Old Testament prophecy as well as from the life, death, and resurrection of Jesus that Jesus uniquely fulfilled the promise for a Messiah. And Jesus the Messiah came to bring in the

---

[12] 2:24-32; 3:15, 26; 4:10, 33; 5:30; 10:40-41; 13:30-31, 33-37; 17:3, 18b, 31-32; 23:6; 24:15, 21; 25:19; 26:8, 15-16, 22-23.
[13] 9:20; see also 2:21, 36; 5:42; 8:32-34; 9:22; 17:3; 18:5, 15, 28; 24:24 [28:23]; 28:31.

kingdom of God, that is, the rule and reign of God (8:12; 19:8; 20:25; 28:23, 31). This is the good news! (5:42; 8:12, 35; 10:36; 13:32; 17:18b).

The people who believed Jesus was the resurrected Messiah were "called Christians first at Antioch" (11:26); the title would have had the significance of "Messianics." At the heart of the disciple's message, then, was the answer to the millenniums-old question, Who is the Messiah? "It is Jesus!" they said. And this has been the unifying theme in our studies. "What is the truth about Jesus?" It is the recognition that, in Jesus, God fulfilled his ancient promise to redeem a people for himself. Jesus came as the Savior, that is, a bringer of salvation (4:12; 5:31; 13:23, 26; 15:11). And he will come again as Judge of the living and the dead (10:42; 17:31; 24:25).

What does it mean for Jesus to be our Savior? The Savior saves us from our sins. He wipes them out and brings forgiveness from God (3:19; 5:31; 10:43; 13:38; 22:16; 26:18). Quoting Moses, Peter warned that anyone who did not listen to this prophet, this Messiah, "will be completely cut off" (3:23; cf. 4:12). The same is true for us today. The early Christians present us with this message: either your sins will be wiped out by Jesus, or you will be wiped out by your sins. There is salvation in no one else.

How did these early Christians say the blessings of salvation come? We must repent,[14] believe,[15] and be baptized,[16] all while calling on Christ's name (2:21; 8:12; 10:43; 22:16). Peter summarized the appropriate response to the gospel as "believ[ing] in the Lord Jesus Christ" (11:17). He and the other disciples did not say "be circumcised." Nor did they say to any non-Jews, "If you want to accept our Jewish Messiah, become Jewish by being circumcised." No, they said turn *from* your sins and *to* God, have faith in him and what he has done in Christ, and be baptized as a symbolic cleansing and confession. This is what the early Christians meant by "testifying to the gospel of God's grace," as Paul put it (20:24).

Two verses in particular well summarize what the early Christians teach us—13:39 and 15:11. First, Paul said to the Jews in the synagogue, "Through [Jesus] everyone who believes is justified from everything you could not be justified from by the law of Moses" (13:39). Justification comes from believing, not from the law of Moses. Paul could not have stated it more clearly.

Second, some of the Jewish Christians at the council at Jerusalem insisted that "The Gentiles must be circumcised and required to obey the law of Moses" (15:5). The apostles and elders considered this proposal, and then Peter addressed the whole council:

---

[14] 2:38; 3:19, 26; 5:31; 17:30; 20:21; 26:18, 20.
[15] 4:4; 8:12; 10:43; 13:39, 48; 15:7, 9; 17:34; 20:21; 21:20; 22:19; 24:24; 26:18.
[16] 2:38; 8:13, 36, 38; 10:47-48; 22:16.

"Brothers, you know that some time ago God made a choice among you that the Gentiles might hear from my lips the message of the gospel and believe. God, who knows the heart, showed that he accepted them by giving the Holy Spirit to them, just as he did to us. He made no distinction between us and them, for he purified their hearts by faith. Now then, why do you try to test God by putting on the necks of the disciples a yoke that neither we nor our fathers have been able to bear? *No! We believe it is through the grace of our Lord Jesus that we are saved, just as they are*" (15:7b-11; verse 11 in italics).

Peter's answer was very different from the solution offered by some today who see faith as a universal religious substance rather than as a disposition of heart that comes to life when it views its true object—Christ!

And notice how 15:11 begins: "No!" "No" is a surprisingly good way to begin a presentation of the gospel, especially if the person with whom you are speaking believes something that contradicts the gospel. No, we are not naturally right with God. No, attending church on Sunday or being nice to your work colleagues will not save you. No, not all paths lead to God. "No! We believe it is through the grace of our Lord Jesus that we are saved."

Goal of the Message

The goal of the disciples' teaching, finally, was for Jesus to be worshiped as God. In the Gospels, Jesus accepted the worship that was reserved for God alone. In Acts, the apostles allowed no one else to be worshiped as God except Jesus. Peter did not let the focus on Jesus be displaced: "As Peter entered the house, Cornelius met him and fell at his feet in reverence. But Peter made him get up. 'Stand up,' he said, 'I am only a man myself'" (10:25-26). Nor do Paul and Barnabas:

In Lystra there sat a man crippled in his feet, who was lame from birth and had never walked. He listened to Paul as he was speaking. Paul looked directly at him, saw that he had faith to be healed and called out, "Stand up on your feet!" At that, the man jumped up and began to walk.

When the crowd saw what Paul had done, they shouted in the Lycaonian language, "The gods have come down to us in human form!" Barnabas they called Zeus, and Paul they called Hermes because he was the chief speaker. The priest of Zeus, whose temple was just outside the city, brought bulls and wreaths to the city gates because he and the crowd wanted to offer sacrifices to them.

But when the apostles Barnabas and Paul heard of this, they tore their clothes and rushed out into the crowd, shouting: "Men, why are you doing this? We too are only men, human like you. We are bringing you good news, telling you to turn from these worthless things to the living God, who made heaven and earth and sea and everything in them. In the past, he let all nations go their own way. Yet he has not left himself without testimony: He has shown kindness by giving you rain from heaven and crops in their seasons; he provides you with plenty of food and fills your hearts with joy." Even with these words, they had difficulty keeping the crowd from sacrificing to them (14:8-18).

But notice how fickle such adoration is: "Then some Jews came from Antioch and Iconium and won the crowd over. They stoned Paul and dragged him outside the city, thinking he was dead" (14:19). In the space of a verse, the crowd changed from a posture of worship to the activity of stoning. Peter, Paul, and Barnabas knew they were neither the Savior nor the promise of salvation. Jesus is.

Luke provides another powerful example of wrongly directed worship in Acts 12. Sycophantic crowds praised Herod as if he were "a god." Herod said nothing to correct them, so "the Lord struck him down, and he was eaten by worms and died" (12:23). Luke then points to the real eternal ruler in the next sentence: "But the word of God continued to increase and spread."

What is the message of the early Christians? What is their good news? It is the same message that we who are evangelicals preach. As Paul says to the Romans, we have sinned and fallen short of the glory of God (3:23). But God, in his great love, has put on human flesh in Christ and died in our place on the cross. He took upon himself the Father's wrath merited by our sins. Then God defeated death and sin by raising Jesus from the dead. Now Jesus invites us to newness of life and the forgiveness of sins through our repenting and trusting in him. This is the message spoken by these early Christians more than nineteen-hundred years ago in the book of Acts.

THE MISSION OF JESUS

What is to be done with this gospel message? Jesus means for it to be taken to all kinds of people everywhere.

That movement, or growth, is a major theme in Acts. In chapter 6, the church encountered complaints of favoritism from one group against another. Once the church worked through this struggle, growth followed: "So the word of God spread. The number of disciples in Jerusalem increased rapidly, and a large number of priests became obedient to the faith" (6:7). Several chapters later, we see that the church continued to grow: "Then the church throughout Judea, Galilee and Samaria enjoyed a time of peace. It was strengthened; and encouraged by the Holy Spirit, it grew in numbers, living in the fear of the Lord" (9:31). And several chapters after that, the growth showed no sign of abating: "the word of God continued to increase and spread" (12:24). There are many passages like these in Acts. The young Christians must have felt as if Jesus' parable of the tiny mustard seed growing into the largest of garden plants (Matt. 13:31-32) was happening right in their midst.

Yet the growth in the book of Acts was not directionless. It involved several movements that were central to Jesus' mission. Specifically, three patterns of growth emerged.

From the Nation (Jews) to the Nations (Gentiles)

The world is Jesus' mission! In the plan of God, the church becomes the new Israel. On the heels of Judas's betrayal and death, the apostles followed Jesus' practice and maintained their number at twelve. In this, they appear to have been fulfilling the role of Israel with its twelve tribes. This does not means God's "A" plan had failed, forcing him to move to plan "B." God had always planned for Israel to be the seed that falls into the ground, dies, and is transformed for the blessing of the nations (cf. John 12:24).

Old Testament. One of the greatest themes in the Old Testament is God's plan to glorify his name in all nations of the earth through his chosen people. The theme begins in Genesis 12 when God promises Abraham that his seed will be a blessing to all nations. The theme rises and falls throughout the Old Testament, sometimes with more strength, sometimes with less, until Jesus recovers it with full clarity and force.

Jesus' ministry. Jesus, the seed of Abraham (Matt. 1:1), commissioned his apostles to preach the good news of forgiveness to all the peoples of the earth.[17] And they, the new Israel in him, were to proclaim that Jesus is Lord of all (Acts 10:36; 17:31). Before the events recorded in Acts even begin, the ministry of Jesus and his followers had already surrendered much of its "Jewishness." Non-Jews, like the Roman centurion (Matt. 8:5-13) or the half-breed Samaritans (John 4), kept coming to faith. Meanwhile, the Jews kept rejecting Jesus.

Pentecost. At Pentecost, the curse of national and linguistic division set upon humankind after the Tower of Babel began to be reversed, as Peter and the Eleven were given the ability to speak in the tongues of many nations (Acts 2:5-12). The emphasis here is not yet on the Gentiles but on the multitude of nations (2:5). Gentiles first become receptive to the gospel a bit later. In chapter 8, "the apostles in Jerusalem heard that Samaria had accepted the word of God" (8:14).

Peter and Cornelius. In chapter 10, Peter preached to the Gentile Cornelius. Peter had traveled to a coastal town where he received a vision

---

[17] Acts 1:8; 10:35, 45; 13:16, 26; 15:11; 20:21; 21:19; 22:21; 26:17, 20, 22-23.

from the Lord. In this vision, a blanket full of ceremonially unclean food was lowered down, and the command was given to eat. Three times, Peter responded by saying, "Surely not, Lord! . . . I have never eaten anything impure or unclean" (Acts 10:14). God responded each time by saying, "Do not call anything impure that God has made clean" (10:15b). Meanwhile, the God-fearing Roman centurion, Cornelius, also received a vision several miles away in another city. He was told to send for this man he had never heard of, Peter, and to have this man tell him some good news. Cornelius sent for Peter, Peter came, and he preached "the good news of peace through Jesus Christ, who is Lord of all" (10:36). Then,

> While Peter was still speaking these words, the Holy Spirit came on all who heard the message. The circumcised believers who had come with Peter were astonished that the gift of the Holy Spirit had been poured out even on the Gentiles (10:44-45).

The circumcised believers may have been surprised, but they could not deny that the Spirit of God had come upon the Gentiles. Peter did not then respond by saying, "They should be circumcised." He said, "Can anyone keep these people from being baptized with water? They have received the Holy Spirit just as we have" (10:47). Explaining what happened to the believing Jews in Jerusalem, he again concluded, "God gave them the same gift as he gave us" (11:17), to which the Jewish believers responded with praise (11:18).

What is interesting is where Peter was located when he receives his vision. He said, "I was in the city of *Joppa* praying, and in a trance I saw a vision" (11:5; cf. 9:36-37; 10:8). Where else in the Bible is Joppa mentioned? One of the few other times the port city is mentioned occurs in the book of Jonah. When Jonah tried to flee from God's call to preach to the Gentile Ninevites, he fled to Joppa. Now God continued this theme: his gospel would go to Nineveh and the world through the work of Peter and the apostles!

Paul and Barnabas. This turn to the Gentiles is the hinge, or turning point, of the book of Acts. It is pre-figured at Pentecost in chapter 2. It is formally introduced at Cornelius's house in chapter 10. And it is reinforced in the ministry of Paul and Barnabas, who in chapter 13 received a welcome from the Gentiles and a rejection from the Jews:

> On the next Sabbath almost the whole city gathered to hear the word of the Lord. When the Jews saw the crowds, they were filled with jealousy and talked abusively against what Paul was saying.
>
> Then Paul and Barnabas answered them boldly: "We had to speak the word of God to you first. Since you reject it and do not consider yourselves worthy of

eternal life, we now turn to the Gentiles. For this is what the Lord has commanded us:

> "I have made you a light for the Gentiles,
>   that you may bring salvation to the ends of the earth."

> When the Gentiles heard this, they were glad and honored the word of the Lord; and all who were appointed for eternal life believed. The word of the Lord spread through the whole region. But the Jews incited the God-fearing women of high standing and the leading men of the city. They stirred up persecution against Paul and Barnabas, and expelled them from their region (13:44-50).

Paul understood that prophets like Isaiah had promised the Gentiles would come into the church. And by Acts 15, James and the rest of the apostles agreed. Quoting from Amos, James argued that the promise was being fulfilled in their own day (15:13-19).

Through his journeys, Paul's ministry continued to fulfill the age-old promise: "when the Jews opposed Paul and became abusive, he shook out his clothes in protest and said to them, 'Your blood be on your own heads! I am clear of my responsibility. From now on I will go to the Gentiles'" (18:6). And his "final statement" in Acts, spoken in Rome, resounds like the thud of the closing door:

> "The Holy Spirit spoke the truth to your forefathers when he said through Isaiah the prophet:
>
> "'Go to this people and say,
> "You will be ever hearing but never understanding;
>   you will be ever seeing but never perceiving."
> For this people's heart has become calloused;
>   they hardly hear with their ears, and they have closed their eyes.
> Otherwise they might see with their eyes,
>   hear with their ears,
> understand with their hearts
> and turn, and I would heal them.'
>
> "Therefore I want you to know that God's salvation has been sent to the Gentiles, and they will listen!" (28:25-28).

From Peter to Paul

As in the first half of Acts, Luke gives his patron Theophilus in the second half a story full of vivid characters:

- the imperious Herod, who examined and summarily executed the guards who failed to prevent Peter's angelic release (chapter 12). Herod was then struck down by God;
- John Mark, Barnabas's nephew, failed companion of Paul on Paul's early missionary journeys, and author of the Gospel of Mark (12:12, 25; 15:37);
- Paul's unnamed nephew who saved the day (23:16ff.);
- the corrupt provincial governor Felix, who frequently asked Paul to come and witness to him, really hoping that Paul would offer him a bribe (24:26);
- the succeeding provincial governor Porcius Festus, who prepared the way for King Agrippa to hear Paul (25:26);

The overriding character, of course, is Jesus. He is the focus of the entire book.

However, on a human level—front and center—are the two dominating figures of Peter and Paul. Peter's character dominates early in the book, while Paul dominates later.

After Peter's boasts, failures, tears, and restoration in the Gospels, he comes out wonderfully in this story of the early church. If you identify with Peter's failures when reading the Gospels, take comfort by how Peter grows up in Acts. He has a clear understanding of the gospel and is willing to give himself for it.

But Luke's interest in Peter is eclipsed by the middle of Acts, where he transitions to the story of someone with whom we believe Luke traveled: Paul. Paul is introduced as Saul in 8:1, 3. Yet we do not learn anything more about him until the story of his conversion in chapter 9. At first, Paul seems to be an unlikely person for accomplishing God's mission in the church. He is an ultra-nationalist, a Pharisee of Pharisees, and one who specializes in cult control and sect extermination, particularly this cult known as "the Way." Then again, God always seems to work through unlikely people and circumstances to glorify himself (e.g., the Savior of the world, born of a virgin and hung on a cross?). Saul was even known and feared as a Christian-killer. When the Lord asked the disciple Ananias to meet with Paul, Ananias answered, "Lord . . . I have heard many reports about this man and all the harm he has done to your saints in Jerusalem. And he has come here with authority from the chief priests to arrest all who call on your name" (9:13-14). Luke records a similar reaction among the other disciples: "When he came to Jerusalem, he tried to join the disciples, but they were all afraid of him, not believing that he really was a disciple" (9:26). Yet Jesus confronted this Christian-killer, converted him, and commissioned him to be "my chosen instrument to carry my name before the Gentiles and their kings and before the people of Israel" (9:15).

Paul was absolutely brilliant. He addressed Greek philosophers at the Areopagus in Athens (Acts 17:19-32). He presented himself as a Jew to the

Jews in Jerusalem and gained their attention by speaking in Aramaic (21:39–22:2). Then he presented himself as a Roman citizen to the Roman guard who was preparing to flog him (22:27-28). Appearing before the Sanhedrin in chapter 23, he brashly insulted the high priest, quickly apologized, and then diverted attention from himself by provoking an argument between the Pharisees and Sadducees over the resurrection (23:1-10).

And Paul was known to be trustworthy. He said to the elders from the Ephesian church, "You yourselves know that these hands of mine have supplied my own needs and the needs of my companions" (20:34). Paul was an amazing tool in the hands of Jesus.

From Jerusalem to Rome

Throughout the book, members of "the Way" of Christ, a term with overtones of the Old Testament Exodus (Ex. 13:21; cf. Isa. 40:3), grew from a few score adherents in Jerusalem to something large enough to be familiar to the Roman governor Felix (24:22) and to the Jews in Rome. Like the movement from nation (Jews) to nations (Gentiles), the fact that Acts is set in Jerusalem at the beginning and in Rome at the end is significant. Rome was the center of the known world and as a result of Paul's having gone there, "people everywhere [were] talking" about the church (28:22). In God's redemptive plan, historic Jerusalem was set aside and the gospel took root in this Gentile city (28:30-31), from which it would eventually spread throughout the Roman Empire and then the world.

THE MEANS FOR THIS MISSION

Acts presents an amazing message and an incredible mission, but how would it ever happen?

God Uses People—Disciples

To perform signs and wonders. God used his disciples to perform healings, signs, and other wonders. In this manner, they continued the ministry of Jesus. As a result of Peter's miracles, "people brought the sick into the streets and laid them on beds and mats so that at least Peter's shadow might fall on some of them as he passed by" (5:15; cf. 9:32-43). As a result of Paul's miracles, "even handkerchiefs and aprons that had touched him were taken to the sick, and their illnesses were cured and the evil spirits left them" (19:12; cf. 14:10; 20:10; 28:8-9). And miracles were not limited to Peter and Paul (2:43; 8:6-7; 11:17-18).

Acts also presents what might be called "reverse healings." For instance, Paul cursed someone with blindness (13:11). And the seven sons of Sceva, trying to emulate a Pauline exorcism, found themselves rebuked by the evil spirit

(19:13-16). In all of this, God specially validated the message of his young church, showing that the church was continuing Christ's ministry by his Spirit.

To live attractive lives. Christians also accomplish their mission by living attractive lives of caring for one another. The first Christians were rightly known for their regular fellowship of breaking bread together, living and sharing everything in common, giving to one another as each had need, and eating with "glad and sincere hearts." Through this, they enjoyed "the favor of all the people" (2:42-47). Yet the Christians cared not only for those who were near, they also cared for those in far away communities, for instance, by working to alleviate hunger (11:29).

And Christians brought peace. Admittedly, throughout Acts, we see non-Christians instigating riots because of Christianity. The riot in Ephesus was caused by the dissatisfied Gentile idol-maker Demetrius (19:23-29). The Jerusalem riots were stirred up by Paul's opponents (21:30; also, 22:22). But Paul calmed them down.

Luke's writing of Acts also functioned to commend Paul. His innocence was evident to the authorities (26:32). He was arraigned before Caesar only because Paul himself appealed to Caesar, not because of any heinous guilt on his part (25:11, 21, 25). He exercised the rights of his Roman citizenship more than once to protect himself (22:25-29). Both a king and a governor conceded that Paul had done nothing wrong (26:30-31).

To preach the Word. The main way the message of the young church spread, however, was through the preaching of the Word. The story of Cornelius in chapter 10 provides one of the clearest examples of this in the Bible, and is worth examining again. Some people have drawn false conclusions from the passage, so we want to observe what they have failed to see:

> At Caesarea there was a man named Cornelius, a centurion in what was known as the Italian Regiment. He and all his family were devout and God-fearing; he gave generously to those in need and prayed to God regularly. One day at about three in the afternoon he had a vision. He distinctly saw an angel of God, who came to him and said, "Cornelius!"
>
> Cornelius stared at him in fear. "What is it, Lord?" he asked.
>
> The angel answered, "Your prayers and gifts to the poor have come up as a memorial offering before God" (10:1-4).

Cornelius is described as devout, God-fearing, and generous to the poor, and these prayers and gifts pleased the Lord. After hearing about Cornelius's visit from the angel, Peter concluded, "I now realize how true it is that God does not show favoritism but accepts men from every nation who fear him and do what is right" (10:34-35). Given God's favor toward him, some people have pointed

to Cornelius as an example of what they call "holy pagans"—individuals outside the visible church whose life of virtue commends them to God and who will
therefore be saved. But did not God go to an extensive amount of trouble to bring
Peter to Cornelius in order to share the Word? God sent one angel to Peter and
another to Cornelius. Then Peter came and shared the gospel of Jesus Christ.
Why would all this be necessary if Cornelius was already saved? Cornelius
needed to have the Word preached to him in order to gain saving faith.

Many times I have heard stories from the Muslim world about God speaking to people in dreams. He does not save them in the dreams, but he tells them
where they can hear the gospel of Jesus. Then the Muslim searches out and
finds the unknown individual, hears the gospel, and is saved.

Why has God made the preaching of the gospel central to his plan of salvation? I do not ultimately know. But in addition to mighty works and attractive lives, God is pleased to give salvation through the preaching of his
message, the message of his holiness, our sin, Christ's atoning death, and the
call upon us to repent and believe.

Paul understood so well the centrality of preaching that on one evening he
talked a man to death! Paul preached so long that Eutychus fell asleep and fell
out a third-story window (20:7-11). Paul enlivened Eutychus with a miracle,
but the rest of us are enlivened by God's word of life.

God Is Sovereign

If we are tempted to place too much responsibility into the hands of Christ's
disciples for accomplishing his mission, Gamaliel's wise words in chapter 5
offer corrective counsel. In the early days of the church, the disciples were again
arrested and hauled before the Sanhedrin, the ruling group of Jews in
Jerusalem. After Peter and the apostles spoke, we read,

> When [the Sanhedrin] heard this, they were furious and wanted to put them to
> death. But a Pharisee named Gamaliel, a teacher of the law, who was honored by
> all the people, stood up in the Sanhedrin and ordered that the men be put outside
> for a little while. Then he addressed them: "Men of Israel, consider carefully what
> you intend to do to these men. Some time ago Theudas appeared, claiming to be
> somebody, and about four hundred men rallied to him. He was killed, all his fol-
> lowers were dispersed, and it all came to nothing. After him, Judas the Galilean
> appeared in the days of the census and led a band of people in revolt. He too was
> killed, and all his followers were scattered. Therefore, in the present case I advise
> you: Leave these men alone! Let them go! For if their purpose or activity is of
> human origin, it will fail. But if it is from God, you will not be able to stop these
> men; you will only find yourselves fighting against God" (5:33-39).

The success of God's mission for taking his message all over the world will not be done without Christian workers. But in a very important sense, it is not left up to us. In other words, God will accomplish his mission through us, yet he is in no way dependent on us. This can be seen in a number of ways in the book of Acts.

Heavenly jailbreaks. On several occasions, angels were sent to release Christ's disciples from prison, providing another subtle reminder of the Exodus. The leaders in Jerusalem attempted to put Peter in prison twice. Both times an angel released him (5:19; 12:7). Paul was eventually released from a Philippian jail after an earthquake shook open the doors and released the chains (16:26).

Fulfillment of Old Testament prophecy. It is amazing how much the disciples understood what had and would happen according to Old Testament prophecy. Perhaps the resurrected Jesus taught them all these things before he ascended. They knew the Old Testament taught that . . .

- one of Christ's disciples would lose his place by betraying Jesus, and would be replaced (1:16-20);
- God would pour out his Spirit (2:16-21);
- this son of David and Son of God would rise from the dead and ascend to heaven as Lord and Messiah (2:25-32);
- diverse leaders would be against him (3:17-18; 13:27);
- God would raise up a prophet like Moses (3:22);
- the Messiah's people would reject him, as they had always rejected God (4:10-11);
- he would be led as a lamb to the slaughter (8:32);
- while Israel would persist in unbelief, the Gentiles would turn to God, and all people would be blessed through the offspring of Abraham (13:26-27; 28:23-28).

God's effectual call. But to be honest, how can we keep from despairing over this great task to which Jesus has called the church: "go to all the world"? If you have read any foreign missions journals, you know how many unreached people groups remain today, two thousand years later! What stops us from giving up and deciding the odds are against us? Isn't it ridiculous in this pluralistic world to continue following Jesus in such single-minded fashion? Not only do many nations remain unreached, some of the "reached" nations offer nothing more than a weak witness to the gospel.

When you read through the book of Acts, you will find this comfort and encouragement: behind it all is God. Oh, weary worker, discouraged disciple, tired Christian, listen to God's Word and see him speak and act with power!

God promises to pour out his Spirit in Peter's Pentecost sermon: "God says, 'I will pour out my Spirit on all people'" (2:17).

God calls people to repentance: "Repent and be baptized, everyone of you. . . . The promise is for you and your children and for all who are far off—for all whom the Lord our God will call" (2:38-39). Who will call on the name of the Lord? "All whom the Lord our God will call."

God grants repentance. Peter says, "God has granted even the Gentiles repentance unto life" (11:18).

God appoints for eternal life: "When the Gentiles heard this, they were glad and honored the word of the Lord; and all who were appointed for eternal life believed" (13:48).

God opens the door of faith: the disciples heard about "all that God had done through them and how he had opened the door of faith to the Gentiles" (14:27).

God opens the hearts of individuals to respond to the gospel: "The Lord opened [Lydia's] heart to respond to Paul's message" (16:14).

God determines the times and places of where people live: God "determined the times set for them and the exact places where they should live" (17:26).

Sometimes the doctrine of election is regarded as discouraging evangelism. But that is not the case in the book of Acts. Faith in God's election is exactly what encourages evangelism. In Corinth, Paul felt discouraged and was about to give up until he was strengthened by a vision: "One night the Lord spoke to Paul in a vision: 'Do not be afraid; keep on speaking, do not be silent. For I am with you, and no one is going to attack and harm you, because I have many people in this city'" (18:9-10). Not many people had yet been converted in Corinth, but God encouraged Paul with the promise that he had many people in the city. Should we not assume God has people in our city and neighborhood who will respond when our own voices speak the gospel?

One of the most remarkable statements in Acts occurred after Peter and John had been imprisoned for a night and interrogated by rulers, elders, and teachers of the law in Jerusalem. Upon release, Peter and John returned to the gathered disciples, who rejoiced and prayed together:

> "Sovereign Lord," they said, "you made the heaven and the earth and the sea, and everything in them. You spoke by the Holy Spirit through the mouth of your servant, our father David:
>
>> "'Why do the nations rage
>>   and the peoples plot in vain?
>> The kings of the earth take their stand
>>   and the rulers gather together
>> against the Lord
>>   and against his Anointed One.'

> Indeed Herod and Pontius Pilate met together with the Gentiles and the people of Israel in this city to conspire against your holy servant Jesus, whom you anointed. They did what your power and will had decided beforehand should happen. Now, Lord, consider their threats and enable your servants to speak your word with great boldness. Stretch out your hand to heal and perform miraculous signs and wonders through the name of your holy servant Jesus" (4:24-30).

Perhaps you are a modern rationalist, and when you read that Herod and Pilate did what God's "power and will had decided beforehand should happen," you wonder, "Doesn't that enervate all action? Doesn't it relieve us of all responsibility? Why should we even bother to act?" All I can say is, that is not how the New Testament characters responded. The reminder of God's sovereignty encouraged and excited Peter, John, and the disciples to persevere. They knew that if God had called them, God would ensure ultimate victory and a successful mission. His ends *will* be met. So if he calls, go!

God sovereignly uses people to spread the good news about Jesus to the entire world. This is the message, the mission, and the means of Acts. There is a way to God, despite our sins, through faith in Jesus. And God will use you and me to spread this good news.

CONCLUSION

What happens when the message of Jesus is accurately taught to people? It is worth observing how the hearers of the ten sermons in Acts responded at the conclusion of those sermons. Though the sermons were all faithful to God's message of Christ, they were received variously.

Peter's sermon at Pentecost ended with the people feeling cut to the heart and crying out, "Brothers, what shall we do?" (2:37).

Peter's sermon at the temple ended when the temple guards seized and imprisoned him (4:3).

Peter's sermon before the Sanhedrin ended when the Sanhedrin ordered him to withdraw (4:15).

Peter's next sermon before the Sanhedrin ended when the Sanhedrin erupted in fury and Gamaliel gave an order for Peter to be taken outside for a time (5:33-34).

Stephen's sermon ended when the crowd became so furious that they covered their ears, yelled at the top of their voices, dragged him out of the city, and stoned him to death (7:54, 57-58, 60).

Peter's sermon before Cornelius ended with the Holy Spirit coming upon Cornelius and his household (10:44).

Paul's sermon before the synagogue in Pisidian Antioch ended, it appears, at the natural conclusion of the sermon. Once finished, Paul received a polite invitation to return and speak again the following week. Some were converted (13:42-43).

Paul's sermon in the Areopagus ended with the sneering of philosophers after Paul mentioned the resurrection of the dead (17:31-32).

Paul's testimonial to the Jerusalem crowd ended when the crowd raised their voices and shouted for Paul's death (22:22).

And Paul's testimonial to King Agrippa and Governor Festus ended when Festus interrupted Paul, shouting, "You are out of your mind, Paul!" when Paul proclaimed that Jesus had risen from the dead (26:23-24).

Those are the different ways people responded to the truth in the book of Acts: conviction, arrest, dismissal, fury and protection, murder, the receiving of the Holy Spirit, polite interest, sneers, shouts, interruptions.

I wonder how *you* respond to this message. Convicted? Dismissive? Furious (at the narrowness of the message)? Converted? Revived? Unconcerned?

Some people hear and become messengers themselves—like me and maybe you. When this happens, the message of Acts continues through us from generation to generation of believers. A good picture of this is found in chapter 5. Some of the early witnesses to Christ had been jailed, hauled before the Sanhedrin, reprimanded, and released. Upon release, "The apostles left the Sanhedrin, rejoicing because they had been counted worthy of suffering disgrace for the Name" (5:41). Does it not seem strange to rejoice over suffering? Did they simply like pain? Did they have a martyr complex?

No, Jesus had promised it would be this way (Luke 21:12). Persecution would come because people neither knew Jesus nor the God who sent him (John 15:21). Yet Jesus had also promised blessing for those who are persecuted:

> "Blessed are those who are persecuted because of righteousness,
>   for theirs is the kingdom of heaven.
>
> "Blessed are you when people insult you, persecute you and falsely say all kinds of evil against you because of me. Rejoice and be glad, because great is your reward in heaven, for in the same way they persecuted the prophets who were before you" (Matt. 5:10-12).

So the apostles left the Sanhedrin "rejoicing" (Acts 5:41).

And the persecution continued. Stephen was arrested and stoned. James, the bother of John, was arrested by Herod and "put to death with the sword" (12:2). Paul was repeatedly beaten. Yes, the word would go forward, but—as the hymn writer put it—"some through the water and some through the flood, some through the fire but all through the blood."[18] We have a hard time understanding this sweet-and-sour combination of suffering then glory. After all, people in the first century had difficulty understanding that the Son of David was also the suffering servant.

Then as now, we are left with this great truth: through Jesus we may have a restored relationship with God. But following him means taking up our cross. I wonder, truly, do you intend to do that? Do you have any idea what it means in your life to do that?

Do you have any idea what it means if you don't?

Let us pray:

Dear God, we thank you for the provision you have given to us through our Lord Jesus Christ. Thank you for your great and costly love. Thank you for calling us to join you in telling the world the truth about themselves and about Christ, in whose name we pray. Amen.

Questions for Reflection

1. We have seen that you can discern what a pastor values by listening to him talk about Jesus. How is that true for you personally? When you talk about Jesus, what personal values might sneak to the surface? What about your church? What aspects of Jesus are emphasized in the public teaching about him? What *should* be determining our views about who Jesus is? How will this happen in your own life? In your church's life?

2. The introduction of this chapter also raises the question of whether you are willing to know the truth, even if the truth is surprising or contrary to what you want. It is easy to imagine ourselves yielding to a truth when it is *proven* to us. But what if the truth is not the sort of thing that can be proven, like a profession of love, or the promise of a friend, or the word of a spouse? Or, we could add, a promise of God? How willing are you to listen to something that you do not want to be true? Would your friends, family, or employers describe you as "teachable"? If you happened to be wrong about the most important matters of life and death, what devices do you have in place for detecting the fact that you are wrong?

3. We see in the section "Witnesses to the Message" that the apostles have the ability to present the gospel in a diversity of ways, yet they always point to the

---

[18] George A. Young, "God Leads His Dear Children Along."

same gospel. Provide two examples of how they do this. Then think of two non-Christians in your own life (if you are a Christian) who might require you to present the *same* gospel in a *different* manner. Furthermore, what are some ways your church can display these same sensitivities?

4. The four Gospels and Acts, all of which present a biography of Jesus of Nazareth, differ from the biographies of most famous people in what peculiar way? What does the book of Acts particularly emphasize? Why is this important? What hope does this give us as Christians? How will this enable us to live lives that are distinct in holiness from the world around us?

5. What does the Bible say the Savior saves us from? How?

6. The book of Acts characterizes Jesus' mission as moving from the nation (Jews) to the nations (Gentiles). At the time, many resisted the church's movement outward. After all, everyone likes the familiar and the comfortable. Consider for a moment how your church receives visitors. Consider what people *you* greet after church or invite to lunch. Consider where your church spends its money. Consider the things your church prays for week after week. Now, would you say that you and your church have an outward-to-the-nations mission? Or are you more inclined to stick with the familiar?

7. What purpose do miraculous signs and wonders play in the book of Acts? What does this mean for the church today?

8. According to the book of Acts, what effect should the doctrine of election have on evangelism? Why might we conclude that the doctrine of the election is in fact one of the most precious doctrines the church has for encouraging missions and evangelism?

9. As we have seen, persecution plays a prominent role in the book of Acts and in the Christian life generally. Following Jesus means taking up our crosses as he did. What would it mean to take up the cross in your life? What things would you have to give up? How much opposition are you willing to endure? Friends rolling their eyes? Disrespect around the office? Missed opportunities for a promotion? Verbal insults? Confiscation of property? Lawsuits? Worse?

PART TWO

KEY IDEAS FOR THE TIMES

THE MESSAGE OF ROMANS: JUSTIFICATION

DO WE HAVE A DIRE PROBLEM?

INTRODUCING ROMANS

THE JUSTIFICATION OF SINNERS IN THE EYES OF GOD

1. *All Need to Be Justified Because All Sin*
2. *None Will Be Justified by What They Do*
3. *Sinners Can Be Justified Only Because of Christ's Person and Work*
4. *Sinners Will Be Justified Only Through Faith in Christ*
5. *All Kinds of Sinners Can Be Justified*
6. *Justification Is by Faith Alone, but Justifying Faith Is Never Alone Application*

THE JUSTIFICATION OF GOD IN THE EYES OF SINNERS

1. *God Himself Has Remained Faithful; Israel Was Unfaithful*
2. *God Has Always Worked by Calling Sinners to Faith*
3. *God Has Not Changed Whom He Intends to Save*
4. *God Has Always Acted for One Ultimate Purpose: His Name's Sake*

CONCLUSION

6

THE MESSAGE OF ROMANS: JUSTIFICATION

DO WE HAVE A DIRE PROBLEM?[1]

Jewish evangelism is one of the most awkward topics that can be addressed in public today. I don't mean Jews trying to proselytize for Judaism. According to my rabbi friends that does not happen much and is not particularly encouraged. No, I mean Christians telling Jewish people that they must accept Jesus as the Messiah of God who was crucified for the sins of all who turn and trust in him—and that, otherwise, they will spend an eternity separated from God. In the view of my rabbi friends, advocating this message about Christ to Jews is the equivalent of advocating what some have called a theological pogrom, a spiritual holocaust.

In recent days the Southern Baptists have entered this socially inflamed area with their usual deftness and aplomb. Preparing for the Jewish High Holy Days—which end with Yom Kippur, the Day of Atonement—the International Mission Board of the Southern Baptist Convention had published a booklet called "Days of Awe: Prayer for the Jews." In this booklet, the reader is daily led through a Scripture passage, a historical illustration, some population information, and particular prayer requests for the day.

Let me cite one day's entry just to give you a sense of it. First, there is a Scripture verse: "September 19. How then can they call on the one they have not believed in, and how can they believe in the one they have not heard? (Romans 10:14)." The entry itself begins, "Although much activity during the days of awe is solemn, there is a festive component focusing on the sweetness of life, or being written in the book of life. A common practice is to take a bowl of sliced apples and honey on a table. People take an apple slice, dip it in the

---

[1] This sermon was originally preached on September 19, 1999, at Capitol Hill Baptist Church in Washington, D.C.

honey, and offer blessings, including 'may it be your will our God and God of your people that the new year be good and sweet for us.'" The entry continues: "Day 9—'Seeking Forgiveness.' Focus group: South Africa. Jewish population: 101,000. Jewish believers: 200. In Cape Town recently a synagogue was bombed in a suburb that used to be mostly Jewish but is now mostly Muslim. Muslim fundamentalists are suspected of initiating the attack." And then the page reads, "Today I pray for," and then it gives you two blank lines for writing in the names of friends or other issues of particular concern to you. After that it lists several specific prayers: "One: Pray the Jewish people have long and fruitful lives in which they have ample opportunity to discover the sweetness of being in Christ. Two: Pray that many respected Christian teachers will be compelled by love to dedicate their lives to sharing the gospel within Jewish communities. Three: As South Africa seeks internal reconciliation, pray that Christians will contribute to an attitude of peace."

I don't know how this sample from the prayer guide strikes you, but it certainly struck a number of people as awkward, to say the least. One Jewish friend telephoned me first thing in the morning when a story about this booklet appeared in the *Washington Post* newspaper. He wanted to know what I knew about it, and whether I would attend a meeting of publicly minded folk to answer a few questions. The article in the *Post* was full of interesting quotes and asides, like this one from Rabbi Eric Yoffie of the Union of American Hebrew Congregations: "We'd like a little less love and a little more respect. There's a kind of theological arrogance that pervades all of this, a certain willingness on their part to play God, and an absence of awareness that these sorts of statements throughout history are associated with coercion, hatred and violence."[2]

Perhaps someone should inform the rabbi that we Baptists mean no disrespect by our love, and that Christians throughout history have never counted submitting themselves to the Word of God as being arrogant. If learning, treasuring, and following God's revealed Word is theological arrogance, then our arrogance should also be ascribed to Moses, Samuel, David, and Isaiah.

Jeff Jacoby, a practicing Jew who published an article in the *Boston Globe* several days later, sprang to the defense of the Southern Baptists. He suggested that Jews should not tell Christians to stop evangelizing (which he acknowledges would be impossible for Christians to do anyway). Instead, he urged Jewish parents to teach their children what to believe. He quoted Binyamin

---

[2] Eric Yoffie, cited in Hanna Rosin, "Prayer Book Provokes Anger; Southern Baptist Conversion Guide Is Timed for Jewish Holidays," *The Washington Post*, Sep. 9, 1999, A02, final edition.

Jolkovsky, who said, "Would that Jewish leaders worried about the souls of confused young Jews as much as the evangelicals do."[3]

Jacoby concluded, "No Christians will offend me by praying that I find my way to their Lord during the Days of Awe. It may surprise them to learn that I—and countless other Jews—annually return the favor. The traditional Rosh Hashanah liturgy several times implores, 'Our God and the God of our fathers, rule the whole world in Your glory . . . and let everyone who breathes proclaim: "The Lord, God of Israel, is king, and His majesty reigns over everything." '"

R. Albert Mohler, Jr., president of the Southern Baptist Theological Seminary, also weighed in on the discussion. On the pages of *The Wall Street Journal,* he defended the prayer guide as simple obedience to Jesus Christ. He wrote openly and honestly, "Southern Baptists have not singled out the Jews as more needful of the gospel than others. But this prayer guide reminds Christians that the Jewish people are not *less* needful, either. . . . We are followers of the one who said: 'I am the Way, the Truth, and the Life.' Southern Baptists didn't invent these words. Rather, we have chosen to believe them—and to follow. We hope and pray that others will too. For us, such a hope is the greatest act of love—not hate—that a Christian can extend to any non-Christian."[4]

Again, I don't know what you make of Christians evangelizing Jews. Yet your response will probably be tied to what you think about the human condition. Are we humans okay by nature, or do we have a dire problem? Your response will also be tied to what you think and feel about God.

Christians today should remember that we are not the first ones to struggle with questions about the spiritual state of our Jewish or other non-Christian neighbors. Christians have long been acquainted with all of these vital issues of salvation.

We should always remember, of course, that Jesus was Jewish. The great early exponents of his gospel, the disciples, were Jewish. And the one-of-a-kind trailblazer into the Gentile world, the Pharisee Saul who became the apostle Paul, was Jewish. Cynics have called Paul the true founder of Christianity. More faithful historians understand that his writings provide the most detailed picture of God's fulfillment of his ancient promises to Abraham.

The letters of Paul are some of the earliest documents we have in the New Testament, and they give us insight into this strange movement that began within Judaism but came to be known as Christianity. Paul wrote to various groups of Christians in the first few decades of Christianity in order to encourage, exhort, warn, rebuke, and generally instruct them. He could draw from

---

[3] Binyamin Jolkovsky, cited in Jeff Jacoby, "Who's Afraid of Baptists?" *Boston Globe,* September 13, 1999.
[4] R. Albert Mohler, Jr., "Houses of Worship," in *Wall Street Journal,* September 17, 1999.

deep wells of knowledge from both the Old Testament and the teachings of Jesus. And these letters, placed in the middle of our New Testaments, should play an incalculably important role in our understanding of Jesus Christ and his mission among us. Our next thirteen studies will cover Paul's thirteen letters. We want to familiarize ourselves with this part of the New Testament so that we can turn to them for the comfort, consolation, teaching, and direction we so badly need.

INTRODUCING ROMANS

In almost every way, Paul's letter to the Romans is chief among these books. Romans is the longest, the most quoted, and the first in order of Paul's letters. Many say that it provides the most systematic presentation of the gospel in the Bible. If you have never read it, read it today.

Not only is Romans an important book, it is unexpectedly useful. I remember one day as an undergraduate discussing Christianity in the college dining hall with a non-Christian friend named Ben. As Ben asked question after question, I remember thinking to myself, "He needs to read Romans 1 . . . he needs to read Romans 2 . . . he needs to read Romans 3 . . ." And so finally I said, "Ben what are you doing for the next three hours?" It was a Saturday, so he replied, "Well, nothing in particular." I then offered, "Look, come back to my room, and let me read you the book of Romans in the New Testament." He said yes and followed me back to my room. It was amazing because as I read through Romans he kept interrupting me with questions. And almost every time, his question anticipated the very next thing Paul would say. Romans is a clear, logical exposition of the gospel of Jesus Christ.

Romans was probably written around A.D. 57, near the end of Paul's life. Paul was a stranger to the church in Rome (see 1:10, 13; 15:22). Unlike some of the other churches to which he had written, he had neither founded nor visited this church. We do not know who established the church in Rome. Perhaps some of the Jews at Pentecost were converted, returned to Rome, and began a church. We know from extra-biblical sources that Christians met together in Rome from a very early period. We don't know much about the Roman church except that Jewish and Gentile believers both belonged to it, which we learn from Paul's letter. Paul explicitly addresses both groups.[5]

Why did Paul write the letter to the Romans? Christians have commonly used this letter sort of as Paul's systematic theology—a timeless and classic statement of the Christian faith, and particularly of the gospel. It is easy to approach Romans like this, in part because Paul does not address specific sit-

---

[5] For example, he addresses Jews in 7:1; Gentiles are addressed in 11:13.

uations or controversies as he does in the letters to the Corinthians or Galatians. While it is true that Romans is a classic statement of the Christian faith, it is not simply a list of unconnected propositions. He makes a sustained argument that explains the Christian gospel, and he uses the argument to introduce himself and to address his readers as in any personal letter. Specifically, he writes to thwart any Judaizing tendencies, in which circumcision and Jewish customs are confused with the gospel. He writes to defuse any tension that might arise between the Jewish and Gentile believers. And he writes to address the question that burns in his soul: the fate of his own people, the Jews. In some ways, this last purpose seems to be the driving force behind the letter to the Romans.

Obviously we cannot cover everything Paul does in this letter. Yet if we wanted to sum up the letter with one word, I would suggest the word "justification." Justification, as it is popularly used, is a defense for why something is the way it is. We often use the word today negatively in the sense of an excuse: "Oh, you're just trying to justify yourself." This means you are trying to explain away something you know is wrong. In the New Testament and in the history of Christian thought, however, the idea of justification refers more particularly to the question, how can a person be right with God? To be *justified* is to be *declared right before God*. And that is the first question Paul addresses in this letter: how can sinners be justified in the eyes of God?

THE JUSTIFICATION OF SINNERS IN THE EYES OF GOD

The beginning of the Christian message about us and about God is that we have sinned and have separated ourselves from God. The first half of Paul's letter is therefore concerned with how we can be reconciled to God, or more to the point, how God can be reconciled to us. This is what we will spend most of our time on, and I think the way to answer this question is to examine six statements about justification.

1. All Need to Be Justified Because All Sin

Paul teaches that all of us need to be justified because all of us have sinned. This is what he argues in the first three chapters of Romans. In chapter 1, he refers to the "godlessness and wickedness of men" (1:18). Humanity is inexcusably guilty because God has revealed himself and his qualities in the natural world and humanity has rejected that revelation. Jew and Gentile alike are addressed here, not just the Jews who have the Mosaic law. All mankind are described as idolaters who pursue debauchery (1:23, 24). A list of increasingly horrible sins follows (1:26-32). In chapter 2, Paul turns specifically to the Jews.

Though they possess the law, they do not obey it (1:17-29). Their bodies might be circumcised, but their hearts are not (1:28-29).[6] In chapter 3, Paul therefore concludes, "Jews and Gentiles alike are all under sin" (3:9). The Psalms prove his point: all need to be justified because all sin.[7]

2. None Will Be Justified by What They Do

Okay, then, how will sinners be justified? If we are sinful and if God is righteous, how can he ever regard us as just? Our second statement tells us how we *cannot* be justified: None of us will be justified by what we do, or in the words of Romans 3, "no one will be declared righteous [that is, justified] in his sight by observing the law" (3:20). Back in chapter 2, Paul says what sounds like the opposite: "it is those who obey the law who will be declared righteous" (2:13). But then he also says no one has obeyed perfectly, as we have seen (2:15-21). In other words, obedience to the law theoretically leads to justification. But since this obedience must be perfect, no one, whether Jew or Gentile, will ever be justified by what he or she does.

3. Sinners Can Be Justified Only Because of Christ's Person and Work

So if sinners will not be justified by what they do, how can they be justified? Our third statement about justification tells us that sinners can be justified only by who Christ is and what he has done. In the words of chapter 3 again, all who are justified "are justified freely by his grace though the redemption that came by Christ Jesus. God presented him as a sacrifice of atonement [literally, a propitiation] through faith in his blood" (3:24-25a). We will never be justified by our own actions; we can only be justified by the actions of Jesus Christ.

John Bunyan illustrates the contrast between how we can and how we cannot be justified in his great allegory *Pilgrim's Progress.* Early in the story, the main character, named Christian, feels the weight of his sin before God and knows he needs to be justified; he needs to be saved. Christian sees Mt. Sinai, which represents Moses' law, and he runs over to it, hoping to climb it and remove the weight of his sin from his back. From a distance the mountain looks easy enough to climb. But as he starts to ascend, he finds it steeper than he expected. He continues, yet it gets steeper and steeper until finally the hill curves over on top of him. Christian discovers that justification cannot be found on Mt. Sinai. He cannot get to salvation by the law. So he descends

---

[6] See Deut. 10:16; 30:6; Jer. 4:4; 9:25.
[7] Rom. 3:10-18; Ps. 5:9; 10:7; 14:1-3; 36:1; 140:3; also Isa. 59:7, 8.

from the mountain, and only then—despairing of the law—does Christian turn and find the gate that leads to salvation. And the gate is Christ. As Paul says, we are "justified freely by his grace through the redemption *that came by Christ Jesus*" (3:24).

How did this redemption come by Christ Jesus? Paul explains, Christ gave himself as a "sacrifice of atonement" (3:25), or as a literal translation will put it, a "propitiation" (ESV). An act of propitiation is an act that assuages the wrath of God. And that is what Christ's sacrifice has done—it has propitiated, or wiped away, the wrath of God. This then is the kernel, the engine, the heart of our salvation! Christ offered himself on the cross as a sacrifice that assuages God's wrath, wrath that God was right to have concerning our wrongs (cf. 3:21-30). As Paul puts it in chapter 4, "He was delivered over to death for our sins and was raised to life for our justification" (4:25). Or as he says in chapter 5, "Christ died for the ungodly" (5:6). Or again several verses later, we are "justified by his blood," and we are "saved from God's wrath through him!" (5:9).

Do you see what is going on here? Paul teaches that Christ bore the wrath of God for us in a way we never could, even if we were to bear his wrath in hell for eternity. The punishment of hell never ends, and God's wrath is infinite, because he himself is infinite. All sin committed against this infinitely good and eternal God is itself an infinite offense. And the punishment against an infinite offense can never be exhausted. Only in the person of Christ—perfectly good and infinite in himself—can the penalty of our transgressions finally be satisfied. So Paul writes,

> For if, when we were God's enemies, we were reconciled to him through the death of his Son, how much more, having been reconciled, shall we be saved through his life! Not only is this so, but we also rejoice in God through our Lord Jesus Christ, through whom we have now received reconciliation (5:10-11).

God can be reconciled to us because of Christ's person and work. Our sins can be dealt with. And we can be freed from our bondage to them. Christ alone was good enough to pay the price of sin's penalty.

Only by Christ can sinners be justified.

4. Sinners Will Be Justified Only Through Faith in Christ

If sinners *can* be justified through Christ's work, how *will* a sinner be effectively justified? Is there a certain ritual we need to perform? Do we need to be circumcised? Do we need to attend Mass? Do we need to walk down the aisle?

Our fourth statement about justification tells us that only faith allows us to receive the benefits of Christ's work. Paul makes this point especially clear through the example of Abraham in chapter 4:

> Under what circumstances was [righteousness] credited? Was it after he was circumcised, or before? It was not after, but before! And he received the sign of circumcision, a seal of the righteousness that he had by faith while he was still uncircumcised. So then, he is the father of all who believe but have not been circumcised, in order that righteousness might be credited to them (4:10-11).

Do you see the significance of the chronological order of Abraham's justification and the command to be circumcised? Certain teachers in the church in the time of the apostles were happy to say salvation comes through Christ's atoning death, so long as one continues to obediently receive circumcision as a sign of God's covenant with Abraham. But Paul notes that Abraham was justified—counted righteous—in Genesis 15 because he trusted God's promise to make him the father of many nations, even though he and his wife were well past child-bearing age; Abraham then received the sign of circumcision in chapter 17, *after* he had been justified. So it was through his faith, or belief, that God "credited" righteousness to him.

Let me repeat this, just to make sure you understand the significance of what Paul is saying: Abraham's belief and consequent justification came *before* he was circumcised. Paul seizes on the chronological order of these two events as crucial for understanding the Old Testament and salvation. Abraham's example is paradigmatic not just for circumcised Jews but for everyone, Jewish or Gentile, circumcised or uncircumcised. Salvation is for "everyone who believes" (1:16)! Justification is gained not by what we do but by "a righteousness that is by faith from first to last" (1:17). Or as Paul puts it in chapter 3, "this righteousness from God comes through faith in Jesus Christ *to all who believe*" (3:22). It is by "faith in his blood" (3:25).

If you want to understand this more, meditate on the latter half of chapter 3. Also, spend time observing Abraham as the supreme example of justification by faith—in chapter 4 of Romans and also in chapter 3 of Galatians. We, like Abraham, have "access by faith into this grace" (5:2). Sinners will be justified only through faith in Christ. That is why Paul can write, "Christ is the end of the law so that there may be righteousness for everyone who believes" (10:4). Christ's work provides the grounds for our justification, while faith provides the means. Sinners will be justified only through faith in Christ.

5. All Kinds of Sinners Can Be Justified

Since faith is the key to justification, wonderful news follows in a fifth statement: all kinds of sinners can be justified. Paul emphasizes this in chapter 3: "there is only one God, who will justify the circumcised by faith and the uncircumcised through that same faith" (3:30). There you have the good news! God has made a way of salvation for all of us alike—alike in our sin—through Jesus Christ. Justification is tied to no ethnically specific ritual. It is tied to faith in God's promise. Paul again uses Abraham to make this point:

> And [Abraham] received the sign of circumcision, a seal of the righteousness that he had by faith while he was still uncircumcised. So then, he is the father of all who believe but have not been circumcised, in order that righteousness might be credited to them. And he is also the father of the circumcised who not only are circumcised but who also walk in the footsteps of the faith that our father Abraham had before he was circumcised (4:11-12).

Notice Paul refers to "our father Abraham." He does not simply mean Abraham as father of the Israelites, he means Abraham as father of all who believe (see also 8:39; 9:7-8).

If you trust in Jesus Christ as the Lamb of God slain for your sins, then you, according to Romans, are a child of Abraham. So Paul recounts God's promise to Abraham, "'I have made you a father of many nations'" (4:17a), and then comments, "He is our father in the sight of God, in whom he believed—the God who gives life to the dead and calls things that are not as though they were" (4:17b). God calls the dead to life. He calls the things that are not as though they were. This is what God did when he made the world. This is what he did when he made Abraham the father of many nations. Abraham was nothing, and then God called him. This is what he did with the children of Israel. He called them out of their bondage in Egypt. This is what he has done with you, if you are Christian. You were lost. You were dead in your sins. You were nowhere, spiritually. God has given you life in Jesus Christ. And this is what God is doing now with the nations.

Paul beautifully sums up his work of bringing the gospel to the Gentiles in chapter 15, where he mentions "the grace God gave me to be a minister of Christ Jesus to the Gentiles with the priestly duty of proclaiming the gospel of God, so that the Gentiles might become an offering acceptable to God, sanctified by the Holy Spirit" (15:15-16).

It makes sense, too, that all kinds of sinners can be saved, because all die through sin. This is Paul's argument in chapter 5: the universality of death proves the universality of sin: "death came to all men, because all sinned"

(5:12). Or again: "just as through the disobedience of the one man the many were made sinners, so also through the obedience of the one man the many will be made righteous" (5:19). The curse and contagion of sin spread to all nations, so the good news of salvation by faith in Christ Jesus is meant for all nations as well. Again, the good news of the gospel is that *all kinds of sinners can be justified.*

6. *Justification Is by Faith Alone, but Justifying Faith Is Never Alone*

There is one last thing to be said about the justification of sinners in the sight of God: The fact that justification is by faith alone, in Christ's work alone, does not mean a justified person can now be licentious (taking moral license) and antinomian (against the law). Justifying faith is never alone. It results in a changed life. If you understand Paul to be saying that, since the law cannot save you it does not matter how you live, you have misunderstood him badly. This is what chapters 6–8 are about. One verse in chapter 6, in fact, sums it up: "You have been set free from sin and have become slaves to righteousness" (6:18). Being freed from sin's penalty and dominion does not mean we are free to do whatever we please. No, "we died to sin, how can we live in it any longer" (6:2). Therefore Paul exhorts us, "do not let sin reign in your mortal body so that you obey its evil desires" (6:12). Sin remains sinful, and it produces death. One who is freed from sin's dominion will want nothing to do with it. It only leads to death: "For the wages of sin is death, but the gift of God is eternal life in Christ Jesus our Lord" (6:23).

In chapter 7, Paul relates this discussion to the law. In the first few verses, he uses the institution of marriage to illustrate our freedom from the law (7:1-6). Just as marital obligations last only as long as both partners are living, so the law no longer has authority over us as Christians, since we have died to the law. We have been bought by Christ and now must serve by his Spirit. Does this mean something is wrong with the law? "Is the law sin?" (7:7). Paul answers: "Certainly not." The problem is not the law. The law is fine for its purpose. The problem is our sin. He writes, "For sin, seizing the opportunity afforded by the commandment [of the law], deceived me, and through the commandment put me to death" (7:11). Do you see what he is saying? The utter sinfulness of sin is shown by sin's insidious ability to use even the law of God to do its dirty work. But even while sin uses the law, the law exposes sin. Both sides of the battle are evident in 7:13: "But in order that sin might be recognized as sin, it produced death in me through what was good, so that through the commandment sin might become utterly sinful." In this life, we struggle. Verses 14 to 24 describe this battle as it rages within our conflicted "body of death" (7:24).

Though we struggle now, we will know a glorious liberation, according to chapter 8. God did for us what the law could not do: "what the law was powerless to do in that it was weakened by the flesh, God did by sending his own Son in the likeness of sinful man to be a sin offering" (8:3, margin). Christians therefore look forward to "the glory that will be revealed in us" (8:18). And then, in what may be the most encouraging verse in the Bible, we find Romans 8:32. If you need an encouraging verse to stick on your refrigerator, mirror, or computer screen, use Romans 8:32: "He who did not spare his own Son, but gave him up for us all—how will he not also, along with him, graciously give us all things?" We can be assured that whatever God knows we need for accomplishing his perfect purposes, he will graciously give.

So, nothing in Paul's wonderful gospel of salvation by faith in Christ means that God does not care about how we live. We are justified by faith in Christ alone. But justifying faith is never alone. It yields a life that hates sin and fights against it.

Do you hear this symphony of God's grace in the first eight chapters of Romans? Because all sin, all need to be justified. None will be justified by what they do. Sinners can be justified only *because of* Christ and only *through* faith in Christ. Therefore, all kinds of sinners can be justified. Justification is by faith alone, but justifying faith is never alone. Jews and Gentiles alike can sing of this wonderful way of salvation made by God in Christ.

Application

I hope you see what this means for you. It means in part that what you may have thought will justify you, won't.

Consider, what do you depend on to justify you before the one who made the heavens and the earth? Really, in the back of your soul, what do you lean on? Your ability to keep some moral guidelines you were taught as a child? The fact that you attend church and perhaps enjoy listening to sermons? The fact that you are doing okay financially and that your health is good? Perhaps you are thinking, "God does not seem to be judging me right now; everything must be fine, right?"

If you should die tonight and stand before God—because one day you certainly will—and he asked you the classic question, "Why should I let you into my heaven?" what would you say? What true answer would your heart allow your lips to say, even if your lips have been taught the right words? Remember, you are looking into the eyes of the one who made you and who knows your every thought. What has your heart truly trusted in?

Christ alone can be trusted. And faith in him alone is the gift that God gives us for salvation. It is all by God's grace. This was Paul's message to the Romans, and it is God's message to us about the justification of sinners in the eyes of God.

Hopefully you understand more of what Christians and the Bible mean by this word "justification." Nineteenth-century theologian James Buchanan defined justification as "man's acceptance with God, or his being regarded and treated as righteous in His sight—as the object of His favour, and not of His wrath, of His blessing, and not of His curse."[8]

Clearly, justification is not just for theologians. Our church's statement of faith, signed by every joining member, reads in article 5, "We believe that the great Gospel blessing which Christ secures to such as believe in Him is Justification; that Justification includes the pardon of sin, and the promise of eternal life on principles of righteousness; that it is bestowed, not in consideration of any works of righteousness which we have done, but solely through faith in the Redeemer's blood; by virtue of which faith His perfect righteousness is freely imputed to us of God; that it brings us into a state of most blessed peace and favor with God, and secures every other blessing needful for time and eternity."[9]

And the doctrine of justification is worth singing about. Eighteenth-century hymn writer William Billings summed it up this way:

> Mercy and Truth have met together;
> Righteousness and Peace have kissed each other.
> Now is the Hour of Darkness come,
> And Jesus waits to hear his Doom;
> The Roman speaks, the Jews reply,
> "His Blood be on us, let him die."
>
> Death and Despair, what do I see?
> The Lamb of God hang on a Tree!
> With rusty Nails his Body tore,
> And bloody Sweat from ev'ry Pore
> Runs plentious down.
>
> Hark! how he groans! his bitter Cries
> The Rocks have split; but see! he dies!

---

[8] James Buchanan, *The Doctrine of Justification: An Outline of Its History in the Church and of Its Exposition from Scripture* (1867; repr. Edinburgh: Banner of Truth, 1997), 17.
[9] Based on the New Hampshire Baptist Confession (1833).

Now is the Hour of Darkness past,
Christ has assum'd his reigning Pow'r;
Behold the great Accuser cast
Down from the Skies to rise no more.

Old Adam the First, excited by Lust,
And Eve the Seducer entailed the Curse;
But Adam the Second, our Saviour and King,
Has made the Atonement and freed us from Sin.

THE JUSTIFICATION OF GOD IN THE EYES OF SINNERS

Another dilemma has loomed behind our discussion thus far. The problem begins with Israel's rejection of Jesus as the Messiah. If we can be justified only by faith in Christ, and Israel has rejected Christ, then it seems that Israel will be rejected. Yet God promised Israel blessing and inheritance through Abraham. Do you see the problem? What shall we say of God's promises? What shall we say about God? This is a very different kind of question about justification. We have been talking about the justification of sinners in the eyes of God, but what about the justification of God in the eyes of sinners? Maybe stating the question like this surprises you at first, yet most of us have asked it in one way or another, at least if we have ever questioned Christianity—either as a Christian or as a non-Christian.

I am not using the word "justification" here in the previous sense of declaring a sinner to be righteous through an act of atonement. Rather, I am using it in the more common way: how do we justify, or make a defense for, God's rejection of Israel (not that God needs me or even Paul to defend him)? Sometimes our vision is clouded and our sympathies are off, even as Christians. We think about God and we are puzzled. Honestly, sometimes we even condemn him.

Paul was tempted to question God as he considered the fate of his own people, the Jews. So in chapters 9–11 he defends God—to himself, to others who would accuse God of injustice, and perhaps to you. The rejection of the Jews does not mean God changed himself or his plan. He and his plan remained, and remain, the same. In order to follow Paul's arguments in the second half of this letter, let us look at four statements about Paul's justification of God.

1. God Himself Has Remained Faithful; Israel Was Unfaithful

The unfaithfulness Israel demonstrated by rejecting God's promised Messiah does not mean that God has changed or has become unfaithful. The whole message of chapters 9–11 is that God is faithful and that he will be glorified.

As Paul says back in chapter 3, the Jews' lack of faith does not nullify God's faithfulness (3:3-4).[10]

Israel's unfaithfulness was clearly a sore trial for Paul. Few sentences in all of his letters reveal his heart more than the beginning of chapter 9, where he mentions the "great sorrow and unceasing anguish in my heart . . . for the sake of my brothers, those of my own race, the people of Israel" (9:2-4). How could the fortunes of God's people have gone so wrong? The question plagued Paul, and, no doubt, it was put to him many times by others. Many assumed that the blame for a problem as grand in scale as the Jews' rejection of the Messiah must be placed not on the individuals but on God himself. Paul mentions this idea, but he will have none of it.

Paul has already reclaimed in the first eight chapters enough of the Old Testament's message to show that many Gentiles will be included in the people of God, just as Jesus taught. In 9:6, he clarifies another portion of Old Testament teaching: many who seem to be a part of God's people are not. He writes, "It is not as though God's word had failed. For not all who are descended from Israel are Israel." They are not Israel now, and they were not Israel then—not spiritually, anyhow. That is the broad argument of chapter 9.

To doubt God's faithful character because of Israel's unbelief is out of the question. So we read, "What then shall we say? Is God unjust? Not at all! . . . It does not, therefore, depend on man's desire or effort, but on God's mercy" (9:14, 16). Now, we should not read this and think Paul is being hard-hearted toward the Jews. Listen to what he says several verses later: "Brothers, my heart's desire and prayer to God for the Israelites is that they may be saved" (10:1). Yet his love for them does not prevent him from seeing their unfaithfulness or from seeing God's continuing faithfulness in saving whomever he intends to save. Paul knew from Old Testament prophecy that Israel would be disobedient (10:18-21). But God himself has remained faithful.

2. God Has Always Worked by Calling Sinners to Faith

Paul knew his Old Testament, and he knew that God has always worked in the same way: by calling sinners to faith in his promise for salvation. He writes in chapter 10, "It is with your heart that you believe and are justified, and it is with your mouth that you confess and are saved" (10:10). He then backs this up by quoting Isaiah: "As the Scripture says, 'Anyone who trusts in him will never be put to shame'" (10:11). Paul resumes his argument: "For there is no difference between Jew and Gentile—the same Lord is Lord of all and richly blesses all who call on him" (10:12). And then he quotes the Old Testament

[10] Really, 3:1-8 seem to act as a precursor of these magnificent chapters 9–11.

again, this time from Joel: "for 'Everyone who calls on the name of the Lord will be saved'" (10:13). Paul uses these quotes from the Old Testament to prove that God has always called sinful human beings to faith. The way of salvation is accessible to all who believe. And if salvation is available to all who believe, all people need to hear the message: "faith comes from hearing the message, and the message is heard through the word of Christ" (10:17). In short, God has not changed his way of working with sinful people. He has always used his word to call his people to faith in him and his way of salvation.

3. God Has Not Changed Whom He Intends to Save

In some ways, the most obvious objection to the character of God is to say his salvation did not work for one group of people so he deserted them and sought another group. Paul takes up this possible objection particularly in chapter 11. He begins, "Did God reject his people? By no means!" (11:1). "At the present time," he says, "there is a remnant chosen by grace" (11:5). God knows—and always has known—exactly what he is doing with his people. Even the Jews' large-scale rejection of Jesus and the Gentiles' acceptance of him serves God's purposes: "because of [Israel's] transgression, salvation has come to the Gentiles to make Israel envious" (11:11). Paul appears to be saying that God planned the hardening of Israel's heart so that Gentiles would be brought to faith. And Moses predicted all of this (10:19)!

Paul argues throughout chapter 11 that God has never guaranteed salvation to every physical descendent of Abraham. The true Israelites have always been the children of the promise. This was true even in the Old Testament. Then as now, many Israelites did not believe God's promises. Yet their unbelief did not somehow make God unfaithful. They were simply exposing their own unfaithfulness. And then as now, some Israelites did believe, like the patriarchs, or Paul himself, or almost all of the earliest Christians.

Eventually, "all Israel will be saved," Paul asserts (11:26). Perhaps he means there will be a great turning to Christ among the physical descendants of Abraham during the last days. Or perhaps he means that all true Israel, the elect of God, will be saved. Perhaps he means both. One thing is clear: God should never be condemned for making promises he has not kept. He has been faithful to his promises and to his people.

4. God Has Always Acted for One Ultimate Purpose: His Name's Sake

Our fourth statement may be the hardest statement of all to accept. It is the crux of the matter, and has been disputed ever since Adam's fall. Romans clearly teaches that God has always acted for one ultimate purpose: his name's sake. We can turn throughout the whole book to see this. In chapter 1, Paul says he was made an apostle to call people to faith from among the Gentiles "for his name's sake" (1:5). In chapter 4, Paul says Abraham's faith "gave glory to God" (4:20). In chapter 9, Paul, quoting Moses, says God raised up Pharaoh "for this very purpose, that I might display my power in you and that my name might be proclaimed in all the earth" (9:17). Even a doctrine as difficult as election, Paul says, makes God's glory known: "What if he [elected some and not others] to make the riches of his glory known to the objects of his mercy, whom he prepared in advance for glory . . . ?" (9:23).

Paul's effort to justify God is not merely an attempt to win his readers to his way of understanding God. Ultimately, Paul's justification of God in the eyes of sinners comes down to a simple declaration of the power, the purposes, and the prerogatives of God as God. Paul does not try to persuade so much as he tries to instruct. He is not interested in placating us with a rationalization, such as, "Will this be okay? Do we have a compromise measure that will pass?" No, Paul tells us what is true. This is God, and there is no other. He alone is God.

No wonder Paul sums up chapters 9–11 by proclaiming, "Oh, the depth of the riches of the wisdom and knowledge of God! How unsearchable his judgments, and his paths beyond tracing out!" (11:33). He continues by reaching for a quote from Isaiah: "'Who has known the mind of the Lord? Or who has been his counselor?'" (11:34; cf. Isa. 40:13). Then he reaches for God's words to Job at the close of the book of Job: "Who has ever given to God, that God should repay him?" (11:35; cf. Job 41:11). And then ascending to the peak of his doxology, Paul declares, "For from him and through him and to him are all things. To him be the glory forever! Amen" (11:36). Now, if all of this is true, who are we to object? As Paul asks rhetorically, "who are you, O man, to talk back to God?" (9:20).

These are challenging truths. When reflecting upon this letter, Luther said, "Only a humble man can receive the word of God."[11] We know something of what Luther means.

What about you? Do you accept God as he has revealed himself? Or do you demand that God play by your rules and sense of fairness? John Piper describes what our response to all of this should be: we should "be deeply sobered by the awful severity of God, humbled to the dust by the absoluteness of our dependence on his unconditional mercy, and irresistibly allured by the

---

[11] Martin Luther, *Romans*, Library of Christian Classics, Wilhelm Pauck, ed. (Philadelphia: Westminster, 1961), 92.

infinite treasury of his glory ready to be revealed to the vessels of glory. Thus we will be moved to forsake all confidence in human distinctives or achievements and we will entrust ourselves to mercy alone. In the hope of glory we will extend this mercy to others that they may see our good deeds and give glory to our Father in heaven."[12]

As a Christian, the longer I reflect on these matters, the more I find that what startles me is not what God does with his creatures considered apart from their sin; it is what God does with his creatures who are sinners. Paul speaks of "God who justifies the wicked" (4:5). People like you and me! He treats us as righteous, thanks to his work in Christ!

Finally, and very briefly, Paul calls us to live transformed lives since God has shown us such mercy. The "indicative" of who we are in Christ in chapters 1–11 is followed by the "imperatives" of chapters 12–16, which describe what these transformed lives should look like. The second half of 12:1 provides the overall imperative: "offer your bodies as living sacrifices, holy and pleasing to God." Why should we do this? Read the first half of the verse: "I urge you, brothers, in view of God's mercy . . ." Chapters 1–11 have highlighted his remarkable mercy.

It is vital for us to understand what God has revealed about his purposes for our lives. He intends our lives of faith to "glorify God for his mercy" (15:9). God's reason for his actions has never changed. He acts for his own name's sake always.

CONCLUSION

Do you remember what Rabbi Eric Yoffie said about Christians praying for Jews to accept the gospel? "We'd like a little less love and a little more respect. There's a kind of theological arrogance that pervades all of this, a certain willingness on their part to play God, and an absence of awareness that these sorts of statements throughout history are associated with coercion, hatred and violence." Well ironically, and with all due respect, Larry Ashbrook had a slightly better understanding of what the Southern Baptists intended. On the evening of September 15, 1999, Ashbrook walked into the Wedgewood Baptist Church in Fort Worth, Texas (a church I have preached at twice in the last two years), during the Wednesday evening service and shot fourteen people, killing eight, including himself. He was a racist, bigoted, hateful, murderer—not the kind of hater that some writers in the press accuse Southern Baptists of being because we pray for people, but the kind of hater that uses bullets. A story in

---

[12] John Piper, *The Justification of God: An Exegetical Study of Romans 9:1-23* (Grand Rapids, Mich.: Baker, 1993, 2nd ed.), 220.

the *Houston Chronicle* the next Friday suggested that Ashbrook's shooting rampage might have been prompted by his anger with the Southern Baptists for their attitudes toward Jewish people. Rabbi Yoffie was not the only one upset by the prayer guide. It seems that Larry Ashbrook truly hated Jews, and he understood better than the rabbi what the Southern Baptists were doing by praying for the Jews. Ashbrook knew, correctly, that the Southern Baptists were loving Jewish people and trying to help them. So he killed the ones praying for them.

May God help us to know the truth about ourselves and about God, so that we will happily spend ourselves praying for others and loving them, telling them this good news of justification by faith in Christ, because God has spent himself so completely in Christ for us.

Why has God done things the way he has? Because this is how he has chosen to display his grace and glory and the fullness of his character to all creation. That is what history is all about. As John Calvin famously said, the world is the theater of God's splendor. That is why God has done things as he has.

Now, here is a more specific question: What is your purpose in living? Does the fact that you have bothered to take up space on the earth today have anything to do with the truths we have been discussing? Does it have anything to do with knowing the one who created you? If you want a life reconciled with God, forgiven of sin, and filled with his Spirit, you must be justified through faith in Christ. Why will you live? Because Christ has died and risen again.

In view of the mercies of God, the final question I have for you is this: why would you die?

Why would you reject God in all his glory, Christ in all his sacrificial love, the Spirit in all his reviving power? Would you reject them in exchange for some tawdry notions of your own about what God should be like, or about the sufficiency of your own goodness?

In view of the mercies of God, why would you die?

Let us pray:

Lord, we hear the words from your ancient prophet Micah: "He has showed you, O man, what is good. And what does the LORD require of you? To act justly and to love mercy and to walk humbly with your God. Listen! The Lord is calling to the city—and to fear your name is wisdom" (Mic. 6:8-9a). And we remember Paul's words as well: "That if you confess with your mouth, 'Jesus is Lord,' and believe in your heart that God raised him from the dead, you will be saved" (Rom. 10:9). O God, we pray that you would make this very place a theater of your glory as you display your goodness to creatures made in your image, but who have turned our backs on you. Lord, conquer our hearts not by coercion of might and power and physical strength, but by your wooing love. For Jesus' sake. Amen.

Questions for Reflection

1. Is it theological arrogance for Christians to preach that repentance and belief in Jesus Christ is the only way to find salvation from our sin and peace with God? Why or why not? Why do so many people in our culture accuse us of arrogance or of "playing God"?

2. What is sin? Is it an action, or something more?

3. Suppose a friend says to you, "Okay, I know everyone makes mistakes. But I know an elderly lady who is so loving and charitable. She honestly seems to take joy in giving to others! She believes in God and even prays sometimes, but she is not a Christian. Are you telling me God is going to send her to hell for eternity because she lied once or twice as a little girl?" How would you respond?

4. The third statement about justifying sinners said that we can be justified *only* because of Christ. Then the fourth statement said that we can be justified *only* through faith. Well, which is it?

5. Why did Jesus the Son of God have to die as our substitute if we were to be saved from hell? Why couldn't God simply overlook our sins and say, "You're forgiven." In other words, why go to all the trouble of sacrificing his Son?

6. Why does Paul, in Romans 4:10-11, make such a big deal about when Abraham *believed* versus when he was *circumcised?*

7. What is meant by the assertion that, "Justification is by faith alone, but justifying faith is never alone"?

8. If you should die tonight and stand before God and he asked you the classic question, "Why should I let you into my heaven?" what would you say? What has your heart truly trusted in?

9. Does Paul try to persuade us of God's prerogatives as God? Should he? Does God owe us an explanation? Consider your friend's statement in question 3

above. Suppose he or she went on to accuse God of being grossly unfair. What would you say?

10. What did Martin Luther mean when he said, "Only a humble man can receive the Word of God"?

11. What responsibility do *you* have to ensure that the gospel of justification by Christ alone through faith alone is the center and heart of your church's teaching and life?

THE MESSAGE OF 1 CORINTHIANS: CHURCH

7

THE MESSAGE OF 1 CORINTHIANS: CHURCH

WHAT'S THE BIG IDEA?[1]

"You only go around once in life, so go for the gusto." Have you ever thought about that slogan? It focuses on *you* and it focuses on *now*, a winning combination for advertisers.

"You deserve a break today."

"Quench your thirst."

"Have it your way, right away."

"Just do it."

Try listing all the ad slogans you know, and you will see that *you* and *today* are their main focus.

These slogans capture in a few words the dominant ideas of our day, namely, individualism and self-indulgence. And because individualism and self-indulgence rule the day, the personal savings rate in America is almost nil. Personal credit card debts soar. And our health care system reels as an affluent and litigious population believes this life is all we have. Don't we all deserve the longest physical life medical technology can give?

Everything from the hours of our workday to the gender of our sexual partner is taken to be a matter of individual preference. The individual conscience is revered and treated as an inviolable demi-deity to whom ultimate allegiance is owed. Even in the Christian religion, the worship of God is in danger of being drowned out by the worship of self-esteem and felt needs. God is praised insofar as he makes us feel better about ourselves.

Big ideas often define an era, like liberty in the eighteenth century, or progress in the nineteenth century, or—I would argue—individualism today.

---

[1] This sermon was originally preached on October 10, 1999, at Capitol Hill Baptist Church in Washington, D.C.

Such ideas provide the mental background noise in a culture, something so pervasive it is almost unnoticeable to those in its midst. These ideas act as the grids through which we interpret everything: our experience of the world, life, relationships, work, even religion. They can help us to see. Even those of us who are Caucasian can discern overt racism in much nineteenth-century literature. Yet a culture's big ideas can also blind us. Some things patently clear to earlier generations are missed by us.

One idea that was prominent in the New Testament and in the history of Christianity, but which is almost imperceptible today, is the idea of the church.

I am not saying that churches in modern America are about to close down. The proportion of church members to non–church members in the United States remained fairly constant through most of the twentieth century. And many individual churches are bursting at the seams. Hundreds, even thousands, of people attend megachurches, where multiple services are offered and programs provide care from the cradle to the grave. In the institutional sense, Christian churches are doing well.

In another sense, however, churches in modern America have nearly vanished. The idea of church, pervasive at different points in Christian history, has dissolved in the acids of the reigning individualism of today's culture. Too often, churches have become no more than expressions of the passing interests of their congregants. Their programs are determined by internal polls. Their services are planned by what leaders perceive outsiders want. And their budgets reflect nothing more than the aggregated desires of the members. Amid all the apparent prosperity of churches today, the church lacks the corporate element whereby it conceives of itself as itself.

By "corporate element" I mean that, when we gather as Christians on Sunday mornings, we do not gather merely to have our personal devotions together. The church service is not just your quiet time. We do not gather to pray, sing, and read Scripture like we do the other days of the week at home except that on Sundays we do it with more people around because it is encouraging. No, we come to participate in the life of our church. And when we come, we come not as individual consumers to do our spiritual shopping for the week, seeing what's of use down this aisle of singing or down that aisle of prayer, looking over the sermon special, browsing through post-service conversations, and taking it all home in our carts for personal use. We actually assemble as a living institution, a viable organism, one body.

I wonder why you come to church.

Let me ask you a question that gets to the nub of the matter: What is the use of the church? If you are a non-Christian, I understand you may have never pondered that question, and you are welcome to continue exploring

Christianity through this study. But if you consider yourself a Christian, what is the use of the church?

Now, if you have answered that question in terms of what the church does for you, you have missed something crucial—something very clear in the New Testament that may be imperceptible to our eyes because of the fog of our culture. The biblical answer to "What is the use of the church?" does not begin with what the church does for *you* as much as it begins with what it does for *God*. What it does for *you* is addressed, but only by putting what it does for God first. When we begin to understand this, we turn the corner from a self-centered involvement in the church to a full-blown, God-centered *life together* to which God calls us for his own purposes. When we get this, the church becomes much more than another item on the list of private virtues we cultivate by moral effort in order to avoid our list of private vices. The church becomes the manifestation of the living God in this world! And he calls us into the church as a way of living with one another. When you get this, the Christian life begins to change.

INTRODUCING 1 CORINTHIANS

In order to see this, we will look at Paul's first canonical letter to the Corinthians (that is, his first letter to them that is included in the canon of Scripture). We will not be able to cover everything in 1 Corinthians in this chapter, but we will try to hit the main points of the letter. In our last chapter, we considered Paul's letter to the church in Rome. Paul had never visited the church in Rome. His experience with the church in Corinth was very different. He founded it, and he knew the church well. According to Acts 18, Paul spent a year and a half at Corinth, laboring to establish and strengthen the church.

Like Rome, Corinth was a very interesting and cosmopolitan city. Located on the main route from Rome to the East, Corinth was a center of business, commerce, travel, and culture. Therefore it was a good place for spreading the gospel.

Paul's first canonical letter to the church in Corinth is particularly interesting because much of it is taken up with his responses to a letter they had apparently written him. You often find the phrases "Now for the matters you wrote about . . ." or "Now about . . ." In the latter half of the letter especially, Paul seems to work his way through the topics the Corinthians had asked him about in their letter, which gives the letter a very different structure than Romans. Unlike Romans, this letter is clearly occasioned by real-life situations in Corinth.

First Corinthians is the second longest of Paul's canonical letters, and can be read aloud in a little less than an hour. It is full of interesting stuff. You may have seen this verse hanging on the wall in the nursery at your church: "Listen, I tell you a mystery: We will not all sleep, but we will all be changed" (15:51). The letter has many other famous passages. Chapter 5 is a famous passage on church discipline. Chapter 7 is often quoted in discussions about marriage. Parts of chapter 11 are read almost every time the Lord's Supper is celebrated. Chapters 12 and 14 are of special interest in discussions about spiritual gifts. Chapter 13, the love chapter, must be one of the most famous chapters in the Bible, read at more weddings than any other part of the Bible. And then there is the sublime chapter 15 on the Resurrection, familiar from being read at countless funerals. It beautifully presents the unique hope we have as Christians.

There are also—for truth in advertising—confusing parts in this letter. In chapter 7, for instance, Paul refers to "the Lord . . . not I" as the one speaking, then two verses later refers to "I, not the Lord" as the one speaking (7:10, 12). Some people have thought this means the text's inspiration starts and stops according to these markers. But if you read the verse in context, you can see Paul is merely indicating whether he is quoting Jesus on a particular matter. Another passage that has been misinterpreted, particularly by the Mormons, occurs in chapter 15: "If there is no resurrection, what will those do who are baptized for the dead? If the dead are not raised at all, why are people baptized for them?" (15:29). Is Paul endorsing baptism for the dead, as some contend? Hardly. He is saying it is silly for the Corinthians to continue practicing this thing called "baptism for the dead"—which we read about nowhere else in the Bible—especially if they do not even believe in the bodily resurrection.

But 1 Corinthians is more than its disparate parts, whether those parts are famous or obscure, clear or confusing. The point of Paul's letter is one we need to hear today: he writes to teach the Corinthians about the church. Particularly, Paul discusses *what* should characterize the church, and *why* these particular characteristics must typify the church.

WHAT SHOULD CHARACTERIZE THE CHURCH

What is the church to be like? What characteristics should we expect of church? According to 1 Corinthians, the church should be holy, united, and loving.

The Church Is to Be Holy

We can begin in 1:2, where Paul greets the church as the people "called to be holy." That is how he defines them. Then in 1:8, he writes that Christ "will keep you strong to the end, so that you will be blameless." Several further characteristics help define what Paul means by "holy."

Strange to the world. First, being holy means being strange! The Christian message and Christian wisdom are different from the world's, and our only hope lies in being estranged from the messages and wisdom of this fallen world. Paul highlights this theme of strangeness in the first two chapters of his letter. He writes in chapter 1, "For since in the wisdom of God the world through its wisdom did not know him, God was pleased through the foolishness of what was preached to save those who believe" (1:21). Christians appear, and will inevitably appear, foolish to the world because, as Paul says in chapter 2, the natural man does not accept God's truth (2:14). Try sharing the whole gospel, being as culturally sensitive as you can—contextualizing perfectly and without error—and still you will find that what Paul writes is true: you will appear foolish to the world. In fact, the more clearly the natural man understands the gospel, the more he will oppose it, at least until God's Holy Spirit begins to work on his heart. Christians are strange and set apart. Strangeness was an inevitable part of holiness in the Old Testament and in the New Testament, and it remains so today.

Special to God. Christians are strange because they have been made special by God, which is why Paul writes, "You yourselves are [God's] temple . . . God's temple is sacred" (3:16-17).

Pure. The holiness of the church also involves its purity. Chapter 5's discussion of church discipline provides one of the classic treatments of the purity of the church. A man in the church had slept with his stepmother, his father's wife. Yet the church was unperturbed by this scandal. They were even proud of their tolerance. Paul responds, "hand this man over to Satan, so that the sinful nature [literally, the flesh] may be destroyed and his spirit saved on the day of the Lord" (5:5). And he warns them about their tolerance of sin: "Don't you know that a little yeast works through the whole batch of dough?" (5:6). In other words, sin spreads! You may want to rethink tolerating sin in the church. Don't think it will have no consequences.

Having reflected on this passage as the pastor of a church, I find it interesting that Paul does not yell at the man who is in adultery. He yells at the church for having tolerated the man's sin. Regarding the man, he simply says to put him out of the church so that he might be saved. In other words, the church makes Paul angrier than the man does. Why? Far worse than a church in which someone commits adultery is a church that says nothing about people committing adultery. One is an individual error. The other is a failure of the entire church. Their tolerance undermines the very life of the church, as if the body's immune system were failing. When that happens, death is imminent.

Ultimately, Paul is concerned that the gospel itself will be subverted by the spreading contagion of sin. If you cannot say what the church is not, you cannot say what it is either. If the morality of the church is no different from the world's morality, how will the world see a distinction between itself and the church? Paul's solution is simple: "Get rid of the old yeast that you may be a new batch without yeast—as you really are" (5:7). And then, "I have written you in my letter not to associate with sexually immoral people" (5:9). He does not mean they should not associate with sexually immoral people in the world—else they would have to leave the world (5:10). No, he is forbidding associating with those who name the name of Christ and yet live worldly, indistinct lives: "You must not associate with anyone who calls himself a brother but is sexually immoral or greedy, an idolater or a slanderer, a drunkard or a swindler. With such a man do not even eat" (5:11).

In the last verse of this chapter, Paul quotes God's words to the people of Israel as they were preparing to enter the Promised Land: "Expel the wicked man from among you" (5:13; quoting Deut. 13:5, etc.). Why does Paul say that? Not because God has decided ultimately to condemn the man sleeping with his father's wife, nor because the church can consign people to hell. It cannot. Rather, the man should be put out of the church so that "his spirit [may be] saved on the day of the Lord" (1 Cor. 5:5). The whole process of discipline is meant as a warning to people. Discipline enables people to see the seriousness of their sin and so averts their condemnation by awaking them to their dire condition (see also 11:32). Discipline also preserves the purity and witness of the church. God has always been concerned that his people be holy. In short, discipline is not meant ultimately to condemn; it is exactly the opposite. For the person caught in sin who will not repent, discipline helps bring repentance.

Paul raises the issue of the church's purity again in chapter 6. He pleads with the Corinthians to lay aside popularity and a sense of entitlement in order to pursue purity: "Do you not know that the wicked will not inherit the kingdom of God? Do not be deceived: . . ." (6:9a). The gospel can easily be twisted. ". . . Neither the sexually immoral nor idolators nor adulterers nor male prostitutes nor homosexual offenders nor thieves nor the greedy nor drunkards nor slanderers nor swindlers will inherit the kingdom of God" (6:9b-10). God's kingdom will not be for the unholy. Christians, on the other hand, have been "washed" and "sanctified" (6:11), and they should use their bodies in holiness. The fact that the body will be raised (6:14) is actually an argument for holiness. Apparently some of the false teachers were saying something like, "You know, it doesn't really matter what you do with your body—it's just going to rot anyway. God's more interested in your soul and spirit." Paul writes back saying, to paraphrase verses 13 and 14, "No, that body is the Lord's! He's going to raise it again on the last day. He cares about your physical body and what you do with it." This is why the resurrection is so important (chapter 15); it shows that God does care what is done with the body in this life.

Holiness is essential to the church's existence. It is an attribute. It is a trademark. It should be common. It should be typical. When someone thinks of the church you or I belong to, they should think, "This is a holy community." That does not mean we are a bunch of self-righteous, prudish people; it means we are a community that holds out in our conduct the hope of a better, more humane, and more God-honoring way of living than the world offers.

That is why we need to be clear about what it means to be a member of a church. That is why biblical teaching is central. That is why the church where I pastor has serious sermons and serious Sunday school classes and Wednesday night Bible studies and small groups throughout the week. We are different from the world—we are holy. We are living in that tension of being in the world but not of it. That is why discipline is important. That is why we must follow 1 Corinthians 5. We are to be holy.

The Church Is to Be United

Not only is the church to be holy, it is also to be united.

Apparently, the Corinthian church was also having a problem with unity. That is not surprising. Once you start tolerating sin, problems with unity follow. From the beginning, Paul appeals for unity:

> I appeal to you, brothers, in the name of our Lord Jesus Christ, that all of you agree with one another so that there may be no divisions among you and that you may be perfectly united in mind and thought. My brothers, some from Chloe's household have informed me that there are quarrels among you. What I mean is this: One of you says, "I follow Paul"; another, "I follow Apollos"; another, "I follow Cephas"; still another, "I follow Christ." (1:10-12).

The separation the Corinthians are supposed to experience is a separation from the world. Instead, they tolerate sin, and so they encourage internal division. Paul then issues a stern rebuke: "You are still worldly. For since there is jealousy and quarreling among you, are you not worldly? Are you not acting like mere men?" (3:3). The church cannot tolerate such unrepentant, unabashed sin. None of us is sinless. But when confronted with those sins, do we want to repent? Do we want to change those things?

Apparently the Corinthians were even suing one another in secular courts, a matter which takes up the first half of chapter 6. Clearly, Paul took a very dim view of Christians suing one another. He asks, why not take your case before other Christians instead of before the ungodly?

> Do you not know that the saints will judge the world? And if you are to judge the world, are you not competent to judge trivial cases? Do you not know that we will judge angels? How much more the things of this life! (6:2-3).

If Christians will judge the world one day with Christ, surely they can sort out these little differences. Such matters should be settled internally. If they cannot settle things in this way, if they must resort to lawsuits, they "have been completely defeated already. Why not rather be wronged? Why not rather be cheated?" (6:7). How many times do you think these questions are asked in law school today? "Why not rather be cheated?"

Now there's an option—choosing to lay down your rights. I do want to be very careful here, considering all the lawyer jokes that go around. Through the work of lawyers, certain rights are preserved in our society that all of us benefit from. Having said that, we as Christians need to be careful not to embody the litigious, self-concerned nature of the culture around us. Once we do this, Paul says, we have already been defeated.

Unity is supposed to be one of the hallmarks of the church, a unity that transcends the old divisions of Jew and Gentile (7:19) as well as every other worldly division. What does this mean for you? It means you begin by noticing the divides in your mind that have made you unwilling to speak to another person at church. Those are the very divides the gospel is meant to overcome. Those are the divides the church repudiates for the sake of unity, giving witness to God. Naturally, then, Paul was upset by the report of divisions in the church. They were dividing even at the feast of their unity—the Lord's Supper. Some of them arrived before the others, and proceeded to abuse the Supper and get drunk (11:18-22).

When churches divide for carnal reasons, they identify themselves with something other than Christ. They become the church of modern music, or the church of this pastor, or the church of the home-schoolers, or the church of the Democrats, or the church of the blue carpet. As soon as this happens, they are no longer the church of Jesus Christ. And though a church may be unified around any such issue, the unity is not a true Christian unity. There will never be a church that is entirely unaffected by the culture around it and by who belongs to it—not in this world. God does not seem to intend otherwise. But all truly Christian churches should reflect the unity of Christ by their unity with each other.

The Church Is to Be Loving

Practically speaking, how are churches to be united? We are to be united in love. Love is the third characteristic Paul uses in this letter to describe the church.

Notice how chapter 8 begins: "We know that we all possess knowledge. Knowledge puffs up, but love builds up" (8:1). Now, this does not mean you need to be ignorant in order to be loving. Paul is not saying that. But he is also certainly not saying that being knowledgeable will make you loving. Knowledge is not the same thing as love.

Paul is quite clear on this point, devoting his large excursus in chapters 8–14 to teaching that love and consideration for others should govern what we do in the church. In chapter 8, Paul teaches that love should determine the Christian's use of various freedoms, such as whether to get married or whether to eat meat sacrificed to idols (a big problem in the first-century church). As Christians, we should not merely exercise our freedom to do whatever we please; we should act according to what is most loving toward others. In chapter 9, Paul discusses his own example of laying aside his right as an apostle to be married. The other apostles are married, he says, but he has refrained from marriage in order to be of greater service to the church (9:5). He has also laid aside his rights to ask for financial support from the church at Corinth, even though both the Old Testament and the Lord Jesus have given him this right (9:9, 14). Paul has sought to love and build up the Corinthians, not to assert his rights. In chapter 10, he tells them to be mindful not only of what is permissible but also of what is beneficial to others (10:23-24). In chapter 11, he chides them for their unloving behavior at the Lord's Table. In chapter 12, he tells them that all of God's various spiritual gifts are given for the building up of the whole church. In chapter 13, Paul teaches that love should be at the heart of every action. And in chapter 14, he distinguishes between the two gifts of prophecy and tongues—gifts that apparently were prominent in the Corinthian church—in terms of what best builds up the church as a whole. Whatever builds up the whole church is far better than what merely builds up the individual.

If you have spent any time in churches, you have probably learned that only love will establish the kind of unity that should mark the body of Christ. Nothing else will. We will never so finely attune our vision or desires that all disagreements will be left behind. That will not happen at our church. And it will not happen at any other church you attend. So what can we do? Well, we can love one another. When two disagreeing sisters or brothers (who concur on the church's essentials) agree to set aside their disagreements and work together, they demonstrate a love for the other over themselves. Yes, you are free to make a decision according to your own preferences. But remember Paul's instruction: "Be careful, however, that the exercise of your freedom does not become a stumbling block to the weak" (8:9). Other Christians can be hurt, even destroyed, by your exercise of personal preference: "So this weak brother, for whom Christ died, is destroyed by your knowledge" (8:11; cf. 8:13). In a Christian church, concern for others is paramount.

From my perspective as a pastor it becomes clear over time which brothers and sisters in a church have an edifying effect on those around them. They do not need to chair a committee. They do not need to teach a Sunday school class. You can simply watch God gradually commit different ministries and opportunities into the hands of certain people because they love him and are willing to quietly give themselves in love for others, without particular concern that they be right or be recognized. And again and again you hear about the blessing they have been to others. That should be typical of every one of us. Paul states his principle of love pretty clearly in chapter 10: "Nobody should seek his own good, but the good of others" (10:24).

It is in the context of the church that the famous chapter 13 of 1 Corinthians is so powerful. I am sure you have enjoyed reading verses from this "love chapter" on store-bought cards and at weddings; they are pretty words. But they take on special power when you insert them back into the context in which God placed them—as the dynamic fuel of the church. Love is what motivates everything else God wants to characterize his church. In the first three verses, Paul lays out how love excels other gifts and virtuous actions: "If I speak in the tongues of men and of angels, but have not love, I am only a resounding gong or a clanging cymbal. If I have the gift of prophecy and can fathom all mysteries and all knowledge, and if I have a faith that can move mountains, but have not love, I am nothing. If I give all I possess to the poor and surrender my body to the flames, but have not love, I gain nothing." Clearly, Paul is saying that more than action is required. We evangelicals are pretty good about saying love is what you do—"Love is an action, not a feeling." And this emphasis does helpfully balance out the imbalances of our culture. But having said that, love is more than what you do. It involves the disposition of the heart toward others and God. Actions like laying down your life, teaching others, giving all you have to the poor are not sufficient in themselves. Paul says such actions can be done without love. And without love, they are worthless. So, while we do not want to suggest that love is mere sentiment, nor do we want to say love is mere action. According to the Bible, love is a disposition of the heart toward God and others which then shows itself in our actions.

Paul characterizes this love in some of the most treasured words in the Bible:

> Love is patient, love is kind. It does not envy, it does not boast, it is not proud. It is not rude, it is not self-seeking, it is not easily angered, it keeps no record of wrongs. Love does not delight in evil but rejoices with the truth. It always protects, always trusts, always hopes, always perseveres (13:4-7).

Could this be more clear? Love is not self-seeking! Christians should not be preoccupied with their own limited, private good. They should actually rejoice in the good of others, as Paul rejoices in the salvation of the Corinthians (e.g., 1:4-6). Love lasts (13:8). And love is supreme: "And now these three remain: faith, hope, and love. But the greatest of these is love" (13:13).

Moving to chapter 14, then, Paul exhorts the Corinthians to "Follow the way of love and eagerly desire spiritual gifts, especially the gift of prophecy" (14:1). If you want to work out the implications of chapter 13 in your life and in the life of your church, read chapter 14. Really, I think chapter 14 could be called the "love chapter" as much as chapter 13. Consider: In 14:3-5, Paul judges the worth of something by whether it edifies others. In 14:12, he encourages the Corinthians to excel in gifts that build up the church. In 14:17, he again expresses a concern for edifying others. In 14:19, he measures the gifts by whether they edify others. In 14:26, he says everything in the church must be done for the strengthening of the church. In 14:31, he says prophecy should be devoted to the instruction and encouragement of everyone. In chapter 14, Paul basically says, "Let me give you a practical example of what I mean by the kind of love described in chapter 13." The priority he gives prophecy over tongues is particularly instructive. Prophecy strengthens and edifies the church, whereas speaking in tongues only edifies the self.

Now if you happen to be charismatic, let me emphasize what Paul is not saying in verse 4: In 14:4, Paul says, "He who speaks in a tongue edifies himself, but he who prophesies edifies the church." He is not saying, "Well, you've got two choices here. You can do things for you own edification, which is fine; or you can do things for the church's edification, which is also fine. Two different things for two different purposes." If you read 14:4 all by itself, that might make sense. But if you read all of chapter 14, you see Paul is saying, "Not this, but that." He does say, "I would like every one of you to speak in tongues"

(14:5a), but then he also says, "but I would rather have you prophesy" (14:5b). Again and again, Paul's driving point is that we should value in the church whatever builds up the church as a whole: "try to excel in gifts that build up the church" (14:12) and do whatever edifies others (14:17).

When was the last time you attended church with the edification of others the primary concern on your heart? Or do you usually anticipate what you personally will find most helpful, like whether a hymn or prayer moves you, or whether you get out on time, or whether you speak to the right people afterward? When was the last time you were genuinely concerned about the edification of others around you? Not in the sense of whether they liked this or that hymn, but in the sense of whether they are being built up in the faith? Do you seek out your close friends after the service or do you look around for visitors and unfamiliar faces? Do you pray before and during the service that God would particularly use the time you have together on Sunday as a church family to work in the hearts of both you and others?

Paul has a special concern for the church's health, and this should not be surprising when we remember his history: "For I am the least of the apostles and do not even deserve to be called an apostle, because I persecuted the church of God" (15:9). The memory of his former ways must have been burned onto his mind, and so his love for the church was great. Surely we can see why God would use such a man to teach us to "Do everything in love" (16:14).

Finally, it is worth noting that Paul says Christian love should be expressed not only within churches but also between churches. In chapter 1, he greets them as the ones growing in the Lord "together with all those everywhere" who follow Christ (1:2). In chapter 4, Paul tells them he is sending his beloved Timothy to them (4:17). And in chapter 16, he writes "about the collection for God's people" (see 16:1-4). Again and again in Scripture we see evidence of the early churches reaching out in concern for other local churches. Are our churches marked by such love?

WHY THESE CHARACTERISTICS SHOULD TYPIFY THE CHURCH

Why should the church be typified by the characteristics of holiness, unity, and love? Simply put, the character of the church should reflect the character of God. We are to be holy and united and loving because God is holy, one, and loving. Paul says to the Corinthians, "Follow my example, as I follow the example of Christ" (11:1).

God intends to display his own reflection in the church. We see this generally in chapters 1 and 2. The gospel possessed by the church is the wisdom of God, not the wisdom of this world (1:17–2:16). Paul writes, "We have not received the spirit of the world but the Spirit who is from God, that we may understand what God has freely given us" (2:12). And several verses later, "we have the mind of Christ" (2:16b). In short, the transforming work of the gospel in the church's life will give it the mind of Christ and make the church look more like God than like the world. And his reflection in the church through proclamation and holy, united, loving lives is the very stuff of its witness. As we think about each of these characteristics, we can see their ultimate end is not to improve the moral health of society, though this might be a by-product: their end is to reflect God.

The Church Is to Be Holy Because God Is Holy

The church is holy first and foremost not because it has lived (or will live) in a holy manner; it is holy because God has declared the church holy in Jesus. We are the ones who are "sanctified in Christ Jesus and called to be holy" (1:2). We have already been "washed," "sanctified," and "justified" in Christ Jesus and through the Holy Spirit (6:11). If we are going to be his, we should be like him—holy. Otherwise, we cannot be his. The world in its rebellion has become strange to God. So we must be strange to the world.

The holiness, righteousness, and wisdom the church gains through God's declaration in Christ, ultimately, begins with the holiness, righteousness, and wisdom of God: "It is because of him that you are in Christ Jesus, who has become for us wisdom from God—that is, our righteousness, holiness and redemption" (1:30). Our holiness comes from the Holy One who has purchased and indwelt us: "Don't you know that you yourselves are God's temple and that God's Spirit lives in you? If anyone destroys God's temple, God will destroy him; for God's temple is sacred, and you are that temple" (3:16-17). Our holiness as Christians is God's holiness in Christ imparted to us.

Part of our task, then, in reflecting the character of God is to reflect his holiness. That's why Paul writes, "Get rid of the old yeast that you may be a new batch without yeast—as you really are. For Christ, our Passover lamb, has been sacrificed. Therefore let us keep the Festival . . ."(5:7-8). God has prepared the church for holiness. He has begun by slaying his own Son, the Passover lamb. And now the unleavened loaf needs to be added, the loaf without sin, which is us, the church. We are the missing half of the Passover celebration (the celebration of liberation from bondage) waiting to join the slain Lamb. As the unleavened loaf, we separate ourselves from sin to honor Christ and to show his character to creation. That is our calling as individuals and as a church. Every local church is called to show God's holiness to this world.

The Church Is to Be United Because God Is One

The church is to be united because God is one. In chapter 8, Paul writes, "There is but one God, the Father, from whom all things came and for whom we live; and there is but one Lord, Jesus Christ, through whom all things came and through whom we live" (8:6). The life of the church depends entirely upon God in Christ, who is one.

In chapter 10, Paul points to the Lord's Supper as representing the church's unity with Christ and among its members: "Because there is one loaf, we, who are many, are one body, for we all partake of the one loaf" (10:17). We in the church are one body, because Christ is one.

In chapter 12, Paul relates the oneness of the Trinitarian God with the unity that should be manifest in the church's gifts and labors:

> There are different kinds of gifts, but the same Spirit. There are different kinds of service, but the same Lord. There are different kinds of working, but the same God works all of them in all men.
>
> Now to each one the manifestation of the Spirit is given for the common good. . . .
>
> All these are the work of one and the same Spirit, and he gives them to each one, just as he determines (12:4-7, 11).

If we are Christians, we have God's Spirit in us. And the Spirit gives each of us gifts for the building up of our oneness with one another in the church. Furthermore, our oneness with each other directly reflects God's oneness. Paul writes, "The body is a unit, though it is made up of many parts; and though all its parts are many, they form one body." Now notice what Paul says: "So it is with Christ" (12:12). You expect him to say, "So it is with the church." But he says, "So it is with Christ." God in Christ is one, and we who are "baptized by one Spirit into one body—whether Jews or Greeks, slave or free—and . . . given the one Spirit to drink" (12:13) are the body of Christ. Our unity with one another as the body of Christ is a gift of Christ's Spirit who makes us his body.

Naturally, then, Paul deals theologically with the ill report of various divisions and factions in the church. Notice the question he asks them in light of their divisions: "Is Christ divided?" (1:13). What a fascinating question. It would not make sense unless Paul regards the church as the body of Christ. Yet division in the church makes as much sense as Christ himself being divided. The question reminds us that, as a church, we have no other basis of being than Christ.

Do you remember where Paul got this idea? He learned it on his first day as a Christian. On the Damascus Road on the way to persecute Christians, Paul, then Saul, was knocked off his horse and was given a vision. Jesus appeared to him and said, "Saul, Saul, why are you persecuting me?" Persecuting the church was tantamount to persecuting Christ. So now, many years later, he argues in this letter to Corinth that dividing the church is tantamount to dividing Christ. When there is disunity in the church, it is as if we are lying to one another and to the world about who God is and what he is like. Our disunity in the church says, "God is divided!" Our responsibility to maintain the unity of love is serious indeed. Paul writes, "You are the body of Christ, and each one of you is a part of it" (12:27). We have been given the task of imaging God! Do you approach your life in the local church with the appropriate amount of gravity and seriousness?

Sometimes we lose our unity through a wrong loyalty to different servants in the church. Perhaps we become attached to one particular leader in the church. But Paul reminds the Corinthians, and us, that all of the work accomplished in the church by various people is the work of God:

> For when one says, "I follow Paul," and another, "I follow Apollos," are you not mere men?
>
> What, after all, is Apollos? And what is Paul? Only servants, through whom you came to believe—as the Lord has assigned to each his task. I planted the seed, Apollos watered it, but God made it grow. So neither he who plants nor he who waters is anything, but only God, who makes things grow. The man who plants and the man who waters have one purpose, and each will be rewarded according to his own labor. For we are God's fellow workers; you are God's field, God's building (3:4-9).

If you attend your church because of the pastor, you are wrongly motivated, and time will reveal that. The pastor will disappoint you. Even if he never disappoints you, he will someday die. Your faith cannot be built upon a person. It cannot be built upon that really neat person who brought you to church, or your Sunday school teacher, or the pastor. True faith is built upon God in Jesus Christ. Paul and Apollos are wonderful, but they are only servants of God. Whatever good they did, or whatever good you see Christians around you do, remember that it is God who is doing the work. When you are grateful for a sermon, or a prayer, or how a service is led, or the work of a deacon, or the work of the nursery staff, or the greetings of others, direct your thanksgiving first to the lovingkindness of God for you. Nobody in the church will ever perfectly image his lovingkindness, although we see bits of it through one another. That is what the church does. We have been brought together as one people around one foundation—Jesus Christ (3:11). And there will be only one judge over us (3:13; cf. 4:5). No idol will finally judge us, nor will a false teacher, nor will our own consciences! Paul writes, "My conscience is clear, but that does not make me innocent." You can have a clear conscience and be quite wrong. "It is the Lord who judges me" (4:4). There is one judge, one foundation, and one who finally does all the work.

The Church Is to Be Loving Because God Is Loving

Finally, the church is to be loving because God is loving. In chapter 2, Paul quotes Isaiah: "No eye has seen, no ear has heard, no mind has conceived what God has prepared for those who love him" (2:9). At the center of our heart should be love for God. Yet our love for him is merely a response to his tremendous love for us. God has taken the initiative. God has loved us in Christ to the point of redeeming us (1:30). So Paul chides the Corinthians for not acting lovingly toward one another.

In chapter 8 Paul writes,

> So this weak brother, for whom Christ died, is destroyed by your knowledge. When you sin against your brothers in this way and wound their weak conscience, you sin against Christ. Therefore, if what I eat causes my brother to fall into sin, I will never eat meat again, so that I will not cause him to fall (8:11-13).

In other words, if I have treated you, a brother or a sister, unlovingly, then I have sinned against Christ. Treating you unlovingly is treating Christ unlovingly. When you fail to suffer with those who suffer and rejoice with those who are honored (12:26), you can say you love God but I am not sure what you mean. Christ so identifies himself with his church that he describes such failures to love as failures toward him.

Consider the love that Christ has shown you and me by pouring out his blood and offering his body for us on the cross (11:23-26). The church has been founded on this sacrifice from the beginning. Paul recounts this as a kind of early church creed: "Christ died for our sins" (15:3).

The church is to be the display of God's love amid this messed up, sinful, selfish world. Do we do that? Do our churches display the love of God to the world around us?

CONCLUSION

So what's the use of the church? To manifest to the world the character of God.

If you want help with understanding and living that out, you must realize that how you relate to the church will say something about the core of your relationship with God. You can tell a lot about people's relationship with God simply by watching how they relate to others in the church.

Yet simply loving one another is not sufficient either. As Paul rhetorically asks in chapter 15, "If I fought wild beasts in Ephesus for merely human reasons, what have I gained?" (15:32). Personally, I cannot preach finally and fundamentally because I love you. I must preach finally because I love God and want to give him glory. First Corinthians 10:31 provides a good summary verse for this letter: "So whether you eat or drink or whatever you do, do it all for the glory of God." This is the church's purpose. This is what God calls us to.

It is easy to see when people begin to understand these things for their own lives. Their prayer requests go beyond concerns for a sick cousin and become a little more personal. They start to ask for prayer concerning themselves. And then they don't just ask for prayer concerning their own physical, financial, or professional concerns; they begin to ask for prayer on matters pertaining to their own spiritual character. And then they don't just ask for prayer about their own spiritual life, like faithfulness in Bible reading or honesty at work; they begin praying for the church—that the church would be marked by holiness, unity, and love. And they begin to be concerned about the clarity and visibility of God's character and whether it is reflected by relationships within the church.

Paul points out in the first chapter that God "chose the lowly things of this world and the despised things—and the things that are not—to nullify the things that are, so that no one may boast before him" (1:28-29). God does not want the church to become a basis for human boasting. That is why he chooses us! He chooses people who at some point in their life have come to realize that they are desperate. That they are destitute. That they have no hope without God. That they have nothing to boast about apart from him. God calls the church to himself because he does not want anything to obscure his own glory. That is what God is all about: the proclamation of his glory for the enjoyment of the nations. That is why—and a part of me hates to tell you this—God lets you get into the desperate situations you find yourself in. He wants to show you he is faithful, in spite of your folly. And he uses your circumstances to accomplish your instruction and his glorification. So, in the very first chapter of this letter, Paul quotes Jeremiah: "Let him who boasts boast in the Lord" (1:31; cf. Jer. 9:24). We are not to boast in ourselves or our own strength.

And so, amid a dying world, God shines his light of life through you and me and this church. He says through Paul,

> the time is short. From now on those who have wives should live as if they had none; those who mourn, as if they did not; those who are happy, as if they were

not; those who buy something, as if it were not theirs to keep; those who use the things of the world, as if not engrossed in them. For this world in its present form is passing away (7:29-31).

We are to be wrapped up in God's glory and his service. All else is futile. Paul writes in chapter 15, "If only for this life we have hope in Christ, we are to be pitied more than all men" (15:19). If you have built your Christian life around what you can get in this life, you have missed the whole thing. If our church has encouraged you to do that, I am so sorry. The Christian life was never meant to be about me, or about one local congregation. It is finally about God. And we have no promise from Scripture that all the imbalanced scales in this life will be leveled. And we should never represent the gospel as if it does.

Is that why we do what we do at our church? For the sake of the gospel and for God's glory? Are our public meetings all held to the glory of God?

It is our *destiny* to reflect God:

As was the earthly man, so are those who are of the earth; and as is the man from heaven, so also are those who are of heaven. And just as we have borne the likeness of the earthly man, so shall we bear the likeness of the man from heaven (15:48-49).

This is the hope by which we live as Christians: "Therefore, my dear brothers, stand firm. Let nothing move you. Always give yourselves fully to the work of the Lord, because you know that your labor in the Lord is not in vain" (15:58). If our hope is in anything else, we are not a church, at least not a biblical church.

At a conference I recently attended, I heard a pastor preach on Paul's understanding of the church. He said, "We are one of God's chief pieces of evidence. Paul's great concern for the church [in Ephesians 4:1-16] is that the church manifest and display the glory of God, thus vindicating God's character against all the slander of demonic realms, the slander that God is not worth living for. God has entrusted to his church the glory of his own name." Furthermore, he said, "The circumstances of your life are the God-given occasion of your displaying and manifesting the attributes of God."

If we cultivate in our churches a sub-Christian holiness that tolerates sin, we deceive people about God's character. If we cultivate a sub-Christian unity that papers over real divisions on matters of doctrine and yet boasts of unity around smaller, secondary matters, we will confuse people about God's person. If we cultivate a sub-Christian love that is no more than mere sentiment and family feeling, then we lie to the world about God's purposes. All of these things lie about God, misrepresenting him and what he is like. True holiness includes discipline. True unity must be around Christ, and the diversity of the church's members will give witness to what unites us. And true love will go deeper than sentiment or pious performance. It will draw us outward to the stranger for Christ's sake, because that is the kind of love God has shown us in Christ.

This is how God's glory will be displayed in the church, whether that church is in Corinth or in the town where you live. It will be displayed in lives of holiness, unity, and love.

This is what our church is devoted to.

Are you?

I wonder why you go to church.

Let us pray:

Lord God, we pray that you would give every one of us the humility that comes from knowing both our sinful state before you and your amazing love for us in Christ. As you chip away pride from our hearts, ship it out the door of our churches, that you would build groups of wise, humble, thankful, and selfless people. O Lord, make us those who show your holiness, your unity, and your love to the world around us. We pray in Jesus' name. Amen.

Questions for Reflection

1. What is the use of the church? On a more personal note, why do you attend church?

2. As we have seen, the first definition provided for the holiness of the church is "strange." List some strange things Christians believe. List some strange things Christians do. How does the strangeness of the church affect its witness? As Christians, shouldn't we downplay our strangeness and try to be more relevant? Why or why not?

3. How does the tolerance of sin in a church eventually cause division? How does legalism (emphasizing rule-keeping to the point where people will begin placing their trust for salvation in their ability to keep rules) cause division in the church? Why is the gospel the only true foundation for unity in the church?

4. Are there people in your church with whom you will not speak? What does this communicate about your understanding of the gospel? Are there issues in your church worth dividing over?

5. The famous "love chapter," 1 Corinthians 13, is popular at "romantic" occasions such as weddings. Yet as we have observed, the context of chapter 13 suggests Paul intends this type of love to characterize relationships within the church. Chapter 14's instructions on prophecy and speaking in tongues show us one way to apply chapter 13 in our churches. What are some other ways our churches can practically live out chapter 13?

6. What is the ultimate end of the church? (In answering this question, pretend you don't know the word "glorify"!) How will it accomplish this end?

7. Why should the church gather at least weekly?

8. We have seen that the church's task is to present a picture of God's holiness to the world, so that the world will know what God is like. How does that change (or at least dramatically supplement) more traditional notions of evangelism and witness?

9. What do divisions in the church teach the world about God? Have you ever done anything that might have been a source of division in the church? What do you presently do to actively promote unity in the church?

10. The statement was made that you can tell a lot about a person's relationship with God by how he or she relates with other members of the church. How is this true?

11. What sorts of things do you pray for concerning your church?

12. What have you learned from this chapter about trying to live the Christian life alone? What does the "Lone-Ranger" Christian miss? Why, as Christians, should we never give up the habit of meeting together on a regular basis (Heb. 10:25)?

THE MESSAGE OF 2 CORINTHIANS: WEAKNESS

8

THE MESSAGE OF 2 CORINTHIANS: WEAKNESS

JUDGING A BOOK BY ITS COVER[1]

Recently, the voters of Alabama were presented with a proposition for establishing a state lottery. To most observers, the proposition's passage was a foregone conclusion. Candidate Don Siegelman had handily defeated Alabama's incumbent governor Fob James, and Siegelman had campaigned on a state lottery platform. Polls were showing an Alabama-wide 60 percent approval rating for a state lottery. Forces for the lottery proposition outspent its opponents three to one. And similar measures had won approval in thirty-seven other states over the previous two decades. Still, the proposition to establish a state lottery was defeated by a vote of 54 to 46 percent.

What do we make of this? Does this represent the beginning of a re-moralization of our society? Are evangelical sensibilities and traditional family values regaining their hold in our consciences? Will the other thirty-seven state governments repeal their gambling provisions and repent of what they have done to cultivate addiction and prey upon the populace they were elected to serve? Even more significantly, can we expect our culture's approval of aborting infants to reverse course?

Time will tell.

Time has a funny way of doing that. It changes a lot of perspectives. With the benefit of hindsight, we can look back through history and find that victories were really defeats and that defeats were sometimes victories. In our own lives, apparent jewels are found to be baubles and things once discounted become the things treasured. There is no way around that bit of proverbial wisdom that appearances are deceiving.

---

[1] This sermon was originally preached on October 31, 1999, at Capitol Hill Baptist Church in Washington, D.C.

"You can't judge a book by its cover," we say. In fact, we tend to be a little suspicious even about our good circumstances. "It's too good to be true," we say. Truth is not always immediately evident, and we know that.

INTRODUCING 2 CORINTHIANS

All this brings us to the subject of this study. There was a church which Paul had founded, and to whom he had written, which was beginning to . . . well, it seems they had begun falling for immediate impressions—for looks, for appearances, for worldly measures of success—particularly in their leaders. It was a natural tendency, and a terribly dangerous one. It is dangerous for us today as well. We can become complacent in perceived political victories or personal strengths. We can begin to believe our own publicity, or that all good things in this life will last forever.

I wonder if this sounds like you, or if you think what I am saying sounds suited to someone else? I think this is a particularly important message if you live in America. We are a country of image-making.

The situation in Corinth seemed to be like that. Corinth was an important city in Greece, located on the main shipping highway from Rome to the East. We read in the book of Acts that Paul labored for many months to plant a church in this strategic city—what some have called the San Francisco of the ancient Mediterranean world.

After his initial visit to Corinth when he established the church there, Paul left to start other churches. Sometime later—we don't know how much later—he got the disturbing news of factional problems and other difficulties in the Corinthian church. So he wrote the letter we call 1 Corinthians. Paul then returned to Corinth a second time to follow up on these problems. That visit, which commentaries call the "painful visit," based on 2 Corinthians 2:1, did not go well. Apparently, Paul flopped. He did not make a good impression. And the problem he went to fix did not get fixed. So he left in discouragement and wrote them what is called "the severe letter," also referred to in our present letter (2 Cor. 2:4; 7:8-9). We do not have a copy of the severe letter, but we know that it was very sharp and that it seems to have had an effect. Apparently, it produced some of the changes Paul wanted. When Paul learned that the severe letter had effected change, in joy he wrote what we call 2 Corinthians. All this history is explained through the course of 2 Corinthians. In the letter, he also describes his desire to make another visit to them in order to share his joy at what has happened.

Second Corinthians is fairly simple in structure. In chapters 1–7 Paul defends his ministry. In chapters 8 and 9 he discusses the collection he is taking up for some poor Christians in (we think) Jerusalem. He then closes the letter with a fresh defense of his apostleship (chapters 10–13). His defense is renewed in these last four chapters with such vehemence that some have wondered if Paul received news from Corinth after writing the first nine chapters that made him worry afresh. Whether he did or not, this book presents, of all Paul's letters, the white-hot personal passion of Paul. It is the emotional climax of his writing. Romans may provide the most comprehensive statement of his understanding of the gospel. Galatians highlights the heart of that gospel. Ephesians also contains marvelous theology. The two letters to Timothy and one to Titus tell us how to live as a church. But in 2 Corinthians we encounter Paul's passion at its boiling point as he defends what God has called him to do. Some people in the church at Corinth were following men Paul calls "super-apostles" (11:5; 12:11). These outwardly impressive teachers had become popular, and they were disparaging Paul's credentials.

What was Paul to do? The most important issue was helping the Corinthians sort out their admirations and inclinations. So Paul wrote them this profound and personal meditation on the very heart of the gospel. The gospel was Paul's best response, because these super-apostles were spiritually deviant. They taught the people to pursue the wrong things, though not things that were obviously wrong. They were tricky, and the people were misled. It is not surprising then that Paul wrote at such length, so personally, so profoundly, and so passionately.

The good news of Jesus Christ is not a message Paul, you, or I would invent. On the surface, it sounds much too strange. Throughout the history of the church, many individuals have tried to say the gospel is something different from what Paul said it is. Our own age is perfectly situated to misunderstanding the gospel as well. We are impatient and make hurried judgments. We love appearances, but we have little concern for the realities that generate them. The letter of 2 Corinthians is a good antidote to all this.

We will look at the letter as we would a landscape or a painting new to our view. We first want to *see* the obvious things, and then we want to *perceive* some of the more subtle and significant aspects of this letter. My goal, just to be up front with you, is to deprogram or reeducate you. Choose whatever word you like, I want 2 Corinthians to be used by God to break the false assumptions common today about the gospel and about what it means to be a Christian, as well as to help you see through some of the devil's deceptions that have worked their way into our own lives.

SEEING THE APPARENT STRENGTH OF THE SUPER-APOSTLES

First, we observe that these new leaders in the Corinthian church had the appearance of strength. You will not understand this letter at all without understanding this basic fact.

A number of teachers "masquerading as apostles" (as Paul describes them in 11:13) had entered the Corinthian church. These men were outwardly so strong and impressive that twice Paul uses the word *huper* (hyper) to refer to them in tongue-in-cheek fashion as "super-apostles" (11:5; 12:11). And, sure enough, they presented themselves as professionals. They were not like old Paul, a man who became fixated on some idea and traveled around passionately telling people about it. No, these were real professionals—educated, certified, and degreed in rhetoric. They produced impressive letters of recommendation that established their identities and qualifications beyond doubt (3:1). They were trained, literally, in eloquence—in how to add up the verbs, adjectives, and nouns to get the most rhetorical punch at the end. After all, your eloquence helps people understand the importance of listening to your advice, skill, and insight. Your persuasiveness helps them accept your instruction (cf. 3:1; 10:12). And for just a tiny fee (11:6-7)!

Now, these men did their boasting in what we think was a fairly affluent city. Boasting in one's strength was common in the world of the first century, even as it is common in our world today. Paul can refer to "boasting in the way the world does" (11:18), because boasting is timeless. These super-apostles' boasts probably fit right into the culture of the church; nothing was unusual about their practices. Perhaps the culture of the church in Corinth even encouraged putting oneself forward. And when the people looked on these super-apostles, the evidence was obvious and irrefutable: "These leaders are impressive. Trust them!"

SEEING THE APPARENT WEAKNESSES OF THE POOR, OF PAUL, AND OF GOD

What a contrast there was between the apparent strength of these super-apostles and the obvious weaknesses of so many others. Not everyone in Corinth lived from strength to strength. Paul, probably writing from Macedonia in northern Greece, was among a group of Christians experiencing common troubles of the body and soul such as sickness, discontentment, and fear. This world has always been full of human weaknesses and unavoidable difficulties, which is why Paul empathetically speaks of his groaning in these bodies that are wasting away (5:2-4). In this world, we will always need a God who comforts us "in all our troubles" (1:4).

The Apparent Weakness of the Poor

One of the most common weaknesses then, as today, was poverty. In chapters 8 and 9, Paul expresses his concerns about poverty among the believers in Jerusalem. He had been encouraging the new assemblies of Christians throughout the Aegean world where he was laboring—Turkey and Greece—to supply the needs of these first Christians in Palestine. As he describes this effort, he refers to the poverty of some of the very Christians to whom he has appealed for help in the collection, such as the Macedonians.

> And now, brothers, we want you to know about the grace that God has given the Macedonian churches. Out of the most severe trial, their overflowing joy and their extreme poverty welled up in rich generosity. For I testify that they gave as much as they were able, and even beyond their ability. Entirely on their own, they urgently pleaded with us for the privilege of sharing in this service to the saints (8:1-4).

These Macedonian churches were marked by "extreme poverty," yet they led the way in giving! Strange, isn't it? The extremely poor ones led the way in giving.

The Apparent Weakness of Paul

Most strikingly, Paul and his weaknesses stand in contradistinction to the apparent strengths of the super-apostles. Paul himself was radically marked by weaknesses.

General statements. Paul's letter is littered with general statements about his difficulties. In chapter 1, Paul mentions his distress, sufferings, hardships, and even despair: "We do not want you to be uninformed, brothers, about the hardships we suffered in the province of Asia. We were under great pressure, far beyond our ability to endure, so that we despaired even of life" (1:8; cf. 6-7, 9). In chapter 4, he refers to himself as "hard pressed on every side," "perplexed," "persecuted," "struck down," and "always carry[ing] around in our body the death of Jesus" (4:8-10). Several verses later he refers to this former list as his "troubles" (4:17). In chapter 7, Paul describes himself as "harassed at every turn—conflicts on the outside, fears within" (7:5). In chapters 11 and 12, he refers very generally to his "weakness" and "weaknesses" (11:30; 12:5). It is interesting that he would write about this so openly. These super-apostles were not people who seemed to have such weaknesses, and even if they did, they certainly would not talk about them. Remember, they were marked by "strength."

Personal characteristics. As we have already mentioned, Paul seems to be responding to fresh criticism in the emotionally charged chapters 10 and 11. Apparently, some of Paul's personal characteristics had come under attack. He

had been negatively presented in striking contrast to the self-appointed, confident, impressive apostles with whom the Corinthians had become enamored.
Paul had been charged with being "timid" and "unimpressive" in person, having a speaking style that "amounts to nothing" (10:1, 10). Maybe that is why
his previous visit had ended in failure. He could not stand up to people. Perhaps
he occasionally avoided conflict. He had also been charged with lacking training as a communicator (11:6). In short, Paul is characterized as (and maybe
was) personally weak.

Physical trials. Not only that, Paul refers to his physical weakness
throughout this letter in two different ways. First, he is acutely aware of his
own physical frailty and mortality. He calls himself a "jar of clay" (4:7) that
is "outwardly . . . wasting away" (4:16). He likens the physical body to a
"tent" that will be "destroyed" (5:1).

Second, Paul has a knack for getting himself into physical trials and difficulties, apparently unlike these super-apostles. Then he talks about the trials!
He is not embarrassed by these "sufferings" (e.g., 1:7). In chapter 11, we find
a stirring list of some of these sufferings, where he brags about his trials in
ironic fashion: "Are they servants of Christ? (I am out of my mind to talk like
this.) I am more. I have worked much harder, been in prison more frequently,
been flogged more severely, and been exposed to death again and again . . ."
(11:23). You see, he is mocking how the super-apostles stand up and say great
things about themselves. So he admits he is crazy to boast about himself, but
he will. And then he begins to boast about the most embarrassing things:

> Five times I received from the Jews the forty lashes minus one. Three times I was
> beaten with rods, once I was stoned, three times I was shipwrecked, I spent a
> night and a day in the open sea, I have been constantly on the move. I have been
> in danger from rivers, in danger from bandits, in danger from my own country-
> men, in danger from Gentiles; in danger in the city, in danger in the country, in
> danger at sea; and in danger from false brothers. I have labored and toiled and
> have often gone without sleep; I have known hunger and thirst and have often
> gone without food; I have been cold and naked (11:24-27).

And he keeps going.

You will find a similar list back in chapter 6. Paul describes himself as having been

> in troubles, hardships and distresses; in beatings, imprisonments and riots; in
> hard work, sleepless nights and hunger . . . through glory and dishonor, bad
> report and good report; genuine, yet regarded as impostors; known, yet regarded
> as unknown; dying, and yet we live on; beaten, and yet not killed; sorrowful, yet

always rejoicing; poor, yet making many rich; having nothing, and yet possessing everything (6:4-5, 8-10).

These are just some of the hardships Paul had faced.

Opposition to ministry. Paul writes openly about these trials, many of which have arisen through opposition to his ministry. Some think he is "out of [his] mind" to live and minister as he does exactly because it provokes such difficulty (5:13). He even provokes the opposition of political authorities (11:32-33). Apparently, the super-apostles leveraged the opposition Paul often faced as an argument against his credibility. They used it to call his character, and perhaps his message, into question. You can almost picture them shrugging their shoulders and nonchalantly asking the Corinthians, "Can you really trust someone who provokes so much opposition?"

Yet the opposition Paul faced should not surprise us. In our study of 1 Corinthians, we saw that the natural man does not accept the things of the Spirit (1 Cor. 2:14). Paul knows that his ministry will be the "smell of death" to some (2 Cor. 2:16). People will despise it like they despise death. Yet he also knows that others will find the same message the "fragrance of life." The gospel does not change, but people either love it or hate it. The ones who hate it are the same ones to whom it is veiled, and "it is veiled to those who are perishing. The god of this age has blinded the minds of unbelievers, so that they cannot see the light of the gospel of the glory of Christ, who is the image of God" (4:3-4).

Thorn in the flesh. Paul captures the whole idea of his weakness in the famous "thorn in the flesh" passage:

> To keep me from becoming conceited because of these surpassingly great revelations, there was given me a thorn in my flesh, a messenger of Satan, to torment me. Three times I pleaded with the Lord to take it away from me (12:7-8).

Whatever affliction his "thorn in the flesh" symbolized—we don't know what it was—it kept him in a state of perpetual weakness.

Now what do you make of all this? Paul was weak because his body was beaten, his reputation was in tatters, and his message was rejected. If you are the type of person who likes to associate with winners, you might not want to attend a place where Paul is speaking. You might not join a group that Paul is starting. He was weak. And that was the difference between him and the sleek, respected, successful ministers, with their smooth and popular messages, whom some in Corinth were following. The latter were strong. They inspired courage.

And let's be honest. If you were on the pastoral search committee at

Corinth, whom would you invite to pastor the church? You are sitting with the committee discussing the resumes of the different candidates for the next pastor of your church, and you have someone like Paul's opponents and someone like Paul. You have to admit, you would stop and think about it. "Well, Paul is the one who first brought us the gospel. We really appreciate that. No doubt he is sincere. Look at everything he has suffered. But, on the other hand, these other people are pretty impressive. Look at where their degrees are from. Man! And look at all the people who are recommending them. And when they speak . . . I could just listen to them forever."

Let me ask you this question: Who best represents Christ? These magnificent ministers, or distressed, suffering, mocked Paul? Weak Paul writes in chapter 5, "We are therefore Christ's ambassadors, as though God were making his appeal through us" (5:20). If he is so weak, how could that be? Would God really choose a weak vessel rather than a strong one?

The Apparent Weakness of God

Another apparent weakness helps answer these questions: the apparent weakness of God. Now you may be surprised that I have even put these two words together—"weakness" and "God." Yet it is worth noticing some intriguing phrases Paul uses when he talks about his own troubles. In chapter 1, Paul characterizes the weight of his hardships by saying, "in our hearts we felt the sentence of death" (1:9). What does he mean? We do not exactly know. Maybe he senses his own mortality? Maybe he feels the danger to which he exposes himself for being faithful to the gospel?

He uses a similar phrase in chapter 4. After referring to some of his difficulties, he writes, "We always carry around in our body the death of Jesus" (4:10). There it is! Paul likens his sufferings to carrying around in his body a public display of the death of Jesus for the entire world to see. Something we have ignored in our considerations of Paul's weaknesses thus far is who Paul claims to be sent *by* and *for*. After all, an apostle is, translated literally, "a sent one." Sent by whom? Sent for what? An apostle is sent to represent the God and Father of our Lord Jesus Christ, and to bear his good news. Representing Christ means representing the "meekness and gentleness of Christ" (10:1). It means representing the one of whom Paul says, "though he was rich, yet for your sakes he became poor, so that you through his poverty might become rich" (8:9).

Christ made himself poor. He suffered (1:5). He died (5:14). He was "crucified in weakness" (13:4). And Paul says he (Paul) puts that on display through his own suffering.

This is not what many people conceive of when they imagine God. If you are having a conversation with someone next to you on an airplane and the topic turns to God, unless that person has been steeped in the Christian faith, he or she will probably say God is some powerful benevolent force that we tap into. It seems like all the books sold in airport bookstores are required, if they are religious, to have this view of God. God is just some impersonal, powerful force that you tap into. Maybe it helps reduce people's tension when they are about to fly. People like to imagine a larger, divinized form of themselves and their values. They imagine a religious superman—invincible and invulnerable—but with a face that always smiles on their decisions. Was it something like this the false apostles preached in Corinth? If so, they did not preach about the God and Father of our Lord Jesus Christ.

Writing from the perspective of a World War I soldier, English Congregational minister Edward Shillito conveyed something of the weakness of God in Christ in his poem "Jesus of the Scars":

> If we have never sought, we seek Thee now;
> Thine eyes burn through the dark, our only stars;
> We must have sight of thorn-pricks on Thy brow,
> We must have Thee, O Jesus of the Scars.
>
> The heavens frighten us; they are too calm;
> In all the universe we have no place.
> Our wounds are hurting us; where is the balm?
> Lord Jesus, by Thy Scars we claim Thy grace.
>
> If when the doors are shut, Thou drawest near,
> Only reveal those hands, that side of Thine;
> We know to-day what wounds are, have no fear,
> Show us Thy Scars, we know the countersign.
>
> The other gods were strong; but Thou wast weak;
> They rode, but Thou didst stumble to a throne;
> But to our wounds only God's wounds can speak,
> And not a god has wounds, but Thou alone.[2]

If you stop and think about these words, you will begin to be deprogrammed from the world's lies and you will begin to be reeducated about what it means to be a Christian.

---

[2] Edward Shillito, "Jesus of the Scars," in James Dalton Morrison, ed. *Masterpieces of Religious Verse* (New York: Harper Brothers, 1958), 235.

The Eyes of Faith

How true is what Paul writes in chapter 5: "we live by faith, not by sight" (5:7). If you want one verse that summarizes all of 2 Corinthians, 5:7 is a good one: we live by faith and not by sight. Paul wants the Corinthians to be able to "answer those who take pride in what is seen rather than in what is in the heart" (5:12). Could it be any clearer? The message of Christianity is not finally in how I can guarantee you a comfortable life in this world. Or how I can guarantee you victory in this world. Or how I can guarantee you esteem in the eyes of the world. If anything, I can almost guarantee you the opposite insofar as you are faithful to follow Christ. The false apostles compare themselves to one another by outward appearance (10:12)—bank accounts, degrees, distinguished admirers, chiseled features, chest-to-waist ratios, vocabulary, powers of persuasion. Paul does not. Paul was known to be a short, large-nosed, bald, timid-in-person man. That was Paul. A fearful writer of sharp letters. Yet he says assessing a man's message by a man's outward appearance is inimical to the Christian faith. It goes against the very faith the Corinthians claimed to promote.

Paul himself once had to learn this same lesson. In chapter 5 he writes, "from now on we regard no one from a worldly point of view. Though we once regarded Christ in this way, we do so no longer" (5:16). Do you see what he is admitting? At one point, he too regarded Jesus from a worldly point of view. Jesus was untrained and itinerant, maligned and mocked, betrayed and crucified, hardly a model that any of these popular Corinthian ministers would want to follow! Yet this is why Paul pursues his ministry differently than these other ministers. He has seen the difference between his former ways and the way of Christ, and so his approach to ministry and the Christian life has changed entirely. Now he can write, "though we live in the world, we do not wage war as the world does. The weapons we fight with are not the weapons of the world" (10:3-4).

It is no wonder, then, that Paul condemns these super-apostles as false apostles dressed up in Halloween costumes with cheap plastic masks of righteousness and wisdom, presenting a nice face to the world but hiding the reality beneath:

> For such men are false apostles, deceitful workmen, masquerading as apostles of Christ. And no wonder, for Satan himself masquerades as an angel of light. It is not surprising, then, if his servants masquerade as servants of righteousness. Their end will be what their actions deserve (11:13-15).

At the same time, in chapters 8 and 9, Paul has pointed us to these Christians living in extreme poverty who were materially generous. And why were they so generous? Because they were better people? The real salt of the earth? No, Christians are not just a bunch of virtuous people. The generous Macedonians gave because they lived by faith and not by sight. They perceived realities with eyes of faith that their eyes of flesh could not see. They lived like the woman in the temple Jesus noticed in Mark 12, who had almost no money but put what she did have into the temple coffers. Using her example, Jesus taught his disciples not to be deceived by the thousands of coins poured into the coffers by the rich. Their many coins did not reveal their hearts. The heart is shown when *everything* is given (Mark 12:41-44).

Do you see why this is important for you? God might just want to reeducate you about the way you look at the world around you. Do you look with the eyes of faith or only with your physical eyes? May God so impress this lesson on your mind and mine that we never forget it.

Are you tempted to try, once more, to be a Christian who lives by sight, rather than by faith? Save your time! It will not work. It never has. You will make a mess of your own life, and, if you are a pastor and lead a church that way, you will build a hellish church that allows for fake Christian lives. These angels of Satan, the super-apostles, did that, masquerading for what people would see of them. The people who genuinely know Christ and live by faith understand the futility of living by sight.

Where in your life do you need to live by faith and not by sight? What corners of your heart have been handed over to valuing the esteem of others, or the pleasure of this world, or all the comforts you think you deserve? If you can locate those corners, you have identified where the battle rages against your faith in Christ.

PERCEIVING THE NATURE OF REAL STRENGTH

Paul's praise of the self-sacrificing poor, his willingness to boast in his own weaknesses, and his desire to display the sufferings of God in Christ in his own body should change the way we think about everything! It certainly should change what we think *real strength* is, including the way God displays his own strength and gives his strength to others (e.g., 2 Cor. 1:4). Paul's understanding of strength includes relying on this God who raises the dead (1:9-10), and standing firm in such faith (1:24). There is no declaration of self-sufficiency in a Christian understanding of strength; it is a different matter. The strength of a Christian is shown in the relinquishment of oneself to God in order to rely on his promises and his provision. That way, God gets the glory.

The late actor Richard Burton once criticized Christianity by saying, "The weak rely on Christ, the strong do not." I guess he was right. But I don't think he understood what he was saying. What we gain by relying on Christ is far more than what we gain by relying on ourselves. In fact, it is ridiculous even to call our own ability "strength" in comparison to what God gives us. God himself becomes active in the Christian's apparent weakness! The false apostles may have impressive letters of commendation. But Paul, as he says in chapter 3, has the Corinthians themselves as letters of commendation. Their very lives are letters of commendation written by the Spirit of God (3:2-3), for God had made them into "new creations" (5:17).

Paul faces his circumstances with calmness and equanimity only because he knows the power and peace that are *not of himself*. He has peace not because he is such a mighty man—a sort of "Navy Seal" for God. No, he has peace *because of God*. As he quotes from Jeremiah, "'Let him who boasts boast in the Lord'" (10:17; cf. Jer. 9:24). The super-apostles had gotten it all wrong. The point was never their power. The point has always been the power of God.

Christian, do you know this? Is this something that is clear to you? Have you been able to recognize the times in your own life when a sneaking self-confidence has quietly—in your own mind—edged you up onto the very throne of God? And have you recognized the way God tenderly and terribly, with wonderful power, sweeps you and your wrongful pride off the throne and gives you a clear view of himself? Like Paul, many of us have seen him do this through our trials and difficulties, our challenges and sicknesses. It is when God presses in on our lives through hardship that we tend to see the insufficiency of our strength and the sufficiency of his. William Gouge, a great London preacher in the seventeenth century, when he was laid aside by what proved to be his final illness, remarked to those around him, "When I look upon myself, I see nothing but emptiness and weakness; but when I look upon Christ, I see nothing but fullness and sufficiency."[3] No matter how impressive we think we are, real strength is not ours. It is God's.

PERCEIVING THE GLORY OF GOD

When God's people live by the real strength that comes from him and belongs to him, he is glorified. Southern Baptist Theological Seminary President R. Albert Mohler, standing in our pulpit, once defined the glory of God as "the intrinsic reality and the outward manifestation of God's power and character." Amazingly, God's power and character are manifested through us, his church, as we learn more and more to rely on his strength in our very weaknesses. What is God's great argument to the world that he alone is God? It is us, his church.

---

[3] William Gouge, cited in James Reid, *Memoirs of the Westminster Divines*, vol. 1 (Paisley: Stephen & Andrew Young, 1811; repr. Carlisle, Pa.: Banner of Truth, 1982), 357.

It is faithful Christians everywhere who gather to hear his Word preached and who live by the power of his Spirit. Can you imagine that? The more you know the truth of your own heart's sinfulness, the more you will be amazed by this idea, that God reveals the truth about himself and his strength through us, his weak church. He does not reveal himself through the self-aggrandizing ways of the masquerading super-apostles. No! We testify to God's glory when, in our weakness, we rely on his promises, which are all "yes" to us in Christ (1:20). God brings himself glory through the gospel Paul preached because that gospel is about God's power and sufficiency and not about Paul's. When the gospel is preached and believed and reflected in the lives of his people, God gets the glory. As Paul writes in chapter 3, "We, who with unveiled faces all reflect the Lord's glory, are being transformed into his likeness with ever-increasing glory, which comes from the Lord, who is the Spirit" (3:18).

How many ways can I say it? I have one basic message here: when we rely on God, and God shows himself to be faithful, he gets the glory. This is what he has always intended. He does not intend for us to be strong, self-reliant, and without need of turning to him, thereby robbing him of the opportunity both to supply our need and to gain glory for himself. He intends for us to be weak and oppressed, and then to turn and rely on him, because then he can provide what we need and thereby be glorified. That is how he has always planned it. Consider again these words in chapter 4:

> The god of this age has blinded the minds of unbelievers, so that they cannot see the light of the gospel of the glory of Christ, who is the image of God. For we do not preach ourselves, but Jesus Christ as Lord, and ourselves as your servants for Jesus' sake. For God, who said, "Let light shine out of darkness," made his light shine in our hearts to give us the light of the knowledge of the glory of God in the face of Christ.
>
> But we have this treasure in jars of clay . . .

And by jars of clay, he means our frail and weak bodies. Why are the treasures stored in such weak vessels as us? Keep reading: ". . . to show that this all-surpassing power is from God and not from us" (4:4-7). This is the point of Paul's letter.

Remember, God did not glorify himself by calling the fruitful patriarch of a large family to be the progenitor of his people. No, he called barren old Sarah and Abraham just to make the point that *he* is the provider. God did not glorify himself by calling the mighty Egyptian nation to be his people. No, he called their slaves, the Israelites. God did not glorify himself by letting the Israelites quickly demolish the Egyptians in battle. No, he hardened the heart and resolve of Pharaoh through ten plagues so that God's glory would be increased in Pharaoh's final defeat. Then he led the slaves out to the edge of the Red Sea, and trapped them between the water and the Egyptian army. He did not then let the Israelites fight and win; he supernaturally parted the sea and let the Israelites pass through, ensuring that all glory was given to him. Jumping ahead to the New Testament, we notice that God did not call twelve renowned, sharp young men to be Jesus' disciples. No, he called twelve obscure, dull men. He did not call a Gentile to be a missionary to the Gentiles, which you or I would have done if we were missions strategists. No, he called an ultranationalist Jew, Paul, to be the missionary to the Gentiles. I could keep going through the whole Bible. This is how God does things. He puts us in hard positions in order to bring glory to himself. Why? Because he is so selfish? No, he does it to teach us that his glory and strength are so much better than anything that our rebellious hearts can muster.

And then, of course, there is Jesus. Who would have planned an intervention by the Creator of the universe to look like the ministry of Jesus? Not you or I.

Just before he was murdered a few years ago, designer Gianni Versace was asked about his religious opinions. He replied, "I believe in God, but I'm not the kind of religious person who goes to church, who believes in the fairy tale of Jesus born in the stable with the donkey. That, no—I'm not stupid. I can't believe that God, with all the power that he has, had to have himself born in a stable. It wouldn't have been comfortable!"[4] But that is exactly the kind of God we do know and worship. He gave up his comfort in order to gain eternal glory. To miss that is to miss the point. Likewise, God has purposed for all those areas of your life where you experience pain and suffering to be the very places where he displays his sufficiency and so brings glory to himself. And not just so that you can see it, but so that the people around you can see it. Everything from looking for a job to facing surgery to working on a difficult marriage, those are the very things God has planned to use for his own glory. Why do you think he has chosen you? Not because you were so virtuous. Why do you think he has chosen us? Not because we have no vice. Not because we have never broken the law. Not because we have never sinned against God. Not because we have never committed adultery or hated or coveted in our hearts. No! He has chosen us because he wants to make his grace to forgive and his power to change clear to the world around us. And to that end, you, if you are a Christian, are exhibit number one. If you fail to recognize this, you will view the church as a "morals club." You will think it is all about being a good

---

[4] Gianni Versace, in an interview by Andre Lee, "The Emperor of Dreams," *The New Yorker*, July 28, 1997, 47.

Baptist, or Presbyterian, or Lutheran. You will think it is about being an upstanding citizen. And you will die in your own self-righteousness, never once having comprehended the gospel of Jesus Christ. He died on the cross in pain, not for his own sin, but for your sin and mine, if you repent and believe in him.

This is why Paul tells the Corinthians his sufferings are "for your benefit, so that the grace that is reaching more and more people may cause thanksgiving to overflow to the glory of God" (4:15). This is also why Paul exhorts them and us to make ourselves pure. Only through lives of purity do we, as God's people living by his power and grace, accurately depict something of the true character of God, particularly his holiness. Likewise, Paul encourages the Corinthians to be generous in the offering he is gathering because their generosity would result "in thanksgiving to God" (9:11). He then says,

> Because of the service by which you have proved yourselves, men will praise God for the obedience that accompanies your confession of the gospel of Christ, and for your generosity in sharing with them and with everyone else (9:13).

God is glorified by our dependence upon him. When we acknowledge our weakness, his strength is displayed.

CONCLUSION

At the beginning of this study, we considered the proposition for a state lottery that was defeated by Alabama voters. On the same day, another significant social vote was held in our country. In Jefferson County, Kentucky, which includes Louisville, a "Fairness Ordinance" was voted on and passed in the county council that forbade "discrimination" in housing or employment on the basis of sexual preference.

Perhaps the Alabama voters' rejection of a state lottery did signal a slowing of the pernicious gambling industry that preys on society's most vulnerable members, but it hardly signaled the moral renewal of our society. Indeed, I would say the Jefferson County council's vote on the so-called Fairness Ordinance was probably the more significant of the two votes. Such local and county initiatives are growing, with the next round expected at the level of state legislatures. Furthermore, if legislators ever classify as "hate language" the biblical teaching that God will judge homosexual activity, then we as evangelical, Bible-believing Christians may witness many so-called "evangelical" churches suddenly changing their views on homosexuality as their pastors face heavy fines, property-ownership difficulties, or worse.

Of course, I do not know how marginalized our constituency will become, if at all. Perhaps it will not happen in legal ways, although it is already hap-

pening socially. A recent issue of *Public Opinion Quarterly* had an article saying that anti-Catholicism and anti-Semitism are no longer socially acceptable
prejudices in our country, but that prejudice against Christian fundamentalists
remained the one prejudice that can be freely espoused in public. This is the
one group that it is politically correct to bash. Consider for a moment, which
tragedy provoked more public outcry by celebrities leading rallies: the October
6, 1998 murder of the gay high school student Matthew Shepherd, or the
September 15, 1999 murder of young Baptists gathered on a Wednesday night
at Wedgewood Baptist Church by a man who deplored what they stood for?

Well, what should our response be to societal disfavor? Some suggest we
should withdraw. Paul did not seem to advocate that. Others suggest we should
engage the public square, mobilize politically, and work to restore our culture.
Well, again, that cannot be our primary goal, though we may be called to this
sort of work secondarily. What, then, should we do? Are we condemned to live
in this world with little peace and contentment, always having to worry about
our own families and society as a whole? Perhaps.

Feeling discontent in even the best of times—let alone in the worst of
times—may not be so much a sign of your stubbornness as it may be the conscience God Almighty has given you reminding you that this world is not
home. "Do not mistake this for home," God tells us through our discontent.
"Do not get too comfortable here. If you think I have gone to the cross and
died to save you just for this, you're crazy. No, I have something for you that's
a lot better than this." Perhaps we are supposed to be discontent and not take
everything on face value. Perhaps we are supposed to long for some more permanent arrangement, with no disease or poverty, no sin or death. Perhaps we
are supposed to be homesick for somewhere else. As Augustine said in the great
opening prayer in the *Confessions*, "You have made us for yourself, and our
heart is restless until it rests in you."[5]

Fundamentally, as we have seen in this second letter to the Corinthians,
we should not be surprised if God chooses to glorify himself in the most awkward corners of our society, the corners where you will find socially mocked
believers and legally marginalized churches. God likes to stack the odds against
himself before he moves. Consider what happened at the door of the Castle
Church in Wittenberg, Germany, more than 480 years ago. There, a paranoid
monk, who could not shed a sense of his own guilt and sin though he confessed
so many times a day that his confessor said, "Brother, if you're going to confess so much, why don't you go do something worth confessing?"[6] posted

---

[5] Augustine, *Confessions*, I.i.
[6] Cited in Timothy George, *Theology of the Reformers* (Nashville: Broadman, 1988), 64-65.

ninety-five theses calling into question several of the pope's practices. God used that man to begin the Reformation. As Martin Luther later said, "I simply taught, preached, wrote God's Word: otherwise I did nothing. And then, while I slept or drank Wittenberg beer with my Philip and my Amsdorf, the Word" did its work. "The Word did it all."[7] God used a single monk's distress about the seriousness of his sin—as well as his serious study of Scripture—to turn a civilization on its ear as he recovered the gospel of Jesus Christ, the gospel of justification by faith alone in Christ alone.

My Roman Catholic friends sometimes playfully taunt me with the question every Protestant has been asked: "Where was your church before Luther?" To which my response is, should we expect that God's followers are going to be in the majority? Where did that happen in the Old Testament? Where did God ever call the largest people group on earth to be his people? When did even a majority of the Jews follow him in the Old Testament? Was it not the Jews who kept killing the prophets God sent? So where do Christians get the idea that we are ever going to be in the majority? We certainly don't find that idea in the Bible.

God makes himself known in ways that we never expect.

So what is our response to all this? What do we do when we begin to see our own weaknesses, failings, transgressions, and sins? Generally, we see them and begin to feel something like sorrow. But as Paul says in chapter 7, there is a "worldly sorrow [that] brings death" (7:10b). You frown awhile, and then you die. But there is another kind of sorrow that leads to a changed life, as the bitter sadness we feel over our sin causes us to finally turn to God in repentance: "Godly sorrow brings repentance that leads to salvation and leaves no regret" (7:10a). That is the sorrow I pray that you and I would know for our sins.

After all, we are called to live for God whatever circumstances bring. This is what Paul says in chapter 5: "For Christ's love compels us, because we are convinced that one died for all, and therefore all died. And he died for all, that those who live should no longer live for themselves but for him who died for them and was raised again" (5:14-15). Christ died for us. And by dying for us, he bought us to live for him. We are therefore to live as those redeemed and bought by his blood. A few verses later, Paul writes, "God made him who had no sin to be sin for us, so that in him we might become the righteousness of God" (5:21). Above all else, God wants us to bring glory to him by trusting in Christ's righteousness completely.

As the Lord said to Paul, "'My grace is sufficient for you, for my power is

---

[7] Martin Luther, *Sermons*, ed. John W. Doberstein, vol. 51 of *Luther's Works* (Philadelphia: Fortress, 1959), 77.

made perfect in weakness.'" And what was Paul's response? "Therefore I will boast all the more gladly about my weaknesses, so that Christ's power may rest on me. That is why, for Christ's sake, I delight in weaknesses, in insults, in hardships, in persecutions, in difficulties. For when I am weak, then I am strong" (12:9-10). This is the way it has always been for those who follow Christ. After all, this is the way it was for Christ himself, who, we read "was crucified in weakness, yet he lives by God's power. Likewise, we are weak in him, yet by God's power we will live with him to serve you" (13:4).

How do you keep going in your life? What do you do if you are facing circumstances today that you think are overwhelming? Maybe you don't even admit to anyone else that you feel overwhelmed because your trials seem small compared to others, but you know they feel big to you. What do you do? Paul provides the answer: "We do not lose heart. Though outwardly we are wasting away, yet inwardly we are being renewed day by day. For our light and momentary troubles are achieving for us an eternal glory that far outweighs them all. So we fix our eyes not on what is seen . . ." (4:16-18). Again, if you try to live by what is seen, you will crash and burn as a Christian. Rather, then, we fix our eyes "on what is unseen. For what is seen is temporary, but what is unseen is eternal."

Paul says this to strong people who need to learn that they are weak. And he says it to weak people who are tempted to look elsewhere for strength. Really, he says this to all people, that all might turn and rely on Christ. He said it then, and he is still saying it today—to me and to you. Can you hear him?

Let us pray:

Lord God, we confess we do not always love as we should. Often, we love the wrong things. And often, we fail to love the right things. We love too much or not enough. As a result, we encounter suffering and trials and stresses in this life. We pray, Lord, that your Holy Spirit would work in our hearts now. Take the masks off our lives, we pray. Help us to see the truth when we look in the mirror. Help us to see the truth of our weakness and the truth of your wonderful strength in Christ. We pray so that you will be glorified through him. Amen.

Questions for Reflection

1. In this study, we considered the fact that the gospel is not something Paul, you, or I would invent. It's much too strange. What is strange about the gospel, and what is strange about those who live by the gospel, according to 2 Corinthians?

2. What are you tempted to boast in? Or, if you are not the type to outwardly brag, in what ways do you compare yourself with others in the dark corners of your mind? Which of your virtues do you secretly think about from time to time in order to boost your self-confidence?

3. Do you feel like people owe you respect? Why, and in what ways?

4. Do you try to hide your weaknesses from others? Do you habitually excuse them to yourself? Do you get depressed, angry, or defensive when others out-perform or out-accomplish you? Or when someone points out your mistakes?

5. Following up on question 8, what practical steps can you take to begin viewing your weaknesses and others' strengths with gratitude because your insufficiency invariably draws your gaze to Christ?

6. According to Paul, where does God most clearly manifest his power in our lives?

7. How do you feel about the prospect of spending Sunday lunch with a first-time visitor, a foreigner with poor English, an older man who smells funny?

8. How were the Macedonians able to give so generously? Where does their example intersect with your life and budget?

9. Naturally, most pastors and churches want to see growth, vibrancy, and strength—all good things. Suppose your church hired three consultants to advise you on how to promote such growth: a successful business CEO, a Hollywood producer, and Paul. Would Paul's advice be any different? How?

10. What is a worldly sorrow for sins as opposed to a godly sorrow (2 Cor. 7:10)? How can you differentiate the one from the other? If you consider yourself a Christian, which of the two has characterized your life? If your sorrow were a worldly sorrow, would you be willing to hear a friend tell you that?

11. Pick some trial you presently face: What would living by sight look like in response to that trial? What would living by faith look like? How will you do the one and not the other?

THE MESSAGE OF GALATIANS: FAITH

9

THE MESSAGE OF GALATIANS: FAITH

EXTRA! EXTRA! READ ALL ABOUT IT[1]

American military forces used nerve gas on U.S. defectors during the Vietnam War. So reported Cable News Network and *Time* magazine. Chiquita Brands International, the noted banana grower and distributor, was riddled with improper business practices for years. So said the *Cincinnati Enquirer* in a series of special reports. Both of these stories ran in major media in 1998.

But, in fact, the American military forces did not use nerve gas on U.S. defectors during the Vietnam War, and Chiquita Brands International did not have improper business practices riddling its organization. So the news organizations who made these reports placed retraction boxes and apologies on the front pages of their newspapers—a very unusual placement for a retraction. One star reporter and three producers at CNN were reprimanded. "The first rough draft of history," as the news has been called, is sometimes pretty rough.

Also in 1998, the *Boston Globe* newspaper fired two columnists for fabrications and plagiarisms. It was not a great year for the news business. And these events came on top of ten years of gradually declining readership numbers. Not that the problem with plagiarism is new to the news media. Two hundred years ago, the great poet and hymn writer William Cowper, many of whose hymns we sing and love, called the newspapers of his days an "ever bubbling spring of endless lies."[2]

So where do we find news that is true, reliable, important, and useful? Well, have you ever thought of the church as a news organization? Fundamentally, that is what we are. We are a news organization.

---

[1] This sermon was originally preached November 7, 1999, at Capitol Hill Baptist Church in Washington, D.C.
[2] William Cowper, "The Progress of Error" (1782), in John D. Baird and Charles Ryskamp, eds., *The Poems of William Cowper*, vol. 1 (Oxford: Clarendon, 1980), 262.

This way of looking at the church may surprise you. For at least twenty years we have been told the news business is overwhelmingly filled with people who never attend church (except to write a story) and have remarkably secular worldviews. Indeed, earlier this year, columnist Robert Novak, a Jewish convert to Catholicism, was quoted in the *Washington Post* as saying that "The news media reflect the culture of Washington. They are very non-spiritual."[3]

Still, I think it is valid to consider the church, spiritual as it is, as a sort of news organization: We have a reliable source, a means of distribution, an audience; and most of all, we have some tremendous news. We are all about getting this news out. But unlike some of the other organizations around, the news we have is in no danger of being recalled. You will find no small-print boxes on our bulletins next week saying, "The church staff regrets to inform you an error was made in last week's sermon. Jesus Christ is not the answer to your problems. He is not the world's savior from sin." There is no danger of that happening.

There are many, many activities in the church that do not fit into the image of a news organization. Yet as you think about what the church is at the core, I want to argue for a moment that at least one appropriate image of the church is that of an organization devoted to publishing glad tidings, as the old hymn says, or to proclaiming good news. That is what we do when we sing, whether proclaiming the tidings in a new hymn or an old chorus. The news is also broadcast in our Scripture readings and in our sermons. And that is what I am doing now. I am proclaiming to you a certain message. And that is what you will do throughout this day and this week as you talk with others about Jesus Christ. You will be someone who is broadcasting this very message that is the reason for the church's existence.

What exactly is the news of Christianity? How would you summarize it? To answer that, we turn to a document that Martin Luther called "my own letter," not because he wrote it but because it was so important in his coming to understand the Christian gospel.

INTRODUCING GALATIANS

We turn, in fact, to one of the earliest written documents of Christianity. Perhaps the earliest. It is a little book—a letter, really—written by Paul to some churches he helped start in what is now Turkey. It is his letter to the Galatians.

Galatians is short enough for me to quickly walk you through in summary form. If you follow along paragraph by paragraph in your NIV translation, I will summarize each paragraph in approximately a sentence. Here it goes: Paul,

---

[3] Robert Novak, quoted by Sally Quinn in the *Washington Post*, July 12, 1999, page C2.

an apostle not from men but from God, to the churches in Galatia (1:1-2). Grace and peace from God our Father and the Lord Jesus Christ, who gave himself for our sins (1:3-5). I am astonished you are being confused by false teachers into believing a false gospel (1:6-9)! And if it has been said that I am a man-pleaser, and that the gospel I preach is meant just to please men, this letter should put an end to that thought (1:10)! The gospel I preach did not come from me, but from Jesus Christ (1:11-12). You have heard my testimony and know this is true—I would not have come up with this (1:13-17). The church leaders in Jerusalem did not make it up either; I heard the gospel years before I even met the leaders in Jerusalem (1:18-24). I went to Jerusalem again fourteen years later specifically to ensure that we all were preaching the same gospel and to defend the freedom we, Jews and Gentiles, have in Christ (2:1-5). The leaders in Jerusalem entirely approved of what I had been preaching to the Gentiles (2:6-10). Now, Peter was confused at one point (2:11-13). But I rebuked him (2:14).

This news to the Gentiles is the only saving message for Jews as well: justification is by faith and not by observing the law (2:15-16). Righteousness cannot be gained by observing the law but only by faith in the crucified Christ (2:17-21). My dear brothers and sisters in Galatia, did you receive the Spirit and see miracles worked among you by observing the law, or by believing what you heard and then by receiving the Spirit (3:1-5)? Let's go back and look at redemption history again: Abraham was justified by faith (3:6-9). The law and the prophets also testify that everyone—from Abraham to Gentile believers—will be justified by faith, not by the law (3:10-14). And this was always the plan. The law, given 430 years after Abraham, was never intended to do away with the promise given to Abraham (3:15-18). The law was merely added to expose sin for what it is until Christ had come (3:19-20). The law has never been able to free sinners from sin—that blessing comes only through faith in Jesus Christ (3:21-22). The law served its purpose by leading us Jews to Christ so that we might be justified by faith (3:23-25). So all of you who believe in Christ are together God's children by adoption, regardless of your nation, gender, or social status (3:26-4:7). But now that you are no longer slaves to the law, why are you turning back, as if you wanted to be enslaved again (4:8-11)? You used to treasure me. What happened (4:12-16)? I am sorry I have to sound like this, but these false teachers just want to abuse you (4:17-20)! Look, if you want to talk law, are you not aware that Abraham had both a slave son born by natural means and a free son born as a result of the promise (4:21-23)? This is a picture for us of those who are enslaved to the law, and of those who are miraculously freed by the promise (4:24-27). You are free children of promise!

That is why you are being persecuted by others, and that is why you should throw them out of your churches (4:28-31).

You have been set free, so don't exchange freedom for slavery again (5:1)! If you cave in and begin to require circumcision, you have given up on grace; you have renounced faith (5:2-6). These false teachers are going to pay (5:7-12)! Now, this freedom is not freedom *to* sin (in self-indulgence) but freedom *from* sin (to love one another) (5:8-15). So follow the Spirit, not its enemy the flesh (5:16-18). People who live in sin will not inherit the kingdom of God (5:19-21). The Spirit's presence will show itself in your life (5:22-26). Care for each other (6:1-5). Care especially for those who teach you the truth (6:6). We don't always see the consequences of sin immediately, but God will make sure that someday everyone will see the real results of sin. (6:7-10). I am writing in big letters to prove that it is I who write these words (6:11). These false teachers are just trying to be well-regarded by others—and at your expense (6:12-16)! Respect my suffering for Jesus (6:17). The grace of our Lord Jesus Christ be with you (6:18).

There you have the letter to the Galatians summarized, and in this little letter is our news! Did you see what Paul says is important, what's at the heart of this message we proclaim?

In our study of this letter, we will divide the answer to that question into four parts. In the first chapter and a half, Paul asserts and defends the idea that his message, or news, is from God: *the news is divine*. In the main doctrinal section of the letter, from the last part of chapter 2 through chapter 4, Paul presents the news itself: *we are justified by faith in Christ*. In the letter as a whole, Paul conveys his horror at the thought of the Galatians deserting this message. After all, *the news is vital*. And finally, in parts of chapter 4 through chapter 6, Paul describes the impact of this news relationally: *the news changes us*.

As we move through these four parts, I hope that you will be left with a clear understanding of what our *news* is, and what a difference it should make.

THE NEWS IS DIVINE

We begin by noticing the nature of this good news, this gospel: It is divine. The gospel of Christianity is not merely a personal disposition. It is not merely a tug on your heart. The gospel is a message from God. And this is what the first chapter and a half of Paul's letter is all about.

We join Paul in this letter mid-controversy. These Galatians had formerly heard Paul's message, and now they were hearing a different message from a group of false teachers. These false teachers, who had shown up in Paul's absence, seemed to insinuate that anywhere Paul's message disagreed with their own, it could not be trusted. Paul made a lot of this stuff up, they said, or at least he got it from a couple of the apostles in Jerusalem. And the apostles in Jerusalem were a bit off. "We are telling you the real story now," these false teachers said.

The Source: God

It is in response to these claims that Paul begins his letter. The message the Galatians initially received from him is not his own. Paul is not the story's "source," God is. "The gospel I preached is not a self-generated, false message," Paul says. "It is the truth from God."

Paul makes this point in the very first sentence: he was "sent not from men nor by man, but by Jesus Christ and God the Father" (1:1). His apostolic mission to the Gentiles was not a human idea. The risen Christ himself called him on the Damascus Road and commissioned him for this enterprise. He states in 1:11-12, "I want you to know, brothers, that the gospel I preached is *not* something that man made up. I did not receive it from any man, nor was I taught it; rather, I received it by revelation from Jesus Christ." So do not accuse Paul of simply trying to be a people-pleaser. A rough paraphrase of 1:10 might read, "If it's been suggested that I am a toadying people-pleaser, this letter should show that it is Christ, and certainly not people, that I am trying to please. My tone here is hardly calculated to win people over by being all sweetness and light."

Paul then recounts his personal testimony to the Galatians and points out the absurdity of claiming that someone like him would suddenly show up on the scene and begin preaching the news of a crucified Messiah to nations of Gentiles. He was an ultra-nationalistic Pharisee. He was successfully climbing the Pharisaical career-ladder. He even persecuted Christians! Therefore the claims against him are just absurd (1:13-17). And in case anyone says Paul was in cahoots with some apostle or teacher in Jerusalem, he points out that three years passed after his conversion before he even met the church leaders in Jerusalem (1:18). Before that, he was unknown to them (1:22). It is true that fourteen years later he did go to meet with the leaders in Jerusalem about questions that had arisen concerning his ministry. But he used that visit as an opportunity to defend the freedom both Jewish and Gentile believers have in Christ (2:1-5). And the leaders in Jerusalem entirely approved of his message:

> For God, who was at work in the ministry of Peter as an apostle to the Jews, was also at work in my ministry as an apostle to the Gentiles. James, Peter and John, those reputed to be pillars, gave me and Barnabas the right hand of fellowship when they recognized the grace given to me. They agreed that we should go to the Gentiles, and they to the Jews (2:8-9; cf. 2:6-10).

This is how Paul begins his letter, by defending the divine veracity of his news.

In recent years there have been some embarrassing examples of award-winning newspaper articles and even books that have turned out to be inaccurate, as we considered at the beginning. Some were deliberately and entirely fabricated. Paul's point here is, "My preaching has not been like that. This story is not made up. Come on! If I were going to make up a story, would I put a crucified Messiah at the center?" Would Saul, who was a Christian-persecuting Pharisee, have concocted a message that encouraged Jews to abandon the cherished mark of their identity, circumcision; invited all the Gentiles to join the party; and so put at jeopardy the survival of his own people as a distinct community! Make no mistake, Paul says. This message is from God.

Recently, at the Ethics and Public Policy Center in Washington, I was giving a defense of the "Southern Baptist Prayer Guide for the Jews" to a gathering of Jewish rabbis and reporters from the secular press. It was an enjoyable time, and we had a good discussion. At one point, we were considering the exclusivity of Jesus Christ, and I noticed that a few people were beginning to appear offended, albeit in a kind and courteous manner. One questioner in particular seemed disconcerted by Christianity's claims. Finally, I simply said to her, "You know, it's not that we Christians sit around and try to think up what will really offend people. We don't go scheme in a corner before lunch and say to ourselves, 'What can we say that's really going to upset people? Let's believe *that!*' No, we don't preach this gospel because we think it is going to be popular. We preach it because it is true. We come to you saying that you are going to hell and that you need this salvation offered by Jesus Christ not because we think it is going to be immediately pleasant to your ears but because we know it is true."

Beware of thinking the truth will always consist of ideas that are immediately appealing to you. Why on earth do you think the truth is something you will like? Who taught you that liking something is good evidence for its factuality? Has every fantasy you have ever had come true? Has everything that has happened to you been exactly what you wanted? What about the "D" you got in that class? Or the hurtful thing your father said to you? I could go on and on: Your most recent evaluation at work. The number on the scales when you look down. Your friend's stinging comment on the phone. Your bank balance or the doctor's advice. None of these things are generated by whether we like them or not. They are simple realities that are diminished in no way because we dislike them. Only our foolish imaginations would make us think that because we do not like something, it must not be true.

Paul says he did not make up this gospel—he would not have done so anyway. It came from God.

The Means of Distribution: A Cognitive Proposition

Before moving on, we need to notice a couple of important implications that come from the fact that the gospel is God's news. First, the Christian message has a specific cognitive content. It can be stated as a proposition.

A particular set of cognitive propositions are essential to the gospel. Paul writes in the first chapter,

> I am astonished that you are so quickly deserting the one who called you by the grace of Christ and are turning to a different gospel—which is really no gospel at all. Evidently some people are throwing you into confusion and are trying to pervert the gospel of Christ. But even if we or an angel from heaven should preach a gospel other than the one we preached to you, let him be eternally condemned! As we have already said, so now I say again: If anybody is preaching to you a gospel other than what you accepted, let him be eternally condemned! (1:6-9).

The fact that Paul tells them they are being confused into believing a false gospel is significant. There could be no false gospel if there were no cognitive content to the gospel in the first place—definite, distinct, definable claims that comprise it. Therefore, the Galatians should regard anything that contradicts this defined content as error. The gospel as given to Paul by Christ supersedes tradition or even angelic revelation. Paul writes, "But even if we or an angel from heaven should preach a gospel other than the one we preached to you, let him be eternally condemned!" (1:8).

When a new message does not match the original, regardless of the identity of the messenger you throw it out. It could be your favorite preacher or Sunday school teacher. It could be the long-standing church in Rome. It could be an earnest Muslim or Mormon or Jehovah's Witness at your door. It could be, as Paul says, an angel from heaven. (Interestingly, Mormons do refer to an angel named Moroni, while Muslims refer to their great prophet Mohammed.) Regardless of who the messenger is, Paul says, it is not the gospel if the message is other than what has already been laid out and what is laid out again in this letter. It is not the truth. In fact, Paul even says we should judge *him* if he preaches something other than this gospel.

Clearly, this is helpful instruction if we expect to sort through all the conflicting truth claims that have been made throughout history and today.

The Fact-Checkers: The Galatian Christians

Because of all these conflicting truth claims, we must understand what exactly the truth looks like—just as bank tellers have been trained to detect counterfeit currency not by learning what the counterfeits look like but by learning well the look of real currency. This leads to a second interesting implication. Paul regards the Galatian Christians as being competent to recognize and expunge the errors. If the gospel is a simple cognitive message, it should be recognizable by common Christians. Therefore, Paul appeals to the Galatians to judge their teachers.

He does not write directly to the false teachers and try to convince them, assuming all the while the laity is incompetent to consider doctrinal definitions. He writes the Galatians themselves. "I am astonished that *you* are so quickly deserting the one who called you!" (1:6). *You* should know better! The gospel is not that complex, he is saying. The fact that you have been a Christian for only a few months or a few years should not hinder you from understanding it. It is not something just for smart people.

These young Christians in Galatia are asked to recall the simple message that Paul had preached to them—the message of trusting in Christ's work on the cross—and to recognize the difference between that message and the false message they are now hearing. They are then to reject whatever message is being preached to them that differs from the true gospel. I am lingering on this point in order to ask the question, is there not a kind of congregationalism implied by the fact that Paul writes this letter to the congregation, urging them to judge their teachers? He is not asking a church council to intervene, or referring the matter to the bishop of Jerusalem. He confronts the congregation and assumes they are competent, even responsible, to handle the matter.

Have you ever considered your own responsibility to guard against false teaching in the church in which you are a member, in which you regularly sit, learn, and give money? I think the way Paul writes this letter suggests you should. The Reformation doctrine of the perspicuity, or clarity, of the Scriptures and of the gospel itself suggests something about how we in the church are to watch over the gospel together.

THE NEWS IS JUSTIFICATION THROUGH FAITH IN CHRIST

From the latter half of chapter 2 through much of chapter 4, Paul goes on to clarify exactly what the gospel is. This is the heart of the letter to the Galatians. What exactly is the gospel message? What's the big news? It is this: Justification is not by the law but through faith in Christ.

If we get nothing else right, we must get this right. The heart of the gospel message, the whole reason the church exists, is that every one of us has sinned and separated ourselves from God. But God, in his tremendous and incredible love, has taken on flesh in Christ, lived a perfect life, and died on the cross in the place of every sinner who turns and trusts in him. And he calls us now to repent and to believe in him.

The Content, Part 1: The Death of Christ

The gospel centers on the fact that Jesus Christ gave himself for our sins, which Paul mentions near the beginning of the letter. He prays that the Galatians would receive grace and peace from "God our Father and the Lord Jesus Christ, who gave himself for our sins to rescue us from the present evil age" (1:3-4). Christ's substitutionary death for sinners is the only hope any of us has for salvation, or "rescue," as he puts it here.

It does not appear that the false teachers who infiltrated the Galatian churches rejected Christ out of hand. They were not what we might think of as Orthodox Jews today, who reject any special role for Jesus. Rather, it seems that they did accept Jesus as the Messiah. And we make that conjecture based on the fact that Paul does not try to correct anyone for saying that Jesus was not the Messiah. In one way, at least, these false teachers were like the people who call themselves Messianic Jews today. They could say, "Yes, Jesus is the Christ. He is the Messiah." But, unlike Messianic Jews today, they also said that all of God's people must continue to observe the law. To be a Christian, you must first become a Jew, particularly through circumcision. So, yes, they said, you must recognize Jesus as the Messiah, but you must do something else as well.

The Content, Part 2: Faith in Christ

The boiling issue among these Galatians seems to have been, "How do the benefits of the salvation obtained by Christ become available to us?" And Paul says clearly that we are justified unto salvation not by observing the law but by faith in Jesus Christ. You could put the question another way: "Do you need to become a Jew first in order to become a Christian?" This is what the false teachers were telling the Galatians, and what Paul addresses in the large middle section of his letter.

Beginning in 2:15 he writes:

> We who are Jews by birth and not "Gentile sinners" know that a man is not justified by observing the law, but by faith in Jesus Christ. So we, too, have put our faith in Christ Jesus that we may be justified by faith in Christ and not by observing the law, because by observing the law no one will be justified.
>
> If, while we seek to be justified in Christ, it becomes evident that we ourselves are sinners, does that mean that Christ promotes sin? Absolutely not! If I rebuild what I destroyed, I prove that I am a lawbreaker. For through the law

I died to the law so that I might live for God. I have been crucified with Christ and I no longer live, but Christ lives in me. The life I live in the body, I live by faith in the Son of God, who loved me and gave himself for me. I do not set aside the grace of God, for if righteousness could be gained through the law, Christ died for nothing!

[Chapter 3] You foolish Galatians! Who has bewitched you? Before your very eyes Jesus Christ was clearly portrayed as crucified. I would like to learn just one thing from you: Did you receive the Spirit by observing the law, or by believing what you heard? Are you so foolish? After beginning with the Spirit, are you now trying to attain your goal by human effort? Have you suffered so much for nothing—if it really was for nothing? Does God give you his Spirit and work miracles among you because you observe the law, or because you believe what you heard?

Consider Abraham: "He believed God, and it was credited to him as righteousness." Understand, then, that those who believe are children of Abraham. The Scripture foresaw that God would justify the Gentiles by faith, and announced the gospel in advance to Abraham: "All nations will be blessed through you." So those who have faith are blessed along with Abraham, the man of faith. All who rely on observing the law are under a curse, for it is written: "Cursed is everyone who does not continue to do everything written in the Book of the Law." Clearly no one is justified before God by the law, because, "The righteous will live by faith." The law is not based on faith; on the contrary, "The man who does these things will live by them." Christ redeemed us from the curse of the law by becoming a curse for us, for it is written: "Cursed is everyone who is hung on a tree." He redeemed us in order that the blessing given to Abraham might come to the Gentiles through Christ Jesus, so that by faith we might receive the promise of the Spirit (2:15–3:14).

Paul clearly argues in the first two verses of this passage that justification by faith in Jesus Christ is not just for the Gentiles; it is not just a special thing God added, saying, "Now I'm going to lower the bar a little bit so that all the nations can come in." No, Paul specifically says it has always been this way, even for the Jews. Faith is the only way for Jews to be justified, too. Otherwise Christ's sacrifice would be useless: "I do not set aside the grace of God, for if righteousness could be gained through the law, Christ died for nothing" (2:21).

And the Galatians should know this. If they were to reflect back on their own experience, they would remember that the Spirit of God came upon them not when they successfully observed the law but when they believed what they heard (cf. 3:1-5). It is interesting how God always seems to associate his Spirit and his Word. With the coming of the Word, we have the coming of the Spirit. The Holy Spirit enters the believer's life through the ear.

Not only do the Galatians' personal histories tell this story, redemption history itself says the same. How did an individual become a believer in Old Testament times? The answer is easy. The father of the Jews, the head of it all, the source of the nation, Abraham, is our great example of one who was justified by faith (3:6). Genesis 15:6 proves the point. Abraham received salvation not by trusting the law, which had not yet been given, but by trusting in the promise of God. Then Paul ushers the law and the prophets into his argument and gives them four opportunities to speak.[4] And they say the same thing: the law justifies no one. It only brings a curse. Justification has always been by faith in Christ (from Abraham to the Gentiles), who removed the curse by becoming the cursed one himself (3:10-14). The law served its purpose by leading the ones who were given the law, the Jews, to Christ so that they might be justified by faith (3:24). So every circumcised or uncircumcised Jew or Gentile who believes in Christ is God's child by adoption (3:26–4:7). Later in chapter 4, Paul reminds the Galatians that Isaac was born as a result of the promise, and that a Christian's situation is like Isaac's. A Christian has been miraculously born by the promise of God (4:21-27), a rebirth that is certainly a gift of grace. Paul concludes his letter, "The grace of our Lord Jesus Christ be with your spirit, brothers. Amen" (6:18). The grace of Christ is central to the gospel.

Now this is news! If you are a non-Christian and have any uncertainty about this, ask a Christian friend or a pastor. This is the reason why Christians are Christians. It is because of this news that we are justified—declared righteous and acceptable before God. By faith alone in Christ alone we are forgiven by God and admitted into his fellowship. It is crucial to get this story straight.

I have been pointing to examples of inaccuracy in the media. Accuracy is always important in reporting. Yet it is particularly important that the news of Christianity be reported accurately. Therefore when you talk to people about Jesus this week, if you have any hope for them at all, you must be clear that their sin can be forgiven by God only by their trusting in Christ and what he has done on the cross. There is no other way. We must get the story straight and not garble the news.

When I began as a pastor at Capitol Hill Baptist, a reporter for the local Baptist newspaper, *Capitol Baptist,* came and interviewed me. He took a picture of me, against my suggestion, and placed it beside the article with a caption underneath. During the interview, he had asked me what my strategy was for helping this church, to which I responded, "Really, I don't have any plans. I'm just going to try and preach the word." What do you think the caption underneath the picture was? "Dever Says, 'Preach the World.'"

I do not think the mistake was deliberate, though it is telling. We garble

---

[4] 3:10, from Deut. 27:26; 3:11, from Hab. 2:4; 3:12, from Lev. 18:5; 3:13, from Deut. 21:23.

the message to great consequence. If you were to watch a movie of your last month, especially the conversations you have had with other people about Jesus Christ and the message of salvation in him, would you hear yourself saying something that is not wholly true? Not that you intended to speak falsely, but were you absolutely clear in your conversations that God saves sinners through faith in Christ alone, or were you saying something slightly different?

The other night, I heard a song that said, "Lord, when it's time to judge me, take a look at these hard-working hands." What an absolutely miserable hope. Can you imagine turning up before the throne of God, looking at him, and saying, "I've had an admirable work ethic"?

What if the Lord began to ask you questions about that work ethic? "Why have you worked so hard and faithfully?"

"Well, Lord, it's been because I wanted to be able to provide for my family."

"Good, that's no bad thing. What else? Why did you want to provide for your family?"

"Well, Lord, it's just the right thing to do."

"Really, is there nothing else in it?"

"Well, Lord, I've never thought about it this much, but, I guess, in providing for my family, it's kind of the best thing for me, too."

"Anything else?"

"No, Lord, not that I can think of. I just kind of thought it was the right thing to do."

Do you realize we draw breath and go to work so that we can give glory to God? He created us. He gives us the gospel of Jesus Christ so that we can bring him honor and glory. Our hard-working hands do not honor God simply by working, though certainly we should work. Ultimately, our work honors him only when the worker trusts him, and him alone. Do you think your work, these things you do and practices you observe, obligates God to save you? Do you think you can do something that makes the Lord of the heavens better disposed toward you?

I haven't heard of many churches today requiring circumcision as the initial step for committing to Christ. So how do we lose the message today? Maybe if I ask the question in a less religious way, it will help: What makes you feel good about yourself? Think about that for a second. What genuinely makes you feel good about yourself? A productive day at work? Your children's growth and success? Your husband's care and affection? The admiration of colleagues? Your parents' approval? Consistent quiet times? The ability to articulate your theology well? If you find the answer to what makes you feel good about yourself, you will be close to finding what causes you to confuse the gospel. And there will be something here for every one of us.

The gospel message, our news, is this: We are saved only by faith in Jesus Christ, who died for us and took our punishment upon himself. Only when we believe and trust in Christ will he apply to our hearts the perfect righteousness and forgiveness he won for us. The point is never what you do. The point is what God has done. The point is for him to get the glory. We do not fight our way into heaven by faithful religious observance. It is God who, in his great love in Christ, reached down low to find you. And in this tremendous love he picked you up in Christ and holds you up for the entire world to see as a testimony, not to your greatness, but to his greatness and love.

THE NEWS IS VITAL

The good news is divine. It is about faith in Christ. And notice a third thing: it is vital. Throughout his letter, Paul expresses his horror at the thought of the Galatians deserting this message.

The idea of forsaking the gospel is inconceivable to Paul. Why would anyone turn away from it?

> I am astonished that you are so quickly deserting the one who called you by the grace of Christ and are turning to a different gospel—which is really no gospel at all. Evidently some people are throwing you into confusion (1:6-7).

It is as though they are turning back to slavery: "Do you wish to be enslaved . . . all over again?" (4:9). Paul therefore pleads with them not to submit to slavery but to live according to the freedom that is theirs for the taking: "It is for freedom that Christ has set us free. Stand firm, then, and do not let yourselves be burdened again by a yoke of slavery. Mark my words! I, Paul, tell you that if you let yourselves be circumcised, Christ will be of no value to you at all. Again I declare to every man who lets himself be circumcised that he is obligated to obey the whole law. You who are trying to be justified by law have been alienated from Christ; you have fallen away from grace" (5:1-4). Given the terrible choice the Galatians were about to make, it is no wonder Paul writes with such urgency.

The gospel is precious enough to divide over. Now, as a pastor, I have a vested interest in keeping divisiveness out of the church. However, let me encourage you to be divisive when it comes to the gospel. In a local church, threats to the gospel must be fought. Indeed, an important part of Paul's ministry was such loving correction. He publicly rebuked Peter for behavior that threatened to confuse the message of the gospel (2:11-14). And he certainly does not shrink back from writing a sharp letter to young, wavering Christians in Galatia. This whole letter is a loving rebuke, in which he essentially says, "Hold tight to the gospel, and warn others about turning loose of it!" The news is to be cherished, and it is to be contested for.

Do you ever do this? Would you? Under what circumstances? Is the gospel rooted well enough, clearly enough, and firmly enough in your heart that you would challenge a friend or someone else in your church about the content of the gospel?

THE NEWS CHANGES US

Finally, as with all of Paul's letters, the letter to the Galatians not only contains propositional truth, it describes what that truth looks like when it is lived out. Christianity carries the great insight that propositional truth and personal relationships are not unrelated topics, nor should they be pitted against each other. The head and the heart should not and indeed cannot be divided. What you think and how you act are integrally related. So we are not surprised that Paul turns in the last chapters to how we live. The good news has practical implications for both our individual lives and our life together.

It Changes Our Relationships with Our Teachers

The hot relational issue among the Galatians is their relationships with their teachers. You see this in chapter 4 and a bit in chapter 6.

Paul and the Galatians. Paul, of course, loves the Galatians, and has been loved by them. He has an openly self-sacrificial concern for them, evident even in the letter's tone and passion. In chapter 4, he recounts with great feeling his first time among them:

> As you know, it was because of an illness that I first preached the gospel to you. Even though my illness was a trial to you, you did not treat me with contempt or scorn. Instead, you welcomed me as if I were an angel of God, as if I were Christ Jesus himself. What has happened to all your joy? I can testify that, if you could have done so, you would have torn out your eyes and given them to me. Have I now become your enemy by telling you the truth? (4:13-16).

Some scholars speculate that Paul had trouble with his eyes, both because of this comment and because of his comment in chapter 6, "See what large letters I use as I write to you with my own hand!" (6:11). Whether Paul had eye problems or not, the Galatians had been quite kind to him. They had cared for him, and he had cared for them.

Paul's motive for caring about them is clear. In the next to the last verse in the letter he writes, "Finally, let no one cause me trouble, for I bear on my body the marks of Jesus" (6:17). In other words, Paul is a servant of Jesus. By serving the Galatians, he was serving God. So he can give himself over entirely for their good.

The false teachers and the Galatians. How different Paul's love is from that of the false teachers, who have exploited the Galatians for their own gain. Paul writes, "Those people are zealous to win you over, but for no good. What they want is to alienate you from us, so that you may be zealous for them" (4:17). The false teachers boast in the flesh, while Paul boasts in Christ:

> Those who want to make a good impression outwardly are trying to compel you to be circumcised. The only reason they do this is to avoid being persecuted for the cross of Christ. Not even those who are circumcised obey the law, yet they want you to be circumcised that they may boast about your flesh. May I never boast except in the cross of our Lord Jesus Christ, through which the world has been crucified to me, and I to the world. Neither circumcision nor uncircumcision means anything; what counts is a new creation (6:12-15).

The false teachers are trying to be well regarded by others, and at the Galatians' expense. Even if their words are sweet, their tongues are treacherous.

Let me be perfectly clear about something we often miss in our culture today: Teaching truth is loving. Teaching error is unloving, even abusive.

It Changes Our Relationship with God

The Galatians' relationship with their leaders may have been the raging issue, but their relationship with God was, of course, the deeper issue. And here Paul's assumption may surprise some of us. He assumes the legalists in Galatia have not seriously considered the consequences of their sin, which may sound like the opposite of what you would expect from legalists. After all, we normally associate legalism with anxiety-producing moral standards and mountains of guilt for the slightest peccadilloes.

Yet Paul has another agenda. He wants people to understand that no amount of legalistic law-keeping can justify sinners before God and save us from his certain judgment. Only Christ's work on the cross satisfies God's just wrath, and only faith in Christ's propitiatory work justifies the sinner: "Clearly no one is justified before God by the law, because, 'The righteous will live by faith' . . . Christ redeemed us from the curse of the law by becoming a curse for us, for it is written: 'Cursed is everyone who is hung on a tree'" (3:11,13). And Christ was hung on a tree, taking the curse of the law upon himself!

The justification we gain through faith in Christ's work changes our relationship with God most remarkably. All the rich blessings God promised to Abraham will "come to the Gentiles through Christ Jesus"[5] (that's us, if we are Christians!). We become the people who bear God's name and know God's presence! We become "heirs according to the promise" (3:29). We become free from the law's condemnation (4:4-7, 21-31; 5:1-5). Like the children of Abraham, we are called sons of God: "You are all sons of God through faith in Christ Jesus, for all of you who were baptized into Christ have clothed yourself in Christ" (Gal. 3:26; cf. Ex. 4:22; Hos. 11:1; Matt. 2:15). Not only that, God gives us his Spirit: "Because you are sons, God sent the Spirit of his Son into our hearts, the Spirit who calls out, 'Abba, Father'" (4:6). Practically speaking, the person who has God's Spirit is the one who lives by the Spirit: "So I say, live by the Spirit, and you will not gratify the desires of the sinful nature" (5:16).

Do you see then why legalism is so dangerous? Ultimately, legalism is simply one form of walking according to the sinful nature and not the Spirit: "For the sinful nature desires what is contrary to the Spirit, and the Spirit what is contrary to the sinful nature. They are in conflict with each other" (5:17). On the one hand, legalism leads to terrible self-deception. It causes us to think we are "pretty good" or "good enough," when really, our least sins condemn us before a perfectly holy God. Borrowing from Deuteronomy, Paul says, "Cursed is everyone who does not continue to do *everything* written in the Book of the Law" (3:10; cf. Dt. 27:26; emphasis added). On the other hand, legalism—and the sinful nature behind it—enables us to pursue all sorts of sin while maintaining this sense of being "good enough":

> The acts of the sinful nature are obvious: sexual immorality, impurity and debauchery; idolatry and witchcraft; hatred, discord, jealousy, fits of rage, selfish ambition, dissensions, factions and envy; drunkenness, orgies, and the like (5:19-21a).

And the end of such actions is dire: "I warn you, as I did before, that those who live like this will not inherit the kingdom of God" (5:21b).

Therefore, any false teaching that offers something other than the true remedy—the forgiveness and new life we have in Christ by faith—must be avoided with all our might. "Get rid" of those who wish to reintroduce the law, Paul says (4:30). After all, "A little yeast works through the whole batch of dough" (5:9), and the church, as the holy, unleavened loaf, must get rid of the leaven that quickly spreads and spoils. As for the false teachers' attempt to

---

[5] 3:14; cf. Gen. 12:1-3; 17:7.

require circumcision, Paul exclaims, "I wish they would go the whole way and emasculate themselves!" (5:12).

The most serious consequence of sin—God's final judgment—is hidden from view in this life. Yet the promise of his judgment is like the gravity that anchors our feet on the ground. Without it, we become morally confused and directionless, like astronauts shorn of their weight in space. Even if his judgment is invisible now, it is certain. Therefore, Paul sharply warns the Galatians not to take the future for granted: "Do not be deceived: God cannot be mocked. A man reaps what he sows. The one who sows to please his sinful nature, from that nature will reap destruction" (6:7-8). Do not think you can continue to sin, believing that you will never face judgment simply because you have not faced it yet. That is not a good argument.

In 1662 Edmund Calamy, a faithful English pastor, was unjustly forced to resign from his church, along with hundreds of other pastors on one dark Bartholomew's day. Preaching on God's promise to judge David for disobediently numbering the Israelites, Calamy told his congregation in his final sermon, "Maybe some will say, I have committed many . . . sins, but am not brought into any strait [difficulty]. Remember, it was nine months after David had numbered the people before he was in this strait; but as sure as God is in heaven, sin will bring straits sooner or later; though one sin a hundred years, yet shall he be accursed; maybe thy prosperity makes way for thy damnation; and this is thy greatest distress, that thou goest on in sin and prosperity."[6] Have you ever noticed in Scripture that God will let some individuals continue in prosperity and wealth in order to prevent them from seeing the judgment that waits just over the next hill? Do not assume your prosperity means that God favors you. Seek the forgiveness that comes by grace alone through faith in Christ alone. Christ's work on the cross is the only thing that will save us from God's terrible judgment.

It Changes Our Relationships with Each Other

The deep issue of the Galatians' relationship with God, Paul says, will show itself in their relationships with one another. The Galatians should live as Christians. And, as in many of his letters, Paul concludes this letter with practical pastoral instruction about what it means to live as a Christian.

The Galatians' freedom in Christ is not a freedom to sin as they please. Self-indulgence and failure to love others are always dangers when people

---

[6] Edmund Calamy, "Farewell Sermon," in *Farewell Sermons: Preached by the Ejected Non-Conformist Ministers of 1662 to the Congregations on the Day of Their Ejection* (London: Gale and Fenner, 1816; repr. Soli Deo Gloria, 1992), 11.

begin to understand grace but do not yet really understand it. Yet Paul is not preaching a libertine, antinomian gospel. Their freedom was a freedom from sin (5:8-15). We must reject the idea that being saved by grace means it doesn't matter how we live. We are to follow the Spirit, not its enemy, the flesh (5:16-18). The Spirit will show himself in our lives through his fruit: "the fruit of the Spirit is love, joy, peace, patience, kindness, goodness, faithfulness, gentleness and self-control" (5:22-23a).

Paul exhorts the Galatians to help one another fight sin and face life's challenges:

> Brothers, if someone is caught in a sin, you who are spiritual should restore him gently. But watch yourself, or you also may be tempted. Carry each other's burdens, and in this way you will fulfill the law of Christ. If anyone thinks he is something when he is nothing, he deceives himself. Each one should test his own actions. Then he can take pride in himself, without comparing himself to somebody else, for each one should carry his own load (6:1-5).

Paul then makes particular mention of the special care they should demonstrate toward faithful teachers: "Anyone who receives instruction in the word must share all good things with his instructor" (6:6).

Paul knows the Lord Jesus taught that we should love one another, and that our love for one another is an important part of our testimony to the world of his love. If you happen to be a theology hound, perhaps you enjoyed reading the earlier parts of this chapter where we discussed justification by faith but have been tempted to "tune out" as we consider chapters 5 and 6. After all, they are all about love and kindness, and everybody believes that; we don't really need any sharp teaching on that stuff, right? Beware. It is possible to mentally affirm and even enjoy doctrine but to not believe it, at least not in the biblical sense where God's love in Christ engulfs your heart and you find yourself beginning to love other people as you have been loved.

Beware of mere cognitive Christianity! Even in a letter where he argues strenuously for a particular propositional message, Paul knows it is possible to get the words right and still have an unregenerate heart. I know people who can argue about doctrine until they are blue in the face yet whose lives lack the tenor of love and tenderness that bespeaks a heart truly familiar with Christ. So beware if you are one of those people. Caring a lot about doctrine is a good thing; it is not a bad thing. But do read the last two chapters of Galatians. And pray that God would grant you the kind of love in your heart that you defend so well with your mouth.

CONCLUSION

I hope you can see that the news of Christianity makes a difference, unlike so much of the news that is consumed in this world today. How do you know if you have Paul's—no, God's—message? First, by *what* you say. The message depends on the right cognitive content. We are not saved by circumcision. We are saved by faith in Christ. Second, you know you have God's message by *how* you say it, and how you live it out. Are you saying the message clearly? Are you living it clearly?

In February 1989, the East German border guards at Potsdamer Platz in Berlin shot to death a man trying to escape from the East into West Berlin. But on November 9 of that same year, after dividing far more than just one city for twenty-eight years and ninety-one days, the Berlin Wall fell. Over the subsequent months, cranes and bulldozers finished tearing down the wall, along with scholars and tourists like my good self who took crumbly bits of the wall away.

Do you remember where you were when you watched the pictures of the mobs of people swarming both ways through the gates, and the bewilderment of the guards? Why were there swarms of delirious joy? Because Germany was reunited? Yes, in part. That is what the media emphasized. But there was another, more mundane answer: the daily lives of millions of people in East Germany would change drastically and immediately, and very rarely does drastic change occur in a single life, let alone in thousands or millions of lives. One hotel porter interviewed the next week said that the people in East Berlin changed immediately. "Now people are standing up straight. They are speaking their minds. Even work is more fun. I think the sick will get up from their hospital beds."[7]

Now imagine if *you* were one of the people who walked away from the nation that had been controlled by wrong-headed communist ideologues, that had justified horrible atrocities in the name of false doctrines, that had dominated its citizenry with the fear of secret police. Now, imagine that, after some time of living in freedom, you tried to get back into that nation, forsaking the freedoms you had struggled for. It doesn't make any sense, does it?

That is what Paul is saying these Galatians were doing, when they traded away the wonderful freedom they knew in the gospel of Christ for some set of standards they were supposed to fulfill in order to know God. Are you in danger of doing that?

Apparently in the last months of the regime, Erich Honecker, the East

---

[7] Cited in Timothy Garton Ash, *We the People: The Revolution of 89 Witnessed in Warsaw, Budapest, Berlin, and Prague* (Cambridge, UK: Granta Books, 1990), 63.

German tyrant prime minister, ordered the East German secret police to quietly round up dissidents, present them with completed application forms to emigrate to the West, and give them the choice of emigration or prison. The political strategy was obvious—deplete the opposition. But personally, can you imagine being faced with that choice? As one dissident said who was arrested and confronted with this choice: "It was like being forced to choose between heaven and hell!"

Is that the choice you need to make today? To live in the freedom we have in Christ or to continue living under your own cobbled-together morality? One woman who recently found Christ and joined our congregation remarked to me that what struck her when considering Christianity through the witness of our church was a phrase we often use—"newness of life." She thought, *What clever writers this church must have!*

Of course we got it from the Bible. But just imagine: you can actually have a new life. That is what all of us who are true children of God have experienced. We have a new life in Christ. Doesn't the news of your sins being forgiven sound too good to be true? If this hits you like a dull thud and all you can think about right now is finishing this study and having a bite to eat, I'm not talking to you. I'm talking to those who are entranced by the thought that their sins can be forgiven by faith in Christ. To them I say, turn from your sins, and trust Christ for what he has promised.

May we hear the urgent message of Galatians: keep hold of the gospel. The gospel was not made up by me or by any church, by some committee or some bishop, by Paul or the apostles. It is from God. And you will certainly give an account to him for having heard it.

So, what laws have you observed, thinking you would thereby gain God's favor? You always put some money in the plate? You never use that word, at least not when he is listening? You are faithful, honest, good, and true? Friend, you must ask yourself, have you constructed your understanding of the world so that you think you are not a sinner? That you have no guilty stains? That you are not vile before God? That you have no need of a Savior?

That is what the Galatians were in danger of doing long ago—and of being hoodwinked into thinking a little surgery could bring salvation. What about you? Have you quietly struck your own deal with God, and worked out some way you can give him a little less than everything and still be his?

You can be certain of your sins. That is a given. But you can be certain of your rescue, as Paul calls it in this letter, only by believing in Jesus Christ as your Savior and by trusting in him. That is what this little letter is all about. That is what the church is all about. And that is supposed to be what your life is all about. Is it?

Let us pray:

Lord God, we pray that you would work in our hearts an awareness of our own sins, as well as a sense of how insufficient our imaginary agreements with you are for dealing with these sins. Work in us an understanding of our state before you and of our need for a Savior. And then, Lord, when you have confined us to despair, show us hope and joy in Christ. Lord, teach us to put all of our hope in him alone. We pray for Jesus' sake. Amen.

Questions for Reflection

1. We know better than to trust any newspaper or magazine entirely, because we have witnessed too many errors. Christianity makes quite a claim when it asserts that the Bible is wholly true and without error. How do you respond to someone who says, "The Bible is just like any other book—part history, part mythology, and full of contradictions"?

2. Have people-pleasing tendencies ever tempted you to soften the message, or leave out certain aspects, when sharing the good news? When?

3. If God is the author of Scripture, and if God is truthful and cannot lie, what does that suggest about the accuracy and truthfulness of Scripture? On the other hand, if God is the author of Scripture and the Scriptures are not accurate, what does that suggest about God?

4. As Christians, what is our motivation for proclaiming a gospel that can be difficult for people to hear?

5. Some suggest that what people are looking for today from churches is not *abstract truths* about God so much as *authentic experiences* of God. How would Paul respond?

6. According to Galatians, what *message* should be at the center of our church gatherings?

7. Following up on questions 5 and 6, we might say that Paul became angry with Peter because the church's most important message did not translate into action in his life (2:12-14). What message was Peter forgetting? How did he fail to put what he knew into practice? What lessons does this central message and Peter's failure have for how you relate to others in the church?

8. When false gospels come, will they be wearing a sign that says "Warning: False Gospel!"? If not, how will they be packaged? How will you recognize them? What structures are in place that will enable your church to detect them?

9. As we have seen, Paul does not address the congregation's leaders about the false teachers. He doesn't even address the false teachers themselves. He addresses the congregation. What implications might this have for how we govern our churches? Whom does Paul treat as having the final authority in the local church?

10. Following up on question 9, Paul's frustration with the congregation at Galatia presumes that they have a clear understanding of the gospel and that they should be able to recognize departures from that gospel. What responsibility does that mean *you* have in your local church?

11. If a friend told you that she was a Christian because she believed Jesus died on the cross on her behalf, but that she was not willing to let go of her sinful lifestyle, how would you respond?

12. What was the main dispute between Paul and these false teachers?

13. Explain what "justification by faith" means without using some form of the word "justification" (see Galatians 2:16, where the phrase is used in context).

14. Christians often wonder how people were saved in Old Testament times. After reading Galatians 3:6-10, can you answer that question?

15. Standing before the throne of God on Judgment Day, what will you say in your defense?

16. What obligation does God have to save you? If your quick answer is "none," consider, are you ever tempted to think otherwise? Do you really believe God has no obligation at all to save you? After your profession of faith and baptism? After your years of "walking by faith"?

17. What makes you feel genuinely good about yourself? A productive day at work? Your children's growth and success? Your husband's care and affection? The admiration of colleagues? Your parents' approval? Consistent quiet times? The ability to articulate your theology well? Finding the answer to that ques-

tion will help you discover what is at the core of your identity, and what you prize above all things. And it will help you see what may cause confusion for you regarding what the gospel is all about.

18. Following up on question 17, if you are a teacher of the Bible in any capacity (for a congregation, for a small group, for your children), what are you consistently teaching people to feel good about? Week after week, they walk away from their time with you feeling encouraged because . . . ?

19. As we have seen, teaching truth is a loving thing to do. Teaching error is unloving, even abusive. In what ways are we tempted to forget this, both in our personal lives and in our church lives with other Christians?

20. Should prosperity and success make us think God's favor is on us? Why or why not?

21. What does it mean to have "freedom" in Christ (as in Galatians 5:1)? Does it mean freedom to sin?

THE MESSAGE OF EPHESIANS: GRACE

GIVE ME MY RIGHTS!

INTRODUCING EPHESIANS

WHAT GOD HAS DONE: UNITED US IN GRACE (CHAPTERS 1–3)

God Elects

God Unites

God Is Gracious

God Gives Faith

WHAT WE MUST DO: LIVE OUT OUR UNITY (CHAPTERS 4–6)

Live a Life Worthy of Our Calling

Build Others Up

Make the Most of Every Opportunity

Stand to the End

Rest in God's Sovereignty

WHAT WE MUST NOT DO: PARTNER WITH DARKNESS (5:3-14)

WHY GOD HAS DONE THIS

For the Praise of His Glorious Grace

For Showing His Grace

For Displaying His Wisdom to All Creation

To God Be Glory in the Church and in Christ Forever

CONCLUSION

10

THE MESSAGE OF EPHESIANS: GRACE

GIVE ME MY RIGHTS![1]

Robert George, professor of politics at Princeton University, wrote a short parody not too long ago on the question of whether it is morally legitimate to kill an abortion doctor.[2] He cleverly decided to adopt the language of moral ambivalence found among pro-choice advocates and then to apply the same language to the question of killing abortionists, a practice that is universally rejected. George writes: "I am personally opposed to killing abortionists. However, inasmuch as my personal opposition to this practice is rooted in a sectarian (Catholic) religious belief in the sanctity of human life, I am unwilling to impose it on others who may, as a matter of conscience, take a different view. Of course, I am entirely in favor of policies aimed at removing the root causes of violence against abortionists. Indeed, I would go so far as to support mandatory one-week waiting periods, and even nonjudgmental counseling, for people who are contemplating the choice of killing an abortionist. I believe in policies that reduce the urgent need some people feel to kill abortionists while, at the same time, respecting the rights of conscience of my fellow citizens who believe that the killing of abortionists is sometimes a tragic necessity—not a good, but a lesser evil. In short, I am moderately pro-choice."

George is not seriously suggesting we should claim a right to kill abortionists. Do not misunderstand him. He is saying that, just as a pro-choice position on killing abortion doctors is absurd, so is saying that we have a right to kill infants absurd and horrendous and tragic.

But then, "rights" are the way we talk about everything these days. I have

---

[1] This sermon was originally preached on November 14, 1999, at Capitol Hill Baptist Church in Washington, D.C.
[2] Robert George, in "Killing Abortionists: A Symposium," in *First Things* 48 (December 1994): 24-31.

the right to do what I want. You have the right to make whatever choices you want.

I wonder, what do you think you are entitled to? When you walk into a church or sit at work or shop at the mall, what rights do you assume you have? Inalienable rights given by your Creator, as Thomas Jefferson said? An ever-growing bill of rights? Historians and cultural observers going all the way back to the famous nineteenth-century Alexis De Tocqueville have observed that even the idea of "America" has a legal ring to it. The United States of America was a quickly assembled nation. It was not a slowly developing, ethnically homogenous culture like the Incas, the French, the Chinese, or the Egyptians. The birth of the United States occurred when a group of colonies formulated agreements about how to live together. Perhaps, then, it was natural that law and rights became a way for us to speak.

Yet most observers, I think, agree that a change occurred in the middle of the twentieth century. In the mid-1950s, many Americans began to assume the way to change society for the better was not by legislation but by judicial review. We cannot say exactly why this change occurred. Perhaps it was frustration with how slow legislators were in changing the local laws that enshrined unjust racial prejudice. But for whatever reason, the civil rights movement soon gave birth to many other rights movements as activist courts attempted to bring justice to the nation by delineating whole classes of rights that had not been previously recognized. Of course, much good has been accomplished through such rulings. Yet for all the good that has been accomplished, problems have emerged. As a nation, we should be reluctant to condition ourselves to relying too often on the coercive power of a court over against the popular will.

As the balance of power between courts and legislators has shifted in the last half-century, something has also changed on a personal, individual level. It would take more time and expertise than I have to explore this idea fully, but let me turn to Mary Ann Glendon, a noted expert and writer on legal matters. "There is no more telling indicator," she writes, "of the extent to which legal notions have penetrated both popular and political discourse than our increasing tendency to speak of what is more important to us in terms of rights, and to frame nearly every social controversy as a clash of rights."[3] We act and talk as if our rights are things that cannot be negotiated. Our rights are innate. They are a given. And we hold that to be self-evident!

I think one of the most disturbing rights people believe they have is *the right of fellowship with God*. I have no poll data on this, only countless pieces

---

[3] Mary Ann Glendon, *Rights Talk* (New York: Free Press, 1991), 3-4.

of anecdotal evidence. Yet I feel sure fellowship with God has increasingly been regarded as a right, even if no one quite states it that way. The thought probably runs something like this: "God made me. He's responsible for me. So it is up to him, in fact, he is obliged, to make sure I have a wonderful existence." End of the argument. Like the German poet Heinrich Heine said in 1856 on his deathbed, "The good God will forgive. That is his job."

Is that what you think? Is God obligated to ensure that you have a happy life, and to offer any forgiveness that needs to be offered? Do you have the right to do whatever you want with your body? To do whatever you want with your life? Should even church members be encouraged to think and act independently—so long as they say they believe in Christ—because this inculcates diversity? Is this world all just for you?

INTRODUCING EPHESIANS

If you think any of these things—and if you are a normal American you probably think at least one or two of them—then the idea of *grace* in Paul's letter to the Ephesians might surprise you.

We are not certain when Paul wrote this little letter, but various things in the letter suggest he was a prisoner at the time. Most people have believed he wrote it during his imprisonment in Rome in the early 60s, toward the end of his life.

Unlike his letters to the churches in Corinth or Galatia, we do not know what particular situations in Ephesus prompted Paul to write this letter. Perhaps it was the tensions that arose from his success in bringing large numbers of Jewish and Gentile believers into the church. Whatever the situation was, it produced a lovely letter that helps us understand better what God has done for us, what he calls us to do, what he does not call us to do, and why he has done all that he has.

WHAT GOD HAS DONE: UNITED US IN GRACE (CHAPTERS 1–3)

If the letter to the Galatians is like a bomb, the letter to the Ephesians is like a jewel. It extraordinarily refracts the grace of God. The first thing we discover in the letter is what God has done for us. Let me summarize chapters 1–3 as I did in the study on Galatians. I will give you one sentence for every paragraph in the NIV translation.

Beginning with chapter 1: Paul, an apostle of Christ Jesus by the will of God (1:1a). To the saints in Ephesus, the faithful in Christ Jesus (1:1b). Grace and peace to you from God (1:2). Praise be to God who chose and predestined us to be redeemed through Christ, to the praise of his glorious grace (1:3-10).

Both you and I have been chosen in Christ and sealed with the Holy Spirit, to the praise of his glory (1:11-14). I thank God and pray for you, that you may know Christ better as well as his power for you (1:15-23).

Moving to chapter 2: You know that we were all dead in our sins, but God graciously made us alive in order to show his grace and end our boasting (2:1-10). Remember, you Gentiles were without God but have now been brought near through the blood of Christ (2:11-13). Christ has made Jewish and Gentile believers one by making them members of his body, giving them access to the Father by one Spirit (2:14-18). Gentile and Jewish believers are now one whole building in which God lives by his Spirit (2:19-22).

And then chapter 3: I, Paul, am in prison for you Gentiles (3:1). You know that God entrusted me with the gospel through which you Gentiles are made sharers in the promise in Christ (3:2-6). So it is not by mistake that I suffer; no, it was God's gracious plan for me to suffer in bringing the message of Christ to the nations, so that God's wisdom would be displayed to all creation (3:7-13). I pray for your strengthening by the Spirit and your grasp of Christ's love, so that you may be filled with the fullness of God (3:14-19). To God be glory in the church and in Christ for ever! Amen (3:20-21)!

In these first three chapters, Paul does not instruct his readers to do anything. He simply *indicates* what God has done, what God is like, and what we are. He lays out the framework for these Christians to help them understand everything from the world to themselves to God.

God Elects

First, Paul introduces himself and addresses his readers in a typically Pauline way: "Paul, an apostle of Christ Jesus by the will of God, to the saints in Ephesus, the faithful in Christ Jesus: Grace and peace to you from God" (1:1-2). Paul usually aims at some target in his introductions. He gives his readers a hint about the letter's main topic even in the way he says hello. It is not by accident that in this letter he introduces himself as "an apostle of Christ Jesus, by *the will of God*." Paul uses this phrase more in his later letters, and it is particularly appropriate in this one.

In 1:3-14, Paul begins the body of the letter by praising God for his election of us for redemption through Christ, the "us" referring to the church. God's sovereignty clearly shines forth in his election. He works "everything in conformity with the purpose of his will" (1:11), which includes the election of sinners. God chooses us. As Paul understands it, our salvation is no "right" that we possess infinitely. God is in no way obligated to elect us because he created us. Election is a privilege we are given because of God's great overflow-ing love for us in Christ.

Paul demonstrates his love for the Ephesians in 1:15-23 by praying for them—one of two places in these first three chapters where he describes his prayers for them. It is worth our noting that if God is as great and sovereign a God as Paul describes, you *will* pray to him. You understand he is the sovereign of the world, and there is no one more effective to whom to pray. So Paul gives himself to prayer. He thanks God for the Ephesians and prays for them to know Christ and his power better—a great model of prayer for us. A second great model for our prayers comes in chapter 3, where Paul prays for the Ephesians to be strengthened by God's Spirit, to grasp the love of Christ, and to be filled with the fullness of God (3:14-19). Notice that both times Paul prays—chapters 1 and 3—he prays that they would have knowledge. He knows that their understanding will provide the basis for their actions. So he prays that their understanding will be enlarged.

God Unites

Paul particularly cares for the Ephesians because, as he recounts for them (3:1-13), his whole calling is to bring the message of Jesus Christ to the Gentiles so that they would become sharers in the promise of God along with the Jews. The obvious point here is unity. At the base of Paul's message is the unity of Jews and Gentiles in Christ, as the latter half of chapter 2 makes clear. The god-less Gentiles have been brought near to God through the blood of Christ (2:11-13). Now, these Gentile believers have been made one with the Jewish believers by being members of one body and by having been given access to the one Father by one Spirit (2:14-18). They are now together one building in which the one God lives by his one Spirit (2:19-22).

God Is Gracious

How could there be such oneness, such unity? This unity is possible because God's grace eliminates the importance of worldly distinctions. Foundational to Paul's message of unity, then, are the first ten verses of chapter 2, where we see that unity is entirely based on grace. We were all dead in the transgressions and sins in which we used to live, he says in verse 1. Is Paul insulting his Gentile readers by saying that? Did he think he was better than they? Not at all. In verse 3 he says, "we all once lived in the passions of our flesh, carrying out the desires of the body and the mind, and were by nature children of wrath, like the rest of mankind" (ESV). All mankind is an object of God's righteous wrath because all mankind is born depraved, to use the word theologians use. It means that something has gone wrong with us, and we are actually kind of happy about that. We have all joined the rebellion against the authority of God, and we are pleased to do so. Of course, we may not like certain consequences, or implications, of our rebellion. But at root we are coconspirators against God and his sovereignty over his own creation. As a result, Paul says, we have been declared dead in our sins and transgressions.

Now I have to mention something that frequently happens in Protestant Christianity. When individuals become more liberal in their theology, that is, when they increasingly set aside their belief that Scripture is inspired by God and begin thinking instead that truth is generated through one's own observations and conclusions, they often begin emphasizing unity in greater and greater measure *while* having less and less ground for that unity. Ironically, however, the *true* gospel always seems to bring the unity that these liberal theologians can only dream of. When we understand that we are all depraved, that we are all dead spiritually, that we are in debt to God and bereft before him, a strange, helpless unity comes over us. A group of confessedly depraved people has nothing to brag about. Therefore it is not surprising when the world's most familiar barriers to unity are brought down in churches that are *not* focused on bringing them down but are focused instead on teaching the gospel faithfully and clearly.

We do not have a right standing with God because we are ethnically Jewish, or because we are Gentile, or because we are more cultured, or because we are of this race, or because we belong to the right economic group. Nothing innate in us and no attribute of ours gives us a right standing with God. If we do have a right standing with God, it is only because he has made us alive, according to his love and great mercy: "But because of his great love for us, God, who is rich in mercy, made us alive with Christ even when we were dead in transgressions" (2:4-5a). Ultimately, he has made us alive in order to reveal his own glory and grace: "And God raised us up with Christ and seated us with him in the heavenly realms in Christ Jesus, in order that in the coming ages he might show the incomparable riches of his grace, expressed in his kindness to us in Christ Jesus" (2:6-7). God's grace is shown further in making us alive through faith, not works: "for it is by grace you have been saved, through faith—and this not from yourselves, it is the gift of God—not by works" (2:8-9a). We are not made right with God by what we do, because what we do is sin. We are made right with God as a privilege God extends to us through faith in Christ. In short, the justification we have before God through our faith is not a right for people who sin. It is a privilege.

God Gives Faith

God must give us faith. We are not going to get it from our ethnic background. We are not going to get it from any attribute of ours. No, God must reveal the mystery of the gospel for it to be understood. The word "mystery," when used in the New Testament, does not refer to a problem that is difficult to understand, like a puzzle. It refers to something *impossible* to understand (see 1:9; 3:3-10; 6:19). The gospel of Jesus Christ is that kind of mystery, and God himself had to reveal it. You and I would not have imagined it. We would not have figured it out. God himself revealed the greatness of his glorious love for us in Christ. And he must make it known to us as individuals. So Paul prays, "I pray also that the eyes of your heart may be enlightened" (1:18). He knows that for his preaching of the gospel to have any effect in the Ephesians, God must give light to their eyes and hearts so that they understand and embrace the gospel. And this makes sense, given the darkness the Gentiles and everyone dwells in (4:18).

In these first three chapters, then, we are given a wonderful picture of unity based on the grace of God. An emphasis on religious works always brings division. But when God's grace is emphasized, thus removing the focus from our own abilities and inclinations, unity follows. This unity is reemphasized even in the way Paul finishes the book (6:23-24). He prays for the Ephesians to know peace and grace, which were the traditional Jewish and Greek salutations, respectively. The Jewish greeting is *shalom,* or peace, and the Greek greeting is *charis,* or grace. He begins with "peace" and then makes a point of also saying "with faith," as if he is reminding the Jews in the congregation that their ultimate peace will be found through faith, not through the law and circumcision. Then he mentions "grace," and makes a point of saying who the grace is for: it is for *"all* who love our Lord Jesus Christ with an undying love." What a beautiful phrase! It is not just for the Jewish people but for all nations—Jew and Gentile alike—who love the Lord Jesus.

God has made Jews and Gentiles—indeed, all believers—one in Christ. That is the fundamental point of this letter.

WHAT WE MUST DO: LIVE OUT OUR UNITY (CHAPTERS 4–6)

In the first three chapters of Ephesians, unity is presented as a fact. God *has made* us one. In the last three chapters, unity is presented as a daily goal. It is something we must live out and work toward. If the first three chapters emphasize what God has done, the last three emphasize what we must do. So Paul shifts from the indicative to the imperative—to commands—in chapters 4–6.

He begins in chapter 4 by exhorting the Ephesians: keep the unity of the Spirit required by your new lives in Christ (4:1-6). Christ has given gifts to every one of us for building us up together toward maturity and the fullness of Christ (4:7-13). These various gifts will bring unity when they do their work in love through Christ, who is our head (4:14-16). So you must no longer live as godless Gentiles (4:17-19). You were taught that knowing Christ involved putting off your old self, having your minds renewed, and putting on the new self (4:20-24). Therefore you must not lie or be angry at one another; instead, you must share (4:25-28). Don't tear others down or grieve God's Spirit by malice, but build each other up with kindness, compassion, and forgiveness, just as, in Christ, God forgave you (4:29-32).

Then chapter 5: imitate God your Father, by living a life of love, just as Christ loved us and gave himself up for us (5:1-2). Don't misunderstand me, says Paul, I am not saying you should partner together with anyone who lies to you by telling you immorality is okay (5:1-7). Don't live as though you were still in darkness; instead, find out what pleases the Lord and live in the light (5:8-14). Be very careful how you live by making the most of every opportunity and always giving thanks to God (5:15-20). Submit to one another out of reverence for Christ (5:21). Wives, submit to your husbands (5:22). Husbands, love your wives just as Christ loved the church and gave himself for her (5:25-32).

Chapter 6 continues: Children, obey your parents (6:1-3). Fathers, bring your children up in the training of the Lord (6:4). Slaves, obey your earthly masters (6:5-8). Masters, treat your slaves as they treat you, with respect and fear, knowing that you have the same master who will show no favoritism (6:9). Put on the full armor of God so that, at the end, you are still standing (6:10-18). Pray that I will declare the gospel fearlessly, as I am an ambassador in chains (6:19-20). I am sending Tychicus with information to encourage you (6:21). Shalom and love with faith from God; and grace to all who love our Lord Jesus Christ with an undying love (6:23-24).

Live a Life Worthy of Our Calling

How then does Paul exhort us in chapters 4–6 to strive toward unity? Fundamentally, we must live a life that is worthy of the calling we have received. Paul opens the second half of his letter by writing, "As a prisoner for the Lord, then, I urge you to live a life worthy of the calling you have received" (4:1). What is that calling? It is a calling to display, through love and light, the unity God has given (4:1-3, 17-25; 4:26–5:2). In the first few verses of chapter 4, a life that is worthy of the calling to unity is specifically characterized as humble, gentle, patient, forbearing in love, and eager to keep the unity of the Spirit (4:2-3).

Build Others Up

Christians must also display their unity by building one another up and putting off sin, particularly the sin of anger. Anger provides a foothold for the devil in the Christian's life whereby he starts to use the Christian as a staging ground for bringing harm into the lives of others (4:26-27). And rather than harming others, God intends for Christians to "share with those in need" (4:28) and build "others up according to their needs" (4:29).

Those areas of Christians' lives inverted to selfishness must be reoriented and retooled toward building others up. Thieves must steal no longer. They must work and do something useful for a change. And Paul is not merely interested in respecting private property; a man should work "that he may have something to share with those in need" (4:28). When I first moved to Washington, I had a number of conversations with a man who frequently stood out on the street near Union Station asking for help. He had some obvious disabilities, yet he also had a wonderful personality. The sixth or seventh time I talked to him, I said, "You know, you can just stand here for the rest of your life asking people for money. But God has given you a great personality. If you want to talk to me further, I am sure our church will pay for you to train to work in computers. You could actually generate money yourself, so that you can help other people." He was not interested in that at all. But that is exactly what we want to see, and not just in outsiders. We want to see in ourselves a zeal for blessing others, so that the body is built up.

The words that come out of a Christian's mouth must also be used for "building others up" (4:29). Thus Paul exhorts the Ephesians not to let any unwholesome talk come out of their mouths (4:29). He warns them against grieving the Holy Spirit through "bitterness, rage and anger, brawling and slander, along with every form of malice" (4:30-31). Positively, Paul says they should "be kind and compassionate to one another, forgiving each other" (4:32). Christians are called to "be imitators of God" (5:1), particularly by living a "life of love" (5:2).

Make the Most of Every Opportunity

After describing further ways the Ephesians should put off sin, in the first half of chapter 5, he turns in verse 15 to exhorting Christians to seek unity by living wisely; and living wisely, among other things, means "making the most of every opportunity" (5:16). So Christians are not to be foolish, but are to understand what the Lord's will is (5:17). They must not get drunk on wine, but be filled with the Spirit (5:18). They should strive to build one another up through speaking psalms, hymns, and spiritual songs to one another (5:19a). By singing to one another for the sake of mutual edification, Christians "make music in your heart to the Lord, always giving thanks to God the Father for everything" (5:19b-20).

Christians should make the most of every opportunity in their homes and workplaces as well, which is where Paul turns in the following verses by exhorting the Ephesians to "Submit to one another out of reverence for Christ" (5:21). All of us must submit to Christ, and we practice our submission to him in several concrete ways. A very specific list of *how* to "submit to one another" follows this headline in the remainder of chapter 5 and beginning of chapter 6. Twice Paul tells wives to submit to their husbands (5:22, 24). Wives should also respect their husbands (5:33). Husbands in turn are told to love their wives (5:25, 28, 33). Children must obey their parents (6:1), and the Ten Commandments are enlisted to support this point: "honor your father and mother" (6:2). Yet fathers are warned not to exasperate their children, but to bring them up in the training of the Lord (6:4). Paul addresses slaves next, by which he does not mean a certain race of people, as we might think today given our historical experience. He means the huge portion of the population who worked as indentured servants. So, Paul is saying, if you are an indentured servant, slave, or employee, you must obey whomever God has placed over you. This is God's will for you at work (6:5-6). Serve wholeheartedly, "as if you were serving the Lord, not men" (6:7). Let me suggest, if you personally struggle with diligence at work, type up Ephesians 6:7, stick it underneath your computer screen, and see if it helps you. Be diligent at work, Paul says, as if you are serving the Lord and not men. Then turning to address masters, or employers, he tells them to remember that God is watching how they treat those over whom he has given them charge. So treat them well and do not threaten them (6:9).

Clearly, this list of "how to submit to one another" distinguishes the submission in 5:21 from a kind of simple egalitarianism. Yes, we are all born in the same state spiritually (2:1-3), but Paul does not expect that the natural authority structures of home and work will be renounced. You cannot reverse the instructions which follow 5:21. For instance, parents are never called to submit to their children, though parents must give themselves sacrificially to their children's best interests.

Stand to the End

Finally, Christian unity will be seen as Christians "stand" to the end, an exhortation Paul gives four times (6:11, 13 [x2], 14). So if you read through chapter 6, expect Paul to stare you in the eye and tell you to "Stand! Stand!" This word probably means more to older members of a church than it means to younger members. The longer you live, the more you realize how central perseverance is in the Christian walk. Some of you might be able to say, "I may not have witnessed to seven hundred people this year, but by the grace of God I am still standing in the faith, sixty years after I accepted it." Every year that goes by is more of a testimony to the grace of God, because standing is not easy. So stand. Stand firm in the faith. Realize that it is a contest.

In order to stand, Paul tells the Ephesians to put on the whole armor of God (6:11, 13). He knows the Christian life is a contest indeed. He has already warned them that Satan wants to get a foothold in the Christian's life through anger. Now he exhorts them to "be strong in the Lord" by taking up the shield of faith, the helmet of salvation, and the sword of the Spirit (6:16-17). These verses provide a wonderfully graphic presentation of the Christian ready to stand his ground in the face of inevitable conflict.[4] How appropriate then are his last words of instruction:

> Pray in the Spirit on all occasions with all kinds of prayers and requests. With this in mind, be alert and always keep on praying for all the saints.
>
> Pray also for me, that whenever I open my mouth, words may be given me so that I will fearlessly make known the mystery of the gospel, for which I am an ambassador in chains. Pray that I may declare it fearlessly, as I should (6:18-20).

Rest in God's Sovereignty

Now doesn't that get your heart? There is Paul in prison, an old man, praying and asking others to pray that God would make him fearless. "Paul," you might ask, "how much more fearless can you get? You are giving your whole life away, choosing to be in prison because you want to reach people like me, a Gentile, with the gospel." Paul knew courage was needed to continue, and he knew God's Spirit had to provide what did not come naturally. So he asked for it. It was plain and obvious that sitting in prison was his duty, given by God. His suffering could not obscure God's design. Indeed, Paul's instructions on submission in this letter were hard-won. Languishing in prison, Paul certainly knew what was involved in submission, as much as any slave. Yet he knew he had the freedom to obey. No authority on earth could take that away from him.

Is it an accident that two of the New Testament's clearest statements on God's sovereignty come from the pens of two older men in captivity—John exiled on Patmos in the book of Revelation, and Paul in a Roman prison here? When this world exerts its fullest powers to oppose the gospel, it only serves

---

[4] For a wonderful meditation on these verses, see William Gurnall's classic *The Christian in Complete Armour* (Carlisle, Pa.: Banner of Truth, 1964).

to reveal the powerlessness of rebellion against God. Invariably, these very exertions have a way of wonderfully exposing God's purposeful hand as he works out all things for the good of those who love him. And with this confidence in God's grace, Christians can restfully abide.

WHAT WE MUST NOT DO: PARTNER WITH DARKNESS (5:3-14)

As we are seeing, the unity that Paul says believers have through God's grace (chapters 1–3) is described in all its practical aspects in chapters 4–6. But we should note one special exception to Paul's call for unity, about which he is both clear and urgent. In the beginning of chapter 5, Paul urges these Christians not to strive toward unity where spiritual grace is absent. We must not partner with immorality, or darkness.

There is a wrong kind of unity. Paul writes,

> Among you there must not be even a hint of sexual immorality, or of any kind of impurity, or of greed, because these are improper for God's holy people. Nor should there be obscenity, foolish talk or coarse joking, which are out of place, but rather thanksgiving. For of this you can be sure: No immoral, impure or greedy person—such a man is an idolater—has any inheritance in the kingdom of Christ and of God. Let no one deceive you with empty words, for because of such things God's wrath comes on those who are disobedient. Therefore do not be partners with them (5:3-7).

Though these Jewish and Gentile believers should exercise their unity regardless of their national identity or their religious past, Paul is not suggesting the church's chief end is diversity for its own sake. In fact, Paul warns against certain kinds of diversity. A congregation should never seek unity in diversity if it means tolerance for greed, impurity, impropriety, or immorality. While many differences should be accepted and even celebrated, coarse and obscene language should not be spoken, even in the name of so-called unity. God's people are to separate themselves from these kinds of immoralities. As I reflected on verse 7, the prohibition rang in my soul: "do not be partners with them."

Paul goes on to justify this divinely commanded *dis*unity as a contrast between light and darkness:

> For you were once darkness, but now you are light in the Lord. Live as children of light (for the fruit of the light consists in all goodness, righteousness and truth) and find out what pleases the Lord. Have nothing to do with the fruitless deeds of darkness, but rather expose them. For it is shameful even to mention what the disobedient do in secret. But everything exposed by the light becomes visible, for it is light that makes everything visible (5:8-14a).

It is hard to miss the vigorous *dis*unity that Paul urges the Ephesians to adopt. On the one hand, Christians are to live as children of light (5:8), and this includes finding out what pleases the Lord (5:10). God's pleasure is associated with light and knowledge. On the other hand, Christians are to have nothing to do with deeds of darkness. Instead, they are to expose them by making such deeds known for what they are (5:11)!

Some people do not like the use of the word "darkness." They particularly didn't like how the International Mission Board of the Southern Baptist Convention used the word in their prayer guide focused on the Hindu celebration of Divali. The guide is titled, "Divali: Festival of Light, Circle of Darkness." It begins, "More than 900 million people are lost in the hopeless darkness of Hinduism, worshiping 330 million gods and goddesses created by the imagination of men and women searching for a source of truth and strength." As you can imagine, this language did not go down well either in the United States or overseas. In New Delhi and Bombay, the prayer guide made front-page news for several weeks, I am told. Jim McDermott, a U.S. congressman from Washington state, wrote a "Dear Colleague" letter to his fellow members of Congress in the aftermath of the prayer guide's publication strenuously objecting to the guide. Here's a sample from McDermott's letter:

> Hinduism is one of the world's oldest and most widely practiced religions. Moreover, it teaches tolerance, respect and diversity towards other ways of life and creeds. India, as the birthplace of Hinduism has made a strong commitment to secularism and has demonstrated its resolve in remaining a shining example of how a multitude of faiths can live in peace.

> This letter only asks the SBC to consider a different theme when attempting to convert Hindus. The SBC has adopted an intolerant view that has inflamed Hindu communities worldwide. This letter asks them to consider a more tolerant and less inflammatory method of proselytizing.[5]

McDermott's choice of words was unfortunate in a number of respects. "Inflammatory" is what he calls the Christian practice of praying for others. I assume his language is figurative, and that he is not suggesting crowds of angry Baptists actually burn Hindus. I also must assume that Mr. McDermott is unaware of the crowd of Hindus in India who burned to death Graham Staines and his young sons just a few months previously. Staines was a Baptist missionary in "tolerant" India. And someone may want to remind McDermott of

---

[5] In an October 28, 1999, "Dear Colleague" letter.

the events surrounding the formation of India and Pakistan as modern nations. Suffice it to say, it was not an exercise in religious tolerance.

When reports of the prayer guide hit the news, one non-Christian friend told me he was astonished anyone would use the language of "darkness" to refer to another religion in our enlightened age. I stopped him and said that if anyone taught my children to pray to stone images, to feed cows while humans starve, and to burn women to death when their husbands died, I too would accuse them of leading people into darkness. After a moment of silence, my friend agreed.

Please do not misunderstand what Paul is saying here. He is *not* saying that Christians are culturally, ethnically, racially, or even morally superior to people from the Indian subcontinent. No! Look again at 5:8, "For *you* were once darkness, but *now you* are light in the Lord." The great divide we as Christians experience is found not in geography but in chronology. The divide is not in place, but in time. It is not that people from this or that place are in darkness. *All* people are born in darkness, Paul says at the beginning of chapter 2. And a time came in each Christian's life when he or she came out of the darkness into the light by the gift of faith that God gives. When we become Christians truly and personally, we move from darkness into light, whatever shade of darkness we happened to dwell in before—Hindu or Jewish, Pentecostal or Baptist, Roman Catholic or secular. We move from the religious and cultural context in which we were raised into the light of God in a personal knowing of Jesus Christ.

Paul says we should no longer partner with the dark ways that characterized our lives before knowing Christ. Nor should we partner with anyone who claims to be a Christian yet continues to live openly and unrepentantly in darkness. We should in no way let them think they are talking about the same good news of the gospel that we proclaim. This is a wrong kind of unity.

We should not be united in the church apart from the true work of God's grace.

WHY GOD HAS DONE THIS

Finally, the letter to the Ephesians prompts us to ask why God has done all this. What is the reason for his grace?

Here in this little letter to the Ephesians, we probably have more clarity on God's ultimate purpose for creation than in any other book of the Bible. It provides one of the clearest statements in the Bible on what God is ultimately doing, even more than in Paul's letter to the Romans or in John's book of Revelation. If you have not read Ephesians, and if you want to know what God is up to, read this little book. It will take you about thirty minutes.

In Ephesians, Paul pulls the camera back to the widest angle. That is evident in small ways. For instance, this is the only letter in which Paul talks more about the universal church than the local church. It is also evident in large ways. There are at least five places in Ephesians where God appears to tell us *why* he created the world (1:3-10; 1:11-14; 2:1-10; 3:7-13; 3:20-21). In short, God has created the world for his own good pleasure (see 1:9). And for his own good pleasure he seeks the praise of his people for his grace and his wisdom.

For the Praise of His Glorious Grace

Immediately following the salutations, Paul begins his letter,

> Praise be to the God and Father of our Lord Jesus Christ, who has blessed us in the heavenly realms with every spiritual blessing in Christ. For he chose us in him before the creation of the world to be holy and blameless in his sight. In love he predestined us to be adopted as his sons through Jesus Christ, in accordance with his pleasure and will—to the praise of his glorious grace, which he has freely given us in the One he loves. In him we have redemption through his blood, the forgiveness of sins, in accordance with the riches of God's grace that he lavished on us with all wisdom and understanding. And he made known to us the mystery of his will according to his good pleasure, which he purposed in Christ, to be put into effect when the times will have reached their fulfillment—to bring all things in heaven and on earth together under one head, even Christ (1:3-10).

In verse 5 we learn that the purpose of our being predestined to adoption as sons of God through Jesus Christ was "in accordance with his pleasure and will." Why? Verse 6 answers, "to the praise of his glorious grace."

Further statements about why God has done what he has done occur in the next verses:

> In him we were also chosen, having been predestined according to the plan of him who works out everything in conformity with the purpose of his will, in order that we, who were the first to hope in Christ, might be for the praise of his glory. And you also were included in Christ when you heard the word of truth, the gospel of your salvation. Having believed, you were marked in him with a seal, the promised Holy Spirit, who is a deposit guaranteeing our inheritance until the redemption of those who are God's possession—to the praise of his glory (1:11-14).

In verse 11, Paul says we who are Christians were chosen, or predestined, according to the purpose of his will. Okay, but why? Why is this his will? Verse 12 answers, "that we . . . might be for the praise of his glory," just like he said in verse 6. Verse 13 goes on to say that we who are in Christ are marked and given a deposit in the Holy Spirit, who guarantees our redemption. Again, why? Verse 14 answers, "to the praise of his glory."

For Showing His Grace

But how is it that our election, our adoption, and our redemption amount to God's praise? Well, they certainly do not amount to *our* praise. We do not save ourselves, as we have already seen in chapter 2 of Ephesians. Let's look there again: "As for you, you were dead in your transgressions and sins, in which you used to live when you followed the ways of this world and of the ruler of the kingdom of the air, the spirit who is now at work in those who are disobedient. All of us also lived among them at one time, gratifying the cravings of our sinful nature and following its desires and thoughts. Like the rest, we were by nature objects of wrath. But because of his great love for us, God, who is rich in mercy, made us alive with Christ even when we were dead in transgressions—it is by grace you have been saved. And God raised us up with Christ and seated us with him in the heavenly realms in Christ Jesus, in order that in the coming ages he might show the incomparable riches of his grace, expressed in his kindness to us in Christ Jesus. For it is by grace you have been saved, through faith—and this not from yourselves, it is the gift of God—not by works, so that no one can boast. For we are God's workmanship, created in Christ Jesus to do good works, which God prepared in advance for us to do" (2:1-10). According to 2:9, our salvation is certainly nothing for us to boast about. Indeed, if you do boast about it, you misunderstand something very fundamental. Paul says in verse 6 that God has raised us up with Christ from death and seated us with him in the heavenly realms. Why? So that we would be glorified and could boast? No, he has done it so that "in the coming ages God might show the incomparable riches of his grace, expressed in his kindness to us in Christ Jesus." Isn't that amazing? God is graciously granting us salvation so that he might show the incomparable riches of his grace.

For Displaying His Wisdom to All Creation

God intends to display not only his grace but also his wisdom. We see this as Paul recounts his own call to the ministry:

> I became a servant of this gospel by the gift of God's grace given me through the working of his power. Although I am less than the least of all God's people, this grace was given me: to preach to the Gentiles the unsearchable riches of Christ, and to make plain to everyone the administration of this mystery, which for ages past was kept hidden in God, who created all things. His intent was that now,

through the church, the manifold wisdom of God should be made known to the rulers and authorities in the heavenly realms, according to his eternal purpose which he accomplished in Christ Jesus our Lord. In him and through faith in him we may approach God with freedom and confidence. I ask you, therefore, not to be discouraged because of my sufferings for you, which are your glory (3:7-13).

Paul says that grace was given to him to preach and make plain the riches of knowing Christ. Okay, but why? Why did God intend for Paul to make these mysteries plain? The answer is in 3:10: that the manifold wisdom of God should be made known through the church.

If you want to know why there is evil and suffering in the world and are looking for an answer in the Bible, you will find it here and maybe in Romans 9: that now through the church, God's great wisdom should be made known. To whom will his wisdom be made known? Paul says in Ephesians 3:10 it will be to the rulers and authorities in the heavenly realms. Who are they? It is difficult to say exactly, but they are certainly creatures of God and probably cosmic intelligences. They are not omniscient, but they are watching. They are probably both good and bad—righteous angels and evil demons. Somehow these creatures whom God has made are watching what he does in his creation.

To God Be Glory in the Church and in Christ Forever

In light of God's glorious display of grace and wisdom before all the heavenly hosts, we cannot help but doxologize with Paul:

> Now to him who is able to do immeasurably more than all we ask or imagine, according to his power that is at work within us, to him be glory in the church and in Christ Jesus throughout all generations, for ever and ever! Amen (3:20-21).

God will be glorified in the church and in Christ Jesus forever in the way we his people are redeemed, in the way we live it out, and in the way we will forever be his. God has decided to bring glory to himself through our redemption—we who are sinners! How many other ways could he have used us to bring glory to himself! Is this not amazing? Consider the people you attend church with. Consider the person you see in the mirror every morning. The all-powerful God of the universe extraordinarily chooses to glorify himself through us, his church. We display the character of God to his creation, and so bring him glory.

Perhaps the last thing Jonathan Edwards wrote as a missionary pastor among the Native Americans in Stockbridge, Massachusetts, before taking the presidency of the college at Princeton was a short dissertation titled, "The End for Which God Created the World." It was first published in 1765, a few years after his death. In it Edwards asks, "Why did God make the world?" He sorts carefully through all kinds of chief ends and ultimate ends. But he determines there is, and can be, only one last and highest end or purpose. What is that? God's own glory, Edwards said. That is, to satisfy himself. God's very nature is revealed to be one that eternally communicates his own fullness. God was not thinking fundamentally of his creatures' good, but of "himself and his own infinite, internal glory."[6]

The great truth that Edwards gleaned from scores of passages in the Old and New Testaments is that God does what he does in order to make himself known.[7] This is why he delivered Israel from Egypt in the Exodus, and why he delivered them again from the exile in Babylon. He created the world and acts in it for his own praise, and it is right and good that he does so. This is why Calvin referred to this world as the theater of God's splendor. Others have referred to history as one great parade culminating in the glory of God.

I do not know why you think you are here in this life, but both you and I—Christian or not—are made in the image of God. We were placed on this planet to be walking pictures of the moral nature and righteous character of God, reflecting him for the universe to see and redounding forever to his glory. God is most glorified in Christ, and in our union with God through him. And he has done all this, and calls us to join together with him, not for our glory but for his own.

CONCLUSION

Today, many Christians around the world are being persecuted for their faith. It is easy for us in the West to forget how much suffering Christians throughout history have undergone in order to spread the gospel to a troubled world. More than thirty-five years ago, a number of popular revolts in what is today the Democratic Republic of the Congo (formerly Zaire) were particularly costly and bloody. In November 1964, hundreds of Americans, Belgians, and other foreigners were trapped and held hostage by a group of rebels who called themselves Simbas (lions). Among them was a twenty-eight-year-old bachelor, Bill McChesney, an evangelist on his first term as a missionary.

"Smiling Bill," as everyone called him, had struggled for several years with what to do with his life until finally concluding that the Lord had called him

---

[6] There are many versions in which you can purchase Edwards's book, but perhaps none is so useful as can be found in John Piper's *God's Passion for His Glory* (Wheaton, Ill.: Crossway, 1998). Piper republishes the whole of Edwards's work, along with an extended introduction of his own. The passage cited here is cited on page 248 of Piper's book.

[7] For example, see Ex. 7:5; Deut. 4:34-35; Job 37:6-7; Ps. 106:8; 22:21-22; Isa. 49:22-23; 64:4; Ezek. 20:34-38, 42, 44; 28:25-26; 36:11; 37:6, 13; John 17:26; Rom. 2:4-7.

to missions. Before leaving for Africa, he printed a poem called "My Choice"
in a World Evangelization Crusade publication:

I want my breakfast served at eight,
With ham and eggs upon the plate
A well-broiled steak I'll eat at one,
And dine again when day is done.

I want an ultramodern home
And in each room a telephone
Soft carpets, too, upon the floors,
And pretty drapes to grace the doors.

A cozy place of lovely things,
Like easy chairs with inner springs,
And then I'll get a small TV—
Of course, "I'm careful what I see."

I want my wardrobe, too, to be
Of neatest, finest quality,
With latest style in suit and vest:
Why should not Christians have the best?

But then the Master I can hear
In no uncertain voice, so clear:
"I bid you come and follow Me,
The lowly Man of Galilee."

"Birds of the air have made their nest,
And foxes in their holes find rest,
But I can offer you no bed;
No place have I to lay My head."

In shame I hung my head and cried.
How could I spurn the Crucified?
Could I forget the way He went,
The sleepless nights in prayer He spent?

For forty days without a bite,
Alone He fasted day and night;
Despised, rejected—on He went,
And did not stop till veil He rent.

A man of sorrows and of grief,
No earthly friend to bring relief;
"Smitten of God," the prophet said—
Mocked, beaten, bruised, His blood ran red.

If He be God, and died for me,
No sacrifice too great can be
For me, a mortal man, to make;
I'll do it all for Jesus' sake.

Yes, I will tread the path He trod,
No other way will please my God;
So, henceforth, this my choice shall be,
My choice for all eternity.[8]

That was written around 1960. Do you think that the average twenty-four-year-old today might write about those things as his or her *rights?* The right to home? The right to physical health? The right to entertainment? Would most twenty-four-year-olds so quickly surrender them to Christ?

Well, one morning in mid-November, Simba soldiers came for young Bill McChesney, who was then sick with malaria. He was thrown into a truck to be taken to a prison. A missionary friend from Britain, Jim Rodgers, jumped on the truck voluntarily when he saw the soldiers take Bill. En route, the soldiers beat malaria-weakened Bill mercilessly. By the time the truck reached the prison, Bill could no longer stand. Jim carried him to a small cell, already crammed with forty other people.

The next morning a Simba colonel ordered the prisoners into the courtyard, where a mob had gathered. He separated the prisoners by nationality. He asked Bill and Jim if they were American. Bill nodded weakly. Jim replied, "British." The colonel pulled Bill away from Jim and prepared to kill Bill, but Jim stepped up next to Bill and said, "If you must die, brother, I'll die with you." Another prisoner yelled out to the colonel not to kill Jim: "He's an Englishman." The colonel again asked Jim what his nationality was. Jim said nothing. "Doesn't matter. American—British—they're all alike," the colonel said, and motioned the mob toward the two missionaries. The two missionaries were beaten. So weak was Bill McChesney that he died almost immediately. Jim caught Bill as he died, and laid him on the ground. The mob then knocked Jim down and trampled upon him until he was dead. By the riot's end, almost

---

[8] Reprinted in James and Marti Hefley, *By Their Blood: Christian Martyrs of the Twentieth Century*, 2nd ed. (Grand Rapids, Mich.: Baker, 1996), 519-520.

thirty people were dead, many of them missionaries. The bodies were taken to the Wamba River and tossed in to be eaten by crocodiles.[9]

Do you think such a horrendous death was really Bill's choice? When that smiling, self-confident twenty-four-year-old man wrote that poem and had it published in his missionary organization magazine, was that his choice? Why would anyone choose that?

Thousands of Christians were killed in the Simba uprisings over thirty-five years ago. At the time, the population of the Belgian Congo, or Zaire, was less than 10 percent evangelical. Today, after thousands of Christians and hundreds of missionaries were killed, the nation is about 25 percent evangelical. A remarkable growth of churches is still reported, even in the last few years.

Do you remember what Paul said to the Ephesians, who may have been discouraged or even ashamed that Paul was in prison for preaching the gospel to the Gentiles? "I ask you, therefore, not to be discouraged because of my sufferings for you, which are your glory" (3:13). Sometime after his Roman imprisonment, Paul was again arrested for preaching the gospel. But this time, according to tradition, he was beheaded. They cut his head off with a sword.

Neither Paul nor Bill McChesney nor his British friend Jim were preoccupied with their rights. Instead, they were ready to surrender their rights for the sake of Christ, the unity we have in him, and the unity we have with one another. Our unity in God's grace brings God glory, so that the very circumstances he has ordered for your life and mine, including suffering, are a special way he has given us to live a life of love and to display his character and glory.

Whatever circumstances you face in your life today, God is calling you to reflect his glory by being united to Christ and to other Christians. You might be mocked by friends when you tell them all humanity is lost in darkness, or you might bring the gospel to people who will kill you, like Bill McChesney and Jim Rodgers.

As with bereft Job, and childless Abraham, and pregnant Mary, and imprisoned Paul, and crucified Jesus, God is calling you and me to show, to display, to demonstrate that God in Christ is sufficient amid plenty and amid suffering, and to show it to the entire world. That which is most important is something that this world can neither give nor take away: God's grace. Grace is not a right, it is the gift of God.

---

[9] Ibid, 531-532.

Let us pray:

Lord God, we pray that you would work in each one of our hearts, showing us what we are truly living for according to the choices we have made, and what you think of those choices. In your great grace, we pray that you would bring our deathbeds before our very eyes to prepare us for them. Help us be prepared to meet you so that we may live every week and month and year in this life you give with a lightness of heart, a deep love for you, and a self-givingness as we work with other people. Give us hearts of gratitude and of world-defying hope. O God, forgive us for each hour this last week that we have defined ourselves in sadness, self-pity, and even anger over our circumstances. God, cause us to look above the small walls around us to you and to your great plan, and to the wonderful privilege you give us of showing your great grace to your creation. Work that in our hearts, Lord, we pray for Jesus' sake. Amen.

Questions for Reflection

1. What rights would you say you have? Have you ever considered where your rights come from? Does anyone have the right to take away your rights? What about God?

2. Do we have a right to election or salvation? If not, is God unfair to those he does not elect? Explain.

3. If God is completely sovereign, why should we pray?

4. In chapter 1, Paul prays, [17] "I keep asking that the God of our Lord Jesus Christ, the glorious Father, may give you the Spirit of wisdom and revelation, so that you may know him better. [18] I pray also that the eyes of your heart may be enlightened in order that you may know the hope to which he has called you, the riches of his glorious inheritance in the saints, [19] and his incomparably great power for us who believe." What does Paul pray that God would give to his readers in verse 17? Why? What does he pray God would do in verse 18? What three reasons does he give in verses 18 and 19 for why he wants God to do this? Are these the things you want for your children? Spouse? Parents? Friends? Pastor? Fellow church members? Ask God to grant them.

5. Based on what we have seen in the book of Ephesians, what effect can we expect teaching God's grace in Christ will have on the unity of a church, assuming the church is comprised of regenerate members?

6. What can we expect will happen when a church stresses unity but sets aside central doctrines of the faith such as the inspiration of the Scripture, the depravity of mankind, or the exclusive atonement of Christ? What are several examples of a wrong kind of unity?

7. We have seen that the longer you live as a Christian, the more you realize how central perseverance is in the Christian walk. It is easy to see how a Christian might live a life distinct from the world in adolescence (refraining from pleasures of the flesh) or middle age (not yielding to ambition and materialism), but what about old age? How does a Christian in life's sunset years live distinctly, and so be a witness?

8. The examples of John writing Revelation from exile on Patmos and Paul writing Ephesians from prison provoke the question, what often happens when the world exerts its fullest power to oppose the gospel? What relevance does this have to your life and ministries?

9. According to Ephesians 3:10-11, what is God's ultimate purpose for the church? How can we carry this purpose into what we do when the church gathers? Does this have any implications for evangelism? If so, what?

10. How does God glorify himself in the lives of sinful human beings?

11. Do the *first* few stanzas or the *last* few stanzas of Bill McChesney's poem better characterize you? How does a person grow from one viewpoint to the other?

12. What rights do you have *as a Christian?* Are you willing to give them up? For what?

13. What are some ways you can actively give up your rights right *now* for your spouse? For your children? For your church?

THE MESSAGE OF PHILIPPIANS: HUMILITY

"I AM THE 'UMBLEST PERSON GOING!"

INTRODUCING PHILIPPIANS

OBSERVATION #1: THE PHILIPPIANS AND PAUL CARE FOR EACH OTHER (2:19-30)

The Philippian Concern: The Example of Epaphroditus (2:25-30)

Paul's Concern: The Example of Timothy (2:19-24)

OBSERVATION #2: PAUL HAS A PATTERN OF LOVING MINISTRY TO THEM (1:1-11)

OBSERVATION #3: PAUL MINISTERS THROUGH HARD CIRCUMSTANCES (1:12-26)

OBSERVATION #4: PAUL EXHORTS THE PHILIPPIANS TO FOLLOW HIS EXAMPLE (1:27-30; 3:7-4:23)

OBSERVATION #5: THE PHILIPPIANS HAD ALSO BEEN PRESENTED WITH THE WAY OF PRIDE (3:1-6, 18-19)

OBSERVATION #6: CHRIST HIMSELF WENT THE WAY OF HUMILITY (2:1-11)

OBSERVATION #7: THE PHILIPPIANS SHOULD RELY ON GOD, EVEN IN SUFFERING (2:12-18)

CONCLUSION

11

THE MESSAGE OF PHILIPPIANS: HUMILITY

"I AM THE 'UMBLEST PERSON GOING!"[1]

"The world will little note nor long remember what we say here." Abraham Lincoln said that in his Gettysburg Address on November 19, 1863, in Gettysburg, Pennsylvania. His speech commemorated one of the bloodiest battles of the Civil War. Thousands of soldiers on both sides had been killed on the battlefield the previous July. A great cemetery had been constructed, and part of it was to be dedicated as a National Soldiers' Cemetery. To solemnize the event, the organizers secured one of the best-known speakers of the day, Edward Everett, former everything—president of Harvard, governor of Massachusetts, U.S. senator, secretary of State—to be the keynote speaker. And, in a surprise acceptance from a rather perfunctory invitation, the organizers also got President Lincoln. Lincoln had determined to travel from Washington, even if to offer only a few dedicatory remarks. Everett spoke for two hours, a normal time for such an address in those days. Sometimes such speeches would last three or four hours. The public was accustomed to it, and they were accustomed to standing for the duration of an address. Lincoln spoke for just three minutes, which was short even for dedicatory remarks.

"The world will little note nor long remember what we say here." That was from his brief address, and I guess he was wrong, wasn't he? The words themselves are now carved in stone in the Lincoln Memorial at one end of Washington, D.C.'s Mall. When I was in school, every student had to memorize the Gettysburg Address and repeat it in front of our seventh-grade history class. Far from being forgotten, this is one of the most well-known speeches in the English language. Everett wrote Lincoln several days after the speech and

[1] This sermon was originally preached on November 21, 1999, at Capitol Hill Baptist Church in Washington, D.C.

said, "I should be glad if I could flatter myself that I came as near to the central idea of the occasion in two hours as you did in two minutes."

And yet there is something attractive about Lincoln's kind of modesty, isn't there? "The world will little note nor long remember what we say here." Even the president of the United States, who had himself exerted considerable effort preparing the text of his brief address, seemed genuinely not to expect his words to be remembered. The crowds were there to hear Edward Everett. Lincoln was simply going to give a few brief dedicatory remarks. What do we call such a turn of mind? Humility, perhaps?

When I say humility, I know the word has positive connotations in a Christian church. We think of appropriate decorum. We think of not tooting our own horn. We think of propriety and deference. All positive things.

But did you know that in the ancient world in which Paul wrote, and from which most of the early Christians came, humility was not considered a virtue? Humility was regarded more like we regard servility. At best, it was obsequiousness, and at worst it was weakness. You might think of the character Uriah Heep in Charles Dickens's great novel *David Copperfield*. At one point, Heep says, "I am well aware that I am the 'umblest person going. . . . My mother is likewise a very 'umble person. We live in a 'umble abode." The falsely humble Heep is a great image of how many in the ancient world perceived "humility."

Today, many people would agree with the ancient attitude. Self-esteem and self-assertiveness are virtues in our culture now in a way they were not one hundred years ago. Today, a certainty of ego and an assurance of one's own greatness are the traits we cultivate, as in Garrison Keillor's storied Lake Wobegon community, "where all the children are above average." People on the street shake their heads in condescending wonder when we Christians sing hymns that express our lostness and frailty, when we confess our sins, or when we speak about deserving death. German philosopher Friedrich Nietzsche wrote that, "The trodden worm curls up. . . . Thus it reduces its chances of being trodden upon again. In the language of morality: Humility."[2]

How about you? What do you think of humility?

Let me ask the question in a different way. In the more difficult challenges of life that you face right now, do you conceive of acknowledging your neediness as a help or a hindrance? Whenever you feel insufficient in yourself, do you reflexively think of that sense of insufficiency as part of the problem or part of the solution?

These questions will probably not feel important to you as long as life is going fine. But I promise, your estimate of these questions will grow when life

---

[2] Source unknown.

becomes difficult, especially when the difficulty results from following Christ: when you cannot cut corners at work because your conscience says no; when you feel embarrassed that people know you are a Christian; when you cannot sleep with whomever you want to; when because you are a Christian you are not promoted; when you are deprived of educational or financial opportunities because of your faith; or maybe when you are imprisoned. When any of these things begin to bother you, you will reconsider the merit of Christian humility and weakness. If you do not leave the faith straight away, you may look for some way to alter your doctrines so that you can preserve your pride, your options, your very self. Many people today—even church members—have done just this.

INTRODUCING PHILIPPIANS

If this sounds like you, or if humility sounds like an irrelevant or minor virtue—certainly not a virtue relevant to a strong, brave follower of Jesus Christ and a disciple-till-you-die kind of faith—then Paul's letter to the Philippians is a brief Bible book you need to consider. Philippians is called one of Paul's "prison letters" because Paul wrote it while in prison. If you are new to the Christian faith, this may come as a surprise. But it is true, and it needs to be borne in mind when reading this letter. When Paul wrote it, he was a convict. Now, convicts are not generally lionized. There were not millions of adoring Christians gathered outside his cell, peering in with awe as the great apostle Paul wrote every line to the Philippians. Anybody looking in would have seen an aging religious gadfly, a troublesome ne'er-do-well. Here was this old man, perhaps with breaking health, sitting and scribbling on a piece of parchment.

We also need to bear in mind the audience to whom Paul was writing: a group of Christians in Philippi, which was located in what we think of as northern Greece. They were discouraged and fearful because of Paul's imprisonment for preaching the gospel. So if you want to know how to read this letter, think of Paul writing to a group of young, scared, and discouraged Christians because he is in prison for preaching the gospel.

We do not know exactly when Paul wrote this letter, but it was clearly during an imprisonment in which Paul was staring, at least in his mind's eye, at the gleam of the executioner's sword. It is amazing what comes into focus when you think that life is about to end.

Turning to the letter, we will divide our study into seven observations about Paul's relationship with the Philippians, Paul's example, and Paul's instructions to them. I pray that by the end we will better understand not only the humility of Paul but also the humility of Christ, as well as the humility we gain through knowing him.

OBSERVATION #1: THE PHILIPPIANS AND PAUL CARE FOR EACH OTHER (2:19-30)

The Philippian Christians' and Paul's care for one another is very apparent in this letter. This is our first observation. We can begin our attempt to understand this letter, as well as this mutual care, by noticing the person with the funny name at the end of chapter 2: Epaphroditus. In order to understand why Epaphroditus is significant, we return to Acts 16, where we find an account of how the church at Philippi got started. Epaphroditus's role is easy to understand, and yet it is typical of what this whole letter is about.

The Philippian Concern: The Example of Epaphroditus (2:25-30)

At the end of Acts 15 and beginning of Acts 16, Paul and Silas set out on Paul's second missionary journey with plans to travel beyond the south central region of Asia Minor (what we know as Turkey) into its northern parts. But God called Paul to cross over into Europe, specifically, into Macedonia, to preach the gospel (Acts 16:6-10). Paul and Silas did, and they immediately went to the leading city—Philippi. The first person we have record of becoming a Christian in Philippi was Lydia, an Asian businesswoman who had settled in the city (16:11-15). Eventually, Paul's preaching of the gospel interfered with the economic well-being of one boisterous citizen, who promptly hauled Paul before the magistrates and began a riot. The magistrates stripped, beat, severely flogged, and imprisoned Paul. At midnight, Paul and Silas sat in prison "praying and singing hymns to God, and the other prisoners were listening to them" (16:25). What an amazing attitude! Paul had been heckled, hauled before a magistrate, and imprisoned, and now he sat in a jail praying and singing hymns at midnight. It was as if Paul knew God was in control and that everything had happened according to God's good plan. Then there was an earthquake, which gave Paul the chance to come under the personal custody of the prison jailer. Paul promptly preached to the jailer, and the jailer was saved, along with his household. The next day, Paul and Silas were asked to leave the city.

The Philippians must have been deeply grateful to Paul. He had brought them the gospel at personal expense to himself. So when they heard about Paul's imprisonment, they sent Epaphroditus to support him. And this is where we pick up the story in the end of Philippians 2, where Paul describes Epaphroditus this way: "my brother, fellow worker and fellow soldier, who is also your messenger, whom you sent to take care of my needs" (2:25). Not all the Philippians could visit Paul, so they sent Epaphroditus (see also 4:18). Apparently, after helping Paul, Epaphroditus himself became quite ill. So Paul is sending him back to the Philippians with this thank-you letter in hand to assure them that both he and Epaphroditus are alright. Paul writes, "Welcome him in the Lord with great joy, and honor men like him, because he almost died for the work of Christ, risking his life to make up for the help you could not give me" (2:29-30). The Philippians clearly cared about Paul, and Epaphroditus embodied that concern. He had risked his life for Paul.

It is remarkable how well the Philippians remembered Paul and cherished him. It raises the question, should we ever stop praying for people? When they move out of our lives, is it okay to stop praying for them? We do not know how many years had passed since Paul planted this church in Philippi. Yet the Philippians continued to care for Paul. And they did so probably because he was their father in the gospel. If you are a Christian, I wonder if you have any idea where the person is who first shared the gospel with you? Are you concerned for him or her? That is how these Philippians cared about Paul. They cherished deeply their father in the gospel.

Paul's Concern: The Example of Timothy (2:19-24)

Paul reciprocated the Philippians' love. A little earlier in chapter 2, he says not only is he sending Epaphroditus to Philippi with the letter, he promises to send Timothy as well. And Paul cares a lot about Timothy! Yet he shows his love by sending this son in the ministry to them. Paul writes,

> I hope in the Lord Jesus to send Timothy to you soon, that I also may be cheered when I receive news about you. I have no one else like him, who takes a genuine interest in your welfare. For everyone looks out for his own interests, not those of Jesus Christ. But you know that Timothy has proved himself, because as a son with his father he has served with me in the work of the gospel (2:19-22).

Paul had seen Timothy work, and he knew Timothy would humbly give himself for others. He could also bring Paul reports of the Philippians. Timothy was the right one to send.

In Timothy, we learn something about the qualifications for ministry. People often speak of public presence or the ability to speak. But notice why Paul sends Timothy: Timothy has a genuine concern for others.

OBSERVATION #2: PAUL HAS A PATTERN OF LOVING MINISTRY TO THEM (1:1-11)

A second observation: we know that Paul's concern for the Philippians was nothing new. His loving ministry began when Paul first preached the gospel to them, as recorded in Acts 16, and it picks up again at the beginning of this letter. Paul writes, "Paul and Timothy, servants of Christ Jesus" (1:1). As we saw in our Ephesians study, his introductions provide a little hint of what he will discuss later in the letter. Here, Paul refers to himself as a "servant." He is hundreds of miles away in prison, and what is he doing? Thinking of the Philippians. Writing to them. Praying for them. Thanking God for them. Sending Epaphroditus and his beloved Timothy to them. Encouraging them. Longing for their good in Christ. In short, he is serving them.

Since the beginning, Paul and the Philippians had worked together with common hopes and ambitions. Paul mentions their "partnership in the gospel from the first day until now" (1:5). They both know God, and their love in Christ overflows into mutual affection and loving care. So Paul writes,

> It is right for me to feel this way about all of you, since I have you in my heart; for whether I am in chains or defending and confirming the gospel, all of you share in God's grace with me. God can testify how I long for all of you with the affection of Christ Jesus (1:7-8).

Paul longs for these Philippians as naturally as a parent longs for a child. He is not one of those people with a grand evangelistic vision who loves all the world in general but never seems to love anyone in particular. No, Paul's heart actually fixes on particular people.

So he does what no prison or chains can bind—he prays for them:

> And this is my prayer: that your love may abound more and more in knowledge and depth of insight, so that you may be able to discern what is best and may be pure and blameless until the day of Christ, filled with the fruit of righteousness that comes through Jesus Christ—to the glory and praise of God (1:9-11).

Paul prays that the Philippians' love may more and more abound in knowledge. And he wants their love to abound in knowledge so that they might discern what is best. Their love should be a discerning love. Sometimes we do not think of love and wisdom together. But Paul knows that wise love makes wise lives and that foolish love makes foolish lives. Or as he says here, they must have wise love *so that* they can have lives marked by moral purity, blamelessness, and righteousness until Christ returns (if you have an NIV, scratch out the "and" halfway through verse 10 and insert "so that," which is what the Greek says—"so that you may be pure"). He wants their relationships with God and with each other to prosper, always maintained with the great final day of Christ in view. Hope in the final day keeps Paul himself going. As he prays for them in that last phrase, he does it all "to the glory and praise of God."

What finally motivates Paul is not his own praise. It is not the Philippians' glory and praise. It is the glory and praise of God.

What a wonderful prayer! Have you ever looked to Paul's prayers as models for your own prayers? Our church encourages its members to pray regularly through the church membership directory, which we print to fit easily into most Bibles. The most frequent negative comment I receive about this practice is always, "I don't know some of these people; how can I pray for them?" The answer is easy. Take the prayers Paul prays in the New Testament, and use them to pray for the other members of the church with whom you have covenanted together.[3]

OBSERVATION #3: PAUL MINISTERS THROUGH HARD CIRCUMSTANCES (1:12-26)

Paul's ambition to see God praised and glorified enabled him to continue ministry through hard circumstances—our third observation. Several of these difficulties are enumerated in the remainder of chapter 1, accompanied by Paul's resolute determination to see Christ glorified.

Verses 12 to 14 refer to Paul's imprisonment. The Philippians may worry that Paul's imprisonment is a defeat for Paul and the gospel. But Paul writes,

> Now I want you to know, brothers, that what has happened to me has really served to advance the gospel. As a result, it has become clear throughout the whole palace guard and to everyone else that I am in chains for Christ. Because of my chains, most of the brothers in the Lord have been encouraged to speak the word of God more courageously and fearlessly.

Paul hardly sees his imprisonment as a defeat. And his words are no morning-after spin of how the lost vote was really a victory. Paul believed it and lived it. Because of his imprisonment, more people had heard of Christ, and fellow Christians had been emboldened to speak about Christ. In our study of Ephesians, we saw that Christians often become more fearless when the enemy executes his plans, because the enemy's powerlessness will be exposed in his very attacks. When we see the saints suffering for the gospel *and* continuing in their faith, we can expect God's grace to use that suffering to spread the gospel. So Paul continues ministering even in prison.

In 1:15-18, Paul refers to the hypocritical preachers who had been taking advantage of people for their own profit. Paul is not starry-eyed. He knows not

---

[3] If you want to know more about using Paul's prayers in your own prayer life, D. A. Carson has a great book called, *Call to Spiritual Reformation* (Grand Rapids, Mich.: Baker, 1992), which we encourage for use in small group Bible studies or one-on-one discipleship. Carson studies Paul's prayers in the New Testament and examines them specifically as models for our prayers.

everyone is a hero. Some people, he says, "preach Christ out of envy and rivalry . . . [and] out of selfish ambition, not sincerely, supposing that they can stir up trouble for me while I am in chains" (1:15, 17). And this is not Paul's idea. Jesus himself taught that some people would teach only for money. Yet, says Paul, so what! "What does it matter? The important thing is that in every way, whether from false motives or true, Christ is preached. And because of this I rejoice" (1:18). God sovereignly uses even hypocrites for his own glory.

We face the same realities today, which raises the question, what do we make of all the hypocrites in the church? If you are a Christian, perhaps you can remember being a non-Christian pointing to the hypocrisy of Christians to avoid becoming a Christian yourself. Perhaps you still hear this from your non-Christian friends: "Forget Christianity! Look at all the hypocrites in the church." Well, as a friend once said to me, "You can't help who agrees with you." The truth is the truth is the truth. People who name the name of Christ and who speak the truth may themselves live in a way that does not commend the gospel. We should recognize that fact. In fact, we can be encouraged that servants who are inept or even insincere cannot ultimately halt God's work. Think about the Christians you know; think about yourself; and you will remember that God is a master at using the unlikely. We serve the God who calls old men to father many nations and lead revolutions, young men to fight experienced warriors and to tell off kings to their faces. We serve the God who chose to bring his Son into the world through a young virgin. He called tax collectors for Rome to be friends with Israel's Messiah, and a middle-aged academic bigot to take the gospel to the Gentiles. He can use you and me. We are well within the scope of his sovereign ability to use us for his glory.

Do not misunderstand me here. God's inability to be defeated by hypocrisy is no excuse for hypocrisy. Paul knows these individuals will be severely judged. As James says, those who teach "will be judged more strictly" (James 3:1). Noble actions cannot hide ignoble motives from the gaze of God.

Still, Paul knows that the furtherance of God's rule and reign is not dependent upon uncertain and insincere servants. In fact, we see from Paul's meditations in Philippians 1:19-26 he was certain that even death could not stop God's plan. In this long paragraph, Paul considers the possibility of his death being near. He concludes that his death means he will be with Christ, "which is better by far" (1:23b). Still, he is convinced he will remain alive, because "it is more necessary for you that I remain in the body" (1:24). Paul sees clearly that "Christ will be exalted in my body, whether by life or by death" (1:20). So he prays that he will have the courage to go whichever way most glorifies God. Honestly, that is amazing. Even amid thoughts of his own death, Paul is concerned for the Philippians. We tend to think our suffering justifies at least a little selfishness. Have you ever thought to yourself, "Times are real tough right now. Maybe under normal circumstances this would not be right. But God understands. I have a lot on my plate." No sign of that in Paul. Paul's chief concern, even when his own life is threatened, is the furtherance of the gospel in the lives of the Philippians.

If you are not willing to work for God in imperfect situations, then you are not willing to work, because that is all we have in this life. Paul is in prison unjustly, but Philippians is no long letter of complaint and whining. It is a letter of encouragement, and not just the encouragement of "Hey, I'll be alright" but the encouragement of "God is purposing and using these very difficulties! Can't you see?" How much of our anxiety has the fear of death behind it? Or the fear that we will be unable to handle whatever God is going to dish out? Of course that is why our Christian discipleship began with Jesus' call to come to him and die to ourselves. Once we die to ourselves, we know that neither imprisonment, nor insincere preachers, nor even death itself can stop God's plan.

OBSERVATION #4: PAUL EXHORTS THE PHILIPPIANS TO FOLLOW HIS EXAMPLE (1:27-30; 3:7–4:23)

Notice that Paul does not stop simply with saying, "Thank you for loving me. I love you too. Oh, and trust God with my difficulties." No, he keeps going, and this is where his letter gets a little harder, bringing us to our fourth observation. Paul tells the Philippians they need to follow his example by loving like he loves, with all the consequences that may bring.

In fact, Paul's instruction for the Philippian Christians to follow his example comprises much of this letter. At the end of chapter 1, he calls them to "conduct yourselves in a manner worthy of the gospel of Christ" and to "stand firm in one spirit, contending as one man for the faith of the gospel" (1:27). Then the last two chapters of the book are largely taken up with Paul exhorting the Philippians to follow his example, and thanking them for their help.

In 3:12-17, Paul sets out the way he is going, and by 3:20-21 he describes where this way will take him. So first he writes,

> Not that I have already obtained all this, or have already been made perfect, but I press on to take hold of that for which Christ Jesus took hold of me. Brothers, I do not consider myself yet to have taken hold of it. But one thing I do: Forgetting what is behind and straining toward what is ahead, I press on toward the goal to win the prize for which God has called me heavenward in Christ Jesus (3:12-14).

Unlike some other teachers, Paul makes no claim to be perfect. Instead he is oriented to the prize, and he keeps straining forward. Then he turns to the Philippians and tells them to follow him: "Join with others in following my example, brothers, and take note of those who live according to the pattern we gave you" (3:17).

I wonder if you think Paul sounds a bit radical at times. Perhaps his dedication suited him as an apostle, but his ministry was unique, not like yours or mine. Well, consider 3:20-21:

> Our citizenship is in heaven. And we eagerly await a Savior from there, the Lord Jesus Christ, who, by the power that enables him to bring everything under his control, will transform our lowly bodies so that they will be like his glorious body.

Paul's citizenship is ours, if we are Christians. His hope is ours—a Savior from heaven. And his expectation is ours—the transformation of our lowly bodies to be like Christ's glorious body. Paul simply presents us with the Christian life, and so he instructs us to follow his example.

In chapter 4, Paul exhorts these fellow Christians to "stand firm" (4:1), just as he has stood firm. To this end, he urges two women in the church who had been destructively quarrelling to agree with each other (4:2), and he urges the others in the church to help those two (4:3). To all of them he says, let your gentleness be evident to all (4:5); do not be anxious, but instead pray (4:6); think about whatever is good (4:8); and finally, "Whatever you have learned or received or heard from me, or seen in me—put it into practice" (4:9).

It is very important that in our ministry for Christ, whether as a pastor or as a member of a church, we present ourselves as visible models and examples to others. I promise you, people will follow your example. And I wonder, how do you feel when you think about the fact that people will follow your example? Does that make you happy and proud? Is it possible you are thinking, "I wish everybody talked like I talked yesterday," or "I wish everyone at church spent their money like I spend my money," or "I wish everyone valued other people exactly like I do"? At least three times in this letter, Paul explicitly urges the Philippians to follow his example. We do not learn only from spoken words. We learn by example. As Christians, we are all part of that learning process.

OBSERVATION #5: THE PHILIPPIANS HAD ALSO BEEN PRESENTED WITH THE WAY OF PRIDE (3:1-6, 18-19)

But honestly, isn't this a little difficult? This is where I think the Philippians might have gotten a little irritated, because Paul asks for some hard things. So I am not surprised by a fifth observation: another way had clearly been presented to the Philippians by some of their teachers: the way of pride.

It is easy to see how false teaching would beguile these young Christians. Perhaps disheartened by Paul's own imprisonment and facing persecution themselves, arguments in the church were becoming heated. Tempers were growing short. Fractures within the fellowship were beginning to show as the pressure mounted. These people were in just the right position to be lured into a brand of Christianity that promised rewards now, cash in hand, with palpable benefits and immediate security. Just manufacture a little righteousness and good feelings. Paul sees that such false teaching promises a high degree of self-satisfaction, and that these believers could be easily stampeded in a wrong direction, like a herd of confused animals. So he warns them,

> Watch out for those dogs, those men who do evil, those mutilators of the flesh.
> For it is we who are the circumcision, we who worship by the Spirit of God, who
> glory in Christ Jesus, and who put no confidence in the flesh (3:2-3).

Apparently, certain teachers in Philippi taught that to be a Christian, one had to first follow the Jewish requirement of circumcision. But this requirement is false and destructive, Paul says. What is being taught in the name of righteousness is evil itself. Teaching people to manufacture their own righteousness is directly at odds with the cross of Christ and everything it accomplished.

Another type of opposition is mentioned a few verses later:

> For, as I have often told you before and now say again even with tears, many live
> as enemies of the cross of Christ. Their destiny is destruction, their god is their stom-
> ach, and their glory is in their shame. Their mind is on earthly things (3:18-19).

Perhaps these enemies are the "mutilators of the flesh" already described; perhaps they are a different group. Whatever the particulars, the common element is a reliance on self and not on Christ. Their confidence rests in their power to achieve and not in God's promise to give. Such teaching has an allure for a little while, but it lasts no longer than the sunshine, because it is false. Only when life's circumstances are favorable can someone think well of himself or herself and follow this way of pride.

Proud people are preoccupied with what goes into the mouth, rather than what comes out of it. In other words, they are ultimately ruled by appetite. Material things take up their minds and hearts. They are consumed with earthly matters. Ironically, proud people glory in what should shame them: their own supposed records of obedience. Pride prevents them from seeing how thin and incomplete that record is.

And consider what happens with such people when life gets difficult. They have no way to deal with it. If your Christianity is wrapped up with the benefits it brings you now, you will not last, and it will become obvious that you are not a Christian. The imprisonment of Paul, to say nothing of the cross of

Christ itself, becomes irrational, senseless, and vain from the standpoint of a proud heart. There is no room for hardship and suffering. Any talk about such things as heavenly treasure has as much value as a ten dollar bill in rural Scotland. It's just not your currency. It is not what you value. But these are the very values that allow Paul to face imprisonment.

What destiny awaits these "enemies of the cross"? Consider 3:19 again: "Their destiny is destruction, their god is their stomach, and their glory is in their shame." They will become like the things they worship—earthly and ignorant of God. These teachers offer no hope because they are already in full possession of what they offer. Yes, maybe the bank account could get a little larger. Maybe the sense of one's own righteousness could get a bit larger when six more people are converted. But that's about it. The proud already have everything these teachers offer. And all they possess will come to nothing; in fact, it will come to destruction.

This was the other path that had been presented to the Philippians, and there must have been tremendous pressure to take it. How could they avoid it? It is the same pressure you feel when you want to go the way of obvious and immediate benefit rather than the way of following Christ. So why not go that way? What will stop you?

OBSERVATION #6: CHRIST HIMSELF WENT THE WAY OF HUMILITY (2:1-11)

Sixth, we observe that Christ himself went the way of humility. This is what Paul presents in the famous first eleven verses of chapter 2: "If you have any encouragement from being united with Christ, if any comfort from his love, if any fellowship with the Spirit, if any tenderness and compassion, then make my joy complete by being like-minded, having the same love, being one in spirit and purpose. Do nothing out of selfish ambition or vain conceit, but in humility consider others better than yourselves. Each of you should look not only to your own interests, but also to the interests of others. Your attitude should be the same as that of Christ Jesus: Who, being in very nature God, did not consider equality with God something to be grasped, but made himself nothing, taking on the very nature of a servant, being made in human likeness. And being found in appearance as a man, he humbled himself and became obedient to death—even death on a cross! Therefore God exalted him to the highest place and gave him the name that is above every name, that at the name of Jesus every knee should bow, in heaven and on earth and under the earth, and every tongue confess that Jesus Christ is Lord, to the glory of God the Father." In the first couple of verses, Paul encourages the Philippians to be united in outlook, in love, in spirit, and in compassion. But this unity will become increasingly difficult the more circumstances turn against them. Pressure causes cracks, fissures, and divisions, as when a nut is slowly squeezed in a nutcracker. The same thing happens to our faith when circumstances turn against us for professing Christ. The cracks begin to show. Paul knows that if these Philippians are to hold together, neither he nor they can rely on favorable circumstances. Events are already difficult and could change for the worse. Circumstances are never good ground for Christian unity. Such unity will last only as long as "everything is just the way I like it!"

Well, if unity is not found in circumstances, where is it found? The Philippians are to find their unity as their lives are shaped by the gospel of Jesus Christ. That is why Paul exhorts them in 2:5, "Your attitude should be the same as that of Christ Jesus."

Really, Paul gives two tests for the authenticity of the Philippians' profession of faith in this chapter: unity and humility. Are they united? And are they humble? Paul knows they cannot be united if they are not humble. Any unity manufactured apart from humility is a fraud. True Christian unity is rooted in our humility before Christ, in our awareness of our need, and in the fact that he meets that need fully and faithfully. Paul also knows the Philippians cannot be humble if they are not following the way of Christ by putting on his mind and being indwelt by his Spirit.

The humility of Christ is then described concisely and penetratingly. He did not grasp for equality with God. He made himself nothing. He took the very nature of a servant. He condescended to being found in appearance as a man. He humbled himself. He became obedient to death. He became obedient to death on a cross. What a striking presentation. The very one whom you and I claim to follow, Christ himself, went the way of perfect humility.

OBSERVATION #7: THE PHILIPPIANS SHOULD RELY ON GOD, EVEN IN SUFFERING (2:12-18)

Ultimately, the example and love of Christ should encourage the Philippians to continue relying on God and rejoicing in him, even through times of suffering. This is our final observation. Immediately following the heart transforming example of Christ in 2:6-11, Paul summarizes his basic message to the Philippians in this letter:

> Therefore, my dear friends, as you have always obeyed—not only in my presence, but now much more in my absence—continue to work out your salvation with fear and trembling, for it is God who works in you to will and to act according to his good purpose.

Do everything without complaining or arguing, so that you may become blameless and pure, children of God without fault in a crooked and depraved generation, in which you shine like stars in the universe as you hold out the word of life—in order that I may boast on the day of Christ that I did not run or labor for nothing. But even if I am being poured out like a drink offering on the sacrifice and service coming from your faith, I am glad and rejoice with all of you. So you too should be glad and rejoice with me (2:12-18).

We see in these verses that fulfilling the example of Christ in our own lives does not finally depend on us. God pours into us the ability to trust in him and his purposes: "it is God who works in you . . ." Paul has already mentioned God's sovereignty as the ground of his confidence and joy, back in chapter 1: "being confident of this, that he who began a good work in you will carry it on to completion until the day of Christ Jesus" (1:6). Now, however, Paul particularly exhorts them to work out their salvation while they rest in God's sovereignty— ". . . to work and to act according to his good purpose."

When Christians discover the doctrine of God's sovereignty, we discover great joy and assurance. We discover assurance of his victory: "He who began a good work in you will carry it on to completion." And we discover the joy of being called to participate with him in that victory: "it is God who works in you to will and to act according to his good purpose." Paul provides an excellent example of this joy when he writes that in all his prayers for the Philippians, "I always pray with joy" (1:4), even though he and the Philippians are both in difficult, even dangerous, situations.

These difficult and dangerous situations, strange as it may seem, provide opportunity for the working out of God's plan of salvation. The opposition the Philippians face is a sign to them that "you will be saved—and that by God. For it has been granted to you on behalf of Christ not only to believe on him, but also to suffer for him" (1:28-29). So when he directly exhorts them, "work out your salvation," he means that they, like Jesus himself, have been called— indeed, granted!—to persevere in not living for themselves but for others.

Friedrich Nietzsche did not understand the Christian idea of humility very well. Christian humility does not require fading out of sight, like a worm underfoot. It requires persevering in distinctiveness from the surrounding world as we give ourselves over to God's purposes by serving others. Jesus gave and gave and gave and gave and then was vindicated. So we should give and give and give and give and trust that one day we will be vindicated.

Furthermore, while working out their salvation, the Philippians are called to unity. "Do everything without complaining or arguing" (2:14), Paul says. He does not want them to be like the grumbling and complaining Israelites whom God delivered from Egypt. By this token, we must not fill up our churches with complaining even while God saves us from hell and sin. Instead, our churches should be filled with people who are thankful to God, and whose hearts are filled with great hope in his wonderful plans. Christian unity and thankfulness is important because it demonstrates we are true children of our heavenly Father, "without fault in a crooked and depraved generation." We are called in Christ to be pure amid the impure, light amid the darkness, life amid death. And what a wonderful image Paul uses to represent how Christians stand out: Christians are to shine like stars in the universe. You might picture the dark night of the world, with Christians reflecting the light of God gloriously sparkling against the black backdrop.

Consider the darkness of our argumentative, acquisitive, and self-assertive age, and then the bright sparkles of the church's witness as it grows in contentment in Christ. In your own life, you might think of the bondage that typifies the lives of your non-Christian friends, and how your own growing contentment in Christ can expose that bondage and point to the path of release. What a powerful ministry he is giving to you and me. What a wonderful ministry of liberation for the people around us who believe in such lies. This giving to others will noticeably mark a Christian life.

Clearly, Paul views his struggles and the Philippians' struggles in a way that is radically different from the way most people view hardship. As he says, "Even if I am being poured out like a drink offering on the sacrifice and service coming from your faith, I am glad and rejoice with all of you. So you too should be glad and rejoice with me" (2:17-18). This is simply a whole different way of thinking about suffering, about which the world has no clue. Paul is content for his labors among the Philippians to be modestly offered to God along with their sacrifice and service, even if these labors should culminate in his death. So too should you be content, he says to the Philippians—you have been called not just to begin the race but to endure it! These Philippian Christians, perhaps confused, perhaps becoming a bit fainthearted, needed to be reminded of the big picture. They needed to have their lives and struggles put in perspective.

Paul regularly goes to the central issues of the faith to instruct people on the most practical matters. Too often we expect our preachers to "Give me some more imperatives so that I know what to do right now." We are concerned with immediate advice, and are impatient with "theological instruction." Yet at the end of the day, no moral imperatives will constrain our obedience like the truth of the gospel of Christ in our hearts. Only in the gospel do we begin to understand more and more who God truly is and the glory he has prepared for us in Christ. When a Christian's heart is captivated by the immense love of Christ, we can preach the Bible's commands comparatively lightly. We can talk about anger management techniques, if you want, or flip through lots of how-to-live Christian books. But I would rather you start by meditating on the costliness of God's love for you in Christ, and on the great things that he has in store for you. Behavioristic techniques might serve some purpose. But I have a different agenda. As a Christian, I want to present the gospel of Jesus Christ to you, and I want to see your heart completely won by it.

The Philippians think they are Christians, but Paul is concerned about their fear. So he says, "No, no, no!" He walks over and grabs hold of the very things they are scared of. He does not try to hide those issues, but sets them down right in front of them and says, "Now, this is what it means for you to be a Christian. Don't go worrying about spending ten more minutes a day in prayer, or three more minutes a day reading the Bible. Work on these things that are consuming you in fear, in anger, in envy, in lust, in worry. Look at these things; then look to Christ and ask how he wishes to use these very things to work out your salvation."

Let me ask you, what are you really struggling with these days? And what are you struggling with that does not seem to have to do with the Incarnation, the Trinity, the inspiration of the Bible, or the Second Coming? Once you have located your struggle, pray that God will give you the wisdom, faith, and strength to pick that struggle up, carry it over to Christ, set it down in the middle of your relationship with him, and ask him what it means for following him. And if you have any doubts about the answer, consider his cross.

Christians should continue relying on God and rejoicing in him even through suffering. In fact, suffering provides the very occasion for our reliance and rejoicing.

CONCLUSION

William Law called humility "nothing else but a right judgment of ourselves." John Flavel, the great Puritan preacher, said that true humility was "knowing God."

In Philippians, we see those ideas brought together. Through the example of Paul and the Philippians, and most supremely through the life and death of Christ himself, we discover that true humility is realizing at the core of your being that you exist for the pleasure of our sovereign God. Entirely and ultimately, from first till last, every day you exist for his pleasure. And remember that in serving a sovereign God, nothing surprises him. Everything from the disheartening stories we hear about others to the difficult circumstances that come our way serves to clarify our allegiance, our purpose, and our love for him.

Have you ever been to the optician to get your eyes checked? You press your face up to a device that allows the doctor to flip through what feels like three hundred lenses. Of course, your sight may not be as bad as mine. As he flips from one lens to the next, your sight gets sharper bit by bit. I think this is what God does in our lives. Like an expert optician, he flips the eyes of our faith through the exact combination of circumstances—one lens after another—necessary for gradually sharpening our spiritual sight. With each passing circumstance, with each flip of the lens, we learn to rely on him a bit more. "Can you learn to display my sufficiency and my glory with this circumstance in your life? Or without that one?" One lens, and then another. "Will you display my glory to my creation even if I take that thing you love away from you? Or if I never give you this other thing that you desire?" Flip, flip. "What if I ask you to go through these difficulties?" And on and on, each flip sharpening the eyes of faith a bit more. That is the call he gives us, and how he works out our salvation. In order to follow that call, we need humility. In fact, we need the humility that Christ himself had on the cross. The warm beating heart of this letter is the contentment Christ had in the Father and in doing the Father's will, and that heart transforms our own. This has always been the key to living the Christian life: finding joy in God himself and God alone. How else could Adoniram Judson have been in prison for seventeen months in Burma as a missionary? How else could John Bunyan survive in prison for twelve and a half years in Bedford and write *Pilgrim's Progress* during his captivity? How else could Paul sing hymns in ancient prisons all around the Mediterranean world? How else could Jesus himself endure?

Dare we think our own circumstances are so dire and deadly, so challenging to the faith, so discouraging to our spirits, that God cannot be in control? No, we must turn our mind's eye to the cross of Christ, and then we must think, "Surely not this! Of all people! Of all trials! On the cross? Bearing all sin?" yet also knowing that on the cross God glorified himself supremely. Here, God showed himself fully sufficient, as subsequently affirmed and proven by the resurrection. Thus the final verses of Paul's hymn proclaim, "Therefore God exalted him to the highest place and gave him the name that is above every name, that at the name of Jesus every knee should bow, in heaven and on earth and under the earth, and every tongue confess that Jesus Christ is Lord, to the glory of God the Father" (2:9-11).

Paul writes to the Philippians because he does not want these young Christians, who were concerned about him, to sell out in order to avoid persecution. Their "price," so to speak, had already been found and paid. It was not the giving up of their freedom to hypocritical teachers. It was not even their lives. Their price had been found and paid by Christ. He had bought them, not with silver or gold, but with his precious blood. So, they needed to live as people not for sale.

What is your struggle right now? Is it circumstances? Frustration with those around you? Fear of the future? Fear of being rejected? Let me ask the question like this: What are you holding onto that stands between you and God? You must trust him and be willing to lose what you are trying to grasp, because in Christ you have all you need. Hear the writer to the Hebrews:

> Let us fix our eyes on Jesus, the author and perfecter of our faith, who for the joy set before him endured the cross, scorning its shame, and sat down at the right hand of the throne of God. Consider him who endured such opposition from sinful men, so that you will not grow weary and lose heart (Heb. 12:2-3).

How will you endure today's trials? How will you endure tomorrow? How will you endure the day after that? Every day until your last day? How will you endure all these trials, if not by submitting everything to him, for his sake and glory? How will you embrace suffering, like Paul singing in prison at midnight, if you are not deeply humble before the sovereign goodness of God, shown in and through the humility of Christ? May our lives together be characterized by such divine humility.

Let us pray:

O God, we would line up all the things that we wrongly feel angry, possessive, or covetousness about, and we would sacrifice them. Show us the way forward through the examples of these Philippians and Paul in prison and the Lord Jesus on the cross. We pray that you would not give us spirits that are resigned to our sins, but a deep joy in the certainty of the hope you have set before us: that beyond the tomb the crown awaits. Teach our hearts what it means to rejoice in you, in who you are, and in your good plans for us. Teach us as only your spirit can. We pray for Jesus' sake. Amen.

Questions for Reflection:

1. In the more difficult challenges you face right now, do you conceive of acknowledging your neediness as a help or as a hindrance? Whenever you feel insufficient in yourself, do you reflexively think of that sense of insufficiency as part of the problem or as part of the solution?

2. What is humility? Why is it considered a Christian virtue? What's the difference between humility and poor self-esteem?

3. What people who once played a large role in your life (Christians or non-Christians) do you continue to pray for, even though you have little contact with them now? Whom could you add to that list?

4. Why must love and discernment go together (1:9-11)? How does love grow in discernment?

5. How is Paul able to continue doing ministry through hard circumstances? How will you be able to continue?

6. What is the gospel that Paul rejoices to hear preached?

7. What older men or women in the faith have set a good example for you? Is there anyone for whom you are consciously setting an example, or do you assume that no one really notices what you do or how you live? What relevance do these questions have to your local church?

8. Why are circumstances never good grounds for Christian unity?

9. Do we work out our salvation, or does God work it out in us? What does it mean to "work out" our salvation?

10. Does God preserve Christians to the end, or must Christians persevere to the end? Explain.

11. We have considered the fact that in our argumentative, acquisitive, and self-assertive age, the church's contentment in Christ sparkles as a great witness. In your own life, has your growing contentment in Christ exposed the bondage that typifies the lives of your non-Christian friends? Has it pointed to the path of release?

12. What do you fear? Specifically, what fears do you have that you think Paul, if he could, would grab and set down right in front of you and then say, "Now, this is what it means for you to be a Christian; look at this thing you fear, then look to Christ and ask how he wishes to use this very thing to work out your salvation"?

13. Why is suffering so central to the Christian faith? How do you "embrace" suffering? *Why* would you "embrace" suffering?

THE MESSAGE OF COLOSSIANS: NEW LIFE

12

THE MESSAGE OF COLOSSIANS: NEW LIFE

CAN PEOPLE REALLY CHANGE?[1]

The gay lobby is furious these days, particularly over claims that gays can change their orientation. There was a battle of advertisements not too long ago in some of the major newspapers in the country, one set showing photographs of people who said they had been liberated from homosexuality, the other showing Mom, Dad, and lesbian daughter touting their "family values."

Amid this battle, a group called "Just the Facts Coalition"—representing, among others, the American Academy of Pediatrics, the National Educational Association, the American Federation of Teachers, the Interfaith Alliance Foundation, and the American Psychological Association—announced it was sending out a twelve-page booklet to the heads of all 14,700 public school districts in the country providing "instructions" on how secondary schools ought to handle the issue of homosexuality.

The coalition said the booklet "provides information that will help school administrators and educators create safe and healthy environments in which all students can achieve to the best of their ability." The booklet, titled "Just the Facts About Sexual Orientation and Youth,"[2] singled out for special concern the potential harm caused by techniques for changing sexual orientation.

Kevin Jennings, executive director of the Gay, Lesbian, and Straight Education Network, a New York organization, was quoted in the *New York Times* as saying, "I think this is a history-changing moment. The entire mainstream education and mental health establishment has said that it isn't lesbian,

---

[1] This sermon was originally preached on November 28, 1999, at Capitol Hill Baptist Church in Washington, D.C.
[2] Available online at http://www.apa.org/pi/lgbc/publications/justthefacts.html.

gay and bisexual students who need to change, it is the conditions in our schools that need to change."[3]

By the time the booklet was released, most of the organizations represented by the Coalition had already passed resolutions of their own condemning what is called "reparative therapy," that is, therapy for helping homosexuals change their orientation. The publication itself states, "Therapy directed specifically at changing sexual orientation is contraindicated, since it can provoke guilt and anxiety while having little or no potential for achieving changes in orientation."[4] The booklet advises school administrators, "Because of the religious nature of 'transformational ministry,' endorsement or promotion of such ministry by officials or employees of a public school district in a school-related context could raise constitutional problems."[5] Interestingly, they did not suggest there might be constitutional problems raised by their information. Instead, these organizations endorsed the need for "safe environments" for gay students.

Bruce Hunter, director of public affairs for the American Association of School Administrators, said in this same *Times* article, "there are many communities in this country that are just too conservative for [this booklet], and I trust superintendents to know their communities." He continued, "On the other hand, when push comes to shove, occasionally you have to stand up, and we would hope they would stand up for tolerance."[6]

By raising this topic, I know I am opening not just a can of worms but *cans* of worms: the nature of our sexual orientation, whether one's orientation can change, the interpretation of various passages in Scripture, the nature of civil rights in America today, who is finally responsible for what children are taught, and a number of other issues.

But the one issue I particularly want to draw your attention to in this study is whether or not people can change. The "Just the Facts Coalition" booklet attempts to head off the whole discussion by insinuating that only pitiably benighted religious folk believe homosexuality represents anything unhealthy. Furthermore, anyone who talks about changing such a fundamental aspect of an individual is, when you boil it down, either a self-satisfied bigot or a sinister manipulator, intent on engineering a kind of psychological eugenics that suits one's own tastes or ideas.

Now, let me be clear. The dog that Christians have in this fight, so to speak,

---

[3] Kevin Jennings, cited in Erica Goode, "Group Sends Book on Gay Tolerance to Schools," *New York Times,* November 23, 1999, 20.
[4] Available online at http://www.apa.org/pi/lgbc/publications/justthefacts.html.
[5] Ibid.
[6] Bruce Hunter, cited in Erica Goode, "Group Sends Book on Gay Tolerance to Schools," *New York Times,* November 23, 1999, 20.

is *not* the idea that conversion to Christ will eliminate homosexual desires for those who struggle with them. While God may do that sometimes—as he may well eliminate all kinds of inclinations in us, whether greed, heterosexual lust, uncontrollable anger, and so forth—we cannot assert that he will always, or even normally, do this. This is a silly position, neither taught in Scripture nor confirmed in the painful experiences of thousands of people around the world today who, as earnest Christians, deeply wish their physical attractions would change.

The stake we have in this fight is a slightly different one. It might sound less interesting, but it is more important eternally, and it is essential for maintaining hope for the despairing in this world. The dispute we have is this: whether God so radically changes individuals that we can rightly refer to them as born again, regenerated, and recipients of new life.

This is the Christian claim, and the claim has been made for two thousand years. More than that, this is the Christian hope. I fear that in some of our nation's current discussions, seeds are being sown that indirectly but deeply prejudice people against the hope that any significant change can occur in their lives.

But this is exactly the outrageous claim we make as Christians: you can have a genuinely new life in Christ. Though many imperfections and difficulties remain, we believe the new life we have in Christ is so different from what we had before that we can understand why the Bible uses radical images such as darkness to light and death to life. So great is the change in us.

Of course, many people make errors when thinking about this new life in Christ. Some regard it as a matter of self-effort. Others present it as a life of private religious devotion and mystical contemplation, a life lived for, by, and of the self. Others regard it as quite the opposite, believing the new life is entirely a matter of visible actions such as attending church, observing religious customs, or serving the poor and needy.

Of course, many others today deny that change is needed, or, if it is needed, that it is impossible. We cannot tackle all these issues here, but amid these discussions I would like to lay down some biblical teaching about this key Christian idea of *new life*. To do that, we turn to Paul's letter to the Colossians.

INTRODUCING COLOSSIANS

We do not know exactly what the situation was that prompted Paul to write this letter. It appears that after Paul preached the gospel in Ephesus on one of his journeys, an individual named Epaphras carried the gospel message from Ephesus up the Lycus Valley to a little town called Colosse. Epaphras, apparently a native of Colosse (4:12), appears to have become a Christian through Paul's ministry while away from home. He then returned to his native town to spread the gospel (1:7). Sometime thereafter, situations arose in Colosse that confused Epaphras and sent him back to his first teacher for further instruction. Paul then sent a letter back up the Lycus Valley to the churches meeting there, particularly to a church meeting in the town of Colosse. And this is what we have as the letter to the Colossians.

Colosse was no Jerusalem, Rome, Athens, Corinth, or Ephesus, and we have no record of Paul ever visiting Colosse. When the letter was written, Colosse was a middling-sized town located on a main road. After the New Testament period, however, a new road was laid farther to the west, which took Colosse off the traveler's path. The town then declined in numbers, eventually becoming entirely depopulated.

The wonderful letter Paul writes to the church in Colosse is composed of four short chapters, and you can read it out loud in fifteen to twenty minutes. In chapter 1, Paul tells the Colossians about his prayers for them, about the person and work of Christ, and about the mission Christ has given him to preach the gospel to people like the Colossians. In chapter 2, Paul contrasts the Christian gospel with other ideas that might tempt this young church. The power of Christ's gospel, he says, can be seen in the changed lives of those who follow Christ. Those who have become captive to false philosophies find themselves unable to restrain sensual indulgence. In chapter 3, Paul reminds the Colossians of the mind-set and the behavior they should adopt as Christians. Then in chapter 4, he sends news and greetings.

Colossians describes the new life we have in Christ as Christians. Therefore, we will use this letter to survey a few important aspects of this new life, even amid the confused discussions about whether true change is even possible.

NEW LIFE BEGINS AND ENDS WITH GOD

The first thing to be said about this new life shared by Paul and these Colossians is that it begins and ends with God. In other words, it is given *by* God. And it is lived *for* and *with* God.

Given by God

The source of our new life is God. Paul begins the letter by praying, "We always thank God, the Father of our Lord Jesus Christ, when we pray for you, because we have heard of your faith in Christ Jesus" (1:3-4a). Paul thanks God because he knows God is the one who gives faith. It is also God who strengthens faith (1:11), who qualifies us to share in the inheritance of the saints in the kingdom of light (1:12), who rescues us from the dominion of darkness and brings us into the kingdom of the Son he loves (1:13) and who redeems and forgives (1:14). All this is the work of God: qualifying, rescuing, bringing, redeeming, forgiving, and strengthening.

If you are a Christian, where do you think your new life came from? Do you imagine you created it out of your wit and resources, using bits of traditions, a few wise sayings, and a dash of religious optimism, like some sort of religious stew? That is not what Paul presents in this letter. The new life he describes is no more self-generated than our physical life is self-generated. New life is a gift from God.

Lived for God

Not only is new life from God, it should be lived for God. Now, it may take a moment to get your mind around this idea if this is the first time you have thought about it. Yet that's what Paul prays in 1:10: "And we pray this in order that you may live a life worthy of the Lord and may please him in every way." He asks for lives "worthy of the Lord." What a phrase! And why should we live such lives? Not to please our parents, our pastors, or even ourselves, but to "please him in every way." God's pleasure should be our delight, our joy, our motive. It should be our unswerving purpose, not because we must but because we may. Christ invites us to stop delighting supremely in ourselves, and to begin delighting supremely in him.

God is no idolater. He calls us to delight supremely in him because he delights supremely in himself. The Father and Son's work in creation, election, redemption, and the recreation of a people who imitate and trust him are all bent on bringing glory to his own name. In short, God is all about his own pleasure.[7] He gives us new life, then, for his own pleasure.

As I said, it can be challenging to get our minds and hearts around the idea that God does everything he does, even saving us, ultimately for himself. But it is right for him to do so. He is God! If God delighted in anything more than he delights in himself, he would be guilty of idolatry, which is impossible. When we become alive to the God-centeredness of Scripture, the self-centered little worlds we create are rocked, and we are strangely freed from bending, ducking, and avoiding a substantial number of words, sentences, and ideas in the Bible. Understanding that the new life God gives us is ultimately for himself—so that we may please him in every way—helps us to be more honest when reading Scripture.

---

[7] A great meditation on these ideas can be found in John Piper's book *The Pleasures of God* (Portland: Multnomah, 2000).

So this new life God gives is given by him and for him.

Lived with God

I once heard Ahmed Deedat, a traveling apologist for Islam, publicly mock Christians for the way we talk about having a "relationship with God." Deedat said that the Bible taught no such thing. The idea of a relationship with God is nothing more than a modern, Western, romantic notion Christians read back into the Bible. Was Deedat right? Does the Bible really teach that we can have a relationship with God?

According to Paul, a relationship *with* God is precisely what characterizes our new lives as Christians. This new life begins when we are "reconciled" to God through Christ.

We have already seen that God has qualified, rescued, brought, redeemed, and forgiven us (1:12-14). And notice where he has brought us: to the kingdom of the Son he loves (1:13). In 1:20, Paul says that through the Son, God was pleased "to reconcile to himself all things, whether things on earth or things in heaven, by making peace through his blood, shed on the cross." In essence, our new life *is* a being-reconciled-to-God. It is having our relationship with our Creator restored.

You and I were originally created to have such a relationship with God. We were created "by him and for him" (1:16). But we threw our relationship with God away for sin instead. "Once you were alienated from God and were enemies in your minds because of your evil behavior" (1:21), Paul says to those who are now Christians. Think about these words graphically. First, we were "alienated," that is, we were made aliens. We were to God what green beings from outer space with antennas are to us. Our sin made us strange to him. Worse yet, we were "enemies." Our thoughts opposed him. Our hearts worked overtime to avoid him and slander him. This evil behavior, obviously, set us apart from him. It excluded us from his presence.

"But now," Paul writes gloriously in 1:22, "he has reconciled you by Christ's physical body through death to present you holy in his sight, without blemish and free from accusation." If we are Christians, God has reconciled and restored our relationship with him. How? By Christ's physical death. To what end? To present us blameless in his sight!

Is that how you would describe the Christian life? Having your relationship with the Creator restored? Is that how you would describe your experience during this past week?

Life is empty apart from knowing God. Perhaps we occasionally feel this emptiness now, but we knew it especially before we were Christians. As the hymn says, we were "weary, and worn, and sad."[8] Then we were given new life in Christ; we were reconciled to God. Being reconciled to God does not mean our circumstances suddenly improve. Our gastrointestinal trouble may continue. We may lose our jobs. We may be sued. And all these things might happen in the same week. But our experience of adversity is different *with* God than it was *without* him. Paul was in prison when he wrote this letter, just as he was when he wrote the letter to the Philippians, and just as he was when he first went to Philippi. But as we saw in our Philippians study, Paul sat in the Philippian jail singing hymns at midnight (Acts 16:25)! Being reconciled to God through Christ did not mean he was somehow not in the jail. He was in the jail. The circumstances were bad. But the quality and tenor of his life had changed because his relationship with God had changed.

I don't know if you have ever had a relationship with a family member or close friend go bad. If you have, you know that few heart pains in life are more exquisite. Being alienated from someone who should be close to you, someone with whom you once knew intimacy, is a painful thing. But have you ever had a broken relationship come back to life? It almost seems too much to hope for. What pleasure is more sublime than the pleasure of being restored to someone you have loved and lost?

The new life we have in Christ is characterized most fundamentally by our restoration to the presence of God with joy and acceptance and love.

NEW LIFE INVOLVES OURSELVES

The new life begins and ends with God, yet it dramatically involves our own lives as well. Paul describes at least three ways this is true.

Changed Radically

This new life radically changes what we are. A great reversal takes place, which Paul writes about succinctly in chapter 2: "When you were dead in your sins and in the uncircumcision of your sinful nature, God made you alive with Christ" (2:13).

If you are a Christian, this describes your experience. You were dead, and now you are alive.

Paul writes about our death-to-life transformation again at the beginning of chapter 3, but this time he turns the images of life and death slightly:

> Since, then, you have been raised with Christ, set your hearts on things above, where Christ is seated at the right hand of God. Set your minds on things above,

---

[8] Horatio Bonar, "I Heard the Voice of Jesus Say."

not on earthly things. For you died, and your life is now hidden with Christ in
God. When Christ, who is your life, appears, then you also will appear with him
in glory (3:1-4).

Specific instructions then follow: "Put to death, therefore, whatever belongs to
your earthly nature: sexual immorality, impurity, lust, evil desires and greed,
which is idolatry" (3:5). Then several verses later: "now you must rid yourselves of all such things as these: anger, rage, malice, slander, and filthy language
from your lips" (3:8). And so on. The Colossian Christians were once dead *in*
sin, and now they are to be dead *to* sin. Their previous connection with sin and
sinning was evidence of their spiritual death. Now their struggle to separate
themselves from sin gives evidence of their new life. Their orientation, incli-
nation, first love, disposition, affection, hearts, and minds have been changed.
So their behavior must change too.

This new life changes us radically. Paul gives a small picture of what the
new life looks like in 3:12: "Therefore, as God's chosen people, holy and dearly
loved, clothe yourselves with compassion, kindness, humility, gentleness and
patience." If you have not experienced this radical change in your life, I testify
that you can. You can have radically new life—at the root! And without such
a change, you cannot be saved.

For too long, churches in our land have been guilty of letting people think
they are saved when their lives clearly demonstrate otherwise. Consider carefully: chapter 3 is not pointing to some super-spiritual super-Christian. It simply defines what it means to be a Christian. To misunderstand this may be to
misunderstand altogether what it means to be a Christian. Setting your heart
on things above is not just what those really strong Christians do. Putting lust
to death and ridding yourself of slander are not just the extra practices of
mature Christians. Displaying compassion, kindness, humility, gentleness, and
patience is not just the job of especially fruitful Christians. Those qualities are
typical of Christians. None of us produces them perfectly. We are all painfully
aware of that. But they are typical of us nonetheless.

Beware of muting this great biblical truth and this great biblical hope in
the name of charity and compassion. God does restore us to himself! God does
change us! Dare we rob people of such hope? Our lives are to be beacons of
hope showing God's ability to change people radically.

Contested Dramatically

Not that this new life is easy! I do not mean to suggest that. Our new life will
face rivals and competitors from within and without (2 Cor. 7:5).

From without: empty promises. For starters, Paul points to the empty promises of worldly philosophies. In chapter 2, Paul exhorts these Colossian Christians, "See to it that no one takes you captive through hollow and deceptive philosophy, which depends on human tradition and the basic principles of this world rather than on Christ" (Col. 2:8). Behind these philosophies are "fine-sounding arguments" (2:4). Scholars have written many books trying to figure out what these arguments were. Whatever they were, Paul regards them as dangerous because they encouraged people to rely on human wisdom and not on Christ. Paul therefore exhorts his readers to continue in Christ: "So then, just as you received Christ Jesus as Lord, continue to live in him, rooted and built up in him, strengthened in the faith as you were taught, and overflowing with thankfulness" (2:6-7). These empty philosophies do not root and build up saints in the Lord. Only living in Christ can do that.

Others, perhaps, are attracted by less obscure alternatives. It appears that some people in Colosse were teaching that submitting to a list of rules completes faith in Christ, and that God's full revelation was reserved for Sabbath-keepers or keepers of food laws. Some insisted that non-Jewish converts to Christ should be circumcised. Would Paul go for that? Affirm his Jewish heritage and incorporate new aspects from Christ?

No way! In 2:11, Paul insists that the Colossians are circumcised in Christ already in every way that matters: "In him you were also circumcised, in the putting off of the sinful nature, not with a circumcision done by the hands of men but with the circumcision done by Christ." Christ had freed them from the law's demands. They must not go backwards, from faith in Christ's righteousness to a sad attempt to manufacture their own.

Religious forms and regulations do not produce new life in God. Even in the Old Testament, the regulations given through Moses merely pointed to Christ's new age. These false worshipers, however, "[delight] in false humility and the worship of angels" (2:18). They go "into great detail" about what they have seen (2:18). They proudly demand, "Do not handle! Do not taste! Do not touch!" (2:21). They craft their own worship, confess humility with their mouths, and treat their bodies harshly (2:23). But do not be fooled, says Paul. Christ plus anything is no Christ. Rely on Christ entirely or not at all.

Paul asks, "Since you died with Christ to the basic principles of this world, why, as though you still belonged to it, do you submit to its rules?" (2:20). It is like a licensed medical doctor going to a witchdoctor! A doctor should know better. And a Christian should know better than to pursue new life in Christ through rules. Rules cannot create new life. It is like trying to use your church pew to travel home after church. It was not made for that. It does not serve that purpose!

Still, we are often tempted to judge ourselves by our abilities to keep rules. We need to recognize that tendency. It is not the way to new life.

I want you to notice one further thing about these worldly philosophies and man-made, rule-bound religions that compete with Christianity. Their proponents never know what to do with Christ, at least as the Bible presents him. They may knock him down a few notches, like the Jehovah's Witnesses do; or drown him out with countless "counterfeit" Christs, like the Mormons do; or make him out to be some ethereally abstracted and crazy rabbi, like some Protestants do. But they have to do something with Christ. If you want to get to the heart of an individual or a church's theology, ask what they believe about Jesus. Is he just a preacher? A principle? A myth?

A few years ago I was talking with a clergyman of another denomination, and I asked him what he thought about something Jesus said in the Bible. The man replied, "I don't know. And I don't think we can know. And I don't think it would matter if we could know." This was an ordained clergyman in a Christian denomination!

Apparently, Paul was aware of the fatal tendency to downplay Christ, and so he prepares for the discussion of Christ's competitors in chapter 2 by gloriously displaying Christ in chapter 1. As much as any passage of Scripture, the famous hymn of chapter 1 sticks in the throats of all who downplay Christ. He writes,

> He is the image of the invisible God, the firstborn over all creation. For by him all things were created: things in heaven and on earth, visible and invisible, whether thrones or powers or rulers or authorities; all things were created by him and for him. He is before all things, and in him all things hold together. And he is the head of the body, the church; he is the beginning and the firstborn from among the dead, so that in everything he might have the supremacy. For God was pleased to have all his fullness dwell in him, and through him to reconcile to himself all things, whether things on earth or things in heaven, by making peace through his blood, shed on the cross (1:15-20).

Truly, no one and nothing can rival this one who is the exact image of God; who created all things, and in whom all things hold together; who contains all the fullness of God; who has reconciled all things to the Father. There is no other. If Christ, the eternal God, has spoken, dare we say, "I don't think it would matter if we could" understand him? The world's claims to rival Christ as a way to new life are false, says Paul.

From within: the old self. In addition to rivals from without, the Christian faces rivals from within, and the competition is intense. As we saw several moments ago, Paul addresses the heart, mind, and will in chapter 3. He exhorts his readers to set their hearts on things above (3:1), and then he tells them to do the same with their minds (3:2). Their hearts have to die to this world. Their minds have to get out of the gutters. And all this involves struggle. But the Christian's motivation is clear: "For you died, and your life is now hidden with Christ in God" (3:3). The temptations of the old self continue, but the Christian should see the folly of these things. The Christian is dead to this world. You can play with dead things, but why? Your worldly life has died. Your new life is now *from, for,* and *with* Christ!

Even though the old self has "died" (3:3), Christians must continue to "put to death" the "earthly nature" that is still alive and kicking (3:5). God has changed us radically, therefore Christians must live radically changed lives:

> Put to death, therefore, whatever belongs to your earthly nature: sexual immoral-
> ity, impurity, lust, evil desires and greed, which is idolatry. Because of these, the
> wrath of God is coming. You used to walk in these ways, in the life you once
> lived. But now you must rid yourselves of all such things as these: anger, rage,
> malice, slander, and filthy language from your lips. Do not lie to each other, since
> you have taken off your old self with its practices and have put on the new self,
> which is being renewed in knowledge in the image of its Creator. Here there is
> no Greek or Jew, circumcised or uncircumcised, barbarian, Scythian, slave or
> free, but Christ is all, and is in all (3:5-11).

The earthly nature, the old self, continues to make threats against our alle-giance to Christ. It shows up in sexual immorality, impurity, lust, evil desires, and greed.

Not long ago a major television network featured a weekly program in prime-time called "Greed." The network could have filled out the entire evening's programming from this list in Colossians 3: "Greed" at 8:00, "Evil Desires" at 8:30, "Lust" at 9:00, "Impurity" at 9:30, and "Sexual Immorality" at 10:00, when only the "mature" audiences stay up to watch!

Surely, our day is no different from Paul's. The old way of life can feel like "second nature" to the Christian. Anger, rage, malice, slander, filthy language, lying, ethnic hatred, prejudice, and bigotry are not unknown among us. But a Christian must rid himself or herself of these things, Paul says. A Christian must put on a different kind of clothing (3:12-17), which we will look at momentarily.

In this world, our new life in Christ does not have a monopoly. It faces competition for the mind, heart, and will. Christians historically have there-fore referred to the church in two parts: the church militant and the church tri-umphant. The church triumphant is the church in heaven, delivered from sins, enjoying God's presence, made pure and holy *in fact*. The church militant is the church on earth, struggling still with sin, beset by difficulties within and without, declared perfectly holy in Christ, showing that holiness in increasing measure through the work of Christ's Spirit in and among its members.

The old nature is strong. It is sort of the Mr. Hyde to our new nature's Dr. Jekyll. Only in our story—and this is crucial—the good guy, Dr. Jekyll, wins!

Lasting Permanently

This new life will not be defeated. Whether someone perseveres in Christ to the end, therefore, becomes an essential component for discerning whether he or she truly has Christ's new life. The new life that is real does last. How does it last? We fight to endure, trusting that God will preserve us. So Paul exhorts his readers to "continue." Look again at chapter 1:

> But now he has reconciled you by Christ's physical body through death to present you holy in his sight, without blemish and free from accusation—if you continue in your faith, established and firm, not moved from the hope held out in the gospel (1:22-23).

We will be presented holy in God's sight if we continue. So continue. Paul commands the same thing in chapter 2: "just as you received Christ Jesus as Lord, continue to live in him" (2:6). And then he prays that the Colossians would have "great endurance and patience" (1:11).

The church where I pastor has always taught, in its statement of faith, the need for perseverance. Article 9, titled "Of the Perseverance of the Saints," reads,

> We believe that such only are real believers as endure unto the end; that their persevering attachment to Christ is the grand mark which distinguishes them from superficial professors; that a special Providence watches over their welfare; and they are kept by the power of God through faith unto salvation.[9]

Real believers endure by striving to endure. Yet real believers are ultimately kept through no effort of their own.

When we fail to understand the necessity and nature of perseverance, our understanding of the new life in Christ can lurch in one of two dangerous directions. On the one hand, we can begin flippantly taking it for granted as a one-time event. On the other hand, we can begin trembling in fear, thinking it will be a grueling test of our own mettle and righteousness. The first danger produces a church full of nominal Christians—people who are Christians in name

---

[9] Based on the New Hampshire Baptist Confession (1833).

only and who will tell you again and again they "prayed the prayer," even though their life looks no different from a non-Christian's. The second danger produces a church full of legalistic people who are blindly sure of their own righteousness. The doctrine of the perseverance of all true Christians, with which Paul sprinkles this little letter, acts as a great protection against both of these errors.

So, on the one hand, if you notice a tendency in yourself to take comfort in the fact that you prayed the prayer once, and if you notice that you do this especially to excuse acts of deliberate sinfulness, pray that God would help you to see the great challenge these verses (1:22-23; 2:6) give you. God calls you to continue in your faith, established and firm, not moved from the hope held out in the gospel, throughout your whole life! Your struggle is not over until the last breath leaves your body. Rethink what spiritual anesthetics you have passed out to others if you have told them otherwise.

On the other hand, if you notice a tendency in yourself to think only about your own sins or, conversely, your own righteousness, Paul offers great grounds for hope. As we saw earlier, God has undertaken the project of restoring you to himself. And if he has undertaken it, you can be sure he will finish it, as Paul promised the Philippians (1:6).

The doctrine of perseverance should also give us charity for others. Whether those "others" are paragons of virtue or have fallen so far they must be excluded from the church, God, if he is savingly at work in them, will bring his work to completion. He will not stop!

That is the great hope we have for ourselves in Christ, and that is our great ground for charity toward others. Our own sins and the sins of the saints we know should compel us to prayer: "Father, finish what you have begun, according to your mercy!" If God has really landed himself in our lives, he is on our side, and he will win. He will continue in us as we continue in him, even amid the unusual difficulties and exquisite pains life may bring. We can humbly rely on Christ, certain of his goodness and of his commitment to complete his work in us.

What a great hope we have in him!

So this new life begins and ends with God, but it also deeply involves ourselves. We really change, we really struggle, and we really persevere, with, as Paul says, "all his energy, which so powerfully works in me" (1:29).

NEW LIFE INVOLVES LIVING FOR OTHERS

Finally, new life involves living for others. Notice that in the Bible, and specifically in this letter to the Colossians, the new life is no mere inner feeling of transforming ecstasy with God, where people see us with closed eyes, a seraphic smile, and the glow of gentle, enraptured piety. When lived out, this new life will always mix our lives up with others.

Exemplified By Paul

Paul presents himself as an example of the new life we are called to in Christ. He continually involves himself in the lives of others.

He writes to them. Just look at this letter! He has not just written some nice, flowery Sunday school lessons. He has written difficult words of warning and rebuke. He has written words of encouragement and instruction and guidance, even though he sits in prison.

He thanks God for them. "We always thank God, the Father of our Lord Jesus Christ, when we pray for you," he says at the letter's beginning (1:3). Why does he thank God for them? "Because we have heard of your faith in Christ Jesus and of the love you have for all the saints—the faith and love that spring from the hope that is stored up for you in heaven and that you have already heard about in the word of truth, the gospel that has come to you" (1:4-6). In short, he thanks God for the faith, hope, and love that the Colossians have been given in Christ through the gospel. Is this what you thank God for in the lives of other Christians?

He prays for them. In 1:9, Paul admits, "since the day we heard about you, we have not stopped praying for you." And what does he pray? That God would fill them "with the knowledge of his will through all spiritual wisdom and understanding." He unceasingly asks God to grow them in faith. Again, is this what you pray for in the lives of other Christians?

He preaches to and suffers for them. In his preaching and suffering, Paul fulfills the commission God has given him to build the church. He writes,

> Now I rejoice in what was suffered for you, and I fill up in my flesh what is still lacking in regard to Christ's afflictions, for the sake of his body, which is the church. I have become its servant by the commission God gave me to present to you the word of God in its fullness (1:24-25).

Paul writes this letter for the same reason he preaches. He loves these people, and God has called him to instruct them and to suffer for them. So he labors through beatings, imprisonments, arguments, angry words, stones, and challenges to his integrity and his sanity. And he rejoices in such service!

He desires their perfection and maturity. He writes,

> We proclaim him, admonishing and teaching everyone with all wisdom, so that
> we may present everyone perfect [or mature] in Christ. To this end I labor, strug-
> gling with all his energy, which so powerfully works in me (1:28).

Paul does not merely declare his love. He labors in his love. And this love for
Christ and for them pushes him forward with this hope fixed in his mind: presenting them perfect in Christ.

Paul writes to these Colossians; he thanks God for them; he prays for
them; he suffers for them; and he has never even met them! They had learned
the gospel from Epaphras, remember? That is amazing. Paul has a love that
pours itself out for others. Should we then praise Paul? Or, conversely, should
we sit back discouraged, thinking we will never measure up to Paul the apostle? No, Paul's new life began and ended with God. God did it. Real change is
real, because God is merciful and mighty.

Lived Out in Every Sphere

What "others" should our new lives pour themselves into? What spheres of
life are affected?

The home. Toward the end of chapter 3, Paul addresses the different members of a household:

> Wives, submit to your husbands, as is fitting in the Lord. Husbands, love your
> wives and do not be harsh with them.
>
> Children, obey your parents in everything, for this pleases the Lord.
>
> Fathers, do not embitter your children, or they will become discouraged
> (3:18-21).

Notice the idea that is repeated twice—"as is fitting in the Lord" and "for this
pleases the Lord." As mentioned earlier, that is why we have this new life—to
please the Lord.

The workplace. The new life will also transform our approach to the
workplace:

> Slaves, obey your earthly masters in everything; and do it, not only when their
> eye is on you and to win their favor, but with sincerity of heart and reverence
> for the Lord. Whatever you do, work at it with all your heart, as working for
> the Lord, not for men, since you know that you will receive an inheritance from
> the Lord as a reward. It is the Lord Christ you are serving. Anyone who does
> wrong will be repaid for his wrong, and there is no favoritism.
>
> Masters, provide your slaves with what is right and fair, because you know
> that you also have a Master in heaven (3:22–4:1).

Paul addresses most of the employees of his day as "slaves," or what we might call "servants" in our culture. As with his instructions for the home, he encourages them to remember what pleases the Lord. Work for Christ, he says. Masters, or employers, likewise, must be fair, remembering that God will judge them.

Everyplace. Consider finally Paul's instructions to everyone:

> Devote yourselves to prayer, being watchful and thankful. And pray for us, too, that God may open a door for our message, so that we may proclaim the mystery of Christ, for which I am in chains. Pray that I may proclaim it clearly, as I should. Be wise in the way you act toward outsiders; make the most of every opportunity. Let your conversation be always full of grace, seasoned with salt, so that you may know how to answer everyone (4:2-6).

Your new life will make the most of *every* opportunity. Your new life is comprehensive. There are no pockets of your life that can be hidden from its effects. It should affect the way you treat everyone around you, in whatever circumstances. Similar to the advice he gives employees in 3:23, Paul says to you, me, and every Christian, "Whatever you do, whether in word or deed, do it all in the name of the Lord Jesus, giving thanks to God the Father through him" (3:17).

Lived Out with One Another

Finally, this new life can be lived out only with one another. Consider the virtues Paul encourages Christians to wear:

> Therefore, as God's chosen people, holy and dearly loved, clothe yourselves with compassion, kindness, humility, gentleness and patience. Bear with each other and forgive whatever grievances you may have against one another. Forgive as the Lord forgave you. And over all these virtues put on love, which binds them all together in perfect unity.
>
> Let the peace of Christ rule in your hearts, since as members of one body you were called to peace. And be thankful. Let the word of Christ dwell in you richly as you teach and admonish one another with all wisdom, and as you sing psalms, hymns and spiritual songs with gratitude in your hearts to God. And whatever you do, whether in word or deed, do it all in the name of the Lord Jesus, giving thanks to God the Father through him (3:12-17).

Compassion, kindness, humility, gentleness, patience, forbearance, forgiveness, and above all love. Sounds like a nice list, doesn't it? Maybe they give you a sort of sweet and religious feeling. You might want to put the words on a placard and hang them on the wall. But stop and think about it: for the most part, only bad circumstances require us to wear these virtues. The occasions in which they are required are really quite messy. When do you need to show compassion? When do you need to show kindness? What circumstances require you to demonstrate humility? Gentleness is appropriate in response to what? When do you need patience? What about forbearance? When is forgiveness needed? And love?

Notice that these virtues, and caring for one another generally, are coupled with Paul's instruction to "teach and admonish one another." In other words, exercising compassion, kindness, humility, and so forth does not mean neglecting instruction. It is just the opposite: these virtues assume instruction is needed, and should be given when the conditions are appropriate. Yet we are not to offer instruction in a bitter or proud way, but with humility—"with gratitude in your hearts to God."

Notice, too, toward the very end of the letter, Paul promises to send Tychicus and Onesimus back to Colosse to share news and to encourage them:

> Tychicus will tell you all the news about me . . . I am sending him to you for the express purpose that you may know about our circumstances and that he may encourage your hearts. He is coming with Onesimus. . . . They will tell you everything that is happening here (4:7-9).

Being born again and experiencing new life in Christ shows itself in how we live with our families, our friends, our colleagues, fellow church members, and even acquaintances. This new life does not consist merely of our private opinions, private practices of prayer, secret giving, and so forth, though Jesus clearly commends such private practices (Matt. 6:1-18). Living out the new life we have in Jesus Christ also involves giving ourselves for others, regardless of the responses we receive from them. They may imprison us. They may slander us. They may shrug us off with indifference. But they must not stop us from living out our new lives in Christ of love toward them.

CONCLUSION

New life, according to the Bible, is from, for, and with God. It involves radical change in who and what we are. And it always involves us in the lives of others. Have you known that kind of change in your life? And don't simply think of what others might say of you. You might die today. What will you say to God? He knows the truth. Have you known that kind of change? Do you know the life that comes to those who know his Son?

Adoniram Judson knew such life. Judson was born in 1788 in Malden,

Massachusetts, not too far from Boston. His father was a minister. Parson Judson, his father, sent his young, bright son to study at Rhode Island College, now known as Brown University. There young Judson distinguished himself, as you would expect from someone who learned to read at age three. While in college, Judson attached himself to a slightly older student from Maine named Jacob Eames. Eames was an outspoken deist and rationalist, meaning he rejected the Bible and Jesus in any traditional Christian sense. Judson adopted Eames's worldview without telling his parents, and both young men determined to pursue literary careers, perhaps as playwrights. Following graduation as valedictorian in 1807, one year after Eames, Judson moved back to his family's home, opened a school (which was not so unusual among college graduates in those days), and wrote two textbooks. After a couple of years, he grew weary of the work as well as living at home and found himself deeply discontent. In one sharp exchange, he let his father know that he did not believe the cardinal doctrines of Christianity, and proceeded to argue his position strongly to his shocked and broken-hearted father. Adoniram then hurriedly packed and left.

Judson headed to New York City. Even two-hundred years ago, apparently, that's what you did! There he joined a company of actors and began to lead, as he later put it, "a reckless, vagabond life, finding lodgings where we could, and running up a score, and then decamping without paying the reckoning."[10] Judson was unable to cope with such a life for more than a few weeks, and decided it was useless. So he departed for home, uncertain of his future. One night during his journey home, he stopped at a village inn for rest. The inn was nearly full, but the inn-keeper offered one room next to a young man who appeared to be dying. Judson confidently assured him that this would cause him no uneasiness.

However, the tramp of the doctor's feet and the sounds of groaning kept him awake for much of the night. As he lay awake, he thought about the prospect of dying and wondered if he was prepared to die and face God. But quickly he remembered his good friend Eames and became ashamed of his puerile thoughts and doubts. What would Eames make of such silliness, after all?

The next morning, while Judson was checking out, almost as an afterthought he asked about the condition of his sick neighbor.

"He is dead," said the innkeeper.

"Dead!"

---

[10] Quoted in John Allen Moore's *Baptist Mission Portraits* (Macon, Ga.: Smyth & Helwys, 1994), 45.

"Yes, he is gone, poor fellow. The doctor said he would probably not survive the night."

"Do you know who he was?" Adoniram inquired.

"Oh, yes," replied the innkeeper. "It was a young man from the college in Providence, a very fine fellow. His name was Jacob Eames."

Judson was shocked. He rode off on his horse, his mind filled with thoughts about Eames. As his horse's hooves fell, Judson thought of the fate of his friend—dead, lost, dead, lost. Amid much internal strife, Judson realized that he did believe that the God of the Bible is the true God, and that Jesus Christ his Son had come to bring new life.

God gave Adoniram Judson a new life as a Christian. And you can be sure it worked a radical change in him. The rest of Judson's life was given for others. Judson became the first Christian missionary from America to a foreign land. In 1812, he left Salem, Massachusetts, for India, and finally ended up in Burma in 1813. In Burma, he endured much opposition from the East India Company as well as the loss of many friends, several children, and two wives to disease. He faced a difficult language that took years to learn, and he was in Burma for more than six years before he saw one person brought to the faith through his ministry. He spent the better part of two years in a Burmese prison in torturous conditions, often being held upside down with his feet in shackles. Except for a two-year furlough, Judson ultimately spent thirty-seven years in Burma caring for a people he had not previously known. He had been given a new life from God. It changed him radically and involved him in loving others and giving himself for them.

Do you want this new life? If you do, turn away from your sins and trust in Christ. Value him and his pleasure more than anything else that beckons.

If you have already experienced something of this new life, then hear Paul's cheering, his urging, his warning, and his promises. Continue on in this new life from God—for God and for his will in the lives of others.

Let us pray:

Lord, we pray that your Holy Spirit would dispel even now any remaining areas of our lives in which we know despair. We pray that your sovereign gift of new life would not discourage us in any way but would only encourage us. Challenge the shallowness of our understanding of our new life. Strengthen us so that we could continue to stand firm. Father, give us strength to fight against all that we need to fight against, and to fight for all that we need to fight for. Give us strength to lay hold of Christ, and give us strength to continue until we are finally and fully in your presence, we pray for Jesus' sake. Amen.

Questions for Reflection

1. Can people really change their fundamental identity? Can they be, as it were, "born again"? How does the world answer this question? How do you?

2. If God is the source of our new life, why are we so quick to become proud like Pharisees? How does our pride as Christians show itself? Can pride adopt religious language? What role can be played by the local church in keeping us from pride?

3. Paul argues that radical change given by God is not only possible, it is necessary for salvation. If you consider yourself a Christian, how has your life exemplified this radical change? How did yesterday exemplify it?

4. As we have seen, for too long churches have been guilty of letting people think they are saved when their lives clearly demonstrate otherwise—there is no change in their lives! What are our churches doing wrong? What should a church do to avoid this?

5. Following up on questions 3 and 4, we have been warned to beware of muting, in the name of charity and compassion, the great biblical truth and the great biblical hope that God radically changes people. Describe an example of how such muting of this truth may occur.

6. How long will the battle against sin last in this life? How should we respond to the claims of some Christian teachers that we can be done with sin entirely in this life?

7. If a friend of yours claims to be a Christian and yet he has given up on the fight against sin, what will you say to him?

8. The difference between a Christian and a non-Christian, generally, is that a Christian takes God's side against his sin, while a non-Christian takes his sin's side against God. Which of the two better describes you?

9. We have seen that when we fail to understand the necessity and nature of perseverance, our understanding of the new life in Christ can lurch in one of two dangerous directions. On the one hand, we can flippantly take it for granted as a one-time event. On the other hand, we can tremble in fear, thinking it will be a grueling test of our own mettle and righteousness. If you are a

teacher of God's Word (to a congregation, a Bible study, or your children), how can you help people avoid these two errors? How does any Christian avoid these two errors?

10. In 1:4-6, Paul thanks God for the faith, hope, and love the Colossians have been given in Christ through the gospel. Is this what you thank God for in the lives of other Christians? In 1:9, Paul prays that God would fill them "with the knowledge of his will through all spiritual wisdom and understanding." Again, is this what you pray for in the lives of other Christians?

11. Looking to Paul as your example, what is the difference between declaring love and laboring in love? What does this mean for your discipleship of others? Do you look for opportunities to mentor others?

THE MESSAGE OF 1 THESSALONIANS: THE SECOND COMING

13

THE MESSAGE OF 1 THESSALONIANS: THE SECOND COMING

DO YOU BELIEVE IN DOOMSDAY?[1]

Not long ago I was enjoying a time with family and friends. At one point, when one friend and I were taking a short walk and were alone for the first time that day, he looked at me and said with utter seriousness, "Mark, there's something I've been wanting to ask you. Do you believe in doomsday?"

It was a strange question, particularly coming from my friend, who holds a very responsible job, is quite intelligent, and is an atheist. He had been speaking with a member of the House of Representatives leadership a few days earlier, and somehow the topic had come up. My friend was shocked when he learned that this prominent member of Congress openly believed, as my friend put it with wide-eyed incomprehension, in "doomsday."

"Do you believe in doomsday?" he asked.

Of course concern about the end times is supposed to be mounting right now. There is a strangeness in the air. In the political world, the Irish Republican Army (Catholic) and the Ulstermen (Protestant), bloody antagonists for decades, have just formed a united government in Northern Ireland. The southern Republic of Ireland also promised to drop its claim to these northern counties from its constitution. In the religious world, Roman Catholics and Lutherans had come to an agreement that many heralded as a major breakthrough in restoring a pre-Reformation unity to the Christian church. Meanwhile, the Lutheran and Episcopal Churches were getting closer to various types of union. And socially, in the United States, while we had been horrified by heinous crimes at Columbine High School, Wedgewood Baptist Church, and elsewhere, the overall crime rates for all serious crimes were

---

[1] This sermon was originally preached on December 5, 1999, at Capitol Hill Baptist in Washington, D.C.

falling, and not by small amounts. Unemployment was at a thirty-year low. The stock market was at an all-time high. And even the District of Columbia was posting its first gains in employment in a decade. Prosperity abounded.

And yet there was unease as the big date approached—January 1, 2000. One article I read at the time said that church attendance had begun to swell as people tried to prepare themselves for what might happen. Many feared, of course, the Y2K computer glitch, which could cause some mayhem. The year 2000 was upon us.

But is doomsday, the end of days, the end of the world, coming? What does the Bible say about this topic?

INTRODUCING 1 THESSALONIANS

That brings us to our study of Paul's first letter to the Thessalonians. The letter was probably written about A.D. 51 from Corinth, and was either the first or second letter Paul wrote. Galatians may have been earlier. The situation for writing the letter was basically this: Paul had made what we call his "first missionary journey" in southern Turkey and was now on his second. He intended simply to revisit the churches he had planted on his first journey and then travel to what today is northern Turkey. Before traveling northward, however, he had the famous vision of the Macedonian man saying, "Come . . . and help us" (Acts 16:9). God was calling Paul over to Macedonia and Greece to spread the gospel.

When Paul answered that missionary call, history was changed. The gospel of Christianity went from Asia to Europe for the first time. Paul traveled first to Philippi, a port city, and then he proceeded west on the main east/west road (that eventually reaches Rome) to the chief city of Macedonia, Thessalonica (Acts 16:12; 17:1). Thessalonica was founded in 316 B.C. and was named for the sister of Alexander the Great. After Alexander's great conquests, it was believed Macedonia needed a new and more prominent city, given its enhanced place in the world. So Thessalonica was built.

If you follow the story of Paul's first visit to Thessalonica in Acts 17, you find he was there for only a few weeks—at most, months—before he was run out of town. Still, his time in Thessalonica may have been his most immediately successful evangelistic tour up to that point. We read in Acts 17, "Some of the Jews were persuaded and joined Paul and Silas, as did a large number of God-fearing Greeks and not a few prominent women" (17:4). Yet he actually encountered persecution, and he was smuggled out at night. He went on to Berea, Athens, and Corinth; but in none of these places did the gospel receive the same positive response it had received in Thessalonica. Always, this band of new Christians was on Paul's mind. When he finally thought it was safe, he sent one of his trusted workers, Timothy, to check on the young church. After a short absence, Timothy caught up with Paul at Corinth and gave him the news: the Thessalonian church had survived, and it was doing well!

It remained a young church, however, and had its share of problems. After all, Paul had basically been interrupted mid-lesson in Thessalonica. He had never finished teaching the basic matters of Christianity, and the church's foundations were not complete and solid. Several strange problems had grown up after his premature departure. Apparently, some individuals in Thessalonica opposed this new religion by accusing Paul of being a money-grubbing self-promoter. As soon as circumstances became difficult, they said, he snuck out of town. There were also doctrinal difficulties. The Thessalonians worried that if a Christian died before Christ returned, he or she would be lost forever.

So Paul wrote this letter, which is among his most autobiographical. It also most clearly points to the real end of days—not merely the coming of antichrist but the second coming of Christ himself. Throughout the letter, Paul teaches that the hope we as Christians have in Christ's second coming is woven through every aspect of life. We will look first at Paul's prayers, then at Paul's recollections of ministry among the Thessalonians, then at Paul's vision of the Christian life together, and finally at Paul's hope in the second coming of Christ. Throughout the letter, we find the beams of that hope that shine into our own lives. What is the truth about the second coming of Christ? Let's look and see.

PAUL'S PRAYERS

Again and again, Paul prays for these young Christians. In fact, his prayers constitute one of the most constant and recurring aspects of the letter. He thanks God for what he has already done in the church, and he asks him to do still more.

Paul Thanks God for the Past

Paul begins by thanking God for what he had already done among the Thessalonians. "We always thank God for all of you, mentioning you in our prayers," he says in the letter's first chapter (1:2). And he thanks God for their work, labor, and endurance, or as Paul puts it, "your work produced by faith, your labor prompted by love, and your endurance inspired by hope in our Lord Jesus Christ" (1:3). Paul does not simply write and thank them for *their* effort in the faith amid difficult circumstances; he thanks *God* because he knows their faith, hope, and love are the work of God. He says in 1:4, "For we know, brothers loved by God, that he has chosen you."

What else does Paul thank God for in connection with the Thessalonians? Surely Paul and his friends would have been thankful to God for how the Thessalonians received God's word. They had accepted the word of God "with power, with the Holy Spirit and deep conviction" (1:5). They had followed Paul's example and the Lord's example; "in spite of severe suffering, you welcomed the message with the joy given by the Holy Spirit" (1:6). These young Christians had actually become "a model" to other believers. Their witness had spread far and wide. The story of their repentance had already become famous (1:8-9). Paul speaks of how believers throughout Macedonia and Achaia "report what kind of reception you gave us. They tell how you turned to God from idols to serve the living and true God, and to wait for his Son from heaven, whom he raised from the dead" (1:9-10a).

The spiritual eyes to recognize the word of God and the spiritual life to respond in repentance and faith are nothing for which the Thessalonians could claim credit. Paul knows that. He says, "We also thank God continually because, when you received the word of God, which you heard from us, you accepted it not as the word of men, but as it actually is, the word of God, which is at work in you who believe" (2:13). Paul knows who deserves credit for the past—for the Thessalonians' initial faith and their survival in the faith even after he was ripped away from them. He does not deserve credit. Neither do they. God does.

Paul Prays to God for the Future

Yet the fact that Paul sees God's hand in all things past does not mean Paul is a fatalist, who simply assumes that "what will be, will be." Throughout the letter, Paul happily and repeatedly prays to God for the future.

First, Paul prays to God regarding himself, that God would make a way for Paul to return to the Thessalonians in order to help, nurture, and further instruct them. He writes, "Night and day we pray most earnestly that we may see you again and supply what is lacking in your faith. Now may our God and Father himself and our Lord Jesus clear the way for us to come to you" (3:10-11).

Second, he prays to God for the Thessalonians:

> May the Lord make your love increase and overflow for each other and for everyone else, just as ours does for you. May he strengthen your hearts so that you will be blameless and holy in the presence of our God and Father when our Lord Jesus comes with all his holy ones (3:12-13).

Notice, he prays for their love and their holiness to increase.

Paul prays for them again at the end of the letter:

> May God himself, the God of peace, sanctify you through and through. May your whole spirit, soul and body be kept blameless at the coming of our Lord Jesus Christ. The one who calls you is faithful and he will do it (5:23-24).

In addition to love and holiness, he wants them to grow in hope. Paul knows that in order for the Thessalonians to live differently than the world as well as differently than their own pasts, they must have a different hope—a different goal in life—one that will inspire them to endure in the faith.

It is this hope that enabled the Thessalonians to live as a model for others, as Paul mentions in the first chapter. They had turned to God "to wait for his Son from heaven, whom he raised from the dead—Jesus, who rescues us from the coming wrath" (1:10). The image of waiting is a great one to meditate upon. The Christian is called to live a waiting life. Everything in our culture tells us to go for things *now*. We are told our immediate experience determines how we should spend our time, our money, and our affections. But Paul says no! Christians should live waiting lives. We wait for our salvation to be completed. We wait for our innocence to be demonstrated. We wait for final gratification and final joy. We wait for Christ to be revealed to the world and to all who hope in him. We wait for the worries and pains of this life to end and the war with sin to end. We wait for God's name to be fully vindicated. In short, we wait for Jesus, the Son of God, to come from heaven and rescue us from the coming wrath.

Paul prayed because he hoped. Without that hope, he would not have prayed. If we want to pray like Paul prays, we must hope like Paul hoped.

PAUL'S RECOLLECTION OF GENUINE MINISTRY AMONG THE THESSALONIANS

Paul's situation is an awkward one. He has been charged with fly-by-night fleecing. The product he is accused of peddling is his message, his entertaining story, his novel teachings. The concern and love he has for the Thessalonians has been called an act. And it has been said Paul came to Thessalonica for only one reason—money.

Naturally, Paul is concerned to disprove such slander. So he carefully contradicts these ideas by recalling his own ministry among them. He reminds the Thessalonians how he had shown himself to be a genuinely concerned servant of God who sought their good and not his own.

Seven Signs of Genuine Ministry

The defense of Paul's ministry occurs in chapters 2 and 3, where we can discern at least seven signs of a genuine ministry. You might want to consider the ministries God has committed to you and ask yourself if these seven signs describe your ministry. And then pray that they would.

1. *Self-sacrifice.* The first sign of genuine ministry is self-sacrifice. In his missionary journeys, and not least in his trip to Macedonia, Paul showed he was willing to sacrifice his own safety. Contrary to the slander, Paul had shared the gospel with the Thessalonians at cost to himself. He did not benefit by it. Instead, he faced opposition and the threat of harm. He writes,

> You know, brothers, that our visit to you was not a failure. We had previously suffered and been insulted in Philippi, as you know, but with the help of our God we dared to tell you his gospel in spite of strong opposition (2:1-2; cf. 2:13-14).

Paul was also willing to sacrifice his own popularity. He writes,

> For the appeal we make does not spring from error or impure motives, nor are we trying to trick you. On the contrary, we speak as men approved by God to be entrusted with the gospel. We are not trying to please men but God, who tests our hearts. You know we never used flattery, nor did we put on a mask to cover up greed—God is our witness. We were not looking for praise from men, not from you or anyone else.
>
> As apostles of Christ we could have been a burden to you (2:3-6).

Paul did not preach the gospel to the Thessalonians with mercenary concern for himself and his own gain, but with pure motives, to please God, not men.

Of course, persevering in the ministry amid unpopularity does not necessarily mean one is persevering for the right thing. But it can suggest good motives. And it certainly refutes what Paul's opponents were saying—that he was in it for personal gain. Far from trying to fleece the flock, Paul had been committed to not being a burden to them. He writes, "Surely you remember, brothers, our toil and hardship; we worked night and day in order not to be a burden to anyone while we preached the gospel of God to you" (2:9). Primarily, I think, Paul means he had not been a financial burden to them. He knew such kind of slander might come, so he deliberately made his own money, leaving such charges without traction. Self-sacrifice is a sign of genuine ministry.

2. *Motherly love.* Motherly love is also a sign of genuine ministry. Paul writes,

> We were gentle among you, like a mother caring for her little children. We loved you so much that we were delighted to share with you not only the gospel of God but our lives as well, because you had become so dear to us (2:7-8).

Paul was not harsh, but gentle. He did not take from them but was delighted to share with them. They are dear to him, like a child to a mother.

3. *Fatherly integrity and encouragement.* Next, Paul says that he exhibited a fatherly integrity among them, and now he encourages them with fatherly counsel:

> You are witnesses, and so is God, of how holy, righteous and blameless we were among you who believed. For you know that we dealt with each of you as a father deals with his own children, encouraging, comforting and urging you to live lives worthy of God, who calls you into his kingdom and glory (2:10-12).

Like a good father, he set an example of holiness, righteousness, and blamelessness in his work. And like a good father, he urges them to live lives worthy of God.

4. *Desire for fellowship.* Then there is Paul's desire to be with them. Paul writes, "But, brothers, when we were torn away from you for a short time (in person, not in thought), out of our intense longing we made every effort to see you" (2:17). In spite of what is being said, Paul's departure was no cowardly "slip out the back, Jack." Several times Paul mentions his desire to return and see them (2:18; 3:6, 10-11). Since he has not been able to visit, he has sent Timothy to strengthen and encourage them, and to bring him news of them (3:1-5). Such a desire for fellowship is another evidence of a genuine ministry.

5. *Joy.* Still another sign is Paul's joy. Several times Paul says that he rejoices because of them. First, in chapter 2, he writes, "For what is our hope, our joy, or the crown in which we will glory in the presence of our Lord Jesus when he comes? Is it not you? Indeed, you are our glory and joy" (2:19-20). Then in chapter 3, he writes,

> Therefore, brothers, in all our distress and persecution we were encouraged about you because of your faith. For now we really live, since you are standing firm in the Lord. How can we thank God enough for you in return for all the joy we have in the presence of our God because of you? (3:7-9).

The Thessalonians' joy in receiving the gospel testifies to the genuineness of their belief (1:6); likewise, Paul's joy over them testifies to the genuineness of his concern.

6. *Prayer.* Another sign Paul gives of genuine ministry to the Thessalonians is his prayers for them, as we have already noted (e.g., 2:13).

7. *Hope.* The last sign of a genuine ministry we will note here is Paul's hope. The first six signs are fed by the hope he has for them. As we have seen, Paul has dealt with them as a father deals with his children, "encouraging, comforting and urging you to live lives worthy of God, who calls you into his kingdom and glory" (2:12). In other words, Paul has dealt with the Thessalonians according to the hope of God's calling in their lives. His work among them in the past had been premised upon his hope in God concerning them, and his expectation of the future is also premised upon this hope in God. As we saw in 2:19 above, "For what is our hope, our joy, or the crown in which we will glory in the presence of our Lord Jesus when he comes? Is it not you?" When Jesus comes, the Thessalonian believers will be Paul's hope, joy, crown, and glory. Hope for the future—hope that God will do what he promises—is crucial to the ministry of caring that Paul has among the Thessalonians.

This hope has implications in the present. Paul prays in chapter 3, "May he strengthen your hearts so that you will be blameless and holy in the presence of our God and Father when our Lord Jesus comes with all his holy ones" (3:13). Hope in the coming of our Lord Jesus leads to holiness in the present.

These are the seven testimonies to Paul's own ministry, and the signs that mark any valid ministry: self-sacrifice, a motherly love, a fatherly integrity and encouragement, a desire to be with one's flock, a joy in them, prayer for them, and hope.

I have to ask, do these characteristics mark my ministry? Do they mark the ministry of those who are over you in the Lord? If you are called to labor as a parent, an elder, a teacher, or a leader of any kind in the church, do these qualities mark your labors? Or is your ministry just a self-centered sham with a religious veneer? That was the charge made against Paul. These seven signs comprise his refutation of the charge, and these signs are what we need to consider with regard to our own ministries. Are we genuinely ministering out of real faith, real hope, and real love to God and his people?

PAUL'S VISION OF THE CHRISTIAN LIFE TOGETHER

Paul does not just talk about his own ministry. He also teaches the Thessalonians how to live as Christians. In the last two chapters of this letter, Paul lays out eight qualities that should typify the lives of Christians. In some ways, it is useful for us that Paul was forced to withdraw from Thessalonica prematurely, because it required him to fully enunciate basic teachings about the Christian life for us. As we note these eight qualities that should mark a Christian's life, you may want to keep a list and see how you are doing.

Eight Signs of a Christian Life

1. *Live in order to please God.* The beginning point of the Christian life, and of Christian ministry, is not living to please *others* but living to please *God:*

> Finally, brothers, we instructed you how to live in order to please God, as in fact you are living. Now we ask you and urge you in the Lord Jesus to do this more and more. For you know what instructions we gave you by the authority of the Lord Jesus (4:1-2).

If we live only to please others, we will not live faithfully. If you are a Christian, God will call you to do some things that will be unpopular with those around you. Yet those around you will never be your final court of appeal. As Christians, we must live fundamentally to please God.

2. *Live a sexually holy life.* Paul devotes what is an entire paragraph in the NIV to exhorting the Thessalonians to live sexually holy lives. He writes,

> It is God's will that you should be sanctified: that you should avoid sexual immorality; that each of you should learn to control his own body in a way that is holy and honorable, not in passionate lust like the heathen, who do not know God; and that in this matter no one should wrong his brother or take advantage of him. The Lord will punish men for all such sins, as we have already told you and warned you. For God did not call us to be impure, but to live a holy life. Therefore, he who rejects this instruction does not reject man but God, who gives you his Holy Spirit (4:3-8).

Pleasing God means doing God's will. And God wills Christians to "be sanctified." How? Avoid sexual immorality. Control your own body. If you want to be holy and honorable before the Lord, lead a sexually moral life.

Paul's instruction to avoid sexual immorality may seem like a no-brainer, and we know it is particularly important in our culture today. Yet if you can imagine, it may have been an even more important instruction in the culture of the ancient Greek world. It has been said that the only new virtue Christianity gave the world was chastity. Sexual promiscuity was even more accepted and practiced in the ancient pagan world than in our own world today. Adultery, prostitution, homosexuality, pederasty, and other sexual perversions were common, so common that two millennia of Christian influence may diminish our ability to comprehend it.

Interestingly, Paul insists the Thessalonians should pursue sexually moral lives not only for their own sakes but for the sake of others as well. He says in 4:6, "no one should wrong his brother or take advantage of him." You might have heard people refer to sexual sin as "private sin." But the Bible does not buy this idea. Sexual sin is not private. It is social and has social implications. A man who sleeps with someone else's wife sins not only in his own body: he causes the woman to sin, he sins against her husband, and he sins against his own wife, if he is married. The damage spreads quickly. An unmarried man who sleeps with an unmarried woman sins not only in his own body: he causes the woman to sin, he sins against the woman's future husband, and he sins against his own future wife.

When you sleep with someone other than your spouse, you greedily and destructively take what is not yours.

Behind a Christian's sexual sin against others is sin against God. Paul refers to "God's will" in 4:3. That in itself should be enough to motivate a Christian to avoid sin. That is also why Paul severely warns the Thessalonians against indifference to these instructions: "he who rejects this instruction does not reject man but God," he says in 4:8.

How many times, when I have confronted people over sexual immorality, have they tried to redefine the words "sexual immorality" to show that what they did was not condemned in the Word of God. Surely, they say, the words must mean something other than what *they* were involved in. Friend, for your own soul's sake, unstop your ears. Hear these words now: God says sexual immorality is typical of the heathen (4:5), and he will punish people for all such sins (4:6). Live a sexually holy life.

3. *Live a life of brotherly love.* In chapter 4, Paul writes,

> Now about brotherly love we do not need to write to you, for you yourselves have been taught by God to love each other. And in fact, you do love all the brothers throughout Macedonia. Yet we urge you, brothers, to do so more and more (4:9-10).

Within the context of their own church, Christians should love one another. Yet Christians should also love the saints in other churches. Paul commends the Thessalonians for loving all the brothers throughout Macedonia, and then encourages them to love them more and more.

In short, the New Testament treats loving people beyond the bounds of our own church as normal. We should have a particular concern for other churches. And we should grow in this love: "do so more and more," says Paul.

4. *Live a respectable life.* Paul writes,

Make it your ambition to lead a quiet life, to mind your own business and to work with your hands, just as we told you, so that your daily life may win the respect of outsiders and so that you will not be dependent on anybody (4:11-12).

Christians should seek to live quiet lives, mind their own business, and work with their hands. Not that these things are ends in themselves. Don't read these verses and think, "Great, I like the sound of a quiet life and minding my own business!" That misses Paul's point, which is stated clearly in 4:12: *so that* you may win the respect of outsiders, and *so that* you will not be dependent on anybody. Part of a Christian's basic mission is to live a life that commends the gospel to others. You do this not so that others will think well of you but so that the gospel will be commended.

5. *Live a life awake to God.* In chapter 5, Paul writes,

But you, brothers, are not in darkness so that this day should surprise you like a thief. You are all sons of the light and sons of the day. We do not belong to the night or to the darkness. So then, let us not be like others, who are asleep, but let us be alert and self-controlled. For those who sleep, sleep at night, and those who get drunk, get drunk at night. But since we belong to the day, let us be self-controlled, putting on faith and love as a breastplate, and the hope of salvation as a helmet. For God did not appoint us to suffer wrath but to receive salvation through our Lord Jesus Christ. He died for us so that, whether we are awake or asleep, we may live together with him (5:4-10).

We are to be awake to God. We do not live in darkness but in the light. We do not live in the night but in the day. We are not asleep but awake, alert, and self-controlled. As Christians, we do not wait for condemnation but for salvation. We wear faith, love, and the hope of salvation, not wrath. We may experience physical death, but not spiritual death. We all will live together with Christ because he died for us.

6. *Live an encouraging life.* Paul continues in chapter 5:

Therefore encourage one another and build each other up, just as in fact you are doing.

Now we ask you, brothers, to respect those who work hard among you, who are over you in the Lord and who admonish you. Hold them in the highest regard in love because of their work. Live in peace with each other. And we urge you, brothers, warn those who are idle, encourage the timid, help the weak, be patient with everyone. Make sure that nobody pays back wrong for wrong, but always try to be kind to each other and to everyone else (5:11-15).

Does this sound like you? Encouraging others; building others up; living in peace; being patient with everyone; never paying back wrong for wrong; always trying to be kind? Have I, without naming your name, just described you? If you are a Christian, this is how you are called to live.

Paul especially calls us to give encouragement in two particular cases. First, care for your leaders. The elders and pastors of your church work hard. They are over you. They admonish you. Do you respect them? Do you hold them in the highest regard in love? This is not just the idea of some pastor who likes authority, although some pastors clearly have abused their authority. This is what God teaches his people. You will be blessed if you respect the authority God has placed over you in the church.

Notice also the second group Paul says to encourage: the stragglers. Warn the idle, he says. He does not say, "be kindly indifferent to them." He says to warn them. He also says we should encourage the timid. He doesn't say, "overlook their shyness and wait for time to pass." He says to actively encourage them. Finally, Paul says to help the weak.

Is your life marked by giving warnings, encouragement, and help? That is the life of a Christian. We are called to give our life for others.

7. Live a God-centered life. In the next verses, Paul writes, "Be joyful always; pray continually; give thanks in all circumstances, for this is God's will for you in Christ Jesus" (5:16-18). How can you be joyful always? Not by centering your life upon circumstances. Circumstances will always change. However, if you center your life on God, regardless of what happens at work, regardless of what happens at home, regardless of what happens at church, you can be joyful. God is at the center of your being, and he does not change!

How then do you center your life on God? First, pray continually, as Paul says in 5:17. Second, give thanks in all circumstances, as he says in 5:18. Ask him for what you need. Thank him for what you have. The Christian life always has God at the center. Is God always at the center of your mind and thoughts?

8. Live a discerning life. Paul concludes the exhortation portion of chapter 5 by writing, "Do not put out the Spirit's fire; do not treat prophecies with contempt. Test everything. Hold on to the good. Avoid every kind of evil" (5:19-22). The center of this small paragraph (in the NIV) is the first two words of 5:21: "Test everything." We should be discerning about prophecy as well as about good and evil. In short, live a discerning life.

How are you doing on the checklist? Does reading it encourage you as you consider your own Christian life? Are you thinking, "Yes, failingly, haltingly, I do seem to be getting it. God's Holy Spirit does seem to be working these things in me: living to please God, being sexually holy, loving the brothers, being respectable, being awake to God, encouraging others, being God-centered and discerning"? Perhaps you could use this list in praying for yourself and for others.

Before we go to the final section, two other matters concerning Paul's vision of the Christian life are worth noting. First, we should know the importance of hope for our lives. Hope prompts us to live sexually holy lives now, knowing that God will judge sexual immorality (4:6). Hope enables us to live lives that are ready, alert, and self-controlled (5:4-6). And hope is connected with living in faith and love (5:8). If you try to practice these Christian virtues without hope (because all that "future" stuff sounds a little strange to you), you will not succeed. You are cutting the very nerve of Christianity. These virtues depend on the hope we have in the future through Jesus Christ.

Second, we should note how Paul's own life exemplified these eight qualities. Paul practiced what he preached! No, not perfectly. He may have made a mistake when he and Barnabas argued over Mark (Acts 15:36-40). Paul had his faults. But I am struck by how these qualities characterized Paul's life. He clearly understood the importance of modeling one's teaching through such life characteristics. A preacher can stand in his pulpit preaching Sunday after Sunday, but a congregation may not really take these qualities to heart until they see individuals they know well living out these qualities. God's Holy Spirit changes us powerfully through such examples.

What kind of life characteristics are you demonstrating for others? Among the people watching you, which characteristics of yours cause them to say, "I'm going to be like that"? What habits are they establishing when following you? Have you devoted yourself to living your life in such a way that encourages others to replicate these eight qualities?

I pray regularly for every member of my church, and I pray that God would cause each life to exhibit these eight qualities more and more. Also, the elders of our church are continually looking for new elders as we pray through the membership directory, and these qualities exemplify what we are looking for: people who strive to cultivate these qualities in their own lives *and in the lives of others*. Has God given you a concern for people beyond your own family? Do you work to see God's character of holiness and love replicated in the lives of others? That is what we should be about as Christians.

PAUL'S HOPE IN THE SECOND COMING OF CHRIST

There is one last thing we should note about this letter: Paul's hope in the second coming of Christ, which should also be the hope of all true Christians. This great hope, described at the end of chapter 4 and the beginning of chapter 5, both encourages us and prepares us.

This Great Hope Encourages Us

The Christian hope in the second coming of Christ encourages us amid the difficulties, the trials, and even the end of this present life. Apparently a number of people in the Thessalonian church were unclear about the fate of Christians who died before Christ's return. Paul had taught the Thessalonians that Christ would return, but apparently he had not addressed the issue of what would happen to those who had already died. Perhaps no one had died while he was with them; then, after his departure, perhaps someone in the church died and everybody worried, "Oh, no! Paul told us these glorious things about the Second Coming. Is that person now just gone? Are those who have died going to miss out?" Paul then heard that the Thessalonians were grieving for their dead no differently than the non-Christians around them, so he writes,

> Brothers, we do not want you to be ignorant about those who fall asleep, or to grieve like the rest of men, who have no hope. We believe that Jesus died and rose again and so we believe that God will bring with Jesus those who have fallen asleep in him. According to the Lord's own word, we tell you that we who are still alive, who are left till the coming of the Lord, will certainly not precede those who have fallen asleep (4:13-15).

You see, the hope these Christians could have was not to be based on their optimistic feelings but on the truth. Truth brings hope. What is the unique Christian hope? "We believe that Jesus died and rose again." That is, we believe in the resurrection. Furthermore, "we believe that God will bring with Jesus those who have fallen asleep in him." That is, the dead in Christ will also be resurrected when he returns. Those who have died in Christ will not miss out, they will be honored! They will precede those of us who are left alive when Christ returns.

After dealing with this particular pastoral problem, Paul proceeds to teach the Thessalonians more generally about the second coming of Christ and the real end of days. He writes in the following verses,

> For the Lord himself will come down from heaven, with a loud command, with the voice of the archangel and with the trumpet call of God, and the dead in Christ will rise first. After that, we who are still alive and are left will be caught up together with them in the clouds to meet the Lord in the air. And so we will be with the Lord forever. Therefore encourage each other with these words (4:16-18).

At the center of the end of days will be not an antichrist but Christ himself. The Lord himself, meaning Christ, will come down from heaven. This is *the fact* about the second coming of Christ. If you know nothing else about the Second Coming, hear this from Scripture: the very center of the Second Coming is Christ coming.

Along with this image you should imagine great noises, like a movie soundtrack. Christ will come with a loud command, the voice of the archangel, and the trumpet call of God. Judgment day will include commanding, attention-arresting, ear-splitting, heart-wrenching sounds.

And certainly, the Christian dead should not be omitted from this picture. After all, that is Paul's point. He says in 4:16, the dead in Christ are in no danger of missing out; they will actually rise first.

Yet the picture is not complete. We must include the living. Verse 17 says the living Christians will be caught up with the resurrected Christians to meet Christ in the air. The living and the dead in Christ will be reunited again as one great family of God. The border of death will no longer be a border that Christians recognize.

Is there anything else to be said about Paul's picture of the last day? Yes, it is not only the last day, it is the beginning of eternity. As Paul says, "We will be with the Lord forever."

The point of Paul's picture, again, is to encourage the Thessalonians. "Therefore encourage each other with these words," he says. And even as he commands them to encourage one another, so he encourages them here.

Does thinking about the great day encourage you? Are you thinking, "Oh, no, what if the great day comes really soon? There goes all my financial planning." Or, "Rats, I just met the girl I thought I was going to marry!" There are other things I could mention that often seize our hearts. What about *your* heart? Are you encouraged by the thought that the Lord will return? Don't quickly utter some Sunday school answer in your head. What is the honest response of your own heart?

Do you welcome the thought of Christ's return, or does Paul's picture genuinely make you think of "doomsday"? Doomsday comes from an old Anglo-Saxon word. It just means "day of judgment." It is the day on which the books of doom, the books of God's judgment, will be opened, and the great inquests will be held. We will all be condemned to hell because of our sins—if we stand outside of Christ. None of us has any hope on that great day, not even the most holy appearing person in the world. From Adolf Hitler to Mother Theresa, none has hope except for those who are in Christ. Christ alone lived the holy and perfect life that no one else has lived. And then he died on the cross as the perfect sacrifice, taking the punishment that we deserve for our sins. He calls us now to trust in him and to give our lives to him. And if we trust in and rely on him, he will give us new life. That is the only hope we have, and it is a great hope. When you have that hope, the second coming of Christ can be your greatest and most encouraging expectation.

This Great Hope Prepares Us

This great hope we have in Christ's coming not only encourages us, it also prepares us. You see, though Christ's return will surprise unbelievers, it will not surprise believers. Sometimes Christians get this wrong. They become fixated on what Jesus says in Mark 13—"No one knows about that day or hour" (Mark 13:32)—and that becomes the only thing they know about the Second Coming. But this hope is actually supposed to cause us to prepare. That is Paul's point in the beginning of 1 Thessalonians 5. He writes,

> Now, brothers, about times and dates we do not need to write to you, for you know very well that the day of the Lord will come like a thief in the night. While people are saying, 'Peace and safety,' destruction will come on them suddenly, as labor pains on a pregnant woman, and they will not escape.
> But you, brothers, are not in darkness so that this day should surprise you like a thief (1 Thess. 5:1-4).

On the one hand, Christ's coming will be a surprise to unbelievers. While people are saying "Peace and safety" and "the lowest unemployment in thirty years," destruction will come on them suddenly. Paul couples two images to drive this point home. In 5:2, he promises that destruction will come like a "thief." And then to enhance the image, he adds, "in the night." That is as secretive as you can get. In 5:3, he uses a second image: "as labor pains on a pregnant woman." If unbelievers have not believed in Christ the first time around, they will surely be surprised by his second coming!

On the other hand, Christ's coming will surprise no one who is in the light: "You, brothers, are not in darkness so that this day should surprise you like a thief." No, nobody knows the time and date exactly, but Christians know Christ is coming. And we are to live every day of our lives in that knowledge. It may occur at any moment. So we should live as those who are ready.

Really, this whole letter waters and feeds our lives with this life-giving, hope-inspiring truth for Christians: Jesus is coming again!

CONCLUSION

I know all this talk of doomsday sounds strange to people today. Even Christians can shy away from it. There are a lot of people who talk, think, and even sing about Christ's second coming in church. But in their conversations with secular friends, they would sooner die than bring up this topic. The second coming of Christ sounds like comic book stuff, or like a great special-effects movie. It doesn't sound like real life.

What about you? Does this sound more like the movies or more like the genuine promises God uses to help produce in us lives of prayer, service, holiness, and love?

The gods that many worship today do not arrive and announce a coming Judgment Day. The gods depicted in the soupy best-selling books on spirituality in bookstore checkout lines are morally indifferent gods. They do not bring the teaching of Jesus or the counsel of Paul. The God of Fatherly discipline is replaced with a god of grandfatherly permissiveness. Yet these gods are as powerless as the wooden and metal idols of old. They are nothing more than creations of their own worshipers' imaginations. The true God does not exist, as one author said recently, "merely to stroke and console our desiring hearts."

In Charles Dickens's *Bleak House*, someone tries to put a nice face on an orphan's plight by referring to him as "a child of the universe." Dickens's character John Jarndyce replies, "The universe makes a rather indifferent parent, I am afraid." The mental slop of the New Age offers nothing more than that— an ultimately indifferent universe that leaves us to pick and choose among meaningless options. All these modern bleached-out imitations of God promise us nothing more than the satisfaction of our most superficial desires.

Alan Jacobs, an English teacher at Wheaton College, put it well in an article he wrote called "The God of the Best Seller List": "Several years ago, when Woody Allen was asked to explain his affair with his wife's adopted daughter, he offered this verbal shrug: 'The heart wants what it wants.' This is a tautology of immense moral significance, because it indicates that there is no power capable of interrogating, much less redirecting, the heart that wants—the heart that does nothing but wants. The God of these books congratulates the heart for wanting and stifles the voice of mind or conscience that would offer dissent or even query. He accomplishes this stifling by proclaiming that He merely echoes—as the entire universe merely echoes—the human heart's howl of appetite."[2]

A god who does not reveal his will gives no wisdom. A god who condemns no sin offers no salvation. Such an indifferent god answers no prayers. Such a flattering god calls for no sacrificial service. Such a false god calls for no holiness. Such a god is no true God.

The biblical God gives faith and calls for prayer. The biblical God gives love and calls for sacrificial service for others. The biblical God gives hope and

---

[2] Alan Jacobs, "The God of the Best Seller List," *Weekly Standard*, December 5, 1999, 35.

demands holiness, because he is coming back. Now, to you, does this sound like a promise or a threat?

Let us pray:

Dear God, we pray that, amid modern madness, our souls would not be distracted from their most important task. Teach us to love you, and show us what it means to be reconciled to you. Enable us to live lives of service to others, lives marked by the things we see taught in this little letter. And we pray, Lord, that we would not do these things according to any kind of despairing legalism or entrapment to a set of rules, but as part of our worship of you. We pray for Jesus' sake. Amen.

Questions for Reflection

1. How much time do you think the average non-Christian today gives to thinking about the end times? To thinking about death? How much time do you give to these matters?

2. Paul prays that the Thessalonians would grow in hope (see 5:23). He knows that in order for them to live differently than the world and differently than their own pasts, they must have a different hope—a different goal in life—one that will inspire them to endure in the faith. Is this how you pray for your Christian friends?

3. Paul ministered to the Thessalonians at great cost to himself. What are some of the sacrifices we in the West today might be called upon to make? Ask God to prepare you for whatever he may have in store for you.

4. A sign of genuine ministry is a ministry driven by hope. What does a ministry driven by hope look like? What does a ministry without hope look like? What are some of the symptoms of a ministry that is slowly being sapped of its hope? How do we prevent this from happening?

5. These are the seven testimonies to Paul's own ministry, and the qualities that mark any valid ministry: self-sacrifice, a motherly love, a fatherly integrity and encouragement, a desire to be with one's flock, a joy in them, prayer for them, and hope. Do these qualities mark the ministry of those who are over you in the Lord? If you are called to labor as a parent, an elder, a teacher, or a leader of any kind in the church, do these qualities mark your labors? (Thank God for where they do.) Or is your ministry a self-centered sham with a religious veneer?

6. Have you observed your love for the fellow members of your church increasing over the last couple of years? Be sure to thank God for the progress that you do see!

7. Does this sound like you? Encouraging others; building others up; living in peace; being patient with everyone; never paying back wrong for wrong; always trying to be kind. Be sure to thank God for the places where this does sound like you!

8. So how did you do on the checklist of living the Christian life? Living to please God, sexually holy, loving the brothers, respectable, awake to God, encouraging others, God-centered, and discerning? As we have suggested, you can use this list in praying for yourself and for others.

9. What kind of life characteristics are you demonstrating for others? What habits will they establish by following you?

10. Do you seek to spend time with people who appear to be further along in their faith and in exhibiting its fruits?

11. How does a Christian prepare for the Second Coming?

THE MESSAGE OF 2 THESSALONIANS: HOPE

14

THE MESSAGE OF 2 THESSALONIANS: HOPE

AS GOOD AS IT GETS?[1]

Every couple of years, I find occasion to mention my friend Secular Sam. I wonder if you know him. Sam is successful. He has a good job, a nice girlfriend, and a beautiful apartment. His car is new, and his health is fine. He is humorous, good with people, and intelligent.

Secular Sam is also a Christian. That is, he affirms the things we believe as Christians. And he is quite active! Young Life, Campus Crusade, and InterVarsity are all in his background. Long ago, of course, he left some of the more embarrassing and immature bits behind. He is not a theological liberal. He affirms the authority of Scripture. But he is not a stereotypical, ghettoized fundamentalist. He has recovered the cultural mandate in Scripture. He understands Genesis, the great story of creation, and what God calls us to do. He understands that all of life should come under the scrutiny of Scripture: not just religion, but business, philosophy, ethics, economics, politics, law, and the arts. He has a thoughtful and refined appreciation for how Scripture gives the most satisfying explanation for all kinds of phenomena in our world—certainly the origin and meaning of life. Sam knows Scripture's awesome explanatory power. It has a first principle—God—who, by definition, needs no previous cause. Sam can honestly examine human foibles with his understanding of human sinfulness. He can confute his skeptical friends by the historical evidence for the resurrection. He seems to have a moral bearing that is the envy of many of his more thoughtful friends.

But Sam is profoundly secular in *this:* he expects to wake up in his bed tomorrow morning. Sam has never even heard of what his grandparents' gen-

---

[1] This sermon was originally preached on December 12, 1999, at Capitol Hill Baptist Church in Washington, D.C.

eration called "the blessed hope." No, his concerns, even about his own spiritual life, are all contained in this age, or *saeculum*, to use the Latin root. For Sam assumes that tomorrow will be just like today. Of course, that has serious implications for how he thinks about today. In a strange way, Sam's hope has all been collapsed into the now, the present, the visible, and the feel-able.

What is your hope fixed on? Humans live by their hopes, you know, as surely as they live by the air they breathe.

INTRODUCING 2 THESSALONIANS

The young Thessalonian church, which we began considering in our study of 1 Thessalonians, had a hope problem like Secular Sam. Sam differs in that he is completely unaware of God's promised future. As we will see, the Thessalonians assume the promised future has been realized *now*. But in both cases, there is a hope problem that leaves heaven looking suspiciously like this life.

Paul had heard about some of the Thessalonians' problems, and so he wrote them another short letter. In our previous study, we noted that this young church had been established by Paul just a few months—at most, a year or two—earlier. The church had been persevering through hard times, facing persecution for the faith in Thessalonica, the leading city of Macedonia. This much we learn from the book of Acts and the first letter to the Thessalonians. Paul alludes to this persecution again in his second letter. He writes,

> Therefore, among God's churches we boast about your perseverance and faith in all the persecutions and trials you are enduring.
>
> All this is evidence that God's judgment is right, and as a result you will be counted worthy of the kingdom of God, for which you are suffering (1:4-5).

This was a noble church undergoing suffering, and enduring in a way you or I might find challenging.

But there was a problem in this noble church, which we want to understand more deeply so that we can learn from it. Specifically, we want to ask three questions. First, what was their problem? Second, how did they fall into this problem? Third, what can we learn from them?

WHAT WAS THE THESSALONIANS' PROBLEM?

The Problem

The problem that caused Paul to write this letter was, simply put, idleness. Paul writes in chapter 3,

In the name of the Lord Jesus Christ, we command you, brothers, to keep away from every brother who is idle and does not live according to the teaching you received from us. For you yourselves know how you ought to follow our example. We were not idle when we were with you, nor did we eat anyone's food without paying for it. On the contrary, we worked night and day, laboring and toiling so that we would not be a burden to any of you. We did this, not because we do not have the right to such help, but in order to make ourselves a model for you to follow. For even when we were with you, we gave you this rule: "If a man will not work, he shall not eat."

We hear that some among you are idle. They are not busy; they are busybodies. Such people we command and urge in the Lord Jesus Christ to settle down and earn the bread they eat (3:6-12).

A number of the Thessalonians had decided they did not need to work anymore, even though Paul had previously taught them, "If a man will not work, he shall not eat" (3:10). Not all of a church's problems can be laid at the pastor's door! Three times Paul refers to the "idle" (3:6, 7, 11). These people are "not busy; they are busybodies" (3:11). Paul seems to have understood this was something of a problem in Thessalonica as early as his first letter to the Thessalonians, when he wrote, "warn those who are idle" (1 Thess. 5:14).

Idleness was not a problem completely unique to the Thessalonian church. A similar situation would later arise in the Ephesian church when widows young enough to remarry or work got into "the habit of being idle and going about from house to house. And not only do they become idlers, but also gossips and busybodies, saying things they ought not to" (1 Tim. 5:13). But something about the Thessalonian situation was more problematic than the later situation at Ephesus. We gather that from the fact that Paul not only teaches against idleness in both letters, he lived out this particular teaching among them by paying for his food. In this second letter to them, he chides them for not living "according to the teaching" he has given and for not following his example (2 Thess. 3:6-7). This was not true in every city he ministered in; in some places he did take support, which he had the right to do. Yet in Thessalonica, Paul seems to have realized that some combination of circumstances and false ideas was leading to an acute problem of idleness.

Paul loved the Thessalonians and didn't want to burden them by asking for financial support. But perhaps more importantly, he also wanted to be an example to them, which was a substantial commitment on his part. It meant working night and day. It meant laboring and toiling, as he says in 3:8. He could have exercised his rights for pay, he says in 3:9. But he wanted to be a model for them over the long haul.

Consider Paul's seemingly meaningless act of purchasing his own food. In that one action, Paul 1) paid for his food, 2) cared for the Thessalonian church by not being a burden, and 3) set an example. In other words, even small actions that seem insignificant have tremendous meaning when rightly considered.

Perhaps you have heard of the man who asked the three bricklayers what they were doing, even though all three were laying bricks. The first worker said he was laying bricks. The second said he was building a wall. The third said he was raising up a cathedral for the glory of God. This third worker had the big picture in mind during his work. Paul was like this third bricklayer. He deliberately worked when he was among the Thessalonians because he knew his small actions would teach them about a much larger end. He knew that the way he conducted his daily affairs was an opportunity to love them. So it is with us. Everything you do this week, or even later today, has significance. You and I should consider Paul's example. He took responsibility for his actions in the present in light of the significance he wanted those actions to have in the future.

The Cause

The cause of the problem in Thessalonica was a terrible misunderstanding. In chapter 2, Paul writes,

> Concerning the coming of our Lord Jesus Christ and our being gathered to him, we ask you, brothers, not to become easily unsettled or alarmed by some prophecy, report or letter supposed to have come from us, saying that the day of the Lord has already come. Don't let anyone deceive you in any way, for that day will not come until the rebellion occurs and the man of lawlessness is revealed, the man doomed to destruction (2:1-3).

The Thessalonian Christians had misunderstood the promise of Christ's coming and the gathering of the saints to him. Apparently, false teachers had told them that Christ had already come. So some of them, perhaps many of them, had stopped working. Paul responds, "Don't panic. Settle down. I have not taught that the day of the Lord is here. Don't let anyone deceive you!" It is not that they believed they had missed the Second Coming, as some speak of the Rapture occurring and individuals being left behind. No, they seemed to think the kingdom of God had come in its fullness and they were already experiencing it.

Now that may sound incredibly strange given the state of this world. But that appears to be what they were thinking. Maybe they thought the persecutions they were experiencing were the persecutions the apostles had predicted would occur before the Lord's return. At least the beginning of the end had come, they thought; so they could give up daily labor. Behind all this, of course, was human nature. If human nature can grab a theological reason not to work, then all the better. Bad theology can be used to justify what people like to do anyway. Probably the Thessalonians were not unwilling to lay down their tools. This idleness was probably caused, in other words, by a combination of their own natures and their misunderstanding of the truth.

The Solution

What solution does Paul propose? His answer is two-fold: knowledge and obedience. Know the truth, and live it out.

Know the truth. Paul begins by teaching the Thessalonians the truth about Christ's return. You see this in the first two chapters. The main thing he wants to be sure they know is that Christ has not yet come back. As we saw at the beginning of chapter 2, he tells them not to be deceived by those who say Christ has returned.

But there is more they must understand. When Christ returns, he will destroy the "man of lawlessness" (2:3). Who is this lawless one? Is it some world leader whose name we know? Paul does not say. He does describe him, though. This lawless one will oppose God: "He will oppose and will exalt himself over everything that is called God or is worshiped, so that he sets himself up in God's temple, proclaiming himself to be God" (2:4). He will also deceive: "The coming of the lawless one will be in accordance with the work of Satan displayed in all kinds of counterfeit miracles, signs and wonders, and in every sort of evil that deceives those who are perishing" (2:9-10a).

Paul does not warn the Thessalonians about the man of lawlessness in order to worry them. After all, God will destroy the man of lawlessness. Paul writes, "Don't let anyone deceive you in any way, for that day will not come until the rebellion occurs and the man of lawlessness is revealed, the man doomed to destruction" (2:3). And then several verses later he adds, "And now you know what is holding him back, so that he may be revealed at the proper time. For the secret power of lawlessness is already at work; but the one who now holds it back will continue to do so till he is taken out of the way. And then the lawless one will be revealed, whom the Lord Jesus will overthrow with the breath of his mouth and destroy by the splendor of his coming" (2:6-8). Jesus will overthrow and destroy the man of lawlessness. But the man of lawlessness will come first.

In short, Paul tells the Thessalonians they will know when the Second Coming happens! Nobody will have to sign up for a seminar to figure it out. Christ will judge all the wicked on that day (2:12), and Christians will "share in the glory of our Lord Jesus Christ" (2:14). If the Lord had already returned, the Thessalonians would not still be experiencing persecution.

Obey the truth. In the meantime, Christians are called to be obedient to the truth. They must follow God's call to work. Paul writes, "In the name of the Lord Jesus Christ, we command you, brothers, to keep away from every brother who is idle and does not live according to the teaching you received from us" (3:6). And then, "Such people we command and urge in the Lord Jesus Christ to settle down and earn the bread they eat" (3:12). In other words, get back to work. And watch out for those who don't!

Paul goes on to say,

> And as for you, brothers, never tire of doing what is right.
>
> If anyone does not obey our instruction in this letter, take special note of him. Do not associate with him, in order that he may feel ashamed. Yet do not regard him as an enemy, but warn him as a brother (3:13-15).

The idle must be warned. If they continue in unrepentance, they are not to be associated with. The matter is that serious.

Beyond that, Paul exhorts the Thessalonians to stand firm and hold to his teachings (2:15). And he prays that God would encourage and strengthen their hearts for every good word and deed (2:16-17).

The Thessalonians were idle because they thought the end had come. Paul tells them that Christ has not already returned, and what they must do now is simple: get back to work.

HOW DID THE THESSALONIANS FALL INTO THIS PROBLEM?

How could the Thessalonians have made the mistake of thinking the Lord had come back? Does that not seem like a strange thing to assume? Can you imagine making that mistake this past week? "Thursday was a really good day. Perhaps Thursday was the Second Coming." I don't think so. Not if you have been instructed as a Christian.

One of the crucial things we need to understand in this little letter is all the language about a relationship with God. I think if we notice God's role in the letter, we will understand better how this misunderstanding could have happened.

Our Relationship with God in the Present

I have mentioned in previous studies that some people are skeptical about the Christian claim that we actually come to know God through Christ. But when you read through this letter you find that Paul unmistakably describes a present relationship with God. This relationship is the context of everything else that Paul writes.

Language of relationship. Notice in chapter 3 the little phrase, "The Lord be with all of you" (3:16). This is a simple phrase of blessing, or what some call a "wish prayer." Yet consider what the prayer is: it is a prayer for God to bless the church by accompanying them with his presence. Not only that, notice what Paul promises God will do: "He will strengthen and protect you from the evil one" (3:3). So God is with them; he strengthens them; and he protects them. Does that sound like a relationship?

There is more. Consider whom God will punish: "He will punish those who do not know God" (1:8). Now that is interesting. I suspect that most people walking down the street today without any particular religious faith assume that if God does exist, we all know him by virtue of our creation. But here Paul says there are humans walking around who were made in the image of God, yet who do not know God. Paul uses explicit language elsewhere about "knowing God," as does the apostle John.[2] In fact, Paul and John seem to have learned this from Jesus himself. On the night before his crucifixion, Jesus prayed,

> "Father, the time has come. Glorify your Son, that your Son may glorify you. For you granted him authority over all people that he might give eternal life to all those you have given him. Now this is eternal life: that they may know you, the only true God, and Jesus Christ, whom you have sent" (John 17:1b-3).

Both Paul and these Thessalonians have come to know God, and they have been given eternal life. That is why Paul can write so openly about being loved by God. Paul refers to "God's love" (3:5). A few verses before, he specifically addresses them as, "You, brothers, loved by the Lord" (2:13). And then he speaks of "God our Father, who loved us" (2:16). So, in spite of the skeptics, I would say that if Paul can write about God's presence with them, God's protection of them, their knowledge of God, and even God's love for them, then it is pretty clear they have a relationship with God.

Language of prayer. Perhaps we can perceive Paul and the Thessalonians' relationship with God most clearly in the language of prayer scattered throughout the letter. We see this in three ways: Paul thanks God, he makes requests of God, and he asks the Thessalonians to pray for him.

First, Paul thanks God for the Thessalonians' faith, hope, and love. He writes at the beginning of the letter,

---

[2] Paul in Gal. 4:8-9; 1 Thess. 4:5; Titus 1:16; John in 1 John 4:8.

> We ought always to thank God for you, brothers, and rightly so, because your
> faith is growing more and more, and the love every one of you has for each other
> is increasing. Therefore, among God's churches we boast about your persever-
> ance and faith in all the persecutions and trials you are enduring (1:3-4).

He thanks God for them—he even boasts about them!—because their faith is
growing, their love for one another is increasing, and their hope is being displayed through the perseverance they exercise in the face of persecutions and
trials. Surely this is the work of God in them!

A little later, Paul says that he should thank God for God's own love for
the Thessalonians and how this love has been realized—in their salvation. In
chapter 2 Paul writes,

> But we ought always to thank God for you, brothers loved by the Lord, because
> from the beginning God chose you to be saved through the sanctifying work of
> the Spirit and through belief in the truth. He called you to this through our
> gospel, that you might share in the glory of our Lord Jesus Christ (2:13-14).

Paul is very specific about how God has loved Christians. He has shown his
love in election, vocation, salvation, sanctification, and the promise of glorification. Or, to use less theological language, God has shown us his love by calling us, inclining us to believe in him, saving us, making us holy, and promises
that he will finally bring us home to be with him and like him. Paul thanks God
for all these things.

Second, Paul asks God to bless the lives of the Thessalonians. In our
church, we regularly encourage members to pray for one another by praying
through one page a day in the church membership directory. People often ask
me how they can pray for people they do not know. Well, here are four ways
Paul prays for the Thessalonians. Perhaps you can write them down and pray
this way for yourself and others.

Paul prays for *grace and peace*. At the very beginning of the letter, he writes,
"Grace and peace to you from God the Father and the Lord Jesus Christ" (1:2).
Then at the very end of the letter, he writes, "Now may the Lord of peace himself give you peace at all times and in every way. The Lord be with all of you. . . .
The grace of our Lord Jesus Christ be with you all" (3:16, 18). Coming from
Paul, these traditional Hebrew (peace) and Greek (grace) greetings are more
than mere wish prayers. He invests them with theological meaning—that God
would continue to sustain them in his undeserved favor, and that he would hold
them in a reconciled state of peace with him and those around them.

Paul prays *that God will guide the Thessalonians into love and perseverance*. He writes, "May the Lord direct your hearts into God's love and Christ's

perseverance" (3:5).[3] The ultimate direction a Christian needs is direction into God's love and Christ's perseverance. Paul knows the Thessalonians' love will have to endure through difficult circumstances.

Paul prays for God's *strength*. Paul writes, "May our Lord Jesus Christ himself and God our Father . . . encourage your hearts and strengthen you in every good deed and word" (2:16a, 17). God's encouragement and strength are not given indiscriminately. They have a purpose: to build us up in Christ-glorifying deeds and words.

Paul also prays for the *success* of the saints:

> With this in mind, we constantly pray for you, that our God may count you worthy of his calling, and that by his power he may fulfill every good purpose of yours and every act prompted by your faith. We pray this so that the name of our Lord Jesus may be glorified in you, and you in him, according to the grace of our God and the Lord Jesus Christ (1:11-12).

Paul wants them to be *immediately* successful: that God would fulfill their "every good purpose" and their "every act prompted by faith." And he wants them to be *ultimately* successful: that the Lord Jesus would "be glorified" in them, and they in him.

Third, Paul asks the Thessalonians to pray for him. He writes, "Finally, brothers, pray for us that the message of the Lord may spread rapidly and be honored, just as it was with you. And pray that we may be delivered from wicked and evil men, for not everyone has faith" (3:1-2). Paul asks that the message of the gospel would prosper, spread rapidly, and be honored. Paul also asks that he would be protected from those who oppose this message (3:2).

So we see Christianity is not mere moralism. Unfortunately, some people are attracted to Christianity merely because it provides a set of values in life. It helps them understand the world and decide how to act in it. And you might think a letter that basically says "Get back to work" would be a moralistic letter about how to behave and act. But when you examine 2 Thessalonians, this is not what you find. You find a letter very much about our relationship with God, with implications for our daily lives. Christianity is not about tapping into some impersonal force or universal Christ-principle. It is about having a relationship with a personal God who made us in his image. All this relationship language and prayer language demonstrates that Christians are *already* in a wonderful relationship with God, which helps us understand how the Thessalonians could have been deceived. They had a genuine relationship with God, and they understood that something unusual and supernatural was hap-

---

[3] The root for "perseverance"—*hupomona*—is also used in 1 Thessalonians 1:3 and 2 Thessalonians 1:4.

pening. Perhaps they could be forgiven for thinking, "Wow! This is better than what I had before in life. Maybe this is it. Maybe this is the whole thing." A relationship with God is reality, and it is a wonderful reality.

Our Relationship with God in the Future

We are already in a relationship with God, but the big thing the Thessalonians needed to hear—and that we need to hear—is that far more lies ahead, more than any of us has ever experienced. God has already loved us, chosen to save us, called us, and given us faith. He gives us encouragement and hope. He is sanctifying us. And yet there is more to come! God will do even more in the future.

We can know nothing about what lies ahead except for what God tells us. And one of the main features of this letter is that it tells us what God will do, because the Thessalonians were confused on exactly this point. Most importantly, we are reminded that Jesus will come again. There will come a day, says Paul, "when the Lord Jesus is revealed from heaven in blazing fire with his powerful angels" (1:7). He has not yet come, but throughout the letter Paul promises the Lord will come (1:10; 2:1, 8).

How will we know when Christ comes? "Oh, you will know," says Paul. Here are three things Paul says Christ will do when he returns.

Christ will defeat the lawless one. Christ will begin his defeat of the lawless one by allowing this mysterious figure's followers to be deceived. Paul writes, "For this reason God sends them a powerful delusion so that they will believe the lie and so that all will be condemned who have not believed the truth but have delighted in wickedness" (2:11-12). Their own deception is the beginning of their judgment. Then Christ will destroy the lawless one himself: "And then the lawless one will be revealed, whom the Lord Jesus will overthrow with the breath of his mouth and destroy by the splendor of his coming" (2:8). Whoever the lawless one will be (and the commentators don't have a clue), the Lord Jesus will overthrow him with the breath of his mouth and the splendor of his coming. We hardly need dozens of end-times books to identify this fellow. Christ will identify him clearly.

Christ will sit in judgment. Paul writes,

> God is just: He will pay back trouble to those who trouble you and give relief to you who are troubled, and to us as well. This will happen when the Lord Jesus is revealed from heaven in blazing fire with his powerful angels. He will punish those who do not know God and do not obey the gospel of our Lord Jesus (1:6-8).

Talk about an amazing idea: Christ will come back to sit in judgment and to punish. Judgment and punishment may not be popular concepts today, but they are hardwired into Christianity. Whom will the Lord punish? Those who have troubled Christians (1:6), as well as those who do not know God and do not obey the gospel (1:8). In chapter 2, Paul promises that God will also punish all "who have not believed the truth but have delighted in wickedness" (2:12).

How will he punish them? Paul speaks of punishment (1:8) and condemnation (2:12). He says God will "pay back trouble" (1:6). Vengeance is wrong for us, but the Bible teaches that the Lord himself must exercise vengeance in order to remain just. He also speaks about "everlasting destruction" (1:9). Everlasting destruction may sound like an oxymoron—being destroyed, but not being destroyed, so that you can continue to be destroyed, and so on forever. But the idea here is of a ruin that never ends. What is that ruin like? The great Italian author Dante presented it as coldness. He pictured Satan in hell frozen in the middle of ice. Others have presented it as a ravenous vacuum that can never be filled. Both ideas might have some justification according to this image in 1:9. Clearly, it will involve being shut out from the presence of the Lord and the majesty of his power.

Christ will save his own people. Amid this coming judgment, Christ will save those who are his own. That is really what Paul describes in chapter 1, even though he uses different terminology. When Christ comes, Paul says, "he comes to be glorified in his holy people and to be marveled at among all those who have believed. This includes you, because you believed our testimony to you" (1:10). What distinguishes Christ's own people from the others? Belief, faith, trust, reliance. It is not our superior moral virtue; it is the recognition of our sinfulness before God. We have done things that God says are wrong. Though we act like it, we are not the lords of our own universe. And one day we will have to give account to the true Creator. When we do, our only hope is to trust what God has done in Christ. We must trust that Christ himself lived a perfect life and died on the cross for the sins of everyone who repents of his or her sin and turns to Christ. We trust that God has accepted Christ's sacrifice.

What do we Christians still have to look forward to? What will Christ accomplish at his return? God will gather his own people to himself (2:1). God will count the Christians as worthy of his kingdom (1:5). God will give relief to Christians who are troubled (1:7).

Again, how could the Thessalonians have believed that Jesus had already returned? The relational language in this letter shows us the Thessalonians had a deep and real relationship with God, something radically different from anything they had known as non-Christians. Yet the relational language in this letter also helps us to understand what they—and we—should be looking forward to as Christians.

WHAT CAN WE LEARN FROM THE THESSALONIANS?

What can we learn from all this? There are different answers to this question.

Some Say We Learn Nothing

Some people might say we learn nothing from this letter, and that we need to wake up and smell the coffee. "This is the problem with you evangelicals," some might say. "You assume the authority of these ancient writings in your lives, when you would be more honest if you just admitted they are irrelevant for life today! They weren't written with you in mind, and they don't have anything in particular to say to you, especially 2 Thessalonians with all that talk about the 'lawless one.'" Mary Ann Beavis of the University of Winnipeg has concluded about this short letter, "If 2 Thessalonians has any ongoing relevance in the Christian canon, it is as a patriarchal artifact reflecting values and attitudes that must be acknowledged and critiqued."[4] Other critics say the only meaning we find is the meaning we import into the ancient document ourselves. After studying this letter and reflecting on it, you will have to decide for yourself whether the critics are right. I, for one, think such skepticism is impatient and ill-considered.

We Should Live Working

One thing we can clearly take from this letter is that we should live working. Created in the image of God, we were made to work. It has been said, "The highest reward for a man's toil is not what he gets for it but what he becomes by it."[5] People have recognized that work is an integral part of what it means to be human. Even Sigmund Freud acknowledged, "Love and work are the cornerstones of our humanness."[6]

Remember, work is not a result of the Fall and sin. Throughout the Bible, God calls people to work and gifts them for that work. God designed work to be the means by which we imitate his own creativity. Work has significance itself, and gives significance to our lives. Refraining from work, rightly understood, is a type of fast done for religious purposes—thus the Sabbath is a weekly fast from purposive work (e.g., Ex. 31:12-17). Idleness and sluggishness, on the other hand, are regularly derided in Proverbs and elsewhere.[7]

I wonder if you feel like work is merely a burden—not your particular job

---

[4] Mary Ann Beavis, "2 Thessalonians," in *Searching the Scriptures, Volume 2: A Feminist Commentary*, ed. Elisabeth Schlüssler Fiorenza (New York: Crossroad, 1994), 270.
[5] Commonly attributed to John Ruskin, English critic, essayist, and reformer (1819–1900).
[6] Source unknown.
[7] E.g., Prov. 31:27; cf. Eccles. 10:18; 11:6.

right now, but work itself. If you do, Paul would challenge you to reconsider what work is. Work is a normal, God-given part of human life, including a Christian's life.

We Should Live Wisely

This letter also teaches that we should live wisely. The Thessalonians erred in their lives because they erred in their understanding. They thought wrongly and so they lived wrongly. Theology is not unrelated to life. What we understand to be the truth impacts how we live.

Living wisely requires a right understanding of God's Word. As Paul exhorts the Thessalonians to recall the teaching he had given when among them, so we must recall the teaching God has inspired in his Word. God has given us his Word for a reason, after all. There is a reason why you and I, if we are Christians, take a few hours to gather weekly to pray, sing, meditate, and hear God's Word read and preached. God has given us his Word to learn and understand, so that we will value and even cherish it. The story is told of how Thomas Goodwin, the Puritan minister, during his undergraduate work at Cambridge, once journeyed to hear John Rogers, a famous preacher of his day:

> having heard much of Mr. Rogers of Dedham . . . [Goodwin] took a journey . . . to hear him preach. . . . Mr. Rogers was . . . on the subject of . . . the Scriptures. And in that sermon he falls into an expostulation with the people telling about their neglect of the Bible; . . . he personates God to the people, telling them, "Well, I have trusted you so long with my Bible; you have slighted it, it lies in such and such houses all covered with dust and cobwebs; you care not to listen to it. Do you use my Bible so? Well, you shall have my Bible no longer." And he takes up the Bible from his cushion, and seemed as if he were going away with it and carrying it from them; but immediately turns again and personates the people to God, falls down on his knees, cries and pleads most earnestly, "Lord, whatever thou dost to us, take not thy Bible from us; kill our children, burn our houses, destroy our goods; only spare us thy Bible, only take not away thy Bible." And then he personates God again to the peoples: "Say you so? Well, I will try you a while longer; and here is my Bible for you. I will see how you will use it, whether you will love it more . . . observe it more . . . practice it more, and live more according to it." By these actions . . . he put all the congregation into so strange a posture that . . . the people generally . . . [were] deluged with their own tears; and he [Goodwin] told me [John Howe, who recorded this story] that he himself, when he got out . . . was fain to hang a quarter of an hour upon the neck of his horse weeping before he had power to mount; so strange an

impression was there upon him, and generally upon the people, upon having been expostulated with for the neglect of the Bible.[8]

Sometimes we do not realize what we have, because we take it for granted. You may think it was extreme for Rogers to suggest by his dramatization that the people might say, "kill our children, only spare us thy Bible." But some of these people may have had memories of living in England with no Bible in the language they could read. They could also remember the smell of burning flesh of the people who were burned at the stake for translating the Bible into their own language. They knew what it meant to live in a world with no access to God's Word, and so they valued it as you or I may never have valued it. They realized that God speaks through the Bible. They understood that living spiritual lives meant living in conformity to God's Word and not to their own imaginations. This was true for a bunch of Essex townsmen and farmers in the 1620s. It was true for a bunch of Thessalonian Christians in the first century. And it is true for us today.

We Should Live Waiting

At the moment, we are in the season many Christians refer to as "Advent." This season is based on the idea of waiting. The Latin word *adventus* means "coming." Christians began to observe the thirty days before Christmas about 1,500 years ago as a time, like Lent, for fasting and spiritual preparation for the anniversary of Christ's birth. Yet December is not the only month in which Christians wait. Christians live waiting for Christ's return twelve months a year. The Thessalonians had forgotten this.

As I prepared for this sermon, I considered the fact that it is unlikely anyone hearing it has ever stopped working because he or she thought the Lord had returned. So I began to wonder how I could demonstrate the relevance of Paul's message for us. Yet the more I thought about it, the more I that saw the analogy for us is really quite penetrating. These ancient Christians were not working because they thought they had it all. They thought they had reached the pinnacle of the faith. The Lord had returned, and they already had everything Christ would give. That is how they were deceived.

Aren't you glad you are not deceived like that? Or are you? If you are a Christian, your life is radically affected because of what God has already given you in Christ. Yet you know that you have not yet received everything God

---

[8] In John Howe, "The Principles of the Oracles of God," in *The Works of Reverend John Howe*, vol. 2, ed. Edmund Calamy (New York: John P. Haven, 1835), 1084-1085. J. I. Packer quotes a large portion of this passage in *A Quest for Godliness: The Puritan Vision of the Christian Life* (Wheaton, Ill.: Crossway, 1990), 47.

will give you in Christ. And hopefully you are waiting for something much greater, and that waiting marks your life.

We are deceived like the Thessalonians when we think and live as though we already have everything Christianity offers. When we think and live as if the great summation has already come, either a wrong liberty (doing things we should not do) or a wrong complacency (leaving undone the things we should do) always follows. In the Thessalonians' case, complacency followed. Secular Sam, whom I talked about earlier, had also stopped waiting.

The Thessalonians show us something of the important balance between the *now* and the *not yet.* We do not want to be so preoccupied with the next life that we become unconcerned, defeatist, or glum about this one. On the other hand, we do not want to be so enamored with this life that we ignore the next. I doubt that many of us struggle with being lopsided by giving too much attention to the next life. But many of us have stopped waiting, like the Thessalonian Christians.

We stop waiting in a number of ways. Our faith in the next life slips into faith in this one. Striving for spiritual health is replaced by striving for good stewardship of our physical bodies. Visions of God are replaced by visions of our earthly future, or our children's future. The hope of heaven is replaced by the hope of the good life. Desire for our Creator God is replaced by desires for creatures.

Unbelief can creep in and gain the upper hand so easily. One begins by believing in this age as well as the next. Concentrating on this age rather than the next. Emphasizing this age rather than the next. Being concerned with this age rather than the next. Thinking less of the next. Deemphasizing the next. Questioning the next. Ignoring the next. Forgetting the next. Eventually, denying the next.

This brand of secularism has grown in our society. And it has grown in our churches, as our churches do more and more to help us cope with this life and do less and less to prepare us for the next.

If you do not believe in Jesus Christ, by recognizing him as the God and Savior who will return and bring history to a close in judgment and salvation, you will certainly not wait for him. Yet if you claim to believe in Jesus Christ but are not waiting for this glorious appearing, then, like Sam and the Thessalonians, you will not live in the way Paul writes about here. If you really believe this life is it, you may well decide to go for the gusto, but only as this world defines it. If you believe there is more and better to come, and that this life must be lived in view of Christ's return, then you can live a self-controlled, godly, and upright life.

As Christians, we no longer live entirely for the fulfillment of all of our desires here and now. We live instead working and laboring honorably. We give ourselves to caring for others even at great personal cost because this life no longer has to bear the weight of all our hopes, desires, and expectations. Without the certainty of Christ's return, it is not at all certain we can live as Paul exhorts us in this little letter.

So what do we learn from these Thessalonian believers? We learn to live working, wise, waiting lives.

CONCLUSION

I wonder what this idea of living a waiting life sounds like to you? What do you imagine it means? What would it mean in your life this coming week, month, or year, if you decided to live such a life?

Eulalia lived a life of fervent waiting.[9] Seventeen hundred years ago, in a town then called Merida, on the Guadiana River in Spain, lived this little girl by the name of Eulalia. Eulalia was a high-spirited, enthusiastic girl, known for being bright and happy. Her parents were well-to-do people who brought her up with every comfort and bestowed great care upon her training. As a little child, Eulalia heard of Jesus, and the Holy Spirit did his blessed work in her heart. She saw herself as a sinner and found in Christ the Savior she knew she needed.

Little Eulalia grew up as the joy of her parents. Her one great fault, however, often made them anxious. She was much too rash and impetuous, always eager to do immediately whatever came into her mind. Even after becoming a Christian, she was much the same in this respect. Her mother spoke to her very seriously about this weakness, and warned her it might bring trouble upon her someday. Eulalia would say how sorry she was and promise to be more careful.

Eulalia lived during the time of the Diocletian persecution. Diocletian was a cruel emperor who ordered that sacrifices must be made to the gods of the empire. Like other parts of the empire, Spain suffered its share of persecution. Here, too, the ground was watered with the blood of many who proved faithful to death. The wave of terror rolled on sporadically, till it reached the province of Lusitania, where Merida lay.

When the persecution began to reach nearby towns, Eulalia's father and mother dreaded their daughter's impetuous nature, fearing it might lead her to some rash act that would cost them their lives. They decided it was best to send Eulalia away to the country where she would be safer and would not hear any more news of the persecutions. On one very sad day for a girl of twelve, Eulalia

---

[9] We learn of Eulalia's story from Aurelius Prudentius, a fourth-century Spanish lawyer, administrator, poet, and hymn-writer, who wrote the hymn "Of the Father's Love Begotten."

had to turn her back upon her dear home, leaving those she most loved when so much danger pressed upon them. She wanted to stay with them even if it meant dying, rather than to go away and know nothing of what was happening. But go she must, so she kissed them goodbye and, with many tears, waved farewell.

Once in the country, Eulalia began to feel very lonely. Her eager soul sorely rebelled at being banished when she longed to be at the front of the battle. Eventually she was completely mastered by an overwhelming desire to publicly confess herself a Christian regardless of what it might cost her. So she made up her mind and laid her plans.

One night she went to bed as usual, but not to sleep. Waiting quietly till everyone in the house was asleep, she slipped into her clothes, crept quietly downstairs, unbolted the door, and walked out into the road. Tremblingly, she hurried on, sometimes running, sometimes walking to regain her breath, till she reached Merida once more.

The very next morning, the cruel governor Dacianus had the Christians in the town rounded up. Among the Christians brought before Dacianus that next morning was Eulalia. Whether her parents were present at her trial or not we do not know. The records are taken up entirely with Eulalia herself.

Dacianus sat on his seat surrounded by his lictors. These were the officers who always attended the Roman magistrates of high authority. Each carried an axe with a bundle of sticks tied around it. It must have seemed a terrible array to this girl of twelve.

But she betrayed no sign of fear. She boldly told the proconsul how wrong it was to make war upon the Christian faith. The judge tried kindness at first; but finding kindly persuasion useless, he resorted to threats of torture, fire, and wild beasts. "Besides," he added, "what trouble will it cost you to escape all this? If you will but touch a grain of salt, a pinch of incense with the tips of your fingers, away goes the punishment."

Eulalia was so indignant with the judge for trying to persuade her to give up Christ that, with a cry of horror, she grabbed the image that stood on the little pagan altar, threw it to the ground, and stamped upon the incense. Dacianus tried persuading her no more. He handed her over to the executioners.

They began to torture her with their instruments. When she felt the marks they were making upon her, she cried, "Lord, they are writing that thou art mine!" Then they brought torches and applied fire to her poor wounded body. As the flames reached her lips, the records say, she opened her mouth, sucked them in, and died.

Eulalia died as a martyr for Christ on the tenth of December, in the year 304. Do you think she made a bad choice? She was twelve. She had her life in front of her. Our world would not understand her choice; you can tell by watching the movies from Hollywood. In the world's eyes, Christians are strange misanthropes who are messed up in the mind anyway. Was Eulalia's expectation of the next life as deranged as the worldview found in most modern Hollywood movies would say it is?

The lives of so many individuals would have been so different if they had stopped waiting. Adoniram Judson would not have spent all those years in Burma as a missionary. John Bunyan would not have written *Pilgrims Progress* while in jail. Martin Luther and John Calvin would have quailed before their opposition. Eulalia would never have confessed Christ before a murdering judge. Paul certainly would not have traveled around and experienced persecution for telling people the good news of Jesus Christ. Even the life of the Lord Jesus, who waited more than thirty years for his time to come, who waited upon the cross as he bore our sin, and who waits now to return and gather his people, would have been different if he had ever stopped waiting. As it was for his first coming in Bethlehem and his crucifixion for our sins, so he waits now to come again. And he will.

Let's get back to your life. What if you found out conclusively—for certain—that the Lord Jesus was not returning today? Would that make any difference in the way you spent the day?

What if you found out that he was never coming back? Would your life look any different at all? My fear is, for many of us, it would make no difference at all.

Some have asked me if Secular Sam is just a made-up character. I wish he were. I fear he is not.

Paul wrote to the Corinthians, "If only for this life we have hope in Christ, we are to be pitied more than all men" (1 Cor. 15:19). How is your hope? What is it fixed on? What are you waiting for?

Nothing? Do you already have it all?

Dear friend, is everything you hold dear found in the small compass of this life? If so, then I know one thing you do not have—you do not have Christ.

Are you waiting for anything beyond this life? Christians are.

Let us pray:

Lord God, we acknowledge you as the Creator of all we have, all we see, all we are. From your creative work alone has come everything that exists. We thank you for calling us to work in imitation of you. We pray that by your Spirit and your Word, you would give us wisdom in our work and in our lives. And enable us to work and live with hearts expectant of your returning, hold-

ing lightly to the things of this world. Help us to live waiting for you, with the joy of the bride who waits for her coming groom. In Jesus' name. Amen.

Questions for Reflection

1. Why does the fact that Secular Sam expects to wake up in his bed in the morning make him "profoundly secular"?

2. We have seen that humans live by their hopes as surely as they live by the air they breathe. How is that true? Paul wrote to the Corinthians, "If only for this life we have hope in Christ, we are to be pitied more than all men" (1 Cor. 15:19). How is your hope? What is it fixed on? What are you waiting for? Do you already have everything you want?

3. What is the difference between idleness and the occasional rest every finite human requires? Are you capable of discerning one from the other in your own life?

4. In spite of the problems that beset the Thessalonian church, Paul thanks God because he perceives that their faith and love for one another is increasing. Their sins may require his rebuke, but he does not fail to perceive evidences of grace in their lives. How hard do you look for evidences of grace in the lives of Christians around you? Do you thank God and verbally encourage them with what you perceive?

5. Paul promises that Christ will sit in judgment and bring punishment to those who oppose him. Does this differ from the conception most people have of Jesus? How? How does it affect your view of Jesus?

6. There are at least two dangers we can fall into regarding our work: we can idolize it, or we can begrudge the fact that we have to work at all. Which of these two sins tempts you most? Have you confessed it as a sin and asked God to change your heart? How can you seek to renew your mind in this matter? Be sure to thank God for ways you have seen progress in your life concerning these matters.

7. We can stop waiting for Christ's coming in a number of ways. Our faith in the next life can slip into faith in this one. Striving for spiritual health can be replaced by striving for good stewardship of our physical bodies. Visions of God can be replaced by visions of our earthly future, or our children's future.

The hope of heaven can be replaced by the hope of the good life. Have you been slipping in any of these areas?

8. Following up on question 7, and considering the flip side, have you seen God increase your hope in his coming over the last year? Be sure to give him praise for your progress!

9. We have also considered the fact that too many churches are doing more and more to help us cope with this life, and less and less to prepare us for the next one. What should churches do to correct this error? What can preachers do?

10. Christians are sometimes accused of being so heavenly minded they are no earthly good. Is this a real risk? Why does the opposite conclusion—"more heavenly minded, more earthly good"—actually better characterize what Paul expects of Christians?

11. Was Eulalia's life a waste? Would you spend your life like hers, even if it meant dying at age 12? At what age would you be willing to let your life be cut off for the sake of the gospel?

THE MESSAGE OF 1 TIMOTHY: LEADERSHIP

15

THE MESSAGE OF 1 TIMOTHY: LEADERSHIP

WHAT MAKES A GOOD LEADER?[1]

"Research confirms common sense about effective leaders. They share crucial attributes. The first, termed surgency, contrasts dynamic agents of authority as sociable, gregarious, assertive, and leaderlike against less competent ones who are quiet, reserved, mannerly, and withdrawn. Potent leaders also manifest emotional stability in their calm self-confidence. Their opposites are possessed by their emotions and show it in their anxiety, insecurity, and worrisomeness. Furthermore, people who exercise authority well are well organized, work hard, and act responsibly. Their conscientiousness makes them the polar opposite of people who are impulsive, irresponsible, undependable, and lazy.

"Good leaders are not hard or tyrannical but rather sympathetic, cooperative, good-natured, and warm. Their agreeableness contrasts with the grumpy, unpleasant, and cold traits of persons who do not lead well. Persons who sit easily in the saddle of authority are found to have a healthy sense of curiosity and to be imaginative, cultured, and broad-minded. Those who experience and give little comfort in work, on the other hand, approach their narrow interests in a concrete-minded and practical manner.

"The observation that a leader at ease with authority gets the most out of others is reinforced by the research conducted on commercial airline flight crews. Breakdowns in team performance are the primary cause of air transport accidents. Flight crew performance—defined in terms of the number and severity of the errors made by the crew—is significantly correlated with the personality of the captain. Crews with captains who are warm, friendly, self-confident, and able to stand up to pressure, that is, those who possess the

---

[1] This sermon was originally preached on December 19, 1999, at Capitol Hill Baptist in Washington, D.C.

characteristics previously listed, make the fewest errors. Conversely, crews with captains who are arrogant, hostile, boastful, egotistical, passive-aggressive, or dictatorial make the most errors."[2]

So say Eugene Kennedy and Sara Charles in their book *Authority: The Most Misunderstood Idea in America.* The authors raise important questions about a crucial issue for us as we face the new year, with decisions to be made in our country, our states, and cities around the nation. In our homes, leadership decisions will be made as some establish new homes and as existing families grow and face new challenges.

In our church, too, many crucial decisions will have to be made in the coming year about elders, staff, and other service positions as various members move away and new members join the church. All of this involves not only decision making, but decision making about the decision makers.

What should leaders look like? What should they believe? How should they live? What should be at the heart of a leader's leading?

INTRODUCING 1 TIMOTHY

To help us consider these questions, we turn to the first letter in the New Testament that Paul wrote to an individual and not to a church. The letter of 1 Timothy, which consists of six short chapters, was written to one of Paul's closest and most trusted disciples, Timothy, who had become the pastor of the important church at Ephesus.

There were clearly problems in the church, and those problems appear to have involved a growing and powerful rogue leadership. These leaders used the law in their teaching, they curried favor from various church members, and they appear to have been paid well. Timothy, however, was still young, and the aging apostle Paul had some concerns about Timothy's ability to handle the situation. He knew that Timothy needed encouragement. Apparently, the church was fraying not just at the edges but at the seams. What should be done? Paul knew that Timothy needed to answer that question, so he wrote this letter.

We will follow Paul as he answers the questions: What should a leader teach? How should a leader live? And what is at the heart of good leadership? As we do, we will find matters to pray about for our nation and for our churches. You should also pray about these things for yourself, that you would be a good leader in whatever way God calls you to lead.

---

[2] Eugene Kennedy and Sara Charles, *Authority: The Most Misunderstood Idea in America* (New York: Free Press, 1997), 143-144.

WHAT SHOULD A LEADER TEACH?

We begin by considering what a leader should teach. What do you think? Perhaps "peace on earth, good will toward men"? That God is the Father of all he has created, and that we are all brothers and sisters under the skin? That our business now as the human race is to face our demons honestly and choose the right? That we must live according to our best lights and how our consciences tell us to live? I shudder to think how many pulpits around the country regularly preach some rendition of these sentiments as the message of Christmas.

Not False Doctrine

The basis of Timothy's leadership in the church at Ephesus, Paul says, must be his opposition to false doctrine and his teaching of the truth about Christ. After greeting Timothy in the beginning of the letter, Paul commands him to withstand false doctrine. He warns him against false teachers and charges him with the responsibility of opposing them. "As I urged you when I went into Macedonia, stay there in Ephesus so that you may command certain men not to teach false doctrines any longer nor to devote themselves to myths and endless genealogies. These promote controversies rather than God's work—which is by faith. The goal of this command is love, which comes from a pure heart and a good conscience and a sincere faith. Some have wandered away from these and turned to meaningless talk. They want to be teachers of the law, but they do not know what they are talking about or what they so confidently affirm" (1:3-7). Paul picks this theme up again in chapter 6: "If anyone teaches false doctrines and does not agree to the sound instruction of our Lord Jesus Christ and to godly teaching, he is conceited and understands nothing" (6:3-4).

Apparently, certain individuals had presented themselves in the Ephesian church as teachers. They had been teaching about the law, but they were doing so wrongly, mixing it up with "myths and endless genealogies" (1:4). And all this was stirring up trouble. These self-appointed teachers might be confident talkers, says Paul, but they do not know what they are talking about.

You see, the news we have to declare as Christians is not fundamentally about *our* law-keeping or *our* obedience. The glad tidings we bear are not for "good people." It is "for lawbreakers and rebels, the ungodly and sinful, the unholy and irreligious; for those who kill their fathers or mothers, for murderers, for adulterers and perverts, for slave traders and liars and perjurers" (1:9b-10a). I doubt you have received many Christmas cards like that. Yet have you realized this is who the Christmas message is for? The Christmas message is not for a bunch of well-dressed, respectable people who attend church to cel-

ebrate a cultural holiday. The Christmas message is a message that brings joy
to people like father-killers and slave-traders! Apparently, some teachers in
Ephesus did not know that. They thought church was for respectable people.

The Gospel

So what should Timothy teach if he wants to lead the church well? Paul's
answer is clear: Timothy should teach the gospel.

> I thank Christ Jesus our Lord, who has given me strength, that he considered me
> faithful, appointing me to his service. Even though I was once a blasphemer and
> a persecutor and a violent man, I was shown mercy because I acted in ignorance
> and unbelief. The grace of our Lord was poured out on me abundantly, along
> with the faith and love that are in Christ Jesus.
>
> Here is a trustworthy saying that deserves full acceptance: Christ Jesus came
> into the world to save sinners—of whom I am the worst. But for that very rea-
> son I was shown mercy so that in me, the worst of sinners, Christ Jesus might
> display his unlimited patience as an example for those who would believe on him
> and receive eternal life (1:12-16).

Paul points Timothy to what he should teach by pointing to his own life. Paul's
calling and conversion were living examples of the truth of this Christian message. If you are going to lead the church well, if you are going to teach well, if
you expect others to understand and follow well, then you *must* understand
the mercy of God in Christ to sinners. Don't end up like Alexander and
Hymenaeus, who let go of their faith and a good conscience and so ship-
wrecked their Christianity (1:19-20).

God obviously chose Paul to do this work because of what Paul's life had
been like. He had been a persecutor, a blasphemer, and a violent man. God did
not choose a man who was immediately responsive to the gospel to be the great
apostle to the nations. He chose a man who knew in his heart what it meant
to commit great wrong. Yet God, by his Holy Spirit, had convicted Paul. So
Christ, who lived a perfect life and died a death on the cross for all of us who
repent and rely on him, became the Savior of this violent, blaspheming, and
persecuting man! Christ could not have been that Savior if Paul did not first
realize that he was a sinner in need of salvation. But he did realize this, by the
grace of God.

Not Deceiving Spirits

The gospel is the great theme in the book of 1 Timothy. Yet Paul warns
Timothy in chapter 4 that he must be careful about the message he preaches

because false teachers will not go away. A pastor can never teach so well that he will stop struggling with false doctrine in the church. People will continue to follow deceiving spirits: "The Spirit clearly says that in later times some will abandon the faith and follow deceiving spirits and things taught by demons" (4:1). There will be more people like Hymenaeus and Alexander who shipwreck their faith. "You," Paul urges Timothy, "must be disciplined not to do that. You need to give attention to your life and teaching."

Now, in all this, do not fail to notice how attractive false teaching is. In chapter 1, we learn the false teaching is about the law, and the law is about right and wrong. That is a good thing to teach, right? Isn't it good to go into our schools and teach students about what we agree is right and wrong? It promotes morality. It condemns the sort of illicit behavior Paul mentions in chapter 1. In chapter 4, we find that the false teaching included asceticism and self-denial for spiritual reasons. Abstaining from sin and some of the physical pleasures of this life are good things, right? What was so bad about this teaching?

Well, whenever we *do things* in order to earn God's favor, we have accepted false teaching. We have fundamentally misunderstood Christianity to be about us and our character when it is fundamentally about God and his character. The gospel exposes God's gracious love and mercy to us in Christ, not our upstanding characters. As Christians, we do not put our hope in our ability to earn salvation. Rather, "we have put our hope in the living God, who is the Savior of all men" (4:10).

Today, this message of Christian hope is less and less popular. But this is the message we must teach, even if members of Congress and presidential candidates in televised debates suggest that proclaiming this hope amounts to "projecting intolerance." God's grace to us in Christ is the Christian gospel. There is no other hope. We are separated from God. It does not matter how many religions we invent. Apart from God's coming himself in Christ and dying on the cross in place of sinners, we have no glad tidings for Christmas. We have no glad tidings for the Christian life. We have no hope.

Your Doctrine and Your Life

Positively, Paul tells Timothy to live as a model for the believers, both in how he conducts his life and in the doctrine he teaches:

> Don't let anyone look down on you because you are young, but set an example for the believers in speech, in life, in love, in faith and in purity. Until I come, devote yourself to the public reading of Scripture, to preaching and to teaching. . . .
>
> Be diligent in these matters; give yourself wholly to them, so that everyone

may see your progress. Watch your life and doctrine closely. Persevere in them,
because if you do, you will save both yourself and your hearers (4:12-13, 15-16).

Right doctrine must be matched by right living. Our words together with our
actions will teach either the truth or something else.

So what should a leader teach? If a leader wants to lead well, he must teach
the truth. A Christmas card theology of "holiday cheer" or of angels with
trumpets singing "Peace on earth, good will toward men" is simply not good
enough in a world that includes real tragedies like the Columbine High School
shootings, the terrorist threat of nuclear weapons, or, truly, the contents of your
heart and mine. If you regard evil only as what those "bad people out there"
do, you will not understand Jesus at all. You must understand this truth first:
there is far more to the Christian gospel than celebrating the mean remnants
of goodness that may remain in us. Timothy needed to know that, and so do
we today. We have one true message of hope: Christ Jesus came into the world
to save sinners. That is the message of Christmas.

HOW SHOULD A LEADER LIVE?

If that is what a leader should teach, then how should a leader live? A real
leader must have the ability to help other people think of more than just themselves; indeed, he must lead others to think of the congregation as a whole.

Christmas is a time of self-indulgence in our culture. We draw up wish lists
for ourselves and try to think of what we would like to do on our breaks. If
we are younger, we dream about all the gifts we want. Such self-focus may be
understandable in young children, but it is tragically out of place in parents.
And such selfishness certainly does not characterize biblical leadership. Paul
tells Timothy that authority is important and that good authority is a blessing—between Christians and the state, between men and women in the church,
and between church leaders and church members. Biblical authority is a blessing for those who are beneath it.

Between Christians and the State

Paul does not say a lot about the relationship between Christians and the state,
but he does begin chapter 2 with the exhortation, "I urge, then, first of all, that
requests, prayers, intercession and thanksgiving be made for everyone—for
kings and all those in authority, that we may live peaceful and quiet lives in all
godliness and holiness" (2:1-2). All of us benefit from the peace kept by the
state, because God is concerned for everyone. God "wants all men to be saved
and to come to a knowledge of the truth" (2:4).

　　When was the last time you prayed for, interceded for, or thanked God for those in authority over our nation? It would be good, according to the Bible, if you did, regardless of whether you are a Democrat, a Republican, or an Independent. Remember, Paul was telling these young Christians to pray for the Roman emperor, who would one day take off Paul's head. Paul exhorted them to pray, to intercede, and to thank God for this very one.

Between Men and Women in the Church

Beginning in 2:8, Paul turns to discussing relationships within the church itself—a discussion he will carry on through the rest of the letter. Though written to an individual, 1 Timothy is a letter primarily for the church and about the church. After some interesting and important comments on appropriate dress and activities for women (2:9-11), Paul instructs Timothy on how to approach the question of placing women in positions of authority. He writes, "I do not permit a woman to teach or to have authority over a man; she must be silent. For Adam was formed first, then Eve. And Adam was not the one deceived; it was the woman who was deceived and became a sinner" (2:12-14). Women are prohibited from teaching and ruling men for two reasons: because God created the man first, and because the woman sinned first. This does not mean that all Christian men have authority over all Christian women at all times. It simply means that in the context of the local church, the position of elder is restricted to men. Was Paul just a misogynist? Hardly.[3] He knows this exercise of authority will be a blessing for both men and women. He also adds, "But women will be saved through childbirth." Interestingly, "childbirth" is in the singular, perhaps referring to "the birth" of Jesus Christ. Before God, Christian women stand equally with Christian men.

Between Church Leaders and Church Members

Paul then turns to instructing Timothy on what type of people will make good leaders in the church. Paul writes at the beginning of chapter 3, "Here is a trustworthy saying: If anyone sets his heart on being an overseer, he desires a noble task. Now the overseer must be above reproach . . ." (3:1-2a). He continues to write about the relationship between church leaders and church members through 3:15, where he concludes with, "if I am delayed, you will know how people ought to conduct themselves in God's household, which is the church of the living God, the pillar and foundation of the truth."

---

[3] Paul makes many appreciative comments about women serving with him as he thanks them at the end of his epistles (e.g., Romans 16). Also, Paul clearly appreciates the role Timothy's mother and grandmother had in his life (see 2 Tim. 1:5).

In chapter 3, Paul sets down qualifications for overseers (elders) and deacons. This helps us know what kind of people should serve in each capacity. He gives instructions for how these leaders should conduct themselves within both the church family and their own families, as well as how they should relate to the wider world. Overseers, or elders, should be irreproachable in their observable conduct. They should have exemplary marriages and family lives. And they should be temperate in all things, self-controlled, respectable, hospitable, able to teach, not violent or quarrelsome or greedy, not recent converts, and well-respected by those outside the church (3:2-7).

Deacons too should be blameless, exemplary in their family lives, temperate in everything, not greedy but respectable, not given to lying but to honestly holding the deep truths of the faith (3:8-13).

This is an impressive catalogue of virtues. The false teachers in the Ephesian church clearly were not living up to such standards. Their lives probably gave evidence of the falseness of their doctrine. But the virtues Paul lists here are necessary for those who shepherd the church of God as elders, and for those who serve God's church as deacons.

In chapter 1, you may recall, Paul talked about God graciously including in the church people who have done terrible things, like murdering fathers and mothers. Then, here in chapter 3 he gives this list of virtues necessary for church leaders. Murderers and lawbreakers and such are the kind of people the gospel comes *to*, but the gospel does not leave us unchanged. It works in our hearts by God's Holy Spirit and changes us! Leaders within the church should be individuals whose lives are particularly marked by a gospel-produced and Holy Spirit–given godliness and others-centeredness.

These lists may present the qualifications of church leaders, but they also point to qualities all Christians can seek, since our focus is on living for others and not for ourselves. Paul calls for leaders who are not lovers of money but lovers of strangers (that is what the Greek word translated "hospitable" means—"lovers of strangers"). As true church leaders live others-centered lives, they will act as models for other Christians, all of whom should desire at least most of these traits.

So, how should a leader live? A leader should live for others. If you seek public office, you should seek that office for the good you will be able to do for others. If you exercise authority in the church, it should be exercised for the good of those over whom you have authority. Authority should not be given to people who are self-focused but to people who reflect the good and kind authority of God, thereby blessing those they serve by leading.

WHAT IS AT THE HEART OF GOOD LEADERSHIP?

Finally, we want to ask, what is at the heart of good leadership? Again, the Christmas season provides a helpful approach to this subject. So often we celebrate the coming of him who relinquished the riches of heaven for our sakes by tempting and indulging materialism. Yes, I know our gift-giving can help teach people about God's great gift to us in Christ. But in real, everyday life, I just wonder if Satan could have developed a more effective tool for obscuring the point of this analogy. We go scurrying through countless malls and department stores in order to show our genuine love for others through genuine generosity. None of this is bad. Yet Satan is a past master at using the *pretty good* to obscure from our view *the best.*

God's Pleasure

Paul clearly tells Timothy that the heart of good leadership is to live not for one's own gain but for God's pleasure. And a good leader urges others to do the same.

Pleasing God is the great motive of a Christian. You see this in chapter 5, where Paul deals with our duties toward each other in the church. In the first couple of verses, Paul tells Timothy how to exhort different kinds of folks, respecting each of them as he speaks to them (5:1-2). The bulk of the chapter is then taken up with practical questions about regulating the church's care of widows (5:3-16). In first-century society, it was the family's role to care for its own widows. Paul does not want people to take advantage of the church but to take care of their own families. They should do this, he says, because "this is pleasing to God" (5:4). He does not say to care for widows because it makes for a solid family and a solid society but because it is pleasing to God.

This must be a leader's reason for leading, and the motive he must encourage in others: doing what is pleasing to God. Living for your own pleasure, Paul says, should be replaced by living for God's pleasure.

If you have never thought much about this idea of being motivated by the pleasure of God, let me encourage you to get a copy of John Piper's book *The Pleasures of God.*[4] It is a wonderful book on a huge theme in the Bible that is largely neglected: what is it that brings God pleasure? Paul says our whole salvation happens because it pleases God: "This is good, and pleases God our Savior, who wants all men to be saved and to come to a knowledge of the truth" (1 Tim. 2:3-4). God saves us because it pleases him. By the same token, Paul regularly instructs Christians to live according to what pleases God. Living

---

[4] John Piper, *The Pleasures of God* (Portland: Multnomah, 1991).

by the sinful flesh "cannot please God," he tells the Romans (Rom. 8:8). Therefore, "find out what pleases the Lord," he says to the Ephesians (5:10; cf. 1 Thess. 4:1). What a great study: to make it your end to find out what pleases the Lord, and to live accordingly. We should start this study when we are young. The Colossian children are told, "Children, obey your parents in everything, for this pleases the Lord" (3:20). The writer to the Hebrews reminds us that all of life should be lived by faith, for "without faith it is impossible to please God" (Heb. 11:6).

Likewise, here in 1 Timothy 5, the relatives of widows should, in love, take responsibility for these women because "this is pleasing to God" (5:4). Paul continues in the following verses to designate which widows should and which widows should not be cared for by the church in the absence of family care (see vv. 9-11). If nobody will care for the eligible widows, the church will most happily care for them.

In the latter half of chapter 5, Paul gives Timothy instructions concerning paying, disciplining, and choosing elders (5:17-22). And then he reminds Timothy that he must obey Paul's instructions. Timothy will answer to God concerning the matters they have discussed (5:21). In the beginning of chapter 6, Paul reminds the slaves, or indentured servants, that their behavior will reflect well or ill on God, since they call themselves his followers.

In short, all these actions—from a Christian family's care for its widows to a Christian slave's obedience—should be done out of the desire to bring God pleasure. That should be the great motive in all our actions.

Not Financial Gain

There are, of course, other things that can motivate a leader. A chief motivation that often shows its ugly head is a desire for financial gain. But leadership in the church, indeed, any kind of service in the church, must not be for financial gain, says Paul. He specifically warns those "who think that godliness is a means to financial gain" (6:5). The culprits here are false teachers who do not teach sound doctrine and do "not agree to the sound instruction of our Lord Jesus Christ and to godly teaching" (6:3). They teach because they love money.

The amount of money does not have to be large for someone to love it. Even small amounts of money can work upon small hearts. That seems to have been the case with these false teachers. They wanted more students in order to have more money. So they changed their doctrine in order to have more students. Wanting to get rich led them astray. Paul writes,

> People who want to get rich fall into temptation and a trap and into many foolish and harmful desires that plunge men into ruin and destruction. For the love

of money is a root of all kinds of evil. Some people, eager for money, have wandered from the faith and pierced themselves with many griefs (6:9-10).

What a contrast Paul draws: some people desire to please God; others desire money. He says in chapter 6, "godliness with contentment is great gain" (6:6), and then several verses later, "the love of money is a root of all kinds of evil" (6:10). Those are two great phrases to set side by side: "godliness with contentment" and "love of money." Take them as the two different directions you can go when it comes to your house and your health, your job and your future prospects, your friends and your family, your looks and your desires, your finances and your physical abilities. What phrase would your friends and colleagues think better describes you? Godliness with contentment, or love of money? Which is really you?

Paul concludes his letter with some personal directions to Timothy (6:11-16) as well as some final instructions for the wealthy, who were clearly a source of problems in the Ephesian church (6:17-19). And then he charges Timothy, one more time, don't worry if the paychecks decrease; persevere in the truth: "Guard what has been entrusted to your care. Turn away from godless chatter and the opposing ideas of what is falsely called knowledge, which some have professed and in so doing have wandered from the faith" (6:20-21).

What is at the heart of good leadership? The heart of good leadership is not a desire for money but a desire to please God and to teach others to do the same. May God give his church leaders like this: leaders committed to the gospel, leaders committed to the good of the church, and leaders committed to pleasing God.

CONCLUSION

Perhaps you are thinking, "Hey, Mark, hasn't anybody told you Christmas is coming up this week? What are you doing preaching a sermon on the church?" Well, I have the radical idea that the One in the manger cares more about the church than he cares about the manger. The significance of his coming has everything to do with the regular gathering of the church, the people he purchased by his life and death. The one born in the manger even calls the church his own body. As Jesus said to Saul when Saul was persecuting the *church,* "Saul, Saul, why do you persecute *me?*" (Acts 9:4). The church is his body. His Spirit indwells us.

If you celebrate Christ's birth, do not ignore his life and death. He lived for you, and, if you repent and believe, he also died for you and was raised for you. To think that Christmas is more about the stable in Bethlehem than about the cross in Jerusalem is to regard the acorn as more important than the oak.

Paul says to Timothy in chapter 1, "Christ Jesus came into the world . . ." (1:15). And that is the message of Christmas; but it is not the whole message. People these days feel very Christian when they speak of Christ's coming to the world. But beware; this acknowledgment can be no more than an historical tip of the hat to something you know is important to many people, like recognizing the birth of Mohammed or of George Washington. We mention it because it is important to people. But that is not the true Christian message, at least without the second half of the verse: "Christ Jesus came into the world *to save sinners*" (1:15). That is the Christmas message! The Christmas message is not merely the fact that God became man by being born of the virgin Mary; the Christmas message is the reason for the Incarnation: "Christ Jesus came into the world to save sinners."

During the Christmas holiday season, people often ask one another about their plans for Christmas day or New Year's Eve. But the far more important question is, Are you one of those sinners for whom Christ came into the world? Are you one of those he came to die for and to save? Nothing more important can absorb your thoughts over the coming days than finding an answer to that question, because that is why Christ came into the world: to save those of us who know ourselves to be sinners, so that we would repent of our sins and rely upon him.

How do the cards you receive at Christmastime depict Christmas? With bright green and red wreaths? With a star, trumpeting angels, and a manger scene? With a scene of snow-covered houses with people peeking out the windows as Santa and his sleigh, silhouetted against the moon, ascend to the heights? Don't feel bad if you have sent cards like these. That is what the stores sell. And all these images get jumbled in together: festive seasonal decorations, children holding teddy bears, fireplaces, stockings, and manger scenes.

But can you picture with the eyes of faith that one quintessential Christmas scene?

> Jesus held by the wood.
> Delivered and delivering,
> Jesus held by the wood.
>
> Witnesses on either side.
> Mary silhouetted,
> quietly gazing
> with great feeling
> on her son,
> the sky dark above.
> As at the beginning,
> so at the end.

Jesus held by the wood.
Delivered and delivering,
Jesus held by the wood.

The scene of Christmas
and of Calvary,
of the cradle
and the cross.

This is the message of Christmas. It is not simply a secular message of peace on earth and good cheer toward all. It does not have the self-focus of gift-giving and receiving. This One we celebrate gives a gift to all of us who repent of our sins and believe. He gives us new life as individuals. And he calls us together to be an assembly, a church. It was not Paul or the other apostles who founded the church. Christ himself founded it. Jesus said, "On this rock I will build my church" (Matt. 16:18). He dedicated his life and death to establishing this church. And he wants the church to be filled with leaders who, like himself, know and teach the truth, love God above their own gain, and are willing to lay down their life for the sheep.

True Christian leadership always involves that kind of love, because such love is the gospel. And the gospel is the true message of Christmas.

Let us pray:

Hear the words of Frank Houghton's great Christmas hymn:

> *Thou who wast rich beyond all splendour,*
> *All for love's sake becamest poor;*
> *Thrones for a manger didst surrender,*
> *Sapphire-paved courts for stable floor.*
> *Thou Who wast rich beyond all splendour;*
> *All for love's sake becamest poor.*
>
> *Thou Who art God beyond all praising,*
> *All for love's sake becamest Man;*
> *Stooping so low, but sinners raising*
> *Heavenwards by Thine eternal plan.*
> *Thou Who art God beyond all praising,*
> *All for love's sake becamest Man.*
>
> *Thou Who art love beyond all telling,*
> *Saviour and King, we worship Thee.*
> *Immanuel, within us dwelling,*

Make us what Thou wouldst have us be.
Thou Who art love, beyond all telling,
Saviour and King, we worship Thee.

Lord God, we do worship you. We pray that you would forgive us for ways that we have washed out your love by thinking that people are not so bad and that loving us has not cost you that much. O Lord, restore the vividness and the vigor of the Christian gospel to our minds, that this Christmas we would see the darkness of our own sin and the brightness of our own hope in Christ. Pierce our indifference, lay aside our distractions, and give us a clear vision of yourself and your love. For your own glory we ask these things, in Jesus' name. Amen.

Questions for Reflection

1. What role does teaching play in the local church?

2. What is the heart of what Christian teachers should teach?

3. Clearly, preachers should teach their congregations how to discern between right and wrong. How then can preachers avoid becoming moralistic?

4. True or false: a preacher should preach the gospel every Sunday. Explain.

5. Is false doctrine a threat to the church today? Where?

6. Do you pray for the political leaders of your nation? Your region? Your city? Your own boss?

7. If you are a woman, how is God calling you to serve in your church? If you are a man, is there any reason you could not serve as an elder? Is that reason something you could address or change?

8. We have seen that a leader should live for others. He practices putting the whole before himself. What are some ways you practice putting the whole before yourself during church prayer meetings? At the conclusion of church services? During Sunday school? Throughout the week? In your giving? In your hospitality?

9. What role does a teacher's life play in his teaching?

10. We have seen that the heart of good leadership is to live not for one's own gain but for God's pleasure. How does a leader who lives for God's pleasure look different from a leader who does not?

11. In our own lives, how do we determine what gives God pleasure?

12. How can a church change its gatherings from being entertainment-driven to being God's-pleasure-driven?

13. Suppose tomorrow morning you woke up and began living entirely for God's pleasure. How would your life look different? Do you think living this way would ultimately bring you more or less pleasure? Would it require more or less self-sacrifice?

14. Presumably, of the leaders in the church who are motivated by money, few realize it. Their financial decisions probably seem rational to them. What are some ways a teachable person might detect whether he is motivated by love of money?

15. How can we cultivate leaders in our churches like the leader Paul exhorts Timothy to become?

16. Following up on question 15, begin praying that God would raise up such leaders!

THE MESSAGE OF 2 TIMOTHY: SUCCESS

16

THE MESSAGE OF 2 TIMOTHY: SUCCESS

WHAT'S YOUR PICTURE OF SUCCESS?[1]

Let's make sure I've got it right: The essence of Christmas, if I understood what Bishop Desmond Tutu and the Queen of England said yesterday, is this: we gather together and feel full, and out of that feeling we turn and share with others. I think that is what these great leaders of the world are telling us. We gather together and think about our national budget surpluses, according to the bishop, and our own rising stock portfolios, according to the Queen; then we share with others. That is what Christmas is all about.

Well, we do enjoy gathering together at Christmas. Some people travel to be with family or friends. Others stay at home because the traveling family comes to them. And nobody likes to be alone on Christmas. Perhaps the bishop and the Queen are right about that much. I remember reading one church sign that said, "Why face depression alone? Come to church." Things don't always come out the way you mean them!

Certainly depression is the downside of cultural celebrations such as Christmas. If you are already feeling a little down, being surrounded by cheery people can just make it worse. Let's say on Christmas day you are sitting alone at home, or maybe with one other person. Playing on the television, or running through your head, are scenes of full houses and presents and big meals from your childhood or your family's early years. Being alone amid such scenes is hard.

One local news station had a special feature on how to deal with the Christmas blues. One of the main causes of the Christmas blues, they said, was loneliness. People expect to share special days like Christmas with family and

---

[1] This sermon was originally preached on December 26, 1999, at Capitol Hill Baptist Church in Washington, D.C.

friends. When the news producers first thought of doing this feature, they were assuming what we all assume: more people struggle with feeling depressed around Christmastime than at any other time of the year.

Loneliness can be a tremendous problem for people. We are social creatures. Different people may require different amounts of social activity, but all of us need people. That is how we're made. Depriving people of their normal associations with others can be as disorienting as depriving them of light or rest. People become disoriented, even disinterested in life.

Being successful and at the same time being alone is barely conceivable. Success is having your family around you at Christmas. It is a dinner party with friends and food aplenty. Without cheerful faces and loving companions, good conversation and warm embraces, what is the point of success? What is the point of anything?

Imagine for a moment an old man who is alone. He is in failing health. He is isolated from family and friends. And he is so poor he cannot afford a winter coat. He changed careers in mid-life, but there is no pension plan or medical benefits with his own start-up organization. Not only that, his new enterprise seems to be faltering. Oh, and one more thing: he is incarcerated under capital charges. If found guilty, he could lose his life. And it looks like he will be found guilty.

Now, is that your picture of success? Is that how you would want to begin a new year? Put yourself in his place.

INTRODUCING 2 TIMOTHY

Unless I have misunderstood the letter, that is pretty much what Paul asks Timothy to do in his second letter to Timothy—put himself in Paul's place. In 2 Timothy, Paul exhorts Timothy to clarify the message that he preaches, warns him that the journey ahead will be difficult, and urges him to follow his own example of faithfully preaching the gospel to the end. So Paul writes Timothy about three things: keeping the message, counting the cost, and continuing to the end.

KEEP THE MESSAGE

First, Paul exhorts Timothy to keep the message clear. He begins by reminding Timothy of the crucial things that Timothy already knew:

> For God did not give us a spirit of timidity, but a spirit of power, of love and of self-discipline.
>
> So do not be ashamed to testify about our Lord, or ashamed of me his prisoner. But join with me in suffering for the gospel, by the power of God, who has

saved us and called us to a holy life—not because of anything we have done but because of his own purpose and grace. This grace was given us in Christ Jesus before the beginning of time, but it has now been revealed through the appearing of our Savior, Christ Jesus, who has destroyed death and has brought life and immortality to light through the gospel. And of this gospel I was appointed a herald and an apostle and a teacher. That is why I am suffering as I am. Yet I am not ashamed, because I know whom I have believed, and am convinced that he is able to guard what I have entrusted to him for that day.

What you heard from me, keep as the pattern of sound teaching, with faith and love in Christ Jesus. Guard the good deposit that was entrusted to you—guard it with the help of the Holy Spirit who lives in us (1:7-14).

The Source of the Message

At the heart of this exhortation is what Timothy already knew and believed: the gospel is from God. Neither he nor Paul made up the good news to which Timothy testifies. God gives us the good news. God saves us and sustains us. God calls us. Man did not invent this religion as a way to approach God. God brought this gospel to man. As Paul says, this gospel has been "given," "revealed," and "brought" (1:9-10). It has been given and revealed like many of the gifts given on Christmas—from another to us. Neither Paul nor Timothy, neither you nor I, have written this message. We have received it. And God has given it "because of his own purpose and grace" (1:9).

The Content of the Message

The message that Paul and Timothy share with others is not just any news. No, it is special. For one thing, look at how God revealed it—through Christ Jesus and Christ's work in history. Paul says this in 1:10: "It has now been revealed through the appearing of our Savior, Christ Jesus, who has destroyed death and brought life and immortality to light through the gospel." This is no mere moralism, like loving your neighbor as yourself—though Christ certainly taught that. Most fundamentally, the gospel of Christianity has to do with specific historical events, namely, the birth, the life and ministry, the death, and the resurrection of Jesus of Nazareth. Jesus taught that he came to lay down his life as a ransom for the sin of whoever would turn and trust him. That is the message the apostles taught. After Christ was crucified and raised again, the apostles were filled with the Holy Spirit and they traveled to much of the known world to teach who Jesus is and what he has done. This is the gospel.

As Christians, we do not have some abstract message of God's predisposition toward love, generosity, or even life. The gospel is not ultimately about giving to one another or loving one another. No, we have a very specific message about God's grace shown through the historical work of Christ: God came to earth in Christ; Christ died to reconcile God and man by paying for the sins of everyone who turns from his or her sins and trusts in him; and God proved Christ to be Savior and Lord by raising him from the dead. That is the good news of Christianity.

The Keeping of the Message

What then is Timothy to do with this message? He is to guard it like a trust. That is the kind of language Paul uses. He tells Timothy, "keep . . . the pattern of sound teaching, with faith and love. . . . Guard the good deposit that was entrusted to you" (1:13-14). These two imperatives—"keep . . . guard"—indicate he has given Timothy this message as a trust.

These are important commands for us too. As with Timothy, the message entrusted to us is unique. If we alter it, we lose it. So we must be careful to guard it. You and I are not called to give out another message; or to come up with something that has more surface appeal; or to craft a gospel better suited to modern needs, as we see them. We are called to give the gospel of Jesus Christ alone. If the gospel of Jesus Christ is altered, it is lost.

A mail carrier's job provides a good illustration of this. Consider his job for a moment. A mail carrier is not hired to visit the store, buy a box of cards, bring them to your front porch, sit down, write in the cards, stuff, lick, seal, address, stamp, and then shove them into your mail box. No, he or she is specifically hired to bring you the messages that *someone else* has written and sent to you. He is not supposed to invent the message. He is just supposed to deliver it. That is what we as Christians are supposed to do. We need not be inventive or original. We do not have to come up with something that will meet the demands of the day. No, we have a much simpler job. Our job is like the faithful mail carrier's: deliver the message entrusted to our care.

There are two particular aspects of the gospel message we must take special care in guarding today, because they are so often challenged or changed. First, we must carefully guard how we present human need. In spite of Bishop Tutu and the Queen's statements, humanity's main need is not a physical need. Most fundamentally, our need is a spiritual need caused by the fact that we have all sinned against God. And those sins deserve his condemnation. Meeting people's physical needs, of course, is no bad thing. In fact, it is very important. Yet according to the gospel of Jesus Christ, that is not humanity's main need. Jesus did teach, as the Queen said, that we are called to love our neighbor as ourselves. Yet that is not the essence of the gospel. Loving others does not save us. We cannot be saved by anything we do, not even by meeting the physical needs of others. We can only be saved by what God offers us in Christ: the forgiveness of sins. Christianity is not a do-it-yourself salvation kit, as if God gives you all the elements except the batteries. You provide the batteries of faith, and then you are saved. No, Christianity is the message of God's salvation in Christ. We are in no shape to save ourselves, even if God gives us all the right ingredients. We must *be saved*. So we must guard a right understanding of our need: we are so spiritually poor that we need God in Christ to save us.

Second, we must also guard how we present God's provision for our need. Christianity does not present Jesus as a moral teacher—someone who has garnered respect from people around the world because of his great teaching. Rather, Christianity presents Jesus as the rejected Messiah of Israel who died as an outlaw on the cross. And by dying on the cross, he bore the sins of everyone who would ever turn and trust in him. Jesus entrusted Paul with this message on the road to Damascus. Paul entrusted it to Timothy. Timothy was called to entrust it to his flock. And now, through this letter, this same message has been entrusted to you, if you are a Christian. Scripture does not exhort you, above all else, to go and preach a gospel of sharing with other people. That is a wonderful ethical teaching and has tremendous importance in our world. But it is far from the heart of the gospel. The heart of the gospel is never what we do; it is what God offers us in Christ through his death on the cross.

Interestingly, Paul tells Timothy to keep this message "with faith and love in Christ Jesus" (1:13). Keeping the truth, keeping orthodox dogma, is not keeping a dry, lifeless thing. It is keeping hold of a vital statement of the love that comes from being with Christ. Also, Timothy is not called to be cantankerous, independent, and self-sufficient. Paul exhorts him to do his work "with the help of the Holy Spirit."

Again, all of this is a trust. And this trust is given to and held by Timothy specifically to give to others. John Piper has written, "No one who knows and loves Christ can be content to come to Him alone."[2] How true this is! When we genuinely come to know God in Christ, albeit haltingly and falteringly, we have something we want others to know. So we share this good news with others.

Many public figures today—from press spokesmen to presidential candidates to congressmen to members of religious councils—might believe that sharing this message with others is intolerant. But in the New Testament, Christianity always entails vocalizing the gospel message to others. It is not something we can leave out. The very nature of this gospel requires it to be verbally spread. The angels over the plains of Bethlehem did not whisper about the Messiah's birth to the shepherds, afraid to raise their voices lest they offend

---

[2] John Piper, *Desiring God* (Sisters, Ore.: Multnomah, 2003), 281.

someone. They shouted the news with trumpets. The apostles proclaimed the death and resurrection of Christ in the same public squares of Jerusalem where the Messiah had just been accused and crucified. They did not even back down from blaming the people for Jesus' death. Yet their speech was not hate speech; it was love speech. The apostles did not desire ill for their audiences. They desired their good, even though it eventually cost the apostles their own lives to proclaim the good. Regardless of how politicians may spin it, gospel speech does not threaten to increase levels of intolerance in our country.

How can Timothy survive the difficulties he will inevitably face as he keeps the message clear? Only by God's power, Paul says:

> God did not give us a spirit of timidity, but a spirit of power, of love and of self-discipline.
> So do not be ashamed to testify about our Lord, or ashamed of me his prisoner. But join with me in suffering for the gospel by the power of God (1:7-8).

Would you want such a "gift" from God? The gift of power to suffer for the gospel? What a strange idea. I am not asking if, masochistically, you want to suffer. Rather, if you knew that God's power and the beauty of the gospel would be displayed by your suffering, would you want such a gift?

What message are you keeping? Is there any message for which you would be willing to suffer?

COUNT THE COST

This brings us to Paul's second reason for writing Timothy. In chapters 2 and 3, he warns Timothy about the difficulty of the road ahead and exhorts him to count the cost. In the first half of chapter 2, Paul again reminds Timothy of the gospel with which he has been entrusted: "Remember Jesus Christ, raised from the dead, descended from David. This is my gospel" (2:8). But now he also charges Timothy to entrust the same message to others: "the things you have heard me say in the presence of many witnesses entrust to reliable men who will also be qualified to teach others" (2:2).

Timothy is given quite a charge. Certainly, it involves knowing the gospel clearly. Every Christian must understand this message. Yet Paul's charge involves more. Timothy must teach this message. He must teach it to people who in turn can teach it to still other people. Paul (generation 1) speaks to Timothy (generation 2), telling him to entrust the gospel to reliable men (generation 3), who will be qualified to teach others (generation 4).

We have no reason for supposing that Paul's charge was a unique apostolic calling of the apostolic age. Paul is simply teaching Timothy what the

Great Commission means in his life. For ourselves, then, we should ask whether we are involved in teaching others who will then be able to teach still others. Those of us who are pastors like Timothy should be directly involved in training future ministers, or elders. Non-pastors should also be busy discipling, evangelizing, attending Bible studies, leading Bible studies, studying the gospel, and encouraging others to know it as well. For the church, this means placing a clear priority on supporting the teaching ministry.

In addition to calling Timothy to entrust the gospel to others, Paul calls him to endure suffering. As we have seen, Paul invites Timothy to "join with me in suffering for the gospel" (1:8). Yet to do this, Timothy must "be strong" (2:1). He must "Endure hardship" (2:3). Three images are used: endure hardship like a good soldier (2:3); compete as an athlete (2:5); work hard like a farmer (2:6). Timothy must consider the example of each.

Paul speaks from experience. He has suffered to "the point of being chained like a criminal" (2:9). Why does he choose to endure such suffering? "I endure everything for the sake of the elect, that they too may obtain the salvation that is in Christ Jesus, with eternal glory" (2:10). Paul has remained faithful, and he calls Timothy to remain faithful, too, despite the suffering that faithfulness entails.

We Christians must be willing to endure suffering and opposition to the truth. When opposition to the gospel comes, we have a choice: we can endure it, or we can avoid it by disowning the gospel. Often in life, we can hold the gospel with one hand and our comfort with the other. We walk around carrying both, saying we value the gospel more than our comfort. Circumstances permit us to carry both, so who's to question our sincerity? Suppose, then, a difficult trial hits you. Maybe your sorority sister or fraternity brother, your coworker or a family member, challenges your Christian faith. The opposition becomes so strong it takes both hands to hold on to one of the two things. You then have a choice. You can be faithful to the gospel or your can hold on to your comfort. Which one are you going to hold on to? Are you going to let go of the gospel in order to keep your comfort? Or are you going to let go of your comfort in order to keep the gospel? Paul tells Timothy he may need to make this choice one day. He tells us the same thing.

If soldiers, athletes, and farmers endure for prizes less glorious and less lasting, can we not endure opposition for the sake of bringing the good news of Christ's reconciling work to the world? Are you and I committed to being "obedient" only when circumstances are favorable? Since when should circumstances be the lord of our lives, determining what we do and do not do? Perhaps you need to reconsider the terms you have given God for your willingness serve him. Do you maintain control of the contract? "Lord, I appreciate the coherence you have given to my worldview, as well as the occasional moral guidance. But I really don't want you involved in *these* aspects of my life. When it comes to *these* things, I am going to assume the Bible is not relevant."

In the second half of chapter 2 and the beginning of chapter 3, Paul continues to warn Timothy about the suffering he will endure, particularly the suffering that will occur when he attempts to fend off godless teachers. Christians face problems not only from outside of the church; many come from the inside (cf. Acts 20:29-30). So Paul spends a good deal of this letter warning Timothy about godless chatter and quarreling. What should Timothy do with godless chattering? Have nothing to do with it (2:23)! Avoid those who do. Not only are they not productive, they "[ruin] those who listen" (2:14), making them "more and more ungodly" and destroying their faith (2:16). A pastor in particular must avoid "foolish and stupid arguments" (2:23).

Be careful what you fight over. Sometimes you must verbally contend for the gospel. Yet at other times, the way of wisdom is to avoid the fruitless argumentativeness of some, even some in the church.

False teaching and the wickedness it produces should especially be avoided. After all, truth does not fit with wickedness. Paul refers to two particular teachers "who have wandered away from the truth. They say that the resurrection has already taken place, and they destroy the faith of some" (2:18). In other words, their false teaching has led to false living. On the other hand, "Everyone who confesses the name of the Lord must turn away from wickedness" (2:19b). Right teaching will lead to right living. Therefore, we must cleanse ourselves from false teaching and the wickedness inherent in it. If you begin to deviate on the reliability of the Scriptures or what Christ has done, it will show itself in your life.

I know of few, if any, cases where individuals who decided to live contrary to the Scriptures did not also make some attempt to square their actions with God. Somewhere in the process, they began distorting who Christ is or what the Bible says. This makes the teacher of the Word all the more important within the church.

Paul knows Timothy will face false teachers in his church. So he clearly describes what a good teacher must be like. He begins by saying, "Do your best to present yourself to God as one approved, a workman who does not need to be ashamed and who correctly handles the word of truth" (2:15). He then says a good teacher must "avoid godless chatter" (2:16), as we have seen. Then several verses later, he adds,

> the Lord's servant must not quarrel; instead, he must be kind to everyone, able
> to teach, not resentful. Those who oppose him he must gently instruct, in the

hope that God will grant them repentance leading them to a knowledge of the truth, and that they will come to their senses and escape from the trap of the devil, who has taken them captive to do his will (2:24-26).

What Paul requires of those who are entrusted with teaching and guarding the gospel in the church is pretty clear. Specifically, he points to six characteristics. First, a good teacher will "cut straight" the word of truth, as the word for "correctly handle" literally means. He does not avoid the difficult passages or twist words to suit the tastes of people. He says what the Bible says. Second, God's servant must be kind. Third, he must be able to teach. Fourth, he must not be resentful. Fifth, he must be a gentle instructor. Finally, he can do all these things because he is always mindful of his ultimate audience: "present yourself to God" (2:15).

This is a daunting list for anyone who wants to be a public teacher of Scripture. Consider what it requires: tenacity without meanness; firmness without harshness; and the ability to both articulately speak and wisely remain silent. This is what a teacher should be like. Actually, this is what all Christians should be like—utterly resolved to sacrifice themselves for the good of others and the glory of God.

As for the people who present themselves as teachers but fail to meet these qualifications, avoid them! The false teachers who oppose Timothy expose their godlessness by living godless lives. Paul writes,

> But mark this: There will be terrible times in the last days. People will be lovers of themselves, lovers of money, boastful, proud, abusive, disobedient to their parents, ungrateful, unholy, without love, unforgiving, slanderous, without self-control, brutal, not lovers of the good, treacherous, rash, conceited, lovers of pleasure rather than lovers of God (3:1-4).

What a list! How many of these things flourish in our own day? Such teachers may appear godly, Paul says, but to no good end; he describes them as "having a form of godliness . . . but denying its power!" (3:5).

I hope you see the warning against hypocrisy here. A person can wear every form of godliness but be filled with rancidness. You can be very involved in religion and church, not even missing church when away with the family on Christmas weekend. But if your heart lacks an honest commitment to God and love for him, you can be sure the nimble fingers of time even now are flipping through the different combinations of your heart to discover what circumstance will expose your true allegiance. If your heart is not right, your Christianity will last only as long as circumstances allow you to have everything you want.

What should we do when such people put themselves forward as leaders and teachers in the church? Paul answers, "Have nothing to do with them" (3:5). He knows that false teachers are dangerous. Often, we are hesitant to speak like this. But Paul knows that bad teaching can spread like gangrene, and with even worse effects (2:17).

Timothy would have to endure suffering himself, and he would have to lead the church in dealing with suffering. And it would be hard. But Paul wanted to be honest with Timothy, as Jesus had been honest with his own disciples: following Jesus means taking up the cross. Paul had taken up his cross to follow Jesus, and now he was calling Timothy to do the same.

In this vein, Amy Carmichael prays,

> From subtle love of softening things,
> From easy choices, weakenings,
> Not thus are spirits fortified,
> Not this way went the Crucified,
> From all that dims Thy Calvary,
> O Lamb of God, deliver me.[3]

CONTINUE TO THE END

Finally, Paul urges Timothy to continue pressing on to the end, just as Paul had done. Timothy was well familiar with the course of Paul's life. Paul observes, "You, however, know all about my teaching, my way of life, my purpose, faith, patience, love, endurance, persecutions, sufferings—what kinds of things happened to me in Antioch, Iconium and Lystra, the persecutions I endured. Yet the Lord rescued me from all of them" (3:10-11). Timothy had been with Paul during some of the most difficult times of his life. He had faced opposition with him. Paul knows what he is talking about, and Timothy knows it.

Yet Paul was not the only Christian who would face persecution: "Everyone who wants to live a godly life in Christ Jesus will be persecuted, while evil men and imposters will go from bad to worse, deceiving and being deceived" (3:12-13). I don't know if you have seen any of the various "Bible Promise" books offered in bookstores. But I am sure you will not find 2 Timothy 3:12-13 in such books. Yet this is a promise. Everyone who wants to live a godly life in Christ Jesus will be persecuted!

On this basis, Paul exhorts Timothy to follow his example:

---

[3] Amy Carmichael, "Flame of God."

> But as for you, continue in what you have learned and have become convinced
> of, because you know those from whom you learned it, and how from infancy
> you have known the holy Scriptures, which are able to make you wise for sal-
> vation through faith in Christ Jesus. All Scripture is God-breathed and is useful
> for teaching, rebuking, correcting and training in righteousness, so that the man
> of God may be thoroughly equipped for every good work (3:14-17).

Timothy knows what kind of people had taught him the gospel. They were not self-serving, ease-loving money-grubbers who made up stories. Incidentally, is it not wonderful that Paul can appeal to examples of people Timothy knows? We learn so much from the lives of those who faithfully follow God. Timothy also knows what these people—such as his mother and grandmother—had taught him. He had been taught the Scriptures from infancy. He knows what the Scriptures *are* and what the Scriptures *do*. The Scriptures are God-breathed, and they make a person wise for salvation.

If you wish to continue to the end, you cannot neglect the Scriptures. This is one of the main ways God has given us to endure to the end. As Thomas Cranmer said, we should read, mark, learn, and inwardly digest God's Word.[4] Our Bible reading should be regular. Our study should be diligent. Our meditation should be thoughtful. Our references to the Bible should be frequent. If we are Christians, this is what we are called to do—feed upon God's Word to us.

Timothy has seen Paul's example; now Paul exhorts him to follow it. Through good times and bad, Timothy must be faithful to the trust he has been given, just as Paul has been. Paul tells Timothy to "Preach the Word" (4:2). Preach. Proclaim. Herald. Don't hide it under a basket. Don't be scared or shy about it. Don't deny or ignore it. Preach it. And what must Timothy preach? The Word. He has no license to preach anything else.

As a preacher, I have no license to preach anything but the Bible. Do not mistake me for a professional speaker. I am a preacher of the Word of God. If I begin to preach something else, I have wandered outside the call God and my local church have given me. I have wandered outside the area of my competence. I have no authority to declare a message other than the Word of God.

Preaching involves more than standing and speaking to a congregation for an hour a week. It may also involve the things Paul mentions next: "be prepared in season and out of season; correct, rebuke and encourage—with great patience and careful instruction" (4:2b). You can just imagine what qualities are needed to fulfill this mandate. Paul not only tells a pastor what

---

[4] From Thomas Cranmer's *Book of Common Prayer* (1549); entry for second Sunday in Advent.

to do, he tells him how to do it: "with great patience and careful instruction." Great patience is required by the very nature of teaching. If you have ever taught Sunday school or your own children, you know what it is like to repeat yourself. You have to be willing to explain something a second time, a third time, a fourth time without remonstrating the students or making them feel bad for needing to ask questions. This is how God is patient with us. He gives wisdom when we ask, and he does not rebuke us for not already possessing it (James 1:5). A teacher of the Word must instruct carefully and with great patience.

As the pastor preaches, he should do so with the Second Coming in view: "in view of his appearing and his kingdom, I give you this charge: Preach the Word" (4:1b-2a). We often plan today's activities based on expectations of tomorrow. So Paul exhorts Timothy to prioritize today in view of Christ's coming. Yet perhaps Paul also has something more immediate in mind. He exhorts Timothy to preach because of what lies in store in the Ephesian church. Some of the Ephesians would begin falling away from the truth. He writes,

> For the time will come when men will not put up with sound doctrine. Instead, to suit their own desires, they will gather around them a great number of teachers to say what their itching ears want to hear. They will turn their ears away from the truth and turn aside to myths. But you, keep your head in all situations, endure hardship, do the work of an evangelist, discharge all the duties of your ministry (4:3-5).

If a pastor wants the gospel to continue spreading tomorrow, preaching must be today's priority. The need is great, and the time to stand up and be counted is now. Timothy must stand up and speak the truth, even when the congregation begins to slip away.

It is interesting how congregational this passage is. Paul does not attack the false teachers. He attacks the people who ask the false teachers to scratch their itching ears. He attributes responsibility to them. If you are a regular member of a church, where you vote, tithe, and pay the pastor's salary, you become partly responsible for what is taught. This is true for every church you will ever join.

Besides the imminence of Christ's return, and the threat of false teaching, Paul also exhorts Timothy to continue to the end because his (Paul's) own race is just about done. Paul writes,

> For I am already being poured out like a drink offering, and the time has come for my departure. I have fought the good fight, I have finished the race, I have kept the faith. Now there is in store for me the crown of righteousness, which

the Lord, the righteous Judge, will award to me on that day—and not only to me, but also to all who have longed for his appearing (4:6-8).

It would be tremendous to have the kind of confidence Paul demonstrates here. He can look back and have confidence in his former purposes and his legacy with Timothy. He can look around his prison cell and see the circumstances that will lead to his death. But he can also look forward beyond his imprisonment and death to the joy that lies in store. Paul knows that one day God will reveal how persevering through trials by faith brings honor and glory to God. That is what Paul is doing as an old man deserted in prison. And that is what he wants Timothy to do one day as well. Yet to do that, Timothy would have to be faithful today by preaching the gospel.

Finally, Paul asks Timothy for help. He writes, "Do your best to come to me quickly" (4:9). This is a plea. Sometimes people think the way to inspire others is to look strong, as if there are no chinks, no problems, no difficulties, and no weaknesses. But that is not correct. If you do too good a job of hiding your weakness, people around you will give up. They know their own weaknesses, and they may not believe they can measure up to the standard you have set. Paul is a model for Timothy exactly because he is willing to be honest. Paul is weak and tired. He realizes his need for a friend at a time like this. Letting people see your weaknesses does not spoil your ability to be an example, it makes your example more realistic and realizable. It sets your example down right next to a person and makes it all the more challenging.

Paul reminds Timothy of his need to be clear with the gospel. He warns him it will not be easy. And he exhorts him to press on, regardless of circumstances, until the race is done. That is Paul's message.

CONCLUSION

Two more of Paul's letters follow 2 Timothy in the canonical order of the New Testament. But chronologically, based on everything we know, 2 Timothy was the last letter from Paul's pen. I wonder if Paul was surprised by how things ended. Consider Paul as a young man in rabbinical school, doing well. Or consider Paul in that incredible moment on the road to Damascus, when a flash of light knocked him off his horse and he was told he would be the apostle to the Gentiles. I wonder if, in his earlier years of ministry, he ever envisioned the emperor of Rome becoming a Christian as the crowning glory and culmination of his faithful ministry. Or did he imagine himself as an old man in a jail alone?

What about you? Are you where you thought you would be at this time in your life? Maybe you are feeling unexpectedly directionless. Maybe you are surprised that you are already married with kids, or that it took this long.

Perhaps you are surprised that you attend church so often. You never planned on being in any church at all. Or perhaps you have yet to realize how rarely you are in church. Possibly you have recently experienced terrible bereavement or physical pain. You may have seen hard things in your family, or struggled with hard things in yourself.

Of course, your circumstances may not be that bad. You may be feeling prosperous. If you are, beware. Good circumstances are like the fog: they cloud your perceptions. In themselves, difficulty and suffering are not good. But they can clear away the clouds and help you to see your heart's true desires. At a recent conference, John Piper gave this warning: "If you don't find your satisfaction in God and in God alone, you will count him as an enemy when he hands you over to the sword."[5]

Friend, there is no guarantee of good circumstances in this life. Be very careful not to convince yourself you are following God when really you are doing nothing of the sort.

Is Paul where you think he should be at the end? Sitting there, alone in a prison? Would you consider him successful? At this point, Paul had been laboring for about thirty years as an itinerant evangelist. In these last words from his pen, he professes to have taught, lived, purposed, believed, had patience, loved, endured, been persecuted, suffered, been rescued, fought the good fight, finished the race, and kept the faith. And now? Now he is being poured out and is ready to depart. He is certain the Lord will bring him safely to heaven.

According to tradition, a few months, weeks, or even days after writing this letter, the emperor Nero gave his verdict on Paul. Paul was taken to one of the main roads leading into Rome, the Ostian Way, and his head was cut off his body. Nero had passed one verdict on Paul, while Christ passed another. Let me ask you again, was Paul successful?

We might also wonder, did Paul's letters to Timothy fail? It appears the Ephesian church continued to struggle after his first letter, so he had to write this second one. What happened to the church after this second letter? We have information about the church from earlier days in Acts, and in Paul's letter to the Ephesians. But we also learn a couple things about the church thirty years later, from the book of Revelation. In Revelation 2, John records Jesus' words to Ephesus:

> "I know your deeds, your hard work and your perseverance. I know that you cannot tolerate wicked men, that you have tested those who claim to be apos-

---

[5] Founders Conference, Birmingham, July 1999.

tles but are not, and have found them false. You have persevered and have
endured hardships for my name, and have not grown weary.

"Yet I hold this against you: You have forsaken your first love. Remember
the height from which you have fallen! Repent and do the things you did at first.
If you do not repent, I will come to you and remove your lampstand from its
place. But you have this in your favor: You hate the practices of the Nicolaitans,
which I also hate.

"He who has an ear, let him hear what the Spirit says to the churches. To
him who overcomes, I will give the right to eat from the tree of life, which is in
the paradise of God" (Rev. 2:2-7).

The Ephesian church obviously continued to struggle. Was it successful?

As we have seen, in this final letter Paul pleads with Timothy to visit him.
We do not know if Timothy was able to visit Paul before Paul was executed.
But tradition has it that Timothy was in Ephesus for many years as the pastor
of the church. He may have been the "lampstand" of the Ephesian church John
refers to in Revelation. Apparently, late in the first century during the reign of
the emperor Nerva (A.D. 96–98), a public celebration for the god Dionysius
was held in Ephesus that included public sinful activity. Timothy was so torn
of heart by the events that he stood up and started shouting in opposition to
this public frenzy. When he did that, the mob became enraged, picked up clubs
and stones, and beat him until he died. Now, was Timothy successful?

Let me bring this home. How can we know if our church was successful
over the past year? How can I know if my ministry as a pastor is a success or
a failure? And how will you determine if you were successful over the past
year? What if your body is aging and your health is failing, or you are separated from family and friends? What if your employment was recently termi-
nated, or your bank account is empty? What if you are cold, imprisoned, and
in danger of losing your life? Then, are you a success?

What if you were born in a barn, your father died when you were young,
you never settled on a career, and you never married or had a family? And what
if you were executed as a terrorist long before reaching the age of forty? Then,
could you still consider yourself a success? Answer that, and I will tell you if
you have understood 2 Timothy, or if you have understood Christmas, or if
you have understood life.

Let us pray:

*Lord God, so many of the good things we look to at this time of year are not
the point. And they confuse us. We put the weight of our hopes upon them in
a way you did not intend. Instead of enjoying the good gifts you have given to*

draw our minds and eyes and hearts back to you, we look at the things them-selves. We focus on the gifts rather than the giver. O Lord, we pray that you would take us where we are, and that in love your Holy Spirit would draw the eyes of our hearts back to you so that we would see the good gift you have given us in Jesus Christ. We praise you for what your gift of Christ as well as your call to repent of sin and trust in you shows of your heart for us. Lord, we pray that that would be the legacy of Christmas in our hearts. For Jesus' sake. Amen.

Questions for Reflection

1. When was the last time you felt alone? What does that feeling teach us about how we have been created? Is there any relationship here on earth that will completely satisfy our longing for fellowship?

2. What is the message that Paul charges Timothy with keeping at all costs?

3. In many areas of life, innovation and originality are prized. Why is this *not* true for the gospel message?

4. As we have seen, there are two particular aspects of the gospel message we must take special care in guarding today: how we present human need, and how we present God's provision for human need. Explain what is at stake here. Why are these two things so important? What implications does this have for preaching? For a church's work generally?

5. Suppose Paul heard someone describe the gospel as "Christ's call for us to share with those in need of food, clothing, shelter, and any other essentials in life." How would he respond? How would you respond?

6. Paul writes Timothy, "God did not give us a spirit of timidity, but a spirit of power, . . . join with me in suffering for the gospel by the power of God" (1:7-8). Would you want such a "gift" from God? Power to suffer for the gospel? Is there any message for which you would be willing to suffer?

7. Paul charges Timothy with teaching men who in turn can teach others. Are you involved in teaching others who in turn can teach still others? As we have considered, those of us who are pastors like Timothy can be directly involved in training future ministers, or elders. Non-pastors can be busy discipling, evangelizing, attending Bible studies, leading Bible studies, teaching their children,

studying the gospel, and encouraging others to know it as well. For the church, this means placing a clear priority on supporting the teaching ministry. So, how are you doing?

8. We have noted that life often allows us to hold the gospel with one hand and our comfort with the other. Nothing immediately forces us to choose one or the other. Yet if you were challenged to do so, which would you give up? How can you prepare yourself *now* for answering correctly *when* the time comes for you to make such a decision? What if the challenge is subtle—will you notice the challenge if you are not preparing yourself now?

9. How are you doing with "godless chatter" and "fruitless argumentativeness"?

10. If a dedication to reading, studying, and learning Scripture is essential to our perseverance in the faith, what would you say your chances are for persevering? How is your church helping you to persevere?

11. We have observed that Paul is not shy about asking Timothy for help. Are you willing to let others see your weaknesses, especially those in positions beneath you?

12. Paul concluded his ministry alone, in prison, and facing the threat of execution. Does this fit with your way of measuring success? By your definition of "success," when do you expect you will be successful?

13. Following up on question 12, how can your church know if it was "successful" over the past year? How would you measure your pastor's success? How will you determine these things over the coming year?

THE MESSAGE OF TITUS: BEGINNINGS

HAPPY "NEW" YEAR!

INTRODUCING TITUS

GET GOOD TEACHERS IN PLACE

The Characteristics of an Elder

His family

His relationships with others

His love of what is good

His blamelessness

His firmness in the truth

The Installation of Elders

Plurality

Appointment

Priority

TEACH THE TRUTH

Teach Whom?

The false teachers

The true believers

Teach How?

Teach What?

CONCLUSION

THE MESSAGE OF TITUS: BEGINNINGS

HAPPY "NEW" YEAR![1]

If ever a week opened with everyone in the world thinking about new beginnings, it would be this one. Perhaps you watched the television coverage showing celebrations around the world on Friday as the clock hit 12:00 A.M., January 1, 2000. Near the stroke of midnight, President Bill Clinton stood on Washington's Mall and told us that it was time to pass the torch on to a new generation, and time to open a new chapter in our history. For many, the changing of the year, the decade, the century, even the millennium is a potent symbol of newness. It causes them to hope other areas of their lives will also find the newness they long for. Somehow, replacing the number 19 with the number 20 on our calendar seems portentous of greater changes.

But then, other things are happening to give us hope. We can almost feel the wind of change the Internet brings to our daily lives: from the way we communicate with family and friends, to the way we shop for Christmas presents, to the way I find quotes for sermons. The stock market continues to climb—new records are almost taken for granted. Consumer confidence is high; unemployment and inflation are low. Even the more stubborn social factors, like crime rates, seem to be dropping in almost every category. And big fears have proven false. Y2K came, but its much-feared glitches did not.

Times seem good. They have for some time now. In this past summer's issue of *The Wilson Quarterly* Paul Berman and Francis Fukuyama both argued that society is getting better, which is what a lot of people are saying.[2]

---

[1] This sermon was originally preached on January 2, 2000, at Capitol Hill Baptist Church in Washington, D.C.
[2] Francis Fukuyama and Paul Berman, "Reconstructing America's Moral Order," in *The Wilson Quarterly* 23, no. 3 (Summer 1999): 31-55 (this article was comprised of two separate articles: Fukuyama, "How to Re-Moralize America" [32-44]; and Berman, "Reimagining Destiny" [45-55].

Of course, not everyone is buying it. Andrew Delbanco, a professor in the humanities at Columbia, wrote back in the following issue and said, "Prompted by these essays to look around, I don't find in our market-driven culture many . . . landmarks by which we might navigate forward, or backward . . . toward a society more fully devoted to responsibility, charity, and genuine self-fulfillment. We may, as Fukuyama believes, be settling down and sobering up; but surely there is in contemporary America . . . an equally evident, and unslaked, longing for something more."[3]

I wonder if you agree with that. Either in your own life, or in the lives of others you know, is there an unslaked longing for something more?

One person greeted me as we passed by one another this last week with an unusually earnest and wistful, "Have a happy new year." And she separated out the words "new" and "year" so that both words stuck in my mind more than they usually do. It made me think about it—"happy . . . new . . . year." As I walked on, I found myself musing, "How many people this coming weekend will place their very serious hopes in this silly reason—the abstract way we represent the movement of time with a change in numbers? How many people believe that calling the month "January" instead of "December," or the year "2000" instead of "1999," will meet our long-standing needs and yield solutions to life's seemingly intractable problems?"

Picture in your mind, for a moment, the image of a man or woman, hopeful in the afternoon of December 31, drunk with their friends by the evening, happy while they are conscious, awake the next morning with the vain hope that a few rearrangements and resolutions will provide the new beginning they desire. These revelers have been told that the movement from one year to another is special. And they believe it. You wonder how they will feel when Saturday afternoon rolls around and then the next day and everyday thereafter, and all the difficulties they faced in 1999 somehow followed them into the "new" year. They survived the passage into the new millennium. Do we tell them to just wait 365,199 more days for the change of the *next* millennium? Is that what they should pin their hope on?

The Bible sometimes uses the image of leaning on a broken reed to describe what relying on a false hope looks like. We are not so familiar with reeds. Perhaps you can better envision a broadsword—a great piece of work with the handle on one end and the sharp point on the other. Now, imagine putting the handle on the ground, holding the tip up, and then leaning on the point! That is what leaning on foolish hopes is like. The more you lean, the

---

[3] Andrew Delbanco, "Correspondence: Overcoming the Great Disruption," in *The Wilson Quarterly* 23, no. 4 (Autumn 1999): 4.

more the sword cuts into you. The more we rely on false hopes, the more they disappoint and hurt. So imagine how people will be feeling in the days and weeks to come.

Many Christian groups have suggested that this great two-thousand-year anniversary of Christ's birth is an unusually important time for Christian witness. Even if the numbers are off by a few years, the birth of Christ is the dividing point in history. Surely we must emphasize this fact, these groups say. And this may be. Still, I think the opportunities we had for evangelizing leading up to the year 2000 will be dwarfed by the opportunities we will have in the weeks and months to come. Once all this hype about newness and change has subsided, people will discover that their normal lives on Mondays, Tuesdays, and Wednesdays are continuing as they always have. People will continue to starve. Debtor nations will continue to drown. And the hearts of humanity will remain mired in the same clutching, grasping selfishness that characterized last year and last century. We need to bring the true hope of newness in Jesus Christ into their everyday world.

Have you read about how optimistic people were at the beginning of the twentieth century? In their lifetimes, they had witnessed the coming of the telegraph, the telephone, the electric light, and a number of medical breakthroughs; and they were just beginning to see the automobile. Optimism was high in 1900. Some people called it the "Christian Century." And what did that Christian century end up containing? Charlie Rose said on his show a few days ago,[4] "If the past is prologue, we have as much to fear as we do to celebrate."

G. G. Findlay, a great theologian who lived a hundred years ago, once said, "Better circumstances do not make better men."[5] Now, if that is the case, then what does make better men? A new year? A new job or a new spouse? A raise or a move? More recognition or more vacation days? More degrees or more children? What makes someone better? If you happen to be stuck in an apparently hopeless situation, do you feel that doing certain religious things will give you hope? Have you been taught that you may somehow save yourself with the right religious instruction or practices?

INTRODUCING TITUS

To consider where our hope for new life should lie, we turn to Paul's letter to Titus. Paul wrote to Titus sometime in the first century, perhaps between A.D. 55 and 60. Titus had been a fellow missionary with Paul until Paul left him on

---

[4] December 20, 1999.
[5] G. G. Findlay, *The Epistle to the Galatians,* The Expositor's Bible, ed. W. Robertson Nicoll (New York: A. C. Armstrong & Son, 1903), 374.

the island of Crete to take care of unfinished business and appoint elders in all the churches. Apparently, some in the churches were advocating false hopes. So in this little letter, Paul instructs Titus about his work, especially about what should be taught in light of the false hopes tempting many.

Paul begins his letter,

"Paul, a servant of God and an apostle of Jesus Christ for the faith of God's elect and the knowledge of the truth that leads to godliness—a faith and knowledge resting on the hope of eternal life, which God, who does not lie, promised before the beginning of time, and at his appointed season he brought his word to light through the preaching entrusted to me by the command of God our Savior,

"To Titus, my true son in our common faith: Grace and peace from God the Father and Christ Jesus our Savior" (1:1-4).

From the get-go, Paul observes that a Christian has a faith and knowledge that rest on the hope of eternal life, a hope that the world does not know.

Paul then proceeds from this introduction to present Titus with two basic challenges: first, get good teachers in place; second, teach the truth. If you want to have an easy way to remember what the book of Titus is about, think of the word "teach." The book is mainly about teaching. So, get good teachers in place, and then teach the truth. We will look at both of these points in turn.

GET GOOD TEACHERS IN PLACE

Paul begins the body of the letter by telling Titus to straighten out what was left unfinished in their previous work and to appoint elders, or teachers. Immediately following the introduction, he writes, "The reason I left you in Crete was that you might straighten out what was left unfinished and appoint elders in every town, as I directed you" (1:5).

The Characteristics of an Elder

Following these basic instructions, Paul goes on to describe what these elders should look like. In fact, he gives fifteen different characteristics, and it is worth taking a moment to notice them:

> An elder must be blameless, the husband of but one wife, a man whose children believe [are faithful] and are not open to the charge of being wild and disobedient. Since an overseer is entrusted with God's work, he must be blameless—not overbearing, not quick-tempered, not given to drunkenness, not violent, not pursuing dishonest gain. Rather he must be hospitable, one who loves what is good, who is self-controlled, upright, holy and disciplined. He must hold firmly to the

trustworthy message as it has been taught, so that he can encourage others by sound doctrine and refute those who oppose it (1:6-9).

His family. Beginning in 1:6, Paul treats a man's leadership within his family as indicative of his capacity for spiritual leadership in the church. While this passage does not say an elder must be married, family life certainly does test and display one's ability and character in a unique way. To begin with, an elder should be the husband of one wife. I do not think Paul means an elder must be married; that would have excluded Paul, not to mention Jesus himself. Nor is it likely that he primarily intends to prohibit polygamy, though that is certainly an implication of what he is saying. Polygamy was not commonly practiced in the Greek culture of Crete. Nor was the practice of divorce common. So again, a prohibition against divorce may be implied, but that is not his primary point. More simply, Paul is probably referring to faithfulness in marriage. An elder must be a man who faithfully keeps to one woman and does not wander in any way.

An elder's ability to lead is also demonstrated through the behavior of his children. Three qualities in particular are mentioned. First, his children must not be open to the charge of being "wild." In context, the word refers to prodigally wasting resources on selfish pleasures and riotous living. Second, his children must not be open to the charge of "disobedience," that is, of openly behaving in a disobedient manner toward their parents. The third quality, and the first to be mentioned, has caused the most discussion. The NIV uses the word "believe," which is a legitimate translation. But I think it is better to translate the word as "trustworthy" or "faithful." In part, it would be strange to guarantee someone's regeneration just because his or her father is an elder. But also, the passage appears to be contrasting a reputation for wild and disobedient behavior with a reputation for being faithful and trustworthy, rather than with "believing" in a religious sense. In all of this, Paul teaches clearly that a man who cannot lead his own family cannot lead the church.

His relationships with others. Paul then turns in 1:7-8 to a person's relationships with others as demonstrating and revealing elder qualities. Negatively in 1:7, he states that an elder should be "not overbearing," that is, self-willed and arrogant. Also, he should be "not quick-tempered." He should not be a hothead who would sooner get angry than work for a solution. An elder should not be inaccessible, rash, and quick-tempered. As someone who has served as an elder, I can affirm Paul's instruction. When you serve as an elder, you find yourself in situations that can be anger provoking, if you tend in that direction. If you do, it is probably best not to serve as an elder. Next, an elder should be "not given to drunkenness." Such self-destructive addiction does not provide an encouraging example or the winsome witness needed by others in the church or by the world. Interestingly, both here and in the comparable list in 1 Timothy 3, the qualification immediately following the prohibition against drunkenness is "not violent." As the KJV reads, he must not be a "striker." An elder must be a leader, but he must not be too aggressive and certainly not given to physical violence. And an elder must not be a man who pursues "dishonest gain." He should not be too fond of money. At some point, that fondness may distort his vision.

Positively in verse 8, Paul tells Titus to look for men who are the opposite of verse 7's picture of self-absorption. Find men who are "hospitable," who, as the word literally means, love strangers. An elder does not regard the church as his own preserve for himself and his six friends. No, he is a man who loves strangers and opens his home to others. Central to an elder's life, after all, is a real devotion to others' welfare and a willingness to be inconvenienced for others. The last four qualities in verse 8 then strike me as two pairs of internal qualities an elder needs to fulfill the requirements of hospitality: he must be "self-controlled" and "disciplined"; and he must be "upright" and "holy." At his core, God's grace has taught the man to control himself and pursue righteousness, and this allows him to live by the other attributes mentioned here.

There are three more characteristics I want to spend a moment observing.

His love of what is good. First, Paul tells Titus that an elder is "one who loves what is good" (1:8). Throughout this letter, Paul uses two Greek words (*agathos* and *kalōs*), which both basically mean "good," in order to emphasize what should characterize the whole church community. Older women should teach what is good (2:3). They should train younger women to be kind, or good (*agathos*, 2:5). Titus himself is to set a good example for the younger men by doing what is good (2:7), and he must remind all the people "to be ready to do whatever is good" (3:1). Devotion to doing good should mark everyone who trusts in God. And again in his closing, Paul writes, everyone must learn to "devote themselves to doing what is good" (3:8). Given that goodness should typify the whole church, it is no wonder that an elder is described as "one who loves what is good."

His blamelessness. Second, an elder must be blameless—the only qualification that is repeated twice on the list (1:6, 7). This does not mean he must be perfect, else we would not have any elders. A blameless life is a life that does not bring the man or the gospel into public reproach. Rather, his life commends the gospel. An elder should not be the sort of man who shows up in a newspaper exposé, to which non-Christians respond with a chortle, "I knew there was nothing to this Christianity thing," and then turn the page. Therefore, a church should dismiss the pastor or elder when the nature of his sin causes people to scorn the gospel. Such a man should not be held up to the world as typifying a follower of Jesus. If I conduct myself in that way, I should be replaced, for the sake of the gospel and my own soul. Do that for any man who serves as an elder or pastor in a church of which you are a member.

His firmness in the truth. Third, an elder "must hold firmly to the trustworthy message as it has been taught" (1:9a). Knowing the message, and holding to the message firmly, are non-negotiables. Why? Paul answers, "so that he can encourage others by sound doctrine and refute those who oppose it" (1:9b). Really, Paul sticks to doing these two things in the rest of the book of Titus: encouraging others by sound doctrine, and refuting those who oppose it.

The Installation of Elders

But before we follow him, I want you to notice a few more things about these elders.

Plurality. Paul instructs Titus to appoint "elders" in every town. The word "elders" occurs in the plural. Biblically, it seems, there is supposed to be more than one elder in a church. Every church should have a number of leaders who are recognized and respected as having the characteristics already discussed. That does not mean a plurality of men the nominating committee likes, or the pastor likes, or who can simply win a church vote. That means a plurality of men who meet these biblical characteristics and are recognized as meeting them. Therefore, local churches should continually pray that God would raise up leaders who are respectable and worthy of being followed.

Appointment. How do you get such leaders? Well, Paul tells Titus to "appoint" them, as the NIV renders it. Some people have concluded the word "appoint" means Titus could act unilaterally, in the same way a president fills certain offices by appointment. But that is not what the word means here. It refers instead to an act of final confirmation, as opposed to how the person is selected in the first place. The word could also be rendered "ordain." In other words, the first order of business is to get a man in place, get him serving, and get him up and running. The various congregations in Crete, working with Titus, would probably have selected the persons. Titus was then charged with appointing, or ordaining, them. Something like this must have been the case, because Titus would have been fairly unfamiliar with many of the churches and individuals in them. Even if he was familiar with them, the members of the congregation would have known much better who the potential leaders among them were.

Priority. Finally, before we move to the subject of teaching, we must note the priority that Paul attaches to finding and installing such men. After all, this is the first thing that Paul tells Titus in this letter. "Look, you need to get reliable leaders who know the gospel and are committed to it. If you don't have that, you're going to have a hard time doing anything else. First, identify those people, and get the church to recognize them." Paul knows this is foundational. And that makes sense, given that most of the letter has to do with teaching. Titus must first concern himself with who will help him teach and who will help regulate the teaching in individual churches.

If our message—the gospel we proclaim—is central to the church's existence and our existence as Christians, then the elders who lead must be faithful in knowing and holding the truth of the gospel. They must also have the kind of lives and personalities, characteristics and qualities, which lend themselves to teaching that truth not only in the church but also in homes, in conversations, in manner, and in everyday life. If you want a good thing to pray for this year, pray that God makes your church rich in such divinely given human resources, and that he builds up the congregation through such men.

TEACH THE TRUTH

The bulk of the book of Titus is taken up with Paul's instruction to teach the truth. On the matter of teaching, we want to ask three questions: Teach whom? Teach how? And teach what?

Teach Whom?

Paul instructs Titus to teach two main groups of people: the false teachers and the true believers in the church.

The false teachers. In the last verses of chapter 1, Paul begins to describe the task of teaching, but he does this by telling Titus what a good teacher should oppose. It is interesting that Paul should start with the negative. If a teacher wants to clarify the gospel message, I guess Paul is saying, he will have to oppose what is false. Paul writes,

> For there are many rebellious people, mere talkers and deceivers, especially those of the circumcision group. They must be silenced, because they are ruining whole households by teaching things they ought not to teach—and that for the sake of dishonest gain. Even one of their own prophets has said, 'Cretans are always liars, evil brutes, lazy gluttons.' This testimony is true. Therefore, rebuke them sharply, so that they will be sound in the faith and will pay no attention to Jewish myths or to the commands of those who reject the truth. To the pure, all things are pure, but to those who are corrupted and do not believe, nothing is pure. In fact, both their minds and consciences are corrupted. They claim to know God,

but by their actions they deny him. They are detestable, disobedient and unfit for doing anything good (1:10-16).

Clearly, there are people in the churches of Crete who are problematic, both in what they teach and—as a result—in how they live. They are "rebellious people." They are "disobedient," not living as they should. They are "mere talkers and deceivers." So, says Paul, do not believe what they say. They are also hypocrites. They claim to know God, but their actions say otherwise. Their minds and consciences have become corrupted. Paul even calls them "detestable." All this is strong language, but look at what he says about them in that final phrase: "they are unfit for doing anything good." The very characteristic that Paul says should be typical of true Christians (3:8), these people lack, even though they present themselves as teachers! Not only are they not devoted to doing good, they are "unfit" for it.

Who are these people? In 1:10, Paul refers to the "circumcision group." Based on what we can piece together from Paul's other letters, these are people who accept Jesus as the Messiah yet require the Jewish laws to be observed, including the law of circumcision. Paul knows that any addition to the gospel is a false gospel. And so he tells Titus in no uncertain terms that it is his duty to oppose such teachers and their teachings. Oppose them for the sake of those around them. Silence them. Tell them to be quiet. Deprive them of their teaching positions. And do not just tell them they are wrong; explain to them *how* they are wrong. Titus must do this, Paul says, both so that the church will not pay attention to these myths and lies and so that it will be "sound in the faith." His goal here is not to stifle freedom of expression but to halt the spread of spiritual disease and to heal sick souls—even the souls of those who teach false doctrine.

Paul picks up the discussion of false teachers again in chapter 3, this time in order to warn Titus about divisions in the church:

> But avoid foolish controversies and genealogies and arguments and quarrels about the law, because these are unprofitable and useless. Warn a divisive person once, and then warn him a second time. After that, have nothing to do with him. You may be sure that such a man is warped and sinful; he is self-condemned (3:9-11).

Titus must protect these churches from divisions. That means not involving himself in wrongful arguments and warning those who do become so involved. Paul's two directives are simple: first, avoid them. Avoid them all—foolish controversies, genealogies, arguments about the law—because they are unprofitable and useless. A pastor must not waste his time engaging in anything unprofitable and useless. Second, warn those who become involved in such things. Warn them once, then twice, and then "have nothing to do" with them. Wow! Have nothing to do with them? Our church has talked a good bit about church discipline. We have had meetings about putting someone out of the church because of sin, and we have talked about not associating with him or her based on 1 Corinthians 5. But I do not believe we have ever gone as far as Paul does here—"have nothing to do" with them—with any sin. Why is Paul so severe? The arguments and controversies condemned here confuse the gospel message, and therefore the people who roil the churches with them are enemies of the gospel. Titus can pray that God will heal their souls, but for the sake of the gospel he must not tolerate their divisiveness. Foolish arguments threaten the clarity of the gospel and therefore the life of the church.

On this particular passage, the British preacher Martyn Lloyd-Jones suggested that the words "have nothing to do with him" literally mean, "have nothing to do with him." Lloyd-Jones thought Paul meant what he said. He went as far as to suggest the church should not even pray for such a person once it had taken disciplinary action—what Paul elsewhere refers to as handing the person over to Satan (1 Tim. 1:20). The church, said Lloyd-Jones, has done all it can in love and prayer already. Once the point of handing a man over comes, his sin is beyond what any human can do. He must simply be handed over. Well, I am not commending Lloyd-Jones's practice. There is no case of church discipline practiced by our own church about which I have ceased praying. Yet I am trying to demonstrate how serious Paul's charge is; and we need to wrestle with what it means. Why is Paul so hard on such people? Because he knows that God values the church, and God charges the pastors and elders to oppose anything that harms the church. The shepherd must protect the sheep.

One of the most important things any pastor or elder will do for you is something you may never notice. It is not visiting hospitals, successfully leading a church to expand its budget, or ensuring that his sermons have clear outlines—all of which are good things. It is this: working hard to know Scripture in order to protect you from false teachings, which are useless, of no benefit, dangerous, and divisive in the church.

Have nothing to do with individuals who are wrongly, inveterately, and unrepentantly divisive!

The true believers. Most of Paul's letter, however, is spent not on the false teachers but on the true believers in the church. Paul mentions four particular groups that require Titus's instruction. First, he tells Titus to teach the *older men* six things that are not unlike his instructions for the elders: "Teach the older men to be temperate, worthy of respect, self-controlled, and sound in faith, in love and in endurance" (2:2). If you are an older man, Scripture speaks clearly to you right here. Isn't that wonderful? You do not have to worry about whether this part of the Bible really applies to you. Pray that these six attributes will characterize you. Your physical body may be slowly deteriorating, but this is the time of life for your spiritual health to shine as an example. Let your life expose the world's lie that all of our eggs must be placed in the basket of physical health. When you go to the hospital for your third surgery this year, show the love of Christ. Your self-control and moderation, even amid incredible difficulties, are to command respect. At this point in your life, your faith and love and endurance are to be evidently robust, regardless of your faltering physical stamina. Your spirit is to be exemplary. You have had decades to work on this.

Next, Paul turns to *older women*. He instructs Titus to teach them five things:

> Likewise, teach the older women to be reverent in the way they live, not to be slanderers or addicted to much wine, but to teach what is good. Then they can train the younger women to love their husbands and children, to be self-controlled and pure, to be busy at home, to be kind, and to be subject to their husbands, so that no one will malign the word of God (2:3-5).

If you are an older women, hopefully you do not flinch at the word "older." Our secular culture encourages you to flinch because it idolizes youth and laments age, when the Bible does the opposite. The Bible associates youth with folly and age with wisdom. Don't buy into Satan's lie, that you should be ashamed of your age. Be proud and thankful for every year that God has given you life and allowed you to persevere. Every year is an honor. By all means, let people know how old you are. If you are going to lie about your age, then inflate it a little! And note these five things as prayer requests for yourself. First, be reverent in the way you live. Second, do not be a slanderer. Third, do not be addicted to much wine. Fourth, teach what is good (notice again the centrality of the good). Find what is good, and teach it to others. Fifth—and Paul spends the most time on this—train the younger women.

Interestingly, Paul does not have any instructions for Titus specific to younger women, even though he does for younger men, as we will see in a moment. Older men and women as well as younger men are specifically addressed. Why not younger women? Don't they matter? Of course they matter, but Paul tells Titus he must teach the older women well, and that they in turn should teach the younger women. Again, if you are an older women, have you stopped to consider that it is your responsibility to teach the younger women in your church? You are charged with teaching them to love their husbands, to love their children, to be self-controlled, to be pure, to be busy at home, to be kind (or good), and to be subject to their husbands. Or did you think that the manner in which the younger ladies in the church live is none of your business? According to Scripture, their lives *are* your business.

If you are a younger woman, have you been learning, from the older women around you, how to do these things? Why is it important for you to learn from them? As Paul says in 2:5, "so that no one will malign the word of God." Younger woman, learn from an older woman so that the loveliness of the fruit of the gospel will be manifest for all to see. If the older women will not take the initiative with you, then risk embarrassing them, go up to them, and ask them to teach you. If they will not initiate fulfilling their biblical responsibilities to you, then, like a child who asks the delinquent parent for some food, risk their love for you, take the initiative, and ask them to fulfill their responsibility. It will be interesting to observe what happens when the young women in the church do this.

Next, Paul turns to the *younger men*. Are you a younger man? Listen to what Paul tells Titus to teach you: "Similarly, encourage the young men to be self-controlled. In everything set them an example by doing what is good" (2:6-7a). Paul basically tells Titus to teach them one thing, and that is not a surprising thing for young men: be self-controlled. And then he tells him to set an example for them in doing good.

The only other group Paul specifically mentions is *slaves:*

> Teach slaves to be subject to their masters in everything, to try to please them, not to talk back to them, and not to steal from them, but to show that they can be fully trusted, so that in every way they will make the teaching about God our Savior attractive (2:9-10).

In one sense, it is ironic I would teach this passage on a New Year's weekend. The most significant January 1 in our nation's history occurred not when a century rolled over but when, on January 1, 1863, Abraham Lincoln issued the Emancipation Proclamation. His proclamation began the process of reversing one of our nation's most egregious practices—slavery. So what am I doing on a January 2, almost a century and a half later, telling slaves to obey their masters? Well, it is helpful to realize that when the New Testament talks about slaves, it is not talking about the racially discriminating slavery America practiced for nearly three centuries. It is talking about a kind of slavery that is surely worse than what we think of as "employment" but which is probably closer to our idea of employment than to our idea of slavery. If we are going to apply this passage to us, we need to think of it applying to us as employees. So what do Paul's five points of instruction say for how you should relate to your boss?

Paul offers two negatives and three positives. Negatively, do not to talk back to your employers, and do not steal from them. Positively, be subject to your bosses in everything (except for sinful things), try to please them, and show them you can be fully trusted. So, imagine such an employee, who does not talk back or steal, who obeys appropriately, who wants to please, and who is trustworthy. That is a good employee to have, and to be! And just why should Christians behave this way on the job? Again, as Paul says in 2:10, we should behave in this way so that we "will make the teaching about God our Savior attractive." Most first-century slaves would have had non-Christian masters, just as most of us today have non-Christian employers. Have you ever thought about God caring for your employers? Have you ever considered God's desire for his gospel to be attractive to them? And have you ever thought about God wanting to use you to reach them? The way you work may be one of the most powerful witnesses God uses to reach them.

So, whom is Titus to teach? He is to teach both the false teachers and the true believers at church, particularly the older men, the older women, the younger men, and any Christian who works for a living.

Teach How?

But how is Titus to teach? "In your teaching show integrity, seriousness and soundness of speech that cannot be condemned, so that those who oppose you may be ashamed because they have nothing bad to say about us" (2:7b-8). The Greek word for "soundness" used in Titus (1:9, 13; 2:1, 2) is the word from which we get "hygiene." Doctrine and teaching should be sound. It should not be maimed, deformed, distorted with errors, or lacking anything. Instead it should be whole, pure, mature, and accurate.

Teachers and pastors should have sound motives, sound manners, and sound matter. Our *motives* should be pure. A preacher of the gospel should never take a pastoral position simply for the financial support it brings. We must be able to stand before you with integrity.

The *manner* of our teaching must be serious. I would not want to ban all humor from the pulpit; humor can occasionally be an appropriate way to communicate something. But preachers must be very careful. It is easy to look for and want an immediate response from listeners. And laughter is culturally acceptable. Laughter lets a preacher know the congregation is engaged and that they are enjoying themselves. Yet using a lot of humor in a sermon does not necessarily help people hear the gospel. Yes, they might enjoy a sermon more, but it can lighten the whole message in such a way that the importance and urgency of the gospel is called into question. If you have opportunity to handle the Word of God in public, do not joke around. You may use a little subtle humor, but be very careful about being lighthearted amid ultimate matters. Richard Baxter, a great Puritan preacher, said of preaching, "Whatever you do, let the people see that you are in good earnest. . . . You cannot break men's hearts by jesting with them."[6]

And the *matter* of the teaching must be healthy, bearing a soundness that cannot be condemned.

So elders are to teach right and to live right. Why? As Paul says in 2:8, "so that those who oppose you may be ashamed." We are to teach and live in such a way that those who oppose the gospel and us have no room for credible attack. We are to shame them by our honest, open trust of the Lord and his teaching in the Word. As Paul says, "These, then, are the things you should teach. Encourage and rebuke with all authority. Do not let anyone despise you" (2:15).

Teach What?

Finally, what was Titus to teach? We have already seen much of what Titus should teach: The false teachers should be rebuked, silenced, and corrected. The older men and women, younger men and slaves are told to do various things. More ethical teaching is presented in chapter 3. For example, Paul writes, "Remind the people to be subject to rulers and authorities, to be obedient, to be ready to do whatever is good, to slander no one, to be peaceable and considerate, and to show true humility toward all men" (3:1-2).

But we have not yet touched on the core of what Titus is called to teach. It is not a command. It does not concern something we have done or can do. And it does not differentiate between friend and foe, young and old, male and female, employers and employees. Rather, at the very heart of what Titus and we are called to teach is what God has done in Christ. Paul writes,

> For the grace of God that brings salvation has appeared to all men. It teaches us to say 'No' to ungodliness and worldly passions, and to live self-controlled, upright and godly lives in this present age, while we wait for the blessed hope—the glorious appearing of our great God and Savior, Jesus Christ, who gave himself for us to redeem us from all wickedness and to purify for himself a people that are his very own, eager to do what is good (2:11-14).

The message we have to preach—whether from Paul to Titus, from Titus to his churches, from me to you, or from you to your friends and family—is about nothing we have done. It is about what God has done.

---

[6] Richard Baxter, *The Reformed Pastor* (Carlisle, Pa.: Banner of Truth, 1981; orig. 1656), chapter 3, section 1, part 2.

You see that beginning in 2:11: "the grace of God that brings salvation has appeared." That is the great message! The grace of God has appeared. This message itself teaches us, negatively, to say no. To what? "To ungodliness and worldly passions." It is not mere moralism that calls us to live, positively, "self-controlled, upright and godly lives in this present age." No, it has to do with our understanding of reality itself, of what is in our best interests, and of what is in the interests of those we love. Finally, it has to do with our delight in God himself. All these things are behind Christian morality. When Christians act for the good and refrain from the bad, it is because of what we understand about reality. So if these ancient Christians on Crete or modern Christians today in America do not have a grasp of that great reality, how can we expect them to live self-controlled, godly, and upright lives? Christian morality does not make sense otherwise. If you want to live a self-controlled and godly life, you must grasp this great hope and reality.

We live as we do "while we wait" (2:13). What a great phrase. What a phrase to stick over your mirror this year. Just write these three words: "While we wait." Waiting is not just what you do in the supermarket checkout line; this state of waiting should characterize your life generally—the way you treat your neighbor, your friends at work, your spouse. You treat them the way you do because you are waiting. Never forget how crucial waiting is for the Christian. And what are we waiting for? "The blessed hope," Paul says. Not the promotion. Not retirement. Not the new medical plan or benefits. Not the new car. We wait for the blessed hope. What hope is that? "The glorious appearing of our great God and Savior Jesus Christ" (2:13).

You see, at the center of our message is Jesus Christ, "who," Paul says, "gave himself for us." Jesus Christ came as the incarnate Son of God, lived a perfect life, and died on the cross, as Paul says, "to redeem us from all wickedness." Christ came to purchase a people, and "to purify for himself a people that are his very own, eager to do what is good" (2:14).

Does this last phrase describe you? If somebody who does not know you watched your life this coming week, would they get to the end of the week and say, "Wow, there is a person who is eager to do what is good"? According to Paul, God bought us so that those who observe us might say just that.

Paul expands on some of these ideas again in chapter 3:

> At one time we too were foolish, disobedient, deceived and enslaved by all kinds of passions and pleasures. We lived in malice and envy, being hated and hating one another. But when the kindness and love of God our Savior appeared, he saved us, not because of righteous things we had done, but because of his mercy. He saved us through the washing of rebirth and renewal by the Holy Spirit,

> whom he poured out on us generously through Jesus Christ our Savior, so that, having been justified by his grace, we might become heirs having the hope of eternal life. This is a trustworthy saying. And I want you to stress these things, so that those who have trusted in God may be careful to devote themselves to doing what is good. These things are excellent and profitable for everyone (3:3-8).

Friend, you are going to devote yourself to something. You are going to have some kind of consuming hope or ambition. I don't care if you think you are too old and near death to be ambitious, or too young to have yet developed ambitions; you will devote yourself to something. Paul says we should be devoted to doing what is good.

After all, that is what the gospel had meant in Paul's own life. He too was once like the false teachers of this letter. "We too were foolish, disobedient, deceived and enslaved by all kinds of passions and pleasures." Not only that, his false doctrines led to divisiveness and hatred—again like the false teachers: "we lived in malice, envy, being hated and hating one another" (3:3). Now maybe you are thinking, "I don't recall ever reading about Paul living a terribly profligate life before his conversion on the Damascus Road. Why is he talking about disobedience and being enslaved to passions and pleasures?" Notice that none of the characteristics listed here demand that sin break out into the open for everyone to see. So much of sin can seethe just below the surface, submarine-like, not surfacing except when it wants to. Paul can refer to disobedience and passion because he knows his own heart.

When Paul was lost in this seething sea of quiet sensuality, deception, and vanity, true hope appeared! True hope appeared not because of anything he had done. Rather, "when the kindness and love of God our Savior appeared, he saved us." This, Paul says, is our real hope. This is our salvation! This is no false hope of circumcision, or obeying the law, or some New Year's resolution, all of which lead us on and then disappoint us. We have actually been rescued from drowning in the consequences of our own stupid and foolish rebellion. Why did God rescue us? "Not because of righteous things we had done." This rescue, this gospel, is not for you if you have already fixed yourself up and you feel that you are righteous. No, remember, it is not about us. It is "because of his mercy."

You must understand this message. It is the very heart of the Christian gospel. Paul writes, "He saved us." God in Christ has done it! We have not done it, whether through circumcision or through obedience to some other set of religious rules. No! Paul says in 3:5, "He saved us through the washing of rebirth and renewal." If you are a true Christian, God has cleansed you from your sin and filth. He has given you new life. It has not happened by some outward rite like circumcision, baptism, or the Lord's Supper. It has happened "by the Holy Spirit, whom he poured out on us generously through Jesus Christ our Savior" (3:6).

Why did God do this? Because he wanted us to have genuine hope! Look again at 3:7: "so that, having been justified by his grace, we might become heirs having the hope of eternal life." What are we to then do? Look at 3:8: We, particularly the pastors and teachers, are to "stress these things." Why? "So that those who have trusted in God may be careful to devote themselves to doing what is good. These things are excellent and profitable for everyone."

If you are truly his, you *are* devoting yourself to doing what is good.

CONCLUSION

That is Titus's—and God's—great gospel of grace in Christ. Perhaps you are still thinking, "But this is a new millennium. Surely everything will change now, right? Look at all the change that has occurred in the last few years." Really? Everything is going to change? Did something change today? Okay, maybe not that quickly, but is everything going to change in the next few years?

Imagine a scene of men and women, children and older people, gathering together in a building specially set aside on a Sunday morning to sing, hear a sermon, and take the Lord's Supper together. I could be describing a scene that occurs in the year 2000. Or, I could also be describing a scene that occurred in the year 1000. Or, should the Lord tarry, it could occur in the year 3000. Contrary to what you read in the press, not everything changes. Some things are pretty unchanging.

Human nature, for instance, does not change. Dr. Edward O. Wilson, professor of zoology at Harvard and winner of two Pulitzer prizes, recently said in an interview, "I think it is safe to say that human nature has not changed in the last 100,000 years, and maybe farther back than that." The interviewer asked, "So there's no reason to think it will change a great deal in the next 1,000 years?" Wilson replied, "No reason to believe it whatsoever."[7]

We Christians have to balance a funny mix of optimism and pessimism. The kind of optimism some people have about the new millennium we call naïve. On the other hand, we are not pessimists. Complete pessimism is atheistic. We understand that God is sovereign, that he acts for his own good purposes, and that he has real hope for us. For everyone. We are never beyond hope. To rule out any real hope is to rule out God himself. Right now what we need is the real stuff. And the most real stuff of all is this message: Christ died on the cross for sinners. And he will come again to rescue all those who repent of their sins and look to him as Savior and Lord. That is the gospel message.

---

[7] Edward O. Wilson, in an interview, *The Wall Street Journal* (special edition), January 1, 2000.

Think of a situation you are facing right now in your own life, one that the millennium has not changed, one that you are going to face on Monday and Tuesday; how will you live in that situation as a Christian? You will do it by knowing this message and having this hope. If you know this message, and if you really have this hope, you will live differently through this day, this week, and this year as a Christian. Only with these certainties can we, by God's grace, stand and live upright.

Martin Luther said, "I live as though Christ died yesterday, rose again today, and is coming again tomorrow."[8] Luther had a good sense of time. We, too, should be people who have faith in the past work of Christ and hope in our coming rescue by Christ. That way, we will live here and now reflecting the character of Christ.

Let us pray:

Lord God, we pray that you would impress these things on our minds and hearts. We pray that you would cause us to know your great gospel and that you would root in our hearts a wonderful hope in Christ that pulls us on to the future—not fearfully, not boastfully, but resting certainly in you and in your goodness. Lord, we pray that you would strengthen our faith as we feed on this hope through our Lord Jesus Christ. Amen.

Questions for Reflection

1. Neither new circumstances nor new years make us better. Why do you suppose so many persist in assuming they will?

2. Why would a man's leadership within his family be indicative of his capacity for spiritual leadership in the church?

3. Why does a quick temper potentially disqualify a man from being an elder?

4. Why do you think "hospitality" is listed among the requisite virtues of an elder? Don't they have more important things to do, like pray and preach?

5. In your own words, what does Paul mean when he says, "an elder must be blameless"? Do you aspire to blameless living? What should be done with an elder who is not blameless?

---

[8] Source unknown.

6. What are some of the benefits of having a plurality of elders?

7. As we have seen, false teachers threaten the clarity of the gospel and cause divisions in the church. So Paul charges Titus with avoiding them and putting them out of the church. Do such false teachers threaten the church today? What do they look like? What do they teach? What is your responsibility with regard to false teachers?

8. One of the most important things any pastor or elder will do for you is work hard to know Scripture in order to protect you from false teachings. Do you and your congregation grant your pastor the ability to fulfill this duty? Do you ensure that he has ample time for study? Would you trust his judgment if he declared a particular teaching to be false?

9. Paul tells older men that their faith, love, and endurance should be plainly robust, regardless of their faltering physical stamina. Their spirits are to be exemplary since they have had decades to work on this. Doesn't this make Paul sound unsympathetic with the difficulties of old age? Couldn't Paul be asking for a bit much? Isn't there some other way for older Christian men (and women) to show they are distinct from non-Christian older men (and women)?

10. Older women, have you considered that it is your responsibility to teach the younger women in your church? Do you?

11. What sort of ministry do you have in the life of your employer? Do you pray for him or her? Does he or she know you are a Christian? Does your work reflect your Christian faith?

12. Why would a lot of humor in a sermon call into question the seriousness and urgency of the gospel?

13. If we Christians are justified by faith alone and not by works, why do we need to be "devoted to doing good"?

14. What is the heart of a Christian's hope for true change?

THE MESSAGE OF PHILEMON: FORGIVENESS

CHRISTIANITY IS ALL ABOUT MY RIGHTEOUSNESS, RIGHT?

INTRODUCING PHILEMON

A PICTURE OF SOMEONE NEEDING FORGIVENESS: ONESIMUS

Onesimus's Escape

Onesimus's Conversion

Onesimus's Return and Need

Of being forgiven

Of making restitution

Of being valued

Of being protected

A PICTURE OF SOMEONE WITH AN OPPORTUNITY
TO FORGIVE: PHILEMON

Philemon's Task: To Forgive

Welcome Onesimus

Transfer his debt

Care for Onesimus

Receive Paul

Philemon's Situation

His role in the church

The difficulty of forgiving

The obligation to forgive

A PICTURE OF SOMEONE WHO ENCOURAGES FORGIVENESS: PAUL

Paul's Appeal

Paul's Method

CONCLUSION: WHAT TRUE CHRISTIAN FAITH WILL LOOK LIKE IN US

We Will Be Peacemakers, Like Paul

We Will Forgive Others, as Philemon Should

We Will Know Our Need for Forgiveness, as Onesimus Did

From others

From God

18

THE MESSAGE OF PHILEMON: FORGIVENESS

CHRISTIANITY IS ALL ABOUT MY RIGHTEOUSNESS, RIGHT?[1]

I heard a fascinating feature on National Public Radio yesterday morning. Somebody recently ferreted out recordings of twelve early sermons by Martin Luther King, Jr. While I was in the car, NPR played about fifteen minutes of the earliest sermon they have of King, from February 28, 1954, at the Second Baptist Church in Detroit, Michigan. In the sermon, King, then a seminary student, preached about absolute values. He suggested that in the increasingly relativistic age of the 1950s, lying is wrong, even if everybody is doing it. And adultery is wrong, even if everybody is doing it. And stealing is wrong, even if everybody is doing it. The real issue that confronts our nation, he said, is the issue of character. We must realize that right and wrong are not relative. It is wrong to hate in Germany. It is wrong to hate in Russia. It is wrong to hate in Canada. And it is wrong to hate in America. Wrong is wrong, wherever it is and whenever it is.

In that sense, everyone from Martin Luther King, Jr., to William Bennett, from James Dobson to Jerry Falwell, can begin to sound alike. They say we need to realize that right is right and wrong is wrong. All of them have told us that the Bible teaches that morality is not negotiable, and that true Christian faith is about absolutes.

In this world where moral boundaries seem to be dissolving, maybe we Christians need to work harder at slowing things down. Perhaps we need to highlight the importance of moral reasoning and to fortify the long-respected behavioral boundaries of our culture—that this is right and that is wrong. Maybe this is what we Christians must make our agendas today.

If we do, that would send the message to the world that true Christian faith

[1] This sermon was originally preached on August 30, 1999, at Capitol Hill Baptist Church in Washington, D.C.

is all about uprightness and propriety; about living the best we can; about being the pillars of our society; and about quietly minding our own business, leaving others to theirs. After all, aren't Christians basically just nice, decent people? Isn't that the sum and substance of Christianity? Isn't propriety the same thing as piety? And isn't being respected the same as being right?

True Christian faith is about righteousness, right? About *my* righteousness? As in going to church and giving to charity?

INTRODUCING PHILEMON

Well, before we go any further with this idea of placing such steely, unwavering virtue at the core of Christianity, I think we should just read the little letter of Paul to Philemon:

> Paul, a prisoner of Christ Jesus, and Timothy our brother,
>
> To Philemon our dear friend and fellow worker, to Apphia our sister, to Archippus our fellow soldier and to the church that meets in your home:
>
> Grace to you and peace from God our Father and the Lord Jesus Christ.
>
> I always thank my God as I remember you in my prayers, because I hear about your faith in the Lord Jesus and your love for all the saints. I pray that you may be active in sharing your faith, so that you will have a full understanding of every good thing we have in Christ. Your love has given me great joy and encouragement, because you, brother, have refreshed the hearts of the saints.
>
> Therefore, although in Christ I could be bold and order you to do what you ought to do, yet I appeal to you on the basis of love. I then, as Paul—an old man and now also a prisoner of Christ Jesus—I appeal to you for my son Onesimus, who became my son while I was in chains. Formerly he was useless to you, but now he has become useful both to you and to me.
>
> I am sending him—who is my very heart—back to you. I would have liked to keep him with me so that he could take your place in helping me while I am in chains for the gospel. But I did not want to do anything without your consent, so that any favor you do will be spontaneous and not forced. Perhaps the reason he was separated from you for a little while was that you might have him back for good—no longer as a slave, but better than a slave, as a dear brother. He is very dear to me but even dearer to you, both as a man and as a brother in the Lord.
>
> So if you consider me a partner, welcome him as you would welcome me. If he has done you any wrong or owes you anything, charge it to me. I, Paul, am writing this with my own hand. I will pay it back—not to mention that you owe me your very self. I do wish, brother, that I may have some benefit from you in the Lord; refresh my heart in Christ. Confident of your obedience, I write to you, knowing that you will do even more than I ask.
>
> And one thing more: Prepare a guest room for me, because I hope to be restored to you in answer to your prayers.

Epaphras, my fellow prisoner in Christ Jesus, sends you greetings. And so
do Mark, Aristarchus, Demas and Luke, my fellow workers.

The grace of the Lord Jesus Christ be with your spirit.

Did you notice that this letter, like the letter to the Colossians, is full of people? You can count twelve different people in the twenty-five verses of this brief
letter. In addition to Paul, Philemon, and Jesus, you have Timothy, Apphia,
Archippus, Onesimus, Epaphras, Mark, Aristarchus, Demas, and Luke. But I
want to focus on the three fullest portraits presented by this New Testament
miniature, this moment of real life, captured in a verbal frozen frame on the
pages of our Bibles between Titus and Hebrews. Here we find the picture of
someone needing forgiveness, the picture of someone with the opportunity to
forgive, and the picture of someone who is encouraging forgiveness. As we consider these pictures, I pray that you might see a living Christian faith both in
the pictures and in yourself.

A PICTURE OF SOMEONE NEEDING FORGIVENESS: ONESIMUS

Onesimus's Escape

The story of Onesimus is something we can reconstruct from the basic parts
of this letter. Paul refers to him as "no longer . . . a slave," suggesting that slavery was his former station (v. 16). In the world of the New Testament, slavery
was not race-specific, as we think of slavery in our own American experience.
Nor were slaves limited to certain types of jobs. In most Hellenic cities of Paul's
day, the majority of the working population were probably considered slaves,
or what might be called indentured servants. So the fact that Onesimus was a
slave actually does not tell us that much. He could have been what we call a
"professional," since many doctors and teachers were indentured servants in
the ancient world. Or he could have been something more indicative of servi-
tude. Either way, Onesimus was clearly a slave. And the whole tone of the letter, especially from verse 14 on, suggests he had been a slave who belonged to
Philemon.

Yet something had gone wrong. In verse 11, Paul refers to the fact that
Onesimus had been "useless" to Philemon. And in verse 14, Paul acknowledges
that Onesimus should not remain with him without Philemon's consent. For
some reason, Paul feels that Philemon needs to agree to Paul's request regarding
Onesimus. He refers to a separation of Onesimus from Philemon in verse 15, as
if it needs explaining. Then in verse 18, Paul is more clear—Onesimus may have
wronged Philemon, or he may be in debt to him. Paul does not get more specific
than that. It seems likely that Onesimus had wronged Philemon by fleeing, since

Paul knows he cannot justify Onesimus's continued absence from Philemon without his consent. Onesimus is AWOL—absent without leave.

Based on the words "if he . . . owes you anything" in verse 18, many have speculated that Onesimus must have stolen something from Philemon and then, in fear of retribution and justice, fled. Whatever the reason, Onesimus left Philemon on bad and unresolved terms.

Onesimus's Conversion

After his escape, Onesimus somehow ended up with Paul. Once in Paul's company, it seems, Onesimus became "useful." More than that, he became a Christian. In verse 10, Paul says that Onesimus "became my son while I was in chains." Paul, ever active in the work of ministry, appears to have helped lead Onesimus to the Lord while in prison. And Onesimus, finding true Christian faith, became "useful" and "very dear" to Paul (vv. 11, 16). Paul's heart had become attached to Onesimus, so much so that Paul refers tenderly to him as "my very heart" (v. 12).

Now, following his conversion, Onesimus needs to redress the wrongs he has committed. Philemon may offer to free him from his obligations, but Onesimus must begin the process of restoration by offering to make restitution for whatever wrongs caused him to flee from Philemon in the first place.

Onesimus's Return and Need

Of being forgiven. Onesimus needs Philemon to welcome him back into his household, his service, and his good graces. The relationship needs restoring. Onesimus needs Philemon to forgive him, so Paul is sending Onesimus back to Philemon.

Of making restitution. There is also the matter of restitution. What can Onesimus do? Apparently, he has stolen property from Philemon. Certainly, he has stolen labor. He needs to pay Philemon back, but how can he? He probably does not have the wherewithal to repay Philemon. I have had more than one friend who became a Christian and decided they needed to right a number of the wrongs previously committed. In the process of their conversion, under the Holy Spirit's conviction of their sins, they have attempted to return to those against whom they had sinned, to confess those sins, and to ask for forgiveness. Sometimes they have written letters or visited in person. Sometimes they have returned money or goods they had stolen. I have seen people make restitution similar to what Paul discusses in the case of Onesimus.

Of being valued. Clearly Paul values Onesimus. He asks Philemon to "refresh my heart in Christ" (v. 20), probably meaning he wants Philemon to welcome Onesimus. If Onesimus is Paul's "very heart," refreshing Onesimus's heart is the same as refreshing Paul's heart. Onesimus needs someone to value him in this way, because he has done things that have caused him to be viewed as less than valued.

Of being protected. I wonder, too, if Paul thinks Onesimus needs a little extra looking after. You see that postscript in verse 22: "And one thing more: Prepare a guest room for me." Paul probably desires to follow up on the situation, and Philemon will recognize this.

So that is Onesimus—the slave who stole, fled, and found Paul; and in finding Paul, he found Christ and found his way back home. Now, Onesimus would turn up at Philemon's house with nothing but a letter from Paul in his hand. Can you imagine the former slave standing in the doorway as his former employer opens the door—needing forgiveness, helpless to repay, cared for only by someone far away in prison. In one sense, the destitution of this former slave is incomparable. He can offer nothing, and he deserves punishment. Yet there he stands, with no excuses to make.

Onesimus is a picture of someone who needs forgiveness.

A PICTURE OF SOMEONE WITH AN OPPORTUNITY TO FORGIVE: PHILEMON

Now, let's look at the picture of someone who has the opportunity to give forgiveness: Philemon. Everything we just said that Onesimus needs, Philemon is called upon to supply.

Philemon's Task: To Forgive

Consider the scope of the forgiveness that Paul asks of Philemon.

Welcome Onesimus. Philemon is being asked to "welcome" Onesimus (v. 17). He is being asked to open his arms to the very one who (possibly) stole from him and then abandoned him. He is being asked to invite this man back into his home. But can this man be trusted? Will Philemon have to count the silverware every day? Will he have to count his change whenever Onesimus returns from the market? Will he have to keep an eye on the chickens?

Transfer his debt. Of course, welcoming Onesimus could also mean Philemon will have to ask Paul to pay off any outstanding debts. Interestingly, Paul does not just say, "forgive and forget, Philemon. It's all in the past. Let go of it." No, he acknowledges a genuine indebtedness that must be reconciled. He says to Philemon, if Onesimus "owes you anything, charge it to me" (v. 18). I wonder if Philemon will take this to mean, "Eat the loss, Philemon." After all, is Philemon actually supposed to send Onesimus's bill to the great apostle who sits languishing in a Roman prison? That sounds like spending your grandmother's social security check on ice cream for all your friends. It is not the kind of thing you want to do! Still, part of forgiving Onesimus, it seems, involves resolving the indebtedness Onesimus has incurred. Whether that means eating the loss or asking an aging apostle to foot the bill, it has to be dealt with; it is part of the problem. Forgiving Onesimus means Philemon will have to take such real issues into account. They cannot simply be swept under the carpet.

Care for Onesimus. Forgiving Onesimus also entails caring for Onesimus. Paul clearly states that he would consider Philemon's kindness to Onesimus as kindness to himself. That means Philemon cannot just begrudgingly let Onesimus back into the house. Paul is asking for more. Philemon will have to let him back into his home and into his heart. He will have to genuinely forgive, from his heart, the multiple wrongs done to him. He will even have to restore affectionate care to the relationship.

Receive Paul. And to top it all off, Philemon can anticipate having Paul check in on him. Not only does he have to forgive, he will have to demonstrate that he has forgiven Onesimus. A certain measure of accountability is going to be implemented. He will have to prepare explanations for his actions or lack of them.

Philemon's Situation

Consider whom Paul is asking to give forgiveness. Philemon's situation is not easy.

His role in the church. Evidently, Philemon has a prominent role in the church. He is probably one of a few who has a personal relationship with Paul. Philemon lives in Colosse, and Paul has never been to Colosse, yet Paul appears to have been instrumental in leading Philemon to the Lord (v. 19), probably when Paul was in nearby Ephesus a number of years earlier. So Philemon is one of the few in the congregation who can brag that he actually knows the great apostle. Paul did not write this letter merely "to the church"; he wrote it particularly to Philemon (v. 1)! Furthermore, we note that Philemon has sufficient economic standing to employ slaves, and he is generous enough to provide his home as the meeting place for the Colossian church (v. 2). Philemon is clearly a leader in the church. And his prominence demands that his actions be exemplary. Philemon *needs* to forgive Onesimus!

The difficulty of forgiving. How difficult can granting forgiveness be? In the ancient world, forgiveness was not something considered honorable. You or I may think, "Come on, Philemon, get on with forgiving him. It's the right thing to do. Stop being recalcitrant." But neither he nor anyone in the world around him would have been raised to think this way. By forgiving Onesimus, he might be regarded as showing weakness. He might bring shame upon himself among his neighbors for treating a runaway employee, or indentured servant, this way. Perhaps he worries that such leniency would encourage Onesimus to view his crime lightly. Perhaps it would also encourage others to follow Onesimus's example and let them think they too would get off lightly.

Furthermore, we cannot guess what will go on inside Philemon's own head. Is Philemon one of those souls who feel every wrong keenly and every injustice like the stroke of the lash? You know how some of us, even if we are not heavily invested in a situation, cry out for justice with every fiber of our being when we perceive someone has wronged us? Maybe the car rental agency overcharges us, or a restaurant server mishandles our order, or we are given short shrift at work. We want everything to be fair and we become indignant when it is not. How much more will Philemon feel that way about someone who has been a part of his own household? Still, he is being asked to forgive.

The obligation to forgive. But after everything is considered, is not Philemon *obliged* to forgive Onesimus? When you consider Paul's pleas, Philemon's public role in the church, and the fact that he has known God's forgiveness in his own life, can Philemon do anything else, as painful as forgiving Onesimus might be? In verse 6, Paul says, "I pray that you may be active in sharing your faith, so that you will have a full understanding of every good thing we have in Christ." This verse is often singled out and used as a reason to evangelize: when you share your faith, you will grow as a Christian. Let me quickly say as an incontrovertible fact, when you do share the good news of the gospel with others, you do grow as a Christian. That is a wonderful blessing of God. Having said that, I do not think this verse is talking about that. In the context, Paul is not talking about proclaiming the gospel to an unbeliever; he is talking about expressing Christian forgiveness to a brother. When Philemon brings Onesimus back and restores him, he will have a fuller understanding of what God has done for him in Christ. He will have a fuller knowledge of the riches of his own Christian faith.

Clearly, Philemon is the picture of someone with an opportunity to forgive.

A PICTURE OF SOMEONE WHO ENCOURAGES FORGIVENESS: PAUL

Finally, we cannot overlook one more picture in this story, the picture of the person encouraging forgiveness—Paul. *Paul* is the one who somehow intercepted Onesimus. *Paul* is the one who shared the gospel with him. And *Paul* is the one who has now sent him back and has written this letter to accompany him. Orchestrating all of this is Paul.

Paul's Appeal

Paul appeals to Philemon in no uncertain terms. He says, "welcome him" (v. 17). Then he adds an important phrase: "as you would welcome me."

That is the only thing Paul directly asks on Onesimus's behalf. In the rest of the letter, he couches all of his requests in the language of asking for himself. He does this in at least three ways. First, he asks Philemon to charge him with any debts that needs to be repaid (v. 18). Paul is willing to foot the bill in order to see forgiveness occur and a relationship restored! Too often today it seems that those who work for healing relationships bill us for the help they give. But Paul says, "Bill me! I am willing to take the time, the trouble, the effort, and the financial investment to see this relationship restored."

Second, as we have already seen, Paul makes himself the object of that appeal by asking Philemon to "refresh my heart" (v. 20). Paul so sincerely identifies with Onesimus that he says to Philemon, "If you do this for the one I love, it will be like you are doing it for me. I care for him that much, and that is how much I care that this relationship be restored." Paul invests himself fully.

Third, he is willing to spend even more pastoral capital to see this forgiveness and restoration occur by asking Philemon to prepare a guest room for him (v. 22). Do you think Paul would just happen to be traveling through this town he has never visited? No, Paul is willing to invest time. So he will visit and find out how the letter has been received.

Paul's Method

We should also notice Paul's method. He is pushy! He certainly pushes the boundaries of what most of us would feel comfortable doing. Paul seems to shamelessly put this church leader on the spot about what to do with an employee who has run away from him. In response, the church leader could feel indignant. He has faithfully served the church, and who is Onesimus? Onesimus is an employee, and an unfaithful one at that. Phrygian slaves, which Onesimus may have been, had a reputation for being useless. Perhaps Paul is playing on this stereotype when he mentions that Onesimus was formerly useless (v. 11). Still, Paul is willing to put Philemon's work and effort on the line for this useless Onesimus. It is not hard to imagine how Philemon might feel offended. He could feel like Paul is being disloyal to him by putting so much pressure on him to care for this wayward and worthless rogue.

Philemon will feel offended if he has understood everything about Christianity except the gospel. In other words, if he understands that right and wrong are absolute, that actions have consequences, and that Christians must live exemplary lives, then, yes, Philemon will understandably feel offended. But if God's Holy Spirit has ever convicted Philemon of his own sin, then he will not take umbrage.

So Paul pulls out all the stops, and look at how he does it. He does not quite pull rank on Philemon in verse 8, but he gets awfully close when he says, "I could be bold and order you to do what you ought to do." In verses 5 and 7, he has encouraged Philemon about the love he has shown for all the saints. So in verse 9, he appeals to Philemon "on the basis of love," as if to say, "Show him love and you will be showing me love." In verse 11, he argues that receiving Onesimus would be beneficial to Philemon. When Paul calls Onesimus his "heart" in verse 12, he leaves no doubt about how important this matter is to him. In verse 13, Paul highlights the sacrifice he once made for Philemon by letting him go, perhaps hinting that Philemon owes him a sacrifice in return. In verse 14, Paul demonstrates that he respects Philemon's rights ("I did not want to do anything without your consent"), and then he encourages him (in verse 15) to realize how the whole situation will turn out for his advantage anyway ("Perhaps the reason he was separated from you for a little while . . ."). The appeal is made in verse 16 on the basis of Christian affection (Paul is sending him back "as a dear brother") while in verse 17 it is made on the basis of a personal obligation ("welcome him as you would welcome me"). In verse 18, Paul offers to take on the debt himself. In verse 19, he even takes up the pen himself, which apparently was difficult for him to do. When Paul does write, his large letters underscore the idea, "LOOK, THIS IS REALLY IMPORTANT TO ME." He makes a direct appeal in verses 20 and 21 ("refresh my heart in Christ"), and in verse 21 he even gets near what some might consider manipulative: "Confident of your obedience, I write to you." Then to top it all off, he basically says in verse 22 that he will be checking up on Philemon! That is the length to which Paul goes to bring about forgiveness and healing in this relationship.

But I do not believe Paul is dishonorable in his methods. If only you or I would expend ourselves in such a manner for the purpose of forgiveness and reconciliation. Does the length to which Paul goes remind you of anyone in particular? Perhaps the great peacemaker himself, Jesus Christ? Paul is following the example of his master, who went to far greater lengths to make peace.

Paul is a picture of someone who encourages—even appeals for—forgiveness.

CONCLUSION: WHAT TRUE CHRISTIAN FAITH WILL LOOK LIKE IN US

Nothing is nearer the heart of Christian faith than the recognition of our own need to forgive because of our own need for forgiveness in Christ. In this little letter, we see three miniature pictures of what true Christian faith will look like in us.

We Will Be Peacemakers, Like Paul

Jesus said, "Blessed are the peacemakers, for they will be called sons of God" (Matthew 5:9). There is something particularly Christlike about peacemaking, which Paul exemplifies so well in this letter.

A couple of movies I saw this summer presented something like a Christian conversion. In *The Apostle,* Robert Duvall actually intends to portray a Christian conversion. In *As Good as It Gets,* which I saw on the airplane, a Christian conversion may have been the furthest thing from Jack Nicholson's mind as he played the lead character (I don't know). But between the two movies, I think Nicholson's character actually does a better job of portraying at least some of the changes that occur in a person's life when he or she becomes a Christian. At the beginning of the film, Nicholson's character is absolutely neurotic: he will not step on cracks in the pavement; he shrinks backward when other people come near him; he avoids physical contamination from others' germs and emotional contamination from others' lives; and so on. Over the course of the movie, however, he becomes deeply involved in the lives of people around him, amid all their problems and pain. By the end of the movie, his neuroses have slipped away. I fear that some of us may have the idea that being a Christian means shrinking back from others' problems and failures as Nicholson does at the movie's beginning. We take great care not to be contaminated by other people's problems. But if you think that is what it means to be a Christian, I fear you will go to hell. That is not what it means to be a Christian at all! Have you found your own soul so pure before God that you are happy to shrink back from others, forgetting that God could have done that with you? Do you think the followers of the One who went to the cross are called to go through life kindly and nicely, neither being bothered nor bothering themselves for anyone? Peacemaking, going out of one's way as Paul does in this letter, striving with all one's might to bring reconciliation, smells like Jesus. If we have a true Christian faith, peacemaking will mark our lives.

We Will Forgive Others, as Philemon Should

If we have true Christian faith, we will also seize opportunities, as Philemon has presented before him, to forgive others. Forgiveness will typify our responses to injustices both large and small. Sometimes, of course, it can be harder to forgive the small things. Teddy Roosevelt liked to tell the story of the Texan who remarked that he might, in the end, pardon a man who shot him on purpose. But he would surely never pardon the man who shot him accidentally. Malicious intent he could stand. But the sheer incompetence of a man who could not handle a gun he could not tolerate. We might laugh at that story, but we can be very small people. It is amazing how we can find it within ourselves to forgive people for huge sins, particularly if they do not affect us. Yet when their incompetencies act like sand in our nicely oiled schedules, well, forgiveness is out of the question. But should sin bother us less than incompetence? As Christians, we must forgive.

Perhaps you read one prominent public official's remarks during a ceremony marking the thirty-fifth anniversary of Martin Luther King, Jr.'s "I Have a Dream" speech. This public official said, "All of you know, I'm having to become quite an expert in this business of asking for forgiveness. It gets a little easier the more you do it. And if you have a family, an administration, a Congress and a whole country to ask—you're going to get a lot of practice. But I have to tell you that in these last days, it has come home to me, again, that in order to get it, you have to be willing to give it. The anger, the resentment, the bitterness, the desire for recrimination against people you believe have wronged you, they harden the heart and deaden the spirit and lead to self-inflicted wounds. And so it is important that we are able to forgive those we believe have wronged us, even as we ask for forgiveness from people we have wronged."[2]

You know that remaining bitter—whether for accidents or actions of ill intent, whether for sins against us large or small—is a contradiction to the confessed Christian faith. Remember what Jesus taught his disciples to pray: "Forgive us our debts, as we also have forgiven our debtors" (Matt. 6:12). Do you really want to pray that? Think carefully about that phrase before you pray the Lord's Prayer next time. Do you really want to be forgiven in the same way you have forgiven others?

We Will Know Our Need for Forgiveness, as Onesimus Did

Finally, if we have true Christian faith, we will know our need for forgiveness.

From others. Like Onesimus, we will know our need to be forgiven by

---

[2] President Bill Clinton, August 28, 1998.

other people. Have you ever heard this saying: "A non-Christian is someone who is wrong. A Christian is someone who is wrong but will not admit it"? The exact opposite should be the case! We do not become Christians simply to wrap a veil of virtue around our evil hearts and lives and to pretend before the world that we are righteous. On the contrary, we pray that God will strip away the veneer—the pretense of our own righteousness—and leave us to rely on Christ's righteousness alone.

So we cannot be offended by the idea that we will sin against others. If we are Christians, like Onesimus, we will necessarily acknowledge that we have not been paragons of virtue, and we will seek the forgiveness of those around us. That is an inevitable part of being a Christian.

From God. How can we seek the forgiveness of others? Fundamentally, by recognizing our need for forgiveness from God. One modern author has written,

> When you get what you want in your struggle for wealth
>   and the world makes you king for a day,
> Then go to the mirror and look at yourself
>   and see what that guy [or gal] has to say.
> For it isn't your father or mother or wife
>   who judgment upon you must pass,
> The fellow whose verdict counts most in your life
>   is the guy staring back from the glass.[3]

Do you believe that? I don't. Not for a moment. At the end of the day, the verdict of the person staring back at you in the mirror doesn't matter at all. Our sins—against others and ourselves—bear a gravity that cannot be explained entirely according to human realities. A few years back, a friend told me of a young woman who came to him in great distress. She was a college student who had had an abortion. In the days after her abortion, she experienced growing feelings of guilt. Her friends said to her, "Don't be silly. This is just some kind of postnatal depression. Snap out of it. You have done nothing to be ashamed of." Her psychologist friends analyzed her guilt feelings. Her social scientist friends assured her that her feelings of guilt were rooted in socially constructed values. But she still felt guilty. Eventually she attempted suicide.

No amount of rationalization could take her guilt away. She had discovered that guilt was not a neurosis to be erased, or to be deprogrammed, or to be eased through reassurance. She wanted to be treated like a responsible human being. She wanted an answer to the guilt that she had incurred, to what she

---

[3] Quoted by Marsha Witten in *All Is Forgiven* (Princeton, N.J.: Princeton University Press, 1993), 111.

knew was an objective stain on her life for which she was personally account-able. Ironically, her conscience cried out for justice to be done against her sin *and* she wanted true forgiveness. Yet she found these two things were irreconcilable, especially from the resources within herself. For we cannot finally forgive ourselves, because all our sin is ultimately against our divine Creator and Judge. He must forgive. Nor can we finally provide a just satisfaction for our own sins. Their offense is too great. Only the sacrifice of Christ can provide such satisfaction and meet the just requirements of God's holy nature.

So what about moral character and absolutes and right and wrong? Christianity is not primarily about any of these things. Primarily, true Christian faith recognizes *not* that we are right but that we are wrong.

> Though Justice be thy plea, consider this,
> That in the course of justice none of us
> Should see salvation. We do pray for mercy . . . [4]

We need God's condescending, self-lowering love in our own lives, offered to us only because Christ has met the demands of justice for all who repent and believe. We need to be forgiven, and we need to forgive, if we would have true Christian faith.

Let us pray:

Lord, we confess that our hearts are often hard, cold, and unyielding—sometimes in what we perceive to be our own righteousness, other times in our sin. But Lord, either way, we need the searchlight of your truth. We need the conviction of your Spirit to act on our hearts, to teach us the truth about ourselves and about you. Lord, do that, we pray, for Jesus' sake. Amen.

Questions for Reflection

1. Is true Christian faith all about my righteousness, as in going to church, not lying, and giving to charity?

2. How was slavery in the biblical world different from slavery in the American experience?

3. Does conversion and new birth in Christ free us of all our moral debt and guilt before God? Does it necessarily free us from all of our earthly debts and liabilities? Explain.

---

[4] Portia to Shylock in William Shakespeare, *Merchant of Venice*, IV.i.198-200.

4. If you are a Christian, you know that your sins have been forgiven through Christ's work on the cross. Still, have you ever found yourself in a situation where it felt difficult, even impossible, to forgive someone who had grieved you? What should we do when that is the case?

5. Have you ever worked hard to forgive someone, and then found that, after some time had passed, you were still bitter, resentful, or angry toward them? Did that mean your first act of forgiveness was false? What should you do in such situations?

6. Did Philemon have an obligation to forgive Onesimus?

7. When was the last time you went out of your way to see two Christians reconciled?

8. Paul tells Philemon that refreshing Onesimus's heart will be like refreshing Paul's own heart. How is Paul able to identify so closely with Onesimus? Where do you think Paul learned how to do this (look in Acts 9)? When was the last time you identified this closely with a sinner or debtor? Would those individuals in your church who are weak or young in the faith say about you, "He (or she) understands. He's been where I'm at. I can talk to him"? Or would they say, "He's not like me. I'll never attain what he has," and avoid you because they become discouraged about themselves when they are around you?

9. Do you shrink back from the failures and problems of others? Or do you press forward, anxious to identify and help? What can you do to help cultivate a culture in your church marked by the latter kind of people and not the former?

10. True or false: you really want to be forgiven in the same way you have forgiven others.

11. When was the last time you sought someone else's forgiveness?

12. Our culture places a lot of emphasis on "forgiving yourself." What role does self-forgiveness play in Philemon? In the Bible?

PART THREE

LIVING IN
THE REAL WORLD

THE MESSAGE OF HEBREWS: STICKING WITH THE BEST

19

THE MESSAGE OF HEBREWS: STICKING WITH THE BEST

I WANT TO KEEP MY OPTIONS OPEN[1]

Everywhere in our lives today is choice. Perhaps choice is even more pervasive than you realize. G. K. Chesterton in his great book *Orthodoxy* writes that "Every act is an act of self-sacrifice. When you choose anything you reject everything else—just as when you marry one woman your give up all the others."[2] Past generations would be startled by some of the choices we have today: choosing our job, choosing where we will live, even choosing our spouse. Not all past generations knew choices like these. Yet we take them for granted.

I remember traveling back from the Soviet Union into the West and being struck when I walked into an American supermarket with all the choices we have about the smallest things in life, from pizza toppings to coffee filters. Not only in supermarkets, our choices proliferate in everything, from TV channels to software programs. And in more serious matters, from schools and jobs to sexual partners. Like good consumers, we check out all our options before choosing a church. Choice is even championed in that great and final issue of this life—death. Increasingly we are told that we have the right to choose our own time and method of death through doctor-assisted suicide. And we have the option of choosing the time and method of the death of others through abortion and euthanasia.

This omnipresence of choice in our world today, of course, reflects our love of choice. As one author puts it, "Trained as consummate consumers, we learn to adopt even religious faiths tentatively, with an eye to new options that may appear around the bend. No wonder we find it less and less credible to think

[1] This sermon was originally preached on May 7, 1995, at Capitol Hill Baptist Church in Washington, D.C.
[2] G. K. Chesterton, *Orthodoxy* (New York: Doubleday Image, 1959), 39.

anything might be worth dying for. But if nothing is worth dying for, is anything worth living for? Devoid of substantive purpose, our lives too easily degenerate into bland avoidance of pain and the unending search for new amusements." So "Shopping," this author suggests, becomes "the highest or essential form of life."[3]

Simply put, too many of us worship at the altar of the god of options. How often I have heard someone utter with a smile, "I just want to keep my options open," assuming that no one would disagree with such self-evident truth. Yet we should not be surprised when the law of diminishing returns afflicts our decisions. The more we choose, the less each choice seems to mean. Buyer's remorse sets in, and we increasingly find ourselves in a state of wondering if something better is still out there. We might insist on having a glut of choices in life's trivial matters—four types of gasoline at the pump, ten kinds of dressing for my salad—but we often find ourselves feeling strangely powerless when standing before life's most important decisions.

In his movie *Annie Hall*, Woody Allen began a commencement address, "More than any other time in history, mankind faces a crossroads. One path leads to despair and utter hopelessness; the other, to total extinction. Let us pray we have the wisdom to choose correctly." Ironically, awash in a sea of choices, we sink into skepticism and cynicism, doubting that any of the choices really matter. And so we become indifferent to all of them.

Besides, in our increasingly managed and regulated lives, the act of choosing does not carry the same risks it once did, since all of our choices are laboratory tested to be safe. The FDA, EPA, OSHA, and all the other government agencies looking out for our best interests have ensured that if real danger is involved, no choice will be allowed, or at least we will find a warning label.

So as our choices proliferate in the mundane, the act of choosing itself, whether directed to the mundane or monumental, becomes an act of self-expression, of vote-casting, of what feels best for right now. We can always change our minds tomorrow.

INTRODUCING HEBREWS

If that is how you feel, the book of Hebrews may come as a shock to you. The book of Hebrews in the New Testament is, as it were, a religious *Consumer Reports* magazine. The author lays out the person of Jesus Christ and what he has done, and then sets him against the Old Testament religious system that was native to most of his audience and to which some were feeling tempted to return.

---

[3] Rodney Clapp, *Families at the Crossroads* (Downers Grove, Ill.: InterVarsity Press, 1993), 64.

Now, there are all kinds of things we do not know about this letter. We do not know who wrote it, or to whom it was written. But we can piece together some things from reading it. We know a little about the struggles the letter's first recipients were facing, as well as what they had done in the past. For example, we learn in chapter 10 that at one time, "you stood your ground in a great contest in the face of suffering. Sometimes you were publicly exposed to insult and persecution; at other times you stood side by side with those who were so treated. You sympathized with those in prison and joyfully accepted the confiscation of your property because you knew that you yourselves had better and lasting possessions" (10:32b-34). Whoever these people were, they had suffered for their faith. They had gone though some hard things to serve the Lord.

We learn in chapter 6 what they were doing at the time the letter was written. The writer says, "God . . . will not forget your work and the love you have shown him as you have helped his people and continue to help them" (6:10). So not only had these people done good things in the past, they continued to live as Christians by helping people at great cost to themselves. They had not apostatized.

And yet, difficulty was brewing. Somewhere a breakdown was beginning to occur: "You need someone to teach you the elementary truths of God's word all over again!" (5:12). They were living as Christians in some ways, but the onset of persecution was prompting them to waver and wonder if the faith was worth all the trouble after all. It appears from the warnings issued in this book that many of these Christians were sorely tempted to desert the faith.

Interestingly enough, the writer does not warn them to come back to the faith by writing a letter merely filled with imperatives and exclamation points. Rather, he gets theological and addresses the fundamental questions of who Jesus is and what he has done. He knows that if his readers are going to endure, they will endure because they believe these truths about Jesus, not because they have risen to the occasion through personal fortitude. Fundamentally, Hebrews addresses two questions, which are then interspersed with a number of warnings. First, who is Jesus? And second, what has he done? After answering these questions, we will look at seven particular dangers the author warns against. By the end I hope you will see that, as the author himself argues, Jesus is the best choice.

WHO IS JESUS?

Jesus Is the Son of God

There were other religious leaders these Christians were tempted to follow. And these other leaders were very impressive. Maybe it would be less morally demanding to follow them; or if it were more morally demanding to follow them, maybe it would be less socially awkward and make for less persecution. Either way, these leaders were hardly false teachers. No, nothing like that. The writer tells us plainly they were "servants of God": prophets of the Old Testament (1:1-3), angels that came as messengers of God (1:4-14), even Moses (chapter 3). In 1:14 the writer says, "Are not all angels ministering spirits sent to serve those who will inherit salvation?" And 3:5 refers to Moses as "a servant in all God's house." These were the people the original readers of Hebrews were tempted to turn toward and follow. Who was this Jesus, after all? Why not just serve these grand religious leaders? They were not as exclusive. Their claims were not as embarrassing.

Well, Jesus is not a servant like the angels, our writer says. He is the *Son of God*. This is made evident in the letter's very first verses:

> In the past God spoke to our forefathers through the prophets at many times and in various ways, but in these last days he has spoken to us by his Son, whom he appointed heir of all things, and through whom he made the universe. The Son is the radiance of God's glory and the exact representation of his being, sustaining all things by his powerful word. After he had provided purification for sins, he sat down at the right hand of the Majesty in heaven. So he became as much superior to the angels as the name he has inherited is superior to theirs.
>
> For to which of the angels did God ever say,
>
> "You are my Son . . ."? (1:1-5a).

Jesus Is Eternal

Okay, Jesus may be the Son, but there is a long line of these prophets and priests stretching back for ages, right?

Yes, it is a long line, the author of our letter admits. *It is long because they were passing.* Aaron, the great high priest and brother of Moses, died. And every other high priest that came after Aaron, however impressive he might have been, also died. That is why there is this long line. As he says in chapter 7, "Now there have been many of those priests, since death prevented them from continuing in office" (7:23).

However, Jesus the Son is *eternal*. He is eternal like Melchizedek and unlike the Aaronic high priest. "Once made perfect, he became the source of eternal salvation for all who obey him and was designated by God to be high priest in the order of Melchizedek" (5:9-10). I am not going to spend a lot of time discussing Melchizedek. The author of Hebrews brings him up in chapters 5, 6, and 7 to demonstrate that Jesus is a priest forever like Melchizedek. Melchizedek is a somewhat mysterious figure mentioned twice in the Old

Testament, first in Genesis and then in Psalm 110.[4] Information about Melchizedek's father or mother and his death are never provided, distinguishing him from priests within Aaron's levitical order. Also, Melchizedek is a priest of a higher and older order than the levitical priests since Abraham, Levi's great grandfather, paid tithes to Melchizedek back in Genesis. Drawing on these ideas, the author of Hebrews describes the Son as eternal. "Jesus . . . has become a high priest forever, in the order of Melchizedek" (Heb. 6:20). And again, "It is declared: 'You are a priest forever, in the order of Melchizedek'" (7:17). Elsewhere, Hebrews describes Melchizedek as being "without father or mother, without genealogy, without beginning of days or end of life, like the Son of God he [Melchizedek] remains a priest forever" (7:3).

Jesus is an eternal Son of God and therefore an eternal priest. The old priests died. But death could not hold Jesus, so he can continue to intercede on our behalf:

> Now there have been many of those priests, since death prevented them from continuing in office; but because Jesus lives forever, he has a permanent priesthood. Therefore he is able to save completely those who come to God through him, because he always lives to intercede for them (7:23-25).

Jesus Is Perfect

Why did these priests pass away while Jesus the Son lives eternally? Because the old priests all sinned:

> Every high priest is selected from among men and is appointed to represent them in matters related to God, to offer gifts and sacrifices for sins. He is able to deal gently with those who are ignorant and are going astray, since he himself is subject to weakness. This is why he has to offer sacrifices for his own sins, as well as for the sins of the people (5:1-3).

But Jesus the eternal Son is *perfect*. He was human, enabling him to be a sympathetic high priest: "Because he himself suffered when he was tempted, he is able to help those who are being tempted" (2:18). Yet he was a human who never sinned: "We do not have a high priest who is unable to sympathize with our weaknesses, but we have one who has been tempted in every way, just as we are—yet was without sin" (4:15). The other leaders whom the Hebrew Christians were tempted to follow were passing servants who passed because they were all sinful. But Jesus is the eternal, sinless Son of God.

---

[4] Gen. 14:18-20; Ps. 110:4. In Matt. 22:41-45 and parallels, Jesus clearly applies this psalm to the Messiah.

WHAT HAS JESUS DONE?

Jesus' eternal and sinless nature brings us to the second issue: what has Jesus done?

Jesus Offered a Permanent Sacrifice

These other leaders were not only impressive for who they were, they were impressive for what they had done. They brought covenants spoken by angels. They proved faithful over God's house. They descended from unbroken lines of high priests stretching back to the beginning of the covenant. They regularly offered sacrifices. And these were well-ordered, impressive ceremonies, no doubt!

Yes, but what were these sacrifices? our writer asks.

They were the repeated offerings of bulls and goats.

Repeated, why? our writer persists, trying to help us see their futility. He then gives us the answer: *they were repeated because imperfect priests can only offer imperfect sacrifices.* As we have seen, the priests were themselves sinners: Every high priest "has to offer sacrifices for his own sins, as well as for the sins of the people" (5:3). And the sacrifices the priests offered were unable to remove the stain of sin: "it is impossible for the blood of bulls and goats to take away sins" (10:4).

But Jesus, as the perfect and sinless high priest, could offer a permanent sacrifice that never had to be repeated. He offered himself. So we read in chapter 7,

> Such a high priest meets our need—one who is holy, blameless, pure, set apart from sinners, exalted above the heavens. Unlike the other high priests, he does not need to offer sacrifices day after day, first for his own sins, and then for the sins of the people. He sacrificed for their sins once for all when he offered himself. For the law appoints as high priests men who are weak; but the oath [Ps. 110:4], which came after the law, appointed the Son, who has been made perfect forever (Heb. 7:26-28).

These other high priests came and went, continually offering sacrifices of bulls and goats. Jesus, the eternal and perfect Son of God, gave himself once forever; he never has to do it again.

Jesus Offered an Effective Sacrifice

And what was the effect of these repeated sacrifices offered up by these high priests of the Old Covenant? our author asks, still persisting. *If they had to be repeated, they must not have been effective.* They must not have "worked." Then again, they were never meant to "work" in that way. We learn this from the Old Testament. Jeremiah is ushered in to testify in the latter half of chapter 8, and Jeremiah tells us the people in the Old Testament were unfaithful: "'they did not remain faithful to my covenant, and I turned away from them, declares the Lord'" (Heb. 8:9, quoting Jer. 31:32). The repeated sacrifices of animals only made the worshipers externally and ceremonially clean. They did not make them truly faithful and clean on the inside before God. Such sacrifices were finally earthly. They were ceremonial reminders of spiritual truths, which is why they had to be repeated. "Day after day every priest stands and performs his religious duties; again and again he offers the same sacrifices, which can never take away sins" (10:11). Animal sacrifices could not remove sin, cleanse hearts, and make atonement with God for unfaithful people like the Israelites or us. They could only point toward something else.

The sacrifice that Jesus, the perfect and eternal Son of God, offered is not only permanent, it is *effective*. It prepares the way for the faithful people Jeremiah promised, whose hearts were engraved with God's law (8:10-12; cf. Jer. 31:33-34). Christ's work inaugurated the creation of these people, because his sacrifice makes God's people truly clean.

> The blood of goats and bulls and the ashes of a heifer sprinkled on those who are ceremonially unclean sanctify them so that they are outwardly clean. How much more, then, will the blood of Christ, who through the eternal Spirit offered himself unblemished to God, cleanse our consciences from acts that lead to death, so that we may serve the living God! (9:13-14).

All of these Old Testament sacrifices pointed toward Christ and the new and better covenant he would mediate: "They serve at a sanctuary that is a copy and shadow of what is in heaven" (8:5). They could not take away sin themselves. They could only remind people of their sins:

> The law is only a shadow of the good things that are coming—not the realities themselves. For this reason it can never, by the same sacrifices repeated endlessly year after year, make perfect those who draw near to worship. If it could, would they not have stopped being offered? For the worshipers would have been cleansed once for all, and would no longer have felt guilty for their sins. But those sacrifices are an annual reminder of sins, because it is impossible for the blood of bulls and goats to take away sins (10:1-4).

But Jesus' sacrifice effectively made people perfect and is effectively making them holy. Therefore, it only had to be offered once. "But when this priest had offered for all time one sacrifice for sins, he sat down at the right hand of God. . . . by one sacrifice he has made perfect forever those who are being made holy" (10:12, 14). His sacrifice is proved perfect by its powerful effect in cleansing the hearts of his people. You and I, if we are Christians, are testimonies to the power of Jesus' sacrifice. As our lives actually change, we show the reality of what he did on the cross.

So, on the one hand, we have the servants who died because of their own sin, and whose endlessly repeated sacrifices of bulls and goats could only make people ceremonially and externally clean. On the other hand, we have the eternal and sinless Son of God, who gave himself once forever to make his people holy. This is the choice the writer of Hebrews presents to us.

SEVEN DANGERS

Along the way, our writer also provides seven particular warnings to these Christians struggling to persevere in the faith. You may not feel that you are presently struggling with all of these dangers, but you might look for where you do struggle.

Ignoring What God Has Done in Christ

Ignoring what God has done in Christ is always a threat, so the writer warns us to "pay more careful attention" (2:1). Why would you listen to angels and prophets, but not to the Son of God! Do not ignore the Word we have from Jesus. Heed his Word, and do not just enjoy some sentimental attachment to the idea of him. Study the New Testament. Seek to understand who he is and what he has done. Do not dare to ignore him but listen to him.

Not Believing God

Having listened, there is still the danger of unbelief. So the writer tells us to believe. "See to it, brothers, that none of you has a sinful, unbelieving heart that turns away from the living God" (3:12). Your hearing needs to be more than ear-hearing. It needs to get into your head, where it can be critically grasped, and then it needs to get into your heart, where it stays. So ask, is this true? And then ask, what implications does it have for my life? That is the kind of real hearing the author is talking about. "We have come to share in Christ if we hold firmly till the end the confidence we had at first" (3:14). Do you ever wonder if you have come to share in Christ? You will know when you have held on to him firmly to the end.

Ceasing to Grow

Having believed, there is still the danger of stopping. Our author mentions this in several warning sections. He laments, "though by this time you ought to be teachers, you need someone to teach you the elementary truths of God's word all over again" (5:12). Then, "let us leave the elementary teachings about Christ and go on to maturity" (6:1). And finally, "show this same diligence to the very end, in order to make your hope sure. We do not want you to become lazy" (6:11b-12a). Many people have the idea that someone can be a "baby Christian"; that somehow a Christian can persist for years and decades in a state of spiritual immaturity. Is that real? There are people I might be tempted to describe that way. But is it a biblical category? You will be hard pressed to find it in the Bible. Rather, severe warnings are given in Scripture to anyone who has heard and claims to believe but who has then stopped and not pressed on. By analogy, we know we are physically alive because we are living, aging, and even growing until our very last breath. The idea that something can be alive even though it has stopped growing is a curious idea, and I am not sure the New Testament is familiar with it.

Not Persevering in Holiness

If you have stopped growing, you will almost inevitably not persevere in holiness. So the author exhorts us, "Let us draw near to God with a sincere heart in full assurance of faith" (10:22a). After all, "If we deliberately keep on sinning after we have received the knowledge of the truth, no sacrifice for sins is left" (10:26). "So do not throw away your confidence. . . . You need to persevere so that when you have done the will of God, you will receive what he has promised" (10:35-36). The writer could not be any clearer. You need to persevere in holiness. That is why his warning is so strong: "If we deliberately keep on sinning after we have received the knowledge of the truth, no sacrifice for sins is left, but only a fearful expectation of judgment and of raging fire that will consume the enemies of God" (10:26-27). One of the most significant things I have gained from studying the book of Hebrews again is the renewed realization of how scary sin is. The book treats it with extreme seriousness— exactly because the sacrifice that Christ offered is considered *effective*. It is the sacrifice to end all sacrifices, and the one that makes us truly holy. So if you say that this sacrifice has been offered for you but you do not persevere in holiness, the author of Hebrews simply warns you of a "fearful expectation of judgment and of raging fire." Deliberate and repetitious sin in the Christian's life is very scary.

This is why the writer is so serious about holiness. He writes, "without holiness no one will see the Lord" (12:14b). If we remain unholy, we show that Christ's sacrifice has been ineffective in our lives; and if Christ's sacrifice has been ineffective in our lives, what hope do we have?

Losing Faith

Amid the above dangers is the danger of losing faith. Therefore we must persevere in faith. The author writes, "Now faith is being sure of what we hope for and certain of what we do not see" (11:1). There is much misunderstanding on this idea of faith, so let me be clear: faith is not the hope that grows to certainty; faith is the reality, or the certainty, that inspires the hope. Do you see the difference? It is not that we have a wish that we cherish and burnish like bronze until it really shines, and then call that our hope and put our faith in it. Nor is faith something we build like we build biceps. These are some of the misconceptions today's secular society has about faith. No, what the author is talking about here is perceiving and believing in the reality of something you cannot yet see. The faith we have which gives us hope, then, is hope in something real. All this is so often misunderstood.

The original recipients of this letter had learned this in their own lives. The author writes, "You sympathized with those in prison and joyfully accepted the confiscation of your property, *because you knew that you yourselves had better and lasting possessions*" (10:34). It was not that their property was confiscated and then they thought to themselves, "Oh, no, we need to find a place for wish fulfillment. We need to project a belief in heavenly things that cannot be taken away. Let us think of that and see if we can build up our faith." No, first they knew they had heavenly possessions. Then they joyfully allowed their earthly possession to be confiscated as they stood true for Christ. Do you see the difference? They had faith, therefore they endured, *not* the other way around. In fact, Jesus—the author tells us—acted in the same manner: "for the joy set before him [he] endured the cross, scorning its shame" (12:2). It was not that Jesus was on the cross needing some sense of joy, so he projected a belief in heavenly things into the future and then had faith. No, his faith saw the joy set before him, and then he had genuine hope. Again, it is not the hope that grows to certainty, but the reality, or the certainty, that inspires the hope. Knowing that is faith. Don't lose faith.

Rejecting Discipline

When we do stop persevering, there is also the danger of rejecting God's discipline. Persevering means accepting discipline. The author writes,

> Our fathers disciplined us for a little while as they thought best; but God disciplines us for our good, that we may share in his holiness. No discipline seems pleasant at the time, but painful. Later on, however, it produces a harvest of righteousness and peace for those who have been trained by it (12:10-11).

If we will not accept God's discipline, we may not know his love. Disciplining children is so important *as a part* of showing them love, concern, and care. It is the same with God and his children. And just as it is important for the child to listen to his or her parents while being disciplined, so it is important to cultivate the ability to hear God when he disciplines you. We need to take the filters off our ears and listen to God even when he says the difficult things we may not want to hear.

Refusing This Warning

Finally, there is the danger of refusing this warning:

> See to it that you do not refuse him who speaks. If they did not escape when they refused him who warned them on earth, how much less will we, if we turn away from him who warns us from heaven? . . . Since we are receiving a kingdom that cannot be shaken, let us be thankful, and so worship God acceptably with reverence and awe, for our God is a consuming fire (12:25, 28-29).

We must heed the warning God has graciously given.

These are the seven dangers: ignoring the word of Christ, developing unbelieving hearts, stopping your growth as a Christian, giving up on holiness, losing faith, rejecting God's discipline, and refusing this warning. We should persevere in this best way, this "new and living way" (10:20). By hearing and believing, by growing and persevering in holiness, by having faith and accepting discipline, and by heeding this warning, we should persevere.

CONCLUSION

An old Dutch proverb says, "He who has a choice has trouble." You can have important choices before you, and then you can choose the wrong way. That is reality. But the writer of Hebrews has laid the best choice before us. I do not know exactly what or who competes with Christ in your life. It may be impressive teachers like the ones the writer of Hebrews talks about. Or it may be something else. I do know this: whatever the others are, Christ is best, because Christ brings what every one of us needs—atonement and peace with God. He is uniquely able to do this. There is no one else like him. There is no other eternal sinless Son of God who gave himself once for us to make us holy.

Persevering means sticking with the best. In Christ, we have the best.

Let us pray:

Lord, we pray that you will help us to wait well. Give us perseverance and strength so that we can wait and prove that the Lord Jesus' sacrifice has not been in vain. And Father, for any person who does not know you and has not found peace with you through Christ, we pray that you will make his (or her) own need clear. In your love, show him great mercy, and open hearts to this sacrifice. Father, we pray that you would teach him to lay his sins upon Jesus, the one effective sacrifice for sin. We ask this all in Jesus' name and for his sake. Amen.

Questions for Reflection

1. The ability to make choices, somehow, seems essential to our humanity. Almost everyone enjoys making choices. What choice do we have concerning matters of truth? Is religion a matter of personal choice? If yes, explain. If no, why do so many people treat it like it is?

2. As we considered at the beginning, the author of Hebrews does not warn his first readers to come back to the faith by writing a letter merely filled with practical advice. Instead, he gets theological and addresses the fundamental questions of who Jesus is and what he has done. Why would the author use this approach? If you are a Christian, what approach do you take when encouraging the fainthearted?

3. Why would following angels, Old Testament prophets, or Moses, as the first readers of Hebrews were tempted to do, seem easier or less socially awkward than following Jesus? What is the lesson in this for us today? In other words, what are some of the things we can do that seem good (and in some sense are good), but if we do them to avoid the cost of being a disciple of Christ, they become bad?

4. What do the New Testament apostles, the early church fathers, the great reformers of the sixteenth century, the heroic missionaries of the eighteenth, nineteenth, and twentieth centuries, and your favorite pastors and church leaders all have in common? Answer: They are all dead, or they will be dead (if the Lord does not return first). Why is it so important that we put our faith and hope in one whom death could not contain but who lives eternally?

5. Jesus Christ faced every temptation we face, yet he was without sin. Why should this encourage and not intimidate us?

6. Hebrews argues strongly that the sacrifice of bulls and goats was not effective, while Jesus' sacrifice was effective. But let's start by asking, why does any sacrifice have to be offered at all? Why can't God simply forgive people's sins? After all, when we forgive people for the things they do against us, we don't require them to sacrifice some poor animal, do we? What's the big deal?

7. Why was Jesus' sacrifice effective?

8. As we have considered, many people have the idea that someone can be a "baby Christian," that somehow a Christian can persist for years and decades in a state of spiritual immaturity. Is that real? There are people we might be tempted to describe that way. But is it a biblical category?

9. If a friend of yours claims to be a Christian but continues to willfully live in a sinful lifestyle, why can you legitimately say to him or her, "In spite of your profession of faith, there are strong reasons for thinking you may not be a Christian"? Should you say this to him or her? Could this be considered "playing God"? What role should churches play in such dilemmas?

10. As we have seen, the author of Hebrews writes, "without holiness no one will see the Lord" (12:14b). Does that mean we have to be holy in order to be saved?

11. Will the true Christian life be characterized by nonstop, dramatic growth in the faith? Explain.

12. What misconceptions does the world have about faith? What, then, *is* faith?

13. Who or what competes with Christ in your life? If your best friend, spouse, parent, or pastor were asked that question about you, what would he or she say?

THE MESSAGE OF JAMES: FAITH THAT WORKS

20

THE MESSAGE OF JAMES: FAITH THAT WORKS

DOES IT WORK?[1]

I often begin sermons with a pithy quote from some great author or philosopher. Well, here is one more: "I've decided," said Charlie Brown, "that life is like an ice cream cone—you have to lick it one day at a time." Now that is good practical advice, isn't it? It is not some heavy idea from Sartre or Nietzsche that is hard to understand. It is very clear. Life is like an ice cream cone. You have to lick it one day at time. You have to divide up your troubles and attack them in manageable sizes. Like Jesus tells us, each day has enough trouble for itself.

The religion that people are looking for today is practical. Do not let all the mystical-sounding talk about spirituality deceive you. By and large, the mystical experiences people want are ones that will give them certainty of purpose when they go to work in the morning. The spirituality people sign up for is the kind that calms their nerves or lowers their blood pressure. People today want a faith that works.

INTRODUCING JAMES

That is what the little letter of James is all about. James provides clear, practical instruction throughout the letter. That is why so many people love this book. Of course, that is why so many people avoid it as well. We want practical advice, and we especially want the kind that agrees with what we already think. But James is not concerned about telling us what we want to hear. No, he lines up one truth, and then he lines up another; and then, having his lis-

---

[1] This sermon was originally preached on May 14, 1995, at Capitol Hill Baptist Church in Washington, D.C.

teners just where he wants them, he delivers a third, hard-hitting truth right to their situation with all the force of the first two points behind it.

And yet, as situationally appropriate and specific as he may be, along the way he provides a searching exposé of perennially popular religious myths. Let's follow James as he lines up these truths, and, in so doing, exposes three myths.

MYTH #1: "TRIALS ARE BAD"

Myth number one is, "trials are bad."

I call that a myth, but there is a lot of obvious truth in the idea that trials are bad. Unless you are a masochist, you want to avoid pain, whether physical or psychological. You want to stay out of situations where you will encounter things that are hard. We all have an instinct for self-preservation, and in one respect that is appropriate.

Behind this natural reaction of ours to say that trials are bad is the assumption that "good" is something immediately apparent to us. And if something appears "bad," it must be bad.

But James wants to work against our natural tendency to avoid trials. In fact, he writes, "Consider it pure joy, my brothers, whenever you face trials of many kinds" (1:2). Trials are reasons for joy! And he says this for four reasons. First, according to 1:3-4, trials are described as the way to maturity. Consider it pure joy when you face trials, he says, "because you know that the testing of your faith develops perseverance. Perseverance must finish its work so that you may be mature and complete, not lacking anything." We have all experienced this. We know, for instance, that testing develops a product. Working out develops the muscles. The challenges of marriage teach us to love someone who is not like us. So trials actually bring us to maturity. Once James has explained himself, we understand what he means, even if his command to "consider it joy" surprises us at first.

Second, trials cause us consciously to depend on God. James teaches in 1:5-8,

> If any of you lacks wisdom, he should ask God, who gives generously to all without finding fault, and it will be given to him. But when he asks, he must believe and not doubt, because he who doubts is like a wave of the sea, blown and tossed by the wind. That man should not think he will receive anything from the Lord; he is a double-minded man, unstable in all he does.

If we do everything in our own strength, we will never learn to rely on God. Yet in his kindness and love, God puts us in trials and circumstances in which we have no option but to trust him. And that is when we learn we can trust him, and we grow.

It has always been this way. When the children of Israel were in slavery in Egypt, oppressed by Pharaoh, what did God do? He promised to rescue them, and then he did. But what did he do next? He led them right to the edge of a sea. Mountains were on the right and left, the sea was in front of them, and Pharaoh's army was right behind them. What option did they have other than to trust in God? And as we know, their trust in God was not in vain: he did part the sea. The whole Bible is filled with such stories. In John's Gospel, Jesus says a number of very hard things that cause many of his disciples to turn away. He then turns to the twelve and says, "You do not want to leave too, do you?" And what do they say? "Lord, to whom shall we go? You have the words of eternal life" (John 6:67-68). In other words, *we have no other option but to trust you!*

How about you? How do you *consider* the things God is calling you to do, including the hard situations that seem to be without a solution? Do you consider them joy? God often, in his love, puts us in hard situations so that we may learn how trustworthy he is.

Third, we can consider trials as joy because this life, its trappings, and its trials will pass. God will ensure that all balances will be leveled in the end, as we see in James 1:9-12:

> The brother in humble circumstances ought to take pride in his high position. But the one who is rich should take pride in his low position, because he will pass away like a wild flower. For the sun rises with scorching heat and withers the plant; its blossom falls and its beauty is destroyed. In the same way, the rich man will fade away even while he goes about his business.
>
> Blessed is the man who perseveres under trial, because when he has stood the test, he will receive the crown of life that God has promised to those who love him.

God's ways of measuring are not like ours.

Finally, trials are reason for joy because we are promised that they are a part of God's good purposes, unlike temptations to evil, which are really temptations to death. James writes in the very next verses,

> When tempted, no one should say, "God is tempting me." For God cannot be tempted by evil, nor does he tempt anyone; but each one is tempted when, by his own evil desire, he is dragged away and enticed. Then, after desire has conceived, it gives birth to sin; and sin, when it is full-grown, gives birth to death (1:13-15)

Temptations do not come from God, and yielding to temptation ultimately produces its own kind of maturity: death. Trials, however, are from God, and in his love he uses them to bring us to a right maturity, the maturity of knowing we can practically rely on him in all of life's circumstances.

Trials strengthen our faith because they cause us to practice putting our trust in God for what we cannot immediately see.

So James calls us to embrace our trials by considering them "all joy." That does not mean we pretend they are not trials. It simply means we do not let our understanding of them ultimately be determined by how they feel at first. If something feels hard or bad at first, we will react to it negatively. That is only natural. But the strange and wonderful thing is, God in his sovereign love again and again uses those things that feel bad at first to teach us to trust him. How many times parents do this with children! Doctors with their patients! Good public servants with the public! You with your friends, if you are a faithful friend!

Our emotional reaction may be negative at first, but that very emotion has its God-given purpose. It forces us to confront the question, *do I really trust God as I say I do?* How easy it is to let our emotions be the all-determining factor. But that gets us nowhere. I often think of our emotions as the jet stream for an airplane pilot. If the jet stream is going in the airplane's direction, it is very helpful. If the airplane turns into headwinds, the winds slow the plane down a good bit. And if the winds blow from the side, flying can be quite dangerous. Emotions are like that for us. On the one hand, emotions can be extremely helpful. On the other hand, trials can produce winds of emotion that feel like headwinds or even crosswinds. So we cannot take our directions from our emotions. We have to take our direction from God and the truth of what he has told us to do in Scripture. And as we see trials strengthen our faith and so prove God's faithfulness, a new emotion, indeed, something deeper than an emotion, will emerge—joy! Now that's a tailwind!

A great illustration of this is found in the life of Sir Norman Anderson of Britain, who died in December 1994. Sir Norman lived a tremendous life for the Lord as a missionary and a servant for the British government in the Middle East, and then as a professor of Oriental law in London for years. He was truly an evangelical statesman. Professor Norman also knew tremendous suffering in his own life. All of his children died before he did, and his wife had a terrible degenerative disease that consumed the last years of his life. And yet I heard Sir Norman say less than a year before his death that he had known God's tremendous blessing through all of this. Not for one moment did he want his children to die prematurely or his wife to be disabled, but even in those very hard things he could see his Father's love. Who knows what greater troubles our heavenly Father has spared us from by the trials he has allowed to come our way.

That is what James is saying here: God in his love gives us trials to test our faith, to develop us, and to mature us. Robert Browning Hamilton's verse captures it well,

> I walked a mile with Pleasure;
>   She chattered all the way,
>   But left me none the wiser
>   for all she had to say.
>
> I walked a mile with Sorrow;
>   and ne'er a word said she;
>   but, oh, the things I learned from her
>   when sorrow walked with me.[2]

MYTH #2: "FAITH IS WHAT I THINK"

If the first myth that James dispels is that trials are bad, the second myth is this: "faith is what I think."

Again, there is an obvious way in which this is true. Faith, or belief, must involve the cognitive. A rock sits. A plant grows. An animal has instincts. But people? We *think!* Much of belief, or faith, is tied up in thinking thoughts.

And yet, James wants to line up a second truth for his readers that makes a further point. Faith, he says, is what you think *and* what you do. The point of hearing God's Word is not to simply know it; the point of hearing God's Word is to do it.

"Humbly accept the word planted in you, which can save you," James says (1:21). And accepting it means trusting it so that you will do it: "Do not merely listen to the word, and so deceive yourselves. Do what it says," he instructs in 1:22 (cf. 1:23-25). Hearing without doing is confusing and potentially self-deceiving.

It is easy to deceive ourselves. It is easy to sit and listen to a sermon or read a Christian book and think that because you have understood something the preacher says, you have moved closer to God. Certainly, understanding something the Bible says is good. Yet hearing and understanding something the Bible says but not making sure that it translates into how you live is quite dangerous. I fear that many religious people in churches have a toxic buildup of religious knowledge that is not lived out. James becomes a terrifying book when

---

[2] Robert Browning Hamilton, "Along the Road," cited in Harry Emerson Fosdick, *Successful Christian Living* (New York: Harper Brothers, 1937), 202.

we consider all the hearers who have not become doers, especially if that includes you.

God desires a righteous life (1:19). "Religion" or "faith" that is cognitively believed but is not lived out is "worthless" (1:26). It is unacceptable to God (1:27).

In chapter 2, James applies this message to a specific situation in the church he is writing to, namely, their problem with favoritism—treating people differently on the basis of external factors like wealth. "As believers in our glorious Lord Jesus Christ," James says, "don't show favoritism" (2:1). After all, believers in our glorious Lord Jesus Christ should live out what they know. Of all people, they should know better—they should live better—than to show respect based on externals like wealth. God did not ask us to fill out a financial application form before bringing us into his kingdom (2:4). He has not measured us by externals that are passing. And neither should *you*, says James, if you want your church to reflect the character of God. Favoritism is insulting to the poor and slanderous to "the noble name of him to whom you belong" (2:3-7). So what could you possibly mean when you claim to have heard God's concern for the poor but you do not reflect that concern in your own life? No, you must "keep the royal law found in Scripture" (2:8a). What is the royal law? "Love your neighbor as yourself" (2:8b), which was spoken back in Leviticus 19:18. Okay, says James, you have heard Leviticus. Now you must obey it. The royal law makes no sense when it is heard but not obeyed. It is about loving, after all. What good is it to hear about love but not do it?

Even a little favoritism is not insignificant: "If you show favoritism, you sin and are convicted by the law as lawbreakers" (2:9). Breaking the law anywhere makes us guilty before God: "For whoever keeps the whole law and yet stumbles at just one point is guilty of breaking all of it" (2:10). Even one trespass shows that you fundamentally disrespect the authority of God! So whatever the particular infraction, whatever the statute broken, you demonstrate a disregard and misunderstanding of who God is and of what your relationship to him is supposed to be.

James then gives his famous warning: there is a kind of faith that is useless and dead:

> What good is it, my brothers, if a man claims to have faith but has no deeds? Can such faith save him? Suppose a brother or sister is without clothes and daily food. If one of you says to him, "Go, I wish you well; keep warm and well fed," but does nothing about his physical needs, what good is it? In the same way, faith by itself, if it is not accompanied by action, is dead.
>
> But someone will say, "You have faith; I have deeds."

Show me your faith without deeds, and I will show you my faith by what I do. You believe that there is one God. Good! Even the demons believe that—and shudder.

You foolish man, do you want evidence that faith without deeds is useless? Was not our ancestor Abraham considered righteous for what he did when he offered his son Isaac on the altar? You see that his faith and his actions were working together, and his faith was made complete by what he did. And the scripture was fulfilled that says, "Abraham believed God, and it was credited to him as righteousness," and he was called God's friend. You see that a person is justified by what he does and not by faith alone.

In the same way, was not even Rahab the prostitute considered righteous for what she did when she gave lodging to the spies and sent them off in a different direction? As the body without the spirit is dead, so faith without deeds is dead (2:14-26).

Faith that is not acted out is not faith at all, and these verses give us three examples. First, says James, are the demons. The demons believe there is one God. They even know in their heart there is one God, and they shudder. But somehow it makes no difference in their lives. It does not translate into repentance and action. So if you want to tell me you have faith, says James, but your faith does not show itself in deeds, your faith is no different from a demon's. The crucial element of relational trust is missing in such "faith."

Second, he points us to the father of the faithful, Abraham, whom we exalt as having great faith. Even Abraham showed his faith by what he did. His faith and action worked together. You might say his faith was made complete by his action, because faith without action is simply not true, saving faith.

This is also true among the most surprising people of God, such as Rahab the prostitute, James's third example. Even Rahab showed her faith by what she did, not simply by what she knew or said!

When glass skyscrapers were first built and popularized in the 1950s, a number of office-workers were scared of working in offices thirty, forty, even fifty stories above the ground with nothing visible stopping them from plunging downward. *Reader's Digest* once carried a story about one of these earliest skyscrapers, describing how a number of people in one office could not work because their desks were too close to the massive windows. The people in the office would sit there looking down hundreds of feet, petrified! They knew there was a glass window between them and the drop, but they were not used to the idea that glass could act as a barrier. It was causing enough trouble in the office that the building manager was contacted. He came up and told them about the design of the frame and thickness of the glass; he explained how it could hold so much stress and even gave an example. But they were still nervous. The building manager was perplexed about what to do. So he brought up a structural engineer who explained it all again. Still, they did not feel comfortable looking down all that distance. Then the engineer said, "I have an idea." He called everyone to stand near the inside wall, which they did. He stepped back, and then ran full speed toward the glass wall, hit it with his full weight, and bounced off. He was fine! He was willing to throw his whole life against the glass wall because he knew it could take it!

That is what James is saying real faith is. It is not the faith of the person who can sit, read a religious document, and say, "I believe this." Saving faith, says James, is the faith that throws its whole life into living out the truth believed. The satisfaction we experience when we *know* or *understand* a truth can actually become dangerous when the *knowing* serves as a substitute for living out the truth.

The problem, in part, is with this English word "believe," because in our vocabulary it refers to an intellectual concept. When I say, "I believe the world is round," I am stating that my mind "believes" the world is round even though I have never seen the earth from outer space or walked around the whole planet. My "belief" refers to an intellectual concept, not necessarily to a deep and abiding trust. But in the Bible, "belief" refers not to just an intellectual recognition but also to a deep and abiding trust. When we fail to understand this, we begin to misinterpret parts of the Bible. For example, John 3:16 reads, "For God so loved the world that he gave his one and only Son, that whoever believes in him shall not perish but have eternal life." We hear that and tend to think it refers simply to a cognitive belief. *The Amplified Bible* captures well what John 3:16 means: "For God so greatly loved and dearly prized the world that He [even] gave up his only-begotten (unique) Son, that whoever believes in (trusts, clings to, relies upon) Him shall not perish (come to destruction, be lost) but have eternal (everlasting) life." Did you catch that? Believing is a clinging to, a relying on, a trusting in. That is the biblical idea of "belief," and that is what James is talking about in chapter 2. A believer is not one who intellectually recognizes God but does not employ his or her faith. Rather, a believer is one who lives out God's Word. We are saved by faith alone, but the faith that saves is never alone. It is always accompanied by visible acts and evidences.

God has made you and me to know him, but we have sinned against him. He is now rightly committed to judging all of us for our sins. Our only hope is to repent of our sins and have real saving faith in Jesus Christ—God incarnate—who was crucified and raised to life for our salvation. Do you believe that? Real faith works.

So the second myth is that "faith is what I think."

MYTH #3: "RELIGION IS A PRIVATE MATTER"

The third myth James dispels is, "religion is a private matter."

Again, this is obviously true in one respect because faith is very *personal*. It has to be personal if it is genuine. Some kinds of public religion are nothing but hypocrisy. But what people usually mean when they say "faith is private" is, "I don't want to talk about faith." In the name of religion or spirituality, then, they justify treating this life as ours to do with as we please. Religion becomes a tool for self-centeredness and control over our own destinies. The playwright Tennessee Williams, explaining why he had given up visiting his psychoanalyst, reportedly said, "He was meddling too much in my private life." We have a tendency these days to think of our religion as a part of our own private lives, on the same level as our ambitions, fantasies, and fears.

But if what James said earlier is true—that faith must be acted out—then saving, Christian faith cannot finally be private. Personal, yes, but not finally private. Both God and his people will be involved with what you do with your words, time, money, and even your desires for pleasure. Any religion that consists of more than thoughts and opinions—one that involves deeds and actions—cannot be completely private.

So now that he has lined up the first two lessons, James gets to his main point. He first established that trials are not bad, but that God means them for good purposes. Then he established that hearing the word of God means obeying it. Real faith is active faith. Saving belief is both mental and behavioral. And now that the reader has both arms pinned to the wall, he makes the final blow: Christianity is a public matter. It is about our life together. James does not say this directly, but that is the clear implication of the very thing he is trying to correct in this stress-ridden, faction-prone church: division.

As you read through this book, the evidence of this division is everywhere. These Christians are boastful about the future, perhaps comparing one another's future prospects (4:13-17; cf. 3:5). They are quick to become angry with one another, and quick to use hurtful words (1:19). They are cursing at one another (3:9-10). They are slandering one another (4:11-12). They are grumbling against one another (5:9). Not only are they showing favoritism to the rich, they are oppressing the poor (5:1-6).

Behind this division in the church, it would seem, is careless teaching: "Not many of you should presume to be teachers, my brothers, because you know that we who teach will be judged more strictly" (3:1). It is interesting that James opens this section with a comment about teaching. It could be that someone was teaching that selfishness is okay. Several verses later, James writes, "if you harbor bitter envy and selfish ambition in your hearts, do not boast about it or deny the truth. Such 'wisdom' does not come down from heaven but is earthly, unspiritual, of the devil" (3:14-15). A true teacher is just the opposite of this, and the teacher's life proves it: "Who is wise and understanding among you? Let him show it by his good life, by deeds done in the humility that comes from wisdom" (3:13).

Along these lines, it is also interesting to note how many of James's cautions focus on words. Our words have tremendous effects on other people: "Likewise the tongue is a small part of the body, but it makes great boasts. Consider what a great forest is set on fire by a small spark" (3:5). We may view our words primarily as a means of self-expression, but our words belong to God: "With the tongue we praise our Lord and Father, and with it we curse men, who have been made in God's likeness. Out of the same mouth come praise and cursing. My brothers, this should not be" (3:9-10). Our speech is not primarily for expressing ourselves, it is for expressing God's character. And in the letter of James, God claims ownership over every word that a believer speaks. Wise speech is from God and brings unity.

What can be done about division and all of its associated problems? James offers at least four responses. First, he identifies the root problems. One of the root problems is selfishness, the same sort of selfishness that pretends religion is a private affair in order to mask ambition: "For where you have envy and selfish ambition, there you find disorder and every evil practice" (3:16). Such selfishness knows no bounds:

> What causes fights and quarrels among you? Don't they come from your desires that battle within you? You want something but don't get it. You kill and covet, but you cannot have what you want. You quarrel and fight. You do not have, because you do not ask God. When you ask, you do not receive, because you ask with wrong motives, that you may spend what you get on your pleasures (4:1-3).

Behind the selfishness, of course, is pride: "That is why Scripture says: 'God opposes the proud but gives grace to the humble'" (4:6).

After identifying these root problems—selfishness and pride—James offers a second response. He tells us to submit to God. Before God, the way up is down:

> Submit yourselves, then, to God. Resist the devil, and he will flee from you. Come near to God and he will come near to you. Wash your hands, you sinners, and purify your hearts, you double-minded. Grieve, mourn and wail. Change your laughter to mourning and your joy to gloom. Humble yourselves before the Lord, and he will lift you up (4:7-10).

Okay, we are to humble ourselves. It is one thing to say it, but how do we do it? We do it by facing the facts about ourselves. To begin with, realize that our lives are not our own. James's readers are living as though their lives were theirs. So he warns them,

> Now listen, you who say, "Today or tomorrow we will go to this or that city, spend a year there, carry on business and make money." Why, you do not even know what will happen tomorrow. What is your life? You are a mist that appears for a little while and then vanishes. Instead, you ought to say, "If it is the Lord's will, we will live and do this or that." As it is, you boast and brag. All such boasting is evil (4:13-16).

Worldly people believe their lives are their own; Christians must not believe that. That is why James calls his readers "adulterous people" (4:4). They are religious bigamists.

James implores you, remember that you and all you have belong to God. Time is not yours; it is God's. Even pleasure is God's to give, not yours to take (e.g., 4:3; 5:4-5).

James's third response to the problem of divisions in the church is to warn that God's judgment is coming as quickly as this world's wealth is passing:

> Now listen, you rich people, weep and wail because of the misery that is coming upon you. Your wealth has rotted, and moths have eaten your clothes. Your gold and silver are corroded. Their corrosion will testify against you and eat your flesh like fire. You have hoarded wealth in the last days. Look! The wages you failed to pay the workmen who mowed your fields are crying out against you. The cries of the harvesters have reached the ears of the Lord Almighty. You have lived on earth in luxury and self-indulgence. You have fattened yourselves in the day of slaughter. You have condemned and murdered innocent men, who were not opposing you (5:1-6).

Everything you might rely on will pass away. What will remain is the fact that God will judge. Among other things, he will judge you for how you spend your money. And God's ownership of your life will be proved beyond doubt when he exercises his judgment. We live best in this world when we remember the next world and live with the next world in view.

I have often heard the statement, "He's so heavenly minded, he's no earthly good." I don't think I have ever met such a person. There is little danger of that today. We evangelical, Bible-believing Christians are so worldly minded, we are of little heavenly good. James tells his readers the same thing when he calls them adulterous: "You adulterous people, don't you know that friendship with the world is hatred toward God? Anyone who chooses to be a friend of the world becomes an enemy of God" (4:4). Clearly, he does not mean they are adulterous because all of them are committing adultery. He means they are adulterous because they are cheating on God by being deeply influenced by the world.

But the Judge is standing at the door (5:9). For some people, that means repenting. For others it means being patient and waiting for the Lord's coming, even as the farmer does:

> Be patient, then, brothers, until the Lord's coming. See how the farmer waits for the land to yield its valuable crop and how patient he is for the autumn and spring rains. You too, be patient and stand firm, because the Lord's coming is near (5:7-8).

Even as James promised back in chapter 1, he again promises that those who persevere in suffering will be blessed:

> Brothers, as an example of patience in the face of suffering, take the prophets who spoke in the name of the Lord. As you know, we consider blessed those who have persevered. You have heard of Job's perseverance and have seen what the Lord finally brought about. The Lord is full of compassion and mercy (5:10-11).

Fourth, James tells his division-riddled readers to love peace:

> But the wisdom that comes from heaven is first of all pure; then peace-loving, considerate, submissive, full of mercy and good fruit, impartial and sincere. Peacemakers who sow in peace raise a harvest of righteousness (3:17-18).

On that same note, he closes his letter by encouraging the readers to treat one another with tender concern: praying for the sick (5:14), confessing sins to one another (5:16a), valuing the prayers of the righteous (5:16b-18), bringing back those who wander (5:19-20).

James knows that so much of our relationship with God will be shown by our relationships with other people. As a Christian, my primary obligation in this life is not to myself. It is to God and to the body of Christ. You and I must realize that our selfishness hurts others, and that God will judge us for it. Really, we are to use ourselves for others. We must learn to cherish the opportunity of living in peace through valuing each other.

I have been in more than one church meeting where someone has made sharp comments about what he or she wants, or what *must* happen in the church for them to be satisfied; and I have feared how little that person must know of Christ. What but a loss of perspective and a lack of love for Christ and his body could lead to that sort of talk? Our Christianity, if it is to live up to its name, must affect other people in a loving and godly way. What does it mean to say we are followers of Jesus Christ, who literally gave his life for others, if we do not live like that ourselves?

Religion is not a private matter. It is personal, yes, but it is also public. It is about life together.

CONCLUSION

What James lays out in his letter is day-by-day practical: how to understand trials, how to live out your faith, and how to seek peace with God and others. So, in the spirit of James, I give you this instruction very seriously: consider your trials joys. Look for how your life makes your beliefs visible. And, especially, watch your words and the divisiveness you sow, or that you allow others to sow, in the body. I exhort you not as a captain who fears his boat may sink, but as an ambassador of the approaching king. We will give account. As James says, "The Lord's coming is near. . . . The Judge is standing at the door!" (5:8-9).

Let us pray:

Our Father, we thank you for every way that you have spoken to us through your Word. We pray, Lord, that you will challenge our attitudes about trials. Show us your goodness in them. Father, we also ask that you would enable us to live out our faith. By your Holy Spirit, fill us and help us to understand your Word. Enliven our hearts to obey you. And Lord, we pray you would grant a heavenly wisdom that would work for peace among us. Grant us the true wisdom that values your body and works for peace so that you will be glorified. Father, teach us to surrender our whole selves to you so that we can truly live for Christ. And it is in his name we ask it. Amen.

Questions for Reflection

1. At the beginning, we considered the fact that the religion most people look for today is practical—a religion that works. They are less interested in a religion that emphasizes old truths and things that happened long ago. Somehow, practicality and truth have become pitted against each other. "He's a truth person," and "she's a practical person," we say. Is this right? Is there a trade-off between truth and practicality?

2. James tells us to consider trials joy for at least four reasons. First, trials are a way to maturity. Can you recall a time when a trial that originally seemed impossible to endure ultimately grew and matured you, so that you are now grateful you faced that trial? What steps can you take for recalling these lessons in future trials?

3. Second, we consider trials as joy because they cause us consciously to depend on God. He puts us into situations that give us no option but to trust him. Why is this a *loving* and *kind* thing for God to do? Where has God shown himself to be trustworthy in your life? Have you thanked him for these occasions?

4. Third, we consider trials as joy because they teach us that the trappings of this life will pass. They focus our hearts on eternity instead. Can you think of something or someone you formerly prized and valued, but a bitter experience with that thing or person turned your heart sour? Not that God delights in conflict or that he cannot bring reconciliation, but would James say that perhaps your bitter experience was an act of God's love and compassion in your life?

5. Fourth, we consider trials as joy because we know they are all a part of God's plans for our lives, unlike the temptation to sin, which leads to death. But knowing that trials are a part of his plans for us is comforting only if we also believe that God is good. Why is it hard sometimes to believe that God is good? What does the Bible say about God's goodness? What can we do to grow in our certainty of God's goodness?

6. When a non-Christian friend turns to you for comfort amid a trial, how can you sensitively use the instruction of James—as prudence and empathy permit—to point him or her to Christ?

7. Describe how "believing" something can deceive you into thinking you live by it. Do you regard yourself as capable of self-deception? Name one occasion when you deceived yourself.

8. Assuming that you believe God saves us through faith in Christ, is it possible that anyone will arrive at Judgment Day and say to Christ, "I *believed* in you, that you died and rose again," and yet be condemned to eternity in hell? Explain.

9. Following up on question 8, what does God require for salvation?

10. What's the difference between a workless faith and a faith that works? Why is a faith that has no deeds so despicable in the sight of God?

11. Can Christianity be lived out only in private? Why not?

12. We have observed that James places a lot of emphasis on how we use our words. Wise speech brings unity. Selfish speech brings division. What are several ways you can use words to bring unity to your local church? To your family? What are several areas of your own speech that could use a little work? Where have you seen God teach you to be more controlled with your tongue? Be sure to thank him for his faithful work.

13. Would your spouse, parents, coworkers, pastor, children, friends, all those with whom you come into contact when running errands, and drivers of other cars say you are a peace lover? How do you actively promote peace? How are evangelism and discipleship forms of peace loving?

14. James promises us that the judge is standing at the door. Does that cause you hope or fear?

21

THE MESSAGE OF 1 PETER: WHEN THINGS GET TOUGH

WHEN THINGS GET TOUGH: INTRODUCING 1 PETER[1]

Let's begin this study by reading several portions of Peter's first letter. As we do, listen for what theme surfaces again and again in these quotations. We begin in chapter 1:

> In his great mercy he has given us new birth into a living hope through the resurrection of Jesus Christ from the dead, and into an inheritance that can never perish, spoil or fade—kept in heaven for you, who through faith are shielded by God's power until the coming of the salvation that is ready to be revealed in the last time. In this you greatly rejoice, though now for a little while you may have had to suffer grief in all kinds of trials. These have come so that your faith—of greater worth than gold, which perishes even though refined by fire—may be proved genuine and may result in praise, glory and honor when Jesus Christ is revealed (1:3-7).

Then we read this in chapter 2:

> It is commendable if a man bears up under the pain of unjust suffering because he is conscious of God. But how is it to your credit if you receive a beating for doing wrong and endure it? But if you suffer for doing good and you endure it, this is commendable before God. To this you were called, because Christ suffered for you, leaving you an example that you should follow in his steps.
>
>> "He committed no sin,
>> and no deceit was found in his mouth."
>
> When they hurled their insults at him, he did not retaliate; when he suffered, he made no threats. Instead, he entrusted himself to him who judges justly. He

[1] This sermon was originally preached on May 21, 1995, at Capitol Hill Baptist Church in Washington, D.C.

himself bore our sins in his body on the tree, so that we might die to sins and live for righteousness; by his wounds you have been healed. For you were like sheep going astray, but now you have returned to the Shepherd and Overseer of your souls (2:19-25).

Then in chapter 4, we read,

Therefore, since Christ suffered in his body, arm yourselves also with the same attitude, because he who has suffered in his body is done with sin. As a result, he does not live the rest of his earthly life for evil human desires, but rather for the will of God. For you spent enough time in the past doing what pagans choose to do—living in debauchery, lust, drunkenness, orgies, carousing and detestable idolatry. They think it strange that you do not plunge with them into the same flood of dissipation, and they heap abuse on you. But they will have to give account to him who is ready to judge the living and the dead. For this is the reason the gospel was preached even to those who are now dead, so that they might be judged according to men in regard to the body, but live according to God in regard to the spirit (4:1-6).

Then skipping down to 4:12, we read,

Dear friends, do not be surprised at the painful trial you are suffering, as though something strange were happening to you. But rejoice that you participate in the sufferings of Christ, so that you may be overjoyed when his glory is revealed. If you are insulted because of the name of Christ, you are blessed, for the Spirit of glory and of God rests on you. If you suffer, it should not be as a murderer or a thief or any other kind of criminal, or even as a meddler. However, if you suffer as a Christian, do not be ashamed, but praise God that you bear that name (4:12-16).

Clearly, all of these passages pertain to suffering as a Christian. Here are some other quotes about suffering, but not from 1 Peter:

"It is the suffering church that is the growing church."

"Scars are the price which every godly believer pays for loyalty to Christ."[2]

"Crushing the church is like smashing the atom: divine energy of high quality is released in enormous quantity and with miraculous effects."

I have found scores of pious quotes about the blessing that persecution is to the church of Christ. But almost every one was spoken by people like me, whose bodies were probably sleek with prosperity and whose skin had never been cut for being a follower of Jesus Christ. For every story we read about

---

[2] John MacArthur, *Keys to Effective Evangelism* (Chicago: Moody, 1988), 28.

the army of noble martyrs in the early church, the Reformation, nineteenth-century Africa, or twentieth-century Asia; for all the deep emotions these stories stir within us; and for all of the ways we admire the people who suffer for their convictions and ours, we have to admit, if we are honest, the church crushed by persecution often has not grown, let alone exploded with atomic power. More often than we care to say, it has been slowly strangled to death.

Take, for example, the church in the Middle East and North Africa. For several centuries after the apostles, these two regions comprised the heartland of Christianity. Some of the church's greatest writings of the first five centuries come from North Africa. Notable persecutions did occur and sometimes strengthen the church in these regions. And the blood of the martyrs did become the seed of the church, as the early church theologian Tertullian said. Yet the persecutions kept coming. In the centuries following the rise of Islam, persecution increased even more dramatically. First, the Christians in North Africa were taxed heavily. Then, beginning in the seventh century, they were killed. Christians often found themselves staring at a sword with a simple demand made of them: renounce Christianity or die. The killing continued until the middle of the twelfth century when, well, the supply of Christians was exhausted. Quite simply, there was a finite number of Christians to murder.

Let's be honest: suffering persecution for your faith is very hard. If you have any doubt of that, you can ask Sharaf el-Din. An Egyptian Muslim by birth, Mr. el-Din converted to Christianity in 1983 after both he and his wife had visions of Jesus (a surprisingly frequent occurrence in Muslim countries). They left Egypt for Kenya in 1988 to search for employment and to avoid the increasing religious persecution they faced at home. Desperate for a job, Mr. el-Din legally returned to Egypt in 1994. But upon his return, his family did not hear from him for five months because he was immediately "detained." A hearing was eventually held in which no charges were raised, yet he continued to be detained. After getting legal permission, his lawyer attempted to visit him in the prisons, but he couldn't find him. The only reason given for his incarceration, informally, was that he converted to Christianity. He was suffering for his faith.[3]

It is clear from Peter's letter that the early Christians knew suffering. Some of their suffering may have been similar to Mr. el-Din's. Yet much of it was less severe. Peter mentions insults, intimidations, grumblings, and threats. Perhaps you can identify with what Peter means, especially if you have experienced the cold shoulders and sharp jokes of people who used to be your friends. Once,

---

[3] Editor's note: at date of publication, no further information on Mr. el-Din could be found.

they really liked you and treated you with goodwill. Now, well, things have changed.

Understandably, these early Christians were beginning to wonder, "What's going on? Maybe we have done something wrong. If we have chosen the right way, why is there so much suffering?" They were also wondering what to do in the face of it all. Those are the two questions Peter addresses in this little letter: *Why do Christians suffer for their faith* if that faith is something good? And *what should suffering Christians do?* Perhaps, as we consider this letter, we will learn what it means for us to be Christians when things get tough.

WHY DO CHRISTIANS SUFFER?

The suffering of Peter's first readers was not what we think of when we talk about suffering. He is not talking about the suffering that comes with natural disasters like floods, famines, or diseases. Nor is he talking about man-made disasters like bombed buildings, lost jobs, or the pressures of a bad economy. His readers faced what might seem like an even worse problem: they were treated badly because of their faith in Christ. Once, these individuals were accepted by everyone as good people. Now that they had become Christians, they suffered "grief in all kinds of trials" (1:6).

What was happening? Were they doing something wrong? Well, says Peter, there are two kinds of suffering. One kind of suffering results from doing evil. If you murder, steal, or even meddle, suffering will follow (2:20; 3:17; 4:15-16). You should never face this kind of suffering, because you should never do such things.

But there is another kind of suffering that comes from doing good, and Peter tells his readers they are experiencing this second kind. Of course this presents another dilemma: doesn't suffering for doing good seem strange? Why would anyone persecute you for doing what is good and right? In order to explain this strange paradox, Peter writes this letter, and he gives two powerful reasons for why Christians will suffer for good.

Because God Has Chosen Us to Be His Special People

First, Christians suffer because God is our Creator and Lord, and he has chosen us to be his special people.

Holy. We are special, first, because we are holy. God has made us holy, meaning *set apart*. Peter writes in chapter 2,

> You are a chosen people, a royal priesthood, a holy nation, a people belonging
> to God, that you may declare the praises of him who called you out of darkness

into his wonderful light. Once you were not a people, but now you are the people of God; once you had not received mercy, but now you have received mercy (2:9-10).

Notice that God has done this. We were not his people, and then he made us his people.

Now that we have been made holy, we are called to live lives of holiness. Peter writes in chapter 1,

> Therefore, prepare your minds for action; be self-controlled; set your hope fully on the grace to be given you when Jesus Christ is revealed. As obedient children, do not conform to the evil desires you had when you lived in ignorance. But just as he who called you is holy, so be holy in all you do; for it is written: "Be holy, because I am holy" (1:13-16).

Our holiness, like God's holiness, combines the idea of "set-apartness" and the idea of Christlike purity. God has loved us by setting us apart as his own people, and he has declared us perfectly pure in Christ. That is, he has *made* us holy. But then he calls us to live lives that are set apart by reflecting his character of holiness.

This means that we live our lives in allegiance to him. We live in reverent fear of him. We take our coordinates from him. We take our bearings from him. He is the audience we play to. We do not take our directions from a pollster but from our heavenly Polestar. We are not simply trying to be popular with those around us, we look beyond our circumstances to the One who created us by his word and set us apart as his people.

Strange. If God's people take their bearings from God and live as a holy people, the world will think they are strange. Throughout this letter, Peter refers to these Christians as "strangers." He addresses them in the very first verse as "God's elect, strangers in the world" (1:1). Later in the same chapter, he tells them to "live your lives as strangers here in reverent fear" (1:17). In the next chapter, he says, "I urge you, as aliens and strangers in the world, to abstain from sinful desires, which war against your soul" (2:11). And since they are strange, he says a little later, their old friends "think it strange that you do not plunge with them into the same flood of dissipation, and they heap abuse on you" (4:4). These Christians, because they have been called out to be the holy people of God, are different!

Since I did some of my graduate work in England, my family celebrated seven Fourth of July holidays—a distinctly American holiday—in England. As you can imagine, the fourth day of July looks different in England than in the United States: nobody is celebrating America's independence from England! So none of the shops are closed. No days off are given from work. No groups of friends and family are gathered around barbeques in parks while children play with fireworks. Yet if you look carefully, you might find groups of Americans gathered here or there doing some of these things. Truly, it was *strange* to celebrate the Fourth of July in England.

However, the changes that occur in a new Christian are far more disturbing to his or her old non-Christian friends than celebrating our national holiday ever was to our British neighbors. The old friends notice the Christian no longer acts the way he or she formerly did. They notice that some of the old habits stop. Nothing makes people feel more uncomfortable than changes like these. You see, Christianity is not fundamentally an argument over doctrine. It is not an argument over the name of your church or what author you like. It is an argument instigated by the way your new life says to your non-Christian friends, "There is a different way to live." People do not like that. And so you, the Christian, appear strange. Peter Berger wrote in his book *A Far Glory,* "It is one of the more facetious illusions of liberal ideology that people will like each other better by getting to know each other."[4] Peter's letter shows us how right Berger is, especially when we're talking about non-Christians getting to know Christians. The Christian is the one who

> does not live the rest of his earthly life for evil human desires, but rather for the will of God. For you have spent enough time in the past doing what pagans choose to do—living in debauchery, lust, drunkenness, orgies, carousing and detestable idolatry. They think it strange that you do not plunge with them into the same flood of dissipation, and they heap abuse on you (4:2-4).

If you have not learned this yet, you are learning it now: it is strange in this world to be a Christian. This does not mean there is nothing the world likes about Christians. This is not a message for paranoid conspiracy theorists. No, I am simply recognizing the fact that, as Peter says, Christians are considered strange in this world because we live in reverent fear of God rather than in conformity to the world. In that sense, we live in two worlds at once. The new world has begun for us because God has given us a new birth. On the other hand, we continue to live within the old world, which is the only world non-Christians see. So our actions and attitudes, our comments and commitments, seem strange, even bizarre, to them, like someone talking into the air or pulling out a chair for a guest who isn't there. Things that excite them bore us, and things that excite us bore them. We see both the passing nature of this world

---

[4] Peter Berger, *A Far Glory* (New York: Anchor, 1993), 38.

and the reality of the coming world. We are strange because we live as those already raised with Christ in the light of the coming judgment and the new age.

Some people may ask, "Isn't being a good Christian simply being a good American citizen?" We can see how this might appear to be the case. In this letter, Peter exhorts us to obey the civil authorities. But Peter does not mean, and we should not think, there has ever been a complete identity between being a citizen of any earthly nation and being a Christian. Thirty or forty years ago, Christian morality was more commonly the morality of the culture at large, and so it was easier to mistake being a good citizen for being a good Christian. While common morality and Christian morality were never identical, the increasing secularization of society has made the two now impossible to confuse.

We can see an example of this in the controversies that rocked the Southern Baptist Convention in the latter part of the twentieth century. One aspect of the conflict that has been overlooked was generational. In many churches, the difference between the older and younger generations came down to how important it is to believe something. A member of the older generation might have said, "Is it really so important that we all believe the same things?" Of course the answer depends on what those things are. For some things, the answer must be yes. Yet the older members did not always understand the fuss over the precise formulation of certain doctrinal beliefs because they grew up in a world where most of the culture assumed that Christian beliefs and doctrines were true. But members of the younger generations had grown up in a culture absolutely opposed to Christian values, so they knew they had to be much clearer about exactly what it means to follow Christ.

Of course this gap between the older and younger generations of Christians has not affected only the SBC. I remember one professor I had as an undergraduate at Duke. He was a winsome fellow and a brother in the Lord who taught the Old and New Testaments. He loved to talk about his relationship with the Lord but he also loved to point out all the things he thought were wrong in the Bible. And he did this with glee, because he thought his willingness to concede that the Bible contained mistakes would help his young students mature in their faith, the way he had back in the 1930s when he had first struggled with problems and overcome them. I spoke with him shortly after graduation and told him that I appreciated what he was trying to do: make the faith realistic. I feared, though, that he was unintentionally destroying the faith of young person after young person. Unlike him, the people he taught did not grow up in rural 1920s Georgia or North Carolina, where everyone believed in the Bible. The people he taught grew up in cities and schools that constantly rejected the Bible as true. And so the things that he found mature and liberating were actually destroying the faith in the very students who sat in his classes.

Our culture thinks our Christianity is strange, because we give allegiance to someone they do not know. That is the message of Peter's first letter. Just as certain movements in the 1960s and 70s were described as "countercultural," so too should Christian lives be countercultural. The Puritan Richard Sibbes saw some of the personal implications of this 350 years ago. When someone asked him how a person could know whether he really loved the world or God, Sibbes answered, "That will be seen by observing the bent of our heart, how it is swayed towards God and his service, and how towards things below. When two masters are parted, their servants will be known whom they serve, by following their own master. Blessed be God, in these times we enjoy both religion and the world together; but if times of suffering should approach, then it would be known whose servants we are. Consider therefore beforehand what thou wouldst do. If trouble and persecution should arise, wouldst thou stand up for Christ, and set light by liberty, riches, credit, all in comparison of him?"[5]

In the end, our love indicates our god. Whatever we love most, whatever we trust most, whatever we fear most, whatever we joy and delight in most, whatever we obey most, that is our god. Because our God is so different from the gods of this world, we are persecuted.

Because We Are Called to Participate in the Sufferings of Christ

Really, Peter says, our suffering and persecution should not surprise us (4:12). Jesus Christ himself suffered rejection when he was in the world, and the world persecutes Christ's followers as it persecuted Christ. In fact, our suffering for his name is how we "participate in the sufferings of Christ" (4:13).

As much as any other book of the Bible, this little letter is replete with references to the suffering of Christ (4:13; 5:1), to his blood (1:2, 19), to his rejection (2:7), and to his death (3:18). Of course, we should remember who wrote this book: Peter, the boastful and eager disciple; Peter, the confessor and then denier of Christ who watched Christ suffer for him. Can you imagine how indelibly Christ's sufferings were marked on Peter's memory?

In the most important sense, Christ's sufferings were unique. He died for our sins. Christ was a substitute, bearing God's right punishment for everyone who would ever repent and believe in him. But in a secondary sense, Peter hears

---

[5] Richard Sibbes, "The Danger of Backsliding," *Miscellaneous Sermons and Indices*, vol. 7 of *Works*, ed. Alexander B. Grosart (repr. Edinburgh: Banner of Truth, 1982; orig. 1862–1864).

a calling and sees an example for the Christian in Christ's sufferings. They present a model for what we Christians are to do as we continually repent of our sins and follow him. Peter writes, "if you suffer for doing good and you endure it, this is commendable before God. To this you were called, because Christ suffered for you, leaving you an example, that you should follow in his steps" (2:20-21). Do not be disoriented or surprised by suffering. Suffering is the very call that has been issued to you in Christ. Do you remember his own words? "If anyone would come after me, he must deny himself and take up his cross and follow me" (Matt. 16:24). Jesus did not tell us to take up our cross at a time in history when the cross was a nice religious symbol. He said it when the cross was a cruel instrument of state execution. And Jesus is not trying to form a special elite core of Christians—"the Cross-Bearers," who are to Christianity what the Navy Seals are to the Navy. No, he is simply saying that he is on his way to the cross; and if we want to follow him, that is the path. The call he has offered to Christians has always been, "Come and follow."

Paul also assumes that Christians will be persecuted. He writes to Timothy, "Everyone who wants to live a godly life in Christ Jesus will be persecuted" (2 Tim. 3:12). Paul is not just being gun-shy or cynical because he had faced so much persecution in his life. No, he can also recall the words of Jesus. As Jesus said in the Gospel of Matthew, "Blessed are those who are persecuted because of righteousness, for theirs is the kingdom of heaven. Blessed are you when people insult you, persecute you and falsely say all kinds of evil against you because of me. Rejoice and be glad, because great is your reward in heaven, for in the same way they persecuted the prophets who were before you" (Matt. 5:10-12). In the Gospel of John, Jesus said,

> "Remember the words I spoke to you: 'No servant is greater than his master.' If they persecuted me, they will persecute you also. They will treat you this way because of my name, for they do not know the One who sent me" (John 15:20-21).

And in the Gospel of Luke, he directly told his disciples, "They will lay hands on you and persecute you" (Luke 21:12).

Is all this sounding a little paranoid? No, charging these men with being paranoid would be justified only if what they said were false or distorting. But Peter, Paul, and Jesus himself not only point us to what has proven true through the history of the church, they have loved us by teaching us truly. Jesus Christ is who he said he is. And the world is opposed to him as he said it would be. What should our response be? We should not threaten the world in return; we should turn around and love the very ones who persecute us, as Jesus did.

The holiness and strangeness of Christians threaten a culture that assumes recognizing differences between people is dangerous. But we are different; we play to a different audience; and we proclaim that a difference exists between saved and unsaved. By recognizing these differences we implicitly proclaim that Christ is Lord over all the earth, and this confronts people right where they live. They don't like that, so they lash out. Still, Christ's words are matters of fact: "Anyone who does not carry his cross and follow me cannot be my disciple" (Luke 14:27). This is the way he went. We must go that way as well.

But suffering is not the only thing the future contains for those who follow Christ. Christ may be our example in suffering but he is also our example in vindication. Don't miss this: our rejection before these rejecters is a passing human verdict. It is not final, and it is not divine. We will be saved through Christ's own vindication. Peter promises, "For Christ died for sins once for all, the righteous for the unrighteous, to bring you to God. He was put to death in the body but was made alive by the Spirit" (1 Pet. 3:18). Noah is also presented as an example of one who was vindicated. In the ark built by Noah,

> only a few people, eight in all, were saved through water, and this water symbolizes baptism that now saves you also—not the removal of dirt from the body but the pledge of a good conscience toward God. It saves you by the resurrection of Jesus Christ, who has gone into heaven and is at God's right hand—with angels, authorities and powers in submission to him (3:20b-22).

Noah is a good example because he and his party were few in number and were saved through the waters of God's judgment; and this is a picture of baptism.

So you, Christian, if you struggle in the face of opposition, wondering if something is wrong because only a few stand with you, then look to the example of Christ. Look also to the example of Noah. God vindicates those who truly follow him.

Not only that, the rejecters will themselves be rejected:

> you also, like living stones, are being built into a spiritual house to be a holy priesthood, offering spiritual sacrifices acceptable to God through Jesus Christ. For in Scripture it says:
>
> > "See, I lay a stone in Zion,
> >   a chosen and precious cornerstone,
> > and the one who trusts in him
> >   will never be put to shame."

Now to you who believe, this stone is precious. But to those who do not believe,

> "The stone the builders rejected
>   has become the capstone,"

and,

> "A stone that causes men to stumble
>   and a rock that makes them fall" (2:5-8a).

Peter also writes,

> It is time for judgment to begin with the family of God; and if it begins with us, what will the outcome be for those who do not obey the gospel of God? And,
>
> > "If it is hard for the righteous to be saved,
> >   what will become of the ungodly and the sinner?" (4:17-18).

So Peter's first readers suffered for two reasons: because they were God's special people, which made them strange to the world; and because they were followers of Christ, who also suffered. Their suffering was nothing to be surprised or dismayed about. Peter writes,

> Dear friends, do not be surprised at the painful trial you are suffering, as though something strange were happening to you. But rejoice that you participate in the sufferings of Christ, so that you may be overjoyed when his glory is revealed (4:12-13).

It is a hard message, but it is true. And I feel bad for people who have been sold a bill of goods they think is Christianity yet the suffering has been cut out and the ostracism has been excised.

WHAT SHOULD SUFFERING CHRISTIANS DO?

Practically, what does Peter call his readers to do? What should we do in the face of suffering and persecution? Peter provides three clear directions.

Be Holy

First, Peter tells us to be holy. "'Be holy, because I am holy,'" God says (1:16). We are a holy people because of our relationship to God. His Holy Spirit lives in us. We must reflect his character as best we can in our lives. Because God is holy, we should be holy. Otherwise, we suffer in vain. Suffering for doing evil is suffering for nothing.

Be Witnesses

Second, Peter tells us to witness to non-Christians. He writes,

> Dear friends, I urge you, as aliens and strangers in the world, to abstain from
> sinful desires, which war against your soul. Live such good lives among the
> pagans that, though they accuse you of doing wrong, they may see your good
> deeds and glorify God on the day he visits us (2:11-12).

Peter actually instructs us to desire the good of those who persecute us. Again,
he learned that from Jesus' example. He writes,

> When they hurled their insults at him, he did not retaliate; when he suffered, he
> made no threats. Instead, he entrusted himself to him who judges justly. He him-
> self bore our sins in his body on the tree so that we might die to sins and live for
> righteousness (2:23-24).

Peter knew firsthand the forgiveness of Christ. He knew firsthand how good
Christ could be even toward one who had denied him. We must also remember how good God has been to us. We deserted him, yet he responded with
incredible love toward us. How then can we treat in any other way those who
mock us? We are not called to withdraw or act paranoid. We are called to give
the same open-handed love that Jesus gave.

Be Loving

Finally, we are to be loving toward each other. This is particularly difficult and
particularly important when the church is suffering through strife and persecution. When stress afflicts the church from the outside, stress on the inside follows. It has always been this way. Just as pressure causes cracks to appear in
pipes, in nuts, and in cement, so it will cause fissures in churches. So Peter
writes very clearly,

> The end of all things is near. Therefore be clear minded and self-controlled so that
> you can pray. Above all, love each other deeply, because love covers over a mul-
> titude of sins. Offer hospitality to one another without grumbling. Each one
> should use whatever gift he has received to serve others, faithfully administering
> God's grace in its various forms. If anyone speaks, he should do it as one speak-
> ing the very words of God. If anyone serves, he should do it with the strength God
> provides, so that in all things God may be praised through Jesus Christ (4:7-11).

Several verses later he writes, "So then, those who suffer according to God's
will should commit themselves to their faithful Creator and continue to do

good" (4:19). We are to *commit* to these things: living for God, trusting ourselves to him, and continuing on. In essence, Peter is telling us, "Give no mind to what is going on around you. Take great mind of what God thinks and says. Live in reverent fear of Him. But to those around you, continue to do good. Don't be dissuaded by any opposition."

As Samuel Rutherford once wrote to a friend, "Duties are ours, events are the Lord's." Or, as the little children's rhyme goes, "Do thy duty; that is best. Leave unto Thy Lord the rest."[6]

CONCLUSION

Commit and continue (4:19). Stay the course. And stand fast, Peter concludes (5:12). Peter himself did that. We do not know this from the Bible, but early sources inform us that Peter died being crucified in Rome as a martyr, because he was living for Christ. Commit yourself to your faithful Creator and continue. Stand fast. Stay the course.

I don't know what God is calling you to. Are you being called to an initial commitment to Christ? To give up a particular sin? To be a witness? To *go* for him? To *stay* for him? What is holding you back? "Commit [yourself] to [your] faithful Creator and continue . . ."

Let us pray:

Father, we do pray that you would speak to us very clearly in our own lives. We pray that you would encourage any who are suffering from persecution and from having abuse heaped upon them because they follow you. We pray, Lord, you would forgive those who heap the abuse. Come to them that they might know the love of the Lord Jesus Christ. And we pray that we would be the instruments of your love.

Father, give us not hearts for vengeance, but hearts for love. Help us to have prayers for mercy, Lord. We trust that you are a just God, but we know in our own lives that you are also a merciful God. So we pray that you would make your mercy clear. Make us living pictures of Your mercy and grace to those around us. Now, by Your Holy Spirit, convict those in our lives who are still in rebellion against you and heap abuse on Christians. By your love, forgive and convict.

Father, for those of us who are your children we pray that you would convict us of any particular sins that we are holding onto—particular compromises with the world we make, perhaps in order to avoid being thought odd or

[6] Henry Wadsworth Longfellow, "The Legend Beautiful," in The Complete Poetical Works of Henry Wadsworth Longfellow (New York: Houghton Mifflin, 1901), 332.

strange. We pray that Your Spirit would convict us of our need to be witnesses for you.

Father, for those of us that you are calling to leave their home, to go and serve elsewhere, we pray you would impress our hearts clearly. If you would call us overseas to serve you, enable us to stop delaying in our response to you, that we would be willing to give up everything to face whatever you would call us to do.

Father, for those of us you are calling quite deliberately to stay here and serve you, we pray you would impress this clearly on our hearts as well. We pray you would give all of us a sense of joy, as Peter writes here, about participating in the sufferings of Christ. Help us, Lord, to commit ourselves to you, and to continue. For Christ's sake we ask this. Amen.

Questions for Reflection

1. What does the fact that Christians are called to holiness (which we have defined as *set apart* and *morally pure*) have to do with being persecuted? Why would the world persecute those who are set apart and growing in moral purity?

2. If being holy means being "set apart," what are we to be set apart *from?* What should we be set apart *to?*

3. How have you seen God change you since becoming a Christian so that the new you would seem strange to the old you? How have you seen God increase your hatred of sin and your love of righteousness since your conversion? Be sure to thank God for his work in your life.

4. Today, many churches work hard at being "relevant," "culturally sensitive," and "with-it" by the standards of their communities. They point to the fact that Jesus told culturally relevant parables about soil, farmers, or lost coins, while Paul spoke of being all things to all men. How can churches exercise an appropriate degree of cultural relevance yet remain willing to be considered strange and even culturally backward by the positions they take and the lives they lead?

5. Would your non-Christian friends call you strange?

6. Peter hears a calling and sees an example for the Christian in Christ's sufferings. They present a model for what we Christians are to do, as we contin-

ually repent of our sins and follow him. Why would suffering be something to which Christians are called? Obedience, sure, but suffering? Why this?

7. We have considered the fact that Jesus promises his followers that they would be persecuted. It is part of our calling as Christians. Was this explained to you either when you first became a Christian or even before you made a profession of faith? Should we tell non-Christians or young Christians who are considering the faith that they can expect persecution, so count the cost? Why or why not?

8. Some Christian teachers today say that if you are suffering, it is because you are sinning. Getting right with God means blessing and prosperity. How would you respond to a friend in Christ who has been sold this false bill of goods?

9. Are you willing to be persecuted?

10. Christians believe a number of strange things that the world finds offensive, such as the fact that repentance and belief in Christ are the only way to be reconciled to God and have eternal life. What are some other areas where Christians believe strange, even offensive, things?

11. As we have seen, Peter tells us to respond to suffering and persecution by being holy, being witnesses, and being loving. Why does living in these three ways make the church more "relevant" to seekers and non-Christians than anything else?

12. Are you being called to an initial commitment to Christ? To give up a particular sin? To be a witness? To *go* for him? To *stay* for him? What is holding you back?

THE MESSAGE OF 2 PETER: CERTAINTY

CERTAINTY: INTRODUCING 2 PETER

BE CERTAIN OF YOUR CALL (1:1-11)

It Is God Who Calls

Not self-generated

Not self-based

Not self-sustained

It Is God's Call on Us

BE CERTAIN OF THE TRUTH (1:12-21)

Peter's Testimony Is Factual

Peter's Testimony Is from God

BE CERTAIN THAT FALSE TEACHERS WILL GIVE FALSE
ASSURANCE (CHAPTER 2)

Characteristics of False Teachers

Spiritually confident

Regularly carnal

The Outcome of False Teachers: God's Judgment

BE CERTAIN THAT GOD WILL JUDGE THE WORLD (CHAPTER 3)

CONCLUSION

22

THE MESSAGE OF 2 PETER: CERTAINTY

CERTAINTY: INTRODUCING 2 PETER[1]

We live in a funny day. The things people used to hold certain are now questioned. And the things people used to question are now held certain.

Not too long ago I attended a huge Promise Keepers meeting in Washington, D.C.'s RFK. Stadium. Fifty thousand men, mostly husbands and fathers, gathered to learn how to be better, well, promise keepers. Fifty years ago, every normal husband and father in the country, let alone every Christian, would have just assumed a man should keep his promises to his wife and children. Family promises used to be certain. Now we have to have an event to remind us.

On the other hand, we are now certain of something of which we used to be uncertain: God's love and acceptance! People used to have great interest in the question of whom God loved, and sought hard for answers in the Bible. For centuries, people puzzled over the question, "Will God accept me?" Now, it is taken for granted that God accepts everyone. The question is not even on the agenda. Ask the question, "Are people sinners?" and you will probably hear the answer, "Hey, nobody's perfect. But God is loving and forgiving. There's no problem here."

Interestingly, in academic circles there is deep uncertainty about the larger questions of truth. You might think that in the place where people learn the most, they would know the most. But they don't. All claims to certainty are regarded as mere conceit. All knowledge is regarded as nothing but guesses.

On the other hand, the average person typically assumes he or she is always right (and that is probably true among academics as well). When a

[1] This sermon was originally preached on May 28, 1995, at Capitol Hill Baptist Church in Washington, D.C.

spouse or a friend or colleague contradicts us in the ordinary matters of life, we do not usually respond, "Well, my understanding of this situation is imperfect. Let's do it your way." No, we usually think the person is wrong, if not less intelligent then we are, and we try to get our own way.

In this study, we are going to work our way through the second letter of the apostle Peter and look at the *four things* Peter tells us we can be certain about if we want to live the life God calls us to live.

BE CERTAIN OF YOUR CALL (1:1-11)

For starters, Peter instructs us to be certain of our calling. Let's look at the letter's first eleven verses:

> Simon Peter, a servant and apostle of Jesus Christ,
>
> To those who through the righteousness of our God and Savior Jesus Christ have received a faith as precious as ours:
>
> Grace and peace be yours in abundance through the knowledge of God and of Jesus our Lord.
>
> His divine power has given us everything we need for life and godliness through our knowledge of him who called us by his own glory and goodness. Through these he has given us his very great and precious promises, so that through them you may participate in the divine nature and escape the corruption in the world caused by evil desires.
>
> For this very reason, make every effort to add to your faith goodness; and to goodness, knowledge; and to knowledge, self-control; and to self-control, perseverance; and to perseverance, godliness; and to godliness, brotherly kindness; and to brotherly kindness, love. For if you possess these qualities in increasing measure, they will keep you from being ineffective and unproductive in your knowledge of our Lord Jesus Christ. But if anyone does not have them, he is nearsighted and blind, and has forgotten that he has been cleansed from his past sins.
>
> Therefore, my brothers, be all the more eager to make your calling and election sure. For if you do these things, you will never fall, and you will receive a rich welcome into the eternal kingdom of our Lord and Savior Jesus Christ (1:1-11).

Verse 10 points us to the first thing we must make certain: "be all the more eager to make your calling and election sure." Fundamentally, making our calling and election sure means making sure we are saved—making sure we are Christians. You should be certain about that! Now, making sure we are Christians requires us to conceptually hold on to two ideas at once: it is God who calls, and it is God's call on us.

It Is God Who Calls

Notice how the first few verses of the letter emphasize the fact that God has called us.

Not self-generated. Our calling is not self-generated or self-empowered. Peter writes, "His divine power has given us everything we need for life and godliness through our knowledge of him who called us by his own glory and goodness" (1:3). We do not call ourselves. And if we are going to be certain of God's calling upon us as Christians, we first have to know that it is his calling!

Not self-based. Our salvation is not based upon ourselves or anything we have done. Peter introduces himself and addresses us in the first line: "Simon Peter, a servant and apostle of Jesus Christ, to those who through the righteousness of our God and Savior Jesus Christ have received a faith as precious as ours" (1:1-2). Our salvation has been won through Christ's righteousness, not ours. If God accepts us on the last day, it will not be because of anything you or I have done. It will be through Jesus Christ and what he has done.

Not self-sustained. Finally, our salvation is not sustained by ourselves. God gives us what we need. As Peter says, "His divine power has given us everything we need for life and godliness through our knowledge of him." We are saved by him, and we are sustained by him. He grants what we need for life and godliness.

So if we are going to make our calling and election sure, the first thing we must recognize is that this calling is fundamentally not of us. It is God's call, based on the righteousness of Christ.

It Is God's Call on Us

Yet it is also God's call on us. Therefore, Peter tells *us* to make our calling sure. "Therefore, my brothers, be all the more eager to make your calling and election sure" (1:10a). *We* make it sure. How do we do that? We make it sure by what we *do*: "For if you do these things, you will never fall, and you will receive a rich welcome into the eternal kingdom of our Lord and Savior Jesus Christ" (1:10b-11). Apparently, we make our calling and election sure by *doing*. We do not *save ourselves* by doing; Peter has been very clear about that. We are saved by God through the righteousness of Christ. Nor do we *sustain ourselves* by doing. His divine power gives us everything we need. Still, we make our calling and election sure by doing these things.

Well, what things are we doing? We are *possessing* certain Christlike qualities in increasing measure. We are adding to them. In 1:5, Peter tells us to "make every effort to add" one quality to another. Then in 1:8-9, he writes,

For if you possess these qualities in increasing measure, they will keep you from being ineffective and unproductive in your knowledge of our Lord Jesus Christ. But if anyone does not have them, he is nearsighted and blind, and has forgotten that he has been cleansed from his past sins.

What are these qualities? Peter tells us in that beautiful list in 1:5-7:

For this very reason, make every effort to add to your faith goodness; and to goodness, knowledge; and to knowledge, self-control; and to self-control, perseverance; and to perseverance, godliness; and to godliness, brotherly kindness; and to brotherly kindness, love.

Peter presents Christian growth as a type of spiral. Christian growth brings Christian assurance of our calling and election. Living as a Christian helps me know that I am a Christian.

So God calls us through grace alone, yet the purity of our lives is an evidence of the reality of our calling. It is a confirmation to others and to ourselves that we are in fact Christians. Here is an example of what I mean. At the Promise Keepers rally, everyone had to wear a wristband. Suppose, for the sake of the example, wearing the wristband was someone else's idea. Someone else paid for the wristband, and someone else put the wristband on me. As I walked about the stadium, the security guards only wanted to know one thing about me: was I wearing the wristband? By wearing it, I was not proclaiming that it was my idea, or that I paid for it, or that I made it. No, it was given to me. They simply wanted to know whether I possessed it and was wearing it. In the same way, we must ask ourselves, is there evidence of our salvation? American Christians tend to associate salvation by grace with salvation as a "one-time" event. Have you noticed that? "Once saved, always saved," we say. So whenever someone hands us a list of qualities that should characterize a Christian life, we quickly respond, "That's salvation by works." Well, not necessarily, says Peter. If we are saved, we are saved because of God's action in our lives. And the action of God is not without effect. Our lives will give evidence of his work. More and more, our lives will be marked by the qualities of faith, goodness, knowledge, and so forth.

If you are reading this as a Christian, you *have* faith. You *are* good. You *have* knowledge. You *exhibit* self-control and perseverance and godliness and brotherly kindness and love. And your life will bear these qualities in increasing measure. If you are not a Christian, your attempt to exhibit any one of these qualities will not make you a Christian. You can be made a Christian only if, by the grace of God, the righteousness of Christ has been imputed to you because you have repented of your sins and believed in him. Do you see what

Peter is saying? Salvation is by grace. But once you have been saved by the grace of God, you will begin to look like someone who is saved. None of us Christians are perfect, but every single one of us who is truly God's child will be marked by these qualities.

Therefore, Peter warns that if you consider yourself a Christian and your life is not marked by these qualities, be careful! You may have gotten hold of some false teaching. Be certain of your calling.

BE CERTAIN OF THE TRUTH (1:12-21)

In order to be certain of their own calling, Peter knows his readers require a second certainty: the certainty of God's truth found in Peter's original testimony.

> So I will always remind you of these things, even though you know them and are firmly established in the truth you now have. I think it is right to refresh your memory as long as I live in the tent of this body, because I know that I will soon put it aside, as our Lord Jesus Christ has made clear to me. And I will make every effort to see that after my departure you will always be able to remember these things (1:12-15).

Daily, we should pray, Lord, help me remember tomorrow what you taught me today.

Peter's Testimony Is Factual

Peter's testimony is not mythical, it is factual:

> We did not follow cleverly invented stories when we told you about the power and coming of our Lord Jesus Christ, but we were eyewitnesses of his majesty. For he received honor and glory from God the Father when the voice came to him from the Majestic Glory, saying, "This is my Son, whom I love; with him I am well pleased." We ourselves heard this voice that came from heaven when we were with him on the sacred mountain.
>
> And we have the word of the prophets made more certain, and you will do well to pay attention to it, as to a light shining in a dark place, until the day dawns and the morning star rises in your hearts (1:16-19).

Unlike many today, we do not hear Peter saying, "I like to look at the world this way" or "I've just always felt that God is . . ." No, he says, "This happened!" He stood on the mount of Transfiguration, where God the Father testified that Jesus is his Son. And now, Peter is simply reporting what the Father himself said about Jesus. This is not Peter's interpretation of the life of Jesus. He did not need to interpret it. The Father interpreted it for him.

Peter's Testimony Is from God

God's Word has always provided God's interpretations of events, not man's interpretation:

> Above all, you must understand that no prophecy of Scripture came about by the prophet's own interpretation. For prophecy never had its origin in the will of man, but men spoke from God as they were carried along by the Holy Spirit (1:20-21).

God has always been truthful, and he has always been interested in letting his people know truth. Peter's testimony, like the words of the prophets, is from God.

I have heard that until the Soviet Union collapsed, the Soviet government would not print accurate maps of Moscow for purchase. Friends of mine who lived in Moscow said the government would deliberately put out maps of Moscow that were false. The false maps would include streets that did not exist, and they would exclude streets that did exist. People who tried driving around the city with one of these maps would constantly find themselves lost.

If you want to know where you are, and how to get where you want to go, you need a truthful map. And Peter understands this. There is no hope of salvation, let alone assurance of salvation, if the Christian message is not true. This issue must be settled first. You will have no certainty of your own salvation if you do not know that the basic message of Christianity is true.[2]

BE CERTAIN THAT FALSE TEACHERS WILL GIVE FALSE ASSURANCE (CHAPTER 2)

Be sure of your calling and be sure you know the truth, Peter says, because you can be certain of something else: false teachers will come and offer false assurance! Peter mentions the prophets of the Old Testament at the end of chapter 1 to prepare us for his warnings about false prophets, which fill up chapter 2. People were claiming to be prophets of God who were not. So he warns his readers,

> But there were also false prophets among the people, just as there will be false teachers among you. They will secretly introduce destructive heresies, even denying the sovereign Lord who bought them—bringing swift destruction on themselves. Many will follow their shameful ways and will bring the way of truth into

---

[2] If you have questions about the truth of the Word of God, a great book is J. I. Packer's *Fundamentalism and the Word of God* (Grand Rapids, Mich.: Eerdmans, 1960). I encourage you to read it.

disrepute. In their greed these teachers will exploit you with stories they have made up (2:1-3a).

Characteristics of False Teachers

What are these false teachers like? Peter describes them in at least two ways.

Spiritually confident. First, they are very confident spiritually. We can see that in their rejection of authority. They

> follow the corrupt desire of the sinful nature and despise authority.
>
> Bold and arrogant, these men are not afraid to slander celestial beings; yet even angels, although they are stronger and more powerful, do not bring slanderous accusations against such beings in the presence of the Lord. But these men blaspheme in matters they do not understand. They are like brute beasts, creatures of instinct, born only to be caught and destroyed, and like beasts they too will perish.
>
> They will be paid back with harm for the harm they have done. Their idea of pleasure is to carouse in broad daylight. They are blots and blemishes, reveling in their pleasures while they feast with you (2:10-13).

These false leaders are not people who state things tentatively. They do not shift back and forth. No, these false teachers are very confident. When any spiritual authority other than their own is mentioned, they mock it.

Regularly carnal. Second, they are regularly carnal. The authority they do acknowledge is the authority of their own desires:

> Their idea of pleasure is to carouse in broad daylight. They are blots and blemishes, reveling in their pleasures while they feast with you. With eyes full of adultery, they never stop sinning; they seduce the unstable; they are experts in greed—an accursed brood! They have left the straight way and wandered off to follow the way of Balaam son of Beor, who loved the wages of wickedness. But he was rebuked for his wrongdoing by a donkey—a beast without speech—who spoke with a man's voice and restrained the prophet's madness.
>
> These men are springs without water and mists driven by a storm. Blackest darkness is reserved for them. For they mouth empty, boastful words and, by appealing to the lustful desires of sinful human nature, they entice people who are just escaping from those who live in error. They promise them freedom, while they themselves are slaves of depravity—for a man is a slave to whatever has mastered him. If they have escaped the corruption of the world by knowing our Lord and Savior Jesus Christ and are again entangled in it and overcome, they are worse off at the end than they were at the beginning. It would have been better for them not to have known the way of righteousness, than to have known it and then to turn their backs on the sacred command that was passed on to

them. Of them the proverbs are true: "A dog returns to its vomit," and, "A sow that is washed goes back to her wallowing in the mud" (2:13-22).

Fundamentally, these false teachers disconnect holiness and salvation in their lives and teaching. "It does not matter how you live," they boast. "Do what you want. You're saved!"

Do you see how dangerous their teaching is? Such teachers continually give people false hope with false stories: "In their greed these teachers will exploit you with stories they have made up" (2:3). How heartbreaking it is, then, to read about whom they exploit! As we just read, "they entice people who are just escaping from those who live in error. They promise them freedom, while they themselves are slaves of depravity." They are like fake doctors who promise healing when they only want the money. They are like Nazi soldiers who promise people showers and then usher them into gas chambers. Is this latter comparison over-the-top? Not if we are talking about eternal life and the salvation of souls. There is a reason, Peter says, that "Blackest darkness is reserved for them" (2:17).

Like Peter's first readers, we need to learn how to detect false teaching today. So look for these two warning signs: false teachers despise the authority of God and his Word, and they live according to their own carnal desires. If you see a teacher who looks like this, you can assume you are looking at a false prophet. Do not listen to such people, Peter says. Instead, look for teachers who understand the Word of God and submit to it in their lives and in their teaching.

The Outcome of False Teachers: God's Judgment

False teachers will be exposed when God judges them. Earlier in the chapter, Peter writes,

> Their condemnation has long been hanging over them, and their destruction has not been sleeping.
>
> For if God did not spare angels when they sinned, but sent them to hell, putting them into gloomy dungeons to be held for judgment; if he did not spare the ancient world when he brought the flood on its ungodly people, but protected Noah, a preacher of righteousness, and seven others; if he condemned the cities of Sodom and Gomorrah by burning them to ashes, and made them an example of what is going to happen to the ungodly. . . .
>
> then the Lord knows how to rescue godly men from trials and to hold the unrighteous for the day of judgment (2:3b-6, 9).

The destruction of these false teachers is as certain as three past acts of judgment. God will judge them like he judged the sinning angels (2:4), the ancient world of Noah's day (2:5), and Sodom and Gomorrah (2:6). Just as God testified to the identity of Jesus at the Transfiguration, he will testify to the identity of these false teachers—in their destruction.

This is an important warning. After all, the false prophets give false assurance. They teach people that they can be called by God yet live confidently and carnally at the same time. Never mind godliness, knowledge, self-control, perseverance, brotherly kindness, and love, they say.

No, Peter says, be certain of your calling and election. Be certain of the truth I have shared with you. Be certain these false teachers will come and mislead believers, and that they will be judged.

BE CERTAIN THAT GOD WILL JUDGE THE WORLD (CHAPTER 3)

Be certain, finally, that God will judge the whole world. That is why Peter exhorts his readers to be certain of their salvation from the get-go.

You see, some will scoff at the prospect of judgment:

> You must understand that in the last days scoffers will come, scoffing and following their own evil desires. They will say, "Where is this 'coming' he promised? Ever since our fathers died, everything goes on as it has since the beginning of creation" (3:3-4).

Do not make the mistake of assuming that because God has graciously held back his judgment, judgment will never come. The world will not continue forever in its present state. That is what these scoffers fail to recognize. "It's been the same since creation," they say. "Why worry?"

God will judge, Peter promises:

> But they deliberately forget that long ago by God's word the heavens existed and the earth was formed out of water and by water. By these waters also the world of that time was deluged and destroyed. By the same word the present heavens and earth are reserved for fire, being kept for the day of judgment and destruction of ungodly men (3:5-7).

God created the heavens and the earth by his word, and he can destroy it by his word. In fact, he already has done so once, with water. Now, God promises to judge the world a second time by the power of his word—not by water but by fire.

Again, dare not think, like the scoffers, "Well, this is all just talk. After all, he hasn't done this." He has, and he will. Do you assume that because God has not done something in your lifetime or your parents' lifetime, he never will? Do you think God is done and finished? The Jews waited thousands of years for the Messiah. During any one of those years, an individual could have scoffed and said the Messiah would never come. But he came, and now the church has been waiting thousands of years for his return. Does the fact he has not yet come mean he will not? Not at all, says Peter.

God is not forgetful, but eternal: "But do not forget this one thing, dear friends: With the Lord a day is like a thousand years, and a thousand years are like a day. The Lord is not slow in keeping his promise, as some understand slowness" (3:8-9a).

What you perceive as God's slowness is his patience with you: "He is patient with you, not wanting anyone to perish, but everyone to come to repentance." (3:9b).

When God's judgment finally comes, it will come suddenly: "But the day of the Lord will come like a thief. The heavens will disappear with a roar; the elements will be destroyed by fire, and the earth and everything in it will be laid bare" (3:10). Of course you do not see it yet; it will be sudden!

CONCLUSION

Given the certainty of God's final judgment, we must know how to live. Therefore, Peter concludes his second letter with an exhortation:

> Since everything will be destroyed in this way, what kind of people ought you to be? You ought to live holy and godly lives as you look forward to the day of God and speed its coming. That day will bring about the destruction of the heavens by fire, and the elements will melt in the heat. But in keeping with his promise we are looking forward to a new heaven and a new earth, the home of righteousness.
>
> So then, dear friends, since you are looking forward to this, make every effort to be found spotless, blameless and at peace with him. Bear in mind that our Lord's patience means salvation, just as our dear brother Paul also wrote you with the wisdom that God gave him. He writes the same way in all his letters, speaking in them of these matters. His letters contain some things that are hard to understand, which ignorant and unstable people distort, as they do the other Scriptures, to their own destruction.
>
> Therefore, dear friends, since you already know this, be on your guard so that you may not be carried away by the error of lawless men and fall from your secure position. But grow in the grace and knowledge of our Lord and Savior Jesus Christ. To him be glory both now and forever! Amen (3:11-18).

Not only will the false teachers face judgment, *you* will face the judgment. And when you face the judgment, your false teachers will not be with you. Nor will I be with you. When you give account for what you have done, you will stand alone. Given the promise of judgment, then, what kind of person ought you to be? If you are a Christian, your life ought to be characterized by looking forward to a home of righteousness. In this world, you will never be perfectly spotless and blameless, but the struggle for spotlessness and blamelessness—what Peter calls "making every effort"—will characterize you. The struggle does not make you a Christian. It is simply what a Christian does.

On that day we will all find we are either at peace with Christ or not. So make sure you are in Christ. "If you do these things, you will never fall, and you will receive a rich welcome into the eternal kingdom of our Lord and Savior Jesus Christ." The whole thrust of this letter is to bring the certainties of truth, false teachers, and judgment into the light so that we can and will make our salvation sure.

Some Christians might say we never need to preach sermons like this one. After all, every person already knows whether or not he is a Christian, right? Can't a Christian just look back to a time in the past when he made a decision for Christ? If he made a decision, then he is a Christian. If he did not, then he needs to.

But Peter never says, "Remember the time you made a decision." Instead, he presses his readers on whether they *now* possess the truth he originally taught them.

Do you see Christian qualities in increasing measure in your life today? Has your life been marked by love, brotherly kindness, godliness, compassion, knowledge, perseverance, and self-control? If it has not been, what comfort do you have concerning your state before God? If it has been, there is comfort, not because you are perfectly good, godly, or loving, but because you can see something of God's activity in your life. You can see him changing you to look more like the Lord Jesus Christ! Peter's message is not, look to what you think you did seventeen years ago. His message is, look to how you are living now. There is hope if you see this fruit in your character; you can make your calling and election sure. We are saved by God's grace through Christ, yet we know we are saved by the evidences in our lives.

Check the map, Peter says. Make sure someone has not given you the wrong map. Make sure that you are on the right way. You have not yet arrived, but make sure you are going in the right direction. If you are not sure you are looking at the right map, talk to a Christian friend or pastor. Search the Scriptures. Make sure that you will be saved *then* by finding the marks of God's presence in your character and life *now*.

Let us pray:

Lord, we know that in the life to come the hours we have spent together will seem like passing moments. We know that you clearly see into us—and in ways

*that we don't even see ourselves. So we know that Peter has to write a letter
like this to encourage us to look clearly at ourselves. Because it's not always
clear to us. So, Lord, we pray that by your Holy Spirit you would teach the
truth of this letter to us. Father, help us to labor to make our calling and election sure. We praise you that salvation is by grace, and we praise you for the
fact that if we are saved by your grace we will live as gracious people. Lord,
give us the help of your Spirit for knowing the truth about ourselves, we ask
it for Jesus' sake. Amen.*

Questions for Reflection

1. The first thing Peter tells us to be certain about is our calling. And that means
making sure we are Christians. Why isn't that as simple as pointing back to
the day you made a profession of faith or were baptized?

2. Does the fact that God calls us to salvation absolve us of responsibility?

3. The task of making our calling and election sure requires a certain measure
of self-examination as we look for the fruits of faith, goodness, knowledge, self-
control, perseverance, godliness, brotherly kindness, and love in our lives—and
in increasing measure. How can you involve your family members and your
church in this process? How would journaling be a benefit to this process?

4. What progress in the faith can you recount over the past year of your life?
Be sure to thank God for the progress you see!

5. Can a person be a Christian and live in open, willful defiance of Scripture?
How do you respond to someone who professes to be a Christian yet lives in
this manner? What role or responsibility does the church have in this?

6. The second thing Peter tells us to be certain about is the truth. If the first certainty focuses on our lives, the second certainty focuses on our beliefs. What
is the source of Christian belief?

7. Is there anything humans need to know about how to be saved, how to live
in a manner pleasing to God, and how to find guidance for their lives that is
not contained in the sixty-six books of the Bible?

8. According to 2 Peter 1:20-21, what makes Scripture different from every
other written text in the world?

9. The third thing Peter tells us to be certain about is that false teachers will come and give false assurance of salvation and peace with God. Is that happening today? Who is giving false assurance today in the church? Outside the church?

10. As we have seen, false teachers display a spiritual confidence that prompts them to mock other authorities and teachers. Yet this same mocking of authority can occur not just in teachers but in all of us. How does your heart tend to respond to the authority of those over you? Are you grateful for their authority? Do you perceive it as a God-given blessing? Or do you secretly condemn them in your mind? How would you characterize your heart, particularly toward leaders in the church? Would you say that you err in the direction of suspiciousness or in the direction of giving them the benefit of the doubt, perhaps too much benefit? Pray that God would grant you humility toward those whom he has placed over you. Pray that he would teach you the submission of Jesus himself.

11. Peter finally tells us we can be certain that God's judgment will come. Spurred on by this sort of biblical teaching, Jonathan Edwards included two pledges in his "Resolutions" to deliberately meditate on the Bible's promise of hell. Resolution Ten states, "Resolved, when I feel pain, to think of the pains of martyrdom, and of hell." Resolution Fifty-five reads, "Resolved, to endeavor to my utmost to act as I can think I should do, if, I had already seen the happiness of heaven, and hell torments." Have you spent much time meditating on God's coming punishment for those who do not believe? Do you believe this would be a beneficial exercise? Why or why not?

12. Why does God delay his judgment? How does this sometimes confuse people?

13. What will you say to God when you stand before his throne and he holds up the record of your sins and rebellion against him? What will be your plea?

14. On the one hand, we have been told that we cannot be saved by what we do, but only through faith in Christ's work. On the other hand, we have been told that we must "make every effort" to add to our faith goodness, and to goodness knowledge, and so forth. So are we saved by faith or by works? How do we make sense of this?

THE MESSAGE OF 1 JOHN: CHRISTIANITY AND THE FLESH

23

THE MESSAGE OF 1 JOHN: CHRISTIANITY AND THE FLESH

THE REAL THING: INTRODUCING 1 JOHN[1]

Edward R. Murrow once said about the Vietnam War, "Anyone who isn't confused doesn't really understand the situation."

Some people may feel this statement applies to Christianity as well. Anyone who is not confused about Christianity does not really understand it. After all, there are so many differences between this church and that church, this theology and that theology, living this way and living that way. We could multiply these distinctions again and again.

From the media, well, who knows what you would think of Christianity if everything you knew about it came from the media? On the one hand, you might think Christians are militant revolutionaries. On the other hand, you might think they are poor, pale reflections of our culture.

Amid all this, what is a real Christian? How do we know if we have gotten hold of the real thing? John wrote his first letter to answer such questions. Many times throughout the letter, John says, "This is how we know." This is how we know who the children of God are. This is how we know what Christian love is. And so forth. His letter is written to people who are confused and who want to know if they have gotten hold of the real thing.

A good way to begin our study of John's letter is by looking at several passages. Beginning in the first chapter, we read, "This is the message we have heard from him and declare to you: God is light; in him there is no darkness at all. If we claim to have fellowship with him yet walk in darkness, we lie and do not live by the truth. But if we walk in the light, as he is in the light, we have fellowship with one another, and the blood of Jesus, his Son, purifies us from

---

[1] This sermon was originally preached on June 4, 1995, at Capitol Hill Baptist church in Washington, D.C.

all sin" (1:5-7). Immediately, John puts our profession of having fellowship with God to the test. Are we really walking in the light?

Other passages in the book have the same tone and provoke the same questions. Consider this passage in chapter 3:

> This is how we know what love is: Jesus Christ laid down his life for us. And we ought to lay down our lives for our brothers. If anyone has material possessions and sees his brother in need but has no pity on him, how can the love of God be in him? Dear children, let us not love with words or tongue but with actions and in truth. This then is how we know that we belong to the truth, and how we set our hearts at rest in his presence whenever our hearts condemn us. For God is greater than our hearts, and he knows everything.
>
> Dear friends, if our hearts do not condemn us, we have confidence before God and receive from him anything we ask, because we obey his commands and do what pleases him. And this is his command: to believe in the name of his Son, Jesus Christ, and to love one another as he commanded us. Those who obey his commands live in him, and he in them. And this is how we know that he lives in us: We know it by the Spirit he gave us (3:16-24).

Or this passage in chapter 5:

> Everyone who believes that Jesus is the Christ is born of God, and everyone who loves the father loves his child as well. This is how we know that we love the children of God: by loving God and carrying out his commands. This is love for God: to obey his commands. And his commands are not burdensome, for everyone born of God overcomes the world. This is the victory that has overcome the world, even our faith. Who is it that overcomes the world? Only he who believes that Jesus is the Son of God (5:1-5).

John's goal in this letter, clearly, is to say, "it is *not this,* it is *that.*" So throughout the letter he intertwines several key themes that help the Christian (or non-Christian) test whether he or she walks in the light and in fellowship with God. Specifically, John provides three tests of whether we have gotten hold of the real thing: a doctrinal test, a moral test, and a test of love.

DOCTRINAL TEST: DO YOU BELIEVE JESUS IS THE SON OF GOD?

God is a God of truth. Twice in this letter John refers to God as the Spirit of Truth (4:6; 5:6). In John's Gospel, Jesus himself says, "I am the truth" (14:6). This does not mean that the Truth is God. It means that God is concerned about truth, and that he is the standard of all truth. The first test for determining whether you have gotten hold of the real thing, then, is a doctrinal test.

John says very clearly, *you must believe Jesus is the Messiah and the Son of God come in the flesh*.

A pernicious untruth was circulating in the church to which John was writing (which many believe was in Ephesus). Apparently, some people were teaching that God never really took on human flesh. They said that human flesh is sinful, evil, and bad. So God may have *appeared* as a human in Jesus, but he did not *really take on* flesh. Basically, these false teachers separated the human Jesus of flesh and the divine Christ of spirit.

Interestingly, Paul had warned the elders of the church in Ephesus decades earlier that false teachers would come. He had said, "I know that after I leave, savage wolves will come in among you and will not spare the flock. Even from your own number men will arise and distort the truth in order to draw away disciples after them" (Acts 20:29-30). Paul alluded to this again in his second letter to Timothy, who was then pastor of the church in Ephesus (2 Tim. 4:3-4).

And now the false teachers had come, teaching that Christ was not fully human. Is this false teaching merely an academic matter? Is this something to leave in the classroom? Not at all. Without a fully human and fully divine mediator, we cannot have the atoning sacrifice for sins that we need.

So John responds with no uncertainty. Jesus had a real human body! John had seen, heard, and even touched the Lord Jesus. He writes,

> That which was from the beginning, which we have heard, which we have seen with our eyes, which we have looked at and our hands have touched—this we proclaim concerning the Word of life. The life appeared; we have seen it and testify to it, and we proclaim to you the eternal life, which was with the Father and has appeared to us. We proclaim to you what we have seen and heard, so that you also may have fellowship with us. And our fellowship is with the Father and with his Son, Jesus Christ (1:1-3).

True and false spirits can be recognized, John says, by whether they recognize these things:

> Dear friends, do not believe every spirit, but test the spirits to see whether they are from God, because many false prophets have gone out into the world. This is how you can recognize the Spirit of God: Every spirit that acknowledges that Jesus Christ has come in the flesh is from God, but every spirit that does not acknowledge Jesus is not from God. This is the spirit of the antichrist, which you have heard is coming, and even now is already in the world (4:1-3)

Not only is Jesus fully human, he is fully God, and those who are the children of God will acknowledge this. John writes,

> And we have seen and testify that the Father has sent his Son to be the Savior of the world. If anyone acknowledges that Jesus is the Son of God, God lives in him and he in God. And so we know and rely on the love God has for us (4:14-16a).

John writes to these young Christians to give them confidence. It is hard to believe something confidently when different teachers are teaching opposite things on matters as fundamental as who Jesus is. John realizes this and wants to clear up the whole mess. So he writes, "Everyone who believes that Jesus is the Christ is born of God, and everyone who loves the father loves his child as well" (5:1). The dividing line is very simple. If you believe Jesus is the Christ (the Greek word for Messiah), then you are a child of God. If you do not, you are not. Several verses later, John says, "Who is it that overcomes the world? Only he who believes that Jesus is the Son of God" (5:5). And then again: "I write these things to you who believe in the name of the Son of God so that you may know that you have eternal life" (5:13).

In short, John says you must believe the right doctrine about who Jesus is. Jesus is fully God and fully man.

People often have negative ideas about doctrine. Decades ago, at the height of the ecumenical movement, people dismissed doctrine as an unnecessary encumbrance on the road to unity. These days, it is regarded more as an interesting artifact, a curious but finally unimportant facet of our diversity. "Of course we all believe different things," many of our contemporaries say. But John knows that the doctrine of the person of Christ is fundamental.

A few years ago a radio interviewer went out on the streets of a major northeastern city to ask this question: "Who is Jesus Christ?" One person said Christ is a "pure essence of energy." Another person said he was "a good man." Another person said, "Our leader." Still another said, "I'm not sure . . . I just don't know."

You see, I do not think the church needs to worry about atheism today. That superstition has never seriously threatened the church of Jesus Christ. As a friend of mine once said, "The real danger is not unbelief, but wrong belief; not irreligion, but heresy; not the doubter, but the deceiver." Wrong belief, heresy, and deceivers are what concern John. So he refutes the idea that Christ was merely a fleshless, impersonal principal that we tap into for higher energy. That is not the language of the New Testament, or of Jesus, or of the disciples. He also refutes the idea that Jesus was merely a teacher who taught the way of God, who became hungry and tired, and who one day bled to death. He was a human who could bleed and get hungry, but he is far more. Jesus is fully God and fully man.

We must get the doctrine of Christ's person right, as John presents it, because our salvation hangs on it. Our salvation depends on the sacrifice of the body of Jesus as the utterly unique God-man. If you take away Jesus' physical body, there is no sacrifice. Only a human can sacrificially stand in place of a human, and so payment for sin could not have been made without Jesus' humanity. On the other hand, if you take away the fact that Jesus was God incarnate, his sacrifice loses its infinite worth and its ability to exhaust God's infinite wrath. Only the infinite God himself could act as the "atoning sacrifice" for "the sins of the whole world" (2:2). The sacrifice of one who is fully God and fully man was necessary for guilty man to be reconciled to a holy God.

It is this most awkward truth of all—Jesus is fully God and fully man in one person—that John pulls together as essential for the gospel. Only with this doctrine does what happened on the cross make sense. Who Christ is and what Christ did are bound together. You cannot change one without changing the other. If you try to parse away who Jesus is, you may have a neater philosophy but you will misunderstand Jesus and forfeit the gospel. You will miss what Jesus taught about himself and what the apostles preached. And if you do not understand who Jesus is, says John, you are not a Christian.

You must know that in his love for us God himself took on flesh, lived a perfect life, died the death sinners deserve, and then arose in victory over sin and death.

When you share the gospel with others, you do not merely share your experience (though we certainly can share something about our own experience). Most fundamentally, you share objective truth. You share particular doctrines that are rooted in history about who Jesus is and what he did. You might decide this is not important, but then you would have to take 1 John out of your Bible. John makes it clear that a person must know that Jesus is fully God and fully man in order to be saved.

Do you believe that Jesus is the Christ, the Son of God? If you do not, or if you are not certain, you may wish to consider further why the identity of Jesus is absolutely central to Christianity. Not only that, you may wish to consider why two thousand years' worth of Christians would tell you this is the most important question you could ever ask. Who is Jesus?

MORAL TEST: DO YOU OBEY THE COMMANDS OF GOD?

Not only does John present a doctrinal test, he presents a moral test as well. If you claim to know Jesus but you do not obey him, your words are false. If you have gotten hold of the real thing, you not only believe in the Son of God, you obey his commands. In other words, true belief in Jesus shows itself in righteousness.

John writes,

> We know that we have come to know him if we obey his commands. The man
> who says, "I know him," but does not do what he commands is a liar, and the
> truth is not in him. . . . This is how we know we are in him: Whoever claims to
> live in him must walk as Jesus did (2:3-4, 5b-6).

In the next chapter, John says the same thing, not positively, in terms of following God's commands, but negatively, in terms of continuing in sin: "You
know that he appeared so that he might take away our sins. And in him is no
sin. No one who lives in him keeps on sinning. No one who continues to sin
has either seen him or known him" (3:5-6).

Earlier, we saw that a pernicious doctrinal untruth was circulating in the
church. Not surprisingly, the church's problems did not stop there. There was
also the problem of sin. People were living in ways that were wrong, thinking
they were beyond good and evil. John points us to their malady when he
exhorts them,

> Do not love the world or anything in the world. If anyone loves the world, the
> love of the Father is not in him. For everything in the world—the cravings of sin-
> ful man, the lust of his eyes and the boasting of what he has and does—comes
> not from the Father but from the world. The world and its desires pass away,
> but the man who does the will of God lives forever (2:15-17).

Certainly these people claimed to love God. They would not have been in a
church if they did not. But they also claimed to love the world. And John is
saying that such a combination of loves is impossible. Two loves like this will
pull your heart in two ways and finally rip it apart. In short, the difference
between obedience and disobedience is the difference between love of God and
love of the world.

Yet so great is the divergence between obedience and disobedience, John
is not content to use just one illustration to display the starkness of the contrast. He also uses the contrast between light and dark. "God is light," he
writes, "in him there is no darkness at all. If we claim to have fellowship with
him yet walk in the darkness, we lie and do not live by the truth. But if we walk
in the light, as he is in the light, we have fellowship with one another, and the
blood of Jesus, his Son, purifies us from all sin" (1:5-7). He does not say, "Light
is God," but "God is light." Walking in darkness is walking in sin. We walk
in darkness when we want to hide from God's presence.

And as if the contrast between light and darkness were not severe enough,
John finds yet one more illustration—children of God versus children of the

devil! "If you know that he is righteous, you know that everyone who does what is right has been born of him. How great is the love the Father has lavished on us, that we should be called children of God!" (2:29–3:1). Those who are obedient, then, are children of God. Several verses later John says this:

> Dear children, do not let anyone lead you astray. He who does what is right is righteous, just as he is righteous. He who does what is sinful is of the devil, because the devil has been sinning from the beginning. The reason the Son of God appeared was to destroy the devil's work. No one who is born of God will continue to sin, because God's seed remains in him; he cannot go on sinning, because he has been born of God. This is how we know who the children of God are and who the children of the devil are: Anyone who does not do what is right is not a child of God; nor is anyone who does not love his brother (3:7-10).

It's very simple. If you are a child of God, you will live like God. If you are a child of the devil, you will live like the devil. That's all there is to it. Now, no Christian perfectly lives like God. And thankfully, no non-Christian lives exactly like the devil. So don't misunderstand what I am saying—Christians will make mistakes and sin. John follows his remarks on the contrast between light and darkness by saying, "But if anybody does sin, we have one who speaks to the Father in our defense—Jesus Christ, the Righteous One" (2:1). Jesus speaks for us; he atones for our sins. Still, the contrasts between love of the world versus love of God, light versus darkness, and children of God versus children of the devil are stark and absolute. Your life will display one general pattern or the other. It will tend in one direction or the other.

So ask yourself, do you obey God's commands? As we have seen, "We know that we have come to know him if we obey his commands" (2:3). Or as John says in chapter 5,

> Everyone who believes that Jesus is the Christ is born of God, and everyone who loves the father loves his child as well. This is how we know that we love the children of God: by loving God and carrying out his commands. This is love for God: to obey his commands. (5:1-3a).

In all of this, John certainly is not pointing to the ever-popular "nice people are Christians" doctrine. All of us know nice people who are *not* Christians. Many of us, before we were Christians, were nice people. No, the moral test is subsequent to the doctrinal test. You might say it is the proof of the doctrinal test. In other words, both tests are necessary.

So John writes to a church filled with people claiming to be Christians, and firstly he exhorts them to believe the right things about Jesus Christ. Then, secondly, he exhorts them to obedience. If they are not obeying Christ's commands, then their "belief" is not real. It is a lie, and they are not Christians. True belief, or what we can call biblical faith, is characterized by believing *and* obeying. You might say it is *really* believing. It is the kind of believing you exercise every time you rest your weight on a church pew. Your believing is confirmed by your *doing,* in this case by your resting your weight. This is the kind of believing John means.

For us today, this means the most orthodox person in the world, who has every point of doctrine correct, is not a Christian if his or her right thinking is not coupled with right living. Let me use a story to illustrate this point. Suppose Bob starts a business and he puts me in charge of it. Then Bob travels to Europe for some business deals and leaves me with very careful instructions. While he is away, Bob sends me a few more letters with further instructions about what should be done in the office. Suppose, then, Bob returns several weeks later and finds the office in ruins. The receptionist sits listening to the local disco station while ignoring the ringing telephone. Everyone else is playing checkers, chess, or cards. There is trash in the halls. And Bob's email is filled with angry notes from canceling customers and clients. So Bob walks up to me and says, "Mark, what happened here? Didn't you get my letters?" I smile and say, "Oh, yeah, I got your letters. Not only did I get your letters, I loved reading them. Bob, those were wonderful letters! You know, those letters were so good that I photocopied them and gave a copy to everybody in the office. And they liked them so much we had letter studies. After work, we gathered to study them together. We also had them framed. There they are, up on the wall! What great letters! Some of us had even begun memorizing parts of them and are having our children memorize them." Well, you can only image what Bob might say at this point. "Mark, why didn't you do what the letters said to do? And what do you mean, you loved the letters? Of course you don't!"[2]

This is what John is saying to these Christians: "You might have all your doctrine right and say you believe in Jesus. But why aren't you obeying his commands?" If we claim to walk in the light, but we walk in the dark, we lie. Words alone, without actions, are empty. You are not a disciple if there are no actions. A disciple is one who follows. You can be as emotionally attached as you want to the word "Christian," but if you are not following Christ you are not a disciple. Besides, why do you think Jesus lived the life he did if the kind of life you live is not important? Why do you think he died the death he did? How you and I live is very important.

---

[2] Illustration adapted from Charles Swindoll, *Improving Your Serve: The Art of Unselfish Living* (Waco, Tex.: Word, 1981), 170.

Do you obey the commands of God? If you do not, pray and repent. Turn away from your sin. John Newton, the one-time slave trader who became a Christian and then wrote the hymn "Amazing Grace," once prayed with his family, "I am not what I ought to be. I am not what I wish to be. I am not what I hope to be. Yet I can truly say, I am not what I once was. By the grace of God I am what I am." When you have gotten hold of the real thing, you believe in the Son of God and you increasingly obey his commands.

LOVE TEST: DO YOU LOVE THE PEOPLE OF GOD?

There is one final test. Do we love one another as God has loved us? John writes, "And he has given us this command: Whoever loves God must also love his brother" (4:21). If you have gotten hold of the real thing, not only will you believe Jesus is the son of God; and not only will you obey the commands of God; you will also love the people of God. John is not commanding his readers to love the people of God. He is simply saying, anyone who has gotten hold of the real thing *will* love the people of God.

Apparently, there was this third problem in the church that concerned John: lovelessness. People disagreed with one another, and love was leaking out of the church like air out of a punctured tire. As the church sunk down to the tire's rim, it was getting hard to keep moving. In response, John writes, "God is love" (4:16). Again, not "Love is God," but "God is love."

Jesus is our greatest example of the love of God. In John's Gospel, Jesus says, "A new command I give you: Love one another. As I have loved you, so you must love one another. By this all men will know that you are my disciples, if you love one another" (John 13:34-35).

John returns to the centrality of love in the Christian life again and again in his first letter.

Anyone who claims to be in the light but hates his brother is still in the darkness. Whoever loves his brother lives in the light, and there is nothing in him to make him stumble. But whoever hates his brother is in the darkness and walks around in the darkness; he does not know where he is going, because the darkness has blinded him (1 John 2:9-11).

We know that we have passed from death to life, because we love our brothers. Anyone who does not love remains in death (3:14).

Dear friends, let us love one another, for love comes from God. Everyone who loves has been born of God and knows God. Whoever does not love does not know God, because God is love. This is how God showed his love among us: He sent his one and only Son into the world that we might live through him. This

is love: not that we loved God, but that he loved us and sent his Son as an atoning sacrifice for our sins. Dear friends, since God so loved us, we also ought to
love one another. No one has ever seen God; but if we love one another, God
lives in us and his love is made complete in us (4:7-12).

We love because he first loved us. If anyone says, "I love God," yet hates his
brother, he is a liar. For anyone who does not love his brother, whom he has
seen, cannot love God, whom he has not seen. And he has given us this command: Whoever loves God must also love his brother (4:19-21).

I once heard a preacher say about these last verses (to paraphrase),

Who knows, maybe God looks like the brother you cannot love. Maybe God
has some of the characteristics that really irritate you about that brother. Not if
they are sins, of course. Still, how can you feel certain that you love God, when
you cannot love a brother whom you have seen?

John's joy is made complete by his readers' fellowship in belief and in love:
"We write this to make our joy complete" (1:4). And God's love is made complete in us through our obedience: "But if anyone obeys his word, God's love
is truly made complete in him" (2:5). And his love is made complete through
our love for one another: "but if we love one another, God lives in us and his
love is made complete in us" (4:12). And love that has been made complete
gives confidence:

God is love. Whoever lives in love lives in God, and God in him. In this way,
love is made complete among us so that we will have confidence on the day of
judgment, because in this world we are like him. There is no fear in love. But
perfect love drives out fear, because fear has to do with punishment. The one
who fears is not made perfect in love (4:16b-18).

Such love also gives assurance: "We know that we have passed from death to
life, because we love our brothers. Anyone who does not love remains in
death" (3:14).

Imagine a church that has correct doctrine and that keeps God's laws. The
people live moral and righteous lives. But then imagine how this church would
look if its members shared little love for one another. How hollow it would all
sound! Their doctrinal exactness. Their moral rigor. Without love, as another
apostle said, "I am nothing" (1 Cor. 13:2).

And this is not a message for non-Christians "out there." People out there
cannot love themselves into the kingdom. If you are not a Christian, you might
find yourself loved into the kingdom by God, but you cannot love yourself into

the kingdom. If you are a Christian, this is John's message: You must love. Really, you will love, as he has loved you.

Have you heard the expression, "If looks could kill . . ." Mercifully, they cannot, because there would be a lot of dead people lying around, even in the church. We need love. We need Christlike consideration for others. We do not just need doctrinal belief and morality, though we need those too! We also need the active love that induces church members to give themselves away for one another. We need to learn to love people who do not look like we do or act as we do. We tend to form friendships with people who are just like ourselves. Yet Jesus responds, "What are you doing more than others? Do not even the pagans do that?" (Matt. 5:47). The most honest test of Christian love is whether we love those with whom we have disagreed or had difficulty. If we simply love those who agree with us, we have no evidence of Christian love. Christian love looks like Christ's love. Whom did Christ love and lay down his life for? Sinners! People in rebellion against him. At the very point of our rebellion, he laid down his life for us. That is Christian love.

Do you love the people of God? I am not asking if you feel *well disposed* toward them. Do you actually and actively love them? Do you use your hands for them? Your money? Your lips? If not, perhaps you have not understood God's love for you.

What then should you do? First look to Christ. Consider his love for you. "This is how we know what love is: Jesus Christ laid down his life for us. And we ought to lay down our lives for our bothers" (3:16). Or as John says a little later,

> This is how God showed his love among us: He sent his one and only Son into the world that we might live through him. This is love: not that we loved God, but that he loved us and sent his Son as an atoning sacrifice for our sins. Dear friends, since God so loved us, we also ought to love one another (4:9-11).

Having begun by looking to the love of Christ for you, consider afresh the person who has injured you or rejected you or has not forgiven you. This is exactly the person you are called to love in Jesus, because this is how Jesus has loved you. This is fundamental to being a Christian.

Knowing who Jesus is—getting our doctrine right—is essential because it affects our ability to love others. The more you understand who Jesus is, the more amazing his love becomes. When you water down your understanding of who Jesus is, you not only destroy your doctrine, you deafen your ears to the love of God. Why else would John begin his letter saying, "I saw, heard, and touched him!" He wants us to know that the perfect and holy God actually took on flesh and loved us to the fullest measure through his death. That is love. And that is the model for our love. You and I work on how to love others by working on our understanding of who Jesus is and what he has done.

CONCLUSION

John concludes his letter with a short verse over which commentators have spilled gallons of ink: "Dear children, keep yourselves from idols" (5:21). That is the final line. There is no benediction; no prayer for God's grace to be upon us. No, he just says, "Dear children, keep yourselves from idols," even though idolatry has not been mentioned once in the letter. People wonder, why on earth does he introduce idolatry now?

We have already seen that for John, faith *is* believing, obeying, and loving. Any faith that does not contain all three elements, John says, is false. And then he concludes with the exhortation, "Dear children, keep yourselves from idols." What he is saying is simple: keep yourselves from a false and distorted Jesus. And you know you have a false and distorted Jesus in one of three ways. First, you might have the wrong doctrine. You might conceive of Christ as an impersonal principle or a spiritual force. Alternatively, you might think he was just a great, human teacher. No, God became incarnate. Keep yourselves from such imposter Christs. Those are just idols to suit your desires.

Second, you might think God is indifferent to sin. No, God incarnate died for our sins. He is deeply concerned for how we live! If you are worshiping a God who is indifferent to sin, you are not worshiping the true God; you are worshiping an idol of your own making.

Third, you might think God is unconcerned with love. Get your doctrine right; don't do anything grossly immoral; go to church. That's enough, right? No, the God incarnate died for our sins because of his love for us. He leads his children to love one another with the same love. If you miss this, you have missed the real God and are worshiping some idol.

"Dear children, keep yourselves from idols." If you keep yourself from those idols, you can know you have gotten hold of the real thing.

Let us pray:

Father, we pray that you would forgive us for our inattention to the truth about the Lord Jesus. Lord, how often we just don't like the way somebody says something, so we feel entitled to ignore it. We thank you, Lord, that you care for the truth and that you are a God of truth. Lord, we ask that you would forgive us for the sin in our lives and for all of the ways we have not lived con-

sistently with the faith we claim. We know that you are light and that in you there is no darkness. We pray, Lord, that you would cleanse us from our sins. And we pray that you would forgive us for our cold hearts. We see in the Lord Jesus an amazing display of your love to those who hate you. We pray that you would teach us of your great goodness to us in Christ and of your amazing love. Father, win our hearts to you. Make our hearts soft in your hands. Teach us to love as you have loved us. We pray for Jesus' sake. Amen.

Questions for Reflection

1. Is believing the right thing necessary to become a Christian? What do you have to believe about who Christ is?

2. What objection do many people today make to the claim that we *must* believe the right doctrine about who Jesus is? How would you respond?

3. Is sharing your personal testimony the same thing as sharing the gospel? Why or why not?

4. In what practical ways have you used the resources offered by your local church to become a person who is obedient to God? In what ways do you try to help others in your church?

5. We have considered the fact that the most honest test of Christian love is whether we love those with whom we have disagreed or had difficulty. If we simply love those who agree with us, we have no evidence of Christian love. Think of somebody in your church right now whom you find difficult to love or get along with. What steps can you take to begin loving that person as Christ calls you to love him or her? Be sure to thank God as he increases the love in your heart!

6. One way to practice loving others in the church is to look for evidences of God's grace in their lives. What evidences of God's grace have you seen in your own life? What evidences of grace have you seen in the life of a close friend? What evidences have you seen in the life of that difficult person you thought about in question 13?

7. Drawing from the doctrinal test, the moral test, and the love test but using your own words, summarize what a Christian is.

8. There are at least three ways, we have observed, that a Christian can fall into idolatry. First, you might have the wrong doctrine. You might conceive of Christ as an impersonal principle, a spiritual force, or a great human teacher. Do you have the right doctrine of who Christ is? On what do you base your doctrine? What does your church teach?

9. Second, you might fall into idolatry by thinking God is indifferent to sin. Yet God incarnate died for our sins because he is deeply concerned for how we live. Is there some behavior, habit, pastime, attitude, person, possession, emotion (anger, bitterness, misdirected love, etc.) you refuse to give up for God's sake? If so, how is it any different from an idol?

10. Third, you might fall into idolatry by thinking God is unconcerned with love, as if getting your doctrine right and not doing anything grossly immoral is enough. Yet God incarnate died for our sins because he loves us. And then he leads his children to love one another with the same love. If the people closest to you were surveyed, would they say you are more concerned with defending the truth, expressing love, or both? If you examine your life over the past several years, assuming you embrace the doctrines of the Christian faith, can you see evidences of God's love growing in your heart through your love for others in the church? How? Praise him for the evidence you do see!

THE MESSAGE OF 2 JOHN: TRUTH AND LOVE

24

THE MESSAGE OF 2 JOHN: TRUTH AND LOVE

LOVE VERSUS TRUTH[1]

"Truth or tact? You have to choose. Most times they are not compatible." The old radio comedian Eddie Cantor said that. Here is a psychologist on the same topic: "The truth is often a terrible weapon of aggression. It is possible to lie, and even to murder, for the truth."[2] Such comments raise the question, is truth a loving thing? From comedians to counselors, many of us feel that it is not. There is a tension between truth and love, we think.

You get something of this in John Gray's best-selling book *Men Are from Mars, Women Are from Venus*. Gray suggests men are more concerned about problem solving and truth telling, while women are more concerned with empathy and relationships. Again, there is a divide. Truth and love seem to exclude one another. If you want to show love, perhaps you will want to ease up on the truth. Love is amendable and soft. Truth, on the other hand, can be harsh, even aggressive. So, if you don't really love someone, well, you can tell them what you really think!

This division is even found among churches. There are love-oriented churches and truth-oriented churches. Truth-oriented churches major in apologetics, doctrine, evangelism, and preaching, while love-oriented churches stress counseling, fellowship, recovery groups, and soup kitchens.

INTRODUCING 2 JOHN

If this division sounds right to you, John's second letter should be of interest. It is short enough for us to begin by previewing the entire letter.

---

[1] This sermon was originally preached on June 11, 1995, Capitol Hill Baptist Church in Washington, D.C.
[2] Alfred Adler, *Problems of Neurosis* (New York: Harper & Row, 1964), 24.

The elder,

To the chosen lady and her children, whom I love in the truth—and not I only, but also all who know the truth—because of the truth, which lives in us and will be with us forever:

Grace, mercy and peace from God the Father and from Jesus Christ, the Father's Son, will be with us in truth and love.

It has given me great joy to find some of your children walking in the truth, just as the Father commanded us. And now, dear lady, I am not writing you a new command but one we have had from the beginning. I ask that we love one another. And this is love: that we walk in obedience to his commands. As you have heard from the beginning, his command is that you walk in love.

Many deceivers, who do not acknowledge Jesus Christ as coming in the flesh, have gone out into the world. Any such person is the deceiver and the antichrist. Watch out that you do not lose what you have worked for, but that you may be rewarded fully. Anyone who runs ahead and does not continue in the teaching of Christ does not have God; whoever continues in the teaching has both the Father and the Son. If anyone comes to you and does not bring this teaching, do not take him into your house or welcome him. Anyone who welcomes him shares in his wicked work.

I have much to write to you, but I do not want to use paper and ink. Instead, I hope to visit you and talk with you face to face, so that our joy may be complete.

The children of your chosen sister send their greetings (2 John 1-13).

One of the first things people ask about this letter concerns this "chosen lady" in verse 1. Who is she? Is this not an unusual way to begin a New Testament letter? At first, you might wonder if this is a first-century love letter that got stuck into the Bible. He does say in verse 5, "I ask that we love one another."

Yet if this were a letter to an individual, we would expect a number of things in the text to be different. For instance, the adjective "chosen" in front of "lady" would probably have an article in front of it in the Greek text. Also, the author probably would not have slipped so easily from the singular "you" to the plural "you" in verses 6, 8, 10, and 12, a feature we can discern, again, in the Greek text. More evidence could be given within the letter, but we should also notice that this kind of language is not without precedent in the New Testament. Paul uses the image of the church as the bride of Christ in Ephesians 5. John does the same in Revelation 21. And Peter closes his first letter by saying, "She who is in Babylon, chosen together with you, sends you her greetings" (1 Pet. 5:13). In short, many Christians from the early centuries of the church, as well as the majority of modern biblical scholars and interpreters, have taken this lady to be John's metaphorical way of greeting a local church and its members. All the domestic language then is really church language. The language of children, then, would refer to children in the faith, like John's references to "my dear children" in his first letter.

As we move beyond the greeting and delve into the letter itself, we discover that John does not treat love and truth as being at odds with each other. Nor does he conceive of them as merely coexisting. In biblical Christianity, love and truth go together. John signals this pairing in the last phrase of verse 3—"truth and love." Real Christianity includes both love and truth.

REAL CHRISTIANITY INVOLVES LOVE

Three things are worth noticing about the love described by John: God commands it, the elder-author personifies it, and obedience characterizes it.

God Commands Love

John does not write to his readers with an idea of his own making. He asks them to remember God's command:

> And now, dear lady, I am not writing you a new command but one we have had from the beginning. I ask that we love one another. And this is love: that we walk in obedience to his commands. As you have heard from the beginning, his command is that you walk in love (vv. 5-6).

The phrase "from the beginning" must mean *from Jesus* and *from the time he established the church*. The command is nothing new, John says. I am not making up my own commands for you to obey. No, I am passing on the commands that God himself has given. And God commands that we walk in love. This is not some recent innovation. It did not originate with me. It came from God.

By relaying God's command and not his own, John is a good model for me as a pastor. What I preach should not come just from me. I should not use the pulpit to tell the church my personal opinions on Scripture. That is not my job. I stand in the pulpit on Sundays to proclaim the Word of God. Whatever things God has commanded, I must pass on to the church. That is the only reason I preach. His commands are my concerns.

John is a good model for all of us. We should not live our own lives according to our own ideas or selfish interests. Instead, we should live in obedience to the commands of God. The way of love, according to John, is the way of obedience. God commands us to love.

The Elder-Author Personifies Love

This elder himself demonstrates his love in the letter he has written. First, notice his manner. He is gentle with them. He has a command of Jesus, but he does not beat them over the head with it. He says in verse 5, quite simply, "I ask." He does not command them. He asks them. His manner demonstrates his love for them.

Again, John is a good model for us. We should speak softly. Over-speaking will turn up the temperature and turn down the reasonability and the love. Speak instead with gentleness, kindness, and love. Do not try to win your own way. Try instead to show what is best for everyone. That is what the elder is doing here. His very manner personifies the kind of love he commands.

The elder also shows us his love by his matter, or his concerns. He does not ask them for something that profits him. His concern is pastoral. His concern is for them. "I am not writing you a new command but one we have had from the beginning. I ask that we love one another." He wants them to learn to live together in love.

If I want to be a good pastor, I too must be concerned for the church's good, not fundamentally for my own. That is the kind of love this elder is showing. I need to follow John's example by making my concerns those things that will be good for the congregation. Why else do you think someone should serve as an elder or a pastor? An elder should not serve, the apostle Peter says, because he is greedy or wants something for himself. He should be *willing* to serve (1 Pet. 5:2). And that is the kind of love all Christians need to show one another in the church generally. We must look not only to our own interests, the apostle Paul says, but to the interests of others (Phil. 2:4).

Obedience Characterizes Love

God commands love. The elder personifies love. But what is this love? John tells us in the first half of verse 6, "And this is love: that we walk in obedience to his commands." Love is, quite simply, walking in obedience to God's commands. And what is God's command? The second half of verse 6 says, "his command is that you walk in love." It is hard to miss the spiraling nature of obedience and love. What is his command? That you walk in love. What is love? That you obey his commands. And so it goes. But this is not just a circle. I have found in my Christian life that as I grow to understand what God has commanded, I am better able to love. And as I practice loving, I have more interest in going back to the Scriptures and seeing how God wants me to keep going forward in obedience.

If we are disciples of Christ, more and more his image will be formed in us as we learn to love as he has instructed us to love. That is why John said in his first letter, "This is how we know that we love the children of God: by loving God and carrying out his commands. This is love for God: to obey his commands" (1 John 5:2-3a).

This love is not a loose love. It is not simple affection. Nor is it a cold and dispassionate obedience. No, it is warm and it desires to give itself for the good of others. That is what John is talking about here. Real Christianity involves love.

REAL CHRISTIANITY INVOLVES TRUTH

The tone of the letter changes in verse 7 when John turns to discussing "deceivers" and the antichrist. What a contrast between verse 5's "love one another" and verse 10's "do not welcome deceivers." Yet holding these two sections together challenges our assumptions that a division exists between love and truth. In verses 7-11, John is adamant: real Christianity involves not only love but also truth.

False Teachers Oppose the Truth

John's adamancy about the truth can be seen primarily in his opposition to those who oppose truth—the false teachers. He writes in verse 7, "Many deceivers, who do not acknowledge Jesus Christ as coming in the flesh, have gone out into the world" (cf. 1 John 2:19). These deceivers seem to be the same ones we found in our study of John's first letter. They deny that God actually became human and took on flesh. Yet they continue to call themselves Christians and attempt to teach people their doctrine. In his first letter John did not mention their attempt to teach others, but it does appear to be the same group.

Consider how these false teachers present their own teaching. John writes in verse 9, "Anyone who runs ahead and does not continue in the teaching of Christ does not have God; whoever continues in the teaching has both the Father and the Son!" Probably, John is echoing their own wording: they are "running ahead"; their doctrine is "progressive." Perhaps they are trying to persuade the congregation, "You came to the faith on that baby talk of God becoming flesh and becoming a man in Jesus. Now, we are going to give you the advanced class on Christianity. Here is the real stuff. God, of course, would never *really* become flesh. He simply put on an appearance of humanness in Jesus. But he was not really human. He just came to teach us."

John, of course, will have none of it. These teachers are deceivers. They are departing from the "teaching of Christ." No, we must *continue* in the teachings of Christ. Whoever does continue will have the Father and the Son. You cannot have the Father and the Son without the teaching Christ has given!

Not all change is bad, but not all change is good. How can you tell which is good and which is bad? Use the Bible as your guide. Contend for the things that are clear in Scripture, and continue in them. John knows it is of great importance whether or not Jesus came in the flesh. And so he writes this letter.

I heard James White, a pastor in North Carolina, recount a story about changes in how evangelicals understand the church's mission. He prefaced the story by citing a study that concluded that 90 percent of all lay people believe the mission of church is meeting their personal needs. Only 10 percent of churchgoers, on the other hand, believe that the church's mission is to win the world. White then told the story of an elderly woman who approached him at the end of a conference in which he had spoken about contemporary music in churches: "She came right up to me and said, 'Young man, I want to have a word with you about what you said today.' I thought to myself, 'Oh, no, here it comes. I can take it from anybody, but not from a grandmother.' She said, 'Are you trying to tell me churches should use contemporary music during the service? Because, young man, I want you to know that Monteverdi is about as contemporary as I get. If I'm feeling particularly feisty—Lawrence Welk.' Then she took her cane and pointed it up right in my face and said, 'If rock and roll is what it takes to get people back in the church, then all I can say is, "Let's boogey!"' I couldn't believe it. I said, 'I got through to you?' Then she looked at me with eyes that reflected communion with Christ and said, 'Son, it's not my style of music, but if it will reach people for my Jesus, I like it. Besides,' she went on, 'the church doesn't exist to meet my needs but to win the world.'"

Not all changes are bad. Some are good, and some are matters of indifference. What should worry us are not changes like the change in musical styles from one generation to the next. Rather, we should be concerned about anyone who tries to alter or "improve" truths such as whether or not God the Son came in the flesh. These false teachers probably presented their change as an improvement. They probably made clever arguments. And how were their hearers to know better? By knowing the Scriptures. By knowing the truth. By caring what Jesus taught about himself.

Christians Must Know the Truth

Few if any truths are as important as whether Jesus is God-come-in-the-flesh. John does not simply argue in his second letter that opponents to "the truth" (that is, truth as a generalized concept) exist. John is adamant about the particular truth of who Christ is. It is certainly true you can take some doctrines and elevate them to a point where they are unhelpful to everybody. Yet some truths are essential for Christianity. Whether or not Jesus is fully God and fully man is such a truth, John says in his first and second letters. If you lose this truth, you lose Christianity.

The sacrifice of Christ's physical body is integral to our salvation, because human sinners require a human substitute in the face of God's just wrath for sin. Jesus exemplified his own teaching by his death, particularly his teaching about love. The death of a less physical Christ would make his love less remarkable and less costly. The death of a less than divine Jesus, on the other hand, would make his love less important and less significant. Really, it would make the satisfaction accomplished by his sacrifice less than divine. Jesus has made a way for sinful humans to be reconciled to the holy Father through his own body, if we will repent of our sins and trust in him. That is why we cannot misunderstand either his full humanity or his full divinity.

Look at verse 8: "Watch out that you do not lose what you have worked for, but that you may be rewarded fully." You do not want to lose what you have worked for here. That is, you do not want to lose the reward to which you have been looking forward. Friend, I promise that you will most definitely lose everything in your life that you can presently hold, feel, taste, and see. There is no question about that. But that is not what John is talking about here. He is telling us how to keep the one thing we can keep and want never to lose—our salvation, our relationship with God through the Lord Jesus Christ. We keep it by knowing that God has come in the flesh in Jesus.

You *will* lose this world. Make sure that you possess *more* that what is contained in this world.

Anyone who opposes this teaching, John says in verse 7, is the deceiver and the antichrist. Their opposition to this teaching is opposition to Christ. In so doing, they deceive and mislead others. And their judgment is clear: "Anyone who runs ahead and does not continue in the teaching of Christ does not have God" (v. 9). That is a sweeping pronouncement! The teaching of Christ is essential to our salvation. Those who do not have Christ and his teaching do not have God. John recounts this same idea in his Gospel when he quotes Jesus as saying to his disciples, "'If you really knew me, you would know my Father as well. From now on, you do know him and have seen him'" (John 14:7). This is the great news the church has: God has actually come in the flesh and, in his great love, lived a perfect life and died a sacrificial death on the cross. Then he rose in victory over death and offered new life to all who turn and believe in him.

That is the great message we have to spread. And in this message we find the union of truth and love. Essentially, John is telling his readers, "Your heart must be stoked by love, because you know that you are loved by God through what he has done in Christ." Show me an unloving person and you show me a person who does not understand how much God has forgiven him or her. The people who best understand who Christ is and what he has done will be the people who are the most gentle and meek, because they best know the love of God. You will love only as well as you know the truth. If you could hear all the critical words and thoughts you had over the last week, would more of them be about yourself or about others?

We love only as well as we understand the gospel.

Implication: Christians Must Be Inhospitable Toward Untruth

A Jewish fable tells of how Abraham thrust an aged wayfarer from his tent because the wayfarer did not ask for God's blessing on his food but said that he was a fire-worshiper. Afterwards, the Lord said to Abraham, "I have suffered him these hundred years, although he dishonored me; and couldst not thou endure him for one night?"

Many verses in the Bible exhort us to be hospitable. Paul commanded the Romans to "Share with God's people who are in need. Practice hospitality" (Rom. 12:13). He told Timothy that widows should be known for showing hospitality (1 Tim. 5:10). The author of Hebrews said, "Do not forget to entertain strangers, for by so doing some people have entertained angels without knowing it" (Heb. 13:2). And Peter wrote, "Offer hospitality to one another without grumbling" (1 Pet. 4:9).

So what could John possibly mean when he writes, "If anyone comes to you and does not bring this teaching, do not take him into your house or welcome him. Anyone who welcomes him shares in his wicked work" (2 John 10-11). Does this mean we should refuse housing to someone who teaches something we disagree with about the Christian life? Should we refuse to house a "holiness teacher" or a cousin who is Jewish? Should we refuse to share a meal with a nonreligious friend or a Jehovah's Witness?

A few observations will help us clarify what John means here. First, when John says, "If anyone comes to you," he does not mean people who do not profess to be Christian. He means people who profess to be Christians, yet who teach this false doctrine. Second, when John refers to someone who "comes and brings this teaching," he does not mean "comes and brings" in a casual sense, as in, "anyone who happens to show up for a service on Sunday morning and tells a couple of people afterward the pastor was wrong." He is referring to someone who comes in an official teaching capacity. Third, when John refers to his readers' "house," remember, he means the church's meeting place. After all, in those days churches met in houses. Fourth, when John forbids them to "welcome" or "share" in this wicked work, he means he does not want them to give their recognition and consent to such a false teacher. Do not let him teach the congregation with his false doctrine, much less install him in a formal teaching position. Allowing him to teach is "sharing" in his wicked work. It is having "koinonia," or fellowship, with it.

We must not have any fellowship with false teaching about the person or work of Christ. We can have open homes, as we understand the word "home" or "house" today. But our pulpits must be closed to false teaching about Christ. Real Christianity involves love, and real Christianity involves truth.

CONCLUSION

Maybe you still do not see what the first half of John's letter has to do with the second half. Maybe the first half seems nice—"love one another." But the second half just seems so hard—"do not take him into your house or welcome him." After all, is not the real danger we face in the church a lack of love, not lack of truth? John says no. Love and truth are intimately related. Real Christianity involves both love and truth. Teachers of truth who live loveless lives will find that people reject their truth, and truth will not be served. But teachers of untruth, no matter how loving they might appear, can destroy lives, and love will not be served.

Let me make an analogy. Last week my wife and I celebrated an anniversary by traveling by car to historic Williamsburg. Neither of us had ever been to Williamsburg. Suppose we were ready to go on our trip and had a map; we knew exactly how to get there. But we had no fuel in the car. How far would we get? Not very far. Let's say on the other hand that the fuel tank was full. We even had several spare tanks of fuel in the trunk. But we did not have a map and did not know how to get to Williamsburg. Let's also say—yes, this is a little silly—there were no street signs. In a certain respect, John is saying that truth is like the map and the street signs, while love is like the fuel. Truth tells us where we should go. Love helps us to get there. It motivates us and pushes us out. Christians must have the map—they must know the truth. They do not want to drive all over the place foolishly spending precious fuel. But Christians must also have fuel—they must love. They do not want to just sit in their cars and study the exact route but fail to ever start the engine. Just as duty is the foundation of freedom, so truth is a prerequisite for godly love.

Biblical truth is not satisfied when simple facts are coldly laid out. And biblical love is not satisfied when we compromise the truth. Biblical truth teaches in biblical love, and biblical love is disposed toward biblical truth. God has loved us by teaching us the truth about ourselves and about him. And we love others most when we share these truths with them.

It is hardly surprising that John connects truth and love. He had spent time with Jesus! Through his life and death, Jesus made the connection between truth and love more clear than anyone else who has ever lived. Jesus told us the truth about ourselves—we are sinners. And then Jesus loved us to the fullest measure by dying for us.

The truth is, this world is ending. And Jesus is the way to God. That's the truth. Now, what are you going to do about it? John says we should know the truth, and then live the truth in love. Claiming that you know the truth without living in love demonstrates that you do not know the truth. But try living in love without knowing the truth. John says you cannot. You will deceive yourself and others. Disobeying this command to love, or denying the truth of God in Christ, *may* be disastrous for others. It *will* be disastrous for you.

Accept the truth. Walk in love.

Let us pray:

Lord, we are thankful for the way those of us who are parents know instinctively that combination of truth and love. We pray that you will humble each one of our proud hearts and teach us the truth about yourself. Father, cause us to be ashamed of our sin for your glory. We pray that you would change us for Jesus' sake. For those of us who do not know you, we pray that you would convict us of our need for you. Show us your love very clearly in Jesus. For those of us who profess to be disciples, we pray that you would humble us with the truth of this message. For those of us who tend to be loveless, we pray you would grow in our hearts a great love as we understand how you have loved us in Christ. And for those of us who have little concern for truth, we pray that you would arrest our attention by how concerned John is for the one particular point of doctrine—who Jesus is. Teach us to value the truth that you have revealed in your Word. Help us to hide it in our hearts and to proclaim it for your glory. We ask it all in Jesus' name. Amen.

Questions for Reflection

1. Is there a real tension between truth and love? Or is it only an apparent tension? Explain.

2. Who is the "lady" to whom John writes?

3. John reminds us that Jesus commanded Christians to love one another. Can you command love? Isn't love, at least in part, a feeling of affection and warm desire to give oneself for the good of others? How can you command a feeling of affection and warm desire? More to the point, how can people obey such a command? How do you?

4. What is the most important thing for a pastor to teach his congregation?

5. Why is John a good model in how he speaks to the congregation? If you were as mature as you wanted to be, how would you want to speak to your church, your spouse, your children or parents, your employees, and your friends? Once you've pictured this, pray for it!

6. We have considered the fact that not all changes are bad. Some are good, and some are matters of indifference. Changes of style are not nearly as worrisome as changes of doctrine. Both the members and the leaders of our churches, therefore, need the wisdom of knowing how to distinguish between matters of importance and matters of indifference. How can individuals in churches go about acquiring such wisdom?

7. Why is it absolutely essential to the Christian gospel and to our salvation that Jesus Christ was God come *in the flesh* and not just in the *appearance* of flesh?

8. Why is it absolutely essential to the Christian gospel and to our salvation that Jesus Christ was *God* come in the flesh and not just a really good man?

9. The statement was made, "We love only as well as we understand the gospel." Explain.

10. With whom should we as Christians share hospitality? With whom should we not share hospitality?

11. How do you practice both truth and love in your home? In your church?

12. What must churches do to cultivate a body of truth lovers? What must churches do to cultivate a body of people who truly love?

THE MESSAGE OF 3 JOHN: WHY GO TO ALL THE TROUBLE?

25

THE MESSAGE OF 3 JOHN: WHY GO TO ALL THE TROUBLE?

WHY GO TO ALL THE TROUBLE?[1]

"We teach hard work and honesty. We teach that prosperity comes to those who learn God's ways." So says Huang Kai, a twenty-nine-year old Protestant who preaches at Yang Ao Church in Wenzhou, a city of 700,000 people on the southeast coast of China. Huang was the subject of an article in *The Wall Street Journal*, "China's Christians Mix Business with God."[2] A number of observers have been struck by the fact that the growth of Christianity in China has been accompanied by the growth of capitalism, and they have concluded that Christianity and capitalism must reinforce one another. Mr. Huang, for one, believes that wealth and devotion grow together.

Is that right? Do wealth and devotion grow together?

I do not know if you have ever thought of the Christian life as a bed of roses, but it is, at least if you include the thorns. Being a Christian is both wonderful and difficult. And if this is true for just being a Christian, how much more is it true for church leadership! Most of what I do as a minister throughout the week is not stand in the pulpit and preach. Aside from preparing sermons, I spend much of my time sitting in meetings, visiting church members, or taking calls from people in distress. In just the last week, I talked to people who were suicidal, who just learned they had terminal illnesses, and who struggle with every kind of problem imaginable. I also have had the joy of sharing Jesus with non-Christians.

I share this not to gain your sympathy but simply to underscore the fact that life is difficult, even for Christians. I can understand why some people

---

[1] This sermon was originally preached on June 18, 1995, at Capitol Hill Baptist Church in Washington, D.C.
[2] *The Wall Street Journal*, June 16, 1995.

would ask the question, "Why go to all the trouble? Why not spend Sundays staying home, watching television, and reading the Sunday paper? You can believe in God in the privacy of your own heart. Why go to all the trouble of being involved in a church? We don't need 'organized Christianity.'" Well, there are two basic answers for why you might go to all the trouble. Depending on whether you are really a believer, you go to the trouble either for God and his gospel or for yourself. In the first case, real truth and real love show themselves as you give yourself to others. You want everyone around you to know the good news about Jesus. In the second case, your life is simply a show, fueled by ambition and directed by self-interest.

INTRODUCING 3 JOHN

Lest you think these two possible motivations are my idea, or a division peculiar to the modern church, listen to John's little third letter. It is the shortest book in the New Testament.

> The elder,
>
> To my dear friend Gaius, whom I love in the truth.
>
> Dear friend, I pray that you may enjoy good health and that all may go well with you, even as your soul is getting along well. It gave me great joy to have some brothers come and tell about your faithfulness to the truth and how you continue to walk in the truth. I have no greater joy than to hear that my children are walking in the truth.
>
> Dear friend, you are faithful in what you are doing for the brothers, even though they are strangers to you. They have told the church about your love. You will do well to send them on their way in a manner worthy of God. It was for the sake of the Name that they went out, receiving no help from the pagans. We ought therefore to show hospitality to such men so that we may work together for the truth.
>
> I wrote to the church, but Diotrephes, who loves to be first, will have nothing to do with us. So if I come, I will call attention to what he is doing, gossiping maliciously about us. Not satisfied with that, he refuses to welcome the brothers. He also stops those who want to do so and puts them out of the church.
>
> Dear friend, do not imitate what is evil but what is good. Anyone who does what is good is from God. Anyone who does what is evil has not seen God. Demetrius is well spoken of by everyone—and even by the truth itself. We also speak well of him, and you know that our testimony is true.
>
> I have much to write you, but I do not want to do so with pen and ink. I hope to see you soon, and we will talk face to face.
>
> Peace to you. The friends here send their greetings. Greet the friends there by name (3 John 1-14)

There is not much in this letter except the good example of Gaius and the troubling example of Diotrephes. When I first began pastoring, I received conflicting advice about what I should do in my first year in a church. Some people told me to change everything I could in the first year, while the congregation still liked me. Other people told me not to change anything in the first year, but to let the congregation get to know me first. You might say I had a choice between taking trouble or making trouble. Interestingly, John's letter is addressed to an individual yet it presents us with two patterns for life in the church: a life that takes trouble for the gospel, and a life that makes trouble for the gospel. Unlike the choice I had in my first year of pastoring, which seemingly had no clear answer, I think we will discover by the end which pattern smells like true Christianity.

TAKING TROUBLE FOR THE GOSPEL—GAIUS (VERSES 1-8)

Let's begin by looking at an example of one who takes trouble for the gospel, Gaius. He is described in the first eight verses.

Loved and Spiritually Prospering

The first thing we learn about Gaius is that John loves him "in the truth" (v. 1). By that, John does not mean he truly and really loves him, though that may be implied. He means he loves him with a love that is grounded in the truth and is consistent with the Christian revelation of God in Christ. John loves Gaius in the way God has loved us in Christ.

Truth and affection go together, even though people often think they are separate. We tend to form two categories in our heads: there are people who care about truth and people who care about love. But again and again in John's letters, truth and love go together.

Not only is Gaius loved, he is spiritually prospering. John writes, "Dear friend, I pray that you may enjoy good health and that all may go well with you, even as your soul is getting along well" (v. 2). John prays that Gaius's physical health would keep up with his spiritual health. In our culture, we worry excessively about physical health and are constantly told to discipline our bodies to be fitter. Here, John gauges Gaius's physical health according to his spiritual health. I hope that you and I can say that—that our spirits are prospering and that we pray for our bodies to catch up.

Walking According to Truth

So how does Gaius take trouble for the gospel? First, Gaius walks in the truth of the gospel. John writes, "It gave me great joy to have some brothers come and tell about your faithfulness to the truth and how you continue to walk in the truth. I have no greater joy than to hear that my children are walking in the truth" (vv. 3-4). Gaius lives according to the truth. That means he faithfully adheres to the doctrine he has been taught: God is holy and perfect. He made us to know him, but we sinned and separated ourselves from him. So he became the enemy. But God the Son became man, lived a perfect life, died on the cross as a substitute for all who would turn to him, and rose in victory over sin and death. He now commands all to repent and believe in him.

In our studies of 1 and 2 John, we considered the fact that Jesus is fully God and fully man. Evidently, Gaius believes that truth and teaches it. More than that, he lives it. Over and over, John has told us through our last two studies to both believe the truth and live it out. Gaius obviously does. He takes trouble for the gospel by walking according to its truth.

Walking According to Love

Gaius also takes trouble for the gospel by walking in the love of the gospel. Not incidentally, this is the main piece of evidence we have that he walks in truth. He lives out his faith! John writes, "Dear friend, you are faithful in what you are doing for the brothers, even though they are strangers to you" (v. 5). Gaius is "faithful" in what he does. Literally, he is doing a thing of faith. And what is this thing of faith he is doing? John continues, "They have told the church about your love. You will do well to send them on their way in a manner worthy of God" (v. 6). Gaius loves these strangers who have visited him. He takes trouble for the gospel by loving the saints.

Whom Gaius loves. There are three things to notice about this love: whom Gaius loves, why he loves, and how he loves. Notice first whom Gaius loves. As verse 5 says, he has been faithful in loving "strangers." He faithfully loves them because these strangers are also "brothers" in the faith. That is all it takes to convince Gaius to treat strangers with love.

It is a sad truth that physical brothers and sisters can become strangers. Sometimes it is just the passing of time. Sometimes one sibling moves to another place. Sometimes one sibling becomes a Christian and begins focusing on new and different things.

Yet if brothers can become strangers, strangers can also become brothers, which is what John writes about here. He commends Gaius for "what you are doing for the brothers even though they are strangers." That is what we experience in the warm relationships of the church. Those of us who are committed to Christ have been adopted by God the Father and become brothers and sisters in a manner most remarkable to the world. People from different nations, different races, different ages, different backgrounds, and different jobs begin to recognize something far more important than all the differences our world observes. And so a kinship—a sisterhood and a brotherhood—is born which is not physical but spiritual. Gaius understands this, which is why he welcomes strangers as brothers.

Why Gaius loves. Why does Gaius love his fellow saints this way? Clearly the answer is, for the sake of the gospel. John writes, "It was for the sake of the Name that they went out" (v. 7a). Of course, the name for whose sake they went out is Jesus. The apostles use the same expression in Acts when they leave the Sanhedrin, "rejoicing because they had been counted worthy of suffering disgrace for the Name" (Acts 5:41). The apostles were moved by the gospel.

Like Gaius and the apostles, that must be our motive and method—being moved by the gospel. That which is not for the sake of the gospel can be set aside. Our lives must be devoted to that which furthers the gospel and *only* that which furthers the gospel.

John continues in verse 8, "We ought therefore to show hospitality to such men so that we may work together for the truth." Insofar as we agree on the truth of the gospel's priority, we will have unity. We must take care about forming divisions in the church that are not for the sake of the Name. In this third letter, John has no hesitation about making Jesus an object of controversy. If people say false things about Jesus, John will wade right into the church and make waves.

We must follow John's example. We should not be afraid of causing strife for the name of Jesus—but we should do it only for the name of Jesus. Gospel truth and unity belong together in a church. That is why you will also find a growing unity in churches where the gospel is clearly preached. People understand why they are there, and they understand what defines them.

How Gaius loves. How then does Gaius love these strangers and fellow saints? He loves them very practically. John writes,

> They have told the church about your love. You will do well to send them on their way in a manner worthy of God. It was for the sake of the Name that they went out, receiving no help from the pagans. We ought therefore to show hospitality to such men so that we may work together for the truth (vv. 6-8).

John encourages Gaius to show hospitality. It is a very practical love he speaks of. In first-century culture, it was traditional for a host to escort guests on the first wave of their journey after a visit. There were no Rand McNally road maps for people to use, and you wanted to make sure your guests knew the way. There were also no Howard Johnsons, Holiday Inns, or Hyatts. You had to show hospitality or people could die. Most importantly, showing hospitality allowed people to come from far away to either teach or hear the gospel.

Do You Walk According to Love?

What does all this mean in our lives? It means that we should be committed to loving and to walking in the love of the gospel.

Whom and why you should love. Consider first, whom do you love? Bring some people before your mind's eye right now whom you love. Now—those people you are imagining—why do you love them? Certainly you would list family and friends. Probably, they are people who like you and agree with you; perhaps people who benefit you. But is there anyone you love purely for the sake of the gospel? In the church, we do not have the luxury of loving people merely because they are attractive to us. Nor do we have the luxury of avoiding people who are not attractive or who are awkward or difficult. The church is not a place exclusively for beautiful people, where we go to find people we are attracted to and want to love. That is not what the church is about. No, we are a cooperative society of garbage takers. We all produce a lot of garbage. That is the nature of fallen creatures. In a Christian church, we volunteer to take one another's garbage because God has taken our garbage. God in Christ has loved us, even though we were not attractive to him in our sin. So that is what we do for one another in the church. We love even the people the world calls unattractive and undesirable.

I mentioned earlier some of the things I did last week. On Tuesday afternoon, I had the opportunity of sharing the gospel with two different people, both of whom had serious degenerative diseases. They were dying and they knew it. The second fellow, in a particularly pathetic way, looked up at me at one point and said, "I don't know why you are talking to me. I'm just a throwaway person. I've lived all my life, and nobody has cared." Well, I was talking to him not because I am a particularly virtuous person but because I have been loved that way by God himself in Jesus.

We should not only love outsiders. We are called to love one another in the church, again because God has loved us. Loving people for the sake of the gospel does not only mean loving them because they need the gospel. It also means loving those who work for the gospel, and John is writing about such people. Jesus himself sent out the twelve apostles saying to them,

> He who receives you receives me, and he who receives me receives the one who sent me. Anyone who receives a prophet because he is a prophet will receive a prophet's reward, and anyone who receives a righteous man because he is a righteous man will receive a righteous man's reward. And if anyone gives even a cup of cold water to one of these little ones because he is my disciple, I tell you the truth, he will certainly not lose his reward (Matt. 10:40-42).

Why do you love people? If you love Christ, you will love his servants.

How you should love. The next question to be answered is, how do you love the saints? In verse 8, John writes that Gaius "ought" to show hospitality to the saints. We do not use the word "ought" much. Yet what is true for John and Gaius is true for every Christian. Again, we are told that Jesus himself, when separating the sheep and the goats, will say, "'Whatever you did for one of the least of these brothers of mine, you did for me'" (Matt. 25:40). Paul exhorts all Christians to, "Share with God's people who are in need. Practice hospitality" (Rom. 12:13). The writer to the Hebrews exhorts Christians not to forget to entertain strangers; by so doing some people have unknowingly entertained angels (Heb. 13:2). And Peter says to some young Christians, "Offer hospitality to one another without grumbling" (1 Pet. 4:9).

In this letter, John gives us at least three compelling reasons why we should practice hospitality, particularly by supporting God's workers. First, we should practice hospitality, like Gaius, "for the sake of the Name." We show hospitality because we love Christ, and therefore we love all those who serve Christ. I am very aware of the fact that the church pays my salary, along with the salaries of several other members of the staff. But neither I nor the others are ultimately the church's servants. We are supported insofar as the church recognizes us as God's servants. Our income constitutes one way the church supports God's work.

Second, John notes that the Christian brothers are "receiving no help from the pagans" (3 John 7). Non-Christians are not going to support the work of God, at least not knowingly. If you are a believer in the Lord Jesus Christ, it is your responsibility and privilege to support the work of God.

Third, it is a privilege to practice hospitality toward God's servants because it signifies our working "together for the truth" of the gospel (v. 8). When you support God's workers, you are joining together with countless others in the same work. Many times people have told me they wish they could be a missionary in the Lord's service, but for some reason they cannot be. But they can, as John exhorts Gaius, show hospitality. They can practically support those whom God has called as pastors and missionaries.

Certainly, hospitality has its difficulties. Christians have always faced this. Even the *Didache,* an early second-century church document, provided rules and regulations for hospitality so that Christians would not be abused by roving so-called Christian workers. The televangelist's line is nothing new. It has been practiced as long as the church has existed. There will always be people who abuse Christian goodwill. We know that. Yet God will judge them. We do not need ultimately to concern ourselves with them.

God calls us to show hospitality, and we can practically do this in a number of ways. First, and this is particularly relevant to fathers, we can open our homes. We often say that a man's home is his castle. Too often that is true. A man comes home from work, and the drawbridge goes up. When the drawbridge is up, the home cannot be a mission station for God's love. Yet if you are a spiritual leader and a father, you should lead your family gently by using your home to show love to others. Make your home a picture of the love this world is starving for—a place where love and authority go together; where truth and affection meet; where holiness and mercy are practiced.

Second, we should give financially to the work of the church. In our church, the older people have done an incredible job of keeping the church open when numbers were down. Many older people have given sacrificially in a way few of us have known. They have done it in war, and with their paychecks. They have done it by going without the things they might have enjoyed or even needed. They have done it out of a love for God and his work. You too must give if you want the work of God to grow in the church.

Third, we should involve ourselves any way we can in the work of the gospel. It is a privilege to be involved in helping those who are spreading the good news of Jesus Christ. Did you notice that phrase in verse 6, where John exhorts Gaius to send them on their way *in a manner worthy of God?* In other words, do not show hospitality stingily. Show it with generosity. If you are going to err, then err on the side of generosity, not on the side of stinginess. Send God's workers on their way in a manner worthy of God, because generosity and love make the truth visible. Gaius's life of loving hospitality for other Christians demonstrated his belief in the truth. Does yours?

MAKING TROUBLE FOR THE GOSPEL—DIOTREPHES (VERSES 9-10)

This little letter presents another pattern for how to live. It is a less comforting and less wholesome way to live, but it is common. Standing across the stage from Gaius is Diotrephes, who makes trouble for the gospel. John writes,

> I wrote to the church, but Diotrephes, who loves to be first, will have nothing to do with us. So if I come, I will call attention to what he is doing, gossiping maliciously about us. Not satisfied with that, he refuses to welcome the brothers. He also stops those who want to do so and puts them out of the church (vv. 9-10).

Now, maybe you wonder if Diotrephes is not as bad as John says. Maybe he is just a young leader who is tired of this old man John badgering him with letter after letter. Perhaps he is a congregationalist who does not accept a bishop's authority over him. Whatever he is, John is clear about one thing: Diotrephes's example is not a good one. He does not take trouble for the gospel, he makes trouble.

Speaking Selfishly

For starters, Diotrephes gossips maliciously. The word for "gossip" here is suggestive of the bubbles at the top of a boiling pot of water. They look big, but then they pop and are meaningless. Diotrephes's words are not only slanderous and evil, they are nonsense, empty, groundless.

These days, we often justify our thoughtless speech by pretending that we are merely wanting to "get something off our chest." We hide behind the idea of self-expression. But really, no one is built up. Everyone within earshot is only torn down. John tells us to consider what our words will do to others. As Christians, we should know better than to speak merely for the sake of self-expression. Compelled by the love of Christ, we should always speak carefully and gently with words that build up those around us.

Living Selfishly

Diotrephes not only makes trouble for the gospel by saying what pleases himself, he does only what pleases himself. John says in verse 9, "I wrote to the church, but Diotrephes, who loves to be first, will have nothing to do with us." Perhaps John had written to the church commending some missionaries he was sending. Yet unlike Gaius, who walks in truth and love, Diotrephes rejects the apostle's authority. He says no. And he does this particularly by refusing "to welcome the brothers" (v. 10). You see, Diotrephes's hostility follows a pattern. He is not just hostile to John, he is hostile to everyone who works for the gospel. Unlike Gaius, who welcomes these workers, Diotrephes rejects them, as well as John's instructions to welcome them. In our study of 2 John, we saw that the problem was the people's willingness to welcome false teachers. In 3 John, the problem is the opposite—refusing to welcome true teachers.

Not only does Diotrephes not welcome these workers, he stops those who do! "He also stops those who want to do so and puts them out of the church," John says (v. 10). He kicks the welcome wagon out of the church. He exercises illegitimate church discipline.

Let it be said, majorities may carry the church vote, but that does not mean their decisions are always right. How should we respond when church decisions are made that are contrary to our own wishes? When nonessential (though not necessarily unimportant) matters in the church develop contrary to our hopes, we can find peace in the fact that although our troubles may be lasting, they are not everlasting. And this peace allows us to deal with the nonessentials with grace and charity. In my own Christian life, when I find myself dealing with difficult situations like these Christians who were put out of the church for doing what was good, I try to concentrate on now and on eternity. I try to forget yesterday and not worry about tomorrow. Instead, I concentrate on now and eternity.

So what is Diotrephes's problem? Is he sympathetic with false teachers? Has he personally fallen out with John the elder? There is much this little letter does not tell us. But it does say Diotrephes "loves to be first" (v. 9). Diotrephes makes trouble for the gospel by loving himself first. Gaius loves the brethren; Diotrephes loves himself. Gaius gives out of his own for the brethren; Diotrephes wants to make sure things go his way. Maybe he is power-hungry. Maybe he enjoys empire building. Certainly, he has ungodly ambition. Certainly, he is selfish and loves to be first.

How does John respond? "If I come, I will call attention to what he is doing" (v. 10). The Bible says we will all ultimately give account to God (Rom. 14:12). In the meantime, he has given certain church leaders responsibility for exercising authority (Eph. 4:11-13). A pastor cannot change people. But he can warn them. As biblical scholar I. H. Marshall says, "It is not Christian to refrain from exercising legitimate authority when there is need to do so."[3]

Diotrephes reminds us of the danger of confusing personal ambition with a zeal for the gospel of Christ. John has made it clear throughout his letters that a lack of Christian character is evidence of a lack of true Christian experience. Now, you may be amazed that a person like Diotrephes ever sat in a Christian church. But what was true in his day is true in ours as well. There will always be problems within the church, as the example of Diotrephes teaches. A. T. Robertson, a famous Greek scholar in the early twentieth century, wrote an article about Diotrephes for a denominational newspaper, calling him the "church boss."[4] In the weeks following publication of Robertson's article, the editor of the newspaper received twenty-five letters from angry deacons canceling their subscriptions. All of them thought the article was a personal attack against them!

It is important for us to think of others first, both with our words and with our actions.

CONCLUSION (VERSES 11-13)

John warns Gaius against the self-centeredness of Diotrephes. Self-centeredness is the basic problem, according to John—the basic sin. Christ, on the other had, though "being in very nature God, did not consider equality with God something to be grasped, but made himself nothing" (Phil. 2:6-7). Clearly, we have

---

[3] I. H. Marshall, *The Epistles of John*, in The New International Commentary on the New Testament, ed. F. F. Bruce (Grand Rapids, Mich.: Eerdmans, 1978), 91.

[4] Archibald Thomas Robertson, *The General Epistles and the Revelation of John*, vol. 6 of *Word Pictures in the New Testament* (Nashville: Broadman, 1933), 263.

two models—two different paths to take. And they smell different from top to bottom, from the way someone talks to how someone walks. John lays out the choice most deliberately in verse 11: "Dear friend, do not imitate what is evil but what is good. Anyone who does what is good is from God. Anyone who does what is evil has not seen God."

Scripture tells us to imitate God. "Be imitators of God," says Paul (Eph. 5:1). Be imitators of Christ, says Peter (1 Pet. 2:21). And insofar as Christians before us have imitated God, we should imitate them. So Paul says, "Follow my example as I follow the example of Christ."[5]

But let me offer a final word of warning. Choose carefully whose example you will follow—Gaius or Diotrephes. Choose carefully. Remember, you are also choosing what kind of example you will be for others.

Let me also give a final word of encouragement. There are Diotrepheses in the church and there will always be. It has been so since the beginning. But there are also Gaiuses. They are the ones who leave vivid, lasting, and inspiring examples for us. And by his love, God keeps those examples fresh in our minds' eyes. The Gaiuses are the ones who fire us up and propel us forward by the example of their love for Christ. In his grace, God gives us Gaiuses.

Now I ask you, why go to all the trouble of being in a church? For God and his gospel, or for yourself? Dear friend, I give you the warning of the elder: "Do not imitate what is evil, but what is good. Anyone who does what is good is from God. Anyone who does what is evil has not seen God."

Let us pray:

Lord God, we praise you that in your love, you do not leave us to be Diotrephes; but in your Word you have warned us to turn from being a Diotrephes to being a Gaius. We praise you that Christ offers this hope for redemption and reconciliation. We thank you for the love you have shown to us when we treated you far worse than anyone could ever treat us. Lord, thank you for your love. We pray that you would take our whole lives as a response of worship to you and your love through Jesus Christ, in whose name we pray. Amen.

Questions for Reflection

1. Is truth or love more important, according to the Bible? What is the relationship between them?

---

[5] 1 Cor. 11:1; see also 1 Cor. 4:16; 1 Thess. 1:6; 2:14; 2 Thess. 3:7; Heb. 6:12; 13:7

2. What is the best evidence that someone is genuinely walking according to the truth? Explain.

3. Real gospel lovers love the gospel in other people so much that divisions in race, age, economic rank, and so forth grow less and less meaningful. Do all of your friends look like you and come from the same background as you? What is the best ministry a church can have to ethnic minorities? To women? To the rich? To the poor? To the old? To youth? To foreigners?

4. Is anything in the church worth dividing over? What?

5. More than anything else, what will bring unity to the church?

6. Given the lack of hotels, cars, and roadmaps, hospitality played an obviously large role in facilitating the teaching and hearing of the gospel message in New Testament times. Does hospitality play a less important role today?

7. What is the gospel message?

8. If you can, think of five to ten people you have known in formal gospel ministry roles: pastors, elders, Bible study leaders, missionaries, and so forth. How have you actively supported these men and women? How have you been leery of them and perhaps made their lives a little more difficult? If all of them were surveyed, would they say you have been a blessing and an encouragement to their ministry or a hindrance and a source of grief?

9. What are several practical ways you can show hospitality? Pray that God would show and equip you.

10. Why are fathers the best ones in the home for taking the lead in showing hospitality?

11. What responsibility does the Bible say Christians have for warning other professing believers in their sin (see Gal. 6:1; Jude 22-23)?

THE MESSAGE OF JUDE: HAVING FAITH IN FAITHLESS TIMES

26

THE MESSAGE OF JUDE: HAVING FAITH IN FAITHLESS TIMES

HAVING FAITH IN FAITHLESS TIMES[1]

"Faith," said Mark Twain, "is believing what you know isn't true."

If George Gallup can be believed, we live in increasingly faithless times. Gallup poll findings from 1991 suggest that 69 percent of people believe "there are few moral absolutes: what is right or wrong usually varies from situation to situation."[2] And Steven Brint, in his book *In an Age of Experts,* says that middle-class professionals are "relatively skeptical about moral certainties."[3]

The increasing faithlessness of our times can be found not only outside the church but inside as well. When so-called Christian ministers dismiss the person and work of Christ, it is not surprising that maintaining faith is difficult. In such circumstances, how can we continue to have faith? What does it mean to have Christian faith in faithless times like these?

INTRODUCING JUDE

As I have been meditating on these final letters in the New Testament for our last few studies, I have been struck by how contemporary they are. The problems we might feel are new or modern were the same problems these early Christians faced. And that is true in the letter of Jude. Jude, the brother of James and the half-brother of Jesus, writes a short, trenchant letter which encourages his first readers, and no less us, to live faithfully in faithless times.

---

[1] This sermon was originally preached on June 25, 1995, at Capitol Hill Baptist Church in Washington, D.C.
[2] Cited in *The National and International Religion Report,* April 6, 1992, 8.
[3] Steven Brint, *In an Age of Experts: The Changing Role of Professionals in Politics and Public Life* (Princeton, N.J.: Princeton University Press, 1994), 86.

Jude, a servant of Jesus Christ and a brother of James,

To those who have been called, who are loved by God the Father and kept by Jesus Christ:

Mercy, peace and love be yours in abundance.

Dear friends, although I was very eager to write to you about the salvation we share, I felt I had to write and urge you to contend for the faith that was once for all entrusted to the saints. For certain men whose condemnation was written about long ago have secretly slipped in among you. They are godless men, who change the grace of our God into a license for immorality and deny Jesus Christ our only Sovereign and Lord.

Though you already know all this, I want to remind you that the Lord delivered his people out of Egypt, but later destroyed those who did not believe. And the angels who did not keep their positions of authority but abandoned their own home—these he has kept in darkness, bound with everlasting chains for judgment on the great Day. In a similar way, Sodom and Gomorrah and the surrounding towns gave themselves up to sexual immorality and perversion. They serve as an example of those who suffer the punishment of eternal fire.

In the very same way, these dreamers pollute their own bodies, reject authority and slander celestial beings. But even the archangel Michael, when he was disputing with the devil about the body of Moses, did not dare to bring a slanderous accusation against him, but said, 'The Lord rebuke you!' Yet these men speak abusively against whatever they do not understand; and what things they do understand by instinct, like unreasoning animals—these are the very things that destroy them.

Woe to them! They have taken the way of Cain; they have rushed for profit into Balaam's error; they have been destroyed in Korah's rebellion.

These men are blemishes at your love feasts, eating with you without the slightest qualm—shepherds who feed only themselves. They are clouds without rain, blown along by the wind; autumn trees, without fruit and uprooted—twice dead. They are wild waves of the sea, foaming up their shame; wandering stars, for whom blackest darkness has been reserved forever.

Enoch, the seventh from Adam, prophesied about these men: 'See, the Lord is coming with thousands upon thousands of his holy ones to judge everyone, and to convict all the ungodly of all the ungodly acts they have done in the ungodly way, and of all the harsh words ungodly sinners have spoken against him.' These men are grumblers and faultfinders; they follow their own evil desires; they boast about themselves and flatter others for their own advantage.

But, dear friends, remember what the apostles of our Lord Jesus Christ foretold. They said to you, "In the last times there will be scoffers who will follow their own ungodly desires." These are the men who divide you, who follow mere natural instincts and do not have the Spirit.

But you, dear friends, build yourselves up in your most holy faith and pray in the Holy Spirit. Keep yourselves in God's love as you wait for the mercy of our Lord Jesus Christ to bring you to eternal life.

Be merciful to those who doubt; snatch others from the fire and save them; to others show mercy, mixed with fear—hating even the clothing stained by corrupted flesh.

To him who is able to keep you from falling and to present you before his glorious presence without fault and with great joy—to the only God our Savior be glory, majesty, power and authority, through Jesus Christ our Lord, before all ages, now and forevermore! Amen (Jude 1-25).

We will look first at what Jude says about the characteristics of a faithless life, and then at the characteristics of the faithful life. Finally, we will look at what answers he provides to several of the most often asked questions about faith.

CHARACTERISTICS OF A LIFE WITHOUT FAITH

What does Jude say characterizes the life without faith? Most of the letter is used to answer this question (vv. 3 to 19). Two basic answers are provided.

Living Immorally

The first thing that characterizes a life without faith is immorality. Jude writes, "For certain men whose condemnation was written about long ago have secretly slipped in among you. They are godless men, who change the grace of our God into a license for immorality" (v. 4). Notice the word "change." Grace is changed into license.

As we continue in the letter, we find that these men, who are false teachers, live brutal lives, as if they were animals. Jude writes, "these dreamers pollute their own bodies" (v. 8). They "speak abusively against whatever they do not understand; and what things they do understand by instinct, like unreasoning animals—these are the very things that destroy them" (v. 10). They commit "ungodly acts" (v. 15). They follow "their own evil desires" (v. 16) and "their own ungodly desires" (v. 18). These men who will divide the church, says Jude, follow "mere natural instincts and do not have the Spirit" (v. 19).

Think about several of these words for a second: "instinct," "natural," "desires." Today, these are very positive words. If you want to justify an action, behavior, or thought, call it instinctive or natural. If you want to characterize a life-decision as good, say it is a product of natural desire. That's your trump card. People today assume that whatever is innate, whatever we naturally desire, must be good.

But look at what Jude says. These false teachers might teach that a

Christian can live however he wants and remain in the church; that a Christian can give full expression to his natural desires and chalk it up to grace. But this is wrong, Jude says. It is dangerously untrue.

I remember one conversation I had with friend who had been a full-time Christian worker but who had fallen away from the Christian faith. As we discussed the state of his faith, I realized he had no way of hearing that God disagreed with anything he wanted. So I asked him, "How will you ever know if something you want is wrong? In the way you now understand your faith, is there any way you are able to hear God if he is against what you want?" If there is no way for us to hear God, if we are deaf to him by the din of our own desires and insulated from him by the imperial sway of own impulses, we will become brutal like the men in this letter, like the animals who cannot hear. We will be unable to learn from God.

Denying the Truth

Jude knows, furthermore, that behind the moral failure of brutish immorality is active moral rebellion, which brings us to the second characteristic of a faithless life: a faithless life denies the truth. Consider verse 4 again:

> For certain men whose condemnation was written about long ago have secretly slipped in among you. They are godless men, who change the grace of our God into a license for immorality and *deny* Jesus Christ our only Sovereign and Lord.

At root, the brutal, impure lives of these false teachers come from their insolence, irreverence, and rebellion. Impure lives are a product of faith*less*ness, of not having faith and denying the truth. Jude focuses particularly on this faithless denial of the truth in the strange middle verses: these dreamers "reject authority and slander celestial beings" (v. 8). Not even the archangel himself would dare speak in such a manner: "But even the archangel Michael, when he was disputing with the devil about the body of Moses, did not dare to bring a slanderous accusation against him, but said, 'The Lord rebuke you!'" (v. 9). Yet these men know nothing of reverence. They "speak abusively against whatever they do not understand" (v. 10). So Jude warns, "Woe to them! They have taken the way of Cain; they have rushed for profit into Balaam's error; they have been destroyed in Korah's rebellion" (v. 11). Like Cain and Balaam and Korah, says Jude, these men have lifted themselves up against God's people, God's truth, God's way, and finally God himself. Several verses later, Jude reports they have "spoken against" God (v. 15). And they "boast about themselves" alone (v. 16). In short, these men exalt themselves to the position reserved for God. They deny Christ and his people, slander angels, and promote only themselves. Jude even recalls an apostolic prediction: "'In the last times there will be scoffers who will follow their own ungodly desires'" (v. 18).

It is such faithlessness that breeds the immorality you read about in this letter. Ungodly lives stem from a denial of God's truth. Moral faithlessness exposes spiritual faithlessness. These false teachers not only teach that a Christian can live however he wants to live, they teach that a Christian can believe whatever he wants to believe and still be a Christian and belong to the church. To this, Jude responds with a clear no! What you believe affects how you live. You cannot maintain that you have a relationship with God and live as these men live or believe as they believe.

The twentieth-century writer Aldous Huxley made an unusually candid mid-life admission as he was in the process of moving from agnosticism to Eastern mysticism: Like many of his contemporaries, he says, he "took it for granted" that life has absolutely "no meaning." This was partly due to his scientific worldview. But he admits it was due "partly also to other, non-intellectual reasons. I had motives for not wanting the world to have a meaning; consequently assumed that it had none, and was able without any difficulty to find satisfying reasons for this assumption." Other, non-intellectual motives? What does Huxley mean? He continues: "The philosopher who finds no meaning in the world is not concerned exclusively with a problem in pure metaphysics; he is also concerned to prove that there is no valid reason *why he personally should not do as he wants to do,* or why his friends should not seize political power and govern in the way that they find most advantageous to themselves." Then Huxley changes to a more personal note and sounds eerily similar to the teachers Jude is warning us about: "For myself, as, no doubt, for most of my contemporaries, the philosophy of meaninglessness was essentially an instrument of liberation. The liberation we desired was simultaneously liberation from a certain political and economic system and liberation from a certain system of morality. We objected to the morality because it interfered with our sexual freedom; we objected to the political and economic systems because it was unjust. . . . There was one admirably simple method of confuting these people and at the same time justifying ourselves in our political and erotic revolt: we could deny that the world had any meaning whatsoever."[4]

Francis Bacon made the same point even more concisely: "Man prefers to believe what he prefers to be true." Faithless lives are marked by immorality and by a denial of the truth.

---

[4] Aldous Huxley, *Ends and Means* (New York: Harper & Brothers, 1937), 269-273.

Result: Barrenness and Punishment

What is the end of all of this faithlessness? Jude says in verses 12 and 13 that faithlessness results in barrenness and punishment.

Barrenness. He begins verse 12 by describing the false teachers as "blemishes at your love feasts, eating with you without the slightest qualm." These "love feasts" were a combination of what we think of as a Communion service and a potluck. As far as we can tell, the early church did not separate Communion from a full meal. When they gathered together for a meal, they would set aside a particular time for taking the bread and wine and remembering Christ's sacrifice on the cross. Remembering this salvific event and proclaiming it has always been the focal point of the Christian community. Yet these men, Jude says, are "blemishes" (or "hidden reefs," as some translations have it) upon that gathering. They mar the feast. They are dangerous obstacles to the church's fellowship.

Jude then uses several images to describe them: shepherds, clouds, trees, waves of the sea, and stars, all of which are pleasant images. But like an Alfred Hitchcock movie that takes normal things—like birds—and scares audiences with them, Jude takes these lovely images and uses them to expose the deceitfulness of these men and the utter barrenness of their lives. So he says they are

"shepherds	who feed only themselves. They are
clouds	without rain, blown along by the wind;
autumn trees,	without fruit and uprooted—twice dead.

They are

| wild waves | of the sea, foaming up their shame; |
| wandering stars, | for whom blackest darkness has been reserved forever" (vv. 12b-13). |

A faithless life is an impotent and barren life. A life not fed and guided by faith is like a shepherd who does not take care of sheep, a cloud with no rain, a tree with no fruit. It foams up nothing but shame. It is as useful as a falling star. It serves no purpose. Faithlessness benefits a life as well as windlessness helps a sailing boat. Without faith, Noah would have drowned. Without faith, Abraham would have stayed in Ur. Without faith, Moses would have remained in the wilderness and the children of Israel would have remained in slavery.

And without faith, what would be different in *your* life? Anything?

Punishment. Notice again that Jude calls the false teachers wandering stars "for whom blackest darkness has been reserved forever." In addition to barrenness, in other words, faithlessness results in punishment.

Given their lives and teaching, these men appear to think they are not accountable to God and that no punishment awaits anyone. Yet Jude is clear: punishment is real, and everyone who forsakes the truth and lives faithlessly will be punished. And like a good preacher, Jude uses three illustrations to make this point—the Israelites who fell in the wilderness, fallen angels, and Sodom and Gomorrah:

> I want to remind you that the Lord delivered his people out of Egypt, but later destroyed those who did not believe. And the angels who did not keep their positions of authority but abandoned their own home—these he has kept in darkness, bound with everlasting chains for judgment on the great Day. In a similar way, Sodom and Gomorrah and the surrounding towns gave themselves up to sexual immorality and perversion. They serve as an example of those who suffer the punishment of eternal fire (vv. 5-7).

Anyone who disbelieves in the face of God's blessings will be punished. Anyone who forsakes the truth will be punished. Anyone who lives contrary to God's way will be punished. God's judgment on sin is real. Jude says no to their immorality and unbelief because God says no.

But Jude takes the threat of punishment a step further. Punishment is not only a *possibility* for these men; they *will* be punished. "These dreamers" know God judged the Egyptians, the fallen angels, and Sodom and Gomorrah. Yet they have not heeded the warning. Imagine the stupidity of having such clear examples set before you and then ignoring them. So, "these are the very things that destroy them," Jude promises (v. 10). He is so certain of their destruction that he writes as if it had already happened: "they have been destroyed" (v. 11). After all, their destruction has been prophesied: their "condemnation was written about long ago" (v. 4). Enoch "prophesied about these men: 'See, the Lord is coming with thousands upon thousands of his holy ones to judge'" (vv. 14-15). Also, "the apostles of our Lord Jesus Christ foretold" of "scoffers who will follow their own ungodly desires" (vv. 17-18). This faithlessness should come as no surprise to Jude's readers.

The eighteenth-century evangelist George Whitefield was renowned for being an incredible orator. He was able to tell his stories with an almost unimaginable vividness. On one occasion, he was in the drawing room of the Countess of Huntingdon, where a number of nobility were gathered to hear him preach, including some famous skeptics. At one point in the meeting, Whitefield described the plight of a sinner who is unaware of his sin as "a blind man on a stormy night, feeling his way along near the edge of a cliff." As he told the story, he walked forward tapping a cane and describing the blind man getting closer and closer to the edge of the cliff. Finally, when a great deal of intensity had built up in the room, one of the most well-known skeptics jumped up and said, "Save the man, Whitefield, save the man." Of course, Whitefield was interested in the real man who stood up. That was the man who was in danger. The blind man was imaginary. The false teachers of whom Jude speaks likewise know the illustrations of fallen angels and Sodom and Gomorrah, yet they fail to recognize it applies to *them*. So too with us. If we see the warnings God has given and do not heed them, we are like the blind man walking toward the edge of the cliff. Only someone hallucinating—only a dreamer—believes otherwise.

Well, this is what Jude says a life without faith is like, and this is where Jude spends most of his time. But not quite all of it. At the end of his letter, Jude returns to what really was his main theme.

CHARACTERISTICS OF A LIFE WITH FAITH

What are the characteristics of a life with faith?

Contending for the Faith

Mainly, a life with faith is marked by contending for the faith. Immediately following his salutation, Jude opens his letter,

> Dear friends, although I was very eager to write to you about the salvation we share, I felt I had to write and urge you to *contend for the faith* that was once for all entrusted to the saints. For certain men whose condemnation was written about long ago have secretly slipped in among you. They are godless men, who change the grace of our God into a license for immorality and deny Jesus Christ our only Sovereign and Lord (vv. 3-4).

He does not tell them to contend for overly short togas, or overly long hair. He does not tell them to contend over the meanings of obscure words, or what color to paint the catacombs. No, Jude tells them to contend for the faith, that is, the truth about the Lord Jesus Christ, his atoning death, and his call to discipleship. He tells them to contend for the faith *once for all* entrusted to Christians. The faith does not change. The gospel does not change. It is final and unchanging, regardless of the latest theological fashions.

The word for "contend" is the word from which we get our word "agonize." It is a strenuous, athletic word. You might think of some sporting event you like. Perhaps you have a favorite player. Imagine how your favorite player looks at the high point of the game or match, straining with every nerve and muscle in the body. Now, says Jude, we are to do *that* for the faith. Contend for the faith not because it is familiar or traditional or conservative. Contend because it is true and it is essential.

When I first became a Christian, I loved the song "I Have Decided to Follow Jesus," particularly the line that says, "Though none go with me, still I will follow." We must have such a determination for the truth. I am determined to contend for the truth of the faith once for all delivered. I contend first with myself but also with my family. I contend among my friends and in my church. I contend in our community and in our convention of churches. As God gives me opportunity, I will contend in our nation and in our world.

Do I say this to dazzle you? Do I preach to exhibit my knowledge? Do I pastor to flatter and impress, or even to satisfy the conditions of my employment? Do I show up on Sunday mornings to entertain or to act as the personal spiritual trainer for members of the congregation, helping each one accomplish the year's spiritual goals? No, I preach, I pastor, I write to contend for the faith once for all delivered to the saints. Contending for the faith is the call of *every* Christian. So just as Jude contends for the faith by writing this letter and exhorting his readers to contend for the faith, I am contending for the faith in this chapter so that *you* will contend for the faith.

Let me encourage you not to be like the crowds that rode out from Washington in carriages to watch the first battle of the Civil War at Bull Run. If you are a Civil War buff you may remember the story. At the first battle of the war, streams of people actually traveled from Washington, spread blankets on a nearby hillside, served tea, and watched while the battle raged. Do not be like that! Do not spread your blankets and serve your tea while there is a faith to contend for. Join me in contending for the faith.

Contending for the faith is not, however, ultimately negative. That is, it is not defined primarily by what we refrain from doing, though that is part of it. Contending is primarily positive and constructive. This becomes clear in the climax of the letter, verses 20 and 21, where Jude tells us what to do positively.

Building One Another Up in the Faith, Not Fomenting Division Through Error

A life marked by faith, then, means building one another up in the faith and not fomenting division through untruth and error. Jude writes, "But you, dear friends, build yourselves up in your most holy faith" (v. 20a). The "yourselves" here is plural. He is not saying to build oneself up. He is saying to build one another up. There is no Lone Rangerism here. *We together* are God's temple, where he dwells (1 Cor. 3:16). These ungodly teachers were dividing the church through error and carnality. We are to build it on the foundation of our most holy faith.

In other words, we have a concern for both truth (the faith) and unity (building one another up). Our concern for the truth should lead to unity. In Scripture, error brings division. All tearing down—unless it is tearing down expressly for the gospel—is *wrong*. I cannot say that strongly enough. Apart from preserving the gospel, all tearing down is wrong. We should build ourselves up in the most holy faith.

Praying by the Spirit, Not Following Unholy Carnality

The life with faith is also marked by Spirit-led prayer and not by unholy carnality. Jude says simply, "pray in the Holy Spirit" (v. 20b). These false teachers, you will notice, "do not have the Spirit" (v. 19). We, on the other hand, are to pray as God's own Spirit leads us into truth by reading his Word.

If you are spiritually alive as an individual, and if your church is alive, you will find God leading you to himself in prayer. You will desire such opportunities. Capitol Hill Baptist Church grew up out of a prayer meeting in a woman's home on Capitol Hill in 1865. If Capitol Hill Baptist Church or any church is to continue, church members must attend church not only to consume. They must also come to pray.

When I first arrived at our church, I received a number of comments about the fact that the Lord's Supper was shared on Sunday morning less frequently than it had been in the past (since we began sharing it more often on Sunday evening). Yet I never heard one complaint about not being able to come and pray together. Scripture nowhere tells us how often we must observe Communion. However, Scripture is very clear that we must gather together to pray as Christians. If you have not made gathering together with other Christians to pray for the church one of your priorities, let me encourage you to do just that. If the work of the church is to prosper, then we must pray it to prosperity by the grace of God.

Living Obediently, Not Rebelliously

The life with faith should be marked by obedience and not by rebellion. That is what Jude means in verse 21 when he says, "Keep yourselves in God's love." We keep ourselves in God's love, Jesus said, when we obey his commandments: "If you obey my commands, you will remain in my love, just as I have obeyed my Father's commands and remain in his love" (John 15:10; cf. 1 John 4:16).

Showing Mercy, Not Selfishness

Finally, the life with faith should be marked by mercy and not by selfishness. "Be merciful to those who doubt," Jude says (Jude 22). We should also be merciful to those who are liable to punishment: "snatch others from the fire and save them" (v. 23a). And we should "show mercy, mixed with fear" to those who are caught in carnal sin, "hating even the clothing stained by corrupted flesh" (v. 23b). We must bear ourselves toward them with both a trembling pity and an abhorrence of their impurities.

Don't just stop the erosion. Begin building by going out and showing mercy to those who need to know God! With some, be patient. With others, explain the faith.

This is the life with faith. It is marked by contending for the gospel, building up the saints, praying in the Spirit, living obediently, and showing mercy. Now, look at your own life. Can you put a check by all five characteristics and say that they mark your life? Contending for the gospel, praying, living obediently? Do you live by faith in God by showing mercy to others when they do not deserve it? Do you strive to build other Christians up in the faith? In other words, are you living a life of Christian faith, or something else?

CONCLUSION: THREE QUESTIONS ABOUT FAITH

In closing, Jude answers three questions on the topic of faith. First, looking to the past, we might ask where our faith comes from. Jude writes in the very first verse, "To those who have been called, who are loved by God the Father and kept by Jesus Christ." In other words, faith comes from God. It is a gift. God has *called* us out from the world and into his body, the church. Jude does not say we call ourselves, or that the church calls us. He says God has called us. God the Father has also *loved* us, which is why he has called us. From before the foundations of the world, we have been the beloved of God! And Jesus Christ, God the Son, has *kept* Christians. We are kept through trials and temptations. We certainly cannot keep ourselves. Christ keeps us with his constant and sure care. So we have been called and loved and kept. Our identity as Christians, as people whose lives are marked by faith, depends ultimately on God. I can exhort you to believe, but I cannot give you faith. Where does faith come from? As Paul says, faith is a gift of God (Eph. 2:8).

Second, looking to the future, who will evaluate and judge this world on the last day? Once again, the answer is God. He is presently keeping the fallen angels "bound with everlasting chains for judgment on the great Day" (v. 6). He formerly destroyed the inhabitants of Sodom and Gomorrah, so that they "serve as an example of those who suffer the punishment of eternal fire"

(v. 7). He is coming again "to judge everyone, and to convict all the ungodly" (v. 15). And he is coming again to bring "the mercy of our Lord Jesus Christ to bring you to eternal life" (v. 21). If we look to the future with faith, we see that God is the final judge and evaluator. He is the beginning of faith and he is its final judge.

Third, while living in the present, how do we keep living by faith in such faithless times? Look at those tremendous last two verses:

> To him who is able to keep you from falling and to present you before his glorious presence without fault and with great joy—to the only God our Savior be glory, majesty, power and authority, through Jesus Christ our Lord, before all ages, now and forevermore! Amen (vv. 24-25).

In these two verses we see that God is our keeper, our promised presenter, and our Savior. He is our keeper. He keeps us from falling into soul-destroying sin. As one Puritan, John Flavel, said, "As God did not at first choose you because you were high, so he will not forsake you because you are now low."[5] He is also our promised presenter. We will be presented in his glorious presence without fault and with great joy. In other words, he is powerful not just to keep but also to cleanse. In the presence of God, Adam hid, Isaiah fell to the ground and confessed his uncleanness, and Job repented in dust and ashes. In *that* presence, we will be presented without fault and with great rejoicing. And Jesus is our Savior, or as Jude says, the "only God our Savior." There is no other God to serve and to rely upon. So how do we continue in the faith in such faithless times? The answer can only be, by God. Faith comes from God. Faith will be judged by God. And our faith persists today because of God. Not only that, our faith ultimately serves his glory—"before all ages, now and forevermore."

When I lived in England, I sometimes went hill-walking. When you go hill-walking, you occasionally find that places that look impassible from a distance often prove to be easily negotiated by following a well-laid path. On the other hand, stretches of land that look easy to traverse might in fact conceal a great ravine. So much of what you can see depends on where you are standing. Sometimes we need to change our position in order to see the truth.

Augustine said that if we do not believe, we will not understand. Perhaps you may need to work more on understanding. Alternatively, you may have worked on understanding and now you believe what Christ said is true: you stand under God's righteous judgment. If this is you, I say, change your position. Flee from the wrath of God. Flee to Christ. Pray to God for this faith we

[5] John Flavel, *Keeping the Heart*, 5.2.4.

read about in Jude's little letter. As Jesus said, "The time has come. The kingdom of God is near. Repent and believe the good news!" (Mark 1:15).

Let us pray:

Lord God, we see in the faithlessness of individuals in this letter something of our own faithlessness. It is so easy for us to fall into a "however we want to live" and "whatever we want to believe" attitude. Yet we see here that the consequences of such an attitude are most serious: spiritual barrenness, impotency, and finally judgment.

Lord, we praise you for the hope we have that comes from faith in you. We praise you that faith is a gift of yours, as Paul said. We praise you that you are the one who sustains our faith. And we praise you that you are the one who will ultimately vindicate our faith. O Lord, give us the ability to repent and believe. Convict us of sin and show us your mercy very clearly. Show it as you did to the disciple Peter, who confessed that you were the Son of God. You told him that he did not figure out who you were on his own but that the Father had revealed it to him. So, we pray that your Holy Spirit would minister to us today by revealing the truth, convicting us of sin, and lifting up the Lord Jesus Christ in our hearts. For Jesus' sake we ask it. Amen.

Questions for Reflection

1. Do you think it is harder to have faith in our days than at other times in history? What challenges to faith particularly characterize our own times?

2. Have you ever been tempted to justify either your own sin or someone else's by saying it was "natural," "hereditary," "chemical," or "that's just me"?

3. How will you ever know if something you want is wrong? In the way you now understand your faith, is there any way you are able to hear God if he is against what you want? How would you know if God opposed what you wanted?

4. We have seen that ungodly lives stem from a denial of God's truth. What you believe affects how you live. What implications does this have for the work of the church? The work of discipleship? Parenting? How should we respond to people who claim to value experience over truth?

5. On a closely related note, Francis Bacon said, "Man prefers to believe what he prefers to be true." In other words, if we want to engage in some behavior,

or live in a certain way, we will figure out how to rationalize it and call it "good" or "true." Can you think of a time when you have done this, only to discover later that you were acting according to sinful motives all along? Think further about the implications this has for evangelism and apologetics. If people *prefer* to believe what they *prefer* to be true, non-Christians might offer a host of intellectual objections to Christianity, but are you truly having a conversation with their intellects—or are you having a conversation with their appetites?

6. The presence of faith in a person's life is often evidenced by spiritual fruit. A lack of faith is evidenced by barrenness. One way of examining the state of your faith is to look for spiritual fruit in your life, and particularly the progress you make over the years (see 2 Pet. 1:8). Well, how are you doing? Ask God to show you evidences of his grace in your progress in the faith, so that you might thank him for them.

7. What examples of punishment has God placed before you, whether in your own life or in the lives of others? How can you practice meditating on those examples in order to learn their lessons?

8. What exactly is the "faith" for which we should contend?

9. Do you contend for the faith? How?

10. When do you gather with other Christians to pray for the work of the church? Do you do it with your own family?

11. This is the life with faith: contending for the gospel, building up the saints, praying in the Spirit, living obediently, and showing mercy. Now, look at your own life. Can you put a check by all five characteristics and say that they mark your life? Contending for the gospel, praying, living obediently? Do you live by faith in God by showing mercy to others when they do not deserve it? Do you strive to build other Christians up in the faith? In other words, are you living a life of Christian faith, or something else?

THE MESSAGE OF REVELATION: WHAT ARE WE WAITING FOR?

27

THE MESSAGE OF REVELATION: WHAT ARE WE WAITING FOR?

WHAT ARE WE WAITING FOR? INTRODUCING REVELATION[1]

It has been said there are two kinds of disappointments in life. The first occurs when you don't get what you want. The second occurs when you do.

It is true, isn't it? Even when we get the things we want so much, we find they are not perfect: they break; they have to be replaced; the batteries wear out. Even the best things in this life have the fine print.

So when people look to the future, they do not know whether to look with hope or worry. And that is where the last book of the Bible, Revelation, finds them.

I have to admit, Revelation is a famously confusing book. I could tell you it is not that difficult, like Mark Twain's comment about Wagner's music, "It's not as bad as it sounds." But when you read Revelation, you will find dragons, angels, beasts, locusts with human faces, scenes set in heaven, and all sorts of images you cannot imagine. Some of these things will be difficult to understand. Other things, however, are not that hard to understand; and these are the most important things in the book.

In order to understand John's message in Revelation, we will look at four arresting images that John sees in the vision he is given. We will begin by looking at the image of a throne in chapters 4 and 5. Then we will observe the image of a storm in chapter 11 and elsewhere. We will then come back to chapter 5 to consider the image of the Lamb. We will finish by looking at the image of a city in the great chapter 21. What does this book tell us about the future? Should we wait with hope or with dread?

---

[1] This sermon was originally preached on July 2, 1995, at Capitol Hill Baptist Church in Washington, D.C.

A THRONE

In Revelation's first three chapters, we read about John's record of the initial vision he is given as well as Jesus' letters to seven churches. These letters make for a great sermon series themselves! For our purposes here, this grand vision really begins in chapters 4 and 5.

The One on the Throne

The first image I want you to notice, right here at the beginning of the vision in chapter 4 and dominating everything else in the future, is a throne and the one upon it. "At once I was in the Spirit," John writes, "and there before me was a throne in heaven with someone sitting on it. And the one who sat there had the appearance of jasper and carnelian" (4:2-3a). Interestingly, not a lot of specifics are given about this indescribable someone sitting on the throne, who had the appearance of jasper and carnelian.

The Scene Around the Throne

John goes on in his vision and talks about the splendor surrounding this throne. He writes,

> A rainbow, resembling an emerald, encircled the throne. Surrounding the throne were twenty-four other thrones, and seated on them were twenty-four elders. They were dressed in white and had crowns of gold on their heads. From the throne came flashes of lightning, rumblings and peals of thunder. Before the throne, seven lamps were blazing. These are the seven spirits of God. Also before the throne there was what looked like a sea of glass, clear as crystal.
>
> In the center, around the throne, were four living creatures, and they were covered with eyes, in front and in back. The first living creature was like a lion, the second was like an ox, the third had a face like a man, the fourth was like a flying eagle. Each of the four living creatures had six wings and was covered with eyes all around, even under his wings (4:3b-8a).

Notice all the brilliant language about a rainbow and flashes of lightning and a crystal sea. It is difficult to know what all of these images mean. Maybe the lamps before the throne are other angelic servants of God. Maybe they point to the presence of the Holy Spirit of God. I do think we can say that all these images, one piled on top of the other, present the superlative splendor of the one who sits on the throne. This is the throne room to end all throne rooms because the king to end all kings dwells here!

The four living creatures around the throne sound like a cross between the cherubim in Ezekiel and the seraphim in Isaiah. Whoever they are, the impression they make is crystal clear: even beings as magnificent as these are given over entirely to the worship of this most magnificent one on the throne. "Day and night," John says of these creatures, "they never stop saying: 'Holy, holy, holy is the Lord God Almighty, who was, and is, and is to come'" (4:8b).

And John keeps going. He next describes the twenty-four elders, who are also wholly devoted to worshiping the one on the throne:

> Whenever the living creatures give glory, honor and thanks to him who sits on the throne and who lives for ever and ever, the twenty-four elders fall down before him who sits on the throne, and worship him who lives for ever and ever. They lay their crowns before the throne and say:
>
> "You are worthy, our Lord and God,
>   to receive glory and honor and power,
>   for you created all things,
>   and by your will they were created and have their being" (4:9-11).

All the descriptions of these heavenly creatures are not given so that one day, when you are circulating in the heavenly menagerie, you will not be embarrassed by forgetting who somebody is. They are not provided so that you can know what the elders do as opposed to the four living creatures, or for getting the kids to draw any of them in Sunday school. No, the purpose is to draw our attention again and again back to the one on the throne. That is why the elders keep falling down! They fall toward the throne, and they cast all their honor and glory to the one on the throne. So often, when Christian writers fill hundreds of pages on what these creatures are, they miss the point of the vision. The point is to throw all glory and honor to the one on the throne, to God Almighty. God himself is the focus. As if to draw our attention away from themselves and back to God, these mighty elders, whoever they are, lay the crowns they have been given before the throne and say, "You are worthy, our Lord and God." They acknowledge that God is the source of all the glory they possess, and he alone is sovereign over the world.

Perhaps you have seen the movie *The Wizard of Oz*. Behind a seemingly massive and powerful wizard is just a little man pulling levers. Worldly power and authority can seem that way. As soon as you get to know someone whom you have admired, you learn that he or she is just human. But there are no small men behind curtains here. Instead, the elders fall to their faces, just as John had fallen to his face "as though dead" in 1:17. Day and night, the four great creatures worship.

The Action Around the Throne

The action around the throne begins to happen when a scroll is brought into the throne room in chapter 5. John writes,

> Then I saw in the right hand of him who sat on the throne a scroll with writing on both sides and sealed with seven seals. And I saw a mighty angel proclaiming in a loud voice, "Who is worthy to break the seals and open the scroll?" But no one in heaven or on earth or under the earth could open the scroll or even look inside it. I wept and wept because no one was found who was worthy to open the scroll or look inside. Then one of the elders said to me, "Do not weep! See, the Lion of the tribe of Judah, the Root of David, has triumphed. He is able to open the scroll and its seven seals" (5:1-5).

In the following chapters we watch as the seven seals are opened and the effects follow one by one. This scroll seems to be the document upon which the rest of history is written out. It contains the decrees and judgments of the sovereign, heretofore sealed so that none could see. God is on his throne. And he is sovereign not only over this throne room but over all history. He executes his decrees through this scroll.

The One on the Throne Alone Deserves Our Worship and Trust

All of this, of course, was vitally important to John and the Christians to whom he was writing. When John heard these heavenly creatures say to God, "You are worthy," he was hearing the same words that were used to worship the emperor of Rome. The emperor Domitian required this phrase to be used as an act of worship when people greeted him in triumphal procession. John was in exile, it appears, because he would not comply. He knew that Yahweh alone is God, and that he alone deserves worship. The Roman government was asking for false worship.

So in this time when the whole civilized world gave homage to a human emperor, John's vision reminded the early believers that the God they worshiped was not just the Lord of their individual hearts while the Roman emperor ruled everything else. No, all creation pays homage to its true sovereign, the Lord God Almighty. Unlike Emperor Domitian, the Lord Almighty was, is, and is to come. Just when circumstances might have beaten the churches into hopelessness, John is given this great vision of the glory and greatness of God to share with all the churches. Certainly this, before anything else, would have breathed new life into many withering believers. The Lord of their lives was indeed the Lord of History!

At the center of history is not an impersonal chemical reaction. At the center of the universe is not chance and randomness. There is a throne, and on that throne there is a sovereign God who rules the world. John goes on to tell us many other things about the future. But he wants us to get this clear at the beginning. At the center of everything is a throne—the throne of God. And we are called to ultimately trust nothing other than God on his throne.

The world and all of us in it are not held in the hand of Caesar. We are not in the hand of any government or boss or family member. If we are Christians who trust in the Lamb who was slain, we are in the hand of the one who bought us with the Lamb's blood. The future is not meaningless. It is not anonymous. It is not foreboding and empty like a soon-to-be occupied casket. No, the future is full and bright. And it is full and bright for Christians because of this throne.

Trust God for his perfect rule.

A STORM

Beginning in chapter 6, the Lamb begins to open the seals of the scroll one by one. When he does, this splendid vision of God's court gives way to the storms of judgment decreed by God. From chapter 6 through chapter 20, God's judgments roll out in repeated peals of thunder. This is the second image I want us to notice in this book: a storm. There are three series of judgments in the book. First, seven seals are opened. Then seven trumpets are sounded by angels. Then seven bowls are poured out. At the conclusion of each series is a storm. After the seventh seal is opened, John writes, "there came peals of thunder, rumblings, flashes of lightning and an earthquake" (8:5). After the seventh trumpet, he records, "And there came flashes of lightning, rumblings, peals of thunder, an earthquake and a great hailstorm" (11:19). The same thing is also said after the seventh bowl is poured out, only this time the earthquake is "severe" (16:18). The seals come first, because the Lamb must open the seals of God's decrees of judgment upon creation. The sounding trumpets then announce God's decrees over creation. Finally, the seven bowls pour his judgment out upon creation. The climax of each is a storm.

The Nature of God's Judgment

These chapters appear to record a progression of events, but it is not a simple progression. Many events seem to repeat, yet they also seem to intensify. So you cannot read the book of Revelation and assume that some event recorded in chapter 17 must occur later in time than some event in chapter 9. The book does not work that way. Instead, you should pay attention to this intensification from one series to the next. For instance, when the second trumpet sounds, one-third of the sea turns to blood and one-third of the sea creatures die (8:8-9). When the second bowl is poured out, however, all the sea turns to blood and all the sea creatures die (16:3). Also, when the sixth seal is opened, natural disasters occur (6:12-17). When the seventh bowl is poured out, however, similar sounding natural disasters occur yet they sound even more severe (16:17-21). Again and again, the vision presents images that recall previous images, as if to underscore, or push a bit further, some kind of judgment previously mentioned. And like the opening of the seals in chapter 6, both of the subsequent series begin in the heavenly throne room (8:1-6; 15:1–16:1). Ultimately, it is like watching the judgment of God on humanity in a spiral. John turns and turns the screws of tension, anticipation, and dreadful awe. God's final judgment on his creation will be presented with a crescendoing, unerring procession.

As humans, we do have an instinctive sense of justice. When someone is able to evade responsibility for his actions, we say, "He could get away with murder." Even if a few academics do not, most of us prefer stories where the bad guys get their comeuppance and the good guys are rewarded. Criminals being brought to justice is an ever-popular political slogan.

Yet when people read about this swirling series of judgments, each culminating in a tremendous storm, they are troubled. And that makes sense. Our justice, as we experience it, is insufficient. The judgments handed down by judges do nothing for the victims. Our justice is uncertain. People go to jail and are made worse. Our justice is often stopgap. We cannot catch those who are guilty; and when we do, they get out and repeat their crimes. And our justice can be mistaken. Innocent people are sentenced and suffer wrongly. In this world, there is no perfect justice. At the root of it all, though, our hesitancy about justice and the punishment of wrong must be related to an awareness of our own vulnerability to just accusation. Did not Jesus himself suggest that, at least sometimes, we are not competent to judge: "If any one of you is without sin, let him be the first to throw a stone" (John 8:7). And if what Jesus says is true, all of us know, deep in our hearts, that none of us would cast any stones.

But the one who spoke these words was the one without sin. And as the one who is just, he is the one who will mete out justice. He is the Lamb who opens the scrolls.

In the book of Revelation, the instinctive sense of justice shared by every human finally meets with the one judge who shares none of our judicial inadequacies, who knows all the facts right down to the motives of the heart, who knows right from wrong precisely, and who is able to execute his judgments perfectly. This is the judge against whom no appeal could ever be raised.

The Certainty of God's Judgment

One of these great series of judgments culminates in chapter 11, and the certainty of God's coming judgment is pronounced. The seventh trumpet sounds, voices in heaven proclaim the coming of Christ's reign forever and ever, and the twenty-four elders fall on their faces and worship, saying,

> The nations were angry;
>   and your wrath has come.
> The time has come for judging the dead, and for
>   rewarding your servants the prophets
> and your saints and those who reverence your name,
>   both small and great—
> and for destroying those who destroy the earth (11:18).

It is made clear throughout these chapters that no power on earth can prevent, hinder, or delay God's judgment. The natural and social forces of the world are at God's disposal. Famine and plague do his bidding (6:8; 11:6; 18:8). All creation, from untamed animals to earthquakes, serves God's call for judgment (6:8, 12; 8:5; 11:13, 19; 16:18). More than once, the fixed points of this world—the sky, the mountains, the islands—are "removed" or "flee" away (6:14; 16:20; 20:11). So complete is God's power that even his extraterrestrial creation acts in concert with his judgment on earth: the sun is blackened, the moon turns red, and the stars fall (6:12-13; 8:12). Not even death itself can hide us from the searching judgment of God (11:18).

God's judgment is certain. Nothing will stop it. Perhaps you have read in the newspaper, or seen at work, or witnessed in a family, or even experienced yourself a situation in which injustice appears to go unanswered. It will not always be so. God draws a line under all such situations and will address them at just the right time. He will say, "Enough!" He will vindicate his people.

The Finality of God's Judgment

God's judgment is also final. His judgments continue "for ever and ever." John writes, "The seventh angel sounded his trumpet, and there were loud voices in heaven, which said: 'The kingdom of the world has become the kingdom of our Lord and of his Christ, and he will reign for ever and ever'" (11:15). Regarding those who worship the beast, John says, "And the smoke of their torment rises for ever and ever" (14:11a). The beast and the false prophet are also tormented eternally (20:10). There is no appeal from God's judgment. When God judges, the only response is the silence of assent and songs of worship.

Surely that must give you some peace. Life is not simply a never-ending circle of struggling and suffering, of joys that end and sorrows that endure. Christianity is different from many of the world's religions in just this way— history does not merely recycle us again and again on a treadmill. It focuses all of history on a particular point of time at the throne of God. And the judgment of that throne is final.

The Horror of God's Judgment

Revelation also reveals the horror of God's judgment. Every kind of human will be horrified on that day. John writes,

> Then the kings of the earth, the princes, the generals, the rich, the mighty, and every slave and every free man hid in caves and among the rocks of the mountains. They called to the mountains and the rocks, "Fall on us and hide us from the face of him who sits on the throne and from the wrath of the Lamb! For the great day of their wrath has come, and who can stand?" (6:15-17).

The torment of those who worship the beast will rise forever, as we have seen. From supernatural prisons to the Abyss, from plagues to earthquakes, and from Hades to the eternal lake of fire, this book is filled with unimaginably horrible images. Some have even called these images unbearable, and I can certainly understand why. But if the images are true, we do not help anyone by trying to make them seem less horrible.

Even in our age of overly-stimulated imaginations, this book produces awe. God's judgment will be horrible. Surely our response should be like Job's: "My ears had heard of you but now my eyes have seen you. Therefore I despise myself and repent in dust and ashes" (Job 42:5-6).

The Rightness of God's Judgment

God's judgment is also right. John writes,

> And the twenty-four elders, who were seated on their thrones before God, fell on their faces and worshiped God, saying:
>
> > "We give thanks to you, Lord God Almighty,
> >   the One who is and who was,
> > because you have taken your great power
> >   and have begun to reign.
> > The nations were angry;
> >   and your wrath has come.
> > The time has come for judging the dead,
> >   and for rewarding your servants the prophets

and your saints and those who reverence your name,
  both small and great
and for destroying those who destroy the earth."

Then God's temple in heaven was opened, and within his temple was seen
the ark of his covenant. And there came flashes of lightning, rumblings, peals of
thunder, an earthquake and a great hailstorm (Rev. 11:16-19).

There is no question of God's judgments being uncertain or ineffective,
inadequate or wrong. No, God's judgments are complete, accurate, and
appropriate.

Certainly neither you nor I know every wrong done in every place at every
time by every one who has ever lived. Nor do we have the moral character to
measure wrong perfectly, or even well. But the God of the Bible does. He stands
as an eternal, ever-present, and ever-truthful witness, as well as an ever-wise,
ever-merciful, and ever-just judge.

Trust God for his perfect justice.

THE LAMB

We have seen a throne and a storm. Much in this picture of judgment is dark.
But rays of light break into the darkness. And in those rays of light we see a
third arresting image: Lamb.

The Person of the Lamb

When we left John in the throne room in chapter 5, he was weeping because
no one was found worthy to open the seals on the scroll of history. But John
continues to write down what he sees: "Then one of the elders said to me, 'Do
not weep! See, the Lion of the tribe of Judah, the Root of David, has triumphed. He is able to open the scroll and its seven seals'" (5:5). John is told
to expect a lion, the kind of creature you or I might expect to break open these
seals. A lion would be mighty enough. Lions are great creatures. Nations often
use them as symbols of national power. All this makes sense. But notice what
John sees when he turns:

> Then I saw a Lamb, looking as if it had been slain, standing in the center of the
> throne, encircled by the four living creatures and the elders. He had seven horns
> and seven eyes, which are the seven spirits of God sent out into all the earth. He
> came and took the scroll from the right hand of him who sat on the throne. And
> when he had taken it, the four living creatures and the twenty-four elders fell
> down before the Lamb. Each one had a harp and they were holding golden bowls
> full of incense, which are the prayers of the saints (5:6-8).

Imagine John's astonishment when he looks and sees not a lion but a Lamb, looking as if it had been slain. A Lamb! A Lamb that had been slain! A slain Lamb standing on the very throne of God! This Lamb, you see, is God and is being worshiped as God.

At this moment, did John recall the words of John the Baptist? "Look, the Lamb of God, who takes away the sin of the world!" (John 1:29). Or the words of the prophet Isaiah? He was "led like a lamb to the slaughter, and as a sheep before her shearers is silent, so he did not open his mouth" (Isa. 53:7). Whether he did or not, this slain, now living Lamb, who is about to reveal God's final judgment upon the sin of the world, is clearly Christ. He had spoken to John back in chapter 1, identifying himself as "the Living One; I was dead, and behold I am alive for ever and ever!" (Rev. 1:18). But now this Lamb stands upright with seven horns and seven eyes—perfect power and perfect wisdom. He stands in the center of the throne, encircled by the four living creatures and the elders. And these angelic beings, who so carefully reject John's worship throughout this book, protesting that worship should be offered only to God, here turn and worship the Lamb. John hears the living creatures, the elders, and angels numbering ten thousands upon ten thousands singing,

> "Worthy is the Lamb, who was slain,
>   to receive power and wealth and wisdom and strength
>   and honor and glory and praise!"

> Then I heard every creature in heaven and on earth and under the earth and on the sea, and all that is in them, singing:

> "To him who sits on the throne and to the Lamb
>   be praise and honor and glory and power, for ever and ever!"

> The four living creatures said, "Amen," and the elders fell down and worshiped (5:12-14).

The Work of the Lamb

What has this Lamb done? Why did the elders worship him? In the heart of chapter 5, John records, "And they sang a new song: 'You are worthy to take the scroll and to open its seals, because you were slain, and with your blood you purchased men for God from every tribe and language and people and nation'" (5:9). Then in chapter 7, John witnesses "a great multitude that no one could count, from every nation, tribe, people and language, standing before the throne and in front of the Lamb" (7:9). He is then told that the ones in white have "'washed their robes and made them white in the blood of the

Lamb'" (7:14). This is why only the Lamb could open the sealed scroll of God in chapter 5—only he had authority to fulfill judgment and redemption. Only he had purchased this redeemed company.

Even unbelievers cry "Why?" in response to tragedy and injustice, as if someone exists to hear them and answer their questions. Intuitively, deep within us, we know the events of our lives have meaning. If you are a non-Christian, or you are a Christian doubting your faith, consider the fact that your sense of justice has a root. On the throne of God is the Lamb who will redeem and who will judge. He has given himself, literally, to be punished for the sins of everyone who repents of their sin and follows him as Lord. These are the ones he redeems. So trust. Flee from your sin and trust him as a child trusts his or her parents—not because the child understands everything the parents do but because the child knows that the parents are good and that they keep their promises.

If you are a Christian, be encouraged that on God's throne is the Lamb. As the writer to the Hebrews says, we do not have a God

> who is unable to sympathize with our weaknesses, but we have one who has been tempted in every way, just as we are—yet was without sin. Let us then approach the throne of grace with confidence, so that we may receive mercy and find grace to help us in our time of need (Heb. 4:15-16).

This God, who sits on a high throne surrounded by a great heavenly host, is not finally a God we cannot approach. He is a God who was slain for us. He calls us to approach him through his blood.

Because of this Lamb, all of God's people will be safe. In chapter 7, the reader first encounters the 144,000 saints from every tribe of Israel. Then several series of judgments occur in the ensuing chapters, as we have seen. Then in chapter 14, do you know how many of these 144,000 saints remain standing around the Lamb? Not 143,999, but 144,000. Twelve tribes times twelve, times one-thousand. The number signifies completeness. None of God's people have been left out. Not one of them is missing. All of God's chosen ones are sealed and protected from God's wrath. The Lamb keeps those whom he has purchased with his blood.

These people who worship the Lamb hold victorious palm branches and cry out in praise to the Lamb for their safety and salvation. If you are a follower of the Lamb, you will stand among this great throng. Nothing that troubles you today will trouble you forever. And there is no small print to that statement. No qualifications. No exceptions. Period! As John observes,

he who sits on the throne will spread his tent over them.
Never again will they hunger;
   never again will they thirst.
The sun will not beat upon them,
   nor any scorching heat.
For the Lamb at the center of the throne will be their shepherd;
   he will lead them to springs of living water.
And God will wipe away every tear from their eyes (Rev. 7:15b-17).

Trust God for his deliverance.

A CITY

That brings us to the final arresting image for us to observe in the book of Revelation: a city. According to the Bible, God's relationship with his people ends not in a garden, where it began, but in a city.

Now, if you were brought up in the country, you might have a slight prejudice against cities. You may not think of cities as attractive places, as compared to the beauties of nature. If you were brought up in a city, you know the many trials of city living. Today's cities face growing homelessness, racial conflicts, escalating crime, and gang warfare. The social and economic infrastructures of many cities are falling apart through a damning combination of unemployment and immorality. Even the Bible presents cities as places of Godforsakenness through his judgments on Babel, Sodom and Gomorrah, Jerusalem itself, and (in the book Revelation) Rome. That is the kind of impression many people have of cities. I recently read a contest-prize announcement that said, "First prize: A week in Cleveland. Second prize: Two weeks in Cleveland."

With all this in mind, it is amazing to read what John sees in this last and perhaps greatest vision in the Bible. He does not see a bunch of disembodied beings inhabiting clouds and reclining in everlasting indolence. No, he sees an entirely new creation, and primarily he sees a new city—the city of good times, the city of God, the city of God's people.

City of Good Times

John writes, "Then I saw a new heaven and a new earth, for the first heaven and the first earth had passed away, and there was no longer any sea. I saw the Holy City, the new Jerusalem, coming down out of heaven from God" (21:1-2a).

In this great city, death will be replaced by life: God "will wipe every tear from their eyes. There will be no more death or mourning or crying or pain, for the old order of things has passed away'" (21:4).

Night will be replaced by light:

> the city does not need the sun or the moon to shine on it, for the glory of God gives it light, and the Lamb is its lamp. The nations will walk by its light, and the kings of the earth will bring their splendor into it. On no day will its gates ever be shut, for there will be no night there (21:23-25).

Corruption will be replaced by purity: "Nothing impure will ever enter it, nor will anyone who does what is shameful or deceitful, but only those whose names are written in the Lamb's book of life" (21:27).

And all the effects of the divine curse in Genesis will be replaced by divine blessing:

> Then the angel showed me the river of the water of life, as clear as crystal, flowing from the throne of God and of the Lamb down the middle of the great street of the city. On each side of the river stood the tree of life, bearing twelve crops of fruit, yielding its fruit every month. And the leaves of the tree are for the healing of the nations. No longer will there be any curse (22:1-3a).

City of God

But do you know what the chief good of this city will be? God himself will be there. John records, "And I heard a loud voice from the throne saying, 'Now the dwelling of God is with men, and he will live with them. They will be his people, and God himself will be with them and be their God'" (21:3).

God's presence in the city is marked in several ways. First, we observe the city's brilliant appearance: "It shone with the glory of God, and its brilliance was like that of a very precious jewel, like a jasper, clear as crystal" (21:11). This brilliance is typical throughout the Bible for describing the presence of God. God comes in a brilliant, multicolored spectacle of sparkling, shining light, as in chapter 4's throne room scene. This city glows with the very glory of God. It is magnificent beyond description!

Second, the city has an unusual shape. An angel measures it to be 12,000 stadia (about 1,400 miles) in length, width, and height (21:16). Now what kind of city would be a cube? John's Jewish readers would have understood immediately the allusion being made: the Most Holy Place, which the high priest entered once a year to represent the people after making a sacrifice, was shaped as a cube (see 1 Kings 6:14-19). And here in the Most Holy Place, above the Ark of the Covenant, God would meet with his people (Ex. 25:22). This cube-shaped heavenly city, to which the cube-shaped Most Holy Place merely pointed, will fulfill God's promises to dwell with his people. But we, his people, will not enter only once a year through a priest. We will live there forever in God's presence through the Lamb. By the same token, John does not see a temple—because the Father and the Son are its temple: "I did not see a temple in the city, because the Lord God Almighty and the Lamb are its temple" (21:22).

Finally and preeminently, the seeing of God will be restored to humanity. John writes, "They will see his face" (22:4). Moses desired to see God's face, but he was denied (Ex. 33:23). Solomon wondered if God could really dwell with men (2 Chron. 6:18). Ezekiel and many others fell facedown when God's presence approached. And Paul said, "Now we see but a poor reflection as in a mirror; then we shall see face to face. Now I know in part; then I shall know fully, even as I am fully known" (1 Cor. 13:12). Here in this passage, the presence of God is finally, fully, and visibly with men. We have reached the climax of this book and, indeed, of the whole Bible! "They will see his face." The effects of the Fall will be fully reversed. God will complete his merciful work by bringing the children of Adam back into fellowship with himself.

I don't know about you, but my favorite thing about Christianity is not necessarily living by faith: sometimes, I get tired of believing without seeing; I long to live by sight. And do you know what you and I are given in this verse? The hope and the promise that one day we (if we have repented and trusted in Christ) will do just that: we will see his face.

City of God's People

In chapter 17, the images of a prostitute and the great defiant city of Babylon are combined as "Babylon the Great, The Mother of Prostitutes" (Rev. 17:5). Her fall is announced in 18:2ff., and in 19:7 the wedding of the Lamb and his bride is announced. Then in chapter 21, the great wedding begins. A formal procession brings the bride to her husband. John writes, "I saw the Holy City, the new Jerusalem, coming down out of heaven from God, prepared as a bride beautifully dressed for her husband" (21:2). The false city has given way to the true city. The false lady has given way to the true lady. The Bible's wedding and marriage imagery, which emphasizes exclusivity and intimacy between God and his people, is fulfilled. She is his only bride, and he will dwell with her forever. Yet this close relationship with God is extended to the whole community through this image of the city. All of God's people together dwell with him.

At the center of what we expect of heaven should not be gold streets or pearl gates. It should not be buildings of glass and Peter sitting at a big desk at the gate. No, at the center of our expectation should be the relationship we will have with God forever. All of God's people will be with him. This is what we wait for.

Trust God for the promise of his presence.

CONCLUSION

The message of the book of Revelation is this: We are waiting for the sovereign God to come, execute his judgments, deliver us through the blood of the Lamb, and bring us into his presence forever. So this is where our trust must lie.

Is this what you are waiting for?

I am sure there are smaller things you are waiting for. You might be waiting for this sermon to end. You might be waiting for lunch, or for a scheduled trip to the mall to get that thing you can no longer do without. Maybe you are waiting for retirement, or for a check to come in the mail. There are lots of things you might be waiting for. But in your heart, more than any anything else, are you waiting for the sovereign God to execute his judgments, save us through the blood of the Lamb, and bring us into his presence forever? The future holds many things. For God's people, it holds his coming above all else.

If you are a Christian, you are not to spend your life worrying, but waiting. The future is not meaningless, anonymous, foreboding, and empty. No, it is full and bright. It is a future with God! So the Christian is not afraid of the future; he is in love with it. When Jesus promises at the end of Revelation, "I am coming soon," John responds, "Amen. Come, Lord Jesus" (22:20). This is the ultimate desire of every saint. If you are waiting for anything else, I have to ask, is your wait worth it? This is the hope we were made to run on.

If you are a non-Christian, you too are in this book. John addresses "Whoever is thirsty." I hope this is where you are. Are you? The whole verse reads, "The Spirit and the bride say, 'Come!' And let him who hears say, 'Come!' Whoever is thirsty, let him come; and whoever wishes, let him take the free gift of the water of life" (22:17). You are giving your life for something. You are waiting for something. What are you waiting for? Is it worth the wait? Whatever it is, will it last?

Domitian, the great emperor of Rome, is dead. The Egyptian pharaohs and the Babylonian emperors are all dead. So too are the German führer of the Third Reich and the general secretaries of the Soviet Union's Communist Party. None of these thrones lasted, because none is the ultimate sovereign of this world. Forces and nations that now seem invincible, and problems that now seem insoluble, will pass. God alone will rule on his throne forever. No might on this earth will remain except his. No majesty will endure except his.

Friend, all the things that look so permanent in this life will vanish—every single one. What are you waiting for? Are you waiting for the Lamb who was slain to come and take his own? That is the only thing that will endure. What else will you let captivate your heart? What else can rival that? Perhaps you want to preserve your youth. Perhaps you want to add a few more years to your life. Maybe you want to find a spouse or a job. To live here or travel there. To buy this or pay off that.

But what about the great promises John mentions in this book? Do they elicit merely polite interest from you? Or do you find yourself homesick for a place you have never been, as John does—"Come, Lord Jesus." Aquinas said we need to know three things in order to be saved: what we ought to believe, what we ought to do, and what we ought to desire. The book of Revelation promises that whoever is thirsty will drink without cost from the spring of the water of life. Whoever is thirsty.

Let us pray:

Lord, we praise you that you are the great God who clearly reveals himself in this vision of John. We pray, Lord, that you would forgive us in our hearts for the great concern we have about things. We pray, Lord, that you would make us greatly concerned over great matters. We pray that you would show yourself to us to be the one who is high and lifted up on his throne—the one who will come in storms of judgment and yet who will save all who will turn and trust in the slain Lamb of God. O Lord, we do pray as the church in Revelation prays, that you would come quickly. Come quickly, we ask in Jesus' name. Amen.

Questions for Reflection

1. We have seen that disappointments come not just when we don't get what we want but when we get what we want and it is found to be wanting. Is it possible that all the disappointments you have encountered in life (both what you have not received and what you have found wanting) might be preparing and shaping you to place your hope entirely in what God has prepared for his children? If so, how does this alter your perspective on those past and present disappointments?

2. Why do you think John uses so few words to describe the one on the throne, in contrast to his colorful descriptions of those around the throne?

3. Who is the most powerful person you can think of? The most beautiful person? The most amazing athlete? The most brilliant intellect? What do the four living creatures and elders teach us that the four people you are thinking of would do if they were in the throne room of God? What would you do? Can you imagine what this one on the throne must be like?

4. In what areas of your life are you tempted to think God is not on his throne?

5. Two main reasons were given for why readers of Revelation often shrink back at its pictures of judgment. First, our experience with human judgment is so unsatisfyingly imperfect. Do you remember the second reason? Does this second reason still apply to Christians?

6. Why should the certainty of God's judgment produce peace and assurance in the Christian?

7. Consider what perfect justice will be like. Have we ever known anything like it on earth? Does the fact that perfect justice awaits us only in heaven do away with the need for Christians to concern themselves too strongly about justice in the courts? In the legislature? In the business boardroom? Between different races? Among the poor? And so on?

8. Why is Jesus pictured as both a lion and a Lamb?

9. Do all people have a sense of justice? Does the fact that people have differing standards of justice suggest that justice is relative? Why or why not?

10. You are waiting for something. What are you waiting for? Is it worth the wait? Whatever it is, will it last?

PERSON INDEX

SCRIPTURE INDEX

God intends to display the glory of His beauty, perfection, and love through the church.

Imagine what this would look like in our local congregations:

- God's name exalted in song and sermon.
- Relationships tied together by love and service.
- Marriages and families built for endurance.
- Christ's sacrifice pictured in the lives of sinful but repenting people!

At 9Marks, we believe that there is no better **evangelistic tool, missions strategy,** or **counseling program** than the image of God displayed through His gathering of imperfect but transforming people. As we learn more about Him, we look more and more like Him.

Neighborhoods and nations will look with wonder. As will the heavenly host!

Church leaders do not need another innovative method or engaging metaphor for growing their churches. They need to (get to!) embrace the biblical theology and priorities that God Himself designed for cultivating health and holiness in the local congregation. Scripture actually teaches church leaders how to build churches that display God's glory.

At 9Marks, we seek to answer the "how-to" question and develop a biblical vision for your congregation.

- Media: downloadable web resources, audio interviews, e-newsletters, educational curriculum
- Study: training weekends, conferences, internships, think tanks.
- Publishing: books, pamphlets, papers.
- Outreach: On-site visits, phone conversations.

To learn more, visit www.9marks.org.